A History of
Latin America

A History of Latin America

Fourth Edition

Volume II
Independence
to the Present

Benjamin Keen

Professor Emeritus
Northern Illinois University

HOUGHTON MIFFLIN COMPANY   Boston   Toronto

Dallas   Geneva, Illinois   Palo Alto   Princeton, New Jersey

Cover credit:

Emiliano Di Cavalcanti, *Pescadores,* 1951, oil on canvas.
Museu de Arte Contemporânea da Universidade de São
Paulo, Brazil.

Maps by Dick Sanderson.
       Patty Isaacs, *Parrot Graphics.*

Sponsoring Editor: John Weingartner
Project Editor: Linda Hamilton
Production Coordinator: Renée Le Verrier
Manufacturing Coordinator: Marie E. Barnes
Marketing Manager: Diane Brow Gifford

Printed in the U.S.A.

Library of Congress Catalog Card Number: 91-71983

ISBN 0-395-60139-8

ABCDEFGHIJ-D-9987654321

Contents

Contents

Contents

List of Maps

Preface

The fourth edition of *A History of Latin America* has two major objectives. First, it seeks to make available to teachers and students of Latin American history a text based on the best recent scholarship and enriched with data and concepts drawn from the sister social sciences of economics, anthropology, and sociology. Because the book is a history of Latin American *civilization,* it devotes considerable space to the way of life at different periods of the area's history. To enable students to deepen their own knowledge of Latin American history on their own, it includes an updated annotated bibliography, "Suggestions for Further Reading," limited to titles in English.

A second objective has been to set Latin American history within a broad interpretive framework. This framework is the "dependency theory," the most influential theoretical model for social scientists concerned with understanding Latin America. Not all followers of the theory understand it precisely the same way, but most probably agree with the definition of *dependency* offered by the Brazilian scholar Theotonio dos Santos: "A situation in which the economy of certain countries is conditioned by the development and expansion of another economy to which the former is subject." In recent years the theory has come under scattered fire from some scholars, mostly North American, who charge its followers with serious faults of omission and commission, such as the claim that capitalist development is impossible on the Latin American periphery. But, as Peter Evans pointed out in a thoughtful survey of several "postdependency" writings (*Latin American Research Review,* 20, No. 2 [1985]), Fernando Henriques Cardoso, himself a founder and leading theoretician of the dependency school, had attacked such claims "with vitriolic effectiveness" more than a decade earlier. Evans concluded that the dependency approach had established itself as one of the "primary lenses through which scholars, both North American and Latin American, analyze the interaction of classes and the state in the context of an increasingly internationalized economy," and that "it is hard to argue that this approach has been or is likely to be replaced by some new overarching paradigm." Since Evans wrote those words, Latin America has experienced deepening economic and social crises that have given new relevance to the dependency approach.

A word about the organization of this text. In its planning, the decision was made to reject the approach that tries to cover the post-independence history of the twenty Latin American republics in detail, including mention of every general who ever passed through a presidential palace. Most teachers will agree that this approach discourages students by miring them in a bog of tedious facts. Accordingly, it was decided to limit coverage of the national period in the nineteenth century to Mexico, Argentina, Chile, and Brazil, whose history seemed to illustrate best the major issues and trends of the period. In addition to these four countries, the survey of the twentieth century broadened to include the central Andean area, with a special concentration on Peru, and Cuba, the scene of a socialist revolution with continental repercussions. The second edition added a chapter on Central America, where a revolutionary storm, having toppled the U.S.–supported Somoza tyranny in Nicaragua, threatened the rickety structures of oligarchical and military rule in El Salvador and Guatemala.

To accommodate alternative course configurations, the fourth edition of *A History of Latin America* is being published in two volumes, as well as in the complete version. Volume 1 includes Latin American history from ancient times to 1910, and volume 2 covers Latin American history from independence to the present.

This present edition recognizes the political and economic importance of the Bolivarian lands of Venezuela and Colombia by including a chapter on the modern history of countries. Venezue-

lan history, like that of Mexico, demonstrates that great oil wealth will not, by itself, ensure escape from dependency and mass poverty. The violent history of Colombia, complicated by its recent emergence as principal supplier of cocaine to the United States, reflects an accumulation of political and social problems that still awaits solution.

The colonial chapters, in particular, have been extensively revised and expanded, with new material on ancient America, the discovery of America in historical perspective, colonial labor struggles, and colonial women, among other subjects. The book has also been updated to cover recent events and to incorporate current scholarship. The chapter on United States–Latin American relations, for example, includes sections on the invasion of Panama and the impact of the Gulf crisis and war on Latin America.

The book has also benefited from the careful scrutiny of the third edition by colleagues who made valuable suggestions for revision:

Margaret Chowning, California State University—Hayward
Donald B. Cooper, Ohio State University
Mariano Diaz-Miranda, University of Rhode Island
René De La Pedraja, Canisius College
Jane M. Rausch, University of Massachusetts, Amherst
John Jay TePaske, Duke University
Thomas Zoumaras, Northeast Missouri State University

Many but not all of these colleagues' suggestions were adopted; they bear no responsibility for any remaining errors of fact or interpretation. I wish to recall, too, the many students, graduate and undergraduate, who helped me to define my views on Latin American history through the give-and-take of classroom discussion and the reading and discussion of their papers and theses. In particular, I wish to thank two former students, Professors Steven Niblo and Keith Haynes, for sharing with me the findings of their important research on the political economy of the *Porfiriato* and the ideology of the Mexican revolution, respectively.

B.K.

Introduction

The Geographical Background of Latin American History

Latin America, a region of startling physical contrasts, stretches 7,000 miles southward from the Mexican-U.S. border to the tip of Tierra del Fuego on Cape Horn. The widest east–west point, across Peru and Brazil, spans 3,200 miles. This diverse geography has helped produce distinctive development of each Latin American nation.

Latin America has two dominant physical characteristics: enormous mountains and vast river systems. The often snow-capped and sometimes volcanic mountain ranges—the three Sierra Madre ranges in Mexico and the 4,000-mile-long Andes in South America making a western spine from Venezuela to Tierra del Fuego—form the backbone of the landmass. Nearly impassable for most of their length, these mountain ranges boast many peaks of over 22,000 feet. The mountains have presented a formidable barrier to trade and communications in Mexico and the nations of the southern continent. Not only do the mountain ranges separate nations from each other, they divide regions within nations.

The enormous rivers most often lie in lightly populated areas. Three mammoth river systems (the Amazon, the Orinoco, and the Río de la Plata) spread over almost the entire South American continent east of the Andes. The size of the Amazon River Basin and the surrounding tropics—the largest such area in the world—have posed another impediment to the development of transportation and human settlement, although some rivers are navigable for long distances. Only with the advent of modern technology—railroads, the telegraph, telephones, automobiles, and airplanes—has geographic isolation been partly overcome, a condition that has helped create markets and forge independent states.

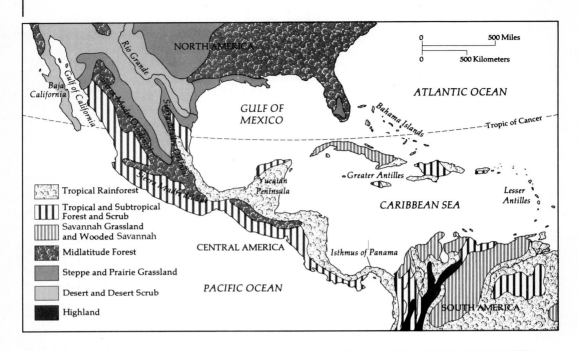

THE MAPS ON THESE FACING PAGES FORM AN OVERALL PICTURE OF THE NATURAL GEOGRAPHIC FEATURES OF LATIN AMERICA; MIDDLE AMERICA (ABOVE) COMPRISED OF MEXICO, CENTRAL AMERICA, AND THE CARIBBEAN REGION; AND SOUTH AMERICA (OPPOSITE).

Latin America encompasses five climatological regions: high mountains, tropical jungles, deserts, temperate coastal plains, and temperate highlands. The first three are sparsely populated, while the latter two tend to be densely inhabited. With the exception of the Mayan, all the great ancient civilizations arose in the highlands of the Andes and Mexico.

The varied climate and topography of South America, Mexico, and Central America have helped produce this highly uneven distribution of population. Three notable examples, the gargantuan Amazonian region of mostly steamy tropical forests and savannah, the vast desert of Patagonia in southern Argentina, and the northern wastelands of Mexico, support few inhabitants. In contrast to these inhospitable regions, a thin strip along Brazil's coast, the plain along the Río de la Plata estuary in Argentina, and the central plateau of Mexico contain most of the people in these countries. Thus these nations are over-populated and underpopulated at the same time.

In western South America the heaviest concentration of people is found on the inland plateaus. None of the major cities—Santiago, Chile; Lima, Peru; Quito, Ecuador; and Bogotá and Medellín, Colombia—are ports; there are few good natural harbors on the west coast. In contrast, in eastern South America the major cities—Buenos Aires, Argentina; Montevideo, Uruguay; and São Paulo–Santos, Rio de Janeiro, Bahia, and Recife, Brazil—are situated on the Atlantic coast. The preponderance of people in Argentina, Brazil, and Uruguay reside on the coastal plains. Mexico City, Guadalajara, and Monterrey, Mexico's largest cities, are inland. Almost all these cities in Latin America have a population of over one million, with Mexico City, the largest, having over fifteen million. (See the Statistical Profile for other data on Latin America on page 575.)

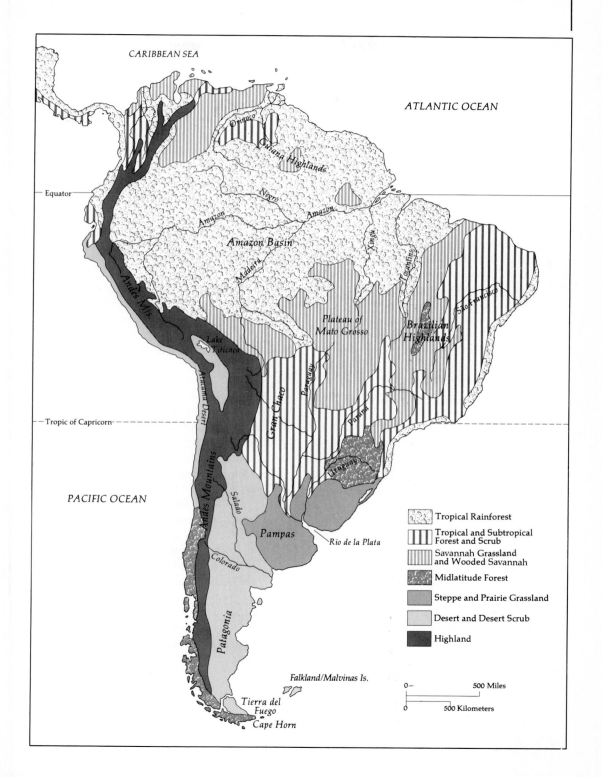

CARIBBEAN SEA

ATLANTIC OCEAN

Orinoco

Guiana Highlands

Equator

Negro

Amazon

Amazon

Amazon Basin

Madeira

Xingu

Tocantins

São Francisco

Andes Mts.

Plateau of
Mato Grosso

Brazilian
Highlands

Lake
Titicaca

Atacama Desert

Gran Chaco

Paraguay

Tropic of Capricorn

Paraná

PACIFIC OCEAN

Andes Mountains

Salado

Uruguay

Pampas

Rio de la Plata

Colorado

Patagonia

Falkland/Malvinas Is.

Tierra del
Fuego

Cape Horn

	Tropical Rainforest
	Tropical and Subtropical Forest and Scrub
	Savannah Grassland and Wooded Savannah
	Midlatitude Forest
	Steppe and Prairie Grassland
	Desert and Desert Scrub
	Highland

0 ___ 500 Miles

0 ___ 500 Kilometers

The number of waterways and the amount of rainfall vary greatly from region to region. Mexico has no rivers of importance, while Brazil contains the huge Amazon network. Lack of rain and rivers for irrigation in large areas makes farming impossible. Barely 10 percent of Mexico's land is fertile enough to farm; rainfall is so uncertain in some cultivable areas that drought strikes often and for years at a time. Mexico, with too little water, contrasts with Brazil with too much. Much of Brazil's vast territory, however, is equally uncultivable as its tropical soils have high acidity and have proved infertile and incapable of sustaining agricultural crops.

On the other hand, Latin America has enormous natural resources for economic development. Mexico and Venezuela rank among the world's largest oil producers. Mexico may have the biggest petroleum reserves of any nation other than Saudi Arabia. Bolivia, Ecuador, Colombia, and Peru also produce oil. Over the centuries, Latin American nations have been leading sources of copper (Mexico and Chile), nitrate (Chile), silver (Peru and Mexico), gold (Brazil), diamonds (Brazil), and tin (Bolivia). Much of the world's coffee is grown on the fertile highlands of Central America, Colombia, and Brazil. Much of the world's cattle have been raised on the plains of northern Mexico, southern Brazil, and central Argentina. Argentina's immense plains, the Pampas, are among the planet's most fertile areas, yielding not only cattle but sheep and wheat as well. Over the past five centuries, the coastal plains of Brazil have produced enormous amounts of sugar. In addition, human ingenuity has converted geographical obstacles into assets. Some extensive river systems have potential for hydroelectric power and provide water for irrigation as well, as has been done in Mexico's arid regions.

The historical record shows that the richness of Latin America's resources has had a significant impact on the economic and political development of Europe and North America. The gold and silver of its New World Empire fueled Spain's wars and diplomacy in Europe for four hundred years. Many scholars trace the origins of the Industrial Revolution in such nations as Great Britain and the Netherlands to resources extracted from Latin America by its colonial masters, Spain and Portugal.

Latin America's resources have affected economic development elsewhere, but how these resources have been developed and by whom and in which ways has profoundly changed the history of the nations in this area. Geography has perhaps narrowed historical alternatives in Latin America, but the decisions of people determined its development. Going back to the colonization by Spain and Portugal, Latin America's history has been marked by exploitation of its peoples and its natural resources. Imperial Spain's policy to drain the lands it conquered of gold, silver, and other resources fixed the pattern for later exploiters. With European dominance came the decisions to subjugate the indigenous peoples and often force them to labor under subhuman conditions in mines and large estates, where many died. In the more recent era, there has been the decision to grow bananas on the coastal plains of Central America, instead of corn or other staples of the local diet; this has made export profitable, usually for North American concerns, but this land-use has left many, like the Guatemalans, without sufficient food.

The book that follows is a history of the development of Latin America's economy, politics, and society viewed primarily from the perspective of ordinary people, who were exploited and oppressed, but who resisted and endured. It is the story of the events and forces that produced the alternatives from which Latin Americans created their world.

Part 2

Latin America in the Nineteenth Century

After winning their independence, the new Latin American states began a long, uphill struggle to achieve economic and political stability. They faced immense obstacles, for independence, as previously noted, was not accompanied by economic and social changes that could spur rapid progress—for example, no redistribution of land and income in favor of the lower classes took place. The large estate, generally operated with primitive methods and slave or peon labor, continued to dominate economic life. Far from diminishing, the influence of the landed aristocracy actually increased as a result of the leading military role it played in the wars of independence and of the passing of Spanish authority.

Economic life stagnated, for the anticipated large-scale influx of foreign capital did not materialize, and the European demand for Latin American staples remained far below expectations. Free trade brought increased commercial activity to the coasts, but this increase was offset by the near destruction of some local craft industries by cheap, factory-made European goods. The sluggish pace of economic activity and the relative absence of interregional trade and true national markets encouraged local self-sufficiency, isolation, political instability, and even chaos.

As a result of these adverse factors, the period from about 1820 to about 1870 was for many Latin American countries an age of violence, of alternate dictatorship and revolution. Its symbol was the *caudillo* (strong man), whose power was always based on force, no matter what kind of constitution the country had. Usually, the caudillo ruled with the aid of a coalition of lesser caudillos, each supreme in his region. Whatever their methods, the caudillos generally displayed some regard for republican ideology and institutions. Political parties, bearing such labels as "conservative" and "liberal," "unitarian" and "federalist," were active in most of the new states. Conservatism drew most of its support from the great landowners and their urban allies. Liberalism typically attracted provincial landowners, professional men, and other groups that had en-

joyed little power in the past and were dissatisfied with the existing order. As a rule, conservatives sought to retain many of the social arrangements of the colonial era and favored a highly centralized government. Liberals, often inspired by the example of the United States, usually advocated a federal form of government, guarantees of individual rights, lay control of education, and an end to special privileges for the clergy and military. Neither party displayed much interest in the problems of the Indian peasantry and other lower-class groups.

Beginning in about 1870, the accelerating tempo of the Industrial Revolution in Europe stimulated a more rapid change in the Latin American economy and politics. European capital flowed into the area, creating the facilities needed to expand and modernize production and trade. The pace and degree of economic progress of the various countries were very uneven, and depended largely on their geographic position and natural resources.

Extreme one-sidedness was a feature of the new economic order. One or two products became the basis of each country's prosperity, making it highly vulnerable to fluctuations in the world demand and the price of these commodities. Meanwhile, other sectors of the economy remained stagnant or even declined through diversion of labor and land to other industries.

The late nineteenth-century expansion had two other characteristics: in the main, it took place within the framework of the hacienda system of land tenure and labor, and it was accompanied by a steady growth of foreign control over the natural and man-made resources of the region. Thus, by 1900 a new structure of dependency, or colonialism, had arisen, called neo-colonialism, with Great Britain and later the United States replacing Spain and Portugal as the dominant power in the area.

The new economic order demanded peace and continuity in government, and after 1870 political conditions in Latin America did, in fact, grow more stable. Old party lines dissolved as conservatives adopted the positivist dogma of science and progress, while liberals abandoned their concern with constitutional methods and civil liberties in favor of an interest in material prosperity. A new type of "progressive" caudillo—Porfirio Díaz in Mexico, Rafael Núñez in Colombia, Antonio Guzmán Blanco in Venezuela—symbolized the politics of acquisition. The cycle of dictatorship and revolution continued in many lands, but the revolutions became less frequent and less devastating.

These are some major trends in the political and economic history of Latin America in the period extending from about 1820 to 1900. Natu-rally, these trends were accompanied by other changes in the Latin American way of life and culture, notably the development of a powerful literature that often sought not only to mirror Latin American society but to change it. In Part 2, we shall present short histories of four leading Latin American countries—Mexico, Argentina, Chile, and Brazil—in the nineteenth century. All four contain themes and problems common to the area in that period, but each displays variations that reflect the specific backgrounds of the different states.

Chapter 9

Dictators and Revolutions

Independence did not bring Latin America the ordered freedom and prosperity that the liberators had hoped for. In most of the new states, decades of civil strife followed the passing of Spanish and Portuguese rule. Bolívar reflected the disillusionment of many patriot leaders when he wrote in 1829: "There is no good faith in America, nor among the nations of America. Treaties are scraps of paper; constitutions, printed matter; elections, battles; freedom, anarchy; and life, a torment." The contrast between Latin American stagnation and disorder and the meteoric advance of the former English colonies—the United States—intensified the pessimism and self-doubt of some Latin American leaders and intellectuals.

The Fruits of Independence

Frustration of the great hopes with which the struggle for liberation began was inevitable, for independence was not accompanied by economic and social changes that could shatter the colonial mold. Aside from the passing of the Spanish and Portuguese trade monopolies, the colonial economic and social structures remained intact. The hacienda, fazenda, or estancia, employing archaic techniques and a labor force of peons or slaves, continued to dominate agriculture; no significant class of small farmers arose to challenge the economic and political might of the great landowners. Indeed, the revolutions strengthened the power of the landed aristocracy by removing the agencies of Spanish rule—viceroys, audiencias, intendants—and by weakening the ingrained habits of obedience to a central authority. In contrast, all other colonial elites—the merchant class, weakened by the expulsion or emigration of many loyalist merchants; the mine owners, ruined by wartime destruction or confiscation of their properties; and the church hierarchy, often in disgrace for having sided with Spain—emerged from the conflict with diminished weight.

To their other sources of influence the landed aristocracy added the prestige of a military elite crowned with the laurels of victory, for many revolutionary officers had arisen from its ranks. The militarization of the new states as a result of years of destructive warfare and postwar instability assured a large political role for this officer group. Standing armies that often consumed more than half of the national budgets arose. Not content with the role of guardians of order and national security, the military became arbiters of political disputes, as a rule intervening in favor of the conservative landowning interests and the urban elites with whom the great landowners were closely linked.

Economic Stagnation

Revolutionary leaders had expected that a vast expansion of foreign trade, which would aid economic recovery, would follow the passing of Spanish commercial monopoly. In fact, some countries, favored by their natural resources or geographic position, soon recovered from the revolutionary crisis and scored modest to large economic advances; they included Brazil (coffee and sugar), Argentina (hides), and Chile (metals and hides). But others, such as Mexico, Bolivia, and Peru, whose mining economies had suffered shattering blows, failed to recover colonial levels of production.

Several factors accounted for the economic stagnation that plagued many of the new states in the first half of the nineteenth century. Independence was not accompanied by a redistribution of land and income that might have stimulated a growth of internal markets and productive forces. The anticipated large-scale influx of foreign capital did not materialize, partly because political disorder discouraged foreign investment, partly because Europe and the United

States, then financing their own industrial revolutions, had as yet little capital to export. Exports of Latin American staples also remained below expectations, for Europe still viewed Latin America primarily as an outlet for manufactured goods, especially English textiles. The resulting flood of cheap, factory-made European products damaged local craft industries and drained the new states of their stocks of gold and silver, creating a chronic balance-of-trade problem. The British conquest of the Latin American markets further weakened the local merchant class, which was unable to compete with its English rivals. By mid-century the wealthiest and most prestigious merchant houses, from Mexico City to Buenos Aires and Valparaíso, bore English names. Iberian merchants, however, continued to dominate the urban and provincial retail trade in many areas.

In their totality, these developments retarded the development of native capitalism and capitalist relations and reinforced the dominant role of the hacienda in the economic and political life of the new states. The deepening stagnation of the interior of these nations, which was aggravated by lack of roads and by natural obstacles to communication (such as jungles and mountains), intensified tendencies toward regionalism and the domination of regions by caudillos great and small, who were usually local large landowners.[1] The sluggish tempo of economic activity encouraged these caudillos to employ their private followings of peons and retainers as pawns in the game of politics and revolution on a national scale. Indeed, politics and revolution became in some countries a form of economic activity that compensated for the lack of other opportunities,

---

[1] The term *caudillo* is commonly applied to politico-military leaders who held power on the national and regional level in Latin America before more or less stable parliamentary government became the norm in the area beginning about 1870. Military ability and charisma are qualities often associated with caudillos, who came in many guises, but not all possessed the same qualities. Since the semifeudal conditions that gave rise to the caudillo still survive in parts of Latin America, it can be said that caudillos and *caudillismo* still exist.

since the victors, having gained control of the all-important customhouse (which collected duties on imports and exports) and other official sources of revenue, could reward themselves and their followers with government jobs, contracts, grants of public land, and other favors.

Politics: The Conservative and Liberal Programs

The political systems of the new states made large formal concessions to the liberal bourgeois ideology of the nineteenth century. With the exception of Brazil, all the new states adopted the republican form of government (Mexico had two brief intervals of imperial rule) and paid their respects to the formulas of parliamentary and representative government. Their constitutions provided for presidents, congresses, and courts; often they contained elaborate safeguards of individual rights.

These facades of modernity, however, poorly concealed the dictatorial or oligarchical reality beneath. Typically, the chief executive was a caudillo whose power rested on force, no matter what the constitutional form; usually, he ruled with the support of a coalition of lesser caudillos, each more or less supreme in his own domain. The supposed independence of the judicial and legislative branches was a fiction. As a rule, elections were exercises in futility. Since the party in power generally counted the votes, the opposition had no alternative but revolt.

Literacy and property qualifications disfranchised most Indians and mixed-bloods; where they had the right to vote, the *patrón* (master) often herded them to the polls to vote for him or his candidates. Whether liberal or conservative, all sections of the ruling class agreed on keeping the peasantry, gauchos, and other "lower orders" on the margins of political life, on preventing their emergence as groups with collective philosophies and goals. The very privileges that the new creole constitutions and law codes granted the Indians—equality before the law, the "right" to divide and dispose of their communal lands—

weakened the solidarity of the native people and their ability to resist the competitive individualism of the creole world. However, especially gifted, ambitious, and fortunate members of these marginal groups were sometimes co-opted into the creole elite and provided some of its most distinguished leaders; two examples are the Zapotec Indian Benito Juárez in Mexico and the mestizo president Andrés Santa Cruz in Bolivia.

At first glance, the political history of Latin America in the first half-century after independence, with its dreary alternation of dictatorship and revolt, seems pointless and trivial. But the political struggles of this period were more than disputes over spoils between sections of a small upper class. Genuine social and ideological cleavages helped to produce those struggles and the bitterness with which they were fought. Such labels as "conservative" and "liberal," "unitarian" and "federalist," assigned by the various parties to themselves or each other, were more than masks in a pageant, although opportunism contributed to the ease with which some leaders assumed and discarded these labels.

Generally speaking, conservatism reflected the interests of the traditional holders of power and privilege, men who had a stake in maintaining the existing order. Hence, the great landowners, the upper clergy, the higher ranks of the military and the civil bureaucracy, and monopolistic merchant groups tended to be conservatives. Liberalism, in contrast, appealed to those groups that in colonial times had little or no access to the main structures of economic and political power and were naturally eager to alter the existing order. Thus, liberalism drew much support from provincial landowners, lawyers and other professional men (the groups most receptive to new ideas), shopkeepers, and artisans; it also appealed to ambitious, aspiring Indians and mixed-bloods. But regional conflicts and clan or family loyalties often cut across the lines of social and occupational cleavage, complicating the political picture.

Liberals wanted to break up the hierarchical social structure inherited from the colonial period. They had a vision of their countries remade into dynamic middle-class states on the model of the United States or England. Inspired by the success of the United States, they usually favored a federal form of government, guarantees of individual rights, lay control of education, and an end to a special legal status for the clergy and military. In their modernizing zeal, liberals sometimes called for abolition of entails (which restricted the right to inherit property to a particular descendant or descendants of the owner), dissolution of convents, confiscation of church wealth, and abolition of slavery. The federalism of the liberals had a special appeal for secondary regions of the new states, eager to develop their resources and free themselves from domination by capitals and wealthy primary regions.

Conservatives typically upheld a strong centralized government, the religious and educational monopoly of the Roman Catholic church, and the special privileges (fueros) of the clergy and military. They distrusted such radical novelties as freedom of speech and the press and religious toleration. Conservatives, in short, sought to salvage as much of the colonial social order as was compatible with the new republican system. Indeed, some conservative leaders ultimately despaired of that system and dreamed of implanting monarchy in their countries.

Neither conservatives nor liberals displayed much interest in the problems of the Indian, black, and mixed-blood masses that formed the majority of people in most Latin American countries. Liberals, impatient with the supposed backwardness of the Indians, regarded their communalism as an impediment to the development of a capitalist spirit of enterprise and initiated legislation providing for the division of communal lands—a policy that favored land grabbing at the expense of Indian villages. Despite their theoretical preference for small landholdings and a rural middle class, liberals recoiled from any program of radical land reform. Conservatives, for their part, correctly regarded the great estate as the very foundation of their power. As traditionalists, however, the conservatives sometimes claimed to continue the Spanish paternalist policy toward the Indians and enjoyed some support among the natives, who tended to be suspicious of all innovations.

This summary of the conservative and liberal programs for Latin America in the first half-century after independence inevitably overlooks variations from the theoretical liberal and conservative norms—variations that reflected the specific conditions and problems of the different states. An examination of the history of four leading Latin American countries in this period, Mexico, Argentina, Chile, and Brazil, reveals not only certain common themes but a rich diversity of political experience.

Mexico

The struggle for Mexican independence, begun by the radical priests Hidalgo and Morelos, was completed by the creole officer Agustín de Iturbide, who headed a coalition of creole and peninsular conservatives terrified at the prospect of being governed by the liberal Spanish constitution of 1812, which was reestablished in 1820. Independence, achieved under such conservative auspices, meant that Mexico's economic and social patterns underwent little change. The great hacienda continued to dominate the countryside in many areas. Although Indian villages managed to retain substantial community lands until after mid-century and even improved their economic and political position somewhat with the passing of Spanish centralized authority, the trend toward usurpation of Indian lands grew stronger as a result of the lapse of Spanish protective legislation. Peons and tenants on the haciendas often suffered from debt servitude, miserable wages, oppressive rents, and excessive religious fees. At the constitutional convention of 1856–1857, the liberal Ponciano Arriaga declared:

With some honorable exceptions, the rich landowners of Mexico . . . resemble the feudal lords of the Middle Ages. On his seigneurial lands, with more or less formalities, the landowner makes and executes laws, administers justice and exercises civil power, imposes taxes and fines, has his own jails and irons, metes out punishments and tortures, monopolizes commerce, and forbids the conduct without his permission of any business but that of the estate.[2]

The church continued to wield diminished but still considerable economic and spiritual power. An anonymous contemporary writer reflected the disillusionment of the lower classes with the fruits of independence: "Independence is only a name. Previously they ruled us from Spain, now from here. It is always the same priest on a different mule. But as for work, food, and clothing, there is no difference."

The Mexican Economy

The ravages of war had left mine shafts flooded, haciendas deserted, the economy stagnant. The end of the Spanish commercial monopoly, however, brought a large increase in the volume of foreign trade; the number of ships entering Mexican ports jumped from 148 in 1823 to 639 in 1826. But exports did not keep pace with imports, leaving a trade deficit that had to be covered by exporting precious metals. The drain of gold and silver aggravated the problems of the new government, which inherited a bankrupt treasury and had to support a swollen bureaucracy and an officer class ready to revolt against any government that suggested a cut in their numbers or pay. The exodus of Spanish merchants and their capital added to the economic problems of the new state.

Foreign loans appeared to be the only way out of the crisis. In 1824–1825, English bankers made loans to Mexico amounting to 32 million pesos, guaranteed by Mexican customs revenues. Of this amount the Mexicans received only a little more than 11 million pesos, as the bankers, Barclay and Company, went bankrupt before all the money due to Mexico from the loan proceeds was paid. By 1843 unpaid interest and principal had

raised the nation's foreign debt to more than 54 million pesos. This mounting foreign debt not only created crushing interest burdens but threatened Mexico's independence and territorial integrity, for behind foreign capitalists stood governments that might threaten intervention in case of default.

Foreign investments, mainly from Britain, however, made possible a partial recovery of the decisive mining sector. Old mines, abandoned and flooded during the wars, were reopened, but the available capital proved inadequate, the technical problems of reconstruction were greater than anticipated, and production remained on a relatively low level.

An ambitious effort to revive and modernize Mexican industry also got under way, spurred by the founding in 1830 of the *Banco de Avío,* which provided governmental assistance to industry. Manufacturing, paced by textiles, made some limited progress in the three decades after independence. Leading industrial centers included Mexico City, Puebla, Guadalajara, Durango, and Veracruz. But shortages of capital, lack of a consistent policy of protection for domestic industry, and a socioeconomic structure that sharply limited the internal market hampered the growth of Mexican factory capitalism. By 1843 the Banco de Avío had to close its doors for lack of funds. The Mexican economy, therefore, continued to be based on mining and agriculture. Mexico's principal exports were precious metals, especially silver, and such agricultural products as tobacco, coffee, vanilla, cochineal, and henequen (a plant fiber used in rope and twine). Imports consisted primarily of manufactured goods that Mexican industry could not supply.

Politics: Liberals versus Conservatives

A liberal-conservative cleavage dominated Mexican political life in the half-century after independence. That conflict was latent from the moment that the "liberator" Iturbide, the former scourge of insurgents, rode into Mexico City on September 27, 1821, flanked on either side by two

[2] Francisco Zarco, *Historia del congreso estraordinario constituyente de 1856 y 1857,* 2 vols. (México, 1857), 1:555.

ATLANTIC OCEAN

MEXICO 1821

San Antonio

Rio Grande

GULF OF MEXICO

Mexico City

Veracruz

BAHAMA IS. (Br.)

CUBA (Sp.)

PUERTO RICO (Sp.)

BR. HONDURAS

HAITI 1804

Guatemala

CARIBBEAN SEA

TRINIDAD (Br.)

UNITED PROVINCES OF CENTRAL AMERICA 1823-1839

Panama

Caracas

BR. GUIANA

DUTCH GUIANA

FR. GUIANA

Bogotá

GRAN COLOMBIA 1819-1830

Quito

GALAPAGOS IS.

Indefinite Boundary

EMPIRE OF BRAZIL 1822

PERU 1821

Lima

Bahia

BOLIVIA 1825

Sucre

PACIFIC OCEAN

PARAGUAY 1813

Asunción

CHILE 1817

UNITED PROVINCES OF LA PLATA 1816

Rio de Janeiro

Santiago

URUGUAY 1828

Buenos Aires

Montevideo

| 0 | 500 | 1000 Miles |
| 0 | 500 | 1000 Kilometers |

LATIN AMERICA IN 1830

insurgent generals, Vicente Guerrero and Guadalupe Victoria, firm republicans and liberals.
The fall of Iturbide in 1823 cleared the way for
the establishment of a republic. But it soon became apparent that the republicans were divided
into liberals and conservatives, federalists and
centralists.

The constitution of 1824 represented a compromise between liberal and conservative interests. It appeased regional economic interests,
which were fearful of a too-powerful central government, by creating nineteen states that possessed taxing power; their legislatures, each
casting one vote, chose the president and vice
president for four-year terms. The national legislature was made bicameral, with an upper
house (Senate) and a lower house (Chamber of
Deputies). By assuring the creation of local civil
bureaucracies, the federalist structure also satisfied the demand of provincial middle classes for
greater access to political activity and office. But
the constitution had a conservative tinge as well:
although the church lost its monopoly of education, Catholicism was proclaimed the official religion, and the fueros of the church and the army
were specifically confirmed.

A hero of the war of independence, the liberal
general Guadalupe Victoria, was elected first
president under the new constitution. Anxious to
preserve unity, Victoria brought the conservative
Lucas Alamán into his cabinet. But this era of
good feeling was very short-lived; by 1825, Alamán was forced out of the government. The liberal-conservative cleavage now assumed the
form of a rivalry between two Masonic lodges,
the York Rite lodge, founded by the American
minister Joel Roberts Poinsett, and the Scottish
Rite lodge, sponsored by the British chargé d'affaires Henry Ward. Their rivalry reflected the Anglo-American competition for economic and political influence in Mexico. The old mining and
landowning aristocracy, which looked to Great
Britain for leadership and assistance in the economic and political reconstruction of Mexico on
a sound conservative basis, formed a pro-British
faction; the liberals and federalists, who regarded

the United States as a model for their own reform
program, formed a pro-American *Yorkino* faction.

The fate of the thousands of Spaniards, including many wealthy merchants who remained in
Mexico after the fall of the colonial regime, soon
became a major political issue. Spain's continued
occupation of the fortress of Veracruz until 1825,
its refusal (until 1836) to recognize Mexican independence, and the discovery of plots against
independence in which Spaniards were implicated created much anti-Spanish feeling. But
conservative leaders like Alamán strongly opposed ouster of the Spaniards as being harmful
to the economy and to the Mexican upper class,
threatened by the ambitions of upstart middle-
class politicians. Nonetheless, in 1827 the liberal
Yorkinos pushed through Congress a decree of
expulsion against the Spaniards. Although not
fully enforced, the decree hastened the transformation of the conservative and liberal factions
into political parties.

The Conservative party represented the old
landed and mining aristocracy, the clerical and
military hierarchy, monopolistic merchants, and
some manufacturers. Its intellectual spokesman
and organizer was Lucas Alamán, statesman,
champion of industry, and author of a brilliant
history of Mexico from the conservative point of
view. The Liberal party represented a creole and
mestizo middle class—provincial landowners,
professional men, artisans, the lower ranks of the
clergy and military—determined to end special
privileges and the concentration of political and
economic power in the upper class. A priest-
economist, José María Luis Mora, presented the
liberal position with great force and lucidity. But
the Liberal party was divided; its right wing, the
moderados, wanted to proceed slowly and sometimes joined the conservatives; its left wing, the
puros, advocated sweeping antifeudal, anticlerical reforms.

The election of 1828 produced the first political
crisis of the republic. The conservatives united
behind Manuel Gómez Pedraza, a leader of the
moderados; the puro candidate was Vicente
Guerrero, a hero of the war for independence

whose popularity should have assured his election. But Gómez Pedraza was secretary of war, and army pressure on the state legislatures produced a vote of ten to nine for him and the conservative vice-presidential candidate, Anastasio Bustamante. Liberal indignation was great, and General Antonio López de Santa Anna, who had overthrown Iturbide and saw another opportunity to make political capital by assuming the role of liberator, rose in revolt against Gómez Pedraza. By January 1829, the liberals had triumphed and Congress declared Guerrero president of the republic. Hoping to promote unity, Guerrero asked Bustamante to remain as vice president—a serious error, as events proved.

An honest but uneducated man who doubted his own ability to govern, a mestizo scorned by the aristocratic creole society of the capital, Guerrero lasted barely one year in office. He coped successfully with a Spanish effort to reconquer Mexico (1829), but was overthrown the next year by an army revolt organized by Bustamante. For two years, a conservative dictatorship dominated by Lucas Alamán used the army to remove liberal governors and legislatures in the states, suppress newspapers, and jail, shoot, or exile puro leaders. The climax of this reign of terror was the execution of the veteran revolutionary Guerrero by a firing squad in 1831.

Growing unrest informed Santa Anna that the political pendulum was swinging toward the liberals, and in 1832 this careerist, a true conservative at heart, led a revolt against Bustamante. Province after province joined the revolt, and by the end of the year Bustamante had been forced into exile. Following congressional elections in March 1833, a new liberal government, dominated by the puros, was formed. Santa Anna, still posing as a liberal, was elected president, and Valentín Gómez Farías, a physician who remained a pillar of the liberal cause for a quarter-century, was chosen vice president. But Santa Anna would not assume responsibility for carrying out the liberal program; pleading ill health, he retired to his hacienda on the Veracruz coast and turned over to Gómez Farías his office.

The year 1833 was a high-water mark of liberal achievement. Aided by José María Luis Mora, his minister of education, Gómez Farías pushed through Congress a series of radical reforms: abolition of the special privileges and immunities of the army and church (meaning that officers and priests would now be subject to the jurisdiction of civil courts), abolition of tithes, secularization of the clerical University of Mexico, creation of a department of public instruction, reduction of the army, and creation of a civilian militia. These measures were accompanied by a program of internal improvements designed to increase the prosperity of the interior by linking it to the capital and the coasts. In their use of the central government to promote education and national economic development, the liberals showed that they were not doctrinaire adherents of laissez faire.

The liberal program inevitably provoked clerical and conservative resistance. Army officers began to organize revolts; priests proclaimed from their pulpits that the great cholera epidemic of 1833 was a sign of divine displeasure with the works of the impious liberals. Santa Anna waited until the time was ripe. Then, in April 1834, he placed himself at the head of the conservative rebellion, occupied the capital, and sent Gómez Farías and Mora into exile. Resuming the presidency, he summoned a hand-picked reactionary congress that repealed the reform laws of 1833 and suspended the constitution of 1824. Under the new conservative constitution of 1836, the states were reduced to departments completely dominated by the central government, upper-class control of politics was assured through high property and income qualifications for holding office, and the fueros of the church and army were restored.

Santa Anna and the conservatives ruled Mexico for the greater part of two decades, 1834 to 1854. Politically and economically, the conservative rule subordinated the interests of the regions and the country as a whole to a wealthy, densely populated central core linking Mexico City, Puebla, and Veracruz. Its centralist trend was reflected in the tariff act of 1837, which restored the alcabala, or sales tax system, inland customhouses, and the government tobacco monopoly, insuring the continuous flow of revenues to Mexico City.

War and Territorial Losses

Conservative neglect and abuse of outlying or border areas like northern Mexico and Yucatán contributed to the loss of Texas and almost led to the loss of Yucatán. Santa Anna's destruction of provincial autonomy enabled American colonists in Texas, led by Sam Houston, to pose as patriotic federalists in revolt against Santa Anna's tyranny. Santa Anna's incompetent generalship contributed to the defeat of his miserable Indian and mestizo conscripts at the battle of San Jacinto (1837), which secured the de facto independence of Texas. In Yucatán, the Caste or Social War of 1839 combined elements of a regional war against conservative centralism and an Indian war against feudal landlords. For almost a decade, Yucatán remained outside Mexico.

After the definitive loss of Texas through annexation by the United States in 1845 came the greater disaster of the Mexican War (1846–1848). Its immediate cause was a dispute between Mexico and the United States over the boundary of Texas, but the decisive factor was the determination of the Polk administration to acquire not only Texas but California and New Mexico. The war ended in catastrophic Mexican defeat, basically due to U.S. superiority in resources, military training, and leadership, but the irresponsible, selfish attitudes of the Mexican aristocracy and church contributed to the debacle.

In 1846, after conservative generals had suffered a series of reverses, a liberal revolt returned the puros to power and re-established the constitution of 1824. Led by Gómez Farías, the puros had a plan for winning the war that produced a curious replay of the events of 1834. The plan called for recalling Santa Anna—still regarded as the best of Mexico's generals—from the exile to which his own conservatives had consigned him. Having been allowed by the Americans to slip through their blockade and re-enter Mexico, Santa Anna was named president and commander in chief of the Mexican armies.

Gómez Farías, meanwhile, undertook to finance the war by seizure of church property. This proposal horrified the clergy and their aristocratic supporters. Some aristocratic militia regiments in the capital, mobilized to fight the Americans, decided it was more urgent to save the church from the puros and rose in revolt against Gómez Farías. At the critical moment, Santa Anna repeated his betrayal of 1834. Returning to the capital, he ousted Gómez Farías, installed the moderado General Pedro María de Anaya as president, then turned to meet the advance of General Winfield Scott from Veracruz. Despite the tenacious resistance of a volunteer army at the approaches to the capital, the American invaders entered Mexico City in September 1847.

Mexican armies had been beaten in the field, but guerrilla warfare, joined with the ravages of disease, was taking a heavy toll of American lives; continued resistance and refusal to admit defeat might have secured a better peace for Mexico. In some regions of the country, peasant revolts broke out that combined demands for division of large haciendas among the peasantry and other reforms with calls for a continued resistance to the invaders. But the aristocratic creoles—some of whom favored a total take-over of Mexico by the United States—and their clerical allies feared the consequences of partisan warfare to their wealth and privileges and hastened to make peace. "The Mexican government," says Leticia Reina, "preferred coming to terms with the United States rather than endanger the interests of the ruling class." While Santa Anna fled to a new exile in Jamaica, a moderado government, formed at Querétaro, opened negotiations with the Americans. By the treaty of Guadalupe Hidalgo (1848), Mexico ceded Texas, California, and New Mexico to the United States; in return, Mexico received $15 million and the cancellation of certain claims against it.

La Reforma, Civil War, and the French Intervention

A succession of moderado administrations, mildly conservative but reasonably honest and efficient, struggled with the myriad problems of postwar Mexico. Meanwhile, the disasters suffered by Mexico under conservative rule had created a widespread revulsion against conservative policies and stimulated a revival of puro liberalism. In 1846, during the war, liberal administrations had come to power in the states of Oaxaca and Michoacán. In Michoacán the new governor was Melchor Ocampo, a scholar and scientist profoundly influenced by Rousseau and French utopian socialist thought, who was described by Justo Sierra as a "man of thought and action, agriculturalist, naturalist, economist, a public man from love of the public good, with no other ambition than that of doing something for his country." In Oaxaca a Zapotec Indian, Benito Juárez, became governor. Aided by a philanthropic creole, Juárez had worked his way through law school and established a law office in the city of Oaxaca. As governor, he gained a reputation for honesty, efficiency, and the democratic simplicity of his manners.

Ocampo and Juárez were two leaders of a renovated liberalism that ushered in the movement called *La Reforma*. Like the older liberalism of the 1830s, the Reforma sought to destroy feudal vestiges and implant capitalism in Mexico. Its ideology, however, was more spirited than the aristocratic, intellectual liberalism of Mora; and its puro left wing included a small number of figures, such as Ponciano Arriaga and Ignacio Ramírez, who rose above the general level of liberal ideology by their attacks on the latifundio, defense of labor and women's rights, and other advanced ideas.

The revived liberal ferment, with its demand for the abolition of fueros and secularization of church property, inspired alarm among the reactionary forces. They feared that the moderado regime of Mariano Arista, who became president in 1850, did not offer adequate insurance against radical change. In January 1853, a coalition of high clergy, generals, and great creole landowners, headed by the aged Alamán, organized a successful revolt against Arista and named Santa Anna, then living in Venezuela, dictator for one year. On his arrival in Mexico City on April 20, Santa Anna was formally proclaimed president.

For Alamán, the old dictator was merely a stopgap for an imported foreign prince. Alamán died on June 2, 1853, and with him died what intelligence and integrity remained in the conservative camp. Free from Alamán's restraining influence, Santa Anna returned to his familiar ways of graft and plunder, looting the public treasury for his own benefit and that of his sycophants. In December he had himself proclaimed perpetual dictator, with the title of His Most Supreme Highness.

Santa Anna's return to power, accompanied by a terrorist campaign against all dissenters, spurred a gathering of opposition forces, including many disgruntled moderados and conservatives. In early 1854, the old liberal caudillo from the state of Guerrero, Juan Álvarez, and the moderado general Ignacio Comonfort issued a call for revolt, the Plan of Ayutla, demanding the end of the dictatorship and the election of a convention to draft a new constitution. Within a year, Santa Anna's regime began to disintegrate, and in August 1855, seeing the handwriting on the wall, he went into exile for the last time. Some days later, a puro-dominated provisional government took office in Mexico City. The seventy-five-year-old Juan Álvarez was named provisional president; to his cabinet he named Benito Juárez as minister of justice and Miguel Lerdo de Tejada as minister of the treasury.

One of Juárez's first official acts was to issue a decree, the *Ley Juárez,* proclaiming the right of the state to limit the clerical and military fueros to matters of internal discipline. The decree raised a storm of conservative wrath, and Comonfort, now minister of war, himself disapproved of the measure. By December, moderado and conservative pressure, wielded through Comonfort, brought a shift to the right in the cabinet.

Melchor Ocampo, the most radical of the puros, was forced out, and a few days later Álvarez himself resigned, turning over the presidency to Comonfort, who proposed to steer a cautious middle course that he hoped would satisfy both liberals and conservatives.

The *Ley Lerdo* (Lerdo Law) of June 1856, drafted by Comonfort's minister of the treasury, Miguel Lerdo de Tejada, was poorly designed to achieve such a reconciliation, for it struck a heavy blow at the material base of the church's power, its landed wealth. The law barred the church from holding land not used for religious purposes and compelled the sale of all such property to tenants, with the rent considered to be 6 percent of the sale value of the property. Real estate not being rented was to be auctioned to the highest bidder, with payment of a large sales tax to the government.

The intent of the law was to create a rural middle class, but since it made no provision for division of the church estates, the bulk of the land passed into the hands of great landowners, merchants, and capitalists, both Mexican and foreign. What was worse, the law barred Indian villages from owning land and ordered that such land be sold in the same manner as church property, excepting only land and buildings used exclusively for the "public use" of the inhabitants and for communal pastures (*ejidos*). As a result, land-grabbers descended on the Indian villages, "denounced" their land to the local courts, and proceeded to buy it at auction for paltry sums. The law provided that the Indian owners should have the first opportunity to buy, but few Indians could pay the minimum purchase price. When the Indians responded with protests and revolts, Lerdo explained in a circular that the intent of his law was that Indian community lands should be divided among the natives, not sold to others. But he insisted that "the continued existence of the Indian communities ought not to be tolerated . . . , and this is exactly one of the goals of the law." He was also adamant on the right of those who rented Indian lands to buy them if they chose to do so. As a result, during the summer and fall of 1856 many Indian pueblos lost crop

and pasturelands from which they had derived revenues vitally needed to defray the cost of their religious ceremonies and other communal expenses. Indian resistance and the liberals' need to attract popular support during their struggle with the conservative counterrevolution and French interventionists in the decade 1857–1867 seem to have slowed enforcement of the Lerdo Law as it applied to Indian villages, but the long-range tendency of liberal agrarian policy was to compel division of communal lands, facilitating their acquisition by hacendados and even small and middle-sized farmers. The result was a simultaneous strengthening of the latifundio and some increase in the size of the rural middle class.[3]

While the provisional government was causing consternation among conservatives with the Ley Juárez and the Ley Lerdo, a constitutional convention dominated by moderate liberals had been completing its work. The constitution of 1857 proclaimed freedom of speech, press, and assembly; limited fueros; forbade ecclesiastical and civil corporations to own land; and proclaimed the sanctity of private property. It restored the federalist structure of 1824, with the same division of Mexico into states, but replaced the bicameral national legislature with a single house and eliminated the office of vice president (the chief justice of the Supreme Court should succeed if the office of president became vacant). An effort by the puro minority to incorporate freedom of religion in the constitution failed; the resulting compromise neither mentioned toleration nor explicitly adopted Catholicism as the official faith.

---

[3] In 1863, in order to finance the struggle against the French intervention, the liberal Juárez issued a decree that authorized the sale of *tierras baldías* (vacant lands) to which there was no valid title. Since the Indians often lacked titles that were regarded as valid, their lands were exposed to "denunciation" and purchase from the state by land-grabbing landlords and speculators. In four years, Juárez issued titles to nearly 4.5 million acres of land, further stimulating the spoliation of Indian lands and the growth of peonage.

A few voices were raised against the land monopoly, peonage, and the immense inequalities of wealth. "We proclaim ideas and forget realities," complained the radical delegate Ponciano Arriaga. "How can a hungry, naked, miserable people practice popular government? How can we condemn slavery in words, while the lot of most of our fellow citizens is more grievous than that of the black slaves of Cuba or the United States?" Despite his caustic attack on the land monopoly, Arriaga offered a relatively moderate solution: the state should seize and auction off large uncultivated estates. The conservative opposition promptly branded Arriaga's project "communist"; the moderate majority in the convention passed over it in silence.

Having completed its work, the convention disbanded and elections followed for the first Congress and president and the members of the Supreme Court. Comonfort, who had already expressed unhappiness with the constitution, was elected president, and Juárez chief justice of the Supreme Court.

Since the new constitution incorporated the Lerdo Law and the Juárez Law, the church now openly entered the political struggle by excommunicating all public officials who took the required oath of loyalty. Counterrevolution had been gathering its forces for months and found an instrument in the vacillating president Comonfort. In December 1857, General Félix Zuloaga "pronounced" in favor of a Comonfort dictatorship, occupied the capital, and arrested Juárez. Pressed by the reactionaries to repeal the Juárez and Lerdo laws, Comonfort refused and finally found the strength to break with his reactionary supporters. He released Juárez, declared the constitution re-established, and himself went into exile, unmolested by the victorious rebels. Meanwhile, the liberals in the provinces had raised an army; proclaiming that Comonfort had violated the constitution and ceased to be president, they declared Juárez president of Mexico. For their part, the conservatives, in control of Mexico City, Puebla, and other major cities, declared the constitution void and the Juárez and Lerdo laws repealed.

Benito Juárez. (Courtesy of the Organization of American States)

The tremendous Three Years' War (1857–1860) had begun. In regional terms, the war pitted the rich central area, dominated by the conservatives, against the liberal south, north, and Veracruz. Controlling extensive regions and enjoying the support of a clear majority of the population, the liberals nevertheless suffered serious defeats in the first stage of the war. The main reason was that most of the permanent army had gone over to the conservatives, while the liberals had to create their own armed forces. The liberal armies, composed of elements of the national guard and guerrilla bands, were at the outset inevitably inferior in discipline and equipment to the conservative troops, which won almost all the pitched battles. In March 1858, conservative troops occupied the important mining center of Guanajuato and approached Querétaro, the seat of Juárez's government. He was forced to move his headquarters, first to Guadalajara and later to Veracruz, which remained the liberal capital until the end of the war.

As the struggle progressed, both sides found themselves in serious financial difficulties. The conservatives, however, had the advantage of generous support from the church. In July 1859, Juárez struck back at the clergy with reform laws that nationalized without compensation all ecclesiastical property except church buildings; the laws also suppressed all monasteries, established freedom of religion, and separated church and state. The reform laws were designed to encourage peasant proprietorship by dividing church estates into small farms, but this goal proved illusory; thanks to the Ley Lerdo, wealthy purchasers had already acquired much of the church land.

By the middle of 1860, the tide of war had turned in favor of the liberals. In August 1860, the best conservative general, Miguel Miramón, was routed at Silao. In October, Guadalajara fell to the liberals. And by the beginning of January 1861, Juárez had re-entered the capital, and the conservative leaders had fled the country. The war was effectively over, although conservative bands in the provinces continued to make devastating raids.

Beaten in the field, the reactionaries looked for help abroad. The conservative governments of England, France, and Spain had no love for the Mexican liberals and their leader Juárez. Moreover, there were ample pretexts for intervention, for both sides had seized or destroyed foreign property without compensation, and foreign bondholders were clamoring for payments from an empty Mexican treasury. The three European powers demanded compensation for damages to their nationals and payment of just debts. Juárez vainly pleaded poverty and noted the dubious nature of some of the claims.

In October 1861, the three powers agreed on a joint intervention in Mexico, and in January 1862, they sent occupation forces to Veracruz. England and Spain, having received assurances of future satisfaction of their claims, soon withdrew, but the French government rejected all Mexican offers, and its troops remained. Napoleon III wanted more than payment of debts. A group of Mexican conservative exiles had convinced the ambitious emperor that the Mexican people would welcome a French army of liberation and the establishment of a monarchy. Napoleon had visions of a French-protected Mexican Empire that would yield him great political and economic advantages. It remained only to find a suitable unemployed prince, and one was found in the person of Archduke Ferdinand Maximilian of Hapsburg, brother of Austrian Emperor Franz Josef.

To prepare the ground for the arrival of the new ruler of Mexico, the French army advanced from Veracruz into the interior toward Puebla. At Puebla, instead of being received as liberators, the interventionists met determined resistance on the part of a poorly armed Mexican garrison and were thrown back with heavy losses. The date—May 5, 1862—is still celebrated as a Mexican national holiday. Reinforced by the arrival of thirty thousand fresh troops, General Elie-Frédéric Forey again besieged Puebla in March 1863, and by May 17 the starving garrison had been forced to surrender. The fall of Puebla and the loss of its garrison of some thirty thousand men left Juárez without an adequate force to defend the capital, and at the end of May his government and the remnants of his army abandoned it and retreated northward. On June 10, the French entered the city to the rejoicing of the clergy; by the end of the year the interventionists had occupied Querétaro, Monterrey, San Luis Potosí, and Saltillo. But the invaders had secure control only of the cities; republican guerrilla detachments controlled most of the national territory.

Meanwhile, in October 1863, a delegation of conservative exiles called on Maximilian to offer him a Mexican crown. As a condition of acceptance, the prince insisted that the Mexican people be consulted, and the French authorities obligingly staged a plebiscite that supposedly gave an overwhelming vote in favor of Maximilian. In April 1864, he accepted the Mexican throne and presently departed with his wife Carlota for their new home.

The conservative conspirators had counted on Maximilian to help them recover their lost wealth and privileges, but the emperor, mindful of realities, would not consent to their demands; the purchase of church lands by native and foreign landlords and capitalists had created new interests that Maximilian refused to antagonize. Confident of conservative support, Maximilian even wooed moderate liberals and won the support of such intellectual lights as the historians José Fernando Ramírez and Manuel Orozco y Berra. These scholars were impressed by Maximilian's good will and they cherished the illusion of a stable and prosperous Mexico ruled by an enlightened monarch.

But the hopes of both conservatives and misguided liberals were built on quicksand. The victories of Maximilian's generals could not destroy the fluid and elusive liberal resistance, firmly grounded in popular hatred for the invaders and aided by Mexico's geography (a rugged terrain with vast, thinly populated territories and few roads). A turning point in the war came in the spring of 1865 in the United States, with the Union triumph over the Confederacy. American demands that the French evacuate Mexico, a region regarded by Secretary of State William Seward as a U.S. zone of economic and political influence, grew more insistent, and American troops were massed along the Rio Grande. Facing serious domestic and diplomatic problems at home, Napoleon decided to cut his losses and liquidate the Mexican adventure.

Marshal Achille François Bazaine, preparing to embark with the remaining French troops, urged Maximilian to abdicate and leave Mexico, but his conservative advisers, who still believed that defeat could be avoided, prevailed on him to stay. With liberal armies converging on Querétaro, the same die-hard conservatives persuaded Maximilian to go there and assume supreme command. Together with the imperialist generals Miguel Miramón and Tomás Mejía, he was captured on May 14, 1867. After a trial by court-martial, all three were found guilty of treason, sentenced to death, and executed by a *Juarista* firing squad.

Postwar Attempts at Reconstruction and the Death of *La Reforma*

Juárez, symbol of the successful Mexican resistance to a foreign usurper, resumed his office of president in August 1867. His government inherited a devastated country. Agriculture and industry were in ruins; as late as 1873, the value of Mexican exports was below the level of 1810. To reduce the state's financial burdens and end the danger of military control, Juárez dismissed two-thirds of the army, an act that produced discontent and uprisings that his generals managed to suppress.

Juárez devoted a considerable part of the state's limited resources to the development of a public school system, especially on the elementary level; by 1874 there were about eight thousand schools with some three hundred and fifty thousand pupils. One of the few material achievements of his administration was the construction of an important railroad line running from Veracruz through Puebla to Mexico City, completed after his death in 1872.

In his agrarian policy, Juárez continued the liberal program of seeking to implant capitalism in the countryside, at the expense not of the hacienda but of the Indian communities. Indeed, the period of the "Restored Republic" (1868–1876) saw an intensified effort by the federal government to implement the Lerdo Law by compelling dissolution and partition of Indian communal lands, opening the way for a new wave of frauds and seizures by neighboring hacendados and other land-grabbers. The result was a series of nationwide peasant revolts, the most serious occurring in the state of Hidalgo (1869–1870). Proclaiming the rebels to be "communists," the hacendados, aided by state and federal authorities, restored order by the traditional violent methods. A few liberals raised their voices in protest, but were ignored; one was Ignacio Ramírez, who condemned the usurpations and frauds practiced by the hacendados with the complicity of corrupt judges and officials and called for suspension of the law. On the other hand, the period saw the first legislative efforts to improve labor conditions and the formation in the cities of numerous trade unions whose leaders combined liberal and trade unionist principles.

Re-elected president in 1871, Juárez was able to put down a revolt by a hero of the wars of the Reforma, General Porfirio Díaz, who charged Juárez with attempting to become a dictator. But Juárez died the next year of a heart attack and was succeeded as acting president by the chief justice of the Supreme Court, Sebastían Lerdo de Tejada. Lerdo scheduled new elections for October 1872, ran against, and easily defeated Díaz, but in turn faced a growing movement of opposition that accused him of violations of republican legality. When Lerdo announced in 1876 that he intended to seek re-election, Díaz again rose in revolt. Aided by a group of Texas capitalists with strong links to New York banks, who financed and armed his rebellion, he defeated troops loyal to Lerdo and sent him into flight.

Díaz had seized power in the name of the ideals of the Reforma. In fact, the year 1876 marked the death of the Reforma and the idealistic principles of natural law that formed its theoretical base. The age of Díaz continued the efforts of the Reforma to construct a bourgeois society, but with new men, new methods, and a new ideology. The libertarian creed to which Juárez subscribed, no matter how often he deviated from it, was replaced by the ideology of positivism as propounded by its French founder, Auguste Comte— ideology that ranked order and progress above freedom.

The Reforma had paved the way for this change by transforming the Mexican bourgeoisie from a revolutionary class into a ruling class that was more predatory and acquisitive than the old creole aristocracy. The remnants of that aristocracy speedily adapted to the ways of the new ruling class and merged with it. The interests of the old and the new rich required political stability, a docile labor force, internal improvements, and a political and economic climate favorable to foreign investments. The mission of the "honorable tyranny" of Porfirio Díaz was to achieve those ends.

Argentina

In 1816 delegates to the congress of Tucumán proclaimed the independence of the United Provinces of the Río de la Plata. "Disunited," however, would have better described the political condition of the area of La Plata, for the creole seizure of power in Buenos Aires in 1810 brought in its train a dissolution of the vast viceroyalty of the Río de la Plata.

The Liberation of Paraguay, Uruguay, and Upper Peru

Paraguay, having repelled efforts by the junta of Buenos Aires to "liberate" it, declared its own independence and fell under the dictatorial rule of the creole lawyer José Gaspar Rodríguez de Francia, who effectively sealed it off from its neighbors. Francia had his reasons for the system of isolation: the rulers of Buenos Aires controlled Paraguay's river outlets to the sea, and isolation and self-sufficiency were the alternatives to submission and payment of tribute to Buenos Aires. Francia did permit a limited licensed trade with the outside world by way of Brazil, chiefly to satisfy military needs.

Francia's state-controlled economy brought certain benefits: the planned diversification of agriculture, which reduced production of such export crops as yerba maté, tobacco, and sugar, insured a plentiful supply of foodstuffs and the well-being of the Indian and mestizo masses. An interesting feature of Francia's system was the establishment of state farms or ranches—called *estancias de la patria*—that successfully specialized in the raising of livestock and ended Paraguay's dependence on livestock imports from the Argentine province of Entre Ríos. The principal sufferers under Francia's dictatorship were Spaniards, many of whom he expelled or penalized in various ways, and creole aristocrats, who were kept under perpetual surveillance and subjected to severe repression.

Uruguay, then known as the Banda Oriental, was led toward independence by the gaucho chieftain José Gervasio Artigas, who resisted the efforts of the junta of Buenos Aires to dominate the area. In 1815 the junta abandoned these efforts, evacuated Montevideo, and turned it over to Artigas. No ordinary caudillo, Artigas not only defended Uruguayan nationality but sought to achieve social reform. In 1815 he issued a plan for distributing royalist lands to the landless, with preference shown to blacks, Indians, zambos, and poor whites. But he was not given the opportunity to implement this radical program. In 1817 a powerful Brazilian army invaded Uruguay and soon had a secure grip on the Banda Oriental. Artigas had to flee across the Paraná River into Paraguay. He received asylum from Francia but was never allowed to leave again; he died in Paraguay thirty years later.

Soon Uruguay again became a battlefield when a small group of Uruguayan exiles, supported by Buenos Aires, crossed over the estuary in 1825 and launched a general revolt against Brazilian domination. Brazil retaliated by declaring war against the United Provinces. The three-sided military conflict ended in a stalemate. Uruguay finally achieved independence in 1828 through the mediation of Great Britain, which was unwilling to see Uruguay fall under the control of either of its more powerful neighbors.

Upper Peru, the mountainous northern corner of the old viceroyalty of La Plata, also escaped the grasp of Buenos Aires after 1810. Three expeditions were sent into the high country, won initial victories, then were rolled back by Spanish counteroffensives. Logistical problems, the apathy of the Indian population, and the hostility of the creole aristocracy, which remained loyal to Spain until it became clear that the royalist cause was doomed, contributed to the patriot defeats. Not until 1825 was Upper Peru liberated by General Antonio José de Sucre, Bolívar's lieutenant.

Renamed Bolivia in honor of the liberator, it began its independent life the next year under a complicated, totally impractical constitution drafted by Bolívar himself.

The Struggle for Progress and National Unity

Even among the provinces that had joined at Tucumán to form the United Provinces of La Plata, discord grew and threatened the dissolution of the new state. The efforts of the wealthy port and province of Buenos Aires to impose its hegemony over the interior met with tenacious resistance. The end of the Spanish trade monopoly brought large gains to Buenos Aires and lesser gains to the littoral provinces of Santa Fe, Entre Ríos, and Corrientes; their exports of meat and hides increased, and the value of their lands rose. But the wine and textile industries of the interior, which had been protected by the colonial monopoly, suffered from the competition of cheaper and superior European wares imported through the port of Buenos Aires.

The interests of the interior provinces required a measure of autonomy or even independence in order to protect their primitive industries, but Buenos Aires preferred a single free-trade zone under a government dominated by the port city. This was one cause of the conflict between Argentine *federales* (federalists) and *unitarios* (unitarians). By 1820 the federalist solution had triumphed; the United Provinces had in effect dissolved into a number of independent republics, with the interior provinces ruled by caudillos, each representing the local ruling class and having a gaucho army behind him.

A new start toward unity came with the appointment in 1821 of Bernardino Rivadavia as chief minister under Martín Rodríguez, governor of the province of Buenos Aires. An ardent liberal, strongly influenced by the English philosopher Jeremy Bentham, Rivadavia launched an ambitious program of educational, social, and economic reform. He promoted primary education, founded the University of Buenos Aires, abolished the ecclesiastical fuero and the tithe, and suppressed some monasteries. Rivadavia envisioned a balanced development of industry and agriculture, with a large role assigned to British investment and colonization. But the obstacles in the way of industrialization proved too great, and little came of efforts in this direction. The greatest progress was made in cattle raising, which expanded rapidly southward into former Indian territory.

In 1822, hoping to raise revenue and increase production, Rivadavia introduced the system of emphyteusis, a program of distribution of public lands through long-term leases at fixed rentals. Some writers have seen in this system an effort at agrarian reform, but there were no limits on the size of grants, and the measure actually contributed to the growth of latifundia. The lure of large profits in livestock raising induced many native and foreign merchants, politicians, and members of the military to join the rush for land. The net result was the creation not of a small-farmer class but of a new and more powerful *estanciero* class that was the enemy of Rivadavia's progressive ideals.

Rivadavia's planning went beyond the province of Buenos Aires; he had a vision of a unified Argentina under a strong central government that would promote the rounded economic development of the whole national territory. In 1825 a constituent congress met in Buenos Aires at Rivadavia's call to draft a constitution for the United Provinces of the Río de la Plata. Rivadavia, who was elected president of the new state, made a dramatic proposal to federalize the city and port of Buenos Aires. The former capital of the province would henceforth belong to the whole nation, with the revenues of its customhouse to be used to advance the general welfare.

Rivadavia's proposal reflected his nationalism and the need to mobilize national resources for a war with Brazil (1825–1828) over Uruguay. Congress approved Rivadavia's project, but the federalist caudillos of the interior, fearing that the rise of a strong national government would mean the end of their power, refused to ratify the constitution and even withdrew their delegates from the congress. In Buenos Aires a similar stand was taken by the powerful estancieros, who had no intention of surrendering the privileges of their province and regarded Rivadavia's program of social and economic reform as a costly folly.

Defeated on the issue of the constitution, Rivadavia suffered a further loss of prestige when his agent signed a peace treaty with Brazil recognizing Uruguay as a province of the Brazilian Empire. Rivadavia rejected the treaty, but popular anger at the agreement combined with opposition to his domestic program had sealed his political doom. In July 1827, he resigned the presidency and went into exile. The liberal program for achieving national unity had failed.

After an interval of factional struggles, the federalism espoused by the landed oligarchy of Buenos Aires triumphed in the person of Juan Manuel Rosas, who became governor of the province in 1829. Under his influence there was forged (1831) a federal pact under which Buenos Aires assumed representation for the other provinces in foreign affairs but left them free to run their own affairs in all other respects. Federalism, as defined by Rosas, meant that Buenos Aires retained the revenues of its customhouse for its exclusive use and controlled trade on the Río de la Plata system for the benefit of its merchants. A network of personal alliances between Rosas and provincial caudillos, backed by use of force against recalcitrant leaders, insured for him a large measure of control over the interior.

Rosas' long reign saw a total reversal of Rivadavia's progressive policies. For Rosas and the ruling class of estancieros, virtually the only economic concern was the export of hides and salted meat and the import of foreign goods. The dictator also showed some favor to wheat farming, which he protected by tariff laws, but he neglected artisans and machine industry. Rosas himself was a great estanciero and owner of a saladero (salting plant) that enjoyed a monopoly on the curing of meat and hides. He vigorously pressed the conquest of Indian territory, bringing much new land under the control of the province of Buenos Aires; this land was sold for low prices to estancieros, and Rivadavia's policy of retaining ownership of land by the state was abandoned. Rosas also discarded Rivadavia's policy of promoting immigration and education. Rosas handed over what schools remained to the Jesuits, who were recalled from exile in 1836 (ultimately, Rosas found the order too independent and expelled it).

By degrees, the press and all other potential dissidents were cowed or destroyed. To enforce the dictator's will there arose a secret organization known as the *Mazorca* (ear of corn—a reference to the close unity of its members). In collaboration with the police, this terrorist organization beat up or even murdered Rosas' opponents. The masthead of the official journal and all official papers carried the slogan "Death to the savage, filthy unitarians!" Even horses had to display the red ribbon that was the federalist symbol. Those opponents who did not knuckle under and escaped death fled by the thousands to Montevideo, Chile, Brazil, or other places of refuge.

Under Rosas, the merchants of the city and the estancieros of the province of Buenos Aires enjoyed a measure of prosperity, although an Anglo-French blockade of the estuary of La Plata from 1845 to 1848, caused by Rosas' mistreatment of English and French nationals and his efforts to subvert Uruguayan independence, resulted in severe losses to both groups. But this prosperity bore no proportion to the possibilities of economic growth; technical backwardness marked all aspects of livestock raising and agriculture, and port facilities were totally inadequate.

Meanwhile, the littoral provinces, which had experienced some advance of livestock raising and agriculture, became increasingly aware that Rosas' brand of federalism was harmful to their interests and that free navigation of the river system of La Plata was necessary to assure their prosperity. In 1852 the anti-Rosas forces formed a coalition that united the liberal émigrés with the caudillo Justo José de Urquiza of Entre Ríos, who was joined by the great majority of the pro-

vincial caudillos, and Brazil and Uruguay. At Monte Caseros, their combined forces defeated Rosas' army and sent him fleeing to an English exile.

Victory over Rosas did not end the dispute between Buenos Aires and the other provinces, between federalism and unitarianism. Only the slower process of economic change would forge the desired unity. A rift soon arose between the liberal exiles who assumed leadership in Buenos Aires and the caudillo Urquiza of Entre Ríos, who was backed by his victorious army. Urquiza, who still sported the red ribbon of federalism, proposed a loose union of the provinces, with all of them sharing the revenues of the Buenos Aires customhouse. But the leaders of Buenos Aires feared the loss of their economic and political predominance to Urquiza, whom they wrongly considered a caudillo of the Rosas type; in fact, Urquiza was a sincere convert to the gospel of modernity and progress.

Within the province of Buenos Aires, opinions were divided. Some favored entry into a new confederation but with very precise guarantees of the interests of their province; others argued for total separation from the other thirteen provinces. After Urquiza had unsuccessfully attempted to make Buenos Aires accept unification by armed force, the two sides agreed to a peaceful separation. As a result, delegates from Buenos Aires were absent from the constitutional convention that met at Santa Fe in Entre Ríos in 1852.

The constitution of 1853 reflected the influence of the ideas of the journalist Juan Bautista Alberdi on the delegates. His forcefully written pamphlet, *Bases and Points of Departure for the Political Organization of the Argentine Republic,* offered the United States as a model for Argentina. The new constitution strongly resembled that of the United States in certain respects. The former United Provinces became a federal republic, presided over by a president with significant power who served a six-year term without the possibility of immediate re-election. Legislative functions were vested in a bicameral legislature, a senate and a house of representatives. The

Catholic religion was proclaimed the official religion of the nation, but freedom of worship for non-Catholics was assured. The states were empowered to elect governors and legislatures and frame their own constitutions, but the federal government had the right of intervention—including armed intervention—to insure respect for the provisions of the constitution. General Urquiza was elected the first president of the Argentine Republic.

The liberal leaders of Buenos Aires, joined by the conservative estancieros who had been Rosas' firmest supporters, refused to accept the constitution of 1853, for they feared the creation of a state they did not control. As a result, two Argentinas arose: the Argentine Confederation, headed by Urquiza, and the province of Buenos Aires. For five years, the two states maintained their separate existence. In Paraná, capital of the confederation, Urquiza struggled to repress gaucho revolts, stimulate economic development, and foster education and immigration. Modest advances were made, but the tempo of growth lagged far behind that of the wealthy city and province of Buenos Aires, which prospered on the base of a steadily increasing trade with Europe in hides, tallow, salted beef, and wool.

Hoping to increase the confederation's scanty revenues, Urquiza began a tariff war with Buenos Aires, levying surcharges on goods landed at the Paraná River port of Rosario if duties had been paid on them at Buenos Aires. Buenos Aires responded with sanctions against ships sailing to Rosario and threatened to close commerce on the Paraná altogether. In 1859 war between the two Argentine states broke out. Defeated at the battle of Cepeda, Bartolomé Mitre, the commander of the Buenos Aires forces, accepted a compromise whereby Buenos Aires would join the confederation after a constitutional reform that protected its special interests. But the peace was short-lived; war broke out again in the presidency of Santiago Derqui, Urquiza's successor and personal rival. In the decisive battle of Pavón (1861), in which Mitre, now governor of the provinces of Buenos Aires, commanded the Buenos

Aires army, the forces of the confederation, led by Urquiza, suffered defeat.

The military and economic superiority of Buenos Aires, the need of the other provinces to use its port, and an awareness on all sides of the urgent need to achieve national unity dictated a compromise. At a congress representing all the provinces, held at Buenos Aires in 1862, it was agreed over the opposition of a die-hard group of Buenos Aires federalists that the city should be the provisional capital of both the Argentine Republic and the province and that the Buenos Aires customhouse should be nationalized, with the proviso that for a period of five years the revenues of the province would not fall below the 1859 level. In conformity with decisions of the congress, elections to choose the first president of a united Argentina were held the same year, and Bartolomé Mitre—distinguished historian, poet, soldier, and statesman—was elected president for a six-year term.

Mitre's term of office saw continued economic progress and consolidation of national unity. The customhouse was nationalized, as had been promised, and plans were made for the federalization of the capital. The construction of railways and telegraph lines that would forge closer links between Buenos Aires and the interior had begun, and European immigrants arrived in growing numbers. Some advances were made in the establishment of a public school system. But great problems remained. The shadow of the provincial caudillo continued to fall on the Argentine Republic; in the north, a revolt by one of Rosas' old allies had to be put down by armed force. The most difficult problem Mitre had to deal with, however, was the long, exhausting Paraguayan War (1865–1870).

The Paraguayan War

On the death of the dictator Francia in 1840, power in Paraguay was assumed by a triumvirate in which Carlos Antonio López soon emerged as the dominant figure. In essence, López continued Francia's dictatorial system but gave it a thin disguise of constitutional, representative government. Since he had inherited a stable, prosperous state, López could afford to rule in a less repressive fashion than his predecessor. More flexible than Francia, too, with a better understanding of the outside world, López made a successful effort to end Paraguay's diplomatic and commercial isolation. After the fall of Rosas, a stubborn enemy of Paraguayan independence, López obtained Argentine recognition of his country's independence, and the Paraná was at last opened to Paraguayan trade. López also established diplomatic relations with a series of countries, including England, France, and the United States. A special diplomatic mission to Europe, headed by his son, Francisco Solano López, also made important economic and cultural contacts, placing orders for ship construction, and inviting specialists to work in Paraguay.

The end of the policy of isolation was accompanied by a major expansion of the Paraguayan economy. Although agriculture (especially the production of such export crops as tobacco and yerba maté) continued to be the principal economic activity, López assigned great importance to the development of industry. One of his proudest achievements in this field was the construction of an iron foundry, the most modern enterprise of its type in Latin America. Transportation was improved with the building of roads and canals, the creation of a fleet of merchant ships, and the construction of a short railroad line.

Continuing Francia's policy, López enlarged the role of the state sector in the national economy. In 1848 he transferred to state ownership forest lands producing yerba maté and other commercial wood products and much arable land. The lucrative export trade in yerba maté and some other products became a government monopoly, and the number of state-owned ranches rose to sixty-four. López promoted education as well as economic growth; by the time of his death, Paraguay had 435 elementary schools with some 25,000 pupils, and a larger proportion of literate inhabitants than any other Latin American country.

At the same time, López took advantage of his position to concentrate ownership of land and various commercial enterprises in his own hands and those of his children, relatives, and associates; thus, there arose a bourgeoisie that profited by its close connection with the state apparatus, which enabled it to promote its own interests. The number of large private estates, however, was small; the private agricultural sector was dominated by small or medium-sized farms cultivated by owners or tenants, sometimes aided by a few hired laborers. By contrast with the situation in other Latin American countries, peonage and debt servitude were rare (slavery had been put in the way of extinction by a gradual manumission law in 1842). The relative absence of peonage and feudal survivals contributed to a rapid growth of Paraguayan capitalism and the well-being of its predominantly Indian and mestizo population. When López died in 1862, Paraguay was one of the most progressive and prosperous states in South America.

His son, Francisco Solano, whom López designated his heir apparent when his death approached, succeeded his father as dictator. The younger López inherited a tradition of border disputes with Brazil that erupted into open war when Brazil sent an army into Uruguay in 1864 to insure the victory of a pro-Brazilian faction in that country's civil strife. López could not be indifferent to this action, which threatened the delicate balance of power in the basin of La Plata. López also feared that Brazilian control over Uruguay would end unrestricted Paraguayan access to the port of Montevideo, which would make Paraguayan trade dependent entirely on the good will of Buenos Aires.

When the Brazilian government disregarded his protests, López sent an army to invade the Brazilian province of Mato Grosso, but this foray into virtually empty territory had no military significance, and he soon withdrew his troops. Hoping to strike a more effective blow at Brazil, López requested President Mitre's permission in January 1865 to cross Argentine territory (the state of Corrientes) en route to Uruguay. López regarded Mitre's refusal as an unfriendly act. In March 1865, the Paraguayan congress declared war on Argentina, and Paraguayan troops occupied the town of Corrientes. On May 1, 1865, Brazil, Argentina, and the Brazilian-sponsored Flores regime in Uruguay concluded a Triple Alliance against Paraguay; a separate secret treaty between Brazil and Argentina provided for the partition of more than half of Paraguay's territory between them. Mitre was named commander in chief of the allied forces. Paraguay thus faced a coalition that included the two largest states in South America, with an immense superiority in manpower and other resources.

Yet the war dragged on for five years, for at its outset Paraguay possessed an army of some 70,000 well-armed and disciplined soldiers that outnumbered the combined forces of its foes. Expelled from the territory that had overrun in Argentina and Brazil, the Paraguayan troops stubbornly defended themselves against the allied forces that crossed the Paraná into Paraguay in mid-April 1866. In August 1868, Fort Humaitá was stormed by Brazilian troops under Marshal Luis Alves de Lima Caxias, at the cost of two thousand men. In January 1869, the allies occupied Asunción. Retreating northward, López attempted to organize a new defense against overwhelming numerical odds. The end came on March 1, 1870. With a few followers, López made his last stand at a point near the Brazilian border. López was slain by a Brazilian soldier. With his death, effective Paraguayan resistance ended.

For Paraguay the war's consequences were tragic. Perhaps as many as 20 percent of the prewar population of some 300,000 perished as a result of military action, famine, disease, and a devastating Brazilian occupation. The peace treaty assigned much Paraguayan territory to the victors and burdened Paraguay with extremely heavy reparations. Brazil, the occupying power, installed a puppet regime composed of former López generals, who began a radical reconstruction of the Paraguayan economy and state. The essence of the new policy was to liquidate the progressive changes made under the Francia and López regimes. Most of the state-owned lands were sold to land speculators and foreign businessmen at bargain prices, with no restriction on the size of holdings. Tenants who could not present the necessary documents were ejected even though they and their forebears had cultivated the land for decades. By the early 1890s, the state-owned lands were almost gone. Foreign penetration of the economy through loans, concessions, and land purchases soon deprived Paraguay of its economic as well as its political independence.

The Paraguayan War caused increased taxes and other hardships; for these reasons, it was unpopular in Argentina. The burdens of the war revived the dying spirit of provincial separatism and compelled Mitre to leave the front to direct the suppression of revolts in different provinces. By 1867 these domestic difficulties had virtually taken Argentina out of the war; when it ended, however, Argentina obtained its share of Paraguayan reparations and territorial concessions (Formosa, Chaco, and Misiones).

Progress and Development Under Sarmiento

At the close of his presidential term, Mitre returned to civilian life. He was succeeded by Domingo Faustino Sarmiento (1868–1874), a gifted essayist, sociologist, and statesman, former Argentine minister to the United States, and an enthusiast for its institutions. Like Mitre, Sarmiento worked for Argentine unity and economic and social progress.

After the Paraguayan War, a flood of technological change began to sweep over Argentina. Railways penetrated the interior, extending the stock-raising and farming area. The gradual introduction of barbed-wire fencing and alfalfa ranges made possible a dramatic improvement in the quality of livestock. In 1876 the arrival of an experimental shipload of chilled carcasses from France prepared the way for the triumph of frozen over salted meat, which led to a vast expansion of European demand for Argentine beef. Labor was needed to exploit the rapidly expanding pasturelands and farmlands; during Sarmiento's administration alone, some three hundred thousand immigrants poured into the country. But Sarmiento taught that it was not enough to build railroads and expand acreage; it was necessary to change people's minds. Believing in the need for an educated citizenry in a democratic republic, he labored to expand and improve the public school system; to this end he introduced to Argentina teacher-training institutions of the kind his friend Horace Mann had founded in the United States.

When Sarmiento left office, Argentina presented the appearance of a rapidly developing, prosperous state. But there were clouds in the generally bright Argentine sky. The growth of exports and the rise in land values did not benefit the forlorn gauchos, aliens in a land over which they had once freely roamed, or the majority of European immigrants. Little was done to provide these newcomers with homesteads. Immigrants who wished to farm usually found the price of land out of reach; as a result, many preferred to remain in Buenos Aires or other cities of the littoral, where they began to form an urban middle class largely devoted to trade. Meanwhile, foreign economic influence grew as a result of increasing dependence on foreign—chiefly British—capital to finance the construction of railways, telegraph lines, gasworks, and other needed facilities. The growing concentration of landownership reinforced the colonial land tenure pattern; the tightening British control of markets and the country's economic infrastructure reinforced the colonial pattern of dependence on a foreign metropolis, with London replacing Seville as commercial center. But Mitre, Sarmiento, and other builders of the new Argentina were dazzled by their success in nation-building and by a climate of prosperity they believed permanent. These men did not suspect the extent of the problems that were in the making nor did they anticipate what problems future generations of Argentines would have to attempt to solve.

Chile

The victories of José de San Martín's Army of the Andes over royalist forces at Chacabuco and Maipú in 1817 and 1818 gave Chile its definitive independence. From 1818 until 1823, Bernardo O'Higgins, a hero of the struggle for Chilean liberation and a true son of the Enlightenment, ruled the country with the title of supreme director. O'Higgins energetically pushed a program of reform designed to weaken the landed aristocracy and the church and promote a rapid development of the Chilean economy along capitalist lines. His abolition of titles of nobility and entails angered the great landowners of the fertile Central Valley between the Andes and the Pacific; his expulsion of the royalist bishop of Santiago and his restrictions on the number of religious processions and the veneration of images infuriated the church. The opposition to O'Higgins was joined by dissident liberals who resented his sometimes heavy-handed rule. In 1823 O'Higgins resigned and went into exile in Lima. There followed seven turbulent years, with presidents and constitutions rising and falling.

Portales and Economic Growth

In Chile, as in other Latin American countries, the political and armed struggle gradually assumed the form of a conflict between conservatives, who usually were also centralists, and liberals, who were generally federalists. The conservative-centralists were the party of the great landowners of the Central Valley and the wealthy merchants of Santiago; the liberal-federalists spoke for the landowners, merchants, and artisans of the northern and southern provinces, who were resentful of political and economic domination by the wealthy central area. The victory of the conservative General Joaquín Prieto over the liberal General Ramón Freire in the decisive battle of Lircay (1830) brought to power a government headed by Prieto as president but dominated by one of his cabinet ministers, Diego Portales.

From 1830 until his death in 1837, Portales, who never held an elective office, placed the enduring stamp of his ideas on Chilean politics and society. A businessman of aristocratic origins, owner of a successful import house, he faithfully served the interests of an oligarchy of great landlords and merchants that dominated the Chilean scene for decades. Although Portales expressed atheist views in private, he supported the authority of the church as an instrument for keeping the lower classes in order. He understood the importance of trade, industry, and mining and promoted their interests. Assisted by his able finance minister, Manuel Rengifo, Portales continued the work of O'Higgins, removing remaining obstacles to internal trade. He introduced income and property taxes to increase the state's revenues and trimmed government spending by dismissing unnecessary employees. Agriculture was protected by high tariffs on agricultural imports. Port facilities were improved, measures were taken to strengthen the Chilean merchant marine, and in 1835 a steamship line began to connect the Chilean ports. Under the fostering care of the conservative regime and in response to a growing European demand for Chilean silver, copper, and hides, the national economy made steady progress in the 1830s.

Measures designed to stimulate economic growth were accompanied by others that fortified the social and political power of the oligarchy. In order to tighten the bond between the conservative government and the church, Portales restored the privileges the church had lost under liberal rule and normalized the troubled relations between Chile and the papacy.

In 1833 a conservative-dominated assembly adopted a constitution that further consolidated the power of the oligarchy. Elections were made indirect, with the suffrage limited to men of twenty-five years or over who could satisfy literacy and property qualifications. Still higher property qualifications were required of members of the lower and upper houses. The constitution restored entails, insuring perpetuation of the latifundio. Catholicism was declared the state religion, and the church was given control over marriage. The president enjoyed an absolute veto over congressional legislation, appointed all high officials, and could proclaim a state of siege. The process of amending the constitution was made so difficult as to be virtually impossible. Since the president controlled the electoral machinery, the outcome of elections was a foregone conclusion. In 1836, Prieto was re-elected president for a second five-year term.

Realizing the futility of legal opposition to the conservative dictatorship, many liberals boycotted the election and later took to arms. This revolt, led by General Freire, was quickly crushed, and Freire was exiled to Australia. The Freire revolt had been organized in Peru, and this fact added to the tensions created by a tariff war between Peru and Chile. Relations between the two countries deteriorated further in 1836 as a result of the formation of a Peruvian-Bolivian confederation under the auspices of the ambitious Bolivian president, Andrés Santa Cruz. Portales saw in this union a threat to Chile's northern borders and obtained a congressional declaration of war on Peru in November 1836. The war lasted three years; it ended with a Chilean victory and dissolution of the confederation. Meanwhile, however, Portales had caused much resentment at home by his highhanded use of the extraordinary powers vested in him in wartime to arrest and jail all critics of the war. In June 1837, mutinous troops seized Portales and killed him before loyal troops could gain his release.

Recovery Under Bulnes

In 1841, Prieto was succeeded in the presidency by General Manuel Bulnes, who was re-elected to a second five-year term in 1846. Victorious at home and abroad, the conservative leadership decided it could relax the strict discipline of the Portales period. Chile's economic life quickly recovered from the strains caused by the war of 1836–1839 and began a renewed advance. Commerce, mining, and agriculture prospered as never before. The Crimean War and the gold rushes to California and Australia of the 1850s created large new markets for Chilean wheat, stimulating a considerable expansion of the cultivated area. In 1840 a North American, William Wheelright, established a steamship line to operate on the Chilean coasts, using coal from newly developed hard coal mines. Wheelright also founded a company that in 1852 completed Chile's first railroad line, providing an outlet to the sea for the production of the mining district of Copiapó. The major Santiago-Valparaíso line, begun in 1852, was not completed until 1863. Foreign—especially British—capital began to penetrate the Chilean economy; it dominated foreign trade and had a large interest in mining and railroads, but national capitalists constituted an important, vigorous group and displayed much initiative in the formation of joint stock companies and banks.

The great landowners were the principal beneficiaries of this economic upsurge; their lands appreciated in value without any effort on their part. Some great landowners invested their money in railroads, mining, and trade. But the essential conservatism of the landed aristocracy and the urge to preserve a semifeudal control over its peons discouraged the transformation of the great landowners into capitalist farmers. A pattern of small landholdings arose in southern Chile, to which German as well as Chilean colonists came in increasing numbers in the 1840s and 1850s. The rich Central Valley, still dominated by the latifundio, reflected inefficient techniques and reliance on the labor of *inquilinos*— tenants who also had to work the master's fields. Thus, alongside an emerging capitalist sector based on mining, trade, banking, intensive agriculture, and some industry, there existed a semifeudal sector based on the latifundio, peonage, and an aristocracy that hindered the development of Chilean capitalism.

Yet Chile at this period presented a more progressive aspect than most other Latin American states. President Bulnes continued the law-and-order system initiated by Portales but tempered its authoritarian rigor. His minister of justice and

instruction, Manuel Montt, established a system of public instruction that included the humanities and technical subjects. In 1842 the University of Chile was founded. Its first rector was the distinguished Venezuelan poet, scholar, and educator Andrés Bello, who helped to train a whole generation of Chilean intellectuals.

One of Bello's disciples was José Victorino Lastarria, historian, sociologist, and a deputy of the Liberal party, which he helped to revive. Dissatisfied with the modest concessions to modernity of the new conservatives, liberals like Lastarria wanted to accelerate the rate of change. They demanded radical revision of the constitution of 1833 and an end to oligarchical rule.

To the left of Lastarria stood the firebrand Francisco Bilbao, author of a scorching attack on the church and the Hispanic heritage, "The Nature of Chilean Society" (1844). Later, he spent several years in France and was profoundly influenced by utopian socialist and radical republican thought. He returned to Chile in 1850 to found, with Santiago Arcos, the Society of Equality, which advocated these advanced ideas. The society carried on an intensive antigovernmental campaign and within a few months had a membership of four thousand.

Montt's Moderate Reforms

The Society of Equality was founded on the eve of the election of 1850, for which President Bulnes had designated Manuel Montt his heir. Despite Montt's progressive educational policies and patronship of the arts and letters, liberals identified him with the repressive system of Portales and the constitution of 1833. Liberals like Lastarria and radical democrats like Bilbao proclaimed the impending election a fraud and demanded constitutional reforms. The government responded by proclaiming a state of siege and suppressing the Society of Equality. Regarding these acts as a prelude to an attempt to liquidate the opposition, groups of liberals in Santiago and La Serena rose in revolts that were quickly crushed. Lastarria was exiled; Bilbao and Arcos fled to Argentina. The conservatives easily elected their candidate; like his predecessor, he served two terms (1851–1861). In the wake of the election, however, the liberals again rose in a large-scale revolt that Montt crushed with a heavy loss of life. Montt had triumphed but immediately took steps to resolve the crisis by granting amnesty to the insurgents; he went on to make concessions to the spirit of the times with two important reforms: the abolition of entails and the tithe.

The abolition of entails, which was designed to encourage the breakup of landed estates among the children of the great landowners, affected a dwindling number of great aristocratic clans. Its effects were less drastic than the anguished cries of the affected parties suggested, for the divided estates were almost invariably acquired by other latifundists, and the condition of the inquilinos who worked the land remained the same. The elimination of the tithe, and Montt's refusal to allow the return of the Jesuits, greatly angered the reactionary clergy. Responding to their attacks, Montt promulgated a new civil code in 1857 that placed education under state control, gave the state jurisdiction over the clergy, and granted non-Catholics the right of civil marriage.

The abolition of entails and the tithe represented a compromise between liberals and conservatives, between the new bourgeoisie and the great landowners. In the process, the bourgeoisie gained little, and the landowners lost almost nothing; the chief loser was the church. Montt's reforms alienated the most reactionary elements of the Conservative party; in Congress these elements combined into a conservative-clerical bloc that formed the right-wing opposition to the government. On the other hand, his reforms gained Montt the support of moderate liberals while he retained the loyalty of the majority of moderate conservatives. In the 1850s, this coalition of moderate liberals and conservatives took the name of the National party. Its motto was the typically positivist slogan "Freedom in Order."

The radical liberals, however, continued to demand the repeal of the constitution of 1833. A leading spokesman for the left wing of the Liberal party was the brilliant historian Benjamín Vicuña Mackenna, who founded a newspaper in 1858 in which he hammered away at the need for drastic political and social change. The government shut the newspaper down and Vicuña Mackenna was exiled.

In the last years of his second term, President Montt faced severe economic and political problems. The depression of 1857 caused a sharp fall in the price of copper and reduced Australian and Californian demand for Chilean wheat. The economic decline fed the fires of political discontent. Montt had designated his energetic and influential cabinet minister, Antonio Varas, to succeed him in 1861. But the radical liberals disliked Varas for his stern suppression of dissidents, while clerical conservatives associated him with Montt's attacks on the church's privileges. Agitation against Varas's candidacy erupted into armed revolt in several Chilean cities in January 1859. Montt managed to quell the revolt, but his political position had been seriously weakened. Hoping to avoid new storms, Montt allowed Varas to withdraw his candidacy and supported a new candidate, José Joaquín Pérez, who was acceptable to moderate liberals and many conservatives. He easily won election as the candidate of the National party but formed a coalition government composed of Nationals, conservatives, and liberals. He served the customary two terms (1861–1871).

By 1861 the depression had lifted, and another boom began, creating new fortunes and bringing large shifts of regional influence. A growing stream of settlers, including many Germans, flowed into southern Chile, founding cities and transforming woodlands into farms.

But Chile's true center of economic gravity became the desert north, rich in copper, nitrates, and guano; the last two, in particular, were objects of Europe's insatiable demand for fertilizers. The major nitrate deposits, however, lay in the Bolivian province of Antofagasta and the Peruvian province of Tarapacá. Chilean capital, supplemented by English and German capital, began to pour into these regions and soon dominated the Peruvian and Bolivian nitrate industries. In the north there arose an aggressive mining capitalist class that demanded a place in the sun for itself and its region. A rich mine owner, Pedro León Gallo, abandoned the liberals to form a new party, called Radical, that fought more militantly than the liberals for constitutional changes, religious toleration, and an end to repressive policies. Under Pérez, liberals and Radicals combined to secure reforms that included toleration for non-Catholics, a curtailment of presidential powers, and a ban on immediate presidential reelection.

Liberal Control

The transition of Chile's political life to liberal control, begun under Montt, was completed in 1871 with the election of the first liberal president, Federico Errázuriz Zañartú. Between 1873 and 1875, a coalition of liberals and Radicals pushed through Congress a series of constitutional reforms: reduction of senatorial terms from nine to six years; direct election of senators; and freedom of speech, press, and assembly. These victories for enlightenment also represented a victory of new capitalist groups over the old merchant-landowner oligarchy that traced its beginnings back to colonial times. By 1880, of the fifty-nine Chilean personal fortunes of over 1 million pesos, only twenty-four were of colonial origin and only twenty had made their fortunes in agriculture; the rest belonged to coal, nitrate, copper, and silver interests or to merchants whose wealth had been formed only in the nineteenth century. Arnold Bauer has observed that the more interesting point is "not that only twenty made their fortune in agriculture, but that the remaining thirty-nine—designated as miners, bankers, and capitalists—subsequently invested their earnings in rural estates. This would be comparable to Andrew Carnegie sinking his steel income into Scarlett O'Hara's plantation." Bauer's comment points to the "powerful social model" that the Chilean agrarian oligarchy continued to

exert. For the rest, the victories of the new bourgeoisie brought no relief to the Chilean masses, the migrant laborers and tenant farmers on the haciendas, and the young working class in Chile's mines and factories.

Brazil

Dom Pedro, Emperor

Brazil took its first major step toward independence in 1808, when the Portuguese crown and court, fleeing before a French invasion of Portugal, arrived in Rio de Janeiro to make it the new capital of the Portuguese Empire. Full national sovereignty came in 1822, when Dom Pedro, who ruled Brazil as regent for his father, João VI, rejected a demand that he return to Portugal and issued the famous Cry of Ipiranga: "Independence or Death!" Dom Pedro acted with the advice and support of the Brazilian aristocracy, determined to preserve the autonomy Brazil had enjoyed since 1808. It was equally determined to make a transition to independence without the violence that marked the Spanish-American movement of liberation. The Brazilian aristocracy had its wish; Brazil made a transition to independence with comparatively little disruption and bloodshed. But separation from Portugal with a minimum of internal dislocation meant that independent Brazil retained not only monarchy and slavery but such other colonial features as the large landed estate and monoculture; a wasteful, inefficient agricultural system; a highly stratified society; and a free population that was 90 percent illiterate and prejudiced against manual labor.

Dom Pedro had promised to give his subjects a constitution, but the constituent assembly that he summoned in 1823 drafted a document that seemed to the emperor to place excessive limits on his power. He responded by dissolving the assembly and assigning to a hand-picked commission the making of a new constitution, which he approved and promulgated by imperial proclamation. This constitution, under which Brazil was governed until the fall of the monarchy in 1889, concentrated great power in the hands of the monarch. In addition to a Council of State, it provided for a two-chamber parliament, a lifetime Senate whose members were chosen by the emperor, and a Chamber of Deputies elected by voters who met property and income requirements. The emperor had the right to appoint and dismiss ministers and summon or dissolve parliament at will. He also appointed the provincial governors or presidents.

Resentment over Dom Pedro's high-handed dissolution of the constituent assembly and the highly centralist character of the constitution of 1824 was particularly strong in Pernambuco, a center of republican and federalist ferment. Here in 1824 a group of rebels, led by the merchant Manoel de Carvalho, proclaimed the creation of a Confederation of the Equator that would unite the six northern provinces under a republican government. A few leaders voiced antislavery sentiments, but nothing was done to abolish slavery, which deprived the movement of the potential support of a large slave population. Within a year, imperial troops had smashed the revolt, and fifteen of its leaders were executed.

Dom Pedro had won a victory but resentment of his autocratic tendencies continued to smolder, and his popularity steadily waned. The emperor's foreign policies contributed to this growing discontent. In 1826, in return for recognition of Brazilian independence and a trade agreement, Dom Pedro signed a treaty with Great Britain that obligated Brazil to end the slave traffic by 1830. Despite this ban and the efforts of British warships to intercept and seize the slave ships, the trade continued with the full knowledge and approval of the Brazilian government. But British policing practices caused the price of slaves to rise sharply. The prospering coffee growers of Rio de Janeiro, São Paulo, and Minas Gerais could afford to pay high prices for slaves, but the cotton and sugar growers of the depressed north could not compete with them for workers and blamed Dom Pedro for their difficulties.

Another source of discontent was the costly and fruitless war with Argentina (1825–1828)

over the Banda Oriental (Uruguay), which the Brazilians called the Cisplatine Province. The war was supported by the ranchers of Rio Grande do Sul, who coveted the rich pasturelands of Uruguay, but it aroused much opposition elsewhere. When it ended in a compromise that guaranteed the independence of Uruguay, its outcome was regarded as a humiliating defeat for Brazil, and Dom Pedro suffered a further loss of prestige. Two other causes of the emperor's growing unpopularity were the favoritism he showed to the corrupt Portuguese courtiers of his entourage and his continued involvement in Portuguese politics, especially his effort in upholding the claims of his daughter Maria to the Portuguese throne.

News of the July Revolution of 1830 in France, a revolution that toppled an unpopular, autocratic king, produced rejoicing and violent demonstrations in Brazilian cities. *Exaltados* (radical liberals) placed themselves at the head of the movement of revolt and called for the abolition of the monarchy and the establishment of a federal republic. In the face of the growing crisis, Don Pedro vacillated; first he made concessions to anti-Portuguese sentiment by appointing a new cabinet of Brazilian-born ministers, then he dissolved it and named a new cabinet that included the most hated figures in his Brazilian entourage. In April 1831, mass demonstrations in the capital were joined by the local garrison. A delegation of city magistrates demanded that he reinstate the former ministry; Dom Pedro refused. The next day, April 7, he abdicated in favor of his five-year-old son Pedro, and two weeks later he sailed for Portugal, never to return.

Regency, Revolt, and a Boy Emperor

The revolution had been the work of radical liberals who viewed Dom Pedro's downfall as the first step toward the establishment of a federal republic, but its fruits were garnered by more moderate men. In effect, the radicals had played the game of the monarchist liberals who guided the movement of secession from Portugal and later lost influence at court as a result of Dom

Pedro's shift to the right. Dom Pedro's departure was a victory for these moderates, and they hastened to restore their ascendancy over the central government and prevent the revolution from getting out of hand.

As a first step, parliament appointed a three-man regency composed of moderate liberals to govern for the child emperor until he reached the age of eighteen. Another measure created a national guard, recruited from the propertied classes, to repress urban mobs and slave revolts. Simultaneously, the new government began work on a project of constitutional reform designed to appease the strong federalist sentiment. After a three-year debate, parliament approved the Additional Act of 1834, which gave the provinces elective legislative assemblies with broad powers, including control over local budgets and taxes. This provision assured the great landowners of a large measure of control over their regions. The Council of State, identified with Dom Pedro's reactionary rule, was abolished. But centralism was not abandoned, for the national government continued to appoint provincial governors with a partial veto over the acts of the provincial assemblies. Centralism was even strengthened by the replacement of the three-man regency with a single regent. To this post parliament named the moderate liberal Diogo Antônio Feijó.

Almost immediately, Feijó had to struggle against a rash of revolts, most numerous in the northern provinces, whose economy suffered from a loss of markets for their staple crops, sugar and cotton. None occurred in the central southern zone (the provinces of Rio de Janeiro, São Paulo, and Minas Gerais), whose coffee economy prospered and whose planter aristocracy had secure control of the central government. These revolts had a variety of local causes. Some were elemental, popular revolts; such was the so-called *cabanagem* (from the word *cabana,* "cabin") of Pará, which originated in the grievances of small tradesmen, farmers, and lower-class elements against the rich Portuguese merchants who monopolized local trade. Others, like the republican and separatist revolt in Bahia

Dom Pedro II. (Courtesy of the Organization of American States)

(1837–1838), reflected the frustrations of the planter aristocracy of this once-prosperous area over its loss of economic and political power.

Most serious of all was the revolt that broke out in 1835 in the province of Rio Grande do Sul. Although it was dubbed the *Revolução Farroupilha* (Revolution of the Ragamuffins) in contemptuous reference to its supposed lower-class origins, the movement was led by cattle barons who maintained a more or less patriarchal sway over the gauchos who formed the rank-and-file of the rebel armies. An intense regionalism, resentment over taxes and unpopular governors imposed by the central government, and the strength of republican sentiment were major factors in producing the revolt of Rio Grande. The presence of considerable numbers of Italian exiles such as Giuseppe Garibaldi, ardent republicans and antislavery men, gave a special radical tinge to the revolt in Rio Grande. In September 1835, the rebels captured the provincial capital of Pôrto Alegre; one year later they proclaimed Rio Grande an independent republic. For almost a decade, two states—one a republic, the other an empire—existed on Brazilian territory.

The secession of Rio Grande and the inability of imperial troops to quell the revolt further weakened the position of Feijó, whose authoritarian temper and disregard for parliamentary majorities in the choice of ministers had caused much discontent. By now the political struggle had begun to assume an organized form, with the emergence of a Liberal party composed chiefly of moderate liberals who favored concessions to federalism, and a Conservative party, which preferred to strengthen the central government. However, on such essential issues as the monarchy, slavery, and the maintenance of the status quo in general, liberals and conservatives saw eye to eye.

In September 1837, Feijó resigned and was succeeded as regent by the conservative Pedro de Araújo Lima. Like his predecessor, Araújo Lima concentrated his efforts on putting down the Rio Grande rebellion and other regional revolts in the north. The Rio Grande experiment in republican government and its offer of freedom to all slaves who joined the republic's armed forces posed an especially serious threat to monarchy and slavery. Among both liberals and conservatives, the idea gained favor of calling the young Pedro to rule before his legal majority in order to strengthen the central government in its war against subversive and separatist movements. By the beginning of 1840, the project had won virtual acceptance, liberals and conservatives differing only with respect to timing and other details. On July 22, in what was in effect a parliamentary coup d'état the two chambers of parliament proclaimed the fourteen-year-old Dom Pedro emperor; he was formally crowned a year later, in July 1841.

In March 1841, after forcing a short-lived liberal ministry to resign, the emperor called the conservatives to power. The new government proceeded to dismantle the federalist reforms in the Additional Act of 1834. The powers of the provincial assemblies were sharply curtailed; locally elected judges were stripped of their judicial and police powers, which were vested in a new national police; and the Council of State was restored. Having consolidated their position, the conservatives decided to change the balance of forces in the new Chamber of Deputies, where the liberals had won a majority and, charging corruption in the elections, persuaded the emperor to dissolve it.

The liberals of São Paulo and Minas Gerais responded with a revolt (1842) that had little popular support, for it was dictated solely by the desire for the spoils of office. Troops led by the conservative leader Baron Caxias swiftly crushed the uprising. But the emperor treated the vanquished rebels leniently; indeed, a short time later he called on the liberals to form a new ministry. Once returned to power, the liberals made no effort to repeal the conservative revisions of the constitution and made use of the broad police powers vested in the central government for their own ends.

With the unity of the ruling class restored, the government undertook to settle scores with the rebels of Rio Grande. As a result of internal squabbles and the cessation of aid from friendly Uruguay when that country was invaded by Rosas' troops in February 1843, the situation of the republic became extremely difficult. Meanwhile, Baron Caxias advanced with large forces against the rebels and wrested town after town from their troops. Facing defeat, the republican leaders accepted an offer from Rio de Janeiro to negotiate a peace, which was signed in February 1845. The peace treaty extended amnesty to all rebels but annulled all laws of the republican regime. The cattle barons won certain concessions, including the right to nominate their candidate for the post of provincial governor and retention of their military titles.

The last large-scale revolt in the series that shook Brazil in the 1830s and 1840s was the uprising of 1848 in Pernambuco. Centered in the city of Recife, its causes included hostility toward the Portuguese merchants who monopolized local trade, the appointment of an unpopular governor by the conservative government, and hatred for the greatest landowners of the region, the powerful Cavalcanti family. The rebel program called for the removal from Recife of all Portuguese merchants, expansion of provincial autonomy, work for the unemployed, and division of the Cavalcanti lands. Even this radical program, however, contained no reference to the abolition of slavery. The movement collapsed after the capture of Recife by imperial troops in 1849. Many captured leaders were condemned to prison for life, but all were amnestied in 1852.

The Game of Politics and the Crisis of Slavery

By 1850, Brazil was at peace. The emperor presided over a pseudo-parliamentary regime that in reality was a royal dictatorship exercised in the interests of a tiny ruling class. He paid his respects to parliamentary forms by alternately appointing conservative and liberal prime ministers at will; if the new ministry did not command a majority in parliament, one was obtained by holding rigged elections. Since the ruling class was united on essential issues, the only thing at stake in party struggles was the spoils of office. An admirer of Dom Pedro, Joaquim Nabuco, described the operation of the system in his book *O abolicionismo:*

The president of the council lives at the mercy of the crown, from which he derives his power; even the appearance of power is his only when he is regarded as the emperor's lieutenant and is believed to have in his pocket the decree of dissolution—that is, the right to elect a chamber made up of his own henchmen. Below him are the ministers, who live by the favor of the president of the council; farther down still, on the third plane, are found the deputies, at the mercy of the ministers. The representative system, then, is a graft of parliamentary forms on a patriarchal government, and senators and deputies only take their roles

seriously in this parody of democracy because of the personal advantage they derive therefrom. Suppress the subsidies, force them to stop using their positions for personal and family ends, and no one who had anything else to do would waste his time in such shadow boxing.[4]

The surface stability of Brazilian political life in the decades after 1850 rested on the prosperity created by a growing demand and good prices for Brazilian coffee. As the sugar-growing northeast and its plantation society continued to decline because of exhausted soil, archaic techniques, and competition from foreign sugars, the coffee-growing zone of Rio de Janeiro, São Paulo, and Minas Gerais gained new importance.

The crisis of the northeast grew more acute as a result of English pressure on Brazil to enforce the Anglo-Brazilian treaty banning the importation of slaves into Brazil after November 7, 1831. Before 1850 this treaty was never effectively enforced; more than fifty thousand slaves a year were brought to Brazil during the 1840s. In 1849 and 1850, however, the British government instructed its warships to enter Brazilian territorial waters if necessary to seize and destroy Brazilian slave ships. Under British pressure, the Brazilian parliament passed the Queiroz anti-slave-trade law, which was effectively enforced. By the middle 1850s, the importation of slaves had virtually ended.

The ending of the slave trade had major consequences. Because of the high mortality among slaves due to poor food, harsh working conditions, and other negative factors, the slave population could not be maintained by natural reproduction, and the eventual doom of the slave system was assured. The passing of the slave trade created a serious labor shortage, with a large flow of slaves from the north to the south because of the coffee planters' greater capacity to compete for slave labor. This movement aggravated the imbalance between the prosperous

[4] Quoted in Benjamin Keen, ed., *Latin American Civilization: The National Era,* vol. 2 (Boston: Houghton Mifflin, 1974), p. 159.

south central zone and the declining north. The end of the slave trade had another important result: large sums formerly expended for the purchase of slaves were now channeled to other uses, partly into coffee agriculture, partly into the building of an infrastructure for the emerging national economy. The first telegraph lines in Brazil were established in 1852; the first railroad line was begun in 1854. In these years, a pioneer of Brazilian capitalism, Irineu Evangelista de Sousa, later the Baron Mauá, laid the foundations of a veritable industrial and banking empire.

By the 1860s, a growing number of Brazilians had become convinced that slavery brought serious discredit to Brazil and must be ended. The abolition of slavery in the United States as a result of the Civil War, which left Brazil and the Spanish colonies of Cuba and Puerto Rico the only slaveholding areas in the Western Hemisphere, sharpened sensitivity to the problem. The Paraguayan War also promoted the cause of emancipation. In an effort to fill the gaps caused by heavy losses at the front, a decree was issued granting freedom to government-owned slaves who agreed to join the army, and some private slave owners followed the official example. Criticism of slavery was increasingly joined with criticism of the emperor, censured for his cautious posture on slavery. The antislavery movement began to merge with the nascent republican movement. In 1869 the left wing of the Liberal party, organized in a Reform Club, issued a manifesto demanding restrictions on the powers of the emperor and the grant of freedom to the newborn children of slaves. The crisis of slavery was fast becoming a crisis of the Brazilian Empire.

Chapter 10

The Triumph
of Neocolonialism

Beginning about 1870, the quickening tempo of the Industrial Revolution in Europe stimulated a more rapid pace of change in the Latin American economy and politics. Responding to a mounting demand for raw materials and foodstuffs, Latin American producers increased their output of those commodities. The growing trade with Europe helped to stabilize political conditions in Latin America, for the new economic system demanded peace and continuity in government.

Encouraged by the increased stability, European capital flowed into Latin America, creating railroads, docks, processing plants, and other facilities needed to expand and modernize production and trade. Latin America became integrated into an international economic system in which it exchanged raw materials and foodstuffs for the factory-made goods of Europe and North America. Gradual adoption of free-trade policies by many Latin American countries, which marked the abandonment of efforts to create a native factory capitalism, hastened the area's integration into this international division of labor.

The New Colonialism

The new economic system fastened a new dependency on Latin America, with Great Britain and later the United States replacing Spain and Portugal in the dominant role; it may, therefore, be called "neocolonial." Despite its built-in flaws and local breakdowns, the neocolonial order displayed a certain stability until 1914. By disrupting the markets for Latin America's exports and making it difficult to import the manufactured goods that Latin America required, World War I marked the beginning of a general crisis the area has not yet overcome.

Although the period from 1870 to 1914 saw a rapid overall growth of the Latin American economy, the pace and degree of progress were uneven, with some countries (like Bolivia and Paraguay) joining the advance much later than others. A marked feature of the neocolonial order was its one-sidedness (monoculture). One or a few primary products became the basis of each country's prosperity, making it highly vulnerable to fluctuations in the world demand and price of these products. Thus, Argentina and Uruguay depended on wheat and meat; Brazil on coffee, sugar, and briefly on rubber; Chile on copper and nitrates; Honduras on bananas; Cuba on sugar.

In each country, the modern export sector became an enclave largely isolated from the rest of the economy; this enclave actually accentuated the backwardness of other sectors by draining off their labor and capital. The export-oriented nature of the modern sector was reflected in the pattern of the national railway systems, which as a rule were not designed to integrate each country's regions but to satisfy the traffic needs of the export industries. In addition, the modern export sector often rested on extremely precarious foundations. Rapid, feverish growth, punctuated by slumps that sometimes ended in a total collapse, formed part of the neocolonial pattern; such meteoric rise and fall is the story of Peruvian guano, Chilean nitrates, and Brazilian rubber.

Expansion of the Hacienda System

The neocolonial order evolved within the framework of the traditional system of land tenure and labor relations. Indeed, it led to an expansion of the hacienda system on a scale far greater than the colonial period had known. As the growing European demand for Latin American products raised the value of land, the great landowners in country after country launched assaults on the surviving Indian community lands. In Mexico the Reforma laid the legal basis for this attack in

the 1850s and 1860s; it reached its climax in the era of Porfirio Díaz.

Seizure of church lands by liberal governments also contributed to the growth of the latifundio. Mexico again offered a model, with its Lerdo Law and the Juárez anticlerical decrees. Following the Mexican example, Colombian liberal governments confiscated church lands in the 1860s, the liberal dictator Antonio Guzmán Blanco seized many church estates in Venezuela in the 1870s, and Ecuadoran liberals expropriated church lands in 1895.

Expansion of the public domain through railway construction and Indian wars also contributed to the growth of great landed estates. Lands taken from the church or wrested from Indian tribes were usually sold to buyers in vast tracts at nominal prices. Concentration of land, reducing the cultivable area available to Indian and mestizo small landowners, was accompanied by a parallel growth of the *minifundio*—an uneconomical small plot worked with primitive techniques.

The seizure of Indian community lands to use immediately or to hold for a speculative rise in value provided great landowners with another advantage by giving them control of the local labor force at a time of increasing demand for labor. Expropriated Indians rarely became true wage earners paid wholly in cash, for such workers were too expensive and independent in spirit. A more widespread labor system was debt peonage, in which workers were paid wholly or in part with vouchers redeemable at the *tienda de raya* (company store), whose inflated prices and often devious bookkeeping created a debt that was passed on from father to son. The courts enforced the obligation of peons to remain on the estate until they had liquidated their debts. Peons who protested low wages or the more intensive style of work demanded by the new order were brought to their senses by the landowner's armed retainers or by local police or military authorities.

In some countries, the period saw a revival of the colonial repartimiento system of draft labor for Indians. In Guatemala, this system—here called *mandamiento*—required able-bodied Indians to work for a specified number of days on haciendas. It was the liberal President Justo Rufino Barrios who issued instructions to local magistrates to see to it "that any Indian who seeks to evade his duty is punished to the full extent of the law, that the farmers are fully protected and that each Indian is forced to do a full day's work while in service."

Slavery survived in some places well beyond mid-century—for example, in Peru until 1855, in Cuba until 1886, in Brazil until 1888. Closely akin to slavery was the system of bondage, under which some ninety thousand Chinese coolies were imported into Peru between 1849 and 1875 to work on the guano islands and in railway construction. The term *slavery* also applies to the system under which political deportees and captured Indian rebels were sent by Mexican authorities to labor in unspeakable conditions on the coffee, tobacco, and henequen plantations of southern Mexico.

More modern systems of agricultural labor and farm tenantry arose only in such regions as southern Brazil and Argentina, whose critical labor shortage required the offer of greater incentives to the millions of European immigrants who poured into those countries between 1870 and 1910.

Labor conditions were little better in the mining industry and in the factories that arose in some countries after 1890. Typical conditions were a workday of twelve to fourteen hours, miserable wages frequently paid in vouchers redeemable only at the company store, and arbitrary, abusive treatment by employers and foremen. Latin American law codes usually prohibited strikes and other organized efforts to improve working conditions, and police and the armed forces were commonly employed to break strikes, sometimes with heavy loss of life.

Foreign Control of Resources

The rise of the neocolonial order was accompanied by a steady growth of foreign corporate control over the natural and man-made resources of the continent. The process went through stages; in 1870 foreign investment was still largely concentrated in trade, shipping, railways, public utilities, and government loans. At that date, British capital enjoyed an undisputed hegemony in the Latin American investment field. By 1914 foreign corporate ownership had expanded to include most of the mining industry and had deeply penetrated real estate, ranching, plantation agriculture, and manufacturing. By that date, too, Great Britain's rivals had effectively challenged its domination in Latin America. Of these rivals, the most spectacular advance was made by the United States, whose Latin American investments had risen from a negligible amount in 1870 to over $1.6 billion by the end of 1914 (still well below the nearly $5 billion investment of Great Britain).

Foreign economic penetration went hand in hand with a growth of political influence and even armed intervention. The youthful U.S. imperialism proved to be the most aggressive of all. In the years after 1898, a combination of "dollar diplomacy" and armed intervention transformed the Caribbean into an "American lake" and reduced Cuba, the Dominican Republic, and several Central American states to the status of dependencies and protectorates of the United States.

The Politics of Acquisition

The new economy demanded a new politics. Conservatives and liberals, fascinated by the atmosphere of prosperity created by the export boom, the rise in land values, the flood of foreign loans, and the growth of government revenues, put aside their ideological differences and joined in the pursuit of wealth. The positivist slogan, "Order and Progress," now became the watchword of Latin America's ruling classes. The social Darwinist idea of the struggle for survival of the fittest and Herbert Spencer's doctrine of "inferior races," frequently used to support claims of the inherent inferiority of the Indian, mestizo, and mulatto masses, also entered the upper-class ideological arsenal.

The growing domination of national economies by the export sectors and the development of a consensus between the old landed aristocracy and more capitalist-oriented groups caused political issues like the federalist-centralist conflict and the liberal-conservative cleavage to lose much of their meaning; in some countries, the old party lines dissolved or became extremely tenuous. A new type of "progressive" caudillo—Porfirio Díaz in Mexico, Rafael Núñez in Colombia, Justo Rufino Barrios in Guatemala, Antonio Guzmán Blanco in Venezuela—symbolized the politics of acquisition.

As the century drew to a close, dissatisfied urban middle-class, immigrant, and entrepreneurial groups in some countries combined to form parties, called Radical or Democratic, that challenged the traditional domination of politics by the creole aristocracy. They demanded political, social, and educational reforms that would give more weight to the new middle sectors. But these middle sectors—manufacturers, shopkeepers, professionals, and the like—were in large part a creation of the neocolonial order, depended on it for their livelihood, and as a rule did not question its viability. The small socialist, anarchist, and syndicalist groups that arose in various Latin American countries in the 1890s challenged both capitalism and neocolonialism, but the full significance of these movements lay in the future.

The trends just described lend a certain unity to the history of Mexico, Argentina, Chile, and Brazil in the period from 1870 to 1914. Each country's history, however, presents significant variations on the common theme—variations that reflect that country's specific historical background and conditions.

Mexican Politics and Economy

Dictatorship Under Díaz

General Porfirio Díaz seized power in 1876 from President Lerdo de Tejada with the support of disgruntled regional caudillos and military personnel, liberals angered by the political manipulations of the entrenched Lerdo machine, and Indian and mestizo small landholders who believed that Díaz would put an end to land seizures. Having installed himself as president, Díaz paid his respects to the principle of no re-election by allowing a trusted crony, General Manuel González, to succeed him in 1880. However, he returned to the presidential palace in 1884 and continued to occupy it through successive re-elections until his resignation and flight from Mexico in 1911. He got rid of the now-inconvenient issue of no re-election by having the constitution amended in 1887 and 1890 to permit his indefinite re-election; in 1904 he obtained an extension of the president's term from four to six years. Thus, Díaz, who had seized power in the name of republican legality, erected one of the longest personal dictatorships in Latin American history.

The construction of the dictatorship, however, was a gradual process. During his first presidential term, Díaz permitted reasonably fair elections, Congress and the judiciary enjoyed a certain independence, and the press, including a vocal radical labor press, was free. The outlines of Díaz's economic and social policies, however, soon became clear. Confronted with an empty treasury, facing pressures from above and below, Díaz decided in favor of the great landowners, moneylenders, and foreign capitalists, whose assistance could insure his political survival. In return, he assured these groups of protection for their property and other interests. Díaz, who had once proclaimed that in the age-old struggle between the people and the haciendas he was on the side of the people, now sent troops to suppress peasant resistance to land seizures. Before taking power, Díaz had denounced Lerdo for his generous concessions to British capitalists; by 1880, Díaz had granted even more lavish subsidies for railway construction to North American companies. Economic development had become for Díaz the great object, the key to the solution of his own problems and those of the nation.

Economic development required political stability; accordingly, Díaz promoted a policy of conciliation that consisted of offering an olive branch and a share of spoils to all influential op-

Beginning in the 1920s, with considerable support from the state, there arose in Mexico a school of socially conscious artists who sought to enlighten the masses about their bitter past and the promise of the revolutionary present. One of the greatest of these artists was David Alfaro Siqueiros, whose painting depicts with satire the former President Porfirio Díaz, who tramples on the Constitution of 1857 as he diverts his wealthy followers with dancing girls. (Reproduccion autorizada por el Instituto Nacional de Bellas Artes y Literatura/Collection Museo Nacional de Historia, I.N.A.H.-S.E.P.)

ponents, no matter what their political past or persuasion—*Lerdistas,* Juaristas, conservatives, clericals, anticlericals. A dog with a bone in its mouth, Díaz cynically observed, neither kills nor steals. In effect, Díaz invited all sections of the upper class and some members of the middle class, including prominent intellectuals and journalists, to join the great Mexican barbecue, from which only the poor and humble were barred. An important instrument of Díaz's law-and-order policy was a force of mounted police, the *rurales,* distinguished by their picturesque dress. The former bandits and vagrants who had composed a good part of this force were gradually replaced by artisan and peasant recruits, who had been dislocated by the large social changes that took place during the *Porfiriato.* Aside from chasing unrepentant bandits, the major function of the rurales was to suppress peasant unrest and break strikes.

There was another side to the policy of conciliation, however, a side described by the formula *pan o palo* (bread or the club). Opponents who refused Díaz's bribes—political offices, monopolies, and the like—suffered swift reprisal. Dissidents were beaten up, murdered, or arrested and sent to the damp underground dungeons of San Juan de Ulúa or the grim Belén prison, a sort of Mexican Bastille. Designed to hold two hundred prisoners, Belén commonly held four to five thousand inmates. One prominent journalist, Filomeno Mata, was jailed thirty-four times.

By such means, Díaz virtually eliminated all effective opposition by the end of his second term (1884–1888). The constitution of 1857 and the liberties it guaranteed existed only on paper. Elections to Congress, in theory the highest organ of government, were a farce; Díaz simply circulated a list of his candidates to local officials, who certified their election. The dictator contemptuously called Congress his *caballada,* his stable of horses. The state governors were appointed by Díaz, usually from the ranks of local great landlords or his generals. In return for their loyalty, he gave them a free hand to enrich themselves and terrorize the local population. Under them were district heads called *jefes políticos,* petty tyrants appointed by the governors with the approval of Díaz; below them were municipal presidents who ran the local administrative units. One feature of the Díaz era was a mushrooming of the administrative and coercive apparatus; government costs during this period soared by 900 percent.

The army, as indispensable to Díaz as it had been to Santa Anna, naturally enjoyed special favor. Higher officers were well paid and enjoyed many opportunities for enrichment at the expense of the regions in which they were quartered. The Díaz army, however, was pathetically inadequate for purposes of national defense. Generals and other high officers were appointed not for their ability but for their loyalty to the

dictator. Discipline, morale, and training were extremely poor. A considerable part of the rank-and-file were recruited from the dregs of society; the remainder were young Indian conscripts. These soldiers, often used for brutal repression of strikes and agrarian unrest, were themselves harshly treated and miserably paid—the wage of ranks below sergeant was fifty cents a month.

The church became another pillar of the dictatorship. Early in his second term, Díaz reached an accommodation with the hierarchy. The church agreed to support Díaz; in return he allowed the anticlerical Reforma laws to fall into disuse. In disregard of those laws, monasteries and nunneries were restored, church schools established, and wealth again began to accumulate in the hands of the church. Faithful to its bargain, the church turned a deaf ear to the complaints of the lower classes and taught complete submission to the authorities. As in colonial times, many priests were utterly venal and corrupt. Only in the closing years of the dictatorship did the church, sensing the coming storm, begin to advocate modest social reforms.

The Díaz policy of conciliation was directed at prominent intellectuals as well as more wealthy and powerful figures. A group of such intellectuals, professional men, and businessmen made up a closely knit clique of Díaz's advisers. Known as *Científicos,* they got their name from their insistence on "scientific" administration of the state and were especially influential after 1892. About fifteen men made up the controlling nucleus of the group. Their leader was Díaz's all-powerful father-in-law, Manuel Romero Rubio, and, after his death in 1895, the new minister of finance, José Yves Limantour.

For the Científicos, the economic movement was everything. Most Científicos accepted the thesis of the inherent inferiority of the Indian and mestizo population and the consequent necessity for relying on the native white elite and on foreigners and their capital to lead Mexico out of its backwardness. In the words of the journalist Francisco G. Cosmes, "the Indian has only the passive force of inferior races, is incapable of actively pursuing the goal of civilization."

But there were differences of opinion within the group. The most distinguished intellectual among the Científicos was the old-time liberal Justo Sierra, a biographer of Juárez who wistfully clung to his libertarian ideas, yet served Díaz, believing that he was preparing Mexico to be free. By contrast with such racists as Francisco Bulnes and José Yves Limantour, Sierra rejected the notion of Indians' racial inferiority and argued that education could correct their seeming dullness and apathy.

Some members of the Díaz establishment even harbored doubts about Díaz's policies and methods. Troubled by the immobility of the regime, fearing revolution, some Científicos urged a variety of reforms, including an end to re-election and the introduction of a multiparty system. But their advice was not heeded and, being practical men, most resigned themselves to the more profitable task of enriching themselves.

Thanks to the devoted efforts of educators like Justo Sierra, the Díaz era saw some advances in public education. In 1887, Sierra secured the adoption of a federal law making primary education obligatory. Despite the law, however, it appears that on the average only one out of three children between the ages of six and twelve were enrolled. The vast majority of these children probably went only through the first year and remained functionally illiterate. The principal beneficiaries of the educational progress under Díaz were the sons of the rich: for every student enrolled in the primary schools in 1910, the state spent about 7 pesos; for every student in the college preparatory schools, it spent nearly 100 pesos.

In the last analysis, however, apologists for the dictatorship rested their case on the "economic miracle" that Díaz had allegedly worked in Mexico. A survey of the Mexican economy in 1910 reveals how modest that miracle was.

Concentration of Landownership

At the opening of the twentieth century, Mexico was still predominantly an agrarian country; 77 percent of its population of 15 million still lived on the land. The laws of the Reforma had already given impetus to the concentration of landownership, and under Díaz this trend was greatly accelerated. There is some evidence of a link between the rapid advance of railway construction, which increased the possibilities of production for export and therefore stimulated a rise in land values, and the growth of land-grabbing in the Díaz period.

A major piece of land legislation was a law of 1883 that provided for the survey of so-called vacant public lands, *tierras baldías.* The law authorized real estate companies to survey such lands and retain one-third of the surveyed area; the remainder was sold for low fixed prices in vast tracts, usually to Díaz's favorites and their foreign associates. The 1883 law required the surveying companies and purchasers to settle at least one person for each five hundred acres surveyed, but a second law (1894) removed this obligation and deleted the clause restricting the amount of land that one individual could purchase.

The 1883 and 1894 laws opened the way for vast territorial acquisitions. One individual alone obtained nearly 12 million acres in Baja California and other northern states. But the land companies were not satisfied with the acquisition of true vacant lands. The law of 1894 declared that a parcel of land to which a legal title could not be produced might be declared vacant land, opening the door to expropriation of Indian villages and other small landholders whose forebears had tilled their lands from times immemorial but who could not produce the required titles. If the victims offered armed resistance, troops were sent against them, and the vanquished rebels were sold like slaves to labor on henequen plantations in Yucatán or sugar plantations in Cuba. This was the fate of the Yaqui Indians of the northwest, defeated after a long, valiant struggle.

Another instrument of land seizure was an 1890 law designed to give effect to older Reforma laws requiring the distribution of Indian village lands among the villagers. The law created enormous confusion. In many cases, land speculators and hacendados cajoled the illiterate Indians into selling their titles for paltry sums. Hacendados also used other means, such as cutting off a village's water supply or simply brute force, to achieve their predatory ends. By 1910 the process of land expropriation was largely complete. More than 90 percent of the Indian villages of the central plateau, the most densely populated region of the country, had lost their communal lands. Only the most tenacious resistance enabled villages that still held their lands to survive the assault of the great landowners. Landless peons and their families made up 9.5 million of a rural population of 12 million.

As a rule, the new owners did not use the land seized from Indian villages or small landholders more efficiently. Hacendados let much of the usurped land lie idle. They waited for a speculative rise in value or for an American buyer. By keeping land out of production, they helped to keep the price of maize and other staples artificially high. The technical level of hacienda agriculture was generally extremely low, with little use of irrigation, machinery, and commercial fertilizer, although some new landowning groups—such as northern cattle raisers and cotton growers, the coffee and rubber growers of Chiapas, and the henequen producers of Yucatán—employed more modern equipment and techniques.

The production of foodstuffs stagnated, barely keeping pace during most of the period with the growth of population, and per capita production of such basic staples as maize and beans actually declined toward the end of the century. This decline culminated in three years of bad harvests, 1907–1910, due principally to drought. As a result, the importation of maize and other foodstuffs from the United States steadily increased in the last years of the Díaz regime. Despite the growth of pastoral industry, per capita consumption of milk and cheese barely kept pace with the growth of population, for a considerable proportion of the cattle sold was destined for the export market.

The only food products whose increase exceeded the growth of population were alcoholic beverages. Some idea of the increase in their consumption is given by the fact that the number of bars in Mexico City rose from 51 in 1864 to 1,400 in 1900. At the end of the century, the Mexican death rate from alcoholism—a common response to intolerable conditions of life and labor—was estimated to be six times that of France. Meanwhile, inflation, rampant during the last part of the Díaz regime, greatly raised the cost of the staples on which the mass of the population depended. Without a corresponding increase in wages, the situation of agricultural and industrial laborers deteriorated sharply.

The Economic Advance

While food production for the domestic market declined, production of food and industrial raw materials for the foreign market experienced a vigorous growth. By 1910, Mexico had become the largest producer of henequen, source of a fiber in great demand in the world market. Mexican export production became increasingly geared to the needs of the United States, which was the principal market for sugar, bananas, rubber, and tobacco produced on plantations that were largely foreign-owned. American companies dominated the mining industry, whose output of copper, gold, lead, and zinc, rose sharply after 1890. A spectacular late development was shown by the oil industry, which was controlled by American and British interests; by 1911, Mexico was third among the world's oil producers. French and Spanish capitalists virtually monopolized the textile industry and other consumer goods industries that had a relatively rapid growth after 1890. Operating behind the protection of tariff walls that excluded foreign competition in cheap goods, they compelled the masses to pay high prices for articles of inferior quality.

Foreign control of key sectors of the economy and the fawning attitude of the Díaz regime toward foreigners gave rise to a popular saying: "Mexico, mother of foreigners and stepmother of Mexicans." The ruling clique of Científicos justified this favoritism by citing the need for a rapid development of Mexico's natural resources and the creation of a strong country capable of defending its political independence and territorial integrity.

Thanks to an influx of foreign capital, some quickening and modernization of economic life did take place under Díaz. The volume of foreign trade greatly increased, a modern banking system arose, and the country acquired a relatively dense network of railways. But these successes were achieved at a very heavy price: a brutal dictatorship, the pauperization of the mass of the population, the stagnation of food agriculture, the strengthening of the inefficient latifundio, and the survival of many feudal or semifeudal vestiges in Mexican economic and social life.

Labor, Agrarian, and Middle-Class Unrest

The survival of feudal vestiges was especially glaring in the area of labor relations. There was some variation in labor conditions from region to region. In 1910 forced labor and outright slavery, as well as older forms of debt peonage, were characteristic of the south (the states of Yucatán, Tabasco, Chiapas, and parts of Oaxaca and Veracruz). The rubber, coffee, tobacco, henequen, and sugar plantations of this region depended heavily on the forced labor of political deportees, captured Indian rebels, and contract workers kidnaped or lured to work in the tropics by a variety of devices.

In central Mexico, where a massive expropriation of Indian village lands had created a large landless Indian proletariat, tenantry, sharecropping, and the use of migratory labor had increased, and living standards had declined. The large labor surplus of this area diminished the need for hacendados to tie their workers to their estates with debt peonage. In the north the proximity of the United States, with its higher wage scales, and the competition of hacendados with mine owners for labor made wages and sharecropping arrangements somewhat more favorable and weakened debt peonage. In all parts of

the country, however, the life of agricultural workers was filled with hardships and abuses of every kind.

Labor conditions in mines and factories were little better than in the countryside. Workers in textile mills labored twelve to fifteen hours daily for a wage ranging from eleven cents for unskilled women and children to seventy-five cents for highly skilled workers. Employers found ways of reducing even these meager wages. Wages were discounted for alleged "carelessness" in the use of tools or machines or for "defective goods"; workers were usually paid wholly or in part with vouchers good only in company stores, whose prices were higher than in other stores. Federal and state laws banned trade unions and strikes. Scores of workers, both men and women, were shot down by troops who broke the great textile strike in the Orizaba (Veracruz) area in 1907, and scores were killed or wounded in putting down the strike at the American-owned Consolidated Copper Company mine at Cananea (Sonora) in 1906. Despite such repressions, the trade union movement continued to grow in the last years of the Díaz era, and socialist, anarchist, and syndicalist ideas began to influence the still small working class.

The growing wave of strikes and agrarian unrest in the last, decadent phase of the Díaz era indicated an increasingly rebellious mood among ever broader sections of the Mexican people. Alienation spread among teachers, lawyers, journalists, and other professionals, whose opportunities for advancement were sharply limited by the monolithic control of economic, political, and social life by the Científicos, their foreign allies, and regional oligarchies. In the United States in 1905 a group of middle-class intellectuals, headed by the Flores Magón brothers, organized the Liberal party, which called for the overthrow of Díaz and advanced a platform whose economic and social provisions anticipated many articles of the constitution of 1917.

Even members of the ruling class began to join the chorus of criticism. These upper-class dissidents included liberal hacendados of a more

Striking workers at the Rio Blanco textile works in Mexico in 1909; the business was controlled by French capital. Troops broke up the strike and much blood was shed. (Brown Brothers)

bourgeois type and national capitalists who resented the competitive advantages enjoyed by foreign companies in Mexico. They also feared that the static, reactionary Díaz policies could provoke the masses to overthrow the capitalist system itself. Fearing revolution, these upper-class critics urged Díaz to end his personal rule, shake up the regime, and institute the reforms needed to preserve the existing economic and social order. When their appeals fell on deaf ears, some of these bourgeois reformers reluctantly prepared to take the road of revolution. Typical of these men was the wealthy hacendado and businessman Francisco Madero, soon to become the Apostle of the Mexican Revolution.

The simultaneous advent of an economic recession and a food crisis sharpened this growing discontent. The depression of 1906–1907, which spread from the United States to Mexico, caused a wave of bankruptcies, layoffs, and wage cuts. At the same time the crop failures of 1907–1910 provoked a dramatic rise in the price of staples like maize and beans. By 1910, Mexico's internal conflicts had reached an explosive stage. The workers' strikes, the agrarian unrest, the agitation of middle-class reformers, the disaffection of some great landowners and capitalists all reflected the disintegration of the dictatorship's social base. Despite its superficial stability and posh splendor, the house of Díaz was rotten from top to bottom. Events proved that only a slight push was needed to send it toppling to the ground.

Argentinian Politics and Economy

In the presidential contest of 1874, Nicolás Avellaneda, a lawyer from Tucumán who had the support of Domingo Sarmiento and powerful provincial bosses, defeated former president Bartolomé Mitre. Mitre, who believed that Buenos Aires must retain control of the republic if it were to stay on a progressive course, promptly organized a revolt. He was defeated and captured but was soon released and continued to enjoy for many years the position of Argentina's most honored elder statesman.

Avellaneda, however, did not represent provincial backwardness and caudillismo. A cultured liberal and a disciple of Sarmiento, in whose cabinet he had held office, he continued his predecessor's work of promoting education, immigration, and domestic tranquillity. In 1876 he inaugurated railroad service between Buenos Aires and his native city of Tucumán. The new line forged stronger economic and political links between the port city and the remote northwest, contributing to the end of the long quarrel between Buenos Aires and the interior.

Consolidation of the State

One more sharp confrontation, however, proved necessary before the quarrel between Buenos Aires and the interior could be finally laid to rest. For almost two decades, Buenos Aires had been both capital of the province of the same name and provisional capital of the republic. In 1880, Carlos Tejedor, governor of the province of Buenos Aires and a fanatical champion of the city's predominance, became a candidate for the presidency against another *Tucumano,* Julio Roca. Roca was Avellaneda's secretary of war and protégé and was supported by a powerful group of provincial politicians known as the Córdoba

League. Tejedor and his supporters responded to Roca's election with a new revolt that government and provincial forces soon crushed.

The victors proceeded to carry out the long-standing pledge to federalize Buenos Aires, which became the capital of the nation, while the provincial capital was moved to the city of La Plata. The interior seemed to have triumphed over Buenos Aires, but that apparent victory was an illusion; the provincial lawyers and politicians who carried the day in 1880 had absorbed the commercial and cultural values of the great city and wished not to diminish but to share in its power. Far from losing influence, Buenos Aires steadily gained in wealth and power until it achieved an overwhelming ascendancy over the rest of the country.

The federalization of Buenos Aires completed the consolidation of the Argentine state. Simultaneously, however, a certain decline appeared in the quality of Argentina's political leadership. The great architects of Argentine national unity—Mitre, Alberdi, Sarmiento—had ardently promoted material progress, which they regarded as the key to the solution of all other problems, but their ultimate goal was a democratic society based on access to land and education for the broad masses. That is why they had sponsored—unsuccessfully—homestead legislation and promoted public education, believing, in the words of Sarmiento, that education would "make the poor gaucho a useful man." Austere idealists, they took pride in their personal integrity; their harshest critics never charged Mitre or Sarmiento with using their high offices to advance their personal fortunes.

With President Roca, a new generation of leaders came to the fore, closely identified with and often recruited from the ruling class of great landowners and wealthy merchants. The "generation of 1880," or the oligarchy, as it was also called, shared the faith of Alberdi and Sarmiento in economic development and the value of the North American and European models, but that faith was now deeply tinged with cynicism, egotism, and a profound distrust for the popular classes. These autocratic liberals prized order and progress above freedom. They regarded the gauchos, the Indians, and the mass of illiterate European immigrants flooding Argentina unfit to exercise civic functions. Asked to define universal suffrage, a leading oligarch, Eduardo Wilde, replied, "It is the triumph of universal ignorance."

The new rulers identified the national interest with the interest of the great landowners, wealthy merchants, and foreign capitalists. Regarding the apparatus of state as their personal property or as the property of their class, they used their official connections to enrich themselves. Although they maintained the forms of parliamentary government, they were determined not to let power slip from their hands and organized what came to be called the *unicato* (one-party rule), exercised by the National Autonomist party, which they formed. Extreme concentration of power in the executive branch and systematic use of fraud, violence, and bribery were basic features of the system.

There are some obvious political and ideological affinities between Argentina's rulers in the period from 1880 to 1910 and Mexico's ruling clique of Científicos in the same period, but also some important differences. Whereas the Díaz government favored the church, Argentine governments displayed a moderate anticlericalism, as indicated by a law of 1884 that barred the church from taking part in public education. This official anticlericalism could have been a tactical maneuver designed to win for the oligarchy a progressive reputation and allay middle-class discontent with its other policies; it may also have reflected the influence of the strong English colony, interested for its own reasons in the secularization of Argentine life. Argentine governments also seem to have made greater efforts than the Díaz regime in the field of public education. By 1914 the Argentine illiteracy rate had been reduced from more than two-thirds in 1869 to a little over one-third (but this improvement was largely concentrated on the coast and in the cities). Finally, the Argentine oligarchy had a better record than the Mexican dictatorship with respect to civil liberties, although suppression of

the press, jailings, and even torture of radical dissidents were far from unknown.

Economic Boom and Inflation

The ominous new trends of the oligarchy emerged in the administration of President Julio Roca (1880–1886) and flowered exuberantly under his political heir and brother-in-law, Miguel Juárez Celman (1886–1890). Roca presided over the beginnings of a great boom that appeared to justify all the optimism of the oligarchy. As secretary of war under Avellaneda, Roca had led a military expedition—the so-called Conquest of the Desert—southward against the pampa Indians in 1879–1880. This conquest added vast new areas to the province of Buenos Aires and to the national public domain. The campaign created a last opportunity for implementing a democratic land policy directed toward the creation of an Argentine small farmer class. Instead, the Roca administration sold off the area in huge tracts for nominal prices to army officers, politicians, and foreign capitalists. The aging Sarmiento, who had seen the defeat of his own effort to acquire and distribute to settlers public land suitable for farming, lamented: "Soon there will not remain a palm of land for distribution to our immigrants."

Coming at a time of steadily mounting European demand for Argentine meat and wheat, the Conquest of the Desert triggered an orgy of land speculation that drove land prices ever higher and caused a prodigious expansion of cattle raising and agriculture. This expansion took place under the sign of the latifundio. Few of the millions of Italian and Spanish immigrants who entered Argentina in this period realized the common dream of becoming independent small landowners.

Some foreign agricultural colonies were founded in the provinces of Santa Fe and Entre Ríos in the 1870s and 1880s. By the mid-1890s, with wheat prices declining and land prices rising, there was a shift from small-scale farming to extensive tenant farming. This was true even in Santa Fe, the heartland of the foreign colonies.

Soaring land prices and the traditional unwillingness of the estancieros to sell land forced the majority of would-be independent farmers to become ranch hands, sharecroppers, or tenant farmers. As sharecroppers or tenants, their hold on the land was very precarious; leases were usually limited to one, two, or three years. The immigrant broke the virgin soil, replaced the tough pampa grass with the alfalfa pasturage needed to fatten cattle, and produced the first wheat harvests but then had to move on, leaving the landowner in possession of all improvements.

As a result, the great majority of new arrivals either remained in Buenos Aires or, having spent some years in the countryside, returned with their small savings to the city, where the rise of meat-salting and meat-packing plants, railroads, public utilities, and many small factories created a growing demand for labor. True, the immigrant workers received very low wages, worked long hours, and crowded with their families into one-room apartments in wretched slums. But in the city barrio they lived among their own people, free from the loneliness of the pampa and the arbitrary rule of great landowners, and had some opportunity of rising in the economic and social scale. As a result, the population of Buenos Aires shot up from 500,000 in 1889 to 1,244,000 in 1909. There arose a growing imbalance between the great city and its hinterland, which held the greater portion of the wealth, population, and culture of the nation, and the interior—particularly the northwest—which was impoverished, stagnant, and thinly peopled. Argentina, to use a familiar metaphor, became a giant head set on a dwarf body.

Foreign capital and management played a decisive role in the expansion of the Argentine economy in this period. The creole elite obtained vast profits from the rise in the price of their land and the increasing volume of exports but showed little interest in plowing those gains into industry or the construction of the infrastructure required by the export economy, preferring a lavish and leisurely lifestyle over entrepreneurial activity.

Just as they left to English and Irish managers the task of tending their estates, so they left to English capital the financing of meat-packing plants, railroads, public utilities, and docks and other facilities. As a result, most of these resources remained in British hands. Typical of the oligarchy's policy of surrender to foreign interests was the decision of Congress in 1889 to sell the state-owned Ferrocarril Oeste, the most profitable and best-run railroad in Argentina, to a British company. Service on a growing foreign debt claimed an ever larger portion of the government's receipts.

Meanwhile, imports of iron, coal, machinery, and consumer goods grew much faster than exports. Combined with the unfavorable price ratio of raw materials to finished goods, the result was an unfavorable balance of trade and a steady drain of gold. New loans with burdensome terms brought temporary relief but aggravated the long-range problem. Under President Miguel Juárez Celman, the disappearance of gold and the government's determination to keep the boom going at all costs led to the issue of great quantities of unbacked paper currency and a massive inflation.

The great landowners did not mind, for they were paid for their exports in French francs and English pounds, which they could convert into cheap Argentine pesos for the payment of local costs; besides, inflation caused the price of their lands to rise. The sacrificial victims of the inflation were the urban middle class and the workers, whose income declined in real value.

The Formation of the Radical Party

In 1889–1890, just as the boom was turning into a depression, the accumulated resentment of the urban middle class and some alienated sectors of the elite over the catastrophic inflation, one-party rule, and official corruption produced a protest movement that took the name *Unión Cívica* (Civic Union). Although the new organization had a middle-class base, its leadership united such disparate elements as urban politicians like

Leandro Além, its first president, who was at odds with the Roca–Juárez Celman machine; new landowners and descendants of old aristocratic families who felt excluded from office and access to patronage by the same clique; and Catholics outraged by the government's anticlerical legislation. Aside from the demand for effective suffrage, the only thing uniting these heterogeneous elements was a common determination to overthrow the government.

The birth of the new party at a mass meeting in Buenos Aires in 1890 coincided with a financial storm: the stock market collapsed, bankruptcies multiplied, and in April the cabinet resigned. Encouraged by this last development, and counting on support from the army, the leaders of the Unión Cívica planned a revolt against Juárez Celman in July. Three days of sharp fighting ended in defeat for the rebels.

The oligarchy now showed its ability to maneuver and divide its enemies. Juárez Celman was forced to resign with an abject confession of his errors; his place was taken by his vice president, Carlos Pellegrini (1890–1892), who moved to appease disgruntled elements of the elite by revising the system of distribution of jobs. Bartolomé Mitre, among other aristocratic dissidents, took the bait and reached an accommodation with the oligarchy that provided for an electoral accord between the National party and his followers. Simultaneously, Pellegrini took steps to improve economic conditions by a policy of retrenchment that reduced inflation, stabilized the peso, and revived Argentine credit abroad. Thanks to these measures and a gradual recovery from the depression, popular discontent began to subside.

The defection of Mitre and other aristocratic leaders of the Unión Cívica isolated Leandro Além and other dissidents who were excluded from Pellegrini's peacemaking scheme. Denouncing the accord between Mitre and Pellegrini as a sellout, Além and his nephew, Hipólito Yrigoyen, formed a new party committed to a "radical" democracy—the *Unión Cívica Radical.* The party named Bernardo de Yrigoyen as its presidential

candidate in 1892 but, knowing that rigged elections made his victory impossible, they also prepared for another revolt—a move that Pellegrini effectively squelched by deporting Além and other Radical leaders until after the election of Luis Sáenz Peña (1892–1895).

On his return from exile, Além organized a new revolt, which began in July 1893. The rebels briefly seized Santa Fe and some other towns, but after two and a half months of fighting, the revolt collapsed for lack of significant popular support. Depressed by his failures and the intrigues of his nephew to seize control of the Radical party, Além committed suicide in 1896.

Between 1896 and 1910, the Radical party, now led by Yrigoyen, proved unable to achieve political reform by peaceful or revolutionary means. The reunited oligarchy continued to win election after election by the traditional methods. The architect of the system of corruption and nepotism, Julio Roca, was re-elected president in 1898 and was succeeded by another oligarch, Manuel Quintana, in 1904; on Quintana's death in 1906, Vice President José Figueroa Alcorta served out the rest of his term. A Radical revolt in 1905 proved to be another dismal fiasco.

In Yrigoyen, however, the Radicals possessed a charismatic personality and a masterful organizer who refused to admit defeat. Yrigoyen was a one-time police superintendent in Buenos Aires, a former minor politician who had maneuvered among various factions in the official party, using his political connections to acquire a considerable wealth, which he invested in land and cattle. As a Radical caudillo, Yrigoyen surrounded himself with an aura of mystery, lived in an ostentatiously modest manner, avoided making speeches, and cultivated a literary style that cloaked the poverty of his thought with turgid rhetoric. "Abstention," refusal to participate in rigged elections, and "Revolutionary Intransigence," the determination to resort to revolution until free elections were achieved, were the party's basic slogans.

The vagueness of the Radical program was dictated by the party's need to appeal to very diverse elements and by its wholehearted acceptance of the economic status quo. The Radical party represented the bourgeoisie, but it was a dependent bourgeoisie that did not champion industrialization, economic diversification, or nationalization of foreign-owned industries. Far from attacking the neocolonial order, the Radical party proposed to strengthen it by promoting cooperation between the landed aristocracy and the urban sectors, which were challenging the creole elite's monopoly of political power. In all respects, it was much more conservative than the contemporaneous reformist movement of José Batlle y Ordóñez in Uruguay.[1]

The Radical party went into eclipse after the debacles of 1890 and 1893, but gradually revived after 1900, due in part to Yrigoyen's charismatic personality and organizing talent. The most important factor, however, was the steady growth of an urban and rural middle class largely composed of sons of immigrants. The domination of the export sector, which limited the growth of industry and opportunities for entrepreneurial activity, focused middle-class ambitions more and more on government employment and the professions—two fields dominated by the creole elite. Signs of growing unrest and frustration in the middle class included a series of student strikes in the universities, caused by efforts of creole governing boards to restrict enrollment of students of immigrant descent.

Electoral Reform and the Growth of the Labor Movement

Meanwhile, a section of the oligarchy, headed by Carlos Pellegrini, had begun to advocate electoral reform. These aristocratic reformers argued that the existing situation created a permanent state of tension and instability; they feared that sooner or later the Radical efforts at revolution would succeed. It would be much better, they believed, to make the concessions demanded by the Radicals, open up the political system, and thereby gain for the ruling party—now generally called Conservative—the popular support and legitimacy it needed to remain in power. Moreover, the conservative reformers were aware of a new threat from the left—from the labor movement and especially its vanguard, the socialists, anarchists, and syndicalists—and hoped to make an alliance with the bourgeoisie against the revolutionary working class.

Pellegrini converted President Figueroa Alcorta to his viewpoint, and Figueroa's disciple and political heir, Roque Sáenz Peña, took office as president in 1910 with a promise that he would satisfy the Radical demands. At his urging, Congress passed a series of measures known collectively as the Sáenz Peña Law (1912). The new law established universal and secret male suffrage for citizens when they reached the age of eighteen. This measure, conceding the Radicals' basic demands, compelled them to abandon their revolutionary posture and operate as a regular party through legal channels. In 1912, having abandoned "Abstention," the Radicals made large gains in congressional and local elections, foreshadowing the victory of Hipólito Yrigoyen in the presidential election of 1916.

The Sáenz Peña Law, "an act of calculated retreat by the ruling class," in the words of David Rock, opened the way for a dependent bourgeoisie to share power and the spoils of office with

---

[1] Under the leadership of José Batlle y Ordóñez (1856–1929), president of Uruguay from 1903 to 1907 and again from 1911 to 1915, Uruguay adopted an advanced program of social reform that made it "the chief laboratory for social experimentation in the Americas and a focal point of world interest." The program included the establishment of the eight-hour day, old-age pensions, minimum wages, and accident insurance; abolition of capital punishment, separation of church and state, education for women, and recognition of divorce; and a system of state capitalism that gradually brought under public ownership banks, railroads, electric systems, telephone and telegraph companies, street railways, and meat-packing plants. Batlle supported labor in its strikes against foreign-owned enterprises. But his advanced welfare legislation was effective only in the port city of Montevideo. Batlle made no effort to challenge the land monopoly of the great estancieros or to apply his social legislation to their peons.

the landed aristocracy. The principal political vehicle for working-class aspirations was the Socialist party, founded in 1894 as a split-off from the Unión Cívica Radical by the Buenos Aires physician and intellectual Juan B. Justo, who led the party until his death in 1928.

Despite its professed Marxism, the party's socialism was of the parliamentary reformist kind, appealing chiefly to highly skilled native-born workers and the lower middle class. The majority of workers, foreign-born noncitizens who still dreamed of returning someday to their homelands, remained aloof from electoral politics but readily joined trade union organizations. Here the Socialist party competed for influence with the anarchists and syndicalists, who in turn competed with each other for leadership of trade unions and strikes. Between 1902 and 1910 wage scales and working conditions deteriorated as surplus immigrant labor accumulated in Buenos Aires; a series of great strikes was broken by the government with brutal repression and the deportation of so-called "foreign agitators." Despite these defeats and the negative consequences of discord among socialists, anarchists, and syndicalists, the labor movement continued to grow and struggle, winning such initial victories as the ten-hour workday and the establishment of Sunday as a compulsory day of rest.

Chilean Politics and Economy

Nitrates and War

In 1876 the official Liberal candidate for the presidency, Aníbal Pinto, defeated two rivals, both distinguished historians—Miguel Luis Amunátegui and Benjamin Vicuña Mackenna. From his predecessor, the new president inherited a severe economic crisis (1874–1879). Wheat and copper prices dropped, exports declined, and unemployment grew. The principal offset to these unfavorable developments was the continued growth of nitrate exports from the Atacama Desert as a result of a doubling of nitrate production between 1865 and 1875. But nitrates, the foundation of Chilean material progress, also became the cause of a major war with dramatic consequences for Chile and her two foes, Bolivia and Peru.

The nitrate deposits exploited by the Anglo-Chilean companies lay, it will be recalled, in territories belonging to Bolivia (the province of Antofagasta) and Peru (the province of Tarapacá). In 1866 a treaty between Chile and Bolivia defined their boundary in the Atacama Desert as the twenty-fourth parallel, gave Chilean and Bolivian interests equal rights to exploit the territory between the twenty-third and twenty-fifth parallels, and guaranteed each government half of the tax revenues obtained from the export of minerals from the whole area. Anglo-Chilean capital soon poured into the region, developing a highly efficient mining-industrial complex. By a second treaty of 1874, Chile's northern border with Bolivia was left at the twenty-fourth parallel. Chile relinquished her rights to a share of the taxes from exports north of that boundary but received in return a twenty-five-year guarantee against increase of taxes on Chilean enterprises operating in the Bolivian province of Antofagasta.

Chile had no boundary dispute with Peru, but aggressive Chilean mining interests, aided by British capital, soon extended their operations from Antofagasta into the Peruvian province of Tarapacá. By 1875, Chilean enterprises in Peruvian nitrate fields employed more than ten thousand workers, engineers, and supervisory personnel. At this point, the Peruvian government, on the brink of bankruptcy as a result of a very expensive program of public works, huge European loans, and the depletion of the guano deposits on which it had counted to service those loans, decided to expropriate the foreign companies in Tarapacá and establish a state monopoly over the production and sale of nitrates. Meanwhile, Peru and Bolivia had negotiated a secret treaty in 1874 providing for a military alliance in the event either power went to war with Chile.

Ejected from Tarapacá, the Anglo-Chilean capitalists intensified their exploitation of the nitrate deposits in Antofagasta. In 1878, Bolivia, counting on her military alliance with Peru, challenged Chile by imposing higher taxes on nitrate exports from Antofagasta, in violation of the treaty of 1874. When the Chilean companies operating in Antofagasta refused to pay the new taxes, the Bolivian government threatened them with confiscation. The agreement of 1874 provided for arbitration of disputes, but the Bolivians twice rejected Chilean offers to submit the dispute to arbitration.

In February 1879, despite Chilean warnings that expropriation of Chilean enterprises would void the treaty of 1874, the Bolivian government ordered the confiscation carried out. On February 14, the day set for the seizure and sale of the Chilean properties, Chilean troops occupied the port of Antofagasta, encountering no resistance, and proceeded to extend Chilean control over the whole province. Totally unprepared for war, Peru made a vain effort to mediate between Chile and Bolivia. Chile, however, having learned of the secret Peruvian-Bolivian alliance, charged Peru with intolerable duplicity and declared war on both Peru and Bolivia on April 5, 1879.

In this war, called the War of the Pacific, Chile faced enemies whose combined population was more than twice its own; one of these powers, Peru, also possessed a respectable naval force. But Chile enjoyed major advantages. By contrast with its neighbors, it possessed a stable central government, a people with a strong sense of national identity, and a disciplined, well-trained army and navy. Although small, the navy included two modern ironclads with revolving turrets and heavy firing power. Chile also enjoyed the advantage of being closer to the theater of operations, since Bolivian troops had to come over the Andes, while the Peruvian army had to cross the Atacama Desert.

All three powers had serious economic problems, but Chile's situation was not as catastrophic as that of its foes. Equally important, Chile had the support of powerful English capitalist interests, who knew that the future of the massive English investment in Chile depended in large part on the outcome of the war. The prospect of Chilean acquisition of the valuable nitrate areas of Antofagasta and Tarapacá naturally pleased the British capitalists. British capital was also invested in Bolivia and Peru, but whereas the Chilean government had maintained service on its debt, Bolivia and Peru had suspended payment on their English loans. Besides, the Peruvian nationalization of the nitrate industry in Tarapacá had seriously injured British interests.

The decisive battle of the war took place on the sea on October 8, 1879, when the two Chilean ironclads, recently acquired from England, forced the surrender of the Peruvian ship *Huáscar,* which had done great damage to Chilean coastal traffic, and severed communications between Santiago and the Chilean forces operating in the Atacama Desert. Having command of the sea, the Chilean forces resumed operations in the Atacama, and in a short time overran the Peruvian provinces of Tarapacá, Tacna, and Arica. By the middle of 1880, Bolivia had effectively been knocked out of the war. In January 1881, a thirty-thousand-man Chilean army under the command of General Manuel Baquedano overcame tenacious Peruvian resistance and occupied the enemy capital of Lima. Meanwhile, the Chilean navy had sunk the last Peruvian warship, the *Atahualpa.* Although scattered fighting between Chilean occupation forces and Peruvian guerrillas continued for over two years, Chile had clearly won the war.

By the Treaty of Ancón (October 20, 1883), Peru ceded the province of Tarapacá to Chile in perpetuity. Tacna and Arica would be Chilean for ten years, after which a plebiscite would decide their ultimate fate. But the plebiscite was never held, and Chile continued to administer the two territories until 1929, when Peru recovered Tacna and Arica went to Chile. An armistice signed in April 1884 by Bolivia and Chile assigned the former Bolivian province of Antofagasta to Chile, but for many years no Bolivian government would sign a formal treaty acknowledging that loss. Meanwhile, Chile remained in de facto possession of the port and province of Antofagasta. Finally, in 1904, Bolivia signed a treaty in which Chile agreed to pay an indemnity and to build a railroad connecting the Bolivian capital of La Paz

228 with the port of Arica. That railroad was completed in 1913.

Aftermath of the War of the Pacific

Chile took advantage of the continued mobilization of its armed forces during the negotiations with Peru to settle scores with the Araucanian Indians, whose struggle in defense of their land against encroaching whites had continued since colonial times. After two years of resistance against very unequal odds, the Araucanians were forced to admit defeat and sign a treaty (1883) that resettled the Indians on reservations but permitted them to retain their tribal government and laws. The Araucanian campaign of 1880–1882, which extended the Chilean frontier to the south into a region of mountain and forest, sparked a brisk movement of land speculation and colonization in that area.

From the War of the Pacific, which shattered Peru economically and psychologically and left Bolivia more isolated than before from the outside world, Chile emerged the strongest nation on the west coast, in control of vast deposits of nitrates and copper, the mainstays of its economy. But the greater part of these riches would soon pass into foreign hands. In 1881 the Chilean government made an important decision: it decided to return the nitrate properties of Tarapacá to private ownership, that is, to the holders of the certificates issued by the Peruvian government as compensation for the nationalized properties.

During the war, uncertainty as to how Chile would dispose of those properties had caused the Peruvian certificates to depreciate until they fell to a fraction of their face worth. Speculators, mostly British, had bought up large quantities of these depreciated certificates. In 1878, British capital controlled some 13 percent of the nitrate industry of Tarapacá; by 1890, its share had risen to at least 70 percent. British penetration of the nitrate areas proceeded not only through formation of companies for direct exploitation of nitrate deposits but through the establishment of banks that financed entrepreneurial activity in the nitrate area and the creation of railways and other companies more or less closely linked to the central nitrate industry. An English railway company with a monopoly of transport in Tarapacá, the Nitrate Railways Company, controlled by John Thomas North, paid dividends of up to 20 and 25 percent, compared with earnings of from 7 to 14 percent for other railway companies in South America.

The Chilean national bourgeoisie, which had pioneered in the establishment of the mining-industrial-railway complex in the Atacama, offered little resistance to the foreign take-over. Lack of strong support from the state, the relative financial weakness of the Chilean bourgeoisie, and the cozy and profitable relationships maintained throughout the nineteenth century between the Chilean elite and British interests facilitated the rapid transfer of Chilean nitrate and railway properties into British hands and the transformation of the Chilean bourgeoisie into a dependent bourgeoisie content with a share in the profits of British companies.

The presidential election of 1881 pitted a conservative military hero of the War of the Pacific, General Manuel Baquedano, against the candidate of a liberal coalition, Domingo Santa María, who won handily. The religious issue, one of the few still separating the new bourgeoisie from the landed aristocracy, dominated his administration (1881–1886). A dispute with the Vatican over its refusal to approve the government's nomination of an archbishop of liberal views led to the expulsion of the apostolic delegate, followed by congressional passage of a series of religious reforms: civil marriage, civil registration of births and deaths, and lay control of some cemeteries. However, the church continued to own extensive properties and receive subsidies from the state. More radical proposals to divorce church and state failed to win approval. In 1884 an electoral reform was adopted; the property qualification for voting was replaced with a literacy test. Since the great majority of Chilean males were illiterate *rotos* (seasonal farm workers) and inquilinos, this change did not materially add to the number of voters; as late as 1915, out of a population of about 3.5 million, only 150,000 persons voted.

The official liberal candidate for president in the election of 1886, José Manuel Balmaceda, had a distinguished record of public service as a diplomat and cabinet minister. As minister of the interior in Santa María's cabinet, he had piloted through Congress the religious reforms just described. Balmaceda took office with a well-defined program of state-directed economic modernization. By the 1880s, factory capitalism had taken root in Chile. The Chilean Society for Industrial Development, which campaigned for state assistance to industrialization in the form of tariffs, subsidies, and other preferential treatment, was founded in 1883. In addition to consumer goods industries—flour mills, breweries, leather factories, furniture factories, and the like—there existed foundries and metal-working enterprises that served the mining industry, railways, and agriculture. Balmaceda proposed to consolidate and expand this native industrial capitalism.

Balmaceda's Nationalistic Policies

Balmaceda came to office when government revenues were at an all-time high (they had risen from about 15 million pesos a year before the War of the Pacific to about 45 million pesos in 1887). The chief source of this government income was the export duty on nitrates. Knowing that the proceeds from this source would taper off as the nitrate deposits diminished, Balmaceda wisely planned to employ those funds for the development of an economic infrastructure that would remain when the nitrate was gone. Hence, public works figured prominently in his program. In 1887 he created a new ministry of industry and public works, which expended large sums on extending and improving the telegraphic and railway systems and on the construction of bridges, roads, and docks. Balmaceda also generously endowed public education, needed to provide skilled workers for Chilean industry. During his presidency, the total enrollment in Chilean schools rose in four years from some 79,000 in 1886 to over 150,000 in 1890. He also favored raising the wages of workers but was inconsistent

in his labor policy; yielding to strong pressure from foreign and domestic employers, he sent troops to crush a number of strikes.

Central to Balmaceda's program was his determination to "Chileanize" the nitrate industry. In his inaugural address to Congress, he declared that his government would consider what measures it should take "to nationalize industries which are, at present, chiefly of benefit to foreigners," a clear reference to the nitrate industry. Later, Balmaceda's strategy shifted; he encouraged the entrance of Chilean private capital into nitrate production and exportation to prevent the formation of a foreign-dominated nitrate cartel whose interest in restricting output clashed with the government's interest in maintaining a high level of production in order to collect more export taxes. In November 1888, he scolded the Chilean elite for their lack of entrepreneurial spirit:

Why does the credit and the capital which are brought into play in all kinds of speculations in our great cities hold back and leave the foreigner to establish banks at Iquique and abandon to strangers the exploiting of the nitrate works of Tarapacá? . . . The foreigner exploits these riches and takes the profit of native wealth to give to other lands and unknown people the treasures of our soil, our own property and the riches we require.[2]

Balmaceda waged a determined struggle to end the monopoly of the British-owned Nitrate Railways Company, whose prohibitive freight charges reduced production and export of nitrates. His nationalistic policies inevitably provoked the hostility of English nitrate "kings" like North who had close links with the Chilean elite and employed prominent liberal politicians as their legal advisers.

But Balmaceda had many domestic as well as foreign foes. The clericals remembered his leading role in the religious reforms and noted his

[2] Harold Blakemore, *British Nitrates and Chilean Politics, 1886–1896: Balmaceda and North* (London, 1974), p. 80.

plans to further curb the powers of the church. The landed aristocracy resented his public works program because it drew labor from agriculture and pushed up rural wages. The banks, whose uncontrolled emission of notes had fed an inflation whose sole beneficiaries were mortgaged landlords and exporters who received payment in foreign currencies, were angered by his proposal to establish a national bank with a monopoly of note issue. The entire oligarchy, liberals as well as conservatives, opposed his use of the central government as an instrument of progressive economic and social change.

Meanwhile, the government's economic problems multiplied, adding to Balmaceda's political difficulties by narrowing his mass base. By 1890 foreign demand for copper and nitrates had weakened. Prices in an overstocked world market fell, and English nitrate interests responded to the crisis by forming a cartel to reduce production. Reduced production and export of nitrates and copper sharply diminished the flow of export duties into the treasury and caused growing unemployment and wage cuts even as inflation cut into the value of wages. The result was a series of great strikes in Valparaíso and the nitrate zone in 1890. Despite his sympathy with the workers' demands and unwillingness to use force against them, Balmaceda, under pressure from domestic and foreign employers, sent troops to crush the strikes. These repressive measures insured much working-class apathy or even hostility toward the president in the eventual confrontation with his foes.

Indeed, Balmaceda had few firm allies at his side when that crisis came. The industrial capitalist group whose growth he had ardently promoted was still weak. The mining interests, increasingly integrated with or dominated by English capital, joined the bankers, the clericals, and the landed aristocracy in opposition to his nationalist program of economic development and independence.

Since the elections of 1888, Balmaceda had lacked a reliable parliamentary majority, a condition that made for a growing deadlock between president and Congress. In October 1890, Bal-

maceda dismissed a cabinet imposed upon him by the congressional majority and appointed one acceptable to himself. Instead of summoning Congress, which was dominated by a coalition of anti-Balmaceda forces, to pass the budget for 1891, the president simply announced that the 1890 budget would continue in force for the next year. In effect, Balmaceda abolished the system of parliamentary government and returned to the traditional system of presidential rule established by the constitution of 1833. His rash act, made without any serious effort to mobilize popular forces, played into the hands of his enemies, who were already preparing for civil war.

On January 7, 1891, congressional leaders proclaimed a revolt against the president in the name of legality and the constitution. The navy, then as now led by officers of aristocratic descent, promptly went over to the rebels, while most army units remained loyal to the president. A junta headed by fleet captain Jorge Montt assumed direction of the revolt. With navy support, the congressionalists seized the ports and customhouses in the north and established their capital at Iquique, the chief port of Tarapacá.

English-owned enterprises actively aided the rebels. Indeed, by the admission of the British minister at Santiago, "our naval officers and the British community of Valparaíso and all along the coast rendered material assistance to the opposition and committed many breaches of neutrality." Many nitrate workers, alienated by Balmaceda's repression of their strike, remained neutral or even joined the rebel army, organized by a German army officer, General Emil Korner. Having gained control of the north and its vast revenues, the congressionalist forces moved south. Victories over Balmaceda's army in the battles of Concón and Placilla opened the way for capture of Valparaíso and Santiago, forcing the president to seek refuge in the Argentine embassy. On September 19, 1891, the day on which his legal term of office came to an end, Balmaceda put a bullet through his head.

The death of Chile's first anti-imperialist president restored the reign of the oligarchy, a coalition of landowners, bankers, merchants, and mining interests closely linked to English capital. A new era began, the era of the so-called Parliamentary Republic. Taught by experience, the oligarchy now preferred to rule through a Congress divided into various factions rather than through a strong executive. Such decentralization of government favored the interests of the rural aristocracy and its allies. A new law of 1892, vesting local governments with the right to supervise elections both for local and national offices, reinforced the power of the landowners, priests, and political bosses who had fought Balmaceda's progressive policies. The presidents of this period, beginning with Jorge Montt (1891–1896), were little more than puppets pulled by strings in the hands of congressional leaders. Corruption, cynicism, and factional intrigue characterized the political life of the Parliamentary Republic. Members of Congress, who received no salaries, paid large sums to secure election, which gave them access to the ample opportunities for graft on the national level.

The Parliamentary Republic, Foreign Economic Domination, and the Growth of the Working Class

The era of the Parliamentary Republic was accompanied by a growing subordination of the Chilean economy to foreign capital, which was reflected in a steady increase in the foreign debt and foreign ownership of the nation's resources. English investments in Chile amounted to 24 million pounds in 1890; they rose to 64 million pounds in 1913. Of this total, 34.6 million pounds formed part of the Chilean public debt. In the same period, North American and German capital began to challenge the British hegemony in Chile. England continued to be Chile's principal trade partner, but United States and German trade with Chile grew at a faster rate. German instructors also acquired a strong influence in the Chilean army, and the flow of German immigrants into southern Chile continued, resulting in the formation of compact colonies dominated by a Pan-German ideology.

The revival of the Chilean economy from the depression of the early 1890s brought an increase of nitrate, copper, and agricultural exports and further enriched the ruling classes, but it left inquilinos, miners, and factory workers as desperately poor as before. Meanwhile, the working class grew from 120,000 to 250,000 between 1890 and 1900, and the doctrines of trade unionism, socialism, and anarchism achieved growing popularity in its ranks.

Luis Emilio Recabarren (1876–1924), the father of Chilean socialism and communism, played a decisive role in the social and political awakening of the Chilean proletariat. In 1906, Recabarren was elected to Congress from a mining area but was not allowed to take his seat because he refused to take his oath of office on the Bible. In 1909, he organized the Workers Federation of Chile, the first national trade union movement. Three years later, he led the founding of the Socialist party, a revolutionary Marxist movement, and became its first secretary.

The growing self-consciousness and militancy of the Chilean working class found expression in a mounting wave of strikes. Between 1911 and 1920, almost three hundred strikes, involving more than 300,000 workers, took place. Many were crushed with traditional brutal methods that left hundreds and thousands of workers dead.

Brazilian Politics and Economy

The Antislavery Movement

From the close of the Paraguayan War (1870), the slavery question surged forward, becoming the dominant issue in Brazilian political life. Dom Pedro, personally opposed to slavery, was caught in a crossfire between a growing number of liberal leaders, intellectuals, and urban middle-class groups who demanded emancipation and slave owners determined to postpone the inevitable as long as possible. In 1870, Spain freed all the newborn and aged slaves of Cuba and Puerto

Rico, leaving Brazil the only nation in the Americas to retain slavery in its original colonial form. Yielding to pressure, a conservative ministry pushed through parliament the Rio Branco Law in 1871. This measure freed all newborn children of slaves but obligated the masters to care for them until they reached the age of eight. At that time, owners could either release the children to the government in return for an indemnity or retain them as laborers until they reached the age of twenty-one. The law also freed all slaves belonging to the state or crown and created a fund to be used for the manumission of slaves.

The Rio Branco Law was a tactical retreat designed to put off a final solution of the slavery problem. The imperial government applied the law with ponderous slowness, the compensation fund was never large enough to buy the freedom of many slaves, and few slave owners came forward to redeem slave children for money. At late as 1884, only 113 had been freed by this means. Given the option of exploiting the labor of these children until they reached the age of twenty-one or exchanging them for government bonds, the great majority of slave owners chose the first course. Regarding them as temporary property, masters often worked these "free" children very hard; even after they reached the age of twenty-one, tradition and lack of education tended to keep them in a condition of semibondage. In effect, the Rio Branco Law gave an indefinite stay of execution to Brazilian slavery.

Abolitionist leaders denounced the law as a sham and illusion and advanced ever more vigorously the demand for total and immediate emancipation. From 1880 on, the antislavery movement developed great momentum. Concentrated in the cities, it drew strength from the process of economic, social, and intellectual modernization under way there. To the new urban groups, slavery was an anachronism, glaringly incompatible with modernization. Among the slave owners themselves, divisions of opinion appeared. In the north, where slavery had long been dying as a result of the sale of the best slaves south and where many of those who remained were aged or dying, a growing number of planters

converted to the use of free labor, drawing on the pool of freedmen made available by the Rio Branco Law and the *sertanejos* (inhabitants of the interior), poor whites and mixed-bloods who lived on the fringes of the plantation economy. Another factor in the decline of the slave population of the northeast was the great drought of 1877–1879, which caused many of the region's wealthier folk to abandon the area. Some sold their slaves before departing for Rio; others brought slaves with them. In states like Amazonas and Ceará, where black slaves were few and most of the work was done by Indians and mixed-bloods, the move to emancipation was relatively easy; in 1884 both of these states declared the end of slavery within their borders. By contrast, the coffee planters of Rio de Janeiro, São Paulo, and Minas Gerais, joined by northern planters who trafficked in slaves, selling them to the coffee zone, offered the most tenacious resistance to the advance of abolition.

The abolitionist movement produced leaders of remarkable intellectual and moral stature. One was Joaquim Nabuco, son of a distinguished liberal statesman of the empire, whose eloquent dissection and indictment of slavery, *O abolicionismo,* had a profound impact on its readers. Another was a mulatto journalist, José do Patrocinio, a master propagandist noted for his fiery, biting style. Another mulatto, André Rebouças, an engineer and teacher whose intellectual gifts won him the respect and friendship of the emperor, was a leading organizer of the movement. For Nabuco and his comrades-in-arms, the antislavery struggle was the major front in a larger struggle for the transformation of Brazilian society. Abolition, they hoped, would pave the way for the attainment of other goals: land reform, public education, and political democracy.

Yielding to mounting pressure, parliament adopted another measure on September 28, 1885, that liberated all slaves when they reached the age of sixty but required them to continue to serve their masters for three years and forbade them to leave their place of residence for five years. These conditions, added to the fact that few slaves lived beyond the age of sixty-five, im-

Slaves drying coffee on a plantation in Terreiros, in the state of Rio de Janeiro, about 1882. (Courtesy, Hack Hoffenburg)

plied little change in the status of the vast majority of slaves. The imperial government also promised to purchase the freedom of the remaining slaves in fourteen years—a promise that few took seriously, in the light of experience with the Rio Branco Law. Convinced that the new law was another tactical maneuver, the abolitionists spurned all compromise solutions and demanded immediate, unconditional emancipation.

By the middle 1880s, the antislavery movement had assumed massive proportions and a more militant character. Large numbers of slaves began to vote for freedom with their feet; they were aided by abolitionists who organized an under-

ground railway that ran from São Paulo to Ceará, where slavery had ended. Efforts to secure the return of fugitive slaves encountered growing resistance. Army officers, organized in a *Club Militar,* protested against the use of the army for the pursuit of fugitive slaves.

In February 1887, São Paulo liberated all slaves in the city with funds raised by popular subscription. Many slave owners, seeing the handwriting on the wall, liberated their slaves on condition that they remain at work for some time longer. By the end of 1887, even the die-hard coffee planters of São Paulo were ready to adjust to new conditions by offering to pay wages to their slaves and improve their working and living conditions; they also increased efforts to induce European immigrants to come to São Paulo. These efforts were highly successful; the flow of immigrants into São Paulo rose from 6,600 in 1885 to over 32,000 in 1887 and to 90,000 in 1888. As a result, coffee production reached record levels. With its labor problem solved, São Paulo was ready to abandon its resistance and even join the abolitionist crusade.

When parliament met on May 3, 1888, to deliberate again on the slavery question, the institution was in its last throes. By overwhelming majorities, both houses of parliament approved a measure whose laconic text read: "Article 1. From the date of this law slavery is declared abolished in Brazil. Article 2. All contrary provisions are revoked." Princess Isabel, ruling as regent for Dom Pedro, who was in Europe for medical treatment, signed the bill on May 13. Contrary to a traditional interpretation, however, the decision of May 1888 was not the climax of a gradual process of slavery's decline and the peaceful acceptance of the inevitable by the slave owners. The total slave population dropped sharply only after 1885, as a result of abolitionist agitation, mass flights of slaves, armed clashes, and other upheavals that appeared to many conservatives to threaten anarchy. In effect, abolition had come not through reform but by revolution.

The aftermath of abolition refuted the dire predictions of its foes. Freed from the burdens of slavery, Brazil made more economic progress in a few years than it had during the almost seven decades of imperial rule. For the former slaves, however, little had changed. The abolitionist demand for the grant of land to the freedmen was forgotten. Relationships between former masters and slaves in many places remained largely unchanged; tradition and the economic and political power of the fazendeiros gave them almost absolute control over their former slaves. Denied land and education, victims of prejudices inherited from the days of slavery, the freedmen were assigned the hardest, most poorly paid jobs. Fazendeiros replaced freedmen with immigrants in the coffee plantations; in the cities, black artisans lost their jobs to immigrants.

The Fall of the Monarchy

Abolition dragged down slavery's sister institution—the monarchy. The empire had long rested on the support of the planter class, especially the northern planters, who saw in the empire a guarantee of the survival of slavery. Before 1888, the Republican party had its principal base among the coffee interests, who resented the favor shown by the imperial government to the sugar planters and wished to achieve a political power corresponding to their economic power. Now, angered by abolition and embittered by the failure of the crown to indemnify them for their lost slaves, those planters who had not previously shifted to the use of free labor joined the Republican movement. The monarchy that had served the interest of the regional elites for the previous sixty-seven years had lost its reasons for existence.

Republicanism and a closely allied ideology, positivism, also made many converts in the officer class, disgruntled by what it regarded as neglect and mistreatment of the armed forces by the imperial government. Many of the younger officers came from the new urban middle class or, if of aristocratic descent, were discontented with the ways of their fathers. Positivism, it has been said, became "the gospel of the military academy," where it was brilliantly expounded by a popular young professor of mathematics, Benjamin Constant Botelho de Magalhães, a devoted disciple of Auguste Comte, the doctrine's founder. The positivist doctrine, with its stress on science, its ideal of a dictatorial republic, and its distrust of the masses, fitted the needs of urban middle-class groups, progressive officers, and businessmen-fazendeiros who wanted modernization but without drastic changes in land tenure and class relations.

In June 1889, the liberal ministry headed by the Viscount of Ouro Prêto made a last effort to save the monarchy by proposing a reform program that included extension of the suffrage, autonomy for the provinces, and land reform. It was too late. On November 15, a military revolt organized and headed by Benjamin Constant and Marshal Floriano Peixoto overthrew the government and proclaimed a republic with Marshal Deodoro da Fonseca as provisional chief of state. Like the revolution that gave Brazil its independence, the republican revolution came from above; the coup d'état encountered little resistance but also inspired little enthusiasm. Although the provisional government included some sincere reformers like Ruy Barbosa, a champion of public education and civil liberties, the radical wing of the abolitionist movement was excluded. Power was firmly held by representatives of the business and landed elites and the military.

The new rulers promptly promulgated a series of reforms. On November 15, 1889, the same day that Brazil was proclaimed a republic, a decree ended corporal punishment in the army; on November 19, a literacy test replaced property qualifications for voting (since property and literacy usually went together, this measure did not significantly enlarge the electorate); and in January 1891, successive decrees separated church and state and established civil marriage.

The New Republic

In November 1891, two years after the revolt, a constituent assembly met in Rio de Janeiro to draft a constitution for the new republic. The draft offered for approval by the assembly provided for a federal, presidential form of government with the customary three branches—legislative, executive, and judicial. The principal debate was between the partisans of greater autonomy for the states and those who feared the divisive results of an extreme federalism. The coffee interests, which dominated the wealthy south central region, sought to strengthen their position at the expense of the central power. The bourgeois groups, represented in the convention chiefly by lawyers, favored a strong central government that could promote industry, aid the creation of a national market, and offer protection from British competition.

The result was a compromise tilted in favor of federalism. The twenty provinces in effect became self-governing states with popularly elected governors, the exclusive right to tax exports (a profitable privilege for wealthy states like São Paulo and Minas Gerais), and the right to maintain militias. The national government was given control over the tariff and the income from import duties, while the president obtained very large powers: he designated his cabinet ministers and other high officers, he could declare a state of siege, and he could intervene in the states with the federal armed forces in the event of a threat to their political institutions. The constitution proclaimed the sanctity of private property and guaranteed freedom of the press, speech, and assembly.

If these freedoms had some relevance in the cities and hinterlands touched by the movement of modernization, they lacked meaning over the greater part of the national territory. The fazendeiros, former slave owners, virtually monopolized the nation's chief wealth, its land. The land monopoly gave them absolute control over the rural population. Feudal and semifeudal forms of land tenure, accompanied by the obligation of personal and military service on the part of tenants, survived in the backlands, especially in the northeast. Powerful *coronéis* (colonels) maintained armies of *jagunços* (full-time private soldiers) and waged war against each other.[3] Banditry flourished in the interior, the bandits sometimes hiring themselves out to the coronéis, sometimes operating on their own, and occasionally gaining the reputation of modern Robin Hoods.

[3] The title *coronel* was often honorary and did not necessarily indicate a military command or landownership; especially after 1870, a coronel might be simply a political boss or even an influential lawyer or priest.

In this medieval atmosphere of constant insecurity and social disintegration, there arose messianic movements that reflected the aspirations of the oppressed sertanejos for peace and justice. One of the most important of such movements arose in the interior of Bahia, where the principal activity was cattle raising. In this area appeared a messiah called Antônio Conselheiro (Anthony the Counselor), who established a settlement at the abandoned cattle ranch of Canudos. Rejecting private property, Antônio required all who joined his sacred company to give up their goods, but he promised a future of prosperity in his messianic kingdom through the sharing of the treasure of the "lost Sebastian" (the Portuguese king who had disappeared in Africa in 1478 but would return as a redeemer) or through division of the property of hostile landowners.

Despite its religious coloration, the existence of such a focus of social and political unrest was intolerable to the fazendeiros and the state authorities. When the sertanejos easily defeated state forces sent against them in 1896, the governor called on the federal government for aid. Four campaigns, the last a large-scale operation directed by the minister of war in person, were required to break the epic resistance of the men of Canudos. A Brazilian literary masterpiece, *Os sertões* (Rebellion in the Backlands) by Euclides da Cunha (1856–1909), immortalized the heroism of the defenders and the crimes of the victors. It also revealed to the urban elite another and unfamiliar side of Brazilian reality.

The Economic Revolution

An enormous historical gulf separated the bleak sertão—in which the tragedy of Canudos was played out—from the cities, the scene of a mushrooming growth of banks, stock exchanges, and corporations. With the economic revolution came a revolution in manners. In Rio de Janeiro, writes Pedro Calmon,

barons with recently acquired titles jostled each other in the corridors of the Stock Exchange or in the Rua da Alfandega, buying and selling stocks; the tilburies [light two-wheeled carriages] that filled the length of São Francisco Street were taken by a multitude of millionaires of recent vintage—commercial agents, bustling lawyers, promoters of all kinds, politicians of the new generation, the men of the day.[4]

A few more years and even the physical appearance of some of Brazil's great urban centers would change. These changes were most marked in the federal capital of Rio de Janeiro, which was made into a beautiful and healthful city between 1902 and 1906 through the initiative and efforts of Prefect Pereira Passos, who mercilessly demolished the narrow old streets to permit the construction of broad, modern avenues, and the distinguished scientist Oswaldo Cruz, who waged a victorious struggle to conquer the endemic malaria and yellow fever by filling in swamps and installing adequate water and sewerage systems.

The economic policies of the new republican regime reflected pressures from different quarters: from the planter class, from urban capitalists, from the military. Many planters, left in a difficult position by the abolition of slavery, required subsidies and credits to enable them to convert to the new wage system. The emerging industrial bourgeoisie, convinced that Brazil must develop an industrial base in order to emerge from backwardness, asked for protective tariffs, the construction of an economic infrastructure, and policies favorable to capital formation. Within the provisional government, these aspirations had a fervent supporter in the minister of finance, Ruy Barbosa, who believed that the factory was the crucible in which an "intelligent and independent democracy" would be forged in Brazil. Finally, the army, whose decisive role in the establishment of the republic had given it great prestige and influence, called for increased appropriations for the armed services.

---

[4] Quoted in Benjamin Keen, ed., *Latin American Civilization: The National Era,* vol. 2 (Boston: Houghton Mifflin, 1974), p. 313.

Their demands far exceeded the revenue available to the federal and state governments.

The federal government solved this problem by resorting to the printing press and allowing private banks to issue notes backed by little more than faith in the future of Brazil. In two years, the volume of paper money in circulation doubled, and the foreign exchange value of the Brazilian monetary unit, the *milréis,* plummeted disastrously. Since objective economic conditions (the small internal market and the lack of an adequate technological base, among other factors) limited the real potential for Brazilian growth, much of the newly created capital was used for highly speculative purposes, including the creation of fictitious companies.

The great boom collapsed in 1891, bringing ruin to many investors and unemployment to workers even as inflation continued to cut into the real value of their wages. Disputes over methods of coping with the crisis contributed to a clash between President Deodoro da Fonseca and Congress when it assembled for its first session in November 1891. When da Fonseca attempted to dissolve Congress and assume dictatorial power, the army and navy turned against him. Faced with a threat from the navy to bombard Rio, the president resigned and was succeeded by his vice president, Marshal Floriano Peixoto.

Under Peixoto, the urban middle-class sector gained even greater influence in the government, and inflation continued unchecked, to the dismay of the planters. The rapid fall in the price of coffee expressed in foreign hard currency brought a decline of real income from exports and a rise in the cost of many imported items to almost prohibitive levels. This hurt the planters but stimulated the growth of Brazilian manufactures: the number of such enterprises almost doubled between 1890 and 1895. The discontent of the "outs" sparked a new revolt with strong aristocratic and monarchical overtones in 1893. The movement began in Rio Grande do Sul and was soon joined by the navy, a stronghold of aristocratic prejudice and influence. Peixoto's firm re-fusal to bow to threats of a naval bombardment of the capital brought a collapse of the fleet revolt and allowed the governments to launch an offensive south against the rebels of Rio Grande; by August 1895, the last insurgents had surrendered.

Peixoto's victory, which won him the name of "consolidator of the republic," was largely due to the loyalty and financial and military support of the state of São Paulo. But this support came at a price; the coffee planters were resolved to end the ascendancy of the urban middle classes, whose policies of rapid industrialization they distrusted and held responsible for the inflation and political instability that had plagued the first years of the republic. In 1893 the old planter oligarchies, whose divisions had temporarily enabled the middle classes to gain the upper hand in coalition with the military, reunited to form the Federal Republican party, with a program of support for federalism and fiscal responsibility. Since they controlled the electoral machinery, they easily elected Prudente de Morais president in 1894. Morais, the first civilian president of Brazil (1894–1898), initiated an era marked by the domination of the coffee interests and the relegation of urban capitalist groups to a secondary role in political life.

Morais' successor, Manuel Ferraz de Campos Sales (1898–1902), continued and expanded his program of giving primacy to agriculture. Campos Sales fully endorsed the system of the international economic division of labor as it applied to Brazil. "It is time," he proclaimed, "that we take the correct road; to that end we must strive to export all that we can produce better than other countries, and import all that other countries can produce better than we." This formula meant the abandonment of the goal of independent economic development—in other words, the acceptance of neocolonialism. Determined to halt inflation, Campos Sales drastically reduced expenditures on public works, increased taxes, and made every effort to redeem the paper money in order to improve Brazil's international credit and secure new loans, which were vital to the coffee interests.

Coffee was king. Around the monarch were grouped his obedient barons: rubber, cacao, cotton, sugar. Whereas in the period from 1880 to 1889, Brazil produced only 56 percent of the world's coffee output, in the period from 1900 to 1904, it accounted for 76 percent of the total production. Its closest competitor, rubber, supplied only 28 percent of Brazil's exports in 1901. Sugar, once the ruler of the Brazilian economy, now accounted for barely 5 percent of the nation's exports. Minas Gerais and especially São Paulo became the primary coffee regions, while Rio de Janeiro declined in importance. Enjoying immense advantages—the famous rich, porous *terra roxa* (red soil), an abundance of immigrant labor, and closeness to the major port of Santos—the *Paulistas* harvested 60 percent of the national coffee production.

Coffee was king, but from the closing years of the nineteenth century its reign was a troubled one. The classic symptoms of overproduction—falling prices and unsalable stocks—had appeared as early as 1896. The problem arose from a vast increase in plantings of coffee trees (from 220 to 520 million between 1890 and 1900). Foreign competition and speculative activity on the part of middlemen added to the difficulties of the planters. These middlemen (usually agents of foreign banks and merchant houses) bought when the coffee harvest flowed into the ports, forcing prices down, and formed reserves that they doled out in periods of shortage, when prices were high.

Responding to the planters' clamor for help, the government of São Paulo took the first step for the "defense" of coffee in 1902, forbidding new coffee plantings for five years. Other steps soon proved necessary. Faced with a bumper crop in 1906, São Paulo launched a coffee price-support scheme to protect the state's economic lifeblood. With financing from British, French, German, and North American banks, and the eventual collaboration of the federal government, São Paulo purchased several million bags of coffee and held them off the market in an effort to maintain profitable price levels. Purchases continued into 1907; from that date until World War I the stocks were gradually sold off with little market disruption. The operation's principal gainers were the foreign merchants and bankers who, since they controlled the Coffee Commission formed to liquidate the purchased stocks, gradually disposed of them with a large margin of profit. The problem, temporarily exorcised, was presently to return in even more acute form.

The valorization scheme, which favored the coffee-raising states at the expense of the rest, reflected the coffee planters' political domination. Under President Campos Sales, this ascendancy was institutionalized by the so-called *política dos governadores* (politics of the governors). Its essence was a formula that gave the two richest and most populous states (São Paulo and Minas Gerais) a virtual monopoly of federal politics and the choice of presidents. Thus, the first three civilian presidents from 1894 to 1906 came from São Paulo; the next two, from 1906 to 1910, came from Minas Gerais and Rio de Janeiro, respectively.

In return, the oligarchies of the other states were given almost total freedom of action within their jurisdictions, the central government intervening as a rule only when it suited the local oligarchy's interest. Informal discussions among the state governors determined the choice of president, with his election a foregone conclusion. No official candidate for president lost an election before 1930. In 1910 the distinguished statesman and orator Ruy Barbosa ran for president on a platform of democratic reform and antimilitarism against the official candidate, Hermes da Fonseca, a conservative military man. Barbosa was beaten by almost two to one; out of a population of 22 million, about 360,000 voted. Similar reciprocal arrangements existed on the state level between the governors and the coronéis, urban or rural bosses who rounded up the local vote to elect the governors and were rewarded with a free hand in their respective domains.

Despite the official bias in favor of agriculture, industry continued to grow in the period from 1904 to 1914. By 1908, Brazil could boast of more than three thousand industrial enterprises. Foreign firms dominated the fields of banking, public works, utilities, transportation, and the export and import trade. Manufacturing, on the other hand, was carried on almost exclusively by native Brazilians and permanent immigrants. This national industry was concentrated in the four states of São Paulo, Minas Gerais, Rio de Janeiro, and Rio Grande do Sul. Heavy industry did not exist; over half of the enterprises were textile mills and food-processing plants. Many of these "enterprises" were small workshops employing a few artisans or operated with an archaic technology, and Brazilians in the market economy continued to import most quality products. The quantitative and qualitative development of industry was hampered by the semifeudal conditions prevailing in the countryside, by the extreme poverty of the masses, which sharply limited the internal market, by the lack of a skilled, literate labor force (as late as 1910, Brazil had an enrollment of only 566,000 pupils out of a population of 22 million, and the great majority received less than two years of formal instruction), and by the hostility of most fazendeiros and foreign interests to industry.

Together with industry there arose a working class destined to play a significant role in the life of the country. The Brazilian proletariat was partly recruited from sharecroppers and minifundio peasants fleeing to the cities to escape dismal poverty and the tyranny of coronéis, but above all it was composed of the flood of European immigrants, who arrived at a rate of 100,000 to 150,000 each year. Working and living conditions of the working class were often intolerable. Child labor was common, for children could be legally employed from the age of twelve. The workday ranged from nine hours for some skilled workers to more than sixteen hours for various categories of unskilled workers. Wages were pitifully low and often paid in vouchers redeemable at the company store. There was a total absence of legislation to protect workers against the hazards of unemployment, old age, or industrial accidents.

Among the European immigrants were many militants with socialist, syndicalist, or social-democratic backgrounds who helped to organize the Brazilian labor movement and gave it a radical political orientation. National and religious divisions among workers, widespread illiteracy, and quarrels between socialists and anarcho-syndicalists hampered the rise of a trade union movement and a labor party.

But trade unions grew rapidly after 1900 in response to unsatisfactory working conditions, with immigrant workers often providing the leadership. In 1906 the first national labor congress, representing the majority of the country's trade unions, met and began a struggle for the eight-hour workday. One result of the congress was the formation of the first national trade union organization, the Brazilian Labor Confederation, which conducted a number of strikes. Repression was the typical answer of the authorities and employers to labor's demands. Police conducted periodic roundups of labor leaders. Immigrants were deported, while native-born leaders were imprisoned or sent to forced labor on a railroad under construction in distant Mato Grosso. The phrase "the social question is a question for the police" was often used to sum up the labor policy of the Brazilian state.

Chapter 11

Society and Culture in the Nineteenth Century

Independence left much of the colonial social structure intact. This fact was very apparent to liberal leaders of the postindependence era. "The war against Spain," declared the Colombian liberal Ramón Mercado in 1853, "was not a revolution. . . . Independence only scratched the surface of the social problem, without changing its essential nature." A modern historian, Charles C. Griffin, comes to much the same conclusion. "Only the beginnings of a basic transformation took place," he writes, "and there were many ways in which colonial attitudes and institutions carried over into the life of republican Spanish America."

How New Was the New Society?

We should not minimize, however, the extent and importance of the changes that did take place. Independence produced, if not a major social upheaval, at least a minor one. It opened wide fissures within the elite, dividing aristocratic supporters of the old social order from modernizers who wanted a more democratic, bourgeois order. Their struggle is an integral aspect of the first half-century after the end of Spanish and Portuguese rule. Independence also enabled such formerly submerged groups as artisans and gauchos to enter the political arena, although in subordinate roles, and even allowed a few to climb into the ranks of the elite. The opening of Latin American ports to foreign goods also established a relatively free market in ideas, at least in the capitals and other cities. With almost no time lag, such new European doctrines as utopian socialism, romanticism, and positivism entered Latin

America and were applied to the solution of the continent's problems. These new winds of doctrine, blowing through what had lately been dusty colonial corridors, contributed to the area's intellectual renovation and promoted further social change.

The Passing of the Society of Castes

Verbally, at least, the new republican constitutions established the equality of all men before the law, destroying the legal foundations of colonial caste society. Since little change in property relations took place, however, the ethnic and social lines of division remained essentially the same. Wealth, power, and prestige continued to be concentrated in the hands of a ruling class that was mainly white, although in some countries, such as Venezuela, it became more or less heavily tinged with individuals of darker skin who had managed to climb the social ladder through their prowess in war or politics.

The Indians

Of all the groups composing the old society of castes, the status of the Indians changed least of all. The Mexican historian Carlos María Bustamante was one of the few creole leaders who recognized that independence had not freed the Indians from their yoke. "They still drag the same chains," he wrote, "although they are flattered with the name of freemen." Even Indian tribute and forced labor, abolished during or after the wars of independence, soon reappeared in many countries under other names. What was worse, Indian communal landholding, social organization, and culture, which Spanish law and policy had to some extent protected in colonial times, came under increasing attack, especially from liberals who believed that Indian communal traditions constituted as much of an obstacle to progress as the Spanish system of castes and special privileges.

Until about 1870, however, large, compact Indian populations continued to live under the traditional communal landholding system in Mexico, Central America, and the Andean region. Then, the rapid growth of the export economy, the coming of the railroads, and the resulting rise in land values and demand for labor caused white and mestizo landowners and landowner-dominated governments to launch a massive assault on Indian lands. The expropriation of Indian lands was accompanied, as noted in Chapter 10, by a growth of Indian peonage and tenantry. Employers used a variety of devices, ranging from debt servitude to outright coercion, to attach laborers to their estates. In some areas, there arose a type of Indian serfdom that closely resembled the classic European model. In the Andean region, for example, Indian tenants, in addition to working the master's land, had to render personal service in his household, sometimes at the hacienda, sometimes in the city. During his term of domestic service, the Indian serf could be given or sold to the master's friends. This and other forms of serfdom survived well into the twentieth century.

The master class, aided by the clergy and local magistrates, sought to reinforce the economic subjection of the Indian with psychological subjection. There evolved a pattern of relations and role-playing that assigned to the patrón the role of a benevolent figure who assured his peons or tenants of a livelihood and protected them in all emergencies in return for their absolute obedience. In countries with Indian populations or peasants descended from Indians, the relations between master and peon often included an elaborate ritual that required the Indian to request permission to speak to the patrón, to appear before him with head uncovered and bowed, and to seek his approval for all major personal decisions, including marriage.

But these relationships and attitudes of submission and servility, more characteristic of resident peons, were not accepted by all Indians. In the Andean area, Mexico, and elsewhere during the second half of the nineteenth century, the surviving Indian landowning communities fought stubbornly to prevent the absorption of their lands by advancing haciendas and to halt the process by which the Indians became land-less laborers. They fought with all the means at their disposal, including armed revolts as a last resort. Such revolts occurred in Mexico in the 1860s and 1870s and were called "communist" by the landowners and government officials who crushed the Indians with their superior military force.

The greater freedom of movement that came with independence, the progressive disappear-ance of Indian communities, and the growth of the hacienda, in which Indians mingled with mes-tizos, strengthened a trend toward Indian accul-turation that had begun in the late colonial pe-riod. This acculturation was reflected in a growth of Indian bilingualism: Indians increasingly used Spanish in dealing with whites, reserving their native languages for use among themselves. To the limited extent that the public school entered Indian regions, it contributed to the adoption of Spanish as a second language or, in the case of the rare Indian whose talents and good fortunes elevated him into the ranks of the white and mestizo elite, sometimes led to total abandon-ment of his native tongue. The Mexican historian Eduardo Ruíz recalled that as a child he spoke only Tarascan but had forgotten it during his twelve years of study at the colegio. "I did not want to remember, I must confess, because I was ashamed of being thought to be an Indian." Some acculturation also occurred in dress, with fre-quent abandonment of picturesque regional styles in favor of a quasi-European style, some-times enforced by legislation and fines. Over much of Mexico, for example, the white trousers and shirt of coarse cotton cloth and the broad-brimmed hat became almost an Indian "uniform."

Yet pressures toward Indian acculturation or assimilation failed to achieve the integration into white society that well-meaning liberals had hoped to secure through education, the growth of Indian wants, and the Indian's entrance into the modern world of industry and trade. At the end of the nineteenth century, the processes of acculturation had not significantly reduced the size of the Indian sector in the five countries with the largest native populations: Mexico, Guate-mala, Ecuador, Peru, and Bolivia. There were var-ious reasons for this. The economic stagnation and political troubles of the first postrevolution-ary decades tended to reinforce the isolation and cultural separateness of Indian communities. When the Latin American economies revived as a result of the expansion of the export sector, this revival was achieved largely at the expense of the Indians and served mainly to accentuate their poverty and backwardness. Their economic mar-ginality, their almost total exclusion from the po-litical process, the intense exploitation to which they were subjected by white and mestizo land-owners, priests, and officials, and the barriers of distrust and hatred that separated them from the white world prevented any thoroughgoing accul-turation, much less integration.

Indian communities made such concessions to the pressures for assimilation as were necessary but preserved their traditional housing, diet, so-cial organization, and religion—which combined pagan and Christian features. In some regions, the pre-Conquest cults and rituals, including oc-casional human sacrifice, survived. The exis-tence in a number of countries of large Indian populations, intensely exploited and branded as inferior by the ruling social Darwinist ideology, constituted a major obstacle to the formation of a national consciousness in those lands. With good reason, the pioneer Mexican anthropologist Manuel Gamio wrote in 1916 that Mexico did not constitute a nation in the European sense but was composed of numerous small nations, differ-ing in speech, economy, social organization, and psychology.

A Question of Color

The wars for independence, by throwing "careers open to talents," enabled a few Indians and a larger number of mixed-bloods of humble origins to rise high in the military, political, and social scale. The liberal caudillos Vicente Guerrero and Juan Álvarez in Mexico and such talented leaders as Juan José Flores of Ecuador, Andrés Santa Cruz of Bolivia, and Ramón Castilla of Peru illustrate the ascent of the mixed-bloods.

The rise of these mestizo or mulatto leaders inspired fears in some members of the creole elite, beginning with Bolívar, who gloomily predicted a race war that would also be a struggle between haves and have-nots. Bolívar revealed his obsessive race prejudice in his description of the valiant and generous Mexican patriot Vicente Guerrero as the "vile abortion of a savage Indian and a fierce African." These fears proved groundless; although some mixed-blood leaders, like Guerrero and Álvarez, remained to one degree or another loyal to the humble masses from which they had sprung, the majority were soon co-opted by the creole aristocracy and firmly defended its interests.

On the other hand, creole politicians of the postrevolutionary era had to take account of the new political weight of the mixed-blood middle and lower classes, especially the artisan groups. The mixed-bloods were exploited politically by white elites who promised to satisfy the aspirations of the masses—promises they failed to fulfill. This happened in Bogotá, where Colombian liberals courted the artisans in their struggle against conservatives, and in Buenos Aires, where Rosas demagogically identified himself with the gauchos and urban artisans—who were mixed-bloods in the great majority—against the aristocratic liberal *unitarios.*

After mid-century, the growing influence of European racist ideologies, especially Spencerian biological determinism, led to a heightened sensitivity to color. From Mexico to Chile, members of the white elite and even the middle class claimed to be superior to Indians and mixed-bloods. A dark skin increasingly became an obstacle to social advancement. Typical of the rampant pseudoscientific racism by the turn of the century is the remark of the Argentine Carlos Bunge, son of a German immigrant, that mestizos and mulattos were "impure, atavistically anti-

Christian; they are like the two heads of a fabulous hydra that surrounds, constricts, and strangles with its giant spiral a beautiful, pale virgin, Spanish America."

Even before the revolutions, black slavery had declined in various parts of Latin America. This occurred in part because of economic developments that made slavery unprofitable and favored manumission or commutation of slavery to tenantry. An even more significant reason, perhaps, was the frequent flight of slaves to remote jungles and mountains, where they formed self-governing communities. In Venezuela, in about 1800, it was estimated that alongside some eighty-seven thousand slaves there were twenty-four thousand fugitive slaves.

The wars of independence gave a major stimulus to emancipation. Patriot commanders like Bolívar and San Martín and royalist officers often offered slaves freedom in return for military service, and black slaves sometimes formed a majority of the fighting forces on both sides. About a third of San Martín's army in the campaign of the Andes was black. Moreover, the confusion and disorder produced by the fighting often led to a collapse of plantation discipline, easing the flight of slaves and making their recovery difficult if not impossible.

After independence, slavery further declined, partly because of its patent incompatibility with the libertarian ideals proclaimed by the new states but even more as a result of the hostile attitude of Great Britain, which had abolished the slave trade in all its possessions in 1807 and henceforth brought pressure for similar action by all countries still trading in slaves: we have seen that British pressure on Brazil contributed to the crisis of Brazilian slavery and its ultimate demise.

Emancipation came most easily and quickly in countries where slaves were a negligible element in the labor force; thus, Chile, Mexico, and the Federation of Central America (1823–1839) abolished slavery between 1823 and 1829. In other countries, the slave owners fought a tenacious rear-guard action. In Venezuela a very gradual manumission law was adopted in 1821, but not until 1854 was slavery finally abolished. Slavery was abolished in Peru in 1855 by Ramón Castilla. The Spanish Cortes decreed the end of slavery in Puerto Rico in 1873 and in Cuba in 1880, but in Cuba the institution continued in a disguised form (the *patronato*) until 1886, when it was finally abolished.

The record of Latin American slavery in the nineteenth century, it should be noted, does not support the thesis of some historians that cultural and religious factors made Hispanic slavery inherently milder than the North American variety. In its two main centers of Cuba and Brazil, under conditions of mounting demand for Brazilian coffee and Cuban sugar and a critical labor shortage, there is ample evidence of systematic brutality with use of the lash to make slaves work longer and harder. The slaves responded with a resistance that varied from slowdowns to flight and open rebellion—a resistance that contributed to the final demise of the institution.

The Process of Modernization

The Landowners

Patriarchal family organization, highly ceremonial conduct, and leisurely lifestyle continued to characterize the landed aristocracy and Latin American elites after independence. The kinship network of the large extended family ruled by a patriarch was further extended by the institution of *compadrazgo,* which established a relationship of patronage and protection on the part of an upper-class godparent toward a lower-status godchild and his or her parents. The lower-class family members in turn were expected to form part of the godparent's following and to be devoted to his interests.

As in colonial times, great landowners generally resided most of the time in the cities, leaving their estates in the charge of administrators (but it must not be assumed that they neglected to scrutinize account books or were indifferent to

considerations of profit and loss). From the same upper class came a small minority of would-be entrepreneurs who challenged the traditional agrarian bias of their society and, in the words of Richard Graham, were "caught up by the idea of capitalism, by the belief in industrialization, and by a faith in work and practicality." Typical of this class was the Brazilian Viscount Mauá, who created a banking and industrial empire between 1850 and 1875 against the opposition of traditionalists. Mauá's empire collapsed, however, partly because the objective conditions for capitalist development in Brazil had not fully matured, partly because of official apathy and even disfavor. The day of the entrepreneur had not yet come; the economic history of Latin America in the nineteenth century is strewn with the wrecks of abortive industrial projects. These fiascos also represented defeats for the capitalist mentality and values.

After mid-century, with the gradual rise of a neocolonial order based on the integration of the Latin American economy into the international capitalist system, the ruling class, although retaining certain precapitalist traits, became more receptive to bourgeois values and ideals. An Argentine writer of the 1880s noted that "the latifundist no longer has that semibarbarous, semifeudal air; he has become a scientific administrator, who alternates between his home on the estate, his Buenos Aires mansion, and his house in Paris." In fact, few estancieros or hacendados became "scientific administrators." They preferred to leave the task of managing their estates to others, but the writer accurately pointed to a process of modernization or Europeanization of elites under way throughout the continent.

The process began right after independence but greatly accelerated after mid-century. Within a decade after independence, marked changes in manners and consumption patterns had occurred. "Fashions alter," wrote Fanny Calderón de la Barca, Scottish-born wife of the Spanish minister to Mexico, who described Mexican upper-class society in the age of Santa Anna in a series of sprightly letters. "The graceful mantilla

The family of an Indian cacique wearing Spanish dress. (From Carl Nebel, *Voyage Pittoresque et Archéologique . . . [au] Mexique,* Paris, 1836. Courtesy of the Newberry Library.)

gradually gives place to the ungraceful bonnet. The old painted coach, moving slowly like a caravan, with Guido's Aurora painted on its gaudy panels, is dismissed for the London-built carriage."

The old yielded much more slowly and grudgingly to the new in drowsy colonial cities like Quito, capital of Ecuador, but yield it did, at least in externals. The U.S. minister to Ecuador in the 1860s, Friedrich Hassaurek, who was harshly critical of Quitonian society and manners, noted that "in spite of the difficulty of transportation, there are about one hundred and twenty pianos in Quito, very indifferently tuned." Another American visitor to Quito in this period, Professor James Orton of Smith College, observed that "the upper class follow *la mode de Paris,* gentlemen adding the classic cloak of Old Spain." He added sourly that "this modern toga fits an Ecuadoran admirably, preventing the arms from doing anything, and covers a multitude of sins, especially pride and poverty."

Under the republic, as in colonial times, dress was an important index of social status. According to Orton, "no gentleman will be seen walking in the streets of Quito under a poncho. Hence citizens are divided into men with ponchos and gentlemen with cloaks." Dress even served to distinguish followers of different political factions or parties. In Buenos Aires under Rosas, the artisans who formed part of the dictator's mass base were called *gente de chaqueta* (wearers of jackets), as opposed to the aristocratic unitarian liberals, who wore dress coats.

By the close of the century, European styles of dress had triumphed in such great cities as Mexico City and Buenos Aires and among non-Indian sectors of the population generally. But attitudes toward clothes continued to reflect aristocratic values, especially scorn for manual labor; dress still made the man. In Buenos Aires, for example, at the turn of the century, a worker's blouse would bar entrance to its wearer to a bank or the halls of Congress. As a result, according to James Scobie, "everyone sought to hide the link with manual labor," and even workingmen preferred to wear the traditional coat and tie.

The Immigrants

After 1880, there was a massive influx of European immigrants into Argentina, Uruguay, and Brazil and of lesser numbers into such countries as Chile and Mexico. Combined with growing urbanization and continued expansion of the export sector, this helped to accelerate the rate of social change. These developments helped to create a small industrial working class of the modern type and swelled the ranks of the middle class and the blue-collar and white-collar workers.

But aside from that minority of the working class that adopted socialist, anarchist, or syndicalist doctrines, the immigrants posed no threat to the existing social structure or the prevailing aristocratic ideology; instead, many were conquered by that ideology. The foreigners who entered the upper class as a rule already belonged to the educated or managerial class. Movement from the middle class of immigrant origin to the upper class was extremely difficult and rare; for the lower-class immigrant it was almost impossible. A few immigrants made their fortunes by commerce or speculation. Their children or grandchildren took care to camouflage the origins of their wealth and to make it respectable by investing it in land. These nouveaux riches regarded Indians and workers with the same contempt as their aristocratic associates.

Women

Independence did not better the status of women. Indeed, their civil status probably worsened as a result of new bourgeois-style law codes that strengthened husbands' control over their wives' property. More than ever, women were relegated to the four walls of their houses and household duties. Church and parents taught women to be submissive, sweetly clinging, to have no wills of their own. The double standard of sexual conduct prevailed; women were taught to deny their sexuality and believe that procreation was the sole end of sexual intercourse. But women's actual conduct did not necessarily conform to the law and ideology. Silvia Arróm has shown, for example, that the restrictions did not deter women in early nineteenth-century Mexico from engaging in extramarital affairs.

The democratic, liberal movements of the first half-century after independence stimulated some developments in favor of women. In Argentina, Sarmiento wrote that "the level of civilization of a people can be judged by the social position of its women"; his educational program envisaged a major role for women as primary-school teachers. In Mexico, the triumph of the Reforma was followed by promulgation of a new school law that called for the establishment of secondary schools for girls and normal schools for the training of women primary-school teachers. In both countries after 1870 there arose small feminist movements, largely composed of schoolteachers, that formed societies, edited journals, and worked for the cultural, economic, and social improvement of women. In the last decades of the century, with the development of industry, women in increasing numbers entered factories and sweatshops, where they often were paid half of what male workers earned, becoming a source of superprofits for capitalist employers. By 1887, according to the census of Buenos Aires, 39 percent of the paid work force of that city was composed of women.

The Church

The church, which in some countries had suffered discredit because of the royalist posture of many clergy during the wars of independence, experienced a further decline in influence as a result of increasing contacts with the outside world and a new and relatively tolerant climate of opinion. In country after country, liberals pressed with varying success for restrictions on the church's monopoly over education, marriage, burials, and the like. Since the church invariably aligned itself with the conservative opposition, liberal victories brought reprisals in the form of heavy attacks on its accumulated wealth and privileges.

The colonial principle of monolithic religious unity was early shattered by the need to allow freedom of worship to the prestigious and powerful British merchants. It was, in fact, the reactionary Rosas, who disliked foreigners and brought the Jesuits back to Argentina, who donated the land on which the first Anglican church in Buenos Aires was built. Despite the efforts of some fanatical clergy to incite the populace against foreign heretics, there gradually evolved a system of peaceful coexistence between Catholics and dissenters, based on reciprocal good will and tact.

The Inquisition, whose excesses had made it odious even to the faithful, disappeared during the wars of independence. In many countries, however, the civil authorities assumed its right to censor or ban subversive or heretical writings. Occasionally, governments exercised this right. In the 1820s, clerical and conservative opposition forced the liberal vice president of Gran Colombia, Francisco de Paula Santander, to authorize the dropping of a textbook by the materialist Jeremy Bentham from law school courses. In Buenos Aires, under Rosas, subversive books and other materials were publicly burned. According to Tulio Halperin-Donghi, however, a reading of the press advertisements of Buenos Aires booksellers suggests that this repression was singularly ineffective. In Santiago in the 1840s, Francisco Bilbao's fiery polemic against Spain and Catholicism was burned by the public hangman. According to Sarmiento, however, it was not the content of Bilbao's book but its violent, strident tone that caused this reaction; Bilbao, he added, had been justly punished for his clumsiness.

After mid-century, with the enthronement of positivism, which glorified science and rejected theology as an approach to truth, efforts to suppress heretical or anticlerical writings diminished or ended completely in many countries. In general, during the last half of the nineteenth century, there existed in Latin America a relatively free market in ideas—free, that is, as long as these ideas were couched in theoretical terms or referred primarily to other parts of the world and were not directed against an incumbent regime. Governments were often quick to suppress and confiscate newspapers and pamphlets whose contents they considered dangerous to their security, but they remained indifferent to the circulation of books containing the most audacious social theories. By way of example, the Díaz dictatorship in Mexico struck at opposition journalists and newspapers but permitted the free sale and distribution of the writings of Marx and the anarchist theoretician Peter Kropotkin.

As a result of the ascendancy of positivism, the church suffered a further decline in influence and power. Conservative victories over liberalism sometimes produced a strong proclerical reaction, typified by Gabriel García Moreno, who ruled Ecuador from 1860 to 1875 and carried his fanaticism to the point of dedicating the republic to the Sacred Heart of Jesus. Rafael Núñez, dictator of Colombia from 1880 to 1894, drafted a concordat with the Vatican that restored to the church most of the rights it had enjoyed in colonial times. But such victories failed to arrest the general decline of the church's social and intellectual influence among the literate classes. Anticlericalism became an integral part of the ideology of most Latin American intellectuals and a large proportion of other upper-class and middle-class males, including many who were faithful churchgoers and observed the outward forms and rituals of the church. However, church influence continued strong among women of all classes, Indians, and the submerged groups generally.

The Romantic Revolt

The achievement of political independence did not end Latin American cultural dependence on Spain and Portugal. The effort of Latin American writers to find their own means of self-expression, to create national literatures, fused with the larger effort to liquidate the Hispanic colonial heritage in politics, economics, and social life. Accordingly, Latin American literature was from the first a literature of struggle; the concept of art for art's sake had little meaning for the writers of the first half-century after independence. Many writers were also statesmen and even warriors, alternately using pen and sword in the struggle against tyranny and backwardness. This unity of art and politics is expressed by the famous comment of Ecuadoran essayist and polemicist Juan Montalvo when he learned that the dictator García Moreno had been assassinated; *"Mi pluma lo mató"* ("My pen killed him"). That unity found its most perfect embodiment in the Cuban José Martí, who devoted himself almost from childhood to the struggle against Spanish rule in Cuba and died in 1895 in action against Spanish troops. He also blazed new trails in Latin American poetry and prose.

Latin American writers took the first step toward literary independence by breaking with Hispanic classic traditions and adopting as their models the great French and English poets and novelists of the romantic school. Romanticism, which Sarmiento once defined as "a true literary insurrection, like the political uprising that preceded it," seemed peculiarly appropriate for the achievement of the tasks the revolutionary young writers of Latin America had set themselves.

Victory over classicism, however, did not come without a struggle. In 1842 a famous debate took place in Chile between the Venezuelan Andrés Bello, conservative arbiter of literary taste, and the Argentine Domingo Sarmiento, who upheld a democratic freedom of expression and the superiority of contemporary French literature over all others. Their opposition was by no means absolute, for Bello was not a true reactionary in politics or literature. A distinguished poet, scholar, and educator, he had made major contributions to the development of Hispanic culture. His Spanish grammar, published in 1857, ended the domination of Latin grammatical rules and forms over the language and won acceptance by the Spanish Academy. His poem "The Agriculture of the Torrid Zone," despite its classic form, stimulated the rise of literary Americanism. He was an admirer of Victor Hugo's romantic writings and had himself translated Hugo and Dumas.

But Bello had a conservative's love for order and decorum and regarded himself as a guardian of the purity of the Castilian language. He was shocked when Sarmiento, in a review of a recently published grammar, wrote that "teachers of grammar are useless, for people learn by practical example and general discussion . . . the people are the real creators of a language, while grammarians are only the maintainers of tradition and compilers of dictionaries." Writing in a conservative journal, Bello retorted with praise of linguistic purity and academic standards; it would make as little sense, he wrote, to allow the people to make their own laws as to permit them to dictate the forms of their language. Sarmiento countered with an ardent defense of democracy in language and style. Bello, who disliked polemic, soon withdrew from the fray, but his disciples continued the debate.

Before the controversy ended, Sarmiento had silenced his opponents and converted Bello's chief disciple, José Victorino Lastarria, to his own beliefs. Romanticism soon triumphed everywhere, but Latin American romanticism was not a simple carbon copy of the European original; it bore its own vigorous stamp, displayed its own distinctive character.

Romanticism in Argentine Writing

By no coincidence, Esteban Echeverría, the founder of Argentine romanticism, gave the name *Dogma socialista* (*Socialist Teaching*) to his first important writing in which *socialism* stood for a nebulous concept of the primacy of the general interest of society over the individual interests. "Association, progress, liberty, equality, fraternity: these sum up the great social and humanitarian synthesis; these are the divine symbols of the happy future of nations and of humanity." By the time *Dogma socialista* was published in 1839, Echeverría had been forced by the Rosas terror to flee from Buenos Aires to Montevideo, where a group of young exiles combined literary activity with plots to overthrow the Rosas regime.

In his short prose masterpiece, *The Slaughterhouse* (published posthumously but probably written about 1840), Echeverría rejects one element of European romanticism, its idealized view of the common people. With unsparing realism, he describes the repellent sights and smells of a slaughterhouse that is also a gathering place of the Mazorca, the band of thugs who terrorize the enemies of Rosas. The story is also a political allegory: the slaughterhouse, with its butchers in gaucho dress and the black and mulatto women who carry away entrails, empty stomachs and bladders, and wade in blood, is a symbol of Rosas' Argentina, in which barbarous lower-class elements are given a free hand to torture and kill. The climax of the story comes when the butchers intercept a passing unitarian, a young man who wears stylish European dress and has his beard cut in the shape of a U. They tie him up, taunt him, and prepare to beat him. He scornfully replies to their taunts, breaks loose with a supreme effort, and dies from a hemorrhage before their very eyes. In the words of Arturo Torres-

Rioseco, "the whole story is a sombre and terrible vignette, against a background of howling curs, bedraggled Negresses, circling vultures—a slaughterhouse that represents the real *matadero* [slaughterhouse] tyranny of Rosas."

A few years after Echeverría's death in 1851, another Argentine émigré, José Marmol, began to publish in serial form in Montevideo the first Argentine novel, *Amalia*. Again, as in *The Slaughterhouse,* literature and political attack fuse. The young unitarian, Eduardo Belgrano, tries to escape from his federalist pursuers; he takes refuge in the house of the widowed Amalia, and the two fall deeply in love. But the dictator's secret police discover Eduardo's hiding place and kill the lovers. Despite a stilted style and the artificiality of some of the characters, its intensity of feeling and the vivid descriptions of various social types and life in Buenos Aires lend portions of the book a genuine power.

Another exile from Rosas' Argentina, Domingo Sarmiento, illustrated his artistic theories in his formless masterpiece, *Life of Juan Facundo Quiroga: Civilization and Barbarism* (1845). Sarmiento offers a geographical and sociological interpretation of Argentine history, showing how the pampa had molded the character and lifestyle of the gauchos, the mass base of the Rosas dictatorship and the petty caudillos who ruled under him. From this tough, self-reliant breed of men springs the "hero" of Sarmiento's book, the provincial caudillo Facundo. Facundo was master of the Argentine western provinces and Rosas' lieutenant until the greater tyrant, who brooked no rival, had him ambushed and killed.

The ambiguity of Sarmiento's posture toward the gaucho—condemnation tempered by recognition of his admirable qualities—gave way to total defense and vindication of the gaucho and his values in the climactic work of gaucho literature, the epic poem *The Gaucho Martín Fierro* (1872) of José Hernández. Written some thirty years after Sarmiento's *Facundo,* its poignant, nostalgic mood reflects the uprooting of the old patriarchal estancia, the unfenced pampa, and the freedom of the gaucho's life by triumphant bourgeois "civilization" championed by Sarmiento. Hernández, a federalist who opposed Mitre and Sarmiento, supported the revolt of the last untamed gaucho chieftain, General López Jordán, and believed that the city, the seat of the central government, was exploiting and strangling the countryside. He portrayed the gaucho as a victim of the forces of "civilization"—judges, recruiting officers, corrupt police. The poem is strongly influenced by the folk songs of the gaucho *payador* (minstrel) and makes restrained but effective use of gaucho dialect.

Mexican National Literature

The beginnings of Mexican national literature are linked to the founding in 1836 of the Academy of Letrán, an informal literary circle whose members met to talk of literature or listen to readings of poetry and prose. Here, according to the Mexican literary historian González Peña, "was incubated the generation which later filled half a century of the history of Mexican literature." One of its founders, Guillermo Prieto, wrote that "the great and transcendent significance of the Academy was its decided tendency to 'Mexicanize' our literature, emancipating it from all other literatures and giving it a specific character." Prieto also noted that the academy "democratized literary studies, recognizing merit without regard to social position, wealth, or any other considerations." The effort to create a Mexican literature was closely linked to the struggle for political and social reform. Most major Mexican literary figures of the first half-century after independence—such men as Guillermo Prieto, Ignacio Altamirano, and Ignacio Ramírez—took an active part in that struggle.

The most serious effort to create a national Mexican literature was made by the Indian comrade-in-arms of Juárez, Ignacio Altamirano. Believing that Mexican poetry and literature should be as completely original as "are our soil, our mountains, our generation," Altamirano rejected the imitation of foreign models. He attempted to offer an example of such originality in his novel *Clemencia* (1869), set in the period of the French intervention. More successful, because of its fresh, unpretentious descriptions of life in a small Mexican village, was his *Christmas in the Mountains* (1870).

From the Academy of Letrán also issued a school of romantic poetry whose most remarkable creation was the "Prophecy of Cuauhtemoc" (1839) of Ignacio Rodríguez Galván. The poem sounds some major themes of Mexican romanticism: nationalism, anti-Spanish sentiment, and the glorification of pre-Cortesian Mexico. The magnificent coloring of the poem, its authentic romantic agony, the restless alternation in the poet's mind between thoughts of his personal sorrow and the woes of his people, make it, in the words of Menéndez y Pelayo, "the masterpiece of Mexican romanticism."

Chilean Writers

Chile lagged behind some of the other republics in the development of a national literature, perhaps—as Sarmiento suggested in his duel with Bello—because the absolute sway of Bello's classicist doctrines had created inertia, or perhaps because the relative stability of Chilean politics and the upward movement of the Chilean economy deprived its writers of the spur that the more dramatic contrasts of Argentine and Mexican life gave to creative literary activity. But if Chile lacked a Sarmiento or an Echeverría, it produced, in José Victorino Lastarria and Francisco Bilbao, two major writers on sociological topics who in their own way promoted the ideal of Chilean cultural emancipation.

Francisco Bilbao threw a bombshell into staid Santiago society with his essay "The Nature of Chilean Society" (1844), in which he declared: "Slavery, degradation: that is the past. . . . Our past is Spain. Spain is the Middle Ages. The Middle Ages are composed, body and soul, of Catholicism and feudalism." Later (1856), in his

America in Danger, Bilbao issued a powerful cry of warning to Latin America to unite under a regime of freedom and democracy. He sounded a special alarm against the expansionist designs of the United States in Latin America. In *The American Gospel* (1864), he offered much the same message: Latin America must throw off its Hispanic heritage of repression and obscurantism, and it must adopt rationalism rather than Catholicism as its guide if the Disunited States of Latin America were to achieve the place the United States had gained among the nations of the earth.

Lastarria, more moderate and scholarly than Bilbao, caused a lesser stir with his address, "Investigations of the Social Influence of the Conquest and the Colonial System of the Spaniards in Chile" (1844). Despite an occasional factual error, it remains an effective summary of the liberal case against the Spanish colonial regime. Andrés Bello undertook to review it. Conceding the general correctness of Lastarria's criticism of Spanish policy and work in Latin America, he offered a partial defense that stressed the mildness of Spanish rule and its civilizing mission in the New World. Whereas Bilbao was profoundly influenced by French left-wing republican and utopian socialist ideas, Lastarria's thought reflected the more conservative positivist teachings of the French philosopher Auguste Comte. Like Bilbao, however, Lastarria waged a consistent struggle against the backwardness he identified with Spanish civilization, which he felt was "the principal cause of our political and social disasters. . . . We cannot remedy these disasters except by reacting frankly, openly, and energetically against that civilization, in order to free our minds and adapt our country to the new form, democracy."

Brazilian Romantic Literature

A strong nationalism characterized the Brazilian romantic literature of the first decades after independence. In contrast with the Argentine writers of the same period, Brazilian writers expressed their nationalism in glorification of the Indian past. This Indianism reflected differences in the historical experience of the two countries: the Brazilian Indian had long ceased to pose a serious threat to white society, and Indian blood was widely diffused throughout the Brazilian people. Indianism, moreover, represented an effort to find roots for Brazilian nationalism—roots that could not be found in Portugal or Europe generally.

The greatest romantic poet of the first generation and the principal exponent of Indianism in poetry was Antônio Gonçalves Dias, in whose veins ran the blood of three races—white, Indian, and black. Basing himself on a careful study of Indian languages and culture, Gonçalves Dias conjured up the image of the defeated Indian with extraordinary emotive power in his *American Poems* (1846) and in the narrative poem "The Timbiras" (1857). He also celebrated the beauty of the Brazilian landscape in poems like the nostalgic "Song of Exile" (1846), which opens with the line: "My land has palm trees where the sabiá sings."

Indianism also found expression in the novels of José de Alencar, whose two most popular novels, *Iracema* (1865) and *The Guarani* (1856), deal with the theme of love between Indian and white. Despite the improbable plots and the sentimentality and artificiality of the dialogue and characters, Alencar's limpid, poetic style successfully evokes, somewhat in the manner of James Fenimore Cooper, the drama of the clash of Indian and white cultures and the grandeur of the Brazilian wilderness, with its majestic rivers, dense forests, and great waterfalls.

After the optimistic nationalism of the first generation of Brazilian romantic poets came the introspection, pessimism, and escapism of the second generation, which perhaps were a reaction to the defeat of the republican revolts of the 1830s and 1840s. In sharp contrast to these second-generation poets, who appeared to be sensitive to their own sufferings and misfortunes only, Antônio de Castro Alves devoted his poetic talent above all to the struggle against slavery. Because of his lofty, impassioned style, he is known as the founder of the *condoreira,* or condor school of poetry. Castro Alves's verses, read at countless abolitionist meetings and frequently published in the abolitionist press, gave a major stimulus to the growth of the abolitionist and republican movements in Brazil.

In 1867, Latin American romanticism, already in decline, produced its finest prose flower, the delicate love story *María* by the Colombian Jorge Isaacs. The story is set in a patriarchal country estate in the Cauca River Valley. Told in a simple, elegiac style, pervaded by a mood of gentle nostalgia, it relates the unfolding of an idyllic romance between a landowner's son and his cousin María. The story ends tragically when María dies during her lover's absence in London.

The Historical Novel

The romantic movement yielded an abundant harvest of historical novels, most of which dealt with episodes from the Spanish Conquest and the colonial era. Often their authors seemed chiefly concerned with exposing Spanish cruelty and the horrors of the Inquisition. Whether or not faithful to the historical facts, they generally lacked originality, talent, and psychological realism.

In 1872, however, Ricardo Palma began to publish his ironic and sparkling evocations of colonial Lima, *The Peruvian Traditions* (1872–1906). With these "traditions," Palma created a new genre: "A short sketch that was not history, anecdote, or satire, but a distillation of all three." Drawing on his immense knowledge of the colonial period (he was director of the National Library of Peru during the latter part of his life), Palma applied his own formula for the traditions: "a little bit, and quite a little bit of lying, a dose of the truth be it ever so infinitesimal, and a great deal of nicety and gloss in the style." From these elements Palma spun a long succession of cheerfully malicious tales that played on the follies and frailties of viceroys, priests, and highborn ladies

as well as lesser folk. Palma's "traditions" evoked the past far more successfully than the typical historical novel of this period.

Literature and Social Change, 1880–1910

By 1880 the romantic movement in Latin American literature had almost completed its tasks and exhausted its creative possibilities. As a result of the economic and political changes that we have surveyed, a new social reality had arisen. The growth of industry, immigration, and urbanization gave a new face to Latin American society. The ruling classes were increasingly acquisitive, arrogant, and philistine; the condition of the masses had not improved and may even have deteriorated. Latin America had become more European; in the process, it had failed to solve some old problems and had acquired some new ones.

In conformity with the specific conditions of their countries and their own backgrounds, writers responded to the new environment in a variety of ways. Generally speaking, romanticism survived as a vital force only in those countries where the old problems had not been solved. (Examples are Ecuador, the scene of a bitter struggle between liberals and conservatives, and Cuba, whose struggle for independence did not reach its climax until the 1890s.)

Poetry and Modernism

In poetry, the most important new phenomenon was the movement called modernism. Because the movement comprises an immense variety of stylistic and ideological tendencies, it is difficult to define. The common feature of modernist poets, however, was their search for new expressive means, for new stylistic forms, in reaction against the outworn language and forms of romanticism. The artistic creed of many modernist poets included rejection of literature as an instrument of social and political struggle. Turning their backs on "a world they never made," the world of shoddy and unstable prosperity ruled, in Rubén Darío's words, by *el rey burgués* (the bourgeois king), these escapists sought refuge in the ivory tower of art.

Most escapist of all was the prodigiously gifted Nicaraguan Rubén Darío (1867–1916), who defined modernism as the rejection of any explicit message in art; stress on beauty as the highest value (in Darío's poems, the swan is the recurrent symbol of beauty as an end in itself); and the determination to free verse from the tyranny of traditional forms. Not unexpectedly, in view of their conception of the artist as an outcast from bourgeois society, Bohemianism, alcohol, and drugs were elements in the lifestyle of many escapist poets, and not a few came to tragically early ends.

In their effort to achieve a renovation of poetry (and prose as well), the modernists drew on a variety of foreign sources (French Parnassianism, impressionism, symbolism, Whitman and Poe, Spain's medieval ballads). But they did not imitate; they appropriated these foreign methods for the creation of poetry and prose that were "entirely new, new in form and vocabulary and subject matter and feeling."

Escapism was a major current of modernism but not the only one. Indeed, before the movement had run its course, some of the leading escapist poets had risen to a new awareness of the continent's social and political problems and the writer's responsibility to the people. Darío himself exemplifies this evolution. If in the first, escapist phase of his poetic career he peopled his verses with satyrs, nymphs, centaurs, peacocks, and swans, in its second phase he gave voice to a powerful public poetry that reflected his new Americanism and concern with political and social themes. Darío's Americanism led him to a search for symbols in both the Spanish and the Indian past, regarded as the sources of a Latin American culture threatened by the aggressive expansionism of the United States.

Literary critics dispute whether the Cuban José Martí was a precursor of modernism or one

Rubén Darío. (Courtesy of the Organization of American States)

of its major figures and creators. Certainly, his spirit was alien to the escapist tendency of many modernist poets. Far from seeking refuge in an ivory tower, he dedicated his life to the struggle for Cuban independence; Cubans of all political faiths still call him "the Apostle." Martí's faith in humanity and progress reflected his links to Enlightenment thought, to romanticism, and to the optimistic evolutionism of the late nineteenth century. "I have faith," he wrote in the preface to his first book of verse (1882), "in the improvement of man, in the life of the future, in the utility of virtue." In a time of rampant racism, he denounced race prejudice of every kind.

From 1881 to 1895, Martí lived in exile in New York. As a correspondent for various Latin American newspapers, he wrote a vast number of articles in which he subjected political, economic, and cultural developments in the United States to searching analysis. Martí fervently admired Lincoln, Emerson, Mark Twain, and the abolitionist Wendell Phillips but expressed growing concern over the rise of monopolistic and imperialist tendencies. He especially feared and disliked the Republican leader James G. Blaine, whom he regarded as the chief exponent of North American imperialist designs on Latin America. He wrote in 1889: "What is apparent is that the nature of the North American government is changing in its fundamental reality. Under the traditional labels of Republican and Democrat, with no innovation other than the contingent circumstances of place and character, the republic is becoming plutocratic and imperialistic." In 1895 he left the United States to launch the Cuban Revolution. On the day before his death on May 19, 1895, while fighting Spanish troops, he set down his fears concerning U.S. policy toward Cuba: "I know the monster because I have lived in its lair, and my sling is that of David."

Martí's artistic ideas reflected his belief in the organic links between art and society, in the social responsibility of the artist. Art should reflect the joys and sorrows of the masses; in that sense it is a collective product. "Poetry is durable when it is the work of all. Those who understand it are as much its authors as those who make it." Simplicity and directness characterize his poems, but he was capable of using vivid, concrete imagery of great symbolic power. The very simplicity of his verse makes it difficult to render into English. In prose he achieved a genuine stylistic revolution. "The style he achieved," writes Pedro Henríquez-Ureña, "was entirely new to the language. He follows no single rhythmical pattern, but constantly varies it . . . he combines words—and meanings—in many unfamiliar ways. The effect is a constantly varied interplay of light and color. In style, as well as in what lies beyond style and becomes expression, his power of invention was inexhaustible." Darío said of Martí: "He writes more brilliantly than anyone in Spain or America."

The Romantic Revolt Continued: Ecuador and Peru

The fires of romantic revolt continued to burn in two Andean republics where small groups of intellectuals battled the rule of reactionary landowners, generals, and the church. In Ecuador, the writer Juan Montalvo, exiled by the fanatical dictator Gabriel García Moreno, leveled polemical attacks against him and claimed credit for García Moreno's assassination. Unhappy with the new rulers of Ecuador, Montalvo spent much of his life in exile from his native country. His *Seven Essays* (1882), reflecting a somewhat old-fashioned liberalism, propose the regeneration of Latin America through the formation of a model elite. His curious *Chapters That Cervantes Forgot,* a continuation of *Don Quijote,* published posthumously, display Montalvo's virtuosity in the use of sixteenth-century Castilian and express his ideas on a wide variety of topics.

The Peruvian writer Manuel González Prada advanced more radical ideas. A member of that generation of Peruvian youth that witnessed with feelings of profound humiliation the swift defeat of their country in the War of the Pacific, he initiated a new era of social unrest and intellectual ferment in Peru. He launched his "prose thunderbolts" against all that was sacrosanct in Peruvian society: the army, the church, the state, the creole aristocracy. In 1886 he founded a *Círculo Literario* (Literary Circle) with the declared aim of creating a nationalistic literature of "propaganda and attack." He proclaimed that "the people must be shown the horror of their degradation and misery; a good autopsy was never made without dissecting the body, and no society can be thoroughly known until its skeleton is laid bare."

González Prada made good his promise of dissecting the Peruvian organism by the ferocity of his attacks. Peru, he wrote, was a great boil: "press down anywhere and the pus comes out." He described the Peruvian Congress as a sewer where all the filth of the country had come together. He called for the creation of a vigorous new literature that would deal with national problems; this required writers to reject tradition and forge a new language: "Archaism implies backwardness: show me an archaic writer and I show you a reactionary thinker."

A woman writer who formed part of González Prada's literary circle and shared many of his progressive ideas, Clorinda Matto de Turner (1854–1909), wrote the first Indianist protest novel, *Birds Without a Nest* (1889). Set in an Indian village of the sierra, the novel denounces the abuses committed against the Indians by the exploitive trinity of judge, priest, and governor. "We were born Indians," declares an Indian woman, "slaves of the parish priest, slaves of the governor, slaves of the cacique, slaves of all those who hold the rod of authority." However, aside from the lesson of the personal charity and benevolence that well-disposed upper-class whites should show to the Indians, the writer offers no solution. As the novel ends, the young married couple who sought to protect the Indians return discouraged and defeated to Lima, leaving the Indians in their former state. With all its weaknesses, however, *Birds Without a Nest* was the forerunner of a genre, the Indianist novel, that had a great future.

Realism and Naturalism

Schools of literary realism and naturalism first arose in lands like Chile, Argentina, and Brazil, where capitalism and capitalist relations had struck firm roots. The Chilean writer Alberto Blest Gana began writing realist novels between 1860 and 1867. Strongly influenced by French realism—especially by Balzac—Blest Gana made the corrosive power of money on human relations the primary theme of his novels, *Arithmetic in Love* (1860), *Martín Rivas* (1862), and *A Good-for-Nothing's Ideal* (1863). Blest Gana painted broad canvases depicting a Chilean society in which merchants, landowners, army officers, and humble provincials struggled to improve their situation by marriage. In 1860, bestowing a literary award to him for *Arithmetic in Love,* a jury

that included José Victorino Lastarria and the historian Miguel Luis Amunátegui praised the novel because "the characters are Chileans, they are very like the people we know, the people we shake hands with and talk to. . . . The novel presents vivid, colorful, and accurate pictures of our national customs."

The boom of the 1880s, which transformed Argentine society, inspired the writing of some naturalist novels whose authors, however, lacked the great talent of Blest Gana. Buenos Aires, with its atmosphere of feverish prosperity and cosmopolitanism, provided the setting for most of these novels. A typical work is *The Bourse* (1890) by José María Miró, which deals with the rise and fall of a financier on the stock exchange. The novel is weakened by poor technique and xenophobic attacks on gold, Jews, and immigrants, regarded as the chief causes of the materialism that was allegedly destroying Argentina. Similar attacks on materialism and the egotism of the ruling classes characterize the naturalist novels of Eugenio Cambaceres (1843–1888).

In the urban novels of Joaquim María Machado de Assis (1839–1908), a master of ironic realism, Brazilian psychological letters display a precocious maturity. Although Machado, a mulatto, shunned involvement in the abolitionist or republican struggles of his time, his work exposes the stifling atmosphere of a society dominated by racism and the race for wealth; cynicism and disillusionment are the typical attitudes of his characters. In *Dom Casmurro* (1900), the principal character ends his melancholy story by congratulating himself that he had no children of his own and thus "transmitted to no one the legacy of his misery." The last words of the narrator of the story "The Attendant," as he is about to die, are a cynical revision of the Sermon on the Mount: "Blessed are they that *possess,* for they shall be comforted." More explicit criticism of Brazilian society appears in the naturalistic novels of Aluizio Azevedo (1857–1913), notably in *The Mulatto* (1881), in which a scheming priest and the relatives of a white girl plan the murder of her well-educated, cultured mulatto sweetheart.

At the turn of the century (1902) appeared an impressive study of rural Brazil, Euclides da Cunha's *Os sertões* (*Rebellion in the Backlands*), which deals, among other things, with the siege of Canudos in 1896–1897, when a handful of wretched backwoodsmen, led by the mystic Antônio Conselheiro, heroically resisted a federal army of some six thousand men. In his style—now lush and sensuous, now rugged; in his unsparing realism; and in his outspoken but unsentimental sympathy with the semibarbarous folk of the backlands, da Cunha blazed a trail for the regional and social novelists who would soon dominate the Brazilian literary scene.

Part 3

Latin America in the Twentieth Century

The complexity of Latin America's political and economic evolution in the twentieth century seems to require an overview of the process that will enable us to comprehend it as a whole. In Part 3, our survey of Latin American history broadens to include three Andean republics with predominantly Indian populations (Peru, Bolivia, and Ecuador); Cuba, the scene of a socialist revolution with continental repercussions; and three Central American countries where social revolutionary movements have recently triumphed or are in progress (Nicaragua, El Salvador, and Guatemala). In addition we look at Mexico, Argentina, Chile, Brazil, and the Bolivarian lands of Venezuela and Colombia.

The struggle of Latin America's peoples to eliminate neocolonialism and *latifundismo,* the chief obstacles to the achievement of a more just economic and social order, gives meaning and direction to the turbulent flow of modern Latin American history. Viewed in the large, that history, with all its contradictory aspects, its gains and setbacks, appears to form a sequence of stages, each representing a higher level of effort to achieve complete economic and political emancipation. Such an overview inevitably ignores the great differences between the Latin American countries but it helps make clear the general unity of problems and the common direction of movement of all the Latin American states.

of rapid capitalist development. Despite the discrepancies between its professed social ideals and its achievements, the Revolution unleashed creative energies in art, literature, and the social sciences that gave Mexico a leading role in the cultural life of Latin America.

World War I seriously disrupted the markets for Latin America's goods and placed difficulties in the way of importing needed manufactured goods. As a result, some local capital and labor were diverted from agriculture to manufacturing in an effort to supply these goods. Although the postwar period saw some revival of the export economy, declines in the price levels of Latin America's exports encouraged a further growth of manufacturing. But at the end of this period, industrialization was still almost completely limited to light consumer goods industries.

The United States, which emerged from World War I as the world's principal industrial and financial power, soon replaced Great Britain as the major source of foreign investments in Latin America. Continuing the "big stick" and "dollar diplomacy" policies of their predecessors, Democratic and Republican administrations used armed intervention and economic pressure to expand United States control over the Caribbean area. By the end of the period, deep Latin American resentment of these strong-arm tactics had forced Republican policy makers to consider a change in dealing with Latin America.

1910–1930

The Mexican Revolution of 1910 and the start of World War I offer two points of departure for this period. The Revolution swiftly developed into the first major effort in Latin American history to uproot the system of great estates and peonage and curb foreign control of the area's natural resources. The famous constitution of 1917 spelled out this social content of the revolution. In the leadership struggle between agrarian and bourgeois revolutionaries, the latter emerged victorious and adopted a program that subordinated the interests of peasants and workers to the goals

1930–1945

The Great Depression dramatically exposed the vulnerability of a neocolonial, monocultural economy: the area's foreign markets collapsed, and the prices of its raw materials and foodstuffs fell much more sharply than those of the manufactured goods it had to import. Latin America's unfavorable balance of trade made necessary exchange controls and other trade restrictions that encouraged the growth of industries to produce goods formerly supplied through importation. World War II, which caused a virtual suspension of imports of manufactured goods, gave further stimulus to the movement for Latin American industrialization.

The nationalist temper of the times also found expression in the formation of state enterprises in such fields as oil exploitation and in efforts to nationalize some foreign-owned utilities and natural resources. The most dramatic example of this trend was the seizure of foreign oil properties in Mexico by President Lázaro Cárdenas in 1938. The new nationalist regimes also made concessions to labor in the form of social legislation but maintained tight control over working-class organizations.

By 1945 the movement for Latin American industrialization could point to some successes. Consumer goods industries had arisen in all the Latin American republics, and some countries had laid the foundations of heavy industry. Industrial development, however, was everywhere hampered by shortages of capital, lack of advanced technology, and the extremely low purchasing power of the masses. Latin American economists often related these deficiencies to such background conditions as latifundismo and its corollary of wretchedly small farms (minifundismo), widespread disease and illiteracy, and absorption of a large part of the area's economic surplus by foreign investors in the form of dividends, interest, and the like. Meanwhile, aside from the massive assault of Lázaro Cárdenas on the Mexican latifundio, little or nothing was done in the way of agrarian reform.

In the same period, the United States, reacting to the diplomatic and economic losses caused by the old-style imperialism and a wave of "anti-Yanqui" feeling throughout the continent, adopted the Good Neighbor Policy, which proclaimed the principle of nonintervention by one American state in the affairs of another. But the policy represented more of a change in form than in content. Washington's friendly, cooperative relations with such tyrannies as those of Anastasio Somoza in Nicaragua, Rafael Trujillo in the Dominican Republic, and Fulgencio Batista in Cuba insured a continuance of North American hegemony in the Caribbean. For the rest, the immense economic power of the United States in Latin America, exercised through investments and its role as the area's main trading partner, usually sufficed to obtain approval of its policies in most parts of the continent.

1945–1959

In the new postwar era, the Latin American drive to industrialize continued, but after 1950 the pace of advance slowed and the industrialization process underwent a certain deformation. Perceiving the changes taking place in the Latin American society and economy as a result of industrialization and the growth of urban markets, foreign firms began to shift the bulk of their new investments from agricultural and mining activities to manufacturing. This shift allowed them to leap over tariff walls and penetrate the Latin American market. The immensely superior resources of foreign firms and their advanced technology gave them a great advantage over national companies. The result was that many small and middle-sized national companies fell or were swallowed up by subsidiaries of foreign firms.

A favorite device of foreign economic penetration was the mixed company, dominated by foreign capital, with native capitalists reduced to the role of junior partners or directors. The huge sums exported annually by foreign companies in profits, dividends, and other types of income led to a process of "decapitalization" that slowed down the rate of Latin American capital accumulation and industrial growth.

The failure to modernize archaic agrarian structures and improve income distribution also held back industrialization. Indeed, the experience of those countries that had the largest growth of capitalism, such as Brazil and Argentina, suggested that the new industrial and financial oligarchies were as fearful of social change, as prone to come to terms with foreign economic interests, as the old landed aristocracy had been. In the 1950s, a number of leading South American countries moved to the right.

A similar rightward swing took place in Mexico, where the conservative successors of President Lázaro Cárdenas pursued policies favorable to big business and large landowners but neglected the peasantry. As a result, a new corporate hacienda arose and soon dominated Mexican agriculture. By the end of the 1950s, the once-fashionable hope that a dynamic entrepreneurial class could lead Latin America out of dependence and underdevelopment had largely faded.

Meanwhile, the discontent of the masses, sharpened by the "revolution of rising expectations," continued to erupt in revolts: a spontaneous rising of Bolivian peasants and miners in 1952; and, in 1944, a revolution in Guatemala whose achievements in democracy and reform made a lasting mark on the country's life. Even more important was the armed struggle begun by Fidel Castro and his comrades against the Cuban dictator Batista in July 1953. Their long guerrilla war ended with the victorious entry of the rebel army into Havana on January 1, 1959.

1959 to the Present

The victory of the Cuban Revolution, soon transformed into a socialist revolution, marks a turning point in Latin American history. The swift, thoroughgoing Cuban agrarian reform and nationalization of foreign enterprises and the revolution's successes in raising the living standards of the people offered Latin America a radical alternative to development along capitalist lines.

Washington responded to the Cuban threat to the old order in Latin America with a variety of tactics. In 1961, President John F. Kennedy proclaimed the establishment of the Alliance for Progress, designed to show that Latin America's social revolution, with United States help, could be achieved peacefully within the framework of capitalism. But within a few years, the failure of the corruption-ridden program to achieve structural change was apparent.

Simultaneously, the United States government sought to undermine and destroy the Castro regime, first by economic blockade and political isolation and then by a CIA-sponsored effort by Cuban exiles to invade Cuba (1961)—an effort that met with a swift and humiliating defeat. The Soviet Union stepped up its flow of arms to Cuba, which led to the Cuban missile crisis (1962). For ten days, a jittery world lived in the shadow of nuclear war between the United States and the Soviet Union. The crisis ended with a pledge on the part of the United States not to invade Cuba in return for the withdrawal of Soviet missiles from the island.

Forced to retreat in Cuba, the United States, supported by the old and new Latin American elites fearful of radical social change redoubled its efforts to prevent a spread of the Cuban "contagion" to other parts of the hemisphere. In 1964 a coalition of reactionary Brazilian military, great landowners, and big capitalists overthrew the mildly progressive government of President João Goulart, whose heresies included a modest program of agrarian and electoral reform. It was succeeded by a heavy-handed military dictatorship that offered large incentives to foreign investors and proclaimed its unswerving loyalty to the United States, which responded with generous financial assistance. The next year, proclaiming the Johnson Doctrine, which authorized the United States to intervene to suppress "communist" activity, President Lyndon B. Johnson sent armed forces into the Dominican Republic to crush a popular revolt led by Colonel Francisco Caamaño and other progressive officers.

But the movement for structural social change and economic independence proved irrepressible. As in the Dominican case, nationalist military sometimes played a leading role in these upheavals, disproving the common assumption that the Latin American officer class is one reactionary group. Thus, the military take-over in Peru in 1968 was quickly followed by nationalization of key foreign-owned industries and land reform that transferred many large estates to peasants and workers, organized into cooperatives. The

Peruvian Revolution—a revolution from above, without significant participation by the masses—soon faltered, however, primarily because of its failure to break with the traditional strategy of development based on foreign loans and export expansion. In 1975 a moderate faction of the military seized power and in 1980 turned it over to a conservative elected civilian government, which attempted to dismantle the major reforms of the previous era.

The struggle against neocolonialism scored a temporary major victory with the triumph of the Marxist presidential candidate Salvador Allende and his Popular Unity coalition in Chile in 1970. In three years, it carried out the nationalization of copper mines and banks and a massive agrarian reform and made significant advances in housing, health, and education. But the Allende government also made serious errors. Most serious was its failure to take preventive action against a coup by reactionary military. In September 1973, military plotters overthrew the Allende government. Published evidence has since confirmed the complicity of the United States in a "destabilization" of his government that prepared the way for the coup.

The new fascist junta not only reversed the progressive policies of the Allende regime but transformed Chile into a concentration camp, torturing and killing thousands of opponents. Its economic policies reduced the living standards of the masses to near-starvation levels.

The destruction of Chilean democracy formed part of a general counteroffensive of Latin American reaction and its foreign allies, designed to halt and roll back the movement for structural economic and social change. By mid-1976 a block of authoritarian states—Brazil, Chile, Bolivia, Uruguay, and Paraguay—had taken shape. Following the deposition of the government of President Isabel Perón by right-wing military in early 1976, they were soon joined by Argentina.

But these regimes, whose policies included the systematic use of torture and assassination against political opponents and the abandonment of the effort to achieve economic independ-

ence, offered no solutions for the deep-seated problems of their countries. Their most shining success, the "Brazilian miracle" of steady economic growth since 1964, was made possible by reducing wages to the subsistence level, an annual inflation rate of about 20 percent, and massive foreign investments that hastened the foreign conquest of Brazilian industry. By the mid-1970s the "Brazilian miracle" was running down; by 1980, Brazil was in deep recession, with factories closing, unemployment rising, and a balance of payments problem growing steadily worse.

Other military regimes, such as Argentina and Chile, faced similarly grave economic problems. But the crisis was not one of dictatorships alone; it confronted all the countries of the region, whatever their political systems, that pursued a strategy of dependent development based on foreign loans and investments.

At the heart of the continuing debt problem lies the unequal exchange between advanced capitalist countries, such as the United States, and the Third World of which Latin America is a part. A major factor in Latin America's balance of payments deficit is the imbalance between the low prices of Latin American export commodities and the high prices of the manufactured goods and oil that most of the countries in the area must buy. Falling commodity prices in recent decades have greatly aggravated the problem. These unfavorable terms of trade help to explain Latin America's mountainous debt, raised still higher by the usurious interest rates often charged by Western bankers.

Certain changes in the Latin American industrialization programs contributed to the growing gap between its exports and imports. Since about 1955, countries like Brazil and Mexico have increasingly stressed production of consumer durables and capital goods that required the importation of expensive machinery, equipment, and technical licenses from countries like the United States. The result was a growing surplus of imports over exports. The transnational companies' take-over of much of the Latin American manufacturing sector contributed to the same result. In the 1970s, for every dollar invested in Latin America, transnationals repatriated approximately $2.20 to their home countries. To cover the deficits in their balance of payments, Latin American countries had to borrow from Western bankers at interest rates that reached double digit figures by 1980.

By 1982, with their national treasuries almost empty of foreign exchange, a number of major Latin American countries faced the prospect of immediate default. This posed immense dangers to the international banking system, for defaults by Mexico and Brazil alone could wipe out 95 percent of the capital of the nine largest U.S. banks. Defaults were averted by emergency aid packages provided by Western governments and bankers in return for agreements by the recipient governments to carry out "austerity" programs that further reduced the living standards of their workers and peasants. Nevertheless the problem had been postponed, not resolved. There was no prospect that even a portion of the huge Latin American debt could be repaid without large write-offs and long delays in payment. Meanwhile the flow of new loans—at higher rates of interest because of increased risk—had sharply declined, while imports were reduced. It seemed that the Latin American model of "dependent development"—in reality a new, streamlined form of neocolonialism—had almost exhausted its potential for generating economic growth.

In the later 1980s, despite populist rhetoric about resisting the tyranny of the International Monetary Fund, which monitored debtor countries' compliance with the austerity programs imposed as a condition for new loans, the new and the old Latin American democracies did little more than demand reschedulings and lower interest payments. Recent efforts by Latin American governments to reduce their debt burdens include debt-bond swaps, in which foreign debt is exchanged at a discount for new government bonds, and debt-equity swaps, in which foreign debt is exchanged for equity, i.e., shares in local companies. None of this has made a serious dent in the region's foreign debt, which stood in 1990

at over $430 billion. To date the sole true dissenter has been Peru's President Alan García, who proclaimed in 1985 that he would limit payments on a $14 billion foreign debt to 10 percent of Peru's export earnings. No country has yet accepted Fidel Castro's conclusion that the foreign debt is *impagable* (unpayable), but in private many governments accept this as true. Major banks have already reduced their Latin American exposure by selling parts of the debt at a discount and setting aside huge reserves to cover possible losses on loans to developing countries. By October 1990 the debt problem appeared to have reached a critical point, with the market value index of foreign debts down to 33 cents on the dollar; it stood at 22 cents for Brazil, the largest debtor, and 14 cents for Argentina.

Ultimately Latin American countries will have to adopt more autonomous, inward-directed strategies of development based on more rational exploitation of human and natural resources. But such strategies cannot be implemented without profound changes in the relations between Latin America and the outside world and in Latin America's economic and social structures, particularly in land tenure and use, ownership of industry, and income distribution. Nor can such strategies be implemented without a democratization of Latin American political life that would allow popular interests and wishes to influence the direction of economic and social policy.

In the early 1980s the reactionary tide of the 1970s began to recede and in country after country—Argentina, Brazil, Bolivia, Uruguay—discredited military regimes gave way to popularly elected governments. By 1990 the last military or personal dictatorships, in Chile and Paraguay, had fallen. The decline of authoritarianism reflected more than popular discontent with the failures and crimes of the military regimes; even the area's elites had become convinced that those regimes tended to destabilize capitalism and damage their class interests.

In view of the long repression of left-wing parties and trade union movements, the divisions within the left, and public nervousness about the possible reaction of the military to radical change, the emerging democratic governments of the 1980s and early 1990s as a rule had a centrist or conservative complexion. None made a clean break with the failed economic policies of the past. This was reflected in their usual acquiescence in payment of the immense foreign debt and in their acceptance of the neoliberal remedies prescribed by the International Monetary Fund and U.S. economic advisers, such as austerity, privatization of state enterprises, and tariff reductions. In particular, the acceptance by Latin America's old and new democracies of privatization and tariff reduction policies represented a virtual abandonment of half a century of struggle to achieve independent capitalist development. To date, the principal results of these policies in countries like Mexico, Brazil, Argentina, and Bolivia have been large increases in unemployment and declines in living standards, relieved in the case of Bolivia by a thriving informal or underground economy based on the production of coca and cocaine.

Not all political signs pointed to the right. In 1988, in Brazilian local elections, socialist or labor parties captured all the major cities, and the following year a conservative candidate for president of Brazil narrowly defeated a trade union leader put forward by the socialist Workers' party. In Uruguay, in 1989, the candidate of a leftist coalition captured the mayoralty of Montevideo, with more than half of the country's pop-

ulation, and in Haiti, in the first democratic election in its history, a left-wing priest was elected president by a landslide in 1990.

More dramatic developments occurred in Central America. In 1990 peace came at last to Nicaragua, whose revolutionary Sandinista government had struggled for almost ten years against the implacable efforts of the United States to topple it. Weary of war and hunger, Nicaraguans in 1990 voted in a conservative president and congress, but the Sandinistas maintained a strong political presence and vowed to defend the structural reforms achieved during their tenure.

In El Salvador, another long struggle continued between a leftist guerrilla army and a repressive regime supported by the United States. In 1989 a formidable guerrilla offensive forced the right-wing government to the bargaining table and for the first time in years there appeared some faint prospect of a peaceful solution and genuinely democratic elections. In Guatemala, where a CIA-organized coup had overthrown a democratic reformist government in 1954, another guerrilla movement revived after temporary defeats and waged a struggle against a military-dominated civilian government that tolerated or was powerless to prevent numerous death squad killings and other human rights abuses. More time is needed to tell whether such developments represent the twilight of the tyrants in Central America.

Chapter 12

The Mexican Revolution—and After

On the eve of the presidential election of 1910, signs of unrest multiplied in Mexico. Peasant risings and workers' strikes became more frequent, and the Mexican Liberal party, founded and led by the exiled revolutionary journalist Ricardo Flores Magón, intensified its conspiratorial activities. Divisions appeared within the oligarchy. Bernardo Reyes, a foe of the Científicos and the powerful governor of Nuevo León whose rule combined iron-fisted repression with reformist trends, announced his candidacy for the post of vice president. Reyes saw this office as a steppingstone to the presidency when Díaz, who was eighty years old in 1910, died or retired.

In an unusual atmosphere of political ferment and debate, there appeared a tract for the times, *The Great National Problems* (1909) by the lawyer Andrés Molina Enríquez. Financed by Reyes, the book combined the customary eulogies of Díaz with incisive criticism of his political system and especially of his agrarian policy. Its denunciation of the latifundio and appeal for land reform anticipated the radical slogans of the coming revolution.

Díaz had contributed to this ferment by announcing in 1908 that Mexico was now ready for democracy and he would welcome the emergence of an opposition party. Francisco Madero, a Coahuila hacendado whose extensive family interests included cattle ranches, wheat farms, vineyards, textile factories, and mines, took Díaz at his word. A member of the elite, Madero was no revolutionary, but he feared that continuance of the existing political order would inevitably breed social revolution. Madero made clear, however, that by democracy he meant control by an elite. "The ignorant public," he wrote, "should take no direct part in determining who should be the candidate for public office." He sought to reassure conservatives by pointing out that even in advanced liberal democracies rulers "are generally . . . drawn from a small number of intellectuals."

Madero criticized Díaz's social policies—his genocidal Indian wars and violent repression of strikes—as counterproductive; in place of those brutal tactics, he proposed a policy of modest concessions to peasants and workers that would reduce mounting tensions and check the growth of radical ideas. Madero regarded democracy as an instrument of social control that would promote the acceptance of capitalism through the grant of limited political and social reforms, with a large stress on education.

In December 1909, Madero began to tour the country, making speeches in which he explained his reform program. In April 1910, an opposition anti-re-electionist party was formed and announced Madero as its candidate for president. Díaz at first refused to take Madero seriously but soon became alarmed by his growing popularity. In early June he had Madero arrested and charged with preparing an armed insurrection; arrests of many of his supporters followed. On June 21 the election was held, and it was announced that Díaz and his hand-picked vice-presidential candidate, Ramón Corral, had been elected by an almost unanimous vote.

After the election, Díaz no longer considered Madero dangerous and allowed him to be released on bail. Convinced that the dictator could not be removed by peaceful means, Madero prepared to resort to armed struggle. On October 7, he fled across the border to Texas and from there announced the Plan of San Luis Potosí. Declaring the recent elections null and void, Madero assumed the title of provisional president of Mexico but promised to hold general free elections as soon as conditions permitted and turn power over to the elected president. The plan made a vague reference to the return of usurped peasant lands, but most of its articles dealt with political reforms. That Madero was allowed to organize the revolution on U.S. soil with little interference by the authorities suggests the United States government's displeasure with Díaz. Fearing that North American domination of investments in Mexico threatened Mexican economic and political independence, the dictator had recently favored British over North American capitalists in the grant of concessions and had given other indications of an anti-U.S. attitude. The administration of President Taft evidently hoped that Madero would display a more positive attitude toward United States interests.

The Great Revolution, 1910–1920

The revolution got off to a shaky start when Madero, having crossed back into Mexico, found only twenty-five supporters waiting for him and hurriedly returned to Texas. But it soon gathered momentum as two major movements of peasant revolt responded to his call. In the huge northern border state of Chihuahua, where peons and small farmers suffered under the iron rule of the Terrazas-Creel clan, masters of a vast landed empire, the rising began under the leadership of Pascual Orozco, a mule driver, and Pancho Villa, a bandit with a reputation for taking from the rich to give to the poor. By the end of 1910, guerrilla armies had seized control of most of the state from federal troops.

Another seat of rebellion was the mountainous southern state of Morelos, where Indian communities had long waged a losing struggle against encroaching sugar haciendas. Here the mestizo insurgent leader Emiliano Zapata, attracted by the promise of land reform in the Plan of San Luis Potosí, proclaimed his loyalty to Madero.

In May 1911, the rebels won two decisive victories. Rather than face an invasion of the poorly defended capital by Zapata's dreaded agrarian rebels, Díaz and his advisers decided to reach an agreement with Madero. Disregarding urgent warnings by the left wing of the revolutionary movement against compromises with the Díaz regime, Madero signed the Treaty of Ciudad Juárez on May 21, which provided for the removal of Díaz but left intact all existing institutions.

It was completely silent on the subject of social change. On May 25, the aged dictator resigned the presidency and a few days later left for Europe. Francisco León de la Barra, the Mexican ambassador to the United States, assumed the interim presidency.

On June 7, 1911, Madero entered Mexico City in triumph, but the rejoicing of the crowds who thronged into the streets to greet the "apostle of democracy" was premature. The provisional president was closely tied to the old regime and had no sympathy with the revolution. The *Porfirista* aristocracy and its allies had not given up hope of regaining power; they regarded the compromise that made León de la Barra provisional president a tactical retreat, a means of gaining time to allow the revolutionary wave to subside so they could prepare a counterblow. Under the interim president, the huge Díaz bureaucracy remained largely intact. The reactionary officer corps remained in command of the federal army and burned for revenge over the revolutionary peasant armies that had defeated it.

Social conditions throughout the country remained largely unchanged, and the provisional government sought a total restoration of the status quo. Efforts were made to disband the revolutionary troops, and León de la Barra sent federal forces into Morelos to initiate hostilities against the Zapatistas, who had begun to confiscate large estates and distribute land to the villages. Madero's ineffective efforts to halt the fighting and mediate between Zapata and León de la Barra only deepened the hatred of the reactionaries for the visionary meddler who had unleashed anarchy in Mexico. But the revolutionary wave was still running strong, and reaction had to bide its time. In October 1911, Madero and his running mate, José María Pino Suárez, were elected president and vice president by overwhelming majorities.

Madero's Presidency: Inadequacy and Revolt

On November 6, 1911, Madero assumed the presidency from León de la Barra. It soon became evident that the "apostle of democracy" had no fundamental solutions for Mexico's grave social and economic problems. Even on the political plane, Madero's thought was far from advanced. His conception of democracy was a formal democracy that would give the masses the illusion of power and participation in political life but would vest all decision making in the hands of an elite.

In regard to economic and social democracy, his vision was even more limited. Madero allowed workers to organize trade unions and to strike and permitted a national workers' center, the *Casa del Obrero Mundial,* to be formed in Mexico City. But his answer to the agrarian problem was a totally inadequate program of purchase of land from large landowners and recovery of national land for distribution among landless peasants. In fact, Madero, who believed that only large landholdings would permit Mexican agriculture to modernize, was totally opposed to land reform at the expense of the haciendas. Madero's retreat on the land issue led to a break with his most faithful ally, Emiliano Zapata. Zapata urged Madero to carry out the agrarian provisions of the Plan of San Luis Potosí. Madero refused, arguing that the treaties that set up the interim government of León de la Barra obliged him to accept the legality of the legal and administrative decisions of the Díaz regime. Madero also demanded the disarmament of Zapata's peasant troops; in effect, he demanded Zapata's total surrender.

Convinced that Madero did not intend to carry out his pledges to restore land to the villages, Zapata announced his own program on November 28, 1911. The Plan of Ayala proclaimed that "the lands, woods, and waters usurped by the hacendados, Científicos, or caciques through tyranny and venal justice" would be returned to their owners, and Zapata began to put the plan into effect. The Zapatista movement soon spread to other states in central and southern Mexico. Madero sent a series of generals against Zapata but failed to crush Zapata and his armies.

Madero's failure to carry out a genuine agrarian reform lost him the trust and support of the

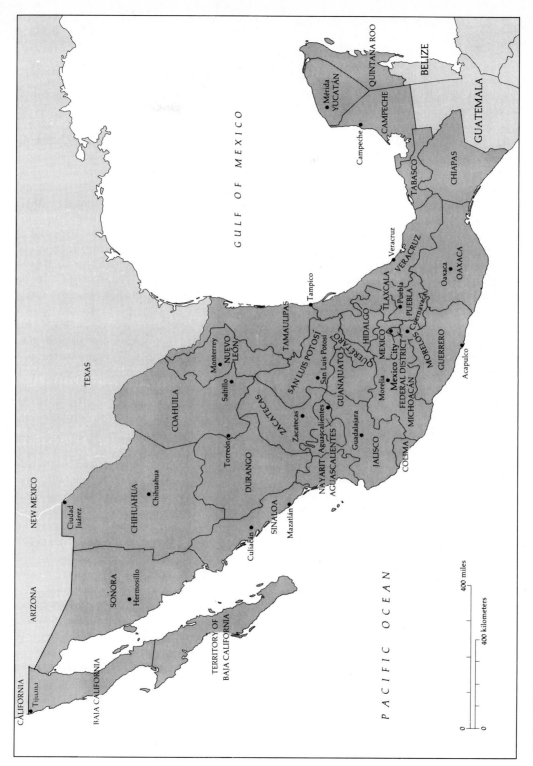

MODERN MEXICO

267

revolutionary peasantry without mollifying the reactionaries, who resented his modest concessions to labor and his efforts to transform Mexico into a bourgeois democracy with freedom of speech and press and the rule of law. They also feared that under pressure from the peasantry and under the influence of urban middle-class reformers like Luis Cabrera, a strong advocate of land reform, Madero might move farther to the left.

The aristocracy, its possessions and influence almost intact, dreamed of restoring the lost paradise of Don Porfirio, when peasants, workers, and Indians knew their place. Almost from the day that Madero took office in November 1911, therefore, counterrevolutionary revolts sprouted in various parts of Mexico. Most serious was a revolt in the north led by Pascual Orozco, who was encouraged and bribed by conservative elements in Chihuahua, especially the Terrazas-Creel clan. Federal troops under General Victoriano Huerta crushed the Orozco revolt in a series of battles, but Huerta's victory, joined with the alienation of Zapata and other of Madero's old revolutionary allies, increased Madero's dependence on an officer corps whose loyalty to his cause was highly dubious.

Abortive revolts followed one after another throughout the rest of 1912. The danger to Madero increased as it became clear that he had lost the support of the United States. Although Madero had made it clear that he favored foreign investments and guaranteed their security, he refused to show special favors to American capitalists and warned foreign investors that the crony system that had operated under Díaz was dead. This independent spirit, plus Madero's legalization of trade unions and strikes, and his inability to cope with the peasant revolution and establish stability, alienated the United States. American foreign policy, originally favorable to Madero, turned against him.

U.S. Ambassador Henry Lane Wilson became increasingly hostile to Madero. In February 1912, a hundred thousand American troops were stationed along the border, and throughout the year Wilson made vehement threats of intervention if the Madero government failed to protect American lives and property.

Meanwhile, preparations for a coup d'état were under way in the capital. Implicated in the conspiracy were General Huerta, the recent conqueror of Orozco; General Miguel Mondragón, former chief of artillery under Díaz; Bernardo and Rodolfo Reyes, father and son; and Félix Díaz, nephew of the old dictator.

The blow fell on February 9, 1913. On that day, the military garrison at Tacubaya "pronounced" against Madero. The rebels marched on the National Palace. Their attack failed, and Bernardo Reyes was killed in an exchange of fire. Díaz then retreated with his troops to the Citadel, a well-fortified army arsenal, and between the rebels and the loyal troops holding the palace there developed a bitter artillery duel. Since the two parties were more than a mile apart, the principal victims of the cannonade were civilians. Meanwhile Huerta, to whom Madero had entrusted command of military operations, only awaited the right moment to dispose of the president.

Meanwhile, the American ambassador, in complete sympathy with the counterrevolutionary revolt, was secretly negotiating with Huerta and Díaz. On February 12, Wilson sent Madero a sharp protest against the conduct of military operations in Mexico City because they threatened American life and property. At his urging, the British, German, and Spanish representatives sent similar demands. As the crisis moved toward a climax, Wilson became feverishly active. On February 14, he demanded that the Mexican government begin negotiations with the other warring parties; otherwise, American marines would be landed in Mexican ports. The same day, Wilson invited other foreign diplomats to a conference at which it was agreed to force Madero to resign. A message to that effect was sent to Madero from the diplomatic corps. Madero firmly rejected the demand. He would rather die, he said, than allow foreign intervention.

Huerta's Dictatorship

Ambassador Wilson's activities were clearly coordinated with those of the conspirators and encouraged Huerta to strike the long-planned blow. On February 18, a detachment of Huerta's troops entered the palace and arrested the president, his vice president, Pino Suárez, and other members of his government. A dispute between Huerta and Díaz over who should head the new regime was settled through Wilson's mediation. At a meeting at the American embassy, agreement was reached that Huerta should head a provisional government, with Díaz to succeed him as soon as an election could be held. Wilson then called a meeting of foreign diplomats to whom he introduced Huerta as the "savior of Mexico."

To give some semblance of legality to his usurpation, Huerta obtained the "voluntary" resignations of Madero and Pino Suárez in return for the promise that they would then be free to leave Mexico. An intimidated Congress accepted the resignations and recognized Huerta as provisional president, almost without dissent. There remained the question of what should be done with Madero. Asked by Huerta for his advice, the American ambassador replied that he should do "what was best for the country." Despite urgent requests by other members of the diplomatic corps and Madero's wife that he intercede to save Madero's life, Wilson refused. On the evening of February 22, Madero and Pino Suárez were murdered as they were being transferred from the National Palace to the penitentiary; the official explanation was that they had been killed during an attempt by armed men to release them. The two assassins, officers of the rurales, were quickly advanced in rank, one being made a general.

Huerta's seizure of power, which was greeted with rejoicing by the landed aristocracy, the big capitalists, and the church, was an effort to set the Mexican clock back, to restore the Díaz system of personal dictatorship. The promise to Félix Díaz that he would succeed Huerta as president was soon broken, and Díaz was shunted aside by sending him off on a diplomatic mission to Japan. On October 10, 1913, preparing for his own election, Huerta arrested 110 congressmen and dissolved both houses. He then installed a new Congress packed with his military followers. The election held on October 26 under these auspices was so fraudulent, the results so obviously falsified, that Huerta's own Congress, with his approval, nullified it and put off a new election until a future date, with Huerta to continue as provisional president. Meanwhile, political assassinations occurred at a rate unknown earlier in Mexican history.

Hoping to broaden the social base of his dictatorship and conceal its reactionary character as long as possible, Huerta for a time continued Madero's labor policies, but as the terrorist nature of the regime became more apparent and labor more and more allied itself with the anti-Huerta movement, he proceeded to arrest its leaders and eventually closed down the Casa del Obrero Mundial.

The Opposition: Zapata, Villa, Carranza, and Obregón

Huerta had counted on a quick victory over the peasant revolutionaries of the south and favorable reception of his coup d'état by conservative economic and political interests in the north. However, the revolutionary wave, still running strong, rose even higher in reaction to Madero's brutal murder and the imposition of Huerta's terrorist regime. Zapata intensified his struggle against local great landowners, Huerta's allies, and federal troops. In the northern border states of Sonora, Chihuahua, and Coahuila, meanwhile, an anti-Huerta coalition of disparate social groups—liberal hacendados, middle classes, miners, industrial workers, vaqueros and peasants—began to take form.

The successive campaigns launched by Huerta against the Zapatistas failed to achieve decisive victories. In mid-1913 the peasant armies laid siege to Cuernavaca, the capital of the state of Morelos, and cut it off from the national capital.

Driven from Morelos in the latter part of 1913, they continued to operate in neighboring states. In April the Zapatistas returned to Morelos and by the end of May had taken all the towns in the state except Cuernavaca. In June they laid siege to Cuernavaca and took it in August 1914.

By forcing Huerta to commit a considerable part of his troops to the campaign in the south, Zapata assured the success of the revolutionary movement that sprang up anew in the north. Pancho Villa assumed leadership of the Constitutionalists, as Huerta's northern opponents called themselves, in Chihuahua (March 1913). Enjoying an immense popularity among the state's vaqueros, he soon recruited an army of three thousand men. By the end of the summer he had won control of almost all Chihuahua except the large cities. In mid-November he captured Ciudad Juárez and went on to capture the state capital, Chihuahua City.

Master of Chihuahua City, Villa imposed a revolutionary new order on the state capital. He employed his soldiers as a civil militia and administrative staff to restore normal life. Villa ordered a reduction of meat prices and distributed money, clothing, and other goods to the poor. Education was a passion with the almost illiterate Villa; according to the U.S. correspondent John Reed, who accompanied him, Villa established some fifty new schools in Chihuahua City.

Clearly, Villa's social policies were more radical than those implemented by the Constitutionalist leaders in the neighboring states of Sonora and Coahuila. In December 1913, he announced the expropriation without compensation of the holdings of the pro-Huerta oligarchy in Chihuahua. His agrarian program, however, differed in significant ways from that of Zapata. Whereas in the area ruled by Zapata confiscated estates were promptly distributed among the peasants, Villa's decree provided that they should remain under state control until the victory of the revolution. The revenues from these estates would be used to finance the revolutionary struggle and support the widows and orphans of the revolutionary soldiers. Once victory had been achieved, they were

to be used to pay pensions to such widows and orphans, to compensate veterans of the revolution, to restore village lands that had been usurped by the hacendados, and to pay taxes left unpaid by the hacendados. Meanwhile Villa turned control of some confiscated haciendas over to his lieutenants; the rest were administered by the state. Cattle were sold in the United States to secure arms and ammunition for Villa's army, and meat was distributed on a large scale to the urban unemployed, to public institutions like orphanages and children's homes, and for sale in the markets. The differences between the agrarian programs of Villa and Zapata may be explained in part by the fact that the economy of the north was based not on agriculture but on cattle raising, which required large economic units. These units had to be administered by the state or on a cooperative basis. In addition, the percentage of peasants in the population was much smaller in the north, and the problem of land hunger much less acute.

In the neighboring state of Coahuila, meanwhile, the elderly Venustiano Carranza, a great landowner who had once served Díaz but joined Madero in 1911 and was appointed by him governor of the state, raised the standard of revolt against Huerta. On March 26, 1913, he announced his Plan of Guadalupe, which called for the overthrow of the dictator and the restoration of constitutional government but did not mention social reforms. Carranza assumed the title of first chief of the Constitutionalist Army. By April he commanded some forty thousand men. He was soon joined by Villa, who placed himself under Carranza's command, but retained much autonomy in Chihuahua; Villa's troops were renamed the Northern Division. Carranza gained another important recruit in the young ranchero Alvaro Obregón, who led the anti-Huerta forces in the state of Sonora. Named commander of the Army of the Northwest, he soon proved his large military gifts by driving the federal troops out of almost all Sonora; in April the state legislature recognized Carranza as first chief of the revolution.

Intervention by the United States

By the beginning of 1914, the Constitutionalist revolt had assumed significant proportions, and Huerta's fall appeared inevitable. Meanwhile, in March 1913, Woodrow Wilson had succeeded Taft as president of the United States. Alone among the great powers, Wilson's government refused to recognize the Huerta regime. Wilson justified his nonrecognition policy with moralistic rhetoric, refusing to recognize a government that had come to power illegally. More important, he was convinced that Huerta could not provide the stable political climate required by U.S. interests in Mexico.

Wilson's concern with a suitable political climate for American investments emerges from a note sent to British officials in November 1913, in which he assured those officials that the United States government "intends not merely to force Huerta from power, but also to exert every influence it can exert to secure Mexico a better government under which all contracts and business concessions will be safer than they have been." On the other hand, Huerta's policy of favoring British capital gained him support in that quarter.

By yielding to a British demand for uniform rates for all shipping using the nearly completed Panama Canal, Wilson obtained an end of British support for Huerta by the end of 1913. As a result, Huerta's financial position became increasingly difficult. Seeking to avert a catastrophe, he suspended payment on the interest on the national debt for six months but that extraordinary measure only increased Huerta's difficulties, however. Foreign creditors began to demand the seizure of Mexican customhouses, and some even clamored for immediate intervention. By February 1914 Wilson decided force must be used. After receiving assurances from Carranza's agent in Washington that the Constitutionalists would respect foreign property rights, including "just and equitable concessions," Wilson lifted the existing embargo on arms shipments to the Carranza forces.

Wilson found a pretext for intervention when a party of U.S. sailors from the cruiser *Dolphin* landed in a restricted area of Tampico and were arrested. They were almost immediately released, with an apology, but the commander of the *Dolphin,* under orders from Washington, demanded a formal disavowal of the action, severe punishment for the responsible Mexican officer, and a twenty-one-gun salute to the American flag. For Huerta to grant these demands might have meant political suicide, and he refused.

President Wilson now sent a fleet into the Gulf of Mexico, and on April 21, 1914, learning that a German merchant ship was bound for Veracruz with munitions, he ordered the seizure of the city. When Mexican batteries at the fortress of San Juan de Ulúa attempted to prevent a landing, they were silenced by answering fire from the U.S. ships. Huerta's forces evacuated Veracruz the same day, but the local population and cadets of the naval academy continued a courageous resistance until April 27, when the American flag was raised over Veracruz. The occupation of Veracruz sent a wave of anti-Yankee sentiment rolling through Mexico; protests were also organized in a number of Latin American countries. Meanwhile Carranza, whom Wilson had hoped to control, bitterly denounced the U.S. action and demanded the immediate evacuation of Veracruz.

The rising storm of Mexican anger and Carranza's defiant stand placed Wilson in a quandary. He sought a way out of his difficult situation by obtaining an offer from Argentina, Brazil, and Chile to mediate the dispute between the United States and Mexico. A conference was convened at Niagara Falls, Canada, in May 1914. Wilson hoped to do more than reduce tensions; he intended to use the mediation as a means of eliminating Huerta and establishing a new provisional Mexican government that he could control. The U.S. candidate to head this provisional government was the moderate Carranza, since the revolutionary peasant leaders Zapata and Villa were obviously unacceptable. But Carranza would not rise to Wilson's bait. The conservative but fiercely nationalist first chief sent representatives to the Niagara Falls conference but did not give them official status, and he refused the mediation of the conference. Mexico, his representatives informed the United States delegates, would settle its own problems without interference from any foreign source.

By this time, the fall of the Huerta regime was imminent. With the northern tier of states securely in Constitutionalist hands, Pancho Villa's Northern Division drove south in March from Chihuahua City toward Torreón, a major railroad center. On April 2, Torreón fell to Villa after twelve days of bitter fighting; the fall of Monterrey, Saltillo, and Tampico followed soon after. Having taken Saltillo, Villa advanced on Zacatecas and took the city by storm on June 23. Meanwhile, Obregón's Army of the Northwest was advancing down the Pacific coast into Jalisco; on July 9, he seized the important railroad and industrial center of Guadalajara. Recognizing that his situation had become hopeless, Huerta took flight for Europe on July 15. On August 15, Obregón's troops entered Mexico City.

Huerta's fall deprived the United States of any pretext for continuing its armed intervention, but President Wilson delayed the evacuation of Veracruz as long as possible in the hope of securing commitments from Carranza that would have effectively prevented any basic changes in Mexico's social and economic structure. Despite hints that "fatal consequences" might follow, Carranza resolutely rejected these demands and continued to insist on the end of the military intervention. U.S. troops finally evacuated Veracruz on November 23, 1914.

Fighting Among the Victors

As the day of complete victory drew near, differences emerged within the Constitutionalist camp, especially between Carranza and Villa. There were personal factors, such as Carranza's jealousy of Villa as a potential rival, but more important was Carranza's failure to define his position on such fundamental issues as the agrarian question, the role of the church, and the new po-

litical order. Villa proposed to incorporate in an agreement a clause drawn up by one of his intellectuals that defined "the present conflict as a struggle of the poor against the abuses of the powerful" and committed the Constitutionalists "to implant a democratic regime . . . to secure the well-being of the workers; to emancipate the peasants economically, making an equitable distribution of lands or whatever else is needed to solve the agrarian problem." Under pressure from his generals, who recognized the potential dangers of an open break with Villa, Carranza permitted his representatives to sign the agreement containing this radical clause, which he personally found unacceptable. Villa, however, continued to distrust Carranza, and his distrust was confirmed by various of Carranza's actions, notably his unilateral occupation of the capital.

Relations also deteriorated between Carranza and Zapata. Zapata had waged war against Huerta independently of Carranza's forces and refused to recognize his leadership; a Zapatista manifesto proclaimed that the Plan of Ayala must prevail, and all adherents of the old regime must be removed.

In October 1914, a convention of revolutionary leaders and their delegates met at Aguascalientes to settle the conflict between Carranza and Villa. At the insistence of the *Villistas,* Zapata was invited to attend, and presently a delegation from "the Liberating Army of the South" arrived. The convention endorsed the Plan of Ayala, assumed supreme authority, called for the resignation of Carranza as first chief, and appointed General Eulalio Gutiérrez provisional president of the nation. Gutiérrez was a compromise candidate pushed by delegates equally opposed to Carranza and Villa. Since Aguascalientes swarmed with Villa's troops, Gutiérrez had no choice but to name Villa commander in chief of the Conventionist Army, as the Northern Division now came to be called.

But Carranza refused to accept the decisions of the Aguascalientes convention, claiming it had no authority to depose him. When he failed to meet the deadline for his resignation, November

In early December, 1914, Pancho Villa met with Emiliano Zapata in Mexico City, where both attended the installation of a new president. Earlier, Villa and Zapata had reached agreement on a course of action for the revolution, but the arrangement soon fell apart. (Culver Pictures)

10, the armies of Zapata and Villa advanced on the capital and occupied it. Carranza retreated with his depleted forces to Veracruz, which had been evacuated by the Americans shortly before. There he established his Constitutionalist government, while Obregón, who had remained loyal to Carranza, rebuilt his army with the aid of arms and munitions purchased abroad.

On December 4, Villa and Zapata held their first meeting and came to full agreement. But although the peasant revolutionaries controlled the capital and much of the country, they could not consolidate their successes. Unskilled in politics, they entrusted state power to the unreliable provisional president, Gutiérrez, a former general in Carranza's army, who sabotaged the Conventionist war effort and opened secret negotiations with Obregón. Meanwhile a conservative wing in the convention strongly opposed land reform, expropriation of foreign properties, and other radical social changes. Villa's sympathies on land reform were with the radicals, but he avoided taking sides in the dispute, probably because he believed that unity was necessary to gain both a rapid military victory and recognition by the United States, which he also regarded as essential to his final triumph. For these and other reasons the convention proved unable to forge a clear national program of socioeconomic reforms that could unite the interests of the peasantry, industrial workers, and the middle class. His later attempts to broaden his program to attract labor, the middle class, and even national capitalists were too little and too late.

The Constitutionalists did not make the same mistake. At the insistence of Obregón and intellectuals like Luis Cabrera, who were aware of the need for broadening the social base of the Constitutionalist movement, the conservative Carranza adopted a program of social reforms designed to win the support of peasants and workers. In December 1914, during the darkest days of the Constitutionalist cause, Carranza issued in Veracruz a decree that promised agrarian reform and improved conditions for the industrial workers. Other decrees followed, the most notable being one of January 6, 1915, which provided for the restoration of lands usurped from the villages and the expropriation of additional needed land from haciendas. (Simultaneously, Carranza secretly promised the hacendados that he would return the haciendas that had been confiscated by revolutionary authorities—promises that in the end he would keep.) Carranza's agrarian decrees, gained him a certain base among the peasantry. Carranza also courted labor support by the promise of a minimum wage law applying to all branches of industry and by affirming the right of workers to form trade unions and to strike.

After Obregón's troops reoccupied Mexico City in January 1915, an alliance was formed between the Carranza government and the Casa del Obrero Mundial, which was restored after the fall of Huerta. Members of the Casa agreed to join "the struggle against reaction"—meaning above all the revolutionary peasantry. Six "red battalions" of workers were formed and made an important contribution to the offensive launched by Obregón against Villa and Zapata in January

1915. Inadequate understanding on the part of the peasant and working-class leaders of their common interests and the skillful opportunism of the middle-class politicians in Carranza's camp contributed to this disastrous division between labor and the peasantry.

As a result, the balance of forces shifted sharply in favor of the Constitutionalists. In early 1915, Carranza's forces won significant victories; having captured Puebla, they threatened the capital. President Gutiérrez, who had long wanted to break with Villa, left the city with a group of his ministers, some troops, and 10 million pesos from the national treasury. Shortly afterward, he submitted his resignation. Following Gutiérrez's flight, the Conventionist government, or what remained of it, designated Roque González Garza as president in his place.

Under pressure from Carranza's troops, Villa was forced on January 19 to evacuate Mexico City, which Obregón soon occupied. A series of complicated movements followed, with Constitutionalists and Conventionists successively occupying and abandoning the city. These maneuvers ended with Obregón in possession of the capital. In April 1915, Obregón advanced toward the important railroad center of Celaya, occupied it, and awaited Villa's attack. Obregón had studied accounts of the great war in progress in Europe and had learned that trenches and barbed wire could stop mass attacks. His army received Villa's furious infantry and cavalry assault with a withering fire from machine-gun emplacements and entrenched infantry. For the first time in his military career, Villa suffered a disastrous defeat, with thousands of men killed or taken prisoner. Fighting a series of battles, he retreated northward. In the hour of his defeat (May 1915), Villa issued a comprehensive, well-thought-out agrarian reform law, providing that all estates above a certain size were to be divided among the peasantry, with some indemnity for the owners, and payment by the peasants in small installments, but the program was never implemented. By the end of 1915, he was back in Chihuahua; here, among his own people, on terrain that he knew perfectly, he was invincible. For three more years he carried on guerrilla warfare but ceased to exist as a major political and military factor. The Constitutionalists had destroyed Villa, whom they regarded as the primary danger.

There remained the Zapatistas, who threatened the capital and who had temporarily occupied it in July. But Zapata's battered forces could not check the advance of General Pablo González's army. In August the Constitutionalists returned to Mexico City to stay, while González, one of Carranza's ablest generals, pursued the Zapatistas into Morelos in a campaign of devastation and plunder.

In October 1915, after unsuccessful efforts to play off the revolutionary chiefs against each other or to achieve a coalition under United States leadership, President Wilson acknowledged Carranza's ascendancy and extended de facto recognition of his regime; equally important, he placed an arms embargo on Carranza's opponents. But the United States had not abandoned its efforts to influence the course of the Mexican Revolution. A memorandum to Carranza dictated the conditions he must meet before he could obtain de jure recognition. They amounted to a claim to determine Mexican policy not only in the area of foreign economic rights but in such internal matters as the role of the church, elections, and the like. These demands were as unacceptable to Carranza in October 1915 as they had been a year before.

In early 1916, relations between the United States and Mexico deteriorated sharply. In part, this resulted from initial efforts by Mexican federal and state authorities to regulate the operations of foreign oil companies. A crisis arose in March when Villa, angered by the arms embargo and wrongly convinced that Carranza had bought United States recognition by agreeing to a plan to convert Mexico into a United States protectorate, raided Columbus, New Mexico, in an apparent effort to force Carranza to show his hand. The Wilson administration responded by ordering General John Pershing to pursue Villa into Mexico. The United States counted on the enmity between Villa and Carranza to secure the latter's neutrality. Carranza denounced the invasion, demanded the immediate withdrawal of American forces, and began to prepare for war with the United States. In a note to other Latin American nations, the Mexican government declared its belief that the basic reason for U.S. intervention was its opposition to the Mexican policy of eliminating privileged treatment of foreign capital and affirmed that the "foreign invasion" must be repelled and Mexican sovereignty respected.

The United States had anticipated an easy victory, but Pershing's hot pursuit of the elusive Villa proved a fiasco, and Wilson accepted Carranza's offer to negotiate a settlement. Wilson was unsuccessful in his efforts to link the evacuation of American forces with acceptance of the United States formula for Mexican domestic policy. In January 1917, influenced by the troubled international scene and his conviction that a war with Mexico would involve at least half a million men, Wilson decided to liquidate the Mexican venture. Mexican nationalism had won a major victory over yet another effort to impose U.S. hegemony.

The Constitution of 1917

In the fall of 1916, Carranza issued a call for the election of deputies to a convention that was to frame a new constitution and prepare the way for his election as president. The convention opened in Querétaro on December 1, 1916. Since the call effectively excluded persons who had not sworn loyalty to his 1913 Plan of Guadalupe, it seemed likely that the constitution would be what Carranza wanted. The draft did not contemplate a radical agrarian reform; for labor, it limited itself to proclaiming the "right to work" and the right of workers to form organizations for "lawful purposes" and to hold "peaceful" assemblies.

These abstract proposals were unsatisfactory to a majority of the deputies, who formed the radical wing of the convention. The principal spokesman for this left wing was Francisco J. Múgica, a young general who helped to make the first land distribution of the revolution. The radicals obtained majority approval to create a commission to revise Carranza's project. Múgica himself was largely responsible for Article 3, which struck a heavy blow at church control of education by specifically forbidding "religious corporations" and "ministers of any cult" to establish or conduct schools.

A most important article was Article 123, dealing with the rights of labor. Carranza had asked only that the federal government be empowered to enact labor legislation. The convention went much further. The finished article, a true labor code, provided for the eight-hour day; abolished the tienda de raya, or company store, and debt servitude; guaranteed the right of workers to organize, bargain collectively, and strike; and granted many other rights and privileges, making it the most advanced labor code in the contemporary world.

Article 27, dealing with property rights, had an equally advanced character. It proclaimed the nation the original owner of all lands, waters, and the subsoil; the state could expropriate them, with compensation to the owners. National ownership of water and the subsoil was inalienable, but individuals and companies could obtain concessions for their exploitation. Foreigners to whom that privilege was granted must agree that they would not invoke the protection of their governments in regard to such concessions. Of prime importance were the same article's agrarian provisions. It declared that all measures passed since 1856 alienating ejidos (communal lands) were null and void; if the pueblos needed more land, they could acquire it by expropriation from neighboring haciendas.

These and other provisions of the constitution of 1917 made it the most progressive law code of its time. It laid legal foundations for a massive assault on the latifundio, for weakening the power of the church, and for regulating the operations of foreign capital in Mexico. But the constitution was not anticapitalist. It sanctioned and protected private property; it sought to control rather than eliminate foreign enterprises, creating more favorable conditions for the development of national capitalism.

The convention completed its work on January 31, 1917, and Carranza ordered promulgation of the new constitution on February 5, 1917. Carranza expressed reservations about the new constitution but promised to uphold it. Then he issued a call for an extraordinary presidential election to be held in March. His election was a foregone conclusion, and on May 1, 1917, he was formally installed as president—the first legally elected president since Madero. On inauguration day, Obregón, his secretary of war, resigned and retired to private life. Obregón, who had been moving to the left, distrusted many of the men around Carranza as reactionaries of Porfirista stamp.

Carranza's Presidency

The three remaining years of the Carranza regime were marked by a sharp swing to the right. Carranza soon made it clear that he did not intend to implement the reform articles of the constitution. Only a trifling amount of land was distributed to the villages. Carranza returned many confiscated haciendas to their former owners; others he turned over to his favorite generals. Official corruption existed on a massive scale. The working class suffered severe repression. Carranza shut down the Casa del Obrero Mundial. The constitution's promise of free education was ignored. Only in Carranza's foreign policy, marked by a genuine revolutionary nationalism, did the spirit of the constitution live. Carranza staunchly resisted U.S. pressure to give guarantees that Article 27 of the constitution would not be implemented against foreign interests. He also kept Mexico neutral in World War I and insisted on an independent Mexican diplomatic position in the hemisphere—postures that the United States regarded as unfriendly.

Meanwhile, Carranza continued to battle the tenacious Zapatista movement in the south and Villa in the north. Against the Zapatistas, Carranza's favorite general, Pablo González, launched campaign after campaign. Zapata's forces diminished and the territory under his control shrank to the vanishing point, but he remained unconquerable, supported by the affection and loyalty of the peasantry. His fall came through treachery. Invited to confer with a Carrancista officer who claimed to have gone over to his side, Zapata was ambushed and slain on April 10, 1919. But his people continued their struggle for *tierra y libertad* (land and liberty).

Carranza's legal term was due to end in 1920, but the president had no intention of relinquishing power. Barred from running again by the constitutional rule of no re-election, he picked as his successor the ambassador to Washington, Ignacio Bonillas, generally regarded as a nonentity. Meanwhile, Obregón, supported by a Labor party formed to further his interests, announced his candidacy for the presidency. As the campaign proceeded, it became clear that Carranza intended to manipulate the electoral machinery to impose Bonillas on the nation. In April 1920, Obregón and the governor of Sonora, Adolfo de la Huerta, issued a call for the removal of Carranza and the appointment of a provisional government until an election could be held. The swift triumph of the revolt revealed the depth of the unpopularity of the distant, aloof Carranza and his policies. In May 1920, Carranza fled from the capital toward Veracruz, taking with him 5 million pesos in gold and silver from the national treasury. On the night of May 21, the mountain village in which he slept was attacked by local guerrillas, and Carranza was slain.

On May 24, Adolfo de la Huerta, the chief of the Liberal Constitutionalist Army, was chosen president at a special session of Congress. He promptly scheduled a presidential election for September 5, with the candidacy and victory of Obregón a certain outcome. Under the interim president, pacification was the order of the day. The Zapatistas, who had joined the uprising against Carranza, obtained confirmation of the agrarian reform for which they had so long fought. Villa, who also aided the anti-Carranza movement, was rewarded with a hacienda, and other lands were given to his men. Villa did not long enjoy his newfound peace and prosperity; he was assassinated in the summer of 1923 under obscure circumstances.

In November 1920, Alvaro Obregón assumed the presidency. At last, peace had come to Mexico, and the work of reconstruction could begin. It would not be an easy task. The great wind that swept Mexico had left a devastated land, with hundreds of thousands dead or missing; the Mexican population had actually declined by 1 million since 1910. The constitution of 1917 offered a blueprint for a new and better social order, but major obstacles to change remained. Not the least were the hundreds of generals thrown up by the great upheaval, men of humble origins who once had nothing and now had an incurable itch for wealth and power. With his characteristic wry humor, Obregón summed up the problem when he said that the days of revolutionary banditry had ended because he had brought all the bandits with him to the capital to keep them out of trouble.

Reconstruction: The Rule of the Millionaire Socialists

Obregón and Reform

With Obregón there came to power a group of northern generals and politicians who began the work of economic and social reconstruction that Madero, Huerta, and Carranza were unable or unwilling to achieve. Of middle-class or even lower-class origins—Obregón had been a mechanic and farmer, his successor Calles, a schoolteacher—both were products of a border region where U.S. cultural influence was strong, where capitalism and capitalist relations were more highly developed than in any other part of Mexico. Obregón and Calles thus possessed a pragmatic business mentality as far removed from the revolutionary agrarian ideology of Zapata as it was from the aristocratic reformism of Carranza. These men

278 deliberately, set out to lay the economic, political, and ideological foundations of a Mexican national capitalism.

Aware that the revolution had radicalized the masses, aware of the appeal of socialism and anti-imperialism to the workers on whose support they counted, Obregón and Calles employed a revolutionary rhetoric designed to mobilize popular support and conceal how modest were the social changes that actually took place. In practice, the Obregonian program was revolutionary only by contrast with the reactionary trend that characterized the last years of Carranza's rule. Far from promoting socialism, Obregón sought accommodation with all elements of Mexican society except the most reactionary clergy and landlords. He allowed exiles of the most varied political tendency to return to Mexico, and radical intellectuals rubbed shoulders with former Científicos in his government. Power was held by a ruling class of wealthy generals, capitalists, and landlords; elections remained a farce; the president was a dictator who kept power by playing regional warlords and various factions against one another. Labor and the peasantry were the government's obedient clienteles, represented by a Labor party and an Agrarian party whose leaders formed part of the establishment and mediated between their clienteles and the all-powerful president.

Regarding agrarian reform as a useful safety valve for peasant discontent, Obregón distributed some land to the pueblos. But the process proceeded slowly, haltingly, against the intense opposition of the hacendados and the church, which condemned the agrarian reform because it did not take account of the "just rights of the landlords." Litigation by landlords, their use of armed force to resist occupation of expropriated land, and the opposition of the clergy, slowed down the pace of the land reform.

Even after a village had received land, its prospect for success was poor, for the government failed to provide the peasants with seeds, implements, and adequate credit facilities or modern agricultural training. Such credit assistance as they received usually came from government rural banks, which exercised close control over land use, intensifying the client status of the peasantry, or from rural loan sharks. The Obregón land reform was neither swift nor thoroughgoing; by the end of his presidency, only some 3 million acres had been distributed among 624 villages, while 320 million acres remained in private hands.

Obregón also encouraged labor to organize, for he regarded trade unions as useful for stabilizing labor-capitalist relations and as an important bulwark of his regime. The principal trade union organization was the *Confederación Regional Obrera Mexicana* (CROM), formed in 1918. Despite the rhetoric of its leaders about "class struggle" and freedom from the "tyranny of capitalism," CROM was about as radical as the American Federation of Labor, with which it maintained close ties. Its perpetual boss was Luis Morones, known for his flashy dress, diamonds, and limousines. As the only labor organization sponsored and protected by the government, CROM had virtually official status. Despite this official protection, Morones's method of personal negotiation with employers yielded scanty benefits to labor; wages barely kept pace with the rising cost of living.

Perhaps the most solid achievements of the Obregón regime were in the areas of education and culture. The creation of a native Mexican capitalism demanded the development of a national consciousness, which meant the integration of the Indian peoples—still made up of so many small nations—into the national market and the new society. From this point of view, the Indians were the key problem of Mexican reconstruction. Because incorporating them into the modern world required a thorough understanding of the Indians' past and their present conditions of life, the revolutionary regimes encouraged scientific study of the Indians. Under Obregón, Manuel Gamio, appointed director of the first government office of anthropology in the Americas in 1917, fused the methods and goals of archaeology and applied anthropology in his famous pilot study of Teotihuacán. Gamio sought not only to preserve and restore a precious cultural heritage but to amass the data needed for a sound plan of economic and social recovery for this area.

An integral part of *indigenismo* was a reassessment of the Indian cultural heritage. To insist on the greatness of the old Indian arts was one way of asserting the value of one's own, of revolting against the tyranny of the pallid, lifeless French and Spanish academicism over Mexican art during the last decades of the Díaz era.

From Europe returned two future giants of the Mexican artistic renaissance, Diego Rivera and David Alfaro Siqueiros, to join another gifted artist, José Clemente Orozco, in creating a militant new art that drew much of its inspiration from the Indians and their ancient art. Believing that "a heroic art could fortify the will to reconstruction," Obregón's brilliant young secretary of education, José Vasconcelos, offered the walls of public buildings for the painting of murals that glorified the Indians, past and present.

The Indianist cult had great political significance. The foes of the revolution, unregenerate Porfiristas, clericals, and reactionaries of all stripes, looked back to Spain as the sole source of enduring values in Mexican life and regarded Cortés as the creator of Mexican nationality; partisans of the revolution tended to idealize Aztec Mexico (sometimes beyond recognition) and elevated the last Aztec warrior-king, Cuauhtémoc, to the status of a demigod.

Convinced that the school was the most important instrument for unifying the nation, that "to educate was to redeem," Vasconcelos, with ample budgetary support from Obregón, launched an imaginative program of cultural missions designed to bring literacy and health to primitive Indian villages. Hundreds of young, idealistic teachers went out to bring the gospel of sanitation and literacy to remote pueblos. Vasconcelos also founded teacher-training colleges, agricultural schools, and other specialized schools. An achievement in which he took special pride was the publication of hundreds of

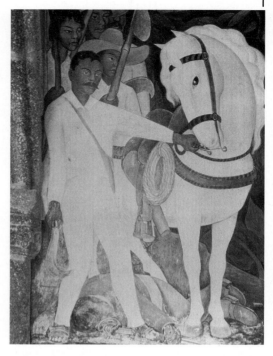

This painting of Emiliano Zapata by Diego Rivera is representative of national themes selected by artists of the Mexican Renaissance. Committed to revolutionary social change, Diego and others like him looked to Mexico's Indian heritage, dramatic events in Mexican history, and the life of the peasant for inspiration. (Laurie Platt Winfrey, Inc.)

classic works in cheap editions for free distribution in the schools.

The new secular, nationalist school provoked clerical anger, for it threatened to supplant the priest with the teacher as the guiding force of the Indian community and to replace the religious world outlook taught by the Catholic church with a scientific world outlook. The church fought back with all the means at its disposal. Some priests denounced secular education from their pulpits and threatened parents who sent their children to state schools with excommunication. As a result of this campaign, many teachers were attacked and some killed by fanatical villagers.

Despite this campaign, Obregón made no effort to implement Article 3 of the constitution, which banned religious primary schools, for he believed that in the absence of enough resources on the part of the state it was better that Mexican children receive instruction from priests than remain illiterate.

The Catholic issue joined with other issues to cause Obregón difficulties in his relations with the United States. For three years, the United States government withheld diplomatic recognition from Obregón in an effort to force him to recognize that Article 27 of the constitution should not apply to mineral concessions obtained by foreigners before 1917. Like Carranza, Obregón was willing to respect the principle of nonretroactivity but refused to formalize it in a treaty, which he considered humiliating.

However, in 1923, with a growing threat of a counterrevolutionary coup to prevent the victory of Obregón's hand-picked successor, Plutarco Elías Calles, Obregón decided to compromise. Mexican diplomats signed the Bucareli Agreement (not a formal treaty), which confirmed that Article 27 was not retroactive, and agreed to pay compensation for damages to American property during the revolution. The United States promptly extended formal recognition to Obregón in August 1923. When the expected revolt broke out in December, the United States allowed Obregón to procure large quantities of war materiel. Together with the help of the organized labor and peasant movements, this aid enabled Obregón to crush the uprising, which was supported by reactionary landowners, clergy, and military. On November 30, 1924, Calles assumed the presidency of Mexico.

Calles's Regime

In and out of office, as legal president or de facto dictator, Calles dominated the next decade of Mexican politics. Building on the foundations Obregón had laid, he continued his work with much the same methods. His radical phraseology tended to conceal the pragmatic essence of his

policy, which was to promote the rapid growth of Mexican national capitalism, whose infrastructure he helped to establish. To strengthen the fiscal and monetary system he created the Bank of Mexico, the only bank permitted to issue money. A national road commission was organized, and a national electricity code was enacted to aid the electric power industry. These measures stimulated the growth of construction and consumer goods industries, in which members of Calles's official family—or the "revolutionary family," as the ruling elite came to be called—were heavily involved. Protective tariffs, subsidies, and other forms of aid were generously extended to industry, both foreign and domestic. In 1925 an assembly plant of the Ford Motor Company began operations in Mexico after Calles and the company negotiated an agreement providing for numerous concessions.

Calles showed more enthusiasm for land reform than Obregón, and the tempo of land distribution increased sharply during his presidency. Like Obregón, Calles regarded land reform as a safety valve for peasant unrest. During the four years of his term, Calles distributed about twice as much land as Obregón.

But less than one-fourth of that amount consisted of arable land, for Calles did not require the hacendados to surrender productive land, and most of the land given up came from pasture or forest lands, or even land that was completely barren. Nor did Calles make a serious effort to provide the peasantry with irrigation, fertilizer, implements, or seed. He established a government bank that was supposed to lend money to the ejidos, promote modern farming techniques, and act as agents for the sale of their produce. But four-fifths of the bank's resources were loaned not to ejidos but to hacendados with much superior credit ratings, and many of the bank's agents took advantage of their position to enrich themselves at the expense of the peasants.

Under these conditions, it is no wonder that the land reform soon appeared to be a failure. By 1930 grain production had fallen below the levels of 1910, and Calles, concluding that peasant proprietorship was economically undesirable, announced the abandonment of land distribution. Meanwhile, on his own large estates Calles introduced machinery and other modern agricultural techniques and advised other large landowners to do the same.

Like Obregón, Calles regarded labor unions as desirable because they helped stabilize labor-capitalist relations and avert radical social change. But by the end of the *Callista* decade, Mexican labor, disillusioned with a corrupt leadership that kept wages at or below the subsistence level, had begun to break away from CROM and form independent unions.

Calles continued the Carranza and Obregón policies of asserting Mexico's right to regulate the conditions under which foreign capital could exploit its natural resources, but he was far from hostile to foreign capital. Indeed, he gave assurances that "the government will do everything in its power to safeguard the interests of foreign capitalists who invest money in Mexico."

But a serious dispute with the United States arose in 1925 when the Mexican Congress passed laws to implement Article 27. The most important of these measures required owners of oil leases to exchange their titles for fifty-year concessions dating from the time of acquisition, to be followed, if necessary, by a thirty-year renewal, with the possibility of yet another extension if needed. No Mexican oil well had ever lasted more than eighty years. Far from injuring the foreign oil companies, the law eliminated the vagueness of their status under Article 27, gave them firm titles emanating from the government, and served to quiet more radical demands for outright nationalization. However, a number of American oil companies denounced the law as confiscatory and threatened to continue drilling operations without confirmatory concessions.

The State Department vigorously protested the restrictive legislation, and the United States ambassador, James R. Sheffield, pursued a hard-line, uncompromising policy. By late 1926 the United States appeared to be moving toward war with Mexico.

Fortunately, the interventionist policy came under severe attack from Progressive Republican senators and from the press, church groups, and the academic world. President Calvin Coolidge and Kellogg, realizing that war with Mexico would have little national support, sought a way out of the impasse; they were aided by U.S. international bankers, who had a clearer understanding of Mexican policies and intentions. The appointment of Dwight Morrow, a partner in the financial firm of J. P. Morgan, as ambassador to Mexico in September 1927 marked a turning point in the crisis. Morrow managed to persuade Calles that portions of the oil law had the potential for injuring foreign property rights, with the result that the Mexican Supreme Court found unconstitutional that portion of the law setting a time period on concessions. As rewritten, however, the law still provided for confirmatory concessions and reaffirmed national ownership of the subsoil.

In addition, a serious domestic dispute arose as a result of the growing opposition of the church to the whole modernizing thrust of the revolution. Under Calles, this opposition assumed the proportions of a civil war. In January 1926, the church hierarchy signed a letter declaring that the constitution of 1917 "wounds the most sacred rights of the Catholic Church" and disavowed the document. Calles responded by enforcing the anticlerical clauses of the constitution, which had lain dormant. The Calles Law, as it was called, ordered the registration of priests with the civil authorities and the closing of religious primary schools. The church struck back by suspending church services throughout Mexico, a powerful weapon in a country so overwhelmingly Catholic.

But neither this strike nor the boycott organized by the church, which urged the faithful to buy no goods or services except absolute necessities, brought the government to its knees. By the end of 1926, militant Catholics, in frequent alliance with local hacendados, had taken to arms. Guerrilla groups were formed, with the mountainous backcountry of Jalisco the main focus of their activity. Government schools and young teachers sent into remote areas were frequent objects of clerical fury; many teachers were tortured and killed. The total number of Catholic guerrillas, known as *Cristeros* from their slogan, *Viva Cristo Rey* (Long Live Christ the King), was small, but federal commanders helped to keep the insurrection alive by the brutality of their repressions. By the summer of 1927, however, the revolt had largely burned itself out, and Calles could turn his attention to the forthcoming presidential election in July 1928.

In an apparent deal between Calles and Obregón, the latter's supporters in Congress amended the constitution to allow a former president to be re-elected after one term, and the presidential term was extended from four to six years. The plan was for Obregón to succeed Calles and Calles to succeed Obregón. Angered by this arrangement, two frustrated presidential hopefuls, General Francisco Serrano and Arnulfo Gómez, began to conspire against Obregón and Calles. Calles acted decisively; the plotters were seized and shot, and Obregón remained the only candidate. In July, Obregón was duly elected, but three weeks later a fanatical Cristero assassinated him in a Mexico City restaurant.

With the passing of the formidable Obregón, Calles became the *jefe máximo,* the maximum chief of the revolution. The presidents who successively held office during what was to have been Obregón's six-year term—Emilio Portes Gil, Pascual Ortiz Rubio, and Abelardo Rodríguez— were Calles's stooges and obediently resigned when they incurred his displeasure. In 1929, after crushing a rebellion that proved to be almost the last hurrah of the regional military caudillos, Calles organized the National Revolutionary party (PNR) as an instrument for pacifying the country and institutionalizing the rule of the "revolutionary family," the military leaders and politicians who had ruled the country since 1920. Under different names and with leaderships of differing composition, the party formed by Calles has been the ruling party of Mexico since 1929. The official party's candidates for president have not lost an election in six decades.

As the "revolutionary family" consolidated its power and its wealth increased, its members became more conservative. Their humble beginnings disposed the revolutionary generals to become even more corrupt and predatory than the old Porfirista aristocracy. As large landowners, they were naturally hostile to agrarian reform; as owners of construction firms and factories, they were naturally hostile to strikes and unions.

Calles and his cronies had never been committed to a radical reconstruction of Mexican society, but after 1928, they retreated from their own modest reform program. To camouflage their shift to the right and validate their revolutionary credentials they indulged freely in anticlerical demagoguery and excesses. Their acts blew new life into the dying Cristero movement, causing a brief but bitter new conflict that took many lives.

This rightward shift of the Callista regime coincided with the beginning in 1929 of the Great Depression, which exposed the bankruptcy of capitalist economics and added to the misery of Mexican peasants and workers. Their growing unrest created fears of a new revolutionary explosion. Rumblings of protest were heard even within the ruling party. A new generation of young, middle-class reformers demanded vigorous implementation of the constitution of 1917. Some were intellectuals influenced by Marxism and the success of the Soviet example, especially by its concept of economic planning, but their basic message was the need to resume the struggle against the latifundio, peonage, and economic and cultural backwardness, that is, to resume the advance of the bourgeois revolution, stalled by the corruption, cynicism, and conservatism of the Callistas.

By 1933 the growing influence of the progressive wing within the PNR had led to a partial reform of the agrarian laws that transferred land distribution from the states to the federal government and to the beginnings of a school reform under the direction of the brilliant Narciso Bassols during his brief tenure as secretary of education under Abelardo Rodríguez.

The acknowledged leader of the reform group within the PNR was General Lázaro Cárdenas, governor of Michoacán. As governor, Cárdenas had established an enviable record for honesty, compassion, and concern for commoners. He had spent almost 50 percent of his budget on education, doubling the number of schools in the state. Despite his progressive ideas, he was close to the inner circle of the "revolutionary family," and the jefe máximo regarded him as a loyal lieutenant. In October 1930, he was chosen chairman of the PNR, a post that made him one of its most powerful figures.

The 1934 presidential elections approached. Aware of the growing strength of the left wing in the PNR, Calles decided to make concessions to the reformers that would leave him in control of the government. With Calles's blessing, Cárdenas was nominated for president at the PNR convention in 1933. With Calles's approval, the convention also drafted a Six-Year Plan (in obvious imitation of the Soviet model) that would give life to the ideals and promises of the constitution of 1917. Although there was no doubt that he would be elected, Cárdenas campaigned vigorously, visiting the most remote areas of the country, patiently explaining to workers and peasants the Six-Year Plan and the need to strengthen the ejidos, build modern schools, and develop workers' cooperatives. In July 1934, he was elected and took office with a cabinet hand-picked for him by Calles. The jefe máximo was confident that the loyal Cárdenas would carry out his orders as the puppet presidents who preceded him had done.

The Years of Cárdenas

Under Cárdenas, the Mexican Revolution resumed its advance. Land distribution to the villages on a massive scale was accompanied by a many-sided effort to raise agricultural productivity and improve the quality of rural life. Labor was encouraged to replace the old, corrupt leadership with militant leaders and to struggle for improved conditions. A spirit of service began to pervade at least a part of the governmental bureaucracy. Cárdenas set an example to subordi-

nates by the democratic simplicity of his manners, by cutting his own salary in half, and by making himself available to the delegations of Indians and workers who thronged the waiting rooms of the National Palace.

These and other policies of the new president—such as the closing down of illegal gambling houses, most of which were owned by wealthy Callistas—angered the jefe máximo. In June 1935, Calles summoned a number of senators to Cuernavaca, denounced the labor movement and its alleged radicalism, and ominously recalled the brief tenure of President Ortiz Rubio. Cárdenas responded by requesting the resignation of all his cabinet members; then he proceeded to form a new cabinet dominated by the left wing but representing a broad coalition of anti-Callista elements, from right to left. There followed a purge of reactionary state governors, acclaimed by peasants' and workers' demonstrations. By the end of 1935, Cárdenas was the undisputed master of Mexico. In April 1936, amid indications that Calles was planning a coup with the aid of a fascist organization, the Gold Shirts, and other reactionary groups, Cárdenas ordered his immediate deportation to the United States.

Land Reform

Having consolidated his political control, Cárdenas proceeded to implement his reform program. He regarded land distribution as of prime importance. Land was distributed to the peasantry in a variety of ways, according to the climatic and soil conditions of the different regions. The principal form was the ejido, the communal landholding system under which land could not be mortgaged or alienated (except under very special conditions), with each *ejidatario* entitled to use a parcel of community land. The ejido was the focal point of the agrarian reform. But Cárdenas also distributed land in the form of the *rancho,* the individual small holding widely prevalent in the northern Mexican states. Finally, in regions where natural conditions favored large-scale cultivation of such commercial crops as sugar, cotton, coffee, rice, and henequen, large cooperative farms (collective ejidos) were organized on a profit-sharing basis. The government generously endowed these enterprises with seeds, machinery, and credit from the *Banco de Crédito Ejidal.*

During the Cárdenas years, some 45 million acres of land were distributed to almost twelve thousand villages. The Cárdenas distribution program struck a heavy blow at the traditional, semifeudal hacienda and peonage, satisfied the land hunger of the Mexican peasantry for the time being, and promoted a general modernization of Mexican life and society. By 1940, thanks to the land reform, supplemented by the provision of villages with schools, medical care, roads, and other facilities, the standard of living of the peasantry had risen, if only modestly. These progressive changes in turn contributed to the growth of the internal market and therefore of Mexican industry. The land reform also justified itself in terms of productivity; average agricultural production during the three-year period from 1939 to 1941 was higher than it had been at any time since the beginning of the revolution.

Granted these benefits and Cárdenas's excellent intentions, the fact remains that the land reform suffered from the first from certain structural defects. To begin with, it was basically conceived as a means of satisfying land hunger rather than as an instrument of dynamic agricultural development. Seeking to satisfy land hunger by the grant or restitution of land to the villages, government agencies overlooked the need to establish agricultural units that would be viable from an economic point of view. In many cases, the *ejidal* parcel, especially in areas of very dense population, was so small as to form a minifundio. Much of the distributed land was of poor quality (the agrarian law always allowed the landowner to retain a portion of his estate, and naturally he kept the best portion for himself), and aid in the form of seeds, technical assistance, and credit was frequently inadequate.

In addition, the peasant received his land from the government and was tied to it through the operations of the *Departamiento Agrario,* the Banco de Crédito Ejidal, and the officially organized Peasant Leagues; thus, he was increasingly dependent on the public authorities. Under Cárdenas, officials of these agencies often worked in a spirit of disinterested service and sought to develop peasant collective initiative and democracy; under his successors in the presidency, they tended to become corrupt and self-seeking, to enmesh the peasantry and its organizations in a bureaucratic network that manipulated them to satisfy its own interests. After 1940, Mexican governments increasingly favored the large private property and neglected the ejido. In concert with the structural defects of the land reform, this produced a gradual decline of the ejido system and a parallel growth of the large landed property, leading to the emergence of a new latifundio.

Labor Reform

Under Cárdenas, the labor movement was revitalized. Aware of the sympathetic attitude of the new regime, workers struck in unprecedented numbers for higher wages and better working conditions; in 1935 there were 642 strikes, more than twice the number in the preceding six years. In 1936 the young radical intellectual Vicente Lombardo Toledano organized a new labor federation, the *Confederación de Trabajadores Mexicanos* (CTM), to replace the dying and discredited CROM. Labor supported and in turn was supported by Cárdenas.

Labor, the peasantry, and the army became the three main pillars of the official party, reorganized in 1938 and renamed the Party of the Mexican Revolution (PRM). The power of the generals was weakened by a policy of raising wages and improving the morale of the rank and file and by the distribution of weapons to the peasantry, formed into a militia. The last important regional caudillo, General Saturnino Cedillo of San Luis Potosí, a foe of Cárdenas's agrarian policy who was linked to the fascist Gold Shirts, launched a revolt in 1938. It was promptly smashed, and Cedillo was killed in a skirmish with federal troops.

Like the land reform, the labor reform had structural flaws that created serious problems for the future. In return for concessions from a paternal government, labor, like the peasantry, was invited to incorporate itself into the official apparatus and to give automatic and obligatory support to a government that in the last analysis represented the interests of the national bourgeoisie. In the domestic and international situation of the 1930s, which was dominated by a struggle between profascist and antifascist forces, the interests of that bourgeoisie and Mexican labor largely coincided, but in the changed conditions after 1940, labor's loss of independence and the meshing of its organizations with the official apparatus led to a revival of corruption and reactionary control of the trade unions.

Economic Reform

Although Cárdenas was sympathetic to labor's demands for better conditions, he was no foe of private enterprise, despite efforts by his foes to link him to socialism and communism. In fact, industrial capitalism made significant strides under Cárdenas. If Cárdenas supported labor's efforts to raise wages where the financial condition of an enterprise warranted it, he also favored Mexican industry with government loans and protective tariffs that insured the creation of a captive market for high-priced consumer goods. In 1934 his government established the *Nacional Financiera,* a government bank and investment corporation that used funds supplied by the federal government and domestic investors to make industrial loans, finance public welfare projects, and issue its own securities. The coming of World War II, which sharply reduced the availability of imports, greatly stimulated the movement toward industrialization and import substitution.

Mexico's struggle for economic sovereignty reached a high point under Cárdenas. In 1937 a dispute between North American and British oil companies and the unions erupted into a strike, followed by legal battles between the contending parties. When the oil companies refused to accept a much-scaled-down arbitration-tribunal wage finding in favor of the workers, Cárdenas intervened. On March 18, 1938—a date celebrated by Mexicans as marking their declaration of economic independence—the president announced in a radio speech that the properties of the oil companies had been expropriated in the public interest. With support from virtually all strata of the population, Cárdenas was able to ride out the storm caused by economic sanctions against Mexico on the part of the United States, England, and the oil companies. The oil nationalization was a major victory for Mexican nationalism. It provided cheap, plentiful fuel for Mexican industry, and the needs of the nationalized oil industries further stimulated industrialization. But the oil nationalization did not set a precedent; some 90 percent of Mexico's mining industry remained in foreign hands.

The Cárdenas government gave firm support to governments resisting the advance of fascism. Mexico and the Soviet Union were the only countries to give significant amounts of aid to the Republicans during the Spanish civil war of 1936–1939. After the Fascist victory in Spain, Mexico opened its doors to Loyalist refugees, including many talented Spanish professionals who made a significant contribution to Mexican culture and economic life. It steadfastly refused to recognize the legality of the Franco regime.

Cárdenas's Growing Moderation and the Election of 1940

Education, especially the rural school system, made considerable progress under Cárdenas, but in the last years of his presidency, in apparent deference to clerical and conservative opposition, he soft-pedaled the so-called socialist character of Mexican education. Of Tarascan Indian origin, Cárdenas displayed much concern for Indian welfare. He created a *Departamiento de Asuntos Indígenas* to serve and protect Indian interests and encouraged the study of Indian culture, past and present, by founding the *Instituto Nacional de Antropología de México.*

Right-wing opposition to Cárdenas's progressive policies grew in the closing years of his presidency. Reactionary groups encouraged and financed by German agents and the Spanish fascist Falange attacked the regime for its supposed communist tendencies. In apparent response to conservative pressure, Cárdenas slowed down the pace of land distribution during the last years of his presidency and displayed a conciliatory attitude toward the entrepreneurial class, assuring its members that he regarded them as part of the *fuerzas vivas* (vital forces) of the country and that they need not fear for the safety of their investments.

On the eve of the presidential election of 1940, right-wingers organized a campaign in favor of General Juan Andreu Almazán, a veteran revolutionary who was now a wealthy industrialist of Monterrey. The left wing of the PRM advanced the candidacy of General Francisco Múgica, author of some of the most advanced provisions of the constitution of 1917 and Cárdenas's close friend and mentor. No man was better qualified to carry out the promises of the second Six-Year Plan, which proposed to continue the rapid pace of agrarian reform; provide the ejidos with cheap credit, irrigation, and roads; and intensify collectivization of ejidos. But the official party was an amalgam of social forces, including increasingly conservative and influential industrialists. Evidently fearing that the nomination of the radical Múgica would be a signal for a rightist revolt, Cárdenas gave him no support, and Múgica soon withdrew. Supported by the powerful CTM, the party gave its nomination to General Manuel Ávila Camacho, who was loyal to Cárdenas. A devout Catholic and a man of generally conservative views, Ávila Camacho was elected with almost 99 percent of the vote.

The defeated Almazán fled to Texas, proclaiming fraud. For a time, it seemed that a revolt would break out, but Almazán soon returned to Mexico and private life. Meanwhile, Ávila Camacho was making statements designed to reassure foreign and domestic capital. He dissociated himself from the radical leadership of the unions, expressed a flexible attitude toward the question of whether the ejido or the small private property was the best form of agrarian organization, and assured the Catholics that he was a *creyente* (believer). In December 1940, Ávila Camacho assumed the presidency without any serious disturbances.

The Big Bourgeoisie in Power, 1940–1976: Erosion of Reform

The Cárdenas era was the high-water mark of the struggle to achieve the social goals of the revolution. Under his successors, there began an erosion of the social conquests of the Cárdenas years. During those years, the material and cultural condition of the masses had improved, if only modestly; peasants and workers managed to secure a somewhat larger share of the total national income. After 1940 these trends were reversed. The new rulers of Mexico favored a development strategy that sharply restricted trade union activity, slowed the tempo of agrarian reform, and reduced the relative share of total income of the bottom two-thirds of the Mexican population.

Ávila Camacho presided over the first phase (1940–1946) of this reversal of policy. Regarding unlimited private profit as the driving force of economic progress, he proposed to create a favorable climate for private enterprise. In practice, this meant the freezing of wages, the repression of strikes, and the use of a new weapon against dissidents—a vaguely worded law dealing with the "crime of social dissolution."

Meanwhile, World War II stimulated both the export of Mexican raw materials and import substitution through industrialization. Significant advances were made in food processing, textiles, and other consumer goods industries, and the capital goods industry, centering in the north, was considerably expanded. Steel production increased, with Monterrey Steel and other companies producing structural and rolled steel for buildings, hotels, highways, and steel hardware. The Nacional Financiera played a leading role in this process of growth through loans to industry for plant construction and expansion. In view of this spontaneous economic growth, the concept of planning was forgotten; the second Six-Year Plan remained on paper. Indeed, a characteristic of the economic expansion was its unplanned character. No effort was made to produce a balanced development of the Mexican regions; most of the development took place in the Federal District and the surrounding area. Meanwhile, land distribution was sharply reduced, and a conservative spirit began to pervade the educational system.

In 1946 the official party changed its name from PRM to the PRI (*Partido Revolucionario Institucional*), and Ávila Camacho was succeeded as president by the lawyer Miguel Alemán (1946–1952), who continued the policies of his predecessor. Alemán made every effort to encourage private investment through tariff protection, import licensing, subsidies, and government loans. A rapid rate of inflation, while wages were virtually frozen by official repression of strikes, supported by corrupt labor leaders, naturally encouraged investment. These policies produced the desired results; during the period from 1940 to 1950, real wages fell in both agricultural and nonagricultural activities, while the real incomes of entrepreneurs rose swiftly. This favorable economic climate attracted domestic and foreign investors looking for outlets for their surplus capital after World War II. A characteristic of the new foreign capital investment was that it flowed primarily into manufacturing rather than the traditional extractive industries.

Under Alemán, land distribution and efforts to increase the productivity of the ejidos were neglected in favor of the large private landholding. To provide an incentive to capitalist entrepreneurs, Alemán had Article 27 of the constitution amended. This "reform" consisted in the grant of certificates of "inaffectibility" to landowners, which exempted them from further expropriation for holdings up to 100 hectares of irrigated land

or 200 hectares of land with seasonal rainfall. For the production of certain specified crops, the size of inaffectible holdings was made even larger.

A massive program of irrigation contributed to the explosion of capitalist agriculture that began in this period. The irrigation projects were concentrated in northern and northwestern Mexico, where much of the land was owned directly or indirectly by prominent Mexican politicians, their friends, and relatives. Alemán presided over a great boom in public works construction, accompanied by an orgy of plunder of the public treasury by entrepreneurs and officials; his was probably the most corrupt administration in modern Mexican history.

Alemán's successor, Adolfo Ruiz Cortines (1952–1958), had to cope with a financial crisis brought on by Alemán's extravagant fiscal policies and the recession imported from the United States. He responded by reducing public spending, which caused a further contraction of the economy. Faced with a steadily deteriorating balance of trade, his administration decided to devaluate the peso in 1954, setting its exchange value at 12.50 to the dollar.

In general, Ruiz Cortines's economic and social policies resembled those of his predecessors. The pace of land distribution was further reduced, and the ejidos suffered a neglect that contributed to the low productivity for which they were criticized. Irrigation works continued to be concentrated in areas dominated by large private landholdings.

Thanks to the new laws of "inaffectibility" and the varied ruses employed by large landowners to violate the agrarian laws, concentration of landownership continued to grow. There arose a new hacienda, technically efficient and often arrayed in modern corporate guise, that soon accounted for the bulk of Mexico's commercial agricultural production and shared its profits with processing plants that were usually subsidiaries of foreign firms. By 1961, fifty years after the revolution began, less than 1 percent of all farms possessed 50 percent of all agricultural land. Increasing numbers of small landholders meanwhile, starved for credit and lacking machinery, had to abandon their parcels of land and become peons on the new haciendas or emigrate to the cities in search of work in the new factories.

Industry continued to grow but was increasingly penetrated and dominated by foreign capital. Direct foreign investments, averaging $26 million a year in the 1940s, rose to an average of $102 million a year in the 1950s. A favorite device for foreign penetration of Mexican industry was the mixed, or joint, company, which had a number of advantages. It satisfied the requirement of Mexican law that Mexican nationals hold 51 percent of most companies operating in Mexico; it camouflaged actual domination of such enterprises by the foreign partners through control of patents, licensing agreements, and other sources of technological and financial dependence; and it formed strong ties between foreign capitalists and the native industrial and financial bourgeoisie.

President Adolfo López Mateos (1958–1964) declared early in his administration that he belonged to the "extreme left within the Constitution," but his social and economic policies did not differ significantly from those of his predecessors. To allay mounting unrest among landless peasants who began to seize uncultivated hacienda lands in different parts of the country, he distributed a large amount of land, but most of it was of inferior quality. He continued the repressive labor policies of his predecessors; thus, he broke a general railroad strike with federal troops and had its leaders arrested and jailed for years.

The colorless, small-minded lawyer Gustavo Díaz Ordaz succeeded López Mateos as president in 1964. During his term of office (1964–1970), discontent among workers mounted as their real income shrank as a result of chronic inflation, a virtual freeze on wages, and official control of trade union organizations. Student unrest also grew in reaction to police brutality against student protesters and violations of the cor titutional autonomy of the national university. The student protest broadened into a nationwide movement demanding democratization of Mexi-

can economic and political life. The government responded with a savage assault by army troops on a peaceful assembly of students and others in the Plaza of Three Cultures in Mexico City (October 2, 1968), leaving a toll of dead and wounded running into the hundreds.

The economic strategy of the Díaz Ordaz administration, like that of his predecessors, centered on providing the greatest possible incentives to private investment, foreign and domestic. The foreign debt grew alarmingly under Díaz Ordaz, with the volume of foreign loans reaching a figure four times that of the Ruiz Cortines era. By 1970 reliance on foreign borrowing to finance Mexico's public-sector investment had reached a point where amortization and interest payments on foreign loans to the Mexican government came close to 30 percent of Mexico's annual export earnings. This heavy influx of loans increased the dependent character of the Mexican economy.

In his foreign policies, however, Díaz Ordaz continued the traditional Mexican posture of diplomatic independence. Despite objections from the United States, Mexico maintained diplomatic relations with revolutionary Cuba, expressed disapproval of U.S. intervention in Cuba (the Bay of Pigs affair), and opposed President Lyndon Johnson's intervention in the Dominican Republic. This independent foreign policy reflected both popular anti-imperialist sentiment and a striving on the part of the Mexican ruling class to achieve a partial independence from Washington.

The official presidential candidate, Luis Echeverría, took office in 1970 amid deepening political, social, and economic storm clouds. Echeverría signaled a tactical shift when he released a large number of students and intellectuals imprisoned after the 1968 student disturbances, promised to struggle against colonialism and corruption, and condemned the unjust distribution of income in Mexico. Impressed by Echeverría's apparent commitment to reform, some of the bitterest academic critics of the regime accepted jobs in his administration—a form of co-optation of political dissenters known in Mexico since the time of Porfirio Díaz.

Echeverría's foreign policies gave some credibility to his liberal image; he hosted a visit by Marxist President Salvador Allende of Chile, opened Mexico's doors wide to Chilean refugees after the fascist seizure of power in Chile, and urged Cuba's full re-entry into the inter-American community. These actions gave Echeverría a reputation for radicalism in certain quarters, especially in the United States.

There seems little doubt that Echeverría began his administration with a genuine desire to achieve reform, to reduce dependency, to spread the fruits of development more widely, and to create a somewhat more open, democratic political system. Conservative Mexican capitalists, closely linked with foreign capital, struck back by withholding investment funds from the market, setting off a serious recession. Under intense pressure from the right, Echeverría retreated. During his last three years in office he reverted to traditional policies and methods, poorly concealed by a populist rhetoric. After an initial thaw in its dealings with labor, his government once again repressed strikes and gave full support to corrupt trade union leaders.

Despite his promise to achieve a more equitable distribution of income, Echeverría rejected a progressive tax on corporate profits on the grounds that such a measure might discourage private investment. He publicly denounced colonialism and multinational corporations, but his government did its utmost to attract foreign investments, especially from the United States. With the investments came growing foreign penetration and domination of Mexican industry, especially of its most strategic sectors. By the mid-seventies, 70 percent of earnings from the capital goods industry went to foreign capital, leaving 20 percent for public firms and 10 percent for national private companies. The share of multinational enterprises in the sale of manufactured goods rose from 38 percent in 1962 to 45 percent in 1970; by 1972 they controlled half the capital in manufacturing. This meant that foreign companies had a significant degree of control over decisions with respect to Mexican development.

As the investments increased, so did Mexico's indebtedness and the drain of its capital in the form of dividends, interest, and other returns on foreign investment. By June 1976, Mexico's foreign debt had reached $25 billion. Mexico and Brazil shared the distinction of having the highest foreign debts among Third World countries. By September of that year the growing trade deficit had forced the government to order a 60 percent devaluation of the peso, causing a sharp rise in inflation and greater hardship for the masses.

When he came to office in 1970, Echeverría promised to provide the ejidos with irrigated land and other aid; in fact, little aid was given. When he left the presidency six years later, the problem of landlessness or inadequate land and rural unemployment and underemployment remained as stubborn as ever. Some 6 million peasants were landless. Perhaps the most oppressed, miserable group in Mexican society were the Indians. Numbering some 7 to 12 million, they suffered from especially severe forms of discrimination, exploitation, and physical aggression at the hands of white and mestizo landowners, merchants, and officials. Their situation has been aptly described as "internal colonialism."

In 1976, prospects for the solution of Mexico's urgent problems through the electoral process appeared dim, because the PRI, dominated by the industrial and financial oligarchy, had an unshakable grip on power. That power rested in the last analysis on a system of institutionalized coercion and fraud. Generally, when the PRI suffered defeat in local elections, either the elections were annulled for one or another technicality by an administrative tribunal, which then ordered new elections to be held, or the elected officials were subjected to severe harassment. But fraud, force, and threat of force were not the only means used by the government and the ruling party to retain control. Other methods included the co-optation of dissidents into the state apparatus; the provision of greater access to medical services, schools, low-cost housing, and other benefits to such strategic groups as state employees, professionals, and organized workers; the paternalistic distribution of goods and services to the urban poor; and a populist rhetoric that identified the ruling party with the great ideals of the Revolution. These policies did little to reduce mass poverty or the growing inequalities of income in Mexican society, but they provided a precarious popular base and legitimacy for the PRI's monopoly of political power. By the mid-seventies, both popularity and legitimacy were threatened by rampant inflation and a stagnant economy.

At the time of the 1976 election, bleak economic conditions might have been expected to produce a major challenge to the ruling party. Discouragement on the part of other parties, however, was so great that the official party candidate, José López Portillo, ran without opposition other than that of an unregistered (that is, officially unrecognized) Communist party candidate. The PRI rolled up the usual huge majority.

López Portillo was reputed to be more conservative than Echeverría, and it seemed unlikely that his administration would break with the long-established policy of favoring the country's elites. In fact, López Portillo soon made it clear that he was opposed to further large-scale land distribution and would not touch efficiently run large estates even if their size exceeded legal limits. In the words of one Mexican weekly, "the constitution is to protect peasants wearing collars and ties, and not those wearing rope sandals."

On the other hand, López Portillo, like Echeverría, appeared to recognize the need to provide a safety valve for growing political dissent and to modernize the monolithic political structure created by Calles in 1929. In October 1977, he offered a constitutional reform bill that eased the requirements for registration of minority political parties and created a system of partial proportional representation designed to insure the presence of opposition elements in Congress. Under the plan the chamber of deputies was expanded from 300 to 400 seats, with the additional seats apportioned to minority parties on the basis of their vote. Nothing in the so-called reform bill, however, threatened the PRI's control over the electoral machinery and its continued domination of the government.

From Oil Boom to Bust, 1977–1991

López Portillo took office on December 1, 1976, amid growing optimism over Mexico's economic prospects as a result of the recent discovery of vast new oil and gas deposits on Mexico's east coast. Figures for the country's estimated and proven oil reserves steadily rose; by January 1980 they were put at 200 billion barrels, and Mexico ranked among the world's major oil producers. With oil prices increasing steeply, government planners counted on the oil and gas bonanza to alleviate Mexico's balance-of-payments problem and to finance the purchase of the goods needed for further development and the creation of new jobs. The resulting expansion of production, however, was largely concentrated in capital-intensive industries—petrochemical factories, steel mills, and the like—that generated relatively few jobs. In agriculture, too, the main growth was in capital-intensive, export-oriented agribusiness operations that created little employment and diverted labor and acreage from staple food production. Indeed, staple food production actually declined during the 1970s; by 1980, one-third of the maize consumed in Mexico came from the United States.

The cost of the imported equipment and technology required to expand oil production came very high and had to be covered by new loans. Despite increasing revenues from oil and gas exports, Mexico's trade deficit rose from $1.4 billion in 1977 to over $2 billion in 1978, and $3 billion in 1979. Inflation again moved upward; Mexican workers lost 20 percent of their purchasing power between 1977 and 1979. Despite these troubling signs, the international bankers appeared eager to lend more, advancing Mexico $10 billion in 1980. Who could question the credit of a country that seemed to float on a sea of oil?

The oil boom and the massive infusions of foreign loans gave a new dimension to the familiar problem of corruption in Mexican political life.[1] One of its signs was a wave of monumental private construction. But "the dance of the billions" was drawing to a close. In the first months of 1981, responding to weakening demand and a developing world oil glut, oil prices fell sharply. This development threw the government into confusion. When the director of Pemex (the national oil industry) cut oil prices $4 a barrel to bring them into line with world prices, he was dismissed, and the new director raised the price. When buyers cancelled contracts, the government lowered prices again; these maneuvers cost the government a loss of $6 to $7 billion in 1981. Mexico's projected earnings in 1982 from oil and gas exports, source of 75 percent of Mexico's foreign exchange, fell from $27 billion to under $14 billion. Many wealthy Mexicans, losing confidence in their currency, hurried to buy dollars and deposit them in U.S. banks. In February 1982, with the government's foreign exchange reserves dwindling at an alarming rate, López Portillo allowed the peso to fall by 60 percent. Fear of further devaluations provoked another flight of dollars. The growing shortage of dollars, vitally needed fuel for Mexican industry, caused a widening recession and unemployment.

In July 1982, Mexicans went to the polls to elect a new president. The PRI, operating with its usual efficiency, gave the official candidate, Harvard-trained economist Miguel de la Madrid, some 74 percent of the vote; the main opposition parties, the Christian Democratic *Partido de Acción Nacional* (PAN) and a coalition of leftist forces, the *Partido Socialista Unificado de México* (PSUM), were allotted 14 percent and 6 percent of the vote, respectively. On the local level there was evidence of growing resistance to efforts to impose official candidates. Yielding to popular pressure, the regime accepted the victory of opposition candidates in a number of towns.

President-elect De la Madrid was not to take office until December 1, and López Portillo had to cope with the growing economic crisis. The peso continued its steady decline, falling to the rate of 95 pesos to one dollar by the end of August, while the cost of imported goods rose sharply. Bankruptcies and closings multiplied as more and more businesses lacked the dollars needed to obtain imported parts and raw materials or to pay debts contracted in dollars. With the Banco de México almost drained of reserves, López Portillo took a dramatic step. On September 1, in his last annual message to Congress, he announced the nationalization of all private (but not foreign) banks and the establishment of stringent exchange controls. The bank nationalization, the most radical measure taken by a Mexican president since the "Mexicanization" of the oil industry by Cárdenas in 1938, was greeted with cries of protest from the private banking sector and great demonstrations of support by the PRI and its client organizations, the trade unions, and the parties of the left.

In Washington, usually so allergic to all measures smacking of collectivism or socialism, the bank nationalization did not arouse the hostility that might have been expected, probably because even conservative United States officials regarded it as a necessary step, given the circumstances. The prime concern of the Reagan administration was to save Mexico, the third largest trading partner of the United States, from a default that could wreck the international banking system and bring down the great American banks to which Mexico owed $25.8 billion—almost a third of its foreign debt. Since July, consultations had been taking place between Mexican finance minister Jesús Silva Herzog and United States officials concerning the details of the rescue operation. The final plan provided for United States aid of $2.9 billion for Mexico's current-account problem; a seven-month freeze on the repayment of principal due to American, Western European, and Japanese bankers; and an eventual IMF (International Monetary Fund) loan of $3.9 billion, which could initiate a new cycle

[1] One Mexican news magazine, *Proceso,* estimated that officials of López Portillo's administration had misused or stolen $3 billion of public funds.

of commercial bank loans to Mexico. The IMF loan was, of course, subject to the usual conditions: Mexico must accept certain austerity measures—reduction of subsidies, restraints on wage increases, and other economies that were bound to hit Mexico's poor the hardest.

Even before he took office on December 1, 1982, President-elect De la Madrid had indicated his approval of the strong financial medicine prescribed by the IMF. To his cabinet he appointed people praised by the *Wall Street Journal* as "conservative young technocrats . . . inclined to take politically unpalatable steps." These "politically unpalatable steps" included price increases of 100 percent and 50 percent on gasoline and natural gas, respectively, and the lifting of price controls and subsidies for consumer items ranging from shoes to television sets. Some three hundred essential items remained under partial control, but even at the controlled prices many were out of reach of a large part of the population—and it was uncertain how long the remaining controls would continue. Another measure was a new devaluation of the peso that was expected to stimulate exports. It would, however, also make imports more costly, increase the burden of foreign debt service, and reduce real wages. Finally, accepting the bank nationalization as "irreversible," De la Madrid clearly indicated that he would not use nationalization to control private credit and investment. He even sent Congress a bill that partially "denationalized" the banks by allowing private investors to purchase 34 percent of their shares.

The solution for the Mexican crisis devised in Washington and accepted by the Mexican political leadership consisted, in essence, of adding new debts to old ones, without the slightest prospect that the huge foreign debt of some $85 billion could ever be paid or even significantly reduced without a large write-off, and of imposing heavy new burdens on already impoverished groups of the Mexican population—a policy that could lead to sharp confrontations with the Mexican working class, peasantry, and even the middle class.

Four years after the rescue operation worked out by Mexico's finance minister Silva Herzog, United States officials, and the banks, the debt problem was more intractable than ever. By the fall of 1986 Mexico's foreign debt had risen to more than $100 billion; the exchange rate of the peso in mid-1987 was about 1,400 to the dollar.

The drain of billions of dollars to service the foreign debt, coupled with the plunge in oil prices and the effects of the IMF-imposed austerity program, had disastrous economic consequences for Mexico. Many businesses, unable to obtain loans from state banks, had to close their doors. The Mexican Confederation of Workers (CTM) estimated that 12 million workers—50 percent of the economically active population—were either unemployed or underemployed. High unemployment and inflation (for the first nine months of 1986 the inflation rate stood at about 104 percent) sharply reduced purchasing power and forced many industries to shut down or to cut production, resulting in more unemployment. By the government's own figures, 1986 was the worst year for the Mexican economy since 1982; in the first nine months almost 1.5 million jobs were lost, gross fixed investment fell by 10.7 percent, manufacturing activity declined by 10.7 percent, and the Gross Domestic Product (GDP) fell by 4 percent. A major natural disaster, the earthquake of September 19, 1985, caused over 20,000 deaths, changed Mexico City's center forever, and created huge reconstruction problems, adding to the public and official woes.

The economic crisis was intertwined with a growing crisis in U.S.–Mexican relations. The Reagan administration, fanatically devoted to a "free market" economy and committed to the overthrow of the Sandinist government in Nicaragua, sought to use negotiations with Mexico over its foreign debt as a means of reshaping Mexico's economic structures and even its foreign policy. While Mexico called for ceilings on interest rates on its foreign debt, a linkage of oil prices to debt payments, and other improved payment conditions, the U.S. economic demands included the opening up of Mexican industry to foreign investments, selling off state-owned enterprises, liberalizing foreign trade, and abandoning regulation of direct foreign investment. Despite the many concessions made by the De la Madrid government in economic policy, the Reagan administration demanded more.

Also, Mexico's independent stance toward Central America caused great anger in Washington. Especially irksome to the United States was Mexico's leading role in the Contadora group of Latin American nations, which sought settlement of Central American problems through dialogue and political agreements and opposed military intervention by outside powers. The displeasure of right-wing elements in the United States with Mexico's independent stance was reflected in a two-day hearing on Mexico in May 1986 by a U.S. Senate Foreign Relations subcommittee, called by ultraright Republican Senator Jesse Helms. Helms attacked Mexico's political system, comparing the PRI to the Communist party of the Soviet Union, while Elliot Abrams, assistant secretary of state for inter-American affairs, criticized the PRI for its domination of Mexican politics and Mexican foreign policy for its alleged support of the Nicaraguan Sandinistas.

Certainly the Mexican political process continued to be tainted by fraud and corruption as was made evident in the 1986 state elections in Chihuahua and Oaxaca. But Helms (a strong supporter of Pinochet's fascist regime in Chile) and Abrams (who was shown in June-July 1987 to have lied to Congress regarding the Iran-Contra scandal) did not attack Mexico's alleged political sins from an attachment to pure democracy. In Mexico the hearings' attack was seen by many as a scheme to destabilize the Mexican government and to destroy the revolutionary nationalist principles the PRI championed.

Thus at the opening of 1987, Mexico faced a profound, many-sided crisis. By mid-1987 a "democratizing faction" within the ruling party grew dissatisfied with the conduct of policy; this led to an open rift with the official leadership. Heading the pro-democracy group was Cuauhtémoc Cárdenas, son of former president and national hero Lázaro Cárdenas. Cuauhtémoc, a former PRI senator and a former governor of Michoacán, was joined by such PRI notables as Porfirio Muñoz Ledo, former Mexican ambassador to the United Nations and secretary of labor and education in previous administrations, and Carlos Tello, former head of Mexico's Central Bank and widely regarded as the author of the 1982 nationalization of the country's banking system. Calling itself "Democratic Current," the group was critical of certain policies of the De la Madrid administration. Specifically the group opposed payment of the foreign debt at the expense of the living standards of the Mexican people; it also called for more grassroots participation in the choice of the 1988 presidential candidate, traditionally selected by the incumbent president.

But the PRI leadership rejected the calls for reform and put forward as its candidate another Harvard-trained economist, Carlos Salinas de Gortari, politically almost a carbon copy of De la Madrid. Cárdenas and other prominent dissenters then withdrew from the PRI and formed a National Democratic Front (FDN) that ran Cárdenas as its presidential candidate; eventually the Front was joined by the Mexican Socialist party and other left-wing parties. Cárdenas's program called for an end to political corruption and electoral fraud, suspension of foreign debt payments and renegotiation of the debt with creditor banks and governments, a mixed economy, and state assistance to the ejido farming sector. His candidacy inspired a wave of popular enthusiasm and mobilization unknown since the election of 1934 that brought his own father to power.

Most political observers believe that Cárdenas actually won the general election of July 6, 1988. Cárdenas and Manuel Clouthier, presidential candidate of the right-wing National Action Party (PAN), claimed that millions of ballots and tally sheets were falsified or destroyed. Since the PRI counted the votes, however, Salinas de Gortari was declared the winner and assumed office on December 1; the official count gave Salinas 50.1 percent of the 19 million ballots cast, 31.1 percent to Cárdenas, and 17 percent to Clouthier.

Still, the election altered Mexican politics in important ways. In the Chamber of Deputies, opposition parties now hold 240 seats and the PRI 260 seats. In the Senate, opposition parties won representation for the first time, with four of the 64 seats. Faced with public anger and the enormous popular mobilization behind Cárdenas, Salinas and the forces he represented within PRI opted to abandon the traditional practice of winning all legislative seats, known as the *carro completo,* in favor of narrower but more plausible victories.

To counter the outcry over the regime's blatant fraud, Salinas promised "electoral reform" and a modernization and democratization of the PRI's structure and methods to make it more responsive to its constituents. More significant was the PRI's new strategy of rapprochement with the conservative PAN, whose economic program, stressing privatization and reduced state intervention, was almost indistinguishable from PRI's own program. One sign of this rapprochement was PAN's approval of a PRI-sponsored proposal for "electoral reform" recently approved by Congress; this misnamed "electoral reform" will leave the government in control of the federal and state bodies that manage elections and certify results. Another sign was PRI's willingness to acknowledge PAN victories, like its sweeping victory in the 1989 gubernatorial election in Baja California, while using traditional fraudulent methods and violence to impose PRI's candidates in local elections won by the newly formed Democratic Revolutionary Party (PRD) in Michoacán and Guerrero. Cárdenas and the PRD correctly viewed this rapprochement as having, among other ends, the goal of splitting the opposition and isolating the new party.

The PRD, however, drawing support from large numbers of workers, peasants, the middle class, and even some businessmen, will probably become a permanent part of the Mexican political landscape. Given the slight difference between the PRI and PAN programs, Cárdenas and the PRD seem to offer the only genuine alternative to the policies of austerity and privatization pursued even more energetically by Salinas de Gortari

than his predecessor. Salinas has slated for privatization almost all of Mexico's 600 state-owned industries. He is presiding over a fire sale of some of Mexico's choicest properties, including mines, sugar mills, a five-star hotel chain, and the national insurance company. Two government-owned airlines, state-owned steel companies, and 70 percent of the petrochemical industry have already been privatized, the Teléfonos de Mexico has been put on the block, and the banks, nationalized in 1982, are to be returned to private hands. Efforts to liquidate or privatize some major industrial enterprises, like the Cananea copper mine in Sonora, were temporarily halted by workers' strikes that gained wide public support, but the process continued, accompanied by widespread layoffs and wage cuts and growing foreign domination of Mexican industry, aided by repeal of the law that restricted foreign control to 49 percent ownership of Mexican businesses.[2]

The denationalization of Mexican industry through privatization and the demise of many small and medium-size domestic businesses as a result of the removal of most tariff barriers (by the first months of 1990 some 400 plastics companies had gone out of business through this cause) reflected a general tendency on the part of Mexico's recent rulers to abandon the struggle for economic independence that had been a major goal of the Mexican Revolution, of Lázaro Cárdenas, and even of the conservative but nationalistic presidents who followed him.

That tendency is reflected in the Mexican government's encouragement of the program that permits U.S. companies to establish plants (called *maquiladoras* or *maquilas*) for production of parts and their assembly on the Mexican side of the border. The program permits duty-free entry of parts and machinery into Mexico and allows total U.S. ownership of the plants. U.S. customs regulations allow the finished products

[2] Observers noted that the state companies are being sold to the same small group of people who already control most of Mexico's economy, with no effort to promote "popular capitalism" through stock offerings in the open market. "'Crony capitalism,'" runs one comment, "is more the current government's style."

to enter the United States with duty paid only on the value of labor, not on that of the goods themselves. The lure of cheap wages (the average hourly wage of maquiladora workers, mostly women, is currently about eighty cents) has caused an explosive growth of maquiladora plants, whose number grew from 455 with 130,000 workers in 1982 to 1,700 with 456,000 workers in November 1989. The shift of U.S. production to Mexico has already caused the loss of many jobs and demands by U.S. unions for congressional action to eliminate the tariff benefit. Mexican officials defend the maquiladora program by arguing that it relieves the heavy Mexican unemployment. But since most of the plants are unorganized and many are true sweatshops, with health and safety problems widespread among the workers, it tends to institutionalize poverty on both sides of the border, for the program inevitably tends to depress wages in the U.S. border zone.[3]

Still on the horizon is a free-trade pact between Mexico and the United States, currently under discussion by the two governments and strongly supported by Presidents Salinas and Bush. The prospect of such a pact, which might loose an avalanche of U.S. goods and capital on Mexico, eliminate whole lines of domestic industry, and create enormous trade deficits, is creating alarm both in Mexico and the United States. Workers in the United States fear the loss of jobs as a result of an accelerated flight of industry to take advantage of Mexico's cheap labor.

The irrationality of the economic policies of the De la Madrid and Salinas administrations, with their stress on austerity, privatization, and the promotion of exports in order to produce revenue to pay the foreign debt, regardless of the social costs, is well illustrated by their agricultural policy. Like his predecessor, Salinas has favored agribusinesses producing meat for middle- and upper-class urban markets and fresh vegetables for the American market but has neglected the needs of *ejidatarios* and other small farmers producing such national staples as maize, beans, and wheat.[4] Public investment in domestic food production has actually declined in the last six years, with the result that thousands of small farmers have given up the struggle for survival and joined the exodus to the overcrowded cities. Sales of fresh agricultural produce to American markets produced about $750 million in the fiscal year 1989, but in the same period Mexico spent $2.3 billion on imported food. The chronic food shortage that results from this skewed agricultural policy has had disastrous social consequences; the World Resources Institute in Washington estimates that 40 percent of Mexico's rural population—some 35 million people—are suffering from malnutrition. Meanwhile inflation continues its steady climb, driving down the living standards of the workers and the middle class; in the spring of 1990 the exchange rate of the peso stood at 2,700 to the dollar. In the past eight years the average worker's real income has been cut in half.

Meanwhile, despite the reformist airs assumed by Salinas, the traditional Mexican abuses in the area of civil liberties and human rights continue unchecked. In June 1990 Americas Watch, the U.S.-based human rights group, issued a report that sharply criticized the Mexican government, complaining of "an array of abuses that have become an institutionalized part of Mexican society," including "killings, torture, and other mistreatments by the police," as well as "disappearances and election-related political violence." The report concluded that "neither President Salinas nor any other official at the highest ranks of government has made it clear to security officers in the field that they must desist from all abuses of internationally recognized human rights or face immediate arrest and prosecution."

[3] In February, 1991, a coalition of 62 labor, environmental, and religious groups in the United States claimed that the maquiladoras, with their low wages and total disregard for the environment, were turning the Mexican side of the border into a "social and economic inferno."

[4] According to Mexico's National Institute of Statistics (1991), more than half of Mexico's *ejidos* lack tractors and other types of modern industrial equipment; about half of all ejidos have no access to credit and are devoted exclusively to the production of maize.

At the heart of the continuing Mexican economic, political, and social crisis was the debt problem—by 1990 the foreign debt had risen to about $110 billion[5]—and the system of dependent capitalism that produced it. North American scholar Peter Evans had presciently written in 1979:

Like Brazil, Mexico has found that dependent development requires a mass of imported inputs even larger than the exports it generates, and that

[5] In February 1989 the Mexican government signed an agreement with its foreign bank creditors in accord with the Brady Plan for debt relief. But the relief was minimal and the agreement seemed likely to increase Mexico's long-term burden. The principal beneficiaries seemed to be the banks, which received "iron-clad guarantees" of payment of the remaining debts (Mexican debt had been selling on the market for fifty-two cents on the dollar).

even when the multinationals cooperate in the promotion of local accumulation they still ship more capital back to the center than they bring in. Mexico's newly discovered oil reserves may alleviate the balance of payments, but Mexico still reinforces the lessons of Brazil. Dependent development does not correct the imbalances in semiperipheral relations with the center; it replaces old imbalances with new ones.[6]

Sooner or later, Mexico has to apply the lessons of its long experience with the model of dependent development that collapsed so ingloriously in 1982.

[6] Peter Evans, *Dependent Development: The Alliance of Multinational, State, and Local Capital in Brazil* (Princeton, N.J.: Princeton University Press, 1979), p. 307.

Chapter 13

Argentina: The Failure of Democracy

After thirty years of explosive economic growth and sustained political stability, Argentina seemed ready to take a place among the developed nations by the first decade of the twentieth century. Argentines could proudly point out that their nation was the world's greatest exporter of grain and one of the most important exporters of meat; they could boast of a railroad network unsurpassed outside western Europe and the United States and of a capital, Buenos Aires, that ranked among the world's most beautiful and cultured cities. Argentines were seemingly prosperous, relatively well educated, and increasingly urban. The burgeoning population (nearly 8 million in 1910) and transportation system promised to create an internal market that would stimulate the rise of native manufacturing and elevate Argentina to the position of one of the world's modern industrialized countries.

The full flowering of democracy, too, seemed close at hand. With the passage of the Saenz Peña reforms in 1912, providing for universal suffrage and the secret ballot, the landed oligarchy, which had long monopolized Argentine politics, at last appeared ready to recognize the aspirations of other social groups and even to share political power with the middle class.

The appearance of prosperity and emerging democracy, however, proved illusory. Stagnation, interspersed with periods of depression and runaway inflation, marked the Argentine economy during succeeding decades. Military coups, disorder, and brutal repression afflicted the nation's politics. At the base of these problems lay Argentina's structural dependence on foreign markets and capital, a dependence that placed the country's economy at the mercy of foreign events and decisions made abroad and helped to perpetuate a deformed social and political system.

The Export Economy

Argentina's dynamic economic development during the last quarter of the nineteenth century and the early twentieth century was due to three factors: the appearance of a large market in Europe for its products—wool, mutton, beef, and wheat; the inflow of millions of immigrants, who provided cheap labor for the expanding agricultural sector; and finally, the influx of large quantities of foreign investment capital, which went to construct railroads, to put more land under cultivation, and to establish food (mainly meat) processing plants. The nation's prosperity depended on its ability to export huge amounts of agricultural commodities, to import the manufactured goods it required, and to attract a steady stream of large-scale foreign investment.

Consequently, Argentina was critically vulnerable to fluctuations in international market and finance conditions. Any reduction in overseas trade reverberated disastrously throughout the economy. Because Argentines usually imported more than they exported—a tendency made worse by the fact that the market price for raw materials remained steady or declined while the prices of manufactured goods rose—the country suffered from large deficits in its balance of payments. To make up the difference, the nation relied heavily on foreign investment.

Foreign investment reached enormous proportions in the first decades of the twentieth century. During the years 1900 to 1929, foreigners came to control between 30 and 40 percent of the nation's fixed investments. Argentina absorbed nearly 10 percent of all foreign investment carried out by capital-exporting nations, one-third of all the foreign investment in Latin America, and more than 40 percent of the total foreign investment of Great Britain, the world's leading capitalist power. Investment was concentrated in railroads and government bonds, the proceeds from which were used to subsidize the construction of railroads and public works.

Although foreign investment unquestionably helped fuel economic development, it simultaneously created immense economic difficulties. Huge interest payments on foreign debts and the profit remittances of foreign-owned companies, often representing between 30 and 50 percent of the value of Argentina's exports, produced serious balance of payments problems. Because government bodies owed much of the foreign debt, a substantial portion of government revenue went to service payments. Rigid interest rates and repayment schedules meant that the burden remained the same, even when state revenues declined because of adverse economic conditions, and that revenues earmarked for debt service could not be diverted to other areas.

Every sector of the Argentine economy depended on exports. Agriculture and livestock raising employed 35 percent of the work force. The nation's greatest agricultural area, the pampas, exported 70 percent of its production. Argentine industry centered on food processing, mainly meat packing. As late as 1935, foodstuff processing accounted for 47 percent of all industrial production, and textiles for another 20 percent. The transportation industry—railroads and coastal shipping—handled mostly export commodities.

Rich and poor alike relied on the export economy for their livelihood. The ruling elite was composed of large landowners, who produced almost entirely for the export trade. Their income and their political power rested squarely on the export economy. In addition to large numbers of farm laborers, many urban and industrial workers depended on exports for their jobs. The major trade and industrial unions in Argentina arose in those industries—coastal shipping, railroads, dock work, and packinghouses—whose workers owed their well-being to overseas trade. Because the government relied on revenues derived from import taxes, significant numbers of white-collar workers and professionals employed by the government also were intimately tied to the export economy.

Foreign control and influence permeated the economy. Most of the large merchant houses,

Argentine Society

299

which carried on the all-important export-import trade, were either owned by or closely affiliated with foreign houses. The major shipping lines (both intercoastal and interoceanic), the railroads, and the *frigoríficos* (meat-packing plants) were owned and operated by British or American companies.

The export economy brought indisputable benefits to Argentina, but those benefits were unequally distributed. There were, for example, sharp differences in economic development among regions. While the pampas and Buenos Aires boomed, most of the interior provinces stagnated. Mendoza and Tucumán with their wine and sugar made some headway, but all the other central and northwestern provinces—Jujuy, La Rioja, Santiago del Estero, and Salta—experienced social and economic decline.

The inequalities of property and income between the various classes were equally glaring. The rich were very rich and growing richer; the poor grew poorer. In the countryside, the estancieros, masters of thousands of acres of rich land, built palaces, while the majority of foreign-born immigrant sharecroppers eked out a miserable living. In Buenos Aires, wealthy landowners, merchants, and lawyers gathered at the sumptuous Jockey Club, while laborers struggled to make ends meet as inflation eroded their already insufficient paychecks.

Argentina's greatest treasure was its land, but only a few Argentines owned sizable portions of it. In 1914, farm units larger than 2,500 acres accounted for only 8.2 percent of the total number of farms but held 80 percent of the nation's farm area. Over 40 percent of farms were worked by tenants, most on terms that were less than favorable. In 1937, 94.8 percent of the active working population in rural areas were landless workers, tenant farmers, sharecroppers, and smallholders. A mere 1 percent of the active rural population controlled over 70 percent of Argentina's farmland, much of which they left idle. Yet the land was fertile and suitable for intensive agriculture. Thousands of immigrants came to Argentina in search of land only to discover that virtually all

had long since been taken up by the estanciero oligarchy.

Income distribution followed the same pattern. Less than 5 percent of the active population garnered 70 percent of the gross income derived from agriculture. Not only did workers and rural laborers receive little benefit from the export system, but the operation of the system's finances and taxation eroded what little return they did receive for their labor. Faced with chronic deficits in the balance of payments and unwilling or unable to tax the land or income of the landed elite, the government had no alternative but to resort to the printing press to finance its costs. The result was inflation. Exporters also demanded a fluctuating currency exchange rate, which had an adverse effect on wage earners. Finally, the tax structure placed its burden squarely on the mass of consumers through such indirect taxes as those on imports.

Argentine Society

Argentine society divided roughly into three classes—upper, middle, and lower. The upper class acquired its wealth and prestige through its ability to capitalize on the opportunities presented by the export economy. Large landholders even before the export boom of the last quarter of the nineteenth century, the upper class used the boom to solidify and enhance its power. The most powerful group within the elite was the cattle fatteners, who supplied beef for both the domestic and the foreign market. This inner circle was composed of approximately four hundred families who were closely allied through social clubs and business associations. Geographically, most of the wealth was located in the cattle and cereal regions of the pampas near Buenos Aires. From 1880 to 1912, the elite class that controlled the nation's land and wealth also controlled its politics. It used its control over the government to promote meat and grain exports, to guarantee easy credit for members, and to provide more

Barranquilla
Cartagena
Puerto Cabello
Caracas
Maracaibo
Orinoco R.
Cd. Guayana
VENEZUELA
GUYANA
Georgetown
SURINAM
Paramaribo
FRENCH GUIANA
Cayenne
Medellín
Bogotá
Buenaventura
Cali
COLOMBIA
Popayán
Esmeraldas
ECUADOR
Quito
Guayaquil
Iquitos
Talara
Manaus
Amazon R.
Belém
B R A Z I L
Natal
Recife
Trujillo
PERU
Cerro de Pasco
Oroya
Callao
Lima
Cuzco
L. Titicaca
Arequipa
Mollendo
Arica
BOLIVIA
La Paz
Oruro
Sucre
Potosí
Santa Cruz
Corumbá
Brasilia
Bahia
Belo Horizonte
Iquique
PARAGUAY
São Paulo
Rio de Janeiro
Antofagasta
Asunción
Tucumán
Florianapolis
Paraná R.
Uruguay R.
Pôrto Alegre
PACIFIC OCEAN
CHILE
Valparaiso
Santiago
Córdoba
Mendoza
Santa Fe
Rosario
Buenos Aires
La Plata
ARGENTINA
URUGUAY
Montevideo
Concepción
Bahia Blanca
Mar del Plata
Valdivia
Puerto Montt
ATLANTIC OCEAN
Comodoro Rivadavia
Falkland/Malvinas Is.
——— International Boundaries
0   500 Miles
0   500 Kilometers

MODERN SOUTH AMERICA

favorable taxation and currency policies. The other great institutions of Argentine society, the military and the church, also reflected the views of the elite.

As the nation grew more urban, its class structure became more complex. An urban middle class arose, which David Rock divides into three categories: rentier (landlords), bureaucratic, and professional groups; entrepreneurs and proprietors; and salaried employees in the private sector. Rock maintains that the urban middle class (unlike its counterparts in the industrialized West) did not challenge the agrarian sector for primacy because its origins lay in the international commercial and service sectors. The middle class, heavily concentrated in the bureaucracy and professions, depended on the export economy. Rock points out that this dependent sector of the middle class almost equaled in numbers the entrepreneurial and white-collar sectors together. It was this dependent group that attached itself to the Radical party. Many members of the entrepreneurial sector were foreign born and thus disfranchised.

The lower class divided into two groups, workers and urban marginals. Most members of the working class lived in Buenos Aires. They labored in small factories, where Argentina's industrial expansion was concentrated until 1914. (The primary exceptions to the predominance of small industries were the frigoríficos.) A considerable number of workers were employed by the railroads and urban tramways and in the Port of Buenos Aires.

Although the Socialist party, born during the 1890s, professed to represent the working class, it failed to achieve a position of leadership because its roots and leaders were mainly middle class. The working class did, nevertheless, organize into unions. The most important unions were those of the railroad workers (*La Fraternidad*) and the dock workers. Numerous strikes occurred after the turn of the century and throughout the first Radical regime (1916–1922). The labor movement, however, was weakened by diverse viewpoints on political activity and by internecine rivalries among Socialists, Anarchists, and Syndicalists.

The Military

In the first decade of the twentieth century, the Argentine military underwent two important transformations: it was professionalized, and it became a national institution. By 1910 seniority and merit were firmly entrenched as the criteria for promotion. The Superior School was established in 1901 to train officers in modern warfare. Also in 1910 a law of conscription was instituted; this greatly expanded the size of the armed forces and required the expansion of the officer corps. As a result, the social make-up of the officer corps changed. In time, men of the middle class, mostly the sons of immigrants, replaced the old officer groups, and the oligarchy gradually lost its predominance. Military personnel developed considerable pride and independence. They resisted political tampering and demanded modern weapons and better pay from the government. As cohesion grew, the military became an important political force. In 1916 it favored the transfer of power from the oligarchy to the Radical party.

The Radical Era, 1916–1930

The Rise of the Radical Party

Amid growing unrest among the urban middle class, university students, and small groups of junior military officers, the Radicals staged their third unsuccessful attempt to overthrow the oligarchy by force in February 1905. Despite their failure, the Radicals attracted growing popular support in the decade that followed. Local party organizations, formed before the February coup, expanded rapidly, drawing heavily from university-educated sons of immigrants. After the adoption of the Saenz Peña Law in 1912, the Radicals abandoned use of the sterile policy of electoral abstention and began to organize the urban middle class from the grassroots level, especially in Buenos Aires.

Radical party strength rested on twin pillars: its local urban organization, which acted to meet the needs of the middle class, and its leader, Hipólito Yrigoyen. Precinct and ward committees, headed by local bosses, dispensed patronage and favors in return for votes. They provided housing, extended loans to businessmen, and helped constituents in minor scrapes with the police. The committees' activities peaked at election time, when they took on the trappings of little social service agencies.

The Radical party was by no means a unified or homogeneous organization, however. Although the party drew most of its popular support and intermediate leadership from the middle class, large landowners dominated its hierarchy. In addition, there were important regional rivalries, most prominently between the provinces and Buenos Aires. Such diverse elements as rural hacendado-caudillos, who brought in the docile peasant vote, urban sons of immigrants, and university-educated professionals joined together under the Radical umbrella. They could come together in part because the Radical program was vague enough to satisfy widely disparate groups and also because of the manipulative skills of Hipólito Yrigoyen.

Yrigoyen played a dual role as the titular head of the Radical party. First, he was the great mediator who managed to reconcile the often conflicting interests of the middle class and large landowners who made up his political coalition. Second, although inarticulate and a recluse, Yrigoyen managed to project an austere democratic image that made him the party's charismatic leader. This clever deal maker and manipulator symbolized for the middle class the Radical dedication to democracy. Despite a checkered past that included shady business deals, he furnished the party with much of its moral appeal.

The Radical propaganda effectively presented the party as a national party, transcending the narrow regional and class interests that had previously governed Argentine politics. The Radical program was purposely vague. It straddled the line between its two major constituencies, the middle class and the landed elite. The Radicals (reflecting the views of both the landowners and the dependent middle class) never challenged the basic premises of the export economy. The party advocated neither land reform nor industrialization.

From 1912 to 1916, the Conservatives failed to construct the broad-based national political party they had hoped would arise as a result of the passage of the Saenz Peña Law. The Socialist party also failed to become a party of national scope. Like the Radicals, the Socialists suffered from a political split personality. The bulk of the party's support came from the working class, but the leaders of the party were middle-class intellectuals. The most serious weakness of the Socialists was their propensity for ruinous bickering that split the party. For the most part, the Socialists could never extend their influence beyond Buenos Aires, nor could they get the group for whom the party had the greatest attraction, the foreign-born workers, to register to vote. The party was, however, strong among skilled workers, particularly those on the railroad.

The Socialists had competition for working-class and union support. Anarchists gained the allegiance of dock workers and of many workers in small industrial and service occupations. They played an important rule in the rise of Argentine unions from the 1890s. After 1906, Syndicalists increasingly influenced the unions. The Syndicalists, who shared the Anarchist ideal of abolishing the state, stressed economic struggle and powerful unions as a means of attaining that goal. They won support among larger workers' groups, such as the coastal shipping workers and railway shop workmen.

Having the advantages of a finely tuned grassroots political organization and a well-known and astute leader as their presidential candidate and untroubled by an ideology or specific program other than the vaguely defined "class harmony," the Radicals won the 1916 presidential elections with 46.5 percent of the vote. Although it was necessary for Yrigoyen to put together a back-room political deal to get a majority of the electoral college, the Radicals had clearly won a great victory. The Progressive Democrats, their nearest rivals, managed to win only 13 percent of the popular vote.

The First Radical Government: Yrigoyen, 1916–1922

The characters of the first and subsequent Radical administrations were determined by the delicate relations between the Radicals and the conservative landowner elite. The elite controlled the military and the major agricultural lobbying groups and had close contacts with the powerful foreign business interests. Yrigoyen continually walked an unsteady tightrope between the middle class, which was clamoring for a piece of the governmental pie, and the oligarchy, which was still wary of the party that had rebelled three times in three decades and that had won an election campaigning against the selfish interests of that oligarchy. He could not push too hard too fast, or the oligarchy would surely overthrow him.

The operating mechanism of the Radical government was a conservative fiscal policy and political stability, in return for which the oligarchy was to allow the middle class wider access to the governmental bureaucracy and the professions. Yrigoyen had little room to maneuver, for there were inherent difficulties in the operation of this arrangement. First, expansion of access to government employment meant that government expenditures necessarily had to increase. But this violated the tenet of fiscal conservatism, unless the economy continued to expand at a rapid rate. Second, Yrigoyen had to maintain the fragile alliance of landowners and members of the middle class within his own party. In sum, the key to the Radicals' staying in power was Yrigoyen's ability to distribute the fruits of Argentine economic development to the middle class without antagonizing the oligarchy.

Nonetheless, the most pressing political problem was that the Radicals did not have control over the government. Although they had won the 1916 election for the presidency, they did not control most of the provinces and were a minority in Congress. Not until 1918 did they win a majority in the Chamber of Deputies. Because Senate terms were for nine years, they did not control that body until 1922. Without complete political control, Yrigoyen faced an impossible task in attempting to meet the conflicting requirements of the elite and the middle class. His first cabinet reflected both the make-up of his party and his eagerness to win the good will of the ruling elite; it was composed entirely of members of the landed oligarchy.

Yrigoyen's balancing act became even more difficult with the emergence of labor agitation for improved wages and working conditions. Wartime demand for Argentine exports had brought on inflation, and as a result, the purchasing power of wages was seriously eroded. Yrigoyen had to move cautiously in attempting to alleviate labor's plight, for the oligarchy might look upon such moves as interference in their economic domain. The problem was complicated by the fact that much of the labor agitation was directed against foreign-owned companies with close ties to the elite. There was growing discontent on the part of the middle class, too, because the decline in government revenues from imports meant fewer government jobs for its members.

From 1913 to 1917, Argentina experienced a serious depression. The prospect of war dried up foreign investment in 1913 and 1914, and the war itself caused a shortage of shipping for export commodities and of imported goods, both of which were critical in an economy based on the export of foodstuffs (bulk commodities) and the import of manufactured goods. To make matters worse, the 1913 harvest failed.

Between 1917 and 1921, however, Argentina again prospered from an export boom. The distribution of the benefits of the new prosperity were decidedly uneven, however, and Yrigoyen again found himself under pressure from his rival constituencies. Europe's mounting demand for cereals and meat exports forced prices for domestically consumed food to rise rapidly. Food prices rose 40 percent, and the cost of living in the cities rose 65 percent. The Radical government was squeezed between the urban community's need for lower prices (wages had not kept pace) and the interests of the landed elite, which insisted on keeping the prices of its products high. The best way to satisfy both constituent groups was to expand job opportunities in government, but this expansion required an increase in government spending, which was severely limited because sources of revenue were limited and the oligarchy was opposed to it. In 1918 the Radicals proposed a modest income tax and a tax on exports, but these proposals met defeat at the hands of a conservative Congress. Some relief came in 1919, when revenues again started to increase.

After becoming president, Yrigoyen sought to broaden his support by making some overtures to the working class. But he had little success, for his fear of antagonizing the landed elite severely limited the concessions he could offer the workers. The use of patronage—a tactic eminently successful with the middle class—failed when applied to the working class. When the strategy of attaching the rank-and-file of the workers to the local Radical political machine failed, Yrigoyen sought to form individual links with the leadership of the trade unions, which at this time were under strong Socialist influence.

From 1916 to the early 1920s, however, Yrigoyen's efforts to form an alliance with organized labor clashed with the Radicals' obligations to the oligarchy, which regarded such an alliance as prejudicial to its interests. Confronted with the bitter opposition of the ruling elite, Yrigoyen backed down and abandoned the workers.

From 1916 to 1919, Yrigoyen had to deal with a wave of large, sometimes violent strikes. Radical policy toward these struggles was clearly determined by expediency and, in the last analysis,

by the degree of pressure exerted by the landed elite. The major strikes occurred against foreign-owned companies engaged in export-related enterprises. The workers sought higher wages to compensate for the erosion of their wages by wartime inflation.

Since Argentine governments often sent in the police and armed forces to break strikes, the attitude of the Yrigoyen regime was decisive. The Maritime Workers' Federation struck twice, in 1916 and 1917, for higher wages. The first strike was timed to coincide with harvest shipments. In both instances the union gained access to Yrigoyen, the government kept out of the dispute, and the union won. But in late 1917, the government abandoned the unions when a general strike began to jeopardize export interests. With the strike threatening the entire harvest, the British government and the elite brought joint pressure on Yrigoyen to intervene, and troops were used. The strike collapsed. The frigorífico strike of 1917–1918 met the same fate when the government sent in marines to subdue the strikers.

The climactic episode came in January 1919 and is known in Argentine history as the *Semana Trágica* (Tragic Week) in reference to the heavy loss of life that followed when Yrigoyen, apparently fearing intervention by the army to topple his government, abandoned his original conciliatory position and sent police and armed forces to break a general strike that had grown out of a strike in a metal works. This violence was accompanied by a wave of brutal pogroms against Russian Jewish immigrants by members of the elite and the middle class, organized in an Argentine Patriotic League. Instead of denouncing the anti-"communist" witch hunt, the Radical government added its voice to the right-wing cry that the strike was a revolutionary conspiracy and even encouraged party members to join the vigilante bands. From that time, the Yrigoyen government gave up efforts to achieve a reconciliation with the workers. Henceforth, it concentrated on catering to its middle-class constituency through the use of patronage and on strengthening Yrigoyen's popular electoral base. The last three years of Yrigoyen's term were a struggle merely to survive.

The Argentine university reform of 1918, which had continental reverberations, reflected Yrigoyen's desire to cater to his middle-class constituency. The series of events leading to this famous reform began with a student strike at the University of Córdoba; the students demanded, among other changes, simplification of the entrance requirements and secularization of the curriculum. When the strike deteriorated into violence, Yrigoyen intervened and acceded to the student demands. But he went further, establishing a series of new universities that increased middle-class access to the professions and the government jobs for which so many middle-class aspirants hungered.

The government also sought to strengthen its electoral position through intervention in the provinces, removing provincial governors on the pretext that they had violated the federal constitution. The government also strove to enhance its popularity by expanding the patronage system.

By 1921 the boom unleashed by the war had ended, and depression followed. The union movement disintegrated. Layoffs eroded union membership, and internal bickering rendered the unions ineffective. The Radicals actually experienced some success in recruiting among the workers during the depression, because their local committees were able to provide charitable services.

The Second Radical Government: Alvear, 1922–1928

Despite adverse economic conditions, the Radicals won the election of 1922. With 48 percent of the vote, Marcelo de Alvear, Yrigoyen's hand-picked successor, became president. Immediately, however, the party began to come apart. Although couched in personal terms—Alvear against Yrigoyen—the division more accurately reflected the growing split between the middle-class and elite sectors of the party. The conflict

arose from the fact that the government was not meeting expenses through revenues but rather through short-term loans from local and overseas banks. Yrigoyen had increased the floating government debt to a staggering 1 billion pesos by 1922, a tenfold increase during his term.

Alvear cut the payroll to trim expenses and hiked tariff rates to increase revenue. The tariff increase was also aimed at reducing imports and alleviating the balance of payments problem. A balanced budget directly contradicted middle-class demands for even more government employment opportunities. In 1924 the Radicals split into two factions. The Radical party's Anti-Personalist wing separated under the leadership of Alvear.

Yrigoyen's Second Term, 1928–1930

Four years later, Yrigoyen made a smashing comeback, winning his second presidential term with an overwhelming 57 percent of the vote. Nonetheless, his political situation was greatly weakened. His local organization had deteriorated during the Alvear years from lack of patronage. In some cases, the local bosses had become gangsters. Yrigoyen set about reviving the patronage system in order to strengthen his underpinnings in the middle class. He also moved to eliminate opposition, and he stepped up intervention in the provinces to assure a majority in the Senate. When grumbling arose in the military, he tried to place loyalists in powerful positions. A Radical paramilitary organization was formed and clashed with its right-wing counterpart.

In October 1929, the depression hit Argentina. The Radicals, whose strength had been increasing, suffered a mortal blow. Exports dropped 40 percent; foreign investment stopped. Unemployment was widespread. Government efforts to spark a recovery served only to induce inflation. The decline in imports severely undermined the government's fiscal position, since it relied on import duties for most of its revenue.

The government incurred a huge deficit, which it tried to cover by borrowing. As a result, it found itself in the position of competing for increasingly scarce credit resources with the landed elite, which desperately needed money to ride out the decline in the export market. Yrigoyen's policy threatened the interests of the landed elite, and he became expendable. Further, his meddling with the military had seriously undercut his standing with that powerful institution. Finally, the depression destroyed his personal popularity in the middle class, his main base.

Yrigoyen became the scapegoat. His enemies pictured him as senile and corrupt, incapable of ruling the nation in a time of crisis. The depression ruined the party apparatus, for there was no patronage to dispense. The political situation continued to disintegrate, and violence increased. Yrigoyen was overthrown by the military on September 6, 1930.

The "Infamous Decade," 1930–1943: The Conservative Restoration

The coup marked the end of Argentina's short experiment with democracy and the entry of the military into the nation's politics; it ushered in a period of harsh repression and corruption, which came to be known as the "infamous decade." Lieutenant General José F. Uriburu, who had led the group of conspirators that overthrew Yrigoyen, became the head of a coalition of widely diverse elements, including traditional Conservatives, right-wing nationalist-fascists, and such center and left parties as the Progressive Democrats, Independent Socialists, and Socialists. There strange bedfellows had agreed on the elimination of Yrigoyen, but little else. Consequently, the loosely built alliance soon fell apart. The military was also divided. One faction, led by Uriburu, sought to establish a regime patterned on the Italian corporate state. A second faction, led by General Agustín P. Justo, desired only a return to the pre-1916 political arrangements.

The split was exacerbated by the long-standing and bitter personal rivalry between Uriburu and Justo.

In the months following the coup, Uriburu conducted a campaign of brutal repression against opponents of his provisional government. At the beginning of 1931, he felt that the opposition was sufficiently cowed and—in the case of the Yrigoyen Radicals—sufficiently discredited to call elections for Buenos Aires Province. The result of the elections was a tremendous victory for the Yrigoyen Radicals. Uriburu quickly annulled the elections. The Conservatives scrambled to find allies and at last found a partner in the Anti-Personalist wing of the Radicals. They formed a coalition known as the *Concordancia*. Their agreement called for the Anti-Personalists to provide a presidential candidate, while the Conservatives would furnish a running mate and control government finances. The alliance soon crumbled when Uriburu refused to permit the ex-president, Alvear, to head the ticket. Alvear took most of his party with him, and the Radicals adopted a policy of electoral abstention until 1935.

What remained of the Concordancia, the conservative National Democratic party and some Anti-Personalists, chose General Justo as their presidential candidate. With the help of fraud, the intimidation tactics of goon squads and gangsters, and the general apathy of an embittered and cynical electorate, Justo won easily. The Concordancia had a very narrow popular base, but its main potential opposition, the Radical party, was deeply fragmented and unable to cooperate with other opposition groups. The regime used its patronage power and benefited from the upturn in the economy after 1934 to consolidate its hold on power.

The Radicals staged several unsuccessful rebellions in the provinces during the early 1930s. Yrigoyen died in 1933, but not before he had been reconciled with Alvear and passed on the mantle of Radical leadership to his old rival. In 1935, Alvear rejoined the main Radical party and led it back into the political arena. In 1937, he opposed the Concordancia ticket composed of the Radical

Roberto M. Ortiz for president and the right-wing Conservative Ramón S. Castillo for vice president. With the aid of widespread vote fraud, Ortiz won.

Hoping to broaden the political base of the Concordancia, Ortiz set about restoring some semblance of free and honest elections. Unfortunately for Argentine democracy, however, Ortiz was a diabetic who was rapidly losing his vision. He therefore had to take an extended leave of absence, handing over the reins of government to Castillo in 1940. Castillo was an archconservative who attempted to undo Ortiz's reforms. The two men fought publicly until Ortiz died in 1942, and Castillo became president. For three years, he maintained an almost constant state of siege and ruled by decree.

Despite his narrowing base of support, Castillo insisted on naming as his successor the unpopular Conservative Robustiano Patrón Costas, a millionaire sugar planter from Salta who was notorious for mistreatment of his Indian laborers. On June 4, 1943, a coup organized by the secret officers' lodge known as the Group of United Officers (GOU) overthrew Castillo and established a ruling junta. Its first head, General Arturo Rawson, lasted only two days; he was followed by General Pedro P. Ramírez, who fell in his turn in 1944; his successor, General Edelmiro Farrell, ruled from 1944 until the elections of 1946.

Before leaving the "Infamous Decade," we should take note of the economic policies pursued by the Conservative administrations. It is an irony of Argentine history that the organizers of the 1930 coup, who proposed to restore the golden age of pre-1916 Argentina, not only failed to prevent far-reaching change in Argentine society but themselves had to abandon the free-trade, laissez-faire economic doctrines on which the prewar export economy was based. Conservative economic policy of the 1930s established state intervention as a decisive factor in the economy. For the most part, the Conservative policies and administration were successful. The men who conducted fiscal matters were extremely competent, sometimes brilliant. The ba-

sic aim of their policy was to protect the nation from the effects of the cyclical nature of the world capitalist economy. To accomplish this, they sought to protect their main foreign market, Great Britain, limit production of farm commodities, and restrict imports through indirect methods, such as the establishment of a currency exchange system that discriminated against non-British imports. They also sought to establish new import-substitution industries primarily through foreign investment.

In this period, finding that they could not export manufactured goods to Argentina on a competitive basis because of high tariffs and the discriminatory exchange system, United States manufacturers established plants in Argentina. As a result, foreign capital played an increasingly important role in the economy during the 1930s, accounting for 50 percent of the total capital invested in Argentine industry. Foreign companies virtually monopolized the meat-packing, electric power, cement, automobile, rubber, petroleum, pharmaceutical, and several other industries.

The British market for beef and grain was critical for the Argentine export economy. During the late 1920s and early 1930s, the British government was under constant pressure to reduce Argentine imports in order to protect producers within the empire. The result of Argentine efforts to secure the British market was the controversial Roca-Runciman Treaty of 1933. By this treaty, Britain guaranteed Argentina a fixed, though somewhat reduced, share of the chilled beef market. It also promised to eliminate tariffs on cereals. Argentina, in return, lowered or eliminated tariffs on British manufactures. It also agreed to spend its earnings from the British market on British goods to be imported into Argentina.

The economy improved after 1934, and by 1936 the crisis had passed. Cereal prices rose gradually on the world market until 1937, when they again dropped. Meat prices rose until 1936 and then remained steady. Industrial investment reached predepression levels. Although real wages declined, unemployment fell sharply as a result of public works and industrial investment.

In general, Argentines were relatively well off during the 1930s. Consumption of consumer goods and food rose considerably.

The nature of Argentine industrialization during the 1930s remains a matter of some controversy. Some historians depict the decade as one of intense expansion of import-substitution manufacturing. However, recent findings suggest that industrial growth did not accelerate during the 1930s but continued to grow at approximately the same rate as previously. In fact, it appears that more industrialization took place during the 1920s than in the 1930s. What did change was the type of products manufactured. Increased foreign investment stimulated the growth of new, technologically more advanced industries, which produced chemicals and electrical and metal products.

The process of industrialization was accompanied by a growth of the native industrialist class and a parallel increase in the size of the working class and its organizations. In 1930 the General Confederation of Labor (CGT) arose from the merger of two large unions. During the first half of the decade, the growth of the trade union movement was seriously hampered by large-scale unemployment and the hostility of employers and the government, which used right-wing thugs to harass the workers. By 1935, however, a degree of recovery had strengthened the workers' bargaining power. Strikes led by the Communist party erupted, and the unions began to grow again. The construction workers, for example, organized and joined the CGT. In 1942 differences over policy and tactics split the CGT, leading to the rise of two organizations, one dominated by Syndicalists, the other by Socialists and Communists. Nevertheless, by 1943 the membership of the trade union movement was estimated to be between three hundred and three hundred and fifty thousand.

The growth of the Argentine industrial bourgeoisie, a class profoundly dissatisfied with the economic policies of the landed oligarchy, and of the working class, still relatively small and unorganized but gaining in self-consciousness and developing new social and political aspirations, heightened the tensions within Argentine society. The military coup of 1943 represented an effort to resolve the gathering crisis.

The Perón Era, 1943–1955

Perón's Rise to Power

The military coup that overthrew Castillo in 1943 had deep and tangled roots. The fraud and corruption that tainted both Conservative and Radical politics in the "Infamous Decade" no doubt offended military sensibilities, and Castillo's choice of the pro-Ally Patrón Costas as his successor also angered some of the military, who were divided in their attitude toward the belligerents in World War II. But the coup of 1943 had deeper causes. During the 1930s, the officer corps of the Argentine armed forces, predominantly middle class in its social origins, developed an ardent nationalism that saw the solution for Argentina's problems in industrialization and all-around technical modernization. The interest of the military in industrialization was closely linked to its desire to create a powerful war machine capable of creating a Greater Argentina that could exercise hegemony in a new South American bloc. To industrialize it was necessary to end Argentina's neocolonial status, to free it from dependence on foreign markets. The pro-German attitude of many officers stemmed in part from the German military instruction that they had received and from their admiration for the supposed successes of the Nazi New Order, but even more, perhaps, from the conviction that England and the United States had conspired to keep Argentina a rural economic colony. Their pro-German attitude was not translated into a desire to enter the war on Germany's side but rather into the wish to keep Argentina neutral in the great conflict.

As concerned domestic policy, the military proposed a massive speedup of industrialization and technical modernization, even though it feared the social changes and forces that such transformations might unleash. In particular, it feared the revolutionary potential of the working class. In effect, the military proposed to build Argentine industrial capitalism with a thoroughly cowed, docile working class. As a result, one of the first acts of the military regime was to launch an offensive against organized labor. The government took over the unions, suppressed newspapers, and jailed opposition leaders. This policy of direct confrontation and collision with labor had disastrous results and threatened to wreck the industrialization program. The military was saved from itself by an astute young colonel, Juan Domingo Perón, who took over the Department of Labor in October, 1943 and promptly raised it to the status of the Ministry of Labor and Welfare.

Born in 1895, the son of immigrant and creole parents of somewhat marginal economic status (his father was a farmer), Perón entered the military college at sixteen and very slowly rose in rank to captain in 1930. He played a minor role in the coup of that year. During the next decade, he spent several years in Europe, where he was much impressed by the German and Italian dictatorships. In 1941, Perón joined the Group of United Officers, although only a junior colonel, and quickly rose to its leadership ranks. He was prominent in the colonels' clique that replaced the GOU in power in 1944. Beginning with a subcabinet post as secretary of labor and welfare, Perón became the indispensable man in the Ramírez government. He subsequently became vice president and minister of war, in addition to secretary of labor and welfare.

Perón's genius lay in his recognition of the potential of the organized and unorganized working class and the need to broaden the social base of the nationalist revolution. He became the patron of the urban proletariat. Workers were not only encouraged to organize but favored in bargaining negotiations, in which his department participated. As a result, workers' wages not only rose in absolute terms but their share of the national income grew. This, of course, increased mass purchasing power and thereby promoted the process of industrialization. Perón also created a state system of pensions and health benefits, with the result that employers' contributions for pensions, insurance, and other benefits rose steadily until the year of Perón's fall (1955). In return for these real gains, however, the unions lost their independence and became part of a state-controlled apparatus in Perón's hands. Meanwhile, Perón was strengthening his position within the military. In February 1944, he led a group of officers in forcing the resignation of President Ramírez, who, as noted previously, was replaced by General Farrell.

Not all of the military was happy with Perón's prolabor policies or with his meteoric rise to power. The end of the war in 1945 also provoked civilian demands for an end to military rule and the restoration of the constitution. In October 1945, Perón's military and civilian foes staged a coup that resulted in his ouster and imprisonment. But the organizers of the coup were divided and unclear about their objectives, and Perón's followers mobilized rapidly. Loyal labor leaders organized the Buenos Aires working class for massive street demonstrations to protest Perón's jailing. The workers virtually took over the city, without opposition from the armed forces. The bewildered conspirators released Perón from prison. Thereupon, he resigned from his various government posts, retired from the army, and began his campaign for the presidency in the 1946 elections.[1]

In preparation for the election of 1946, Perón, taking due account of the defeat of fascism in Europe, cast himself in the role of a democrat ready to abide by the result of a free election. He created a Labor party to mobilize the working class, the principal component in a class alliance whose other major elements were the national industrial bourgeoisie and the army. Perón's

[1] Myth has it that Perón's mistress (later his wife) Eva Duarte almost singlehandedly mobilized the *descamisados* to rescue him from prison. She in fact had little influence. Perón's supporters in organized labor brought him back.

chief opponent was José Tamborini, candidate of the *Unión Democrática* (Democratic Union), a heterogeneous coalition of conservative landed elite, the bureaucratic and professional middle class that traditionally supported the Radical party, and even the Socialist and Communist parties. Perón defeated Tamborini, by 300,000 votes out of 2.7 million. He was helped in the election by the blundering foreign policy of the United States, whose State Department issued a Blue Book blasting Perón for his fascist ties. Perón countered by circulating a Blue and White Book (blue and white being Argentina's national colors) that stressed the theme of Yankee imperialism.

Postwar Economics

The postwar boom enabled Perón to keep his coalition together. The export sector produced large surpluses in the balance of payments, making available funds for industrialization, mainly in labor-intensive manufactures. Between 1945 and 1948, real wages for industrial workers rose 20 percent. Personal consumption also rose. Since there was only a slight decline in the share of the national income that went to profits, the redistribution of income to the working class did not come at the expense of any other segment of the alliance. Industrialists kept profits up and benefited from increased domestic consumption, which provided a growing market for their products. The only sector of the economy that was slighted was agriculture.

Perón managed to win over a considerable sector of the dependent middle class through his use of government patronage, just as Yrigoyen had done before. He kept the military happy by his commitment to industrialization, which was an important aspect of the military's desire for national self-sufficiency and by providing it with generous salaries and the latest equipment for modern warfare.

One of Perón's greatest assets was his beautiful and stylish wife Eva Duarte de Perón, known affectionately by Argentines as "Evita" (little Eva),

who acted as his liaison to the working class. Evita, a former dance hall girl and radio and movie star, headed a huge charitable network that dispensed tremendous amounts of money and patronage. So beloved was she that when she died in 1952 at the age of thirty-two, Perón led a movement to get the Catholic church to canonize her. The president's popularity with the working class suffered after her death. Evita strongly advocated women's suffrage, which was granted in 1947. Consequently, women supported Perón in large numbers.

After 1948, however, the economic picture changed drastically. With the exception of a short-lived recovery during the Korean war, Argentina entered a period of severe recession, which included several drought-induced bad harvests. The late 1940s brought the first signs that Argentina would face serious long-term economic difficulties. Its export commodities began to confront increased competition from the United States and from revitalized Western European agriculture. Later, the advent of the Common Market worsened Argentina's position. Balance of payments deficits replaced the large surpluses that had financed the nation's import-substitution industrialization. Industrial production fell, as did per capita income. Real wages dropped 20 percent from the 1949 level in 1952–1953. It was in this decline that Perón's political failure was rooted.

Whatever one may think of Perón's economics, the fact remains that he solved none of the country's major economic problems. The main roadblocks remained. Transportation continued to be inadequate and obsolete, and a scarcity of electric power stood in the way of industrial modernization. Argentina did not produce enough fuel to meet domestic needs, and this created an enormous drain on the balance of payments. The nation's industry remained limited for the most part to import-substitution light industry. Despite his anti-imperialist rhetoric, Perón did not nationalize such key foreign-owned industries as meat packing and sugar refining. Most serious of all, Perón did nothing to break the hold of the lati-

Juan and Evita Perón, 1952. (UPI/Bettmann Newsphotos)

fundio on the land. As a result, agriculture was marked by inefficient land use, which impeded long-range development.

Perón's Downfall

After his re-election in 1952 and in response to the economic crisis of the early 1950s, Perón formulated a new plan (the Second Five-Year Plan, 1953–1957) that, to a great extent, reversed his previous strategy. He tried to expand agricultural production by paying higher prices to farmers for their produce and by buying capital equipment for this sector (tractors and reapers). He sought to increase the agricultural production available for export by means of a wage freeze, which he hoped would restrict domestic consumption. Although real wages declined, workers did not suffer proportionately more than other groups. But the industrial bourgeoisie was unhappy, for labor productivity declined while the regime's prolabor policies propped up wages. The industrialists, supported by a considerable portion of the army, wanted deregulation of the economy so they could push down wages. But the major problem of the industrial sector was lack of capital, since the agricultural sector no longer generated a large surplus.

In order to solve the capital shortage, Perón abandoned his previously ultranationalistic stand and actively solicited foreign investment. In 1953 the government reached an agreement with a North American company, the Standard Oil Company of California, for exploration, drilling, refining, and distribution rights in Argentina. Perón hoped thereby to reduce the adverse effect oil purchases abroad had on the balance of payments. Foreign capital, however, used the most modern technology and machines, which required fewer workers and tended to create unemployment in the affected industrial sectors.

In order to maintain government expenditures and a bloated bureaucracy in the face of declining revenues, Perón printed more money. The amount in circulation increased from 6 to 45 billion pesos during his two terms. By 1954 he had had some success in stabilizing the economy; he achieved a balance of payments surplus, and capital accumulation showed an upward curve. But his new economic strategy had alienated key elements of his coalition of workers, industrialists, and the armed forces. Perón then sought to divert attention from economic issues—with disastrous results.

Perón adopted two new strategies. First, he attempted to enhance his moral and ideological appeal. Second, he began to employ greater coercion to suppress a growing opposition. The vehicle for his ideological and moral appeal was *justicialismo,* Perón's ideal of justice for all—a third route to development that was neither communist nor capitalist.

Perón's strategy included attacking the church. Starting in 1951, the regime grew more repressive. The government suppressed and took over Argentina's most famous newspaper, *La Prensa* (1951). Further, Perón used his National Liberating Alliance, a private army of thugs, and the thirty-five-thousand-man federal police force to intimidate the political opposition. Torture, imprisonment, censorship, purges, and exile became the order of the day. After 1954, even the General Confederation of Labor became a coercive force, whose prime function seemed to be to suppress opposition within the labor movement.

Perón's reluctance to go along with the industrialists' desire to push down wages and increase productivity alienated that group; the industrial bourgeoisie then joined forces with the agrarian interests, which had long and bitterly opposed Perón. This desertion ended Perón's once highly successful coalition. Inevitably, Perón's hold on the working class loosened as the wage freeze and inflation reduced the value of their wages. The death of Eva Perón in 1952 contributed to the deterioration in the relations between Perón and the working class. She had served as her husband's ambassador to the workers. With Evita no longer at the head of the Social Aid Foundation, a vast philanthropic organization that distributed food, clothing, and money to the needy, Perón's relations with labor did not go so smoothly.

Despite economic adversity, Perón could not have been overthrown had not the military abandoned him. For the better part of a decade, he had masterfully balanced, divided, and bribed the military. Most of the senior officers owed him both their rank and their prosperity. The army was heavily involved in industrial production, and this provided an excellent means to become rich. In addition, to win its allegiance, Perón had showered the military with expensive military hardware and excellent wages. However, his relations with the armed forces began to disintegrate when he altered his economic policy to lessen emphasis on industrialization and self-sufficiency. On this score, his concession to Standard Oil in 1953 was the last straw for the nationalist military. The military was also affronted by the dictator's personal behavior (he had an affair with a teenage girl), and it objected to his virulent attacks on the Catholic church, a pillar of traditionalism, during 1954 and 1955. It also resented Perón's efforts to indoctrinate the military in the tenets of justicialismo.

Thus, in struggling to extricate the nation from an economic quagmire, Perón undermined the multiclass coalition that had brought him to power and sustained him there. When the final successful revolt took place in September 1955, after a failure in June, enough of the working class was alienated to assure the military's success. Perón briefly threatened to arm his working-class supporters, the *descamisados* (the shirtless ones), but instead fled into exile.

The Shadow of Perón, 1955–1973

Economic Stagnation

Chronic, sometimes violent, economic fluctuations characterized the post-1955 period. At the base of these difficulties lay continuous balance of payments deficits, which were caused by the decline in agricultural production. The nation could not earn enough from its exports to pay for the large expenditures necessary to fuel domestic industry. Periods of rapid economic growth were invariably followed by acute depressions, which wiped out all previous gains. Runaway inflation accompanied these cyclical conditions. Between 1958 and 1967, retail prices increased on the average of 27 percent a year. From 1958 to 1962, the cost of living in Buenos Aires rose 323 percent. (It rose 100 percent between 1961 and 1963.) Inflation, of course, redistributed income away from the urban working class. The prevailing economic conditions meant the end to Perón's brand of populist politics. Such politics were predicated on the ability of the economy to expand, which then permitted distribution of benefits to several groups at the same time. This enabled multiclass alliances to form.

Outright class conflict was avoided because the unions were able to beat back repeated attempts by the government to suppress working-class organizations, and the upper and middle classes soon divided over divergent economic interests. The military, too, was divided over whether or not it should rule or should return the reins of government to civilians. Agrarian and industrial groups were the first to split, for they disagreed over government actions concerning currency, credit, and taxation. Furthermore, the industrialist sector split into two groups—old, traditional industrialists and the newer import-substitution industrialists. The latter opposed

the inflow of foreign investment as a development strategy.

Development initiated by foreign investment had severe drawbacks (which were experienced by virtually all noncommunist underdeveloped nations). Foreign companies tended to monopolize credit opportunities, certain key industries became concentrated in foreign hands, and profits earned by foreign subsidiaries and remitted to the home company added to the balance of payments deficits. Finally, foreign investment was usually technologically intensive and therefore created unemployment. It was during the post-Perón era of development spurred by foreign capital that Argentina saw the emergence of large numbers of underemployed and unemployed urban workers.

At various times during the period, the Argentine government had dealings with the International Monetary Fund (IMF), an agency that was supposed to help nations overcome their economic difficulties through advice and loans. The IMF's main concern was to control inflation. Its recommended stabilization programs invariably led to downturns in the business cycle, and unemployment and business failures ensued at an awesome rate. Such austerity programs were politically unpalatable because they held down real wages and therefore elicited labor opposition. During the presidential term of Arturo Frondizi (1958–1962), the IMF had a great deal of influence, and the result was disastrous. Inflation proved unconquerable, and the fund's economic "medicine" was too bad-tasting for Argentines to tolerate.

The Military in Politics

The major political contradiction of the period from 1955 to 1973 was the position of the army regarding Peronism. To win the presidency and a majority in Congress, it was necessary to garner working-class support. The Peronists controlled much of the working-class vote, but the army was unwilling to permit any of the civilian political parties to dicker with either Perón or his best-known henchmen.

General Eduardo Lonardi succeeded Perón. He favored conciliation with the Peronists, but his attempt to implement this policy ran afoul of a large segment of the army, which overthrew him in November 1955, after a tenure of scarcely two months. General Pedro Aramburu replaced Lonardi and set about to sweep away the vestiges of Perón, destroy the power of the trade unions, and deregulate the economy. The government took over the Peronist-led unions and arrested their leaders. Aramburu also eliminated Perón's subsidy of foodstuffs. These blows against the working class had an effect exactly opposite of what was intended. The severely fractured working class found new solidarity in common adversity, and the exiled Perón regained his popularity. The effort to destroy Peronism in the unions failed, and the period from 1956 to 1958 was marked by numerous strikes, accompanied by violence.

Politics became fragmented to an almost incomprehensible degree. The provisional government tried in 1957 to hold a constitutional convention to modernize the 1853 constitution. No fewer than forty parties ran candidates. This did not include the Peronists, who abstained. The convention was a shambles.

Facing rampant inflation, labor unrest, and political fragmentation, the military permitted a return to the game of electoral politics and again stepped into the background. In February 1958, Arturo Frondizi, the head of the Radical party's Intransigent wing and long an adamant opponent of Perón, became president, capturing 45 percent of the vote. The Intransigents also won a wide majority in Congress. Frondizi at first advocated an anti-Perón, anticlerical, antiforeign investment program that favored economic nationalism and state intervention.

During the election campaign, however, he struck an agreement with Perón, promising to deal leniently with the Peronists in return for their support. His first move was to grant labor a 60 percent wage increase. Then, although he had campaigned as an economic nationalist, Frondizi proceeded to borrow vast sums from various foreign governments and the IMF. Frondizi, who had denounced Perón's Standard Oil contract, also signed oil contracts with eight oil companies, provoking a general strike in protest, and opened the doors wide to foreign capital, removing all restrictions on profit remittances. Seeking to stimulate business and agriculture, he removed controls on the economy. Finally, he embarked on a program of trimming the government bureaucracy and the excess labor force, especially in government-owned enterprises like the railroads.

Frondizi, however, proved unable to solve Argentina's most pressing problems—inflation and unemployment. In one year, 1959, the retail price index rose over 130 percent. Workers suffered immensely from the loss of real wages. Despite an upturn in 1960 and 1961, unemployment remained very high. His failure to revive the economy meant that his political strategy was bound to fail as well, since he could not hope to attract wide-based support without an expanding economy. From the beginning, he had been unable to achieve a political consensus and was forced to rule by decree or by proclaiming a state of siege. In the face of escalating violence, his inability to retain high-level government officials, and repeated coup attempts (there were thirty-five during his term), it is a wonder that Frondizi managed to survive as long as he did. Finally, he alienated the military by allowing Peronist participation in elections. The Peronists won a large bloc of seats in the Congress and ten governorships in the spring 1962 elections. The armed forces demanded that Frondizi annul the results, but he consented to cancel only some and was soon overthrown.

During the next year, José Mario Guido headed a provisional government that was a front for the military. Guido ruled by decree, and his term coincided with another depression. The period was tumultuous because the armed services were badly split over whether or not to hold elections and return to civilian rule. In September the dispute became so intense that civil war erupted. In April 1963, the navy revolted. Nevertheless, new elections were held in June. The Peronists, now called the *Unión Popular* (Popular Union), were permitted to run candidates for Congress and provincial congresses only.

Arturo Illia and his Popular Radical party won the presidency, but with a weak 25 percent of the vote. Illia was on shaky ground; not only had he failed to gain anything near to a majority of the popular vote, but he had to share Congress with no fewer than twenty-four different parties. His primary strategy was to unite anti-Peronist groups among the urban middle class and the rural sector. He continued extensive government intervention in the economy and sought to find new markets for Argentine exports. He also tried to divide the labor unions with a policy of rewarding cooperative unions. On all fronts, his program failed. Although the economy did improve during his first two years, inflation continued its upward spiral and agricultural production declined. His only economic measure of importance, and his only popular move, was the cancellation of foreign oil concessions in 1963.

Illia's liberalism was of the Yrigoyen brand, cautious and conciliatory toward the oligarchy, but it was enough to arouse disquiet among the hard-liners of the military. They were discontented with his failure to crack down on Peronists and left-wingers and with his reluctance to support the intervention by the United States in the Dominican Republic and proposals for an inter-American peace force to cope with hemispheric subversion. They were alarmed most of all by the sweeping victory of the Peronist Popular Union in the congressional elections of March 1965, which opened up the frightening possibility of a Peronist victory in the presidential election of 1969.

Determined to prevent such an outcome, the military ousted Illia in June 1966 and installed General Juan Carlos Onganía as president. This time it appeared that the military had come to stay. The government abolished political parties and purged the universities of left and center elements. The trade union movement, meanwhile, suffered from internal divisions owing to differences in policy and personal rivalries over the successor to Perón after his anticipated death. This split enabled Onganía to crack down on the militant wing of the labor movement with the cooperation of its moderate wing.

As minister of the economy Onganía appointed Adalbert Krieger Vaseña, who presided over a program of spurring foreign investment to revive the lagging economy. To attract foreign capital, Krieger Vaseña removed all restrictions on profit remittances; he also stimulated the process of industrial denationalization by devaluating the peso by 40 percent. Devaluation of the peso meant that many local companies could no longer afford expensive capital imports and royalty payments to owners of foreign technology. These local companies disappeared, leaving their share of the market to the remaining firms. In this way, Coca-Cola and Pepsi gained control of 75 percent of the soft-drink market. Bankruptcies grew from 1,647 in 1968 to 2,982 in 1970. In other cases, devaluation encouraged the process of acquisition of national companies by foreign firms, a process that had grown almost uninterruptedly since Frondizi's time. Between 1963 and 1971, foreign interests bought out fifty-three Argentine companies representing almost every industrial sector, particularly the automotive, chemical, petrochemical, metallurgical, and tobacco industries. Meanwhile, wages were frozen, although prices continued their steady rise.

Growing outrage on the part of workers and students over the government's economic program, especially its policy of industrial denationalization and the wage freeze, erupted into violence in the interior in the spring of 1969. Major riots took place in Rosario, Corrientes, and Córdoba. In Córdoba, the most industrialized city of Argentina, workers and students rose in revolt, occupying major sectors of the city until they were ousted by troops. At the same time, there was an upsurge of urban guerrilla activity by a number of groups, of which the most important was the Montoneros, who represented the left wing of the Peronist movement. Their tactics included raids on police stations, assassinations, and robberies. In May 1970, the Montoneros kidnaped and later killed former President Aramburu.

Onganía's failure to cope with the mounting wave of guerrilla activity precipitated the military coup of June 1970, which deposed him and installed General Roberto M. Levingston as president. An expert in military intelligence and counterinsurgency, Levingston decreed the death penalty for terrorist acts and kidnapings; his repressive decrees were answered with fresh acts of violence by the guerrillas. Meanwhile, to make things worse, the economy, after some recovery under Onganía, turned down again in 1970–1971. Industrial production declined and unemployment increased.

The Return of Perón

Displeased with a resurgence of labor unrest, the military ousted Levingston in March 1971. His replacement, General Alejandro Lanusse, carried out a dual policy combining brutal repression of leftist guerrillas with a general liberalization of the political climate. In effect admitting the military's failure to renovate Argentine politics, Lanusse undertook negotiations that led to the restoration of political activity and the return of the Peronists to full electoral participation for the first time since 1955.

The military briefly held out hope that the moderate political parties would unite to stand against the Peronists, but the latter's superior organization and their leader's unchallenged popularity assured their victory. The Peronists formed the FREJULI party (*Frente Justicialista de Liberación* or Justicialist Liberation Front), which nominated Héctor J. Cámpora, a leader of the Peronist left wing, as its presidential candidate. Cámpora handily won the March 1973 election with 50 percent of the vote against 21 percent for Radical party candidate Ricardo Balbín. In a series of fast-moving events during the spring and summer, Cámpora took office in May, Juan Perón returned from exile in June, and Cámpora resigned in July to pave the way for Perón. Perón, with his wife Isabel Martínez de Perón as his running mate, was overwhelmingly elected president in September.

At the heart of the Peronist program were formal agreements with labor and industry that pledged compliance with a wage and price freeze. (These included the so-called Social Contract, or *Pacto Social,* with the labor unions and the *Acto Compromiso del Campo* with industrialists.) This cooperation lasted for about a year, while the Argentine economy, buoyed by high world market prices for beef and grain, boomed. The agreements disintegrated in mid-1974 with the onset of renewed inflation brought on by a huge increase in international oil prices.

Even before these economic arrangements ended, the Peronist movement had begun to disintegrate, divided between left and right wings. By the time Perón died in July 1974, the regime had already veered rightward. With the rise of Welfare Minister Jóse López Rega during the first months of President Isabel Perón's administration, the shift to the right quickened. The level of violence increased. (In 1975 left- and right-wing thugs reportedly killed 1,100 people.) Rightist "death squads" roamed the streets. Left-wing terrorists staged spectacular kidnapings. In the face of escalating violence and economic chaos, the military stepped in again, overthrowing Isabel Perón in March 1976 and installing General Jorge Rafael Videla as president of a three-man junta composed of the three commanders of the armed forces.

Military Rule

In the ensuing years, the military presided over a roller-coaster economy that tore the guts out of Argentine industry and a reign of terror unprecedented in the nation's history. The Videla government managed to reduce inflation from over 300 percent in both 1975 and 1976 to an average of 170 percent from 1977 to 1979 and 100 percent in 1980. By the summer of 1982, however, the annual rate of inflation shot up to a catastrophic 500 percent, the highest in the world. Economic growth fluctuated wildly: the gross domestic product (the total of all the goods and services produced) grew in 1977 and 1979 and fell in 1978 and 1980. During the first six months of 1982, the

GDP fell a dismaying 7 percent. Worst of all, the free market policies of finance minister José Alfredo Martínez de Hoz led to record numbers of bankruptcies and bank failures. By eliminating tariffs on imported industrial goods and reducing government involvement in the economy, Martínez de Hoz presided over the destruction of many of Argentina's largest corporations. The real wages of Argentine workers plummeted 40 percent between 1976 and 1979, before recovering in 1980 and falling again in the severe crisis of 1982. The Catholic church set up soup kitchens in order to feed the needy in Buenos Aires. Many professionals, desperate for work, drove taxis or sold gum on the streets.

Unlike in its previous coups of 1955 and 1966, the military for the first five years of its dictatorship seemed determined to maintain itself in power in order to effect a "Process of National Reorganization." To this end the junta banned all normal political activity and embarked on a "dirty war" against the left. Under military rule, an estimated 6,000 to 15,000 (some calculate as high as 24,000) Argentines disappeared, many victims of illegal rightist death squads. Argentines came to fear the knock on the door at midnight, after which unknown kidnapers would take family and friends, who were never to be heard from again.

Retired Major General Roberto Viola succeeded Videla as president in October 1980. He was unable to manage the growing economic crisis and deepening criticism from landowners and industrialists, who had ranked among the regime's firmest backers. With the "dirty war" won by 1980, the military itself was split into hardliners (*duros*) and moderates (*blandos*) over whether or not to ease repression.

In response to intensifying criticism, Viola opened his cabinet to representatives of critical groups. This came too late, however. The military ousted Viola in November 1981, replacing him with the commander-in-chief of the army, General Leopoldo Galtieri.

The unpopularity of the military widened as the economy continued to deteriorate and the full extent of its butchery was gradually revealed to the Argentine people. The persistent marches of mothers of the *desaparecidos* (the disappeared ones) in Buenos Aires and the revelations of newspaper editor Jacobo Timerman brought the junta international notoriety.[2]

The Malvinas War

In April 1982, Galtieri took a desperate gamble to divert the nation from its economic woes and unite Argentines behind the regime. He sent Argentine forces to capture the Malvinas Islands (known also as the Falklands) in the South Atlantic, three hundred miles off the coast. Argentina and Great Britain had both claimed the islands for 150 years. For the previous seventeen years the two nations had conducted on-and-off negotiations to turn them over to Argentina, but each time agreement seemed imminent talks had broken off. On April 2, Galtieri sent 9,000 troops to settle the matter once and for all.

The invasion was the culmination of a series of colossal miscalculations by the Argentine military. First, Galtieri had not expected Britain to fight to retain the islands. The British, however, sensitive to their position as a declining world power, chose to fight as a matter of national honor. The Argentines also misjudged the position of the United States. They believed that the United States, which had recently made a number of friendly overtures, would remain neutral in the conflict. Instead, after an initial period during which it tried to mediate a peaceful agreement, the United States actively supported the British.

The war was a disaster for Argentina. Although the air force acquitted itself well, inflicting heavy casualties on the British, the navy stayed in port after the tragic loss of the *Belgrano* (300 men died) and, most importantly, the army disgraced itself. Poorly trained, atrociously led Argentine troops offered little resistance to the

---

[2] Timerman was imprisoned and tortured. His memoir, *Prisoner Without a Name, Cell Without a Number*, accused the junta of virulent anti-Semitism.

318

British. Some Argentine commanders actually abandoned their soldiers. In the ten-week war the British recaptured the islands and took the Argentine army prisoner. There were nearly 2,000 casualties in all, about 600 Argentines died.

The military compounded its devastating losses on the battlefield by misleading Argentines with false reports of victory. Thoroughly humiliated and discredited, the military faced an unprecedented political and economic crisis. Inevitably, the generals had to yield power to a civilian government. Galtieri was forced out and replaced in July by another retired general, Reynaldo Benito Antonio Bignone.

Renewed Democracy

Argentina ended nine years of nightmarish military rule in the fall of 1983 with the landslide victory of Radical party candidate Raul Alfonsín. Alfonsín thus became the first democratically elected majority president since Perón in 1946. For the first time, too, Peronism was defeated in an open election.

During Alfonsín's first year and a half in office the Argentine economy deteriorated badly. Inflation soared to 566 percent during 1984 and to 1,200 percent in June 1985. That month, however, Alfonsín instituted the "austral plan." This established wage and price controls, introduced new currency (the austral replaced the peso), and reduced government spending. Almost overnight currency stabilized. Inflation fell to a manageable 25 percent.

Though the immediate crisis ended, the nation's economic problems remained manifold and profound. Argentina's industrial base was technologically backward, its foreign debt exceeded $50 billion by the late 1980s, and it was still dependent on primary export markets plagued by low prices. Unemployment in 1985 was the highest in twenty years.

Alfonsín faced the difficult problem of the trials of the military accused of atrocities during the

In this picture, "Mothers of the Square of May" wear white kerchiefs in silent protest against the disappearance of their loved ones, and distribute newspapers that report the trials of those held responsible for the "dirty war." (Carlos Carrion/Sygma)

so-called "dirty war" of the 1970s and failures during the war with Great Britain. When the military refused to try officers in its own courts, the president transferred the cases to civilian jurisdiction. Shortly after taking office in 1983, he appointed a commission headed by Ernesto Sábato, an internationally known author, to investigate military terrorism. The commission's report, aptly titled *Nunca mas* (Never Again), revealed the full extent of the horror. The commission found the armed forces responsible for 8,971 disappearances; it documented torture, kidnaping, and other crimes, and labeled the acts as "the greatest and most savage tragedy in our history."

In the trials that followed the commission's report, several generals were convicted and awarded long prison sentences. Alfonsín confronted the problem of what to do with lower-ranking officers and enlisted men who actually carried out the crimes. In early 1987, against overwhelming public opposition, Alfonsín ended prosecutions of most lower-rank military for human rights abuses on the grounds that they had simply carried out orders. Despite this lenient attitude, Alfonsín faced a series of mutinies by sections of the divided and disgruntled armed forces. They had no popular support and were quickly crushed by loyal troops, but the light punishments meted out to the ultrarightist leaders of these mutinies by military courts contributed to a continuing atmosphere of indiscipline and turmoil in the armed forces.

Alfonsín had to deal with an economic crisis of unprecedented proportions; by 1989 Argentina's per capita gross product had fallen more than 15 percent since 1981. To cope with the crisis he resorted to traditional conservative remedies, seeking to push exports and enacting the austerity measures—cuts in government services and wage restraints—demanded by the IMF as a condition for new foreign loans to keep the Argentine economy afloat. By spring 1989 the foreign debt stood at about $60 billion. Payment on the debt took some $6 billion a year, but the country's earnings in 1988 were below $3 billion. The deficit had to be made up by new loans, which only increased the country's dependency. The policy of austerity and faithful service of the foreign debt meant that little capital was available for development; new austerity measures announced in 1989 included a 50 percent cut in all major development programs. The economy program contributed to a deterioration of the infrastructure, with long daily blackouts and energy rationing.

By May 1989, as the country prepared to go to the polls to elect a new president, it had the worst of all economic worlds: a profound recession marked by declining production and rising unemployment and an annual inflation rate of

12,000 percent, with prices rising four times a day. In the last forty-five days real wages had dropped 35 percent. The situation sparked a week of food riots that spread across the country, with desperate thousands of people taking over supermarkets, cleaning out the shelves but usually leaving the cash in the registers. The government responded by declaring a nationwide state of emergency and banning all demonstrations and strikes.

Against this background of economic collapse, the election in mid-May of the Peronist candidate, Carlos Saúl Menem, who had campaigned on a program featured by the invitation to "Follow Me" and vague promises of a "productive revolution," was a foregone conclusion. With the situation worsening daily, Alfonsín decided to cut short his term and hand power over to Menem in July, five months early. Menem's followers, including the powerful Peronist-controlled trade unions, naturally expected him to repudiate the policies that had led to an unprecedented economic and social crisis. What followed was a stunning surprise. Contrary to all expectations, Menem included in his cabinet many conservatives, including representatives of big business like the great firm of Bunge and Born, and announced a program of privatization of state-owned companies, the elimination of state monopolies, and cuts of billions in government spending over the next year. Menem's "shock therapy" on the way to his goal of a free-market economy provoked not only surprise but strong disapproval and resistance. The Peronist trade union movement, once his strong supporter, split into pro- and anti-Menem wings, followed by a series of strikes to which Menem responded by firing strike leaders and seeking to curb the right to strike by law or decree. By the last months of 1990 the benefits that Menem had predicted would flow from his new course had not materialized. By Menem's own admission, in the past ten years wages had lost half their value. According to the Ministry of Labor, out of an economically active population of 12 million, 4,300,000 were unemployed or underemployed. Inflation, after

320   a brief decline, again rose sharply, combining with a deep recession to produce the phenomenon of "stagflation." In March 1991 an official report revealed that key branches of Argentine industry, such as auto and steel, were practically paralyzed, and that industry as a whole was operating at only 30 percent of capacity.

As controversial as his economic policies was Menem's handling of the problem of human rights abuses during the "dirty war." Although polls showed that 80 percent of the population opposed such a step, Menem, pleading the need for national reconciliation, pardoned nearly 200 military officers convicted or accused of such abuses, and in December 1990 pardoned the top military commanders and two presidents who continued to serve sentences. Despite this show of good will toward the military, on the eve of President Bush's visit to Argentina in December

Menem suffered the embarrassment of having to quell an uprising by some 300 mutinous officers and soldiers. Behind the revolt was widespread discontent with military salaries, which had fallen far behind inflation. The affair evoked much popular disgust and comments that Argentina was becoming a "banana republic."

The economic crisis, reflected in a 30 percent rise in the cost of living in the first week of February 1991 alone, reduced Menem's popularity to an all-time low. Two separate polls put his popularity rating in February at 17.7 percent and 21.7 percent. With only five months remaining before municipal, state, and congressional elections, there was widespread speculation that "Menemism" was approaching its end and that Menem, like his predecessor Alfonsín, might be forced to resign.

Chapter 14

The Chilean Way

For a century and a half, Chile set a high standard
of political behavior on a continent notorious for
its turmoil and dictatorships. Compared to its
neighbors, Peru, Bolivia, and Argentina, Chile
was a model of domestic tranquility, rarely dis-
turbed by popular unrest, regional conflicts, or
meddlesome military. The nation seemed for the
most part to have escaped the harsh class and
ideological confrontations that had led other
Latin American countries to flirt with fascism
during the 1930s and fall under the rule of extreme right-wing military regimes during the
1960s. Chilean democracy appeared so firmly
rooted that it permitted the election and installation of a Marxist head of state, President Salvador Allende Gossens, in 1970. Only three years
later, however, amid growing economic and political chaos, military rebels overthrew Chile's legitimate government, killed President Allende,
and established a right-wing dictatorship whose
rule was characterized by brutal oppression.

How could Chile maintain its parliamentary
democracy so long when the rest of Latin America could not? Why, after almost a hundred and
fifty years of respect for parliamentary democracy, did it crumble so swiftly? The answers to
these questions lie in the nature of the Chilean
political process and its socioeconomic underpinnings. In retrospect, the bounds of Chilean democracy were narrowly drawn; the elite never allowed political freedom and the practice of
politics to endanger its basic interests. Instead of
seeking to solve the nation's desperate economic
and social problems, successive governments
merely evaded them. When, finally, a coalition
government headed by Chile's working-class parties came to power in 1970 and inaugurated
structural reforms that threatened oligarchical

privilege, the elite responded by calling in the army, abolishing parliamentary democracy, and establishing a reactionary dictatorship.

An Economic History, 1900–1970

The Export Sector in the Twentieth Century

The export sector played a crucial and basically detrimental role in Chilean history. Raw material exports generated enormous profits, but relatively few benefits flowed to the nation as a whole. Instead of stimulating balanced economic growth, the lucrative export sector tended to stunt the country's social and political development. Like the "banana republics" of Central America and the sugar islands of the Caribbean, Chile relied for its revenues on one export commodity, first nitrate and then copper, making it extremely vulnerable to cyclical world market demands for its products. Moreover, the copper industry, which produced the nation's major export in the twentieth century, was operated as an enclave, almost totally isolated from the rest of the economy. Finally, and most importantly, the presence of an export sector that produced sufficient revenue to operate the government and provide employment for a growing middle class enabled the Chilean oligarchy to retain political power and maintain an obsolete system of land tenure and use; these conditions severely hampered the growth of democracy and economic development.

Until World War I, nitrate was Chile's primary export, but after the war a cheaper, synthetic product displaced it on the world market; copper then became Chile's leading export. Initially, small-scale, low-technology operations mined most of Chile's copper, but shortly after 1900 a downturn in copper prices forced many of these producers to close. At the same time, the introduction of improved methods for the extraction of low-grade ore and the lower transportation costs promised by the opening of the Panama Canal attracted large North American companies, which soon dominated the industry. From 1904 to 1923 giant United States–based corporations such as Guggenheim, Kennecott, Anaconda, and Braden purchased the largest and most productive copper mines, including the three mines of the *Gran Minería.*

In 1960 the three great mines of the Gran Minería, all owned by the foreign giants Anaconda and Kennecott, accounted for 11 percent of the country's gross national product, 50 percent of its exports, and 20 percent of government revenues. But the millions of dollars in sales, profits, and tax revenues generated by copper mining provided little stimulus for Chilean commerce and industry. Copper extraction was capital-intensive and required relatively few employees. The Gran Minería, for example, employed only seventeen thousand workers in 1960 (including miners and white-collar staff). Employment in the mines declined steadily in the post–World War II era, and the surplus of miners made it possible for the companies to pay the largely unskilled labor force relatively low wages. Until the 1950s, machinery, equipment, and technical skills were imported entirely from abroad.

The copper companies earned huge profits, which they remitted to their parent corporations in the United States, adding to the outflow of capital from the country. Chile's modest share in copper's riches took the form of taxes, wages, and other limited economic linkages. The Chilean government did not impose an income tax on profits until 1925, when the levy was set at 6 percent. Subsequently, the tax rate was raised to 18 percent in 1931, to 33 percent in 1938, and to 60 percent in 1953.

A brief history of the copper industry since 1929 illustrates Chile's vulnerability to world market cycles. In 1929, the price of copper dropped precipitously. Since the government relied heavily on copper taxes for revenue, the depression forced it to curtail daily operations severely and default on its large foreign debt. In

1932, the United States, Chile's main market for copper, adopted a high tariff on copper imports, which caused mine closings and severe unemployment.

Copper prices recovered in 1935, however, and by 1937 copper production exceeded the pre-depression level. World War II brought a new copper boom, although profits and revenues were limited by price ceilings imposed by the United States. After the war, with the elimination of controls, prices skyrocketed. The Korean war (1950–1953) brought new price controls by the United States, but on somewhat better terms for Chile. In 1953, world market prices again plummeted, and Chile was rescued only by the United States government's purchase of a hundred thousand tons of copper for its military reserve. By the mid-1950s, copper boomed again, and the boom continued through the 1960s. A new down cycle, however, occurred during the last two years of the Allende administration (1971–1973).

The revenues generated from copper taxes enabled the government to avoid taxing large landholdings. Without the spur of equitable taxes, latifundists continued to leave vast tracts of fertile land uncultivated or underutilized. Although it had the potential to feed its own people, Chile had to import foodstuffs—a policy that drained the nation of foreign exchange that would have been better used to purchase capital goods for industrialization or to build roads and harbors.

An equitable tax on idle or underutilized land might have led to the breakup of the latifundia, the modernization of agriculture, and the emergence of a class of small peasant proprietors. Thanks to government policy in favor of the latifundia, however, none of this happened. Chilean agriculture remained relatively backward and inefficient. Such commercialization of agriculture as occurred resulted in further proletarianization of the peasantry.

With its coffers swelled by revenue from the export sector, the Chilean government expanded its role in the economy. A large bureaucracy developed, staffed by an emerging middle class. As the government became the major employer of the middle class and the nation's most important venture capitalist, Chile grew ever more dependent for its economic development on factors beyond its control.

Foreign Domination of the Chilean Economy

After World War I, the United States replaced Great Britain as the major foreign investor in Chile. Guggenheim and Anaconda accounted for better than 80 percent of the copper production, Bethlehem monopolized iron ore, and Guggenheim held 70 percent of the nitrate industry through its *Compãnía de Salitres de Chile* (Chilean Nitrate Company, or COSACH).

Although depression and war slowed the inflow, foreign capital surged into Chile in the postwar period—not only into the extractive sector but into manufacturing and commerce as well. From 1954 to 1970, foreigners invested $1.67 billion in Chile. U.S. companies continued to dominate copper, nitrate, and iodine production. Foreign companies conducted approximately half the nation's wholesale trade, monopolized the telephone and telegraph industries, and had important stakes in electric utilities and banking. Even the major advertising agencies were foreign subsidiaries or affiliates. Foreign investment centered in the largest companies, controlling the administration of forty of the one hundred largest Chilean corporations and substantial blocks of stock in twenty-one others.

Chile depended not only on direct investment from abroad but on loans as well. Payment of interest and amortization on the national debt consumed an increasing share of its revenue from the export sector. The country also relied on foreign sources for industrial technology.

Because most foreign investment, like the copper enclave, was capital-intensive, it provided little employment and few linkages to the rest of the economy. The benefits to Chile's long-range economic development were minimal. Without doubt, Chile was not the master of its own economic fate.

The Concentration of Land and Wealth

In 1964, on the eve of the first serious effort in Chile's history to reform its agrarian structure, there was an extreme concentration of land-ownership, the condition of rural laborers was wretched, and the inefficient great landed estates were clearly incapable of providing enough food to feed Chile's growing urban centers. By contrast with the situation in most underdeveloped nations, Chile's agricultural sector played only a small role in the economy. It accounted for less than 10 percent of the gross national product and employed less than 25 percent of the work force. The inability of agriculture to provide employment, on the one hand, and sufficient food, on the other, resulted in an overurbanized, underemployed, and undernourished population.

The statistics of landholding indicate that there was little change in these patterns between 1930 and 1970. In 1930, holdings of over 2,500 acres composed only 2 percent of the total number of farms but comprised 78 percent of the cultivable land. Eighty-two percent of all farms were under 125 acres but held only 4 percent of the land. By the 1960s, 11,000 units, accounting for 4.2 percent of the farms, composed 79 percent of the land. Farms under 100 acres—77 percent of all farms—held 10.6 percent of the land. Over 700,000 people, the majority of the rural labor force, had no land at all. The living and working conditions of agricultural laborers were appalling—and getting worse. Agricultural wages had consistently declined since the 1940s, falling 23 percent from 1953 to 1964.

Government credit and tax policies before 1964 assured that the maldistribution of land and agricultural income would continue. Small landholders, having no access to bank or government loans, had to rely on moneylenders or store owners, who charged outrageous interest. Smallholders and agricultural laborers also bore a disproportionate burden of taxes. The Chilean tax structure was such that taxes on sales and other transactions (turnover taxes) exacted a higher toll from lower-income groups, because most of their transactions involved the purchase of foodstuffs. Taxes on land, capital, income, and inheritance, on the other hand, were light. The large estates, especially those that were not farmed, went virtually untaxed.

Despite unused land and plentiful manpower, production of food did not keep pace with population growth from the mid-1930s. The deficit had to be made up by imports, which aggravated the balance of payments problem and contributed to Chile's chronic inflation. As a result, the poor were undernourished, and even large portions of the middle class suffered from inadequate diet.

Land was not the only sector of the Chilean economy concentrated in a very few hands. A few powerful clans controlled a wide variety of industrial and financial enterprises and thus exerted a decisive influence on the national economy as a whole. In 1967, 12 companies out of 2,600 transacted nearly half the total wholesale business in the country. One bank, Banco de Chile, furnished 32 percent of the nation's private bank credit; the five largest banks furnished 57.4 percent.

These facts, however, tell only part of the story, for control of the economy was even more concentrated. According to Stefan De Vylder, fifteen large economic groups controlled the Chilean economy. The most powerful of the clans, the Edwards family, controlled one commercial bank, seven financial and investment corporations, five insurance companies, thirteen industries, and two publishing houses and was closely associated with North American companies active in the country. The family's newspaper chain accounted for over half the circulation of daily newspapers in Chile; together with another publishing house, it virtually controlled the entire market for periodicals.

A Political History, 1891–1970

The Parliamentary Republic, 1891–1920

The defeat and suicide of President José Manuel Balmaceda during the civil war of 1891 ushered in the era of the so-called Parliamentary Republic. It was a time of political stagnation, in sharp contrast to the rapid social change. The contradiction between an immobile political structure and a rapidly changing society became increasingly apparent in the first two decades of the twentieth century. The dominant political parties, the Liberal and Conservative parties, represented the great landowners of the Central Valley and supplied the nation's presidents and congressmen. The six presidents who served during the period of the Parliamentary Republic were little more than puppets manipulated by congressional leaders.

A third major party, the Radicals, founded in 1861 by dissident Liberals, enjoyed the support of low-level professionals, bureaucrats, teachers, artisans, and other middle-class groups, as well as that of large landowners on the southern frontier around Concepción, northern mine owners from the Copiapó region, and businessmen from Santiago, the capital. A fourth party, the Democrats, had some base in the lower middle class and among workers.

The only issue separating the major parties was the role of the church in education. The chief concerns of the parties appeared to be the preservation of the status quo and the distribution of the spoils of office. Corruption and inefficiency pervaded the political life of the era.

While politics stagnated in an atmosphere of fraud and apathy, Chilean society underwent profound transformation. The nation grew increasingly urbanized and industrialized, and new classes emerged from these processes. An industrial working class rose in the mining regions of the north, first in the nitrate fields and then in the copper mines. Although their wages were higher than elsewhere in the country, the miners suffered from low pay, inadequate housing, the tyranny of company stores, and unsafe working conditions. In the cities, where wages were even lower, workers lived in wretched slums and were periodically battered by epidemic disease.

After the turn of the century, workers began to struggle against these dismal conditions. The first major strike broke out in Iquique in the northern mining region in 1901 and lasted for two months. In 1907 the nitrate workers of Iquique again struck against inhuman living and working conditions; the government responded by sending in troops who slaughtered two thousand workers. The wave of strikes continued, with a notable upsurge during World War I. Unrest increased at the war's end, for the nitrate industry collapsed, leaving thousands of miners unemployed and plunging the entire country into a severe depression. In 1919, faced with growing unrest, the government declared a state of siege (suspending civil liberties) in the mining areas.

Labor had meantime begun to organize in the effort to achieve better conditions. Luis Emilio Recabarren played a leading part in establishing the Workers' Federation of Chile (*Federación de Obreros de Chile,* or FOCH) in 1909. Three years later he founded the first workers' party, the Socialist, or Socialist Labor, party. In 1922 it became the Communist party and joined the Third (Communist) International. By contrast with the Argentine Socialist party, with its large middle-class base, Chile's first working-class party grew directly out of the labor movement.

In the same period, the middle class became larger and more diverse. The growth of industry and commerce and the expansion of the state created many new white-collar jobs. This growing middle class displayed few of the entrepreneurial traits commonly associated with the North American and European middle classes. The domination of decisive sectors of the economy by large-scale enterprise effectively barred small and medium-size entrepreneurs from playing an important role in economic life. The inflationary policies pursued by oligarchical governments, which eroded the savings needed to finance middle-class business, further discouraged such ventures. Aristocratic control of choice government jobs through clientele and kinship ties also restricted the sphere of middle-class activity. As the twentieth century opened, the middle class began to agitate for a place in the sun.

Meanwhile, the composition of the oligarchy was also changing, for it began to incorporate new elements from among industrialists and businessmen. More completely than elsewhere in Latin America, the Chilean landed elite fused with the new urban upper and upper-middle classes. They intermarried, and the urban rich acquired land, adopting the values of the traditional elite. This elite, instead of investing its wealth from the land in industry, often preferred to spend it on conspicuous consumption. The ability of the state to provide salaried jobs to many members of the middle class, and the elite's policy of forming kinship and social ties with the new industrialist and business class, meant that conflicts between the oligarchy and the bourgeoisie were kept to a minimum, save in times of serious economic crisis. This was a serious impediment to reform. Missing in Chile, too, were the large number of immigrants who in some measure challenged the values and hegemony of the elite in Argentina. The relatively few immigrants who came to Chile preferred to emulate rather than challenge the oligarchy.

Alessandri, the Military Radicals, and Reform

By 1920, even sections of the oligarchy were aware that they could no longer ignore the needs of the rest of Chilean society. It was apparent that some concessions to the working and middle classes had to be made, but the elite appeared incapable of devising a solution for the country's grave economic and social problems. In 1918 the Liberal Alliance, which included Radicals, Liberals, Democrats, and *Balmacedistas,* achieved control of the Chamber of Deputies in the election of that year, and in 1920 it offered a possible "savior" of the country, nicknamed the "Lion of Tarapacá," Arturo Alessandri, as its candidate for president.

A former corporation lawyer turned populist politician, Alessandri appealed to the lower and middle classes with promises to reform the constitution and relieve the bleakness of working-class life. He promised a social security system, a labor code, cheap housing, educational reform,

women's rights, and state control of banks and insurance companies. With considerable support from sections of the oligarchy, which hoped that he could placate the restless masses with a minimum of effective social change, Alessandri defeated the candidate of the conservative National Union in the election of 1920.

During the first four years of Alessandri's term, he proved unable to make good his campaign pledges. The Liberal Alliance, which had supported his election, split and failed to give him the support he needed in Congress. Moreover, although the Liberal Alliance controlled the Chamber of Deputies, it did not control the Senate, where conservative opposition blocked passage of reform legislation. The postwar depression also forced Alessandri to lay aside reform projects while he wrestled with economic problems. Widespread unemployment in Santiago and Valparaíso caused general strikes to erupt in those cities, bringing them to a standstill. Strikes and lockouts plagued the economy. The president issued ever more paper currency to pay unemployment benefits; the result was runaway inflation. The only reform measures secured by Alessandri were a minimum wage law and a trifling tax reform.

Congress, representing entrenched oligarchical interests, stood squarely in the way of any meaningful social and political reforms. Accordingly, Alessandri urged the passage of laws that would restore the balance of power between Congress and the executive branch—a balance destroyed after the civil war of 1891. He also sought such social reforms as a shorter workday, labor laws to protect women and children, the right of workers to strike, and health insurance. These modest proposals certainly did not threaten the status quo, but they would require money. In view of the catastrophic decline of the nitrate industry, this money could be raised only by taxing the oligarchy's land and income—a solution the elite found unthinkable. As a result of the parliamentary deadlock, the Chilean government could not cope with the mounting economic and social crisis.

The Liberal Alliance won a majority in both houses of Congress in 1924, but the new Congress, ignoring the pressing need for reform legislation, proceeded to vote themselves salaries for the first time in Chilean history. The innovation was entirely proper, for congressmen no longer came exclusively from the oligarchy and needed salaries to support themselves, but in a time of depression, when many public employees had not been paid for many weeks, it gave great offense.

The Chilean military, predominantly of middle-class origins, had observed the unfolding crisis with growing impatience and resentment. Many junior and middle-grade officers favored the enactment of Alessandri's social and political reform program; they also felt that Congress had neglected the needs of the armed forces. For these officers, the salary episode was the last straw. Organized in a military junta, they staged a coup in September 1924 and compelled Congress to enact in rapid succession all of Alessandri's reform proposals and, in addition, to raise the size of the army and its pay scale. Alessandri, however, refused to share power with the military and left the country.

Growing tension between progressive junior and middle-grade officers on the one hand and conservative generals on the other produced another coup in January 1925, which brought to power a reform-minded group of officers, led by Carlos Ibáñez del Campo and Marmaduke Grove. The new junta promptly invited Alessandri to return, which he did in March.

On his return, Alessandri set about accomplishing the political reforms for which he had campaigned. The result was the constitution of 1925, which ended the Parliamentary Republic and restored the balance of power between Congress and the president. It provided that the president would be elected by direct vote, serve a six-year term, be ineligible for immediate re-election, and have control over his cabinet and government finance. The constitution proclaimed the inviolable right of private property but stated that this right could be limited in the interest of social needs. Other measures included a new and extensive labor code, the grant of the vote to literate males over twenty-one, the establishment of an electoral registry to reduce electoral fraud, a nominal income tax on income over ten thousand pesos a year, and the establishment of a central bank.

In September, a plebiscite approved the constitution. Soon thereafter, Alessandri again resigned, citing unbearable military pressure. The ensuing election brought to the presidency the weak and colorless Emilio Figueroa Larrain. However, Ibáñez, who became interior minister in the new administration, gradually emerged as a strong man. Blaming the country's problems on communism, Congress, and the leadership of all political parties, he proceeded to jail or deport Communists and key members of Congress who dared to challenge his power. In May 1927, placed in an untenable position by Ibáñez's inroads on his authority, Figueroa resigned the presidency. Less than two weeks later, Ibáñez, running unopposed, was elected president in a special election.

Ibáñez and the Great Depression

The military reform movement of 1924, which for a time appeared to be forging an alliance with the working and middle classes for the achievement of structural reforms, ended in the military dictatorship of Ibáñez (1927–1931). The only fruits of that movement for social change were the social legislation adopted since 1924 and provided for in the constitution of 1925.

To implement that legislation and secure the position of state employees, which was necessary to maintain political stability, Ibáñez needed substantial amounts of money; his program of welfare, public works, and modernization was based above all on huge loans from foreign bankers. Between 1927 and 1931, the government borrowed and spent approximately $250 million on various public works and government projects. The armed forces were a special beneficiary of government largesse, obtaining generous promotions and salary increases.

Ibáñez also spent large sums on education—five times as much as had been spent in 1920—and the number of schools, teachers, and students increased steadily from 1924 to 1931. Educational reform failed, however, because too few teachers were available and because Ibáñez saw education primarily as a propaganda tool. Meanwhile, all opposition was suppressed, political foes were jailed or deported, and efforts were made to split the Communist-led labor movement by the sponsorship of government-backed unions.

Aided by a temporary revival of copper and nitrate sales and massive foreign loans, the Chilean economy prospered for the first two years of Ibáñez's rule. But the Wall Street crash of 1929 cut off the all-important flow of capital and loans, and by the following year the nitrate and copper markets had both collapsed. Unemployment spread throughout the nation. In a vain effort to find a solution for the economic crisis, the government tried to limit nitrate sales to push up prices. Ibáñez trimmed social services and his public works program and hiked taxes, but the financial situation grew increasingly desperate.

In July 1931, confronted by a general strike that involved not only workers but professionals, white-collar employees, and students and faced with growing doubts about the army's loyalty to him, Ibáñez resigned and went into exile in Argentina. The next seventeen months brought a succession of military coups. One such coup, led by Marmaduke Grove, commander of the air force, led to the proclamation of a Socialist Republic of Chile, which lasted barely twelve days before it was overthrown by a new military revolt. The socialist republic was the last gasp of a small group of officers who had been radicalized by the crisis of the 1920s. Ironically, the program of the socialist republic was not socialist; it proposed, rather, to create jobs through public works financed by the issue of paper money.

Finally in September 1932, a new coup led by

General Bartolomé Blanche installed a caretaker regime that presided over new elections and a return to civilian government. In the presidential election, Arturo Alessandri, supported by Radicals, Liberals, Democrats, and even some Conservatives, defeated five rivals, including the Socialist Grove.

The Return of Alessandri

Alessandri began his second term in the depths of the depression, with a hundred and sixty thousand people unemployed in Santiago alone, while a typhoid epidemic ravaged the country. Income from nitrates was one-twentieth the 1927 figure; public employees, including soldiers and policemen, had not been paid for months. In the succeeding five years, 1932 to 1937, the president and his finance minister, Gustavo Ross, presided over an economic recovery that reflected a partial revival and stabilization of the world market. Exports more than tripled, nitrate and industrial production rose, unemployment was eliminated, and the budget was balanced. During the last years of Alessandri's term, the government actually had a budget surplus. As the economy revived, government revenues increased, and Alessandri had more money to implement social legislation already on the books.

But Alessandri had no greater success in solving Chile's structural problems in the 1930s than he did in the 1920s. Foreign capital controlled the lucrative mining sector of the economy, and the inefficient latifundio continued to dominate Chilean agriculture. The urban and rural working class received few benefits from the economic revival; those social reforms that touched urban areas did nothing for Chile's tenant farmers and farm laborers. The government's devaluation of the peso, designed to stimulate exports, sharply increased the cost of living while wages remained stable. Workers' strikes for better wages and living conditions were often brutally suppressed.

Middle-class critics of the regime fared little better. Following the example of Ibáñez, Alessandri closed down hostile newspapers, exiled political critics, and dealt highhandedly with Congress. These conditions produced a major new effort to mobilize workers, peasants, and the urban middle sector to defend democracy and promote social progress. This effort was called the Chilean Popular Front.

The Rise of the Left and the Popular Front

The Chilean left had its roots in the Socialist Labor party, founded by Luis Emilio Recabarren in 1912; ten years later, it joined the Third (Communist) International and became the Communist party. During the 1920s, the Communists won considerable support among organized labor, particularly the railroad workers' union and the Confederation of Chilean Workers (FOCH), which claimed two hundred thousand members. Later, however, the Communists suffered a series of severe setbacks. Recabarren killed himself in 1924, apparently from despair over the military dictatorship that replaced Alessandri. Although they had had a part in framing the constitution of 1925, Communist leaders were imprisoned and exiled during the Ibáñez regime. After the fall of Ibáñez in 1931, however, the party began to revive under the leadership of Carlos Contreras Labarca, and it gained considerable popularity among workers and intellectuals.

The communists' principal rival on the left was the Socialist party. Its predominantly middle-class leadership, though it advocated a leftist program that included revolution, was highly opportunistic, especially the charismatic Marmaduke Grove, who repeatedly left and re-entered the party. From the first, the party was an uneasy alliance of left and right wings.

Chile in the 1930s was fertile ground for the growth of left-wing parties and ideologies because the working class was excluded from the benefits of economic recovery and Alessandri harshly suppressed working-class dissent. Between 1935 and 1937 the Chilean Communist party, at the urging of the Third International, alarmed at the growing threat of fascism, joined with left and moderate parties to form the Chilean Popular Front. The Communists, Socialists, and Radicals united for the elections of 1938, nominating Radical Pedro Aguirre Cerda as their presidential candidate.

The Popular Front's electoral platform called for the restoration of constitutional rule and civil liberties and basic social reforms, summed up in the slogan *pan, techo, y abrigo* (bread, clothing, and a roof). Despite the advantages enjoyed by Alessandri's candidate, Gustavo Ross, including control of the electoral machinery and the support of the large state bureaucracy, Aguirre Cerda gained a razor-thin victory, receiving 50.3 percent of the vote.

The short, stormy life of the Popular Front— it officially ended in 1941 when first the Socialists and then the Radicals withdrew, but was reformed in 1942 as a "Democratic Alliance" of Communists, Radicals, and miscellaneous groups that lasted until 1947—yielded some achievements. In 1938 the State Development Agency, CORFO, was formed to foster industrialization. Aided by a virtual cessation of imports as a result of World War II and by governmental policies of subsidies, low taxes, and protective tariffs on imported consumer goods, native manufacturing made steady progress between 1940 and 1945.

The policy of state-supported industrialization also promoted the growth of the Chilean industrial working class; between 1940 and 1952, the number of workers employed in manufacturing rose from 15 percent of the work force to 19 percent. The industrialization process was accompanied, at least until 1945, by improvement in workers' real purchasing power—up 20 percent between 1940 and 1945—while that of white-collar workers increased 25 percent. After 1945, as Radical administrations moved to the right and the basis of the Popular Front strategy disintegrated, the working class's relative share of the national income declined.

The Popular Front era produced no structural changes in the Chilean economy or society. Chilean governments were unable to institute basic economic and social reforms because the members of the coalition had irreconcilable differences over domestic and foreign policy.

In the 1946 election, the Socialist party ran its own candidate, but Radical Gabriel González Videla (1946–1952) won with the support of the Communist party. His first cabinet was a curious mix of three Radicals, three Communists, and three members of the Liberal party. Soon, responding to the pressures of the cold war, González Videla moved to the right, ousted the Communist members of his cabinet, broke a strike of Communist-led coal miners (with Socialist support), and the following year pushed through the Law for the Defense of Democracy, known unofficially as the *Ley Maldita,* or the Accursed Law, which outlawed the Communist party and eliminated Communists from Congress. González Videla also established a concentration camp for Communist party members and other left-wing militants in an abandoned mining camp in the northern desert. The Socialist party split into the Socialist party of Chile, which endorsed González Videla's repressive measures, and the Popular Socialist party, which denounced the president's anti-Communist drive.

Massive discontent with skyrocketing inflation, the freezing of workers' wages, and González Videla's repressive policies paved the way for a comeback by the old ex-dictator Carlos Ibáñez del Campo in 1952. Offering repeal of the Ley Maldita, a minimum salary, a family allowance for workers, and a sympathetic hearing for just wage demands, Ibáñez defeated several rival candidates, including Salvador Allende Gossens of the Socialist party, who had Communist support. But the decline in Chilean copper revenues following the end of the Korean war made it impossible for Ibáñez to make good on his populist promises. To stabilize the economy he sought loans from North American banks and the International Monetary Fund; meanwhile, he sought to force the working class to absorb inflation through cuts in real wages. Threatened with labor unrest, Ibáñez embarked on a course of harsh repression. By the end of his term, he had alienated all sectors of the Chilean people.

New Alignments: The Emergence of Christian Democracy

Between 1953 and the presidential election year of 1958, the parties of the left restored their unity by forming the *Frente de Acción Popular* (Popular Action Front, or FRAP), which included the reunited Socialist party and the Communists. Simultaneously, a new Christian Democratic party emerged, led by Eduardo Frei; it appealed to Catholic workers, especially white-collar sectors, with a vague ideology that claimed to be neither capitalist nor socialist. In its first try for office in 1958, this party demonstrated its electoral force.

Four major candidates contested the presidency in 1958. They were the Conservative Jorge Alessandri, a son of the former president and a leading industrialist; Eduardo Frei, a Christian Democrat; Salvador Allende, of FRAP; and Luis Bossay, a Radical. Surprisingly Alessandri beat Allende by a threadbare margin of only 33,500 votes. Allende would probably have won if an obscure minor-party candidate had not drawn away some slum and rural poor votes.

Alessandri had no more success than his predecessors in coping with Chile's problems of inflation and economic stagnation. His formula for recovery was to restore the free market, end state intervention in the economy, and employ foreign loans and investment as the basis for economic development. In effect, Alessandri's policy was a replay of Ibáñez's effort between 1927 and 1932 to solve Chile's economic problems through an endless cycle of loans and repayments. By 1962, however, the injections of foreign capital had lost their capacity to stimulate the nation's economy. A serious balance of payments problem arose, and inflation began to increase again.

Politics in Chile during the early 1960s were profoundly affected by changes in United States policy in response to the Cuban Revolution (1959). The United States sought to bolster reform movements throughout Latin America as an alternative to social revolution. As part of this policy, it covertly financed the Christian Democrats. Combined with the backing of the conservative parties, which were badly scared by

Allende's near-election six years earlier, U.S. support enabled Frei to win the 1964 election with 56 percent of the vote.

Frei and Christian Democracy, 1964–1970: A "Revolution in Freedom" Unfulfilled

Eduardo Frei came to the presidency with promises of a "revolution in freedom" that would correct the extreme inequities of Chilean society without a violent class struggle. The problems he faced were familiar ones: inflation and stagnation, a domestic market too narrow to support an efficient mass industry, and an industry and an agriculture incapable of supplying the basic needs of the population. In order to create the market needed for a modern mass industry, Frei proposed agrarian reform, tax reform, and other measures to redistribute income to the lower classes. Agrarian reform was bound to anger the traditional landed elite, but Frei counted on support from progressive industrialists, who understood that cheap production of food could hold down wage increases. He also counted on massive foreign economic aid from the United States.

Frei's plan for the Chileanization of the copper industry was designed both to appease widespread nationalist sentiment and to obtain new government revenue through increased copper production. The plan required the government to buy 51 percent of the shares in the foreign-owned mines. In return for a promise to increase production and refine more ore in Chile, the foreign companies retained control of management and obtained new concessions with respect to taxation and repatriation of profits. The agreement proved quite profitable for the companies concerned. However, the plan failed to expand production significantly or to increase government revenues.

Frei's program of agrarian reform also had mixed results. He began by attempting to improve conditions in rural areas by increasing wages, establishing peasant unions, and instituting a more equitable system of taxation; he also redistributed some land to the peasants, but in-

flation eroded wage gains and land redistribution fell far short of what was promised. As a gradualist, Frei shied away from precipitous or widespread expropriations. Peasants who received land faced a difficult time, for the government did not provide them with credit needed to start off as independent farmers. In July 1967, the Christian Democrats pushed through a fundamental land reform law empowering the government to expropriate landholdings of over 80 hectares (approximately 190 acres) in fertile areas and the equivalent elsewhere, but Frei never implemented the law.

Frei lost labor support when he adopted a tough line toward strikes and wage demands and tried to undermine the country's major labor federation. Increased worker militancy made Socialist and Communist union leadership more influential.

As early as 1965, the president had decided on an economic policy that would attract foreign and domestic investors; as a result, he abandoned the redistributive efforts of his first year and froze wages. During 1966, the government reacted harshly to strikes in the copper mines, at one point sending in troops.

The need to appease his political constituency and the economic decline after 1966 defeated Frei's efforts at reform. Upper-class Catholic intellectuals had founded and provided the leadership of the Christian Democratic party. Its membership was overwhelmingly middle class, including urban professionals, white-collar workers—especially from the public sector—skilled workers, and managers—groups that had emerged during the preceding two decades as the Chilean economy diversified. The party did well in the larger towns, among urban slum dwellers, and among women. In 1964, Frei got considerable support from industrialists and bankers who feared the election of Allende. These were hardly the elements of a revolutionary party. Like the Argentine Radical party under Yrigoyen, the Christian Democrats could not risk alienating their main constituency in an attempt to better the condition of the working class. Their program of reform depended entirely on a healthy, expanding economy that would enable the government to distribute benefits to the lower class without injuring the middle class or altering the basic economic and social structures.

When Frei came to office in 1964, the economy was expanding rapidly, for the Vietnam war kept copper prices high. Frei's moderate reform goals insured good relations with the United States and a resulting flow of loans and private investment. Even Chile's chronic inflation slowed. Two good years, however, were followed by four bad ones. After 1967 the economy stagnated while inflation surged again. From 1967 to 1970, inflation rose steadily, averaging almost 30 percent a year. Income inequalities increased, and living standards declined sharply. Frei's rhetoric brought hope to Chileans, but he fulfilled few of his promises. During his term, the working class grew increasingly restive. Groups like *pobladores* (urban slum dwellers) and rural workers organized for the first time. As the Christian Democrats proved less and less capable of dealing with Chile's economic woes, these newly organized groups and the trade unions moved further to the left. Inflation, wage and salary controls, rising taxes, shortages of consumer goods, and the costly but unsuccessful and unpopular copper policy further eroded Christian Democratic support and pushed the electorate leftward.

This leftward move was reflected within the Christian Democratic party itself. In 1969 disillusioned progressives split off to form the Movement for United Popular Action (MAPU), which later joined the Popular Unity Coalition. This break left Frei the leader of the right wing of the party and Radomiro Tomic the head of what remained of the left wing after the secession of MAPU. Since Frei was ineligible to run again under the constitution, and the party could not risk further erosion of its social base by running a hard-liner, it advanced Tomic as its presidential candidate in 1970. He ran on a platform almost indistinguishable from that of Allende, the candidate of the left coalition, *Unidad Popular* (Popular Unity, or UP), whose main elements were the Socialist, Communist, and Radical parties.

The right backed ex-President Jorge Alessandri, the standard-bearer of the National party (formed in 1966 through the merger of the Conservative and Liberal parties). The right, already alienated by Frei's agrarian reform, found Tomic totally unacceptable and refused to join forces with the Christian Democrats as it had in 1964. Allende won the election with 36 percent of the vote, while Alessandri got 35 percent and Tomic 28 percent. Since Allende failed to receive a majority, the election went to Congress which, after much-publicized maneuvering, approved Allende as president.

The Chilean Road to Socialism

The Opposition

When Allende took office in 1970, political conditions appeared favorable to his program for the achievement of socialism in Chile within a framework of legality and nonviolence. The assassination in October 1970 of General René Schneider, the commander in chief of the army, who had kept the army neutral during the period after the election just before Allende assumed the presidency, had discredited the right. Prospects were excellent that the Popular Unity would receive the cooperation of the left wing of the Christian Democratic party in Congress. For the time being, the UP coalition remained united behind a program that called for the progressive take-over of large foreign companies and monopolies in the fields of commerce, industry, and land distribution and expropriation of all landholdings over 80 hectares.

Nonetheless, the forces against the UP were formidable. It did not have a majority in Congress. Both the judiciary and the *Controlaría General* (the government's fiscal arm) opposed Allende's policies. The entire domestic economic establishment, foreign interests (the most prominent of which was the International Telephone and Telegraph Company), much of the officer

Salvador Allende, president of Chile, died during the military coup of September 1973. (Bruno Barbey/ Magnum Photos, Inc.)

corps of the military and national police, and the Catholic church were also aligned against the UP. The anti-UP political coalition, the *Confederación Democrática* (Democratic Confederation) controlled virtually all of the nation's media— two of the three television stations, 95 percent of the radio stations, 90 percent of the newspaper circulation, and all of the weekly magazines.

On its side, the UP had 36.3 percent of the voters, who made up the best-organized and most politically active sector of the electorate. However, most of the labor force was unorganized (only 2 percent belonged to unions) and unsympathetic with the left. Wide disparities in the economic conditions of various sectors of the work-

ing class made it difficult to construct a program that would satisfy all interests. White-collar workers were much better off than blue-collar workers and therefore tended toward conservatism, seeking to maintain what they had. There were sharp differences among blue-collar workers also. For example, copper miners were among the most highly paid workers, while coal and nitrate miners received very low wages. Similar differentials existed in the various industrial and craft unions. The UP also had trouble organizing in the countryside, for most campesinos were firmly attached to the Christian Democrats, who still controlled the state bureaucracy that dealt with agrarian affairs.

A lack of internal cohesion also hindered the UP. At the moment of victory, its leadership was not fully prepared for the task of governing. Many had doubted that it could win the election. Later, a schism arose within the coalition when the Leftist Revolutionary Movement (*Movimiento Izquierdista Revolucionario,* or MIR) demanded a more radical land program. This split reflected the variety of viewpoints within the UP on the strategy and tactics of the transition to socialism. The old problem of how to satisfy the claims of both the working class—even more militant than during the Popular Front days—and the middle sectors—who worried that their interests were being threatened by the structural reforms undertaken by the UP—was never fully resolved.

The First Year, 1971

The UP's immediate problems were to better the living standard of the working class and get the economy moving. The government accomplished this goal by bringing about an enormous increase in purchasing power, which in turn stimulated demand and industrial production. During the first year of Allende's term, worker income rose a startling 50 percent. The government instituted a massive program of public spending, especially for labor-intensive projects such as housing, education, sanitation, and health. At the same time, the government established price controls, which were backed up by local, housewife-operated price and supply committees. The rate of inflation fell to 22.1 percent in 1971 from 34.9 percent in 1970 and, as a result, real income rose 30 percent.

The short-term policies of the UP government, which aimed to stimulate the dormant economy, alleviate unemployment, improve living standards, and increase popular support for a minority regime, were highly successful—a success reflected in the municipal elections of April 1971, in which the Popular Unity won over 50 percent of the vote. In the long run, however, the depletion of stocks, the outflow of foreign exchange to pay for the import of consumer goods, and the

fall of profits in what was still basically a market economy proved very damaging to the government's economic program.

For the first year, middle-class businessmen, industrialists, and peasants fared very well and cooperated with the Allende regime. There were scattered cases of larger owners sabotaging their own property but, for the most part, business was not hostile. The government also employed coercion to gain cooperation from industry, threatening companies with intervention if they did not agree to increase production. Coercion and increased demand combined to bring about an expansion of industrial production and employment.

Allende's first problems arose when copper prices declined sharply, leading to an imbalance in terms of trade and the depletion of foreign exchange reserves. In addition, the expropriation of the Gran Minería in July 1971 virtually halted the flow of private investment capital from the United States and put an end to the extensive credit that had been forthcoming from such agencies as Agency for International Development (AID), the Export-Import Bank, the Inter-American Development Bank, and the World Bank. The Soviet bloc, Western European nations, and other Latin American countries provided credit, but not enough to compensate for the loss of U.S. loans. The fall of copper prices and the resulting deficit in the balance of payments led Allende to stop servicing the national debt. He eventually managed to reach satisfactory agreements with all of Chile's creditors except the United States, whose continued opposition posed a serious impediment to economic development.

The Left's Old Dilemma: Caught in the Middle, 1972–1973

The first year's gains gave way to economic stagnation and resurgence of inflation. Although Allende's popularity remained high in 1971, he struggled unsuccessfully to reach a delicate balance between needed structural reform demanded by the working class and special interests of the capitalistic-minded middle class. The government's policy of expropriating large enterprises benefited few workers and alienated owners of small and medium-size businesses, who employed 80 percent of the working population. To make matters worse, workers began occupying and operating factories. State enterprises were badly mismanaged.

The socialist government was also unable to solve the agricultural crisis. Chile's inefficiently managed agricultural production was perhaps the biggest economic roadblock, for it neither raised enough to feed the country's inhabitants nor provided employment for the large pool of rural labor. A hostile Congress forced Allende to operate with reform laws inherited from the Frei administration; nonetheless, by the end of 1972, Allende had effectively liquidated the latifundio system. Expropriation and redistribution proceeded, but with considerable cost to production. The amount of land under cultivation decreased by 20 percent, and the harvest of 1972–1973 was poor.

The Allende administration faced a full-fledged economic and political crisis by the fall of 1972. The inevitable disruptions that accompany revolutionary conditions were exacerbated by the mistakes and shortcomings of the UP government and the conflicts within the coalition. Moreover, the Chilean oligarchy and its North American allies were formidable, unrelenting opponents.[1] Although the upper class lost much of its economic base due to the nationalization of large industries and expropriation of large landholdings, it retained control over much of the mass media, the judiciary, a majority in Congress, and the armed forces.

The struggle hinged, finally, on the middle sec-

tors. Soaring inflation eroded their economic position. All of Allende's efforts to reassure and win over the middle class failed to overcome its traditional hostility toward socialism and its association with the bourgeoisie. This middle class provided the mass base for the coup that overthrew the Popular Unity.

Allende's opponents took advantage of the growing economic crisis in late 1972 to embark on a program of sabotage and direct action that included an employers' strike in October, a strike of truck drivers (subsidized by the CIA), which developed into a full-scale lockout by a majority of Chilean capitalists.

The strike ended when Allende made major concessions to his opponents, guaranteeing the security of small and medium-size industries. He also agreed to the inclusion of generals in his cabinet to insure law and order and to supervise the congressional election scheduled for March 1973. The opposition hoped to gain a sweeping victory in that election, a victory that would give it the two-thirds majority needed to impeach Allende and legally oust his government. Instead, the UP vote rose from 36 percent (in 1970) to 44 percent—proof that its socialist policies had substantially increased its support among the working class and peasantry. However, the opposition still commanded a majority in Congress and it redoubled efforts to create economic and political chaos by disruptive strikes, the organization of terrorist bands, and calls on the armed forces to intervene.

When Popular Unity came to power in 1970, the Chilean officer class was divided into two factions: a sizable conservative wing and a moderate wing sympathetic to reform of the kind advocated by the Christian Democrats. General René Schneider, commander in chief of the Chilean army, who was assassinated by reactionary military in 1970, and General Carlos Prats, who succeeded Schneider and held various cabinet posts in the Allende government, were among the moderates. Unquestionably, the Chilean military was greatly influenced by the United States military. Many Chilean officers had counterinsurgency

[1] The United States was deeply involved in Chilean politics. We know from the testimony of William Colby, the director of the Central Intelligence Agency (CIA), before a U.S. Senate subcommittee that the CIA spent $11 million between 1962 and 1970 to help prevent Allende from being elected president and that the CIA, with authorization from Secretary of State Henry Kissinger, spent $8 million between 1970 and 1973 to "destabilize" the Chilean economy.

training either in the United States or in the Panama Canal Zone. Throughout the Allende presidency, even after the United States had cut off all forms of economic aid to Chile and successfully exerted pressure on international banks to cut off loans, U.S. military aid continued. The United States even doubled its usual contribution in 1973. Chile and Venezuela were the principal beneficiaries of U.S. military aid in Latin America. The rigid anti-Communist stance of much of the military was bolstered significantly by material support from the United States, which enabled them to maintain their intransigent opposition to Allende.

By the spring of 1973, the balance of forces within the military had shifted in favor of the conservative wing, and preparations for a coup were well advanced. On June 29 a premature coup was put down by loyal troops under the direction of General Prats. Following the defeat of the coup, workers called for occupation of the factories and distribution of arms among them. Instead, Allende renewed his efforts to achieve a compromise with the Christian Democrats, relying on the armed forces to maintain law and order. The armed forces raided factories in search of illegal weapons, while making no effort to disarm the rightist paramilitary groups. Control of many localities effectively passed from the UP administration to the armed forces. In the face of the growing danger from the right-wing military, the government seemed paralyzed. In August, General Prats, under great pressure from his colleagues, resigned from the cabinet and as commander in chief; Allende, acceding to the requests of the generals, appointed General Augusto Pinochet as Prats's successor.

The coup began on September 10, 1973. The next morning, after Allende rejected a demand by the armed forces that he resign, the army and the air force attacked the presidential palace; Allende, who had promised not to leave the palace alive, committed suicide after broadcasting a final message to the Chilean people. Despite scattered resistance, the left was crushed within a week.

The Junta

After the coup, Chileans endured a brutal and large-scale repression. The four-man military junta headed by General Augusto Pinochet set about to "regenerate" Chilean society. To this end they abolished civil liberties, dissolved the national congress, banned union activities, prohibited strikes and collective bargaining, and erased the Allende administration's agrarian and economic reforms. The junta jailed, tortured, and put to death thousands of Chileans. The dreaded secret police, DINA (*Dirección de Inteligencia Nacional*)—with guidance from Colonel Walter Rauff, a former Nazi who supervised the extermination of Jews at Auschwitz—spread its network of terror throughout Chile and carried out assassinations abroad. The junta also set up at least six concentration camps. It is estimated that one of every one hundred Chileans has been arrested at least once since the coup.

The dictatorship outlawed or suspended left and center political parties and suspended dissident labor and peasant leaders and clergymen. Eduardo Frei and other Christian Democratic leaders initially supported the coup. Later, they assumed the role of a loyal opposition to the military rulers, but soon lost most of their influence. Meanwhile, left-wing Christian Democratic leaders like Radomiro Tomic were jailed or forced into exile. The church, which at first expressed its gratitude to the armed forces for saving the country from the danger of a "Marxist dictatorship," became increasingly critical of the regime's social and economic policies.

With Pinochet there came to power in Chile a group of economists known as the Chicago Boys because many of them had studied at the University of Chicago under Milton Friedman and espoused his free-market doctrines. The Chicago Boys made Chile a laboratory for the testing of Friedman's doctrines. Public spending was cut drastically, almost all state companies privatized, the peso devalued, and import duties sharply reduced. The social consequences of the "shock

In 1983, Chile's four great copper mines were placed under military control. In response, members of the Confederation of Copper Workers voted to strike, leaving the mine shown here at El Teniente and others, deserted. (Carlos Carrion/Sygma)

treatment" soon became apparent. Gross domestic product fell 16.6 percent in 1975. Manufacturing suffered particular injury, with some industries, like the textile industry, devastated by foreign imports. Wages had fallen by 1975 to 47.9 percent of their 1970 level. Unemployment stood at 20 percent, or 28 percent if the people working on government emergency programs were included.

A recovery partly based on export products—minerals, timber, and fish—but above all on a speculative spree of immense proportions began in 1977 and turned into a boom that lasted until 1980, with annual growth rates averaging 8 percent. The Chilean "economic miracle," however, was superficial and short-lived. Hoping to attract heavy foreign investment that would turn Chile into a South Korea or Taiwan, the Chicago Boys deliberately kept interest rates high. Foreign capital did pour in, but almost all of it was in the form of loans to Chilean banks, which made enormous profits from interests on loans to the private sector. Chilean banks borrowed abroad for 12 percent and loaned it out at 35 to 40 percent. The borrowing companies, belonging to a few huge conglomerates, did not invest in production, which the high interest rates made unprofitable but used the loans for speculation in real estate or to buy up at fire sale prices the state companies sold under the privatization program. The bubble began to burst in 1980. By the end of 1981 the government, in violation of its own free-market principles, was forced to step in to take over the nation's largest banks in order to forestall economic calamity. Bankruptcies multiplied. Production declined sharply. Between 1982 and 1986 unemployment rose to more than 30 percent and real wages fell by as much as 20 percent. An earthquake in 1985 added to the country's economic woes.

A recovery began in 1986 and turned into another boom that continues to the present, causing some observers to regard the Chilean economy as a showcase for free-market doctrines. But a closer look at Chile's "prosperity" reveals how precarious are its foundations and how inequitably its fruits are distributed. The economy is heavily dependent on foreign loans. With a population of 12.5 million, the foreign debt stands at $17 billion, in per capita terms one of the heaviest debt burdens in the world. In recent years the Pinochet regime has pursued a policy of swapping debt for ownership of Chilean industries and natural resources, with a resulting growth of foreign control of the economy. Moreover, the current boom, like the previous one, is heavily based on such export products as seafood, timber, fruit, and agricultural products. The unchecked exploitation of Chile's marine and forest resources has produced an ecological disaster.

Exports of fruit and agricultural products have sharply increased in the last five years. But the modernization and expansion of Chilean agriculture has benefited not the mass of the rural population, which lost most of the land and other gains made under the Allende land reform and suffered police repression and chronic unemployment, but the great landowners who control the production, commercialization, and export of agricultural products. Farm workers, prevented from forming labor unions and denied welfare benefits, work no more than three or four months at a time and often live in intolerable conditions.

Conditions are even worse in urban areas, with high levels of unemployment and underemployment among workers who live with their families in shantytowns in squalid, overcrowded conditions. Even the middle class has suffered a sharp decline in its standard of living. Between 1978 and 1988 the wealthiest 20 percent of the population increased their share of the national income from 51 to 60 percent. The next 60 percent, which includes Chile's large middle class, suffered a substantial drop in income, their share falling from 44 to 35 percent. And the poorest 20 percent continued to receive a meager 4 percent.

In January 1978, the military dictatorship held a plebiscite, which—unsurprisingly—overwhelmingly approved General Pinochet, who subsequently proclaimed that there would be no more elections for ten years. In September 1980, Chileans, again faced with little choice, endorsed a new constitution that would keep Pinochet in power at least until 1989 and perhaps 1997. The military was to choose a new president and to elect a legislature in 1989.

For much of the era of the dictatorship the opposition to Pinochet was fragmented. The left distrusted the Christian Democrats because they had cooperated with the military in 1973. The Christian Democrats remained wary of the left, which in their view had nearly destroyed the nation. Nonetheless, Pinochet's harsh repression and unsuccessful economic policies gave rise to mass opposition in 1983 and 1984. Labor and the middle class protested the worsening economic conditions. One poll taken in Santiago in 1985 indicated that only 15 percent of the population supported the government. The first indication that the opposition had begun to close old wounds was in 1983, when the Socialist party joined the Christian Democrats and other center parties to form the Democratic Alliance. Pinochet talked with the AD for a time. However, he de-

Mass opposition to the economic policies and repressive tactics of President Augusto Pinochet erupted in 1983 and 1984. In this picture, thousands of Chilean youths march through Santiago calling for democracy and jobs for unemployed copper workers. (José Manuel Donoso/Camera Press London/Globe Photos)

clared a state of siege in late 1984 that ended only in July 1985. In August 1985 a loose coalition of eleven parties signed an accord for "the transition to full democracy." Even the major rightist parties distanced themselves from Pinochet in 1985, leaving the general with little more than his military in support.

Pinochet's growing isolation reflected changes within Chile and the continent-wide movement away from authoritarian military rule. Even the United States, which had connived the 1973 military coup in Chile and steadfastly supported Pinochet, began to pressure the dictator to make a transition to democracy. The party favored by the United States to guide Chile in the coming democratic era was the moderate Christian Democratic party, led by Patricio Aylwin, who had supported the 1973 military coup but later had a change of heart.

Under growing pressure from the swelling democratic movement, sections of the military, and the United States, Pinochet made limited concessions to the demands for liberalization and amnesty for political prisoners and exiles, even as the repression sometimes intensified. Maneuvering to remain in power, Pinochet called a plebiscite for October 1988, in which Chileans would vote "yes" or "no" on a proposal to grant him eight more years as president. On the eve of the plebiscite, Pinochet permitted a large number of political exiles to return to Chile. On the day of the plebiscite, Chileans voted by a resounding 54.6 percent to 43 percent to deny Pinochet a new term as president. But the old dictator had fallback positions. By the terms of the undemocratic constitution imposed on the country in 1980, even if the "no" vote prevailed Pinochet was to remain in power for one more year and then call general elections. Whatever the outcome of those elections, he would then preside over a military council with broad powers, be able to appoint one-third of the new Senate, and become himself a senator for life.

The pro-democratic forces now began to prepare for the general elections for president and the national Congress to be held in December 1989. Eventually, despite their differences, left and center parties agreed on a single presidential candidate, Aylwin, whose principal opponent was Pinochet's finance minister, Hernan Buchi. Despite an electoral law designed to favor the regime and some efforts by security forces to intimidate the voters, the elections gave a clear majority to Aylwin and the congressional list of his Democratic Accord coalition, consisting of seventeen parties headed by the Christian Democratic and Socialist parties. The influential Communist party, although itself banned from running by the regime, had thrown its support to Aylwin.

The new president assumed office on March 11 1990 with a cabinet dominated by the Christian Democrats and Socialists. The first democratically elected government since 1970 faced enormous problems. One was the challenge posed by the continued existence of a military junta presided over by Pinochet, in effect creating a dual government. A confrontation between Aylwin and Pinochet ended with the latter's agreement to dissolve the junta, but he remained chief of the armed forces and solidly entrenched in other parts of the state apparatus, including the judiciary and the security forces.

Other problems involved the need to revise or scrap the regime's 1980 constitution, which made it a crime even to think Marxist thoughts, to obtain the release of the remaining political prisoners, to dissolve the security forces and put a final end to torture and other human rights abuses, and to bring to justice the officials who had committed such abuses. Here a major obstacle was the amnesty decreed by Pinochet for acts committed during the so-called internal war between 1973 and 1978, but that amnesty did not cover the many brutal murders committed after that date. The discovery in the first months of 1990 of secret cemeteries, generally located near armed forces bases, containing the remains of numerous victims who had frequently been tortured before being murdered, brought home to all Chileans the full horror of the regime under which they had suffered for seventeen years. One year later, the report of a "Commission of Truth and Reconciliation," released by President Aylwin, provided a partial record of the human rights violations committed under the Pinochet dictatorship between 1973 and the beginning of 1990. The report gave a figure of 2,279 known deaths and disappearances, assigned direct responsibility for these crimes to the armed forces, and charged the courts with negligence for failing to respond properly to such violations of human rights. In releasing the report, Aylwin promised material compensation to the families of the victims and a reform of the court system. Insisting that the amnesty issued by Pinochet in 1978 did not apply to offenses punishable under civil and criminal law, he ordered the supreme court to initiate action to bring to justice the individuals responsible for such crimes. The report provoked widespread demands for the resignation of Pinochet as commander in chief.

Not the least of the problems faced by the new democratic government was the need to change the economic and social policies of the old regime, which benefited foreign transnationals and their domestic allies at the expense of long-range national interests and the welfare of Chilean workers. It remained to be seen how swiftly or how far the conservative Aylwin, who had promised to make no major changes in the old regime's free-market policies, would move to change these conditions. He is already committed to changes in the labor law, and his minister of the economy, the Socialist Carlos Ominami Pascual, has stressed the need to repair the disastrous situation in health, education, and housing. In the present delicate situation, with Pinochet still in command of the armed forces and fear of a return to the dreadful past still gripping many Chileans, predictions concerning the speed of change are dangerous. But one can say with some degree of certainty that a clear majority of Chileans favor democratic political, economic, and social reform. The present world situation, marked by relaxation of tensions and rejection of authoritarianism, east and west, should contribute to the attainment of that objective.

Chapter 15

Republican Brazil

On the eve of World War I, Brazil's economic, political, and social structures showed growing strain and instability. Between 1910 and 1914, the Amazonian rubber boom began to fade as a result of competition from the new and more efficient plantations of the Far East. The approaching end of the rubber cycle revealed the vulnerability of Brazil's monocultural economy to external factors beyond its control and heightened its dependence on coffee. The coffee industry was itself plagued by recurrent crises of overproduction that required periodic resort to valorization—governmental intervention to maintain coffee prices by withholding stocks from the market or restricting plantings.

Violence was endemic over large areas of the country. In the backcountry, feudal coronéis with private armies recruited from dependents and jagunços maintained a patriarchal but frequently tyrannical rule over the peasantry. Over large areas of the country, the peasants lived in feudal bondage, obligated to give one or more days per week of free labor as homage to the landowners. Lacking written contracts, they could be evicted at any moment, and could find work elsewhere only on the same conditions. The interior was also the scene of mystical or messianic movements that sometimes assumed the character of peasant revolts. Banditry, especially widespread in the northeast, was another response to the tyranny of rural coronéis and the impotence of officials. A few *cangaceiros* (outlaws) took the part of the peasantry against their oppressors; most, however, served as mercenaries in the coronéis's private wars.

Violence was not confined to the countryside. Even in the growing cities, proud of their European culture and appearance, popular anger at the arbitrary rule of local oligarchies, or divisions within those oligarchies, sometimes flared up into civil war. Intervention by the federal government in these armed struggles on the side of its local allies greatly enlarged the scale of violence.

Decline and Fall of the Old Republic, 1914–1930

Economic Impact of World War I

The outbreak of World War I in August 1914 had a negative initial impact on Brazil. Exports of coffee, a nonessential product, declined, and in 1917 the government came to the rescue of the planters with a new valorization (price maintenance) program. However, the growing demand of the Allies for sugar, beans, and other staples had by 1915 sparked a revival that turned into a boom. Brazil's expanding trade with the Allies exposed its shipping to German reprisals, and in October 1917, after German submarines had torpedoed a number of Brazilian merchant ships, Brazil declared war on Germany. Brazil's major contribution to the Allied war effort continued to be the supply of goods, but its navy assisted an English squadron in patrolling south Atlantic waters.

The war accelerated some changes under way in Brazilian economic life. It weakened British capitalism and therefore strengthened the North American challenge to British financial and commercial pre-eminence in Brazil. The virtual cessation of imports of manufactured goods also gave a strong stimulus to Brazilian industrialization. Profits derived from coffee, an industry protected by the state, provided a large part of the resources needed for industrialization. Favored by its wealth, large immigrant population, and rich natural resources, the state of São Paulo led the movement, replacing Rio de Janeiro as the foremost industrial region. Brazil doubled its industrial production during the war, and the number of enterprises (which stood at about 3,000 in 1908) grew by 5,940 between 1915 and 1918. But these increases were concentrated in light industry, especially food processing and textiles, and most of the new enterprises were small shops.

The advance of industry and urbanization enlarged and strengthened both the industrial bourgeoisie and the working class. In response to wartime inflation that eroded the value of workers' wages, the trade union movement grew, and strikes became more frequent. In 1917 a general strike—the first in Brazilian history—gripped the city and state of São Paulo. The strikers' demands included a wage increase of 30 percent, the eight-hour workday, improved working conditions, and the release of political prisoners. The strike brought the city of São Paulo to a standstill. The federal government sent troops to crush the strike but recalled them when the soldiers refused to fire on the workers. Although the strike wave of the years 1917–1920 forced many employers to grant higher wages, the living conditions of most workers did not permanently improve. The labor movement, composed largely of foreign-born workers, remained small and weak, without ties with the peasantry, who formed the overwhelming majority of the Brazilian people.

Postwar Industry and Labor

Industrialization and urbanization weakened the foundations of the neocolonial order, which was based on the primacy of agriculture and dependence on foreign markets and loans, but it emerged from the war essentially intact, although its stabilization proved temporary and precarious. A chronically adverse balance of trade and a declining rate of exchange against foreign currencies gave Brazilian industry a competitive advantage in goods of popular consumption. It continued to grow, but it had little support from a central government dominated by the coffee interests. Bitter debates between the friends and foes of tariff protection for industry marked the political life of the 1920s.

As that decade opened, Brazil remained an overwhelmingly rural country. A few export products—coffee, sugar, cotton—dominated Brazilian agriculture; food production was so neglected that the country had to import four-fifths of its grain needs. There was an extreme concentration of landownership: 461 great landowners held more than 27 million hectares of land, while 464,000 small and medium-sized farms occupied only 15.7 million hectares. Archaic techniques prevailed in agriculture: the hoe was still the principal farming instrument, and the wasteful slash-and-burn method the favored way of clearing the land. Even relatively progressive coffee planters gave little attention to the care of the soil, selection of varieties, and other improvements. As a result, the productivity of plantations rapidly declined, even in regions of superior soil.

In the cities, most workers toiled and lived under conditions that recalled those of the early Industrial Revolution in Europe. In 1920 the average industrial worker in São Paulo earned about 4 milréis (60 cents) a day; for this wage he or she worked ten to twelve hours, six days a week. A system of fines for "imperfect" work further reduced this miserable wage, and the need for advances kept many workers in perpetual debt to employers. About one-third of the work force was female, and child labor was widespread, with half of all workers under eighteen. Women and children were paid less than men for the same tasks. Rural laborers were somewhat worse off: in the 1920s, workers in the sugar plantations of Pernambuco toiled from dawn to dusk for 2½ to 4½ milréis a day.

Malnutrition, parasitic diseases, and lack of medical facilities limited Brazilians' average life span in 1920 to twenty-eight years. In the same year, more than 64 percent of the population over the age of fifteen was illiterate. Since literacy was a requirement for voting, the general lack of schools kept the people not only ignorant but politically powerless. The peasantry, vegetating in poverty and ignorance, could not initiate a struggle to transform Brazilian society.

Political Unrest

The task of transforming society fell to the rapidly growing urban bourgeois groups, and especially to the middle class, which began to voice ever more strongly its discontent with the rule of corrupt rural oligarchies. In the early 1920s, there arose a many-faceted movement for the renovation of Brazilian society and culture. Intellectuals, artists, junior military officers, professional men, and a small minority of radical workers participated in this movement. But they had no common program and did not comprehend the convergence of their aims and work.

Three seemingly unrelated events of 1922 illustrate the diverse forms that the ferment of the times assumed. First, in February of that year, the intellectuals of São Paulo organized a Modern Art Week to commemorate the centenary of Brazilian independence. The young poets, painters, and composers who presented their works there laid a common stress on independence from old forms and content, on the need to develop an indigenous Brazilian culture. Then, in March, after the appearance of Marxist groups in a number of cities, the Brazilian Communist party was founded at a congress in Rio de Janeiro and began a struggle against the anarcho-syndicalist doctrines that still dominated much of the small labor movement. Last, in July, *tenentes* (junior officers) at the Copacabana garrison in Rio de Janeiro rose to prevent the seating of Artur da Silva Bernardes, who had been elected president according to the agreement between the two dominant states of São Paulo and Minas Gerais. The rebel program denounced the rule of the coffee oligarchy, political corruption, and electoral fraud. Government forces easily crushed the revolt, but it left a legend when a handful of insurgents refused to surrender and fought to the death against overwhelming odds.

The officers' revolt signaled the beginning of a struggle by the Brazilian bourgeoisie to seize power from the rural oligarchy. Given the closed political system, it inevitably assumed the character of an armed struggle; that is why its spearhead was the nationalist young officer group, mostly of middle-class origins, which called for democratic elections, equal justice, and similar political reforms.

President Bernardes (1922–1926) took office amid growing economic and political turmoil. As a result of a massive increase in coffee plantings between 1918 and 1924, the industry again suffered from overproduction and falling prices. Bernardes added to his unpopularity by an armed intervention in the state of Rio de Janeiro, the political base of Nilo Peçanha, his opponent in the 1922 election; by his insistence on trying and punishing the young officers who had rebelled against him; and by his severe repression of strikers and leftists.

In 1924 another military revolt, headed by retired General Isidro Dias Lopes, broke out in São Paulo. It was again organized by junior officers whose program called for the restoration of constitutional liberties and curbs on the executive power but made no reference to economic and social reform. The large working class of São Paulo was sympathetic to the revolt, but its conservative leaders rejected the workers' request for arms.

The rebels held the city for twenty-two days before evacuating it under pressure from greatly superior numbers of government troops. Meanwhile, the revolt had spread to other states. Another group of rebels in Rio Grande do Sul, led by Captain Luís Carlos Prestes, moved north to join the insurgents from São Paulo, and their combined forces, known in history as the Prestes column, began a prodigious march through the interior. The tenentes hoped to enlist the peasantry in their struggle against Bernardes. But they knew little of the peasants' problems and offered no program of agrarian reform. The peasants, for their part, had no interest in fighting the "tyrant" Bernardes in distant Rio de Janeiro. Beating off or eluding attacks by government forces and bands of cangaceiros in the government's employ, the Prestes column covered fourteen thousand miles before reaching Bolivia, where the rebels dispersed.

The long march had much educational value for the officers who took part in it. For the first time in their lives, many of these young men came face to face with the reality of rural Brazil and began to reflect on its problems. As a result, the tenente reform program acquired an economic and social content. It began to speak of the need for economic development and social legislation, including agrarian reform as well as minimum wages and maximum working hours.

Bernardes had survived a second military crisis, but he continued to be plagued by economic problems, with the coffee problem paramount. Bernardes applied the now orthodox remedy of valorization, but gave it a decentralized form. The central government turned over the supervision of the scheme to the individual coffee-producing states. The state of São Paulo established an agency, the Coffee Institute, which undertook to control the export trade in coffee by regulating market offerings to maintain a balance between supply and demand. This was done by withdrawing unlimited stocks of coffee, storing them in warehouses, and releasing them according to the needs of the export trade. The plan required financing the producers whose coffee was withheld from the market. The program appeared to work, for prices rose and remained stable until 1929. But the burdens of valorization steadily grew, for high prices stimulated production, requiring new withdrawals and new loans to finance the unsold output. To make matters worse, Brazil's competitors—especially Colombia—were attracted by the high prices and expanded their own output.

Economic Crisis

In 1926, Bernardes turned over the presidency to the Paulista Washington Luís Sousa de Pereira (1926–1930). He had been elected, without opposition, according to the agreement that usually rotated the presidency between São Paulo and Minas Gerais. During his administration, a series of new loans was made to support the valorization program. As a result, Brazil's foreign debt had risen to $1,181 million by 1930, and debt service in that year amounted to $200 million—one-third of the national budget. By 1930, U.S. investment in Brazil had reached a figure of $400 million, considerably larger than the British total, and the United States had supplanted England as Brazil's chief trading partner.

Brazil's heavy dependence on foreign markets and loans made it extremely vulnerable to the crisis that shook the capitalist world after the New York stock market collapsed in October 1929. Coffee quotations at once fell 30 percent, and the subsequent decline was even sharper; between 1929 and 1931, coffee prices fell from 22.5 to 8 cents a pound, and immense stocks of coffee piled up in the warehouses. By the end of 1930, Brazil's gold reserves had disappeared, and the exchange rate plummeted to a new low. As foreign credit dried up, it became impossible to continue the financing of withheld coffee, and the valorization program collapsed, leaving behind a mountain of debt.

The presidential campaign and election of 1930 took place against a background of economic crisis whose principal burdens—unemployment, wage cuts, and inflation—fell chiefly on the working classes. But the crisis sharpened all class and regional antagonisms, especially the conflict between the coffee oligarchy and the urban bourgeois groups, who regarded the depression as proof of the bankruptcy of the old order. A rift even appeared within the coffee oligarchy, and the traditional alliance of São Paulo and Minas Gerais fell apart as a result of the selection by Washington Luís of another Paulista, Júlio Prestes, governor of São Paulo, as his successor. Angered by this violation of the agreement to rotate the presidency between the two states, many politicians from Minas Gerais joined the opposition to the official candidate.

As a result of these alignments and realignments, two coalitions took shape and confronted each other in the election of 1930. One united the coffee planters of São Paulo, their rural allies in other areas, and the commercial bourgeoisie engaged in the export-import trade. The other coalition, called the Liberal Alliance, joined the bulk of the urban groups, groups of great landowners—like the ranchers of Rio Grande do Sul, who resented São Paulo's dominant position—and disaffected politicians from Minas Gerais and other states. The conservative coalition nominated the Paulista Júlio Prestes for president; the Liberal Alliance named Getúlio Vargas, a wealthy rancher and politician from Rio Grande do Sul, as its candidate.

The working class was not a participant in the Liberal Alliance, but many workers sympathized with its program. The most ardent supporters of Vargas were the veterans of the revolt of 1924, but their former leader, Luís Carlos Prestes, an exile in Buenos Aires, would not endorse Vargas or his program. Prestes, now a Marxist, issued a manifesto in May 1930 in which he proclaimed that the chief task before the Brazilian people was to struggle against the latifundio and Anglo-American imperialism. A few years later, he would join the Communist party and become its leader.

During the campaign, both candidates made vague promises and statements, but Júlio Prestes clearly represented the latifundist and neocolonial interests. Vargas, although careful not to give offense to his latifundist supporters, spoke of the need to develop industry, including heavy industry, advocated high tariffs to protect Brazilian industry using local raw materials, and called on Brazilians to "perfect our manufactures to the point where it will become unpatriotic to feed or clothe ourselves with imported goods." Reflecting the influence of the tenentes, he advanced a program of social welfare legislation and political, judicial, and educational reform. He even made a cautious pledge of "action with a view to the progressive extinction of the latifundio, without violence, and support for the organization of small landed property through the transfer of small parcels of land to agricultural laborers."

In any event, Prestes defeated Vargas in the election of March 1930 by a supposed margin of some three hundred thousand votes. Since both sides cheated on a large scale, the outcome merely proved that the government and its rural allies had control of the electoral machinery in decisive areas. In May, Congress, which was dominated by the administration, refused to seat opposition deputies from Minas Gerais and Paraíba. Political tension ran high and reached the explosive point in July with the murder of Vargas's running mate, João Pessoa, a deed regarded by the opposition as a political assassination.

Vargas's lieutenants now convinced him of the need to overthrow the Washington Luís government. The uprising began simultaneously in Rio Grande do Sul, Minas Gerais, and Paraíba on October 3. Perceiving that the collapse of the discredited regime was probably inevitable, senior army officers deposed Washington Luís on October 24, forming a ruling junta, and ordered the army to lay down its arms; one week later, they turned their power over to Getúlio Vargas as head of the provisional government. The Old Republic, born in 1889 and dominated since 1894 by the coffee oligarchy, was dead. A new era had begun that may with fair accuracy be called the era of the bourgeois revolution. The political career of its chieftain, Getúlio Vargas, faithfully mirrored its advances, retreats, and ultimate defeat.

Vargas and the Bourgeois Revolution, 1930–1954

The liberal revolution of 1930 represented a victory for the urban bourgeois groups who favored industrialization and the modernization of Brazil's economic, political, and social structures. But the bourgeoisie had gained that victory with the aid of allies whose interests had to be taken into account. Getúlio Vargas presided over a heterogeneous coalition that included conservative fazendeiros—who had joined the revolution from jealousy of the overweening Paulista power but feared radical social change—and intellectuals and tenentes who called for agrarian reform, the formation of cooperatives, and the nationalization of mines. On the sidelines was the working class, vital to the development of Brazilian capitalism but a potential threat to its very existence. Finally, Vargas had to take account of foreign capital interests, temporarily weakened but capable of applying great pressure on the Brazilian economy when the capitalist world emerged from the depths of the Great Depression. Vargas's strategy of attempting to balance and reconcile these conflicting interests helps to explain the contradictions and abrupt shifts of course that marked his career.

Vargas's Economic and Political Measures

The most pressing problem facing the new government was to find some way out of the economic crisis. Vargas did not abandon the coffee industry, the base of his political enemies, to its fate; he attempted to revive it by such classic valorization measures as the restriction of plantings and the purchase of surplus stocks and the more drastic expedient of burning the excess coffee, but the level of coffee exports and prices remained low throughout the 1930s. The government had more success with efforts to diversify agriculture. Production of cotton, in particular, grew with the aid of capital and labor released by the depressed coffee industry, and cotton exports rose steadily until 1940, when the outbreak of war interrupted their advance. But diversification of agriculture could not compensate for the steep decline in Brazil's import capacity. The key to recovery was found in import substitution through industrialization.

The Great Depression did not create Brazilian industrialization, but it created the conditions for a new advance. Beginning as a spontaneous response to the loss of import capacity that resulted from the catastrophic decline of exports and a falling rate of exchange, industrialization received a fresh impetus from Vargas, who encouraged industry through exchange controls, import quotas, tax incentives, lowered duties on imported machinery and raw materials, and long-term loans at low interest rates. Thanks to

During a long and complex political career, Getúlio Vargas struggled to create an autonomous Brazilian capitalist state. Here President Vargas is shown watching a military parade on the 116th anniversary of Brazilian independence. (Wide World Photos)

the combination of favorable background conditions and the Vargas policy of state intervention, Brazilian industrialization, based entirely on production for the home market, made notable strides in a few years: industrial production doubled between 1931 and 1936. As early as 1933, when the United States was still in a deep depression, Brazil's national income had begun to increase, which indicated that for the moment, at least, the economy no longer depended on external factors but on internal ones.

Meanwhile, Vargas pursued an uncertain political course that now appeared to favor the left wing of the revolutionary coalition, the tenentes, and now its conservative fazendeiro wing. The tenentes appeared to have considerable influence over Vargas during the first two years of the provisional government; he used them as his po-

litical lieutenants in various capacities, especially as interventors, or temporary administrators, in the states, replacing unreliable elected governors. Believing that a strong centralized government was needed to carry out the necessary structural reforms and fearing that premature elections would enable the oligarchies to frustrate those reforms, the tenentes urged Vargas to remain in power indefinitely.

The Paulistas demanded the removal of João Alberto, and asked for a return to constitutional government through immediate elections, preferably under the old federal constitution of 1891, which would most likely enable them to regain power in their own state. Vargas sought to appease the Paulistas with concessions: he replaced João Alberto with a civilian from São Paulo, appointed a conservative banker from the same state as his first minister of finance, and announced a date for the holding of a constituent assembly.

Emboldened rather than appeased, the Paulistas launched a counterrevolutionary "constitutionalist revolt" in July 1932. Lacking popular support either in São Paulo or in other parts of the country, it collapsed after three months of halfhearted combat. But Vargas neither punished nor humiliated the vanquished rebels. Determined to maintain and strengthen his ties with the São Paulo establishment, he made new concessions to it: he pardoned 50 percent of the bank debts of the coffee planters and ordered the Bank of Brazil to take over the war bonds issued by the rebel government. After mid-1932 the influence of the tenente group over Vargas rapidly waned, although individual tenentes of moderate tendency continued to hold important positions in the regime.

In February 1932, Vargas had promulgated an electoral code that established the secret ballot, lowered the voting age from twenty-one to eighteen, and extended the vote to working women, but the code still denied the vote to illiterates, who formed the majority of the adult population. A constituent assembly elected under this code drafted a new constitution, which was promulgated on July 16, 1934. This document retained the federal system but considerably strengthened the powers of the executive. The assembly, constituting itself the first Chamber of Deputies, elected Vargas president for a term extending to January 1938.

The section of the constitution on the "economic and social order" stressed the government's responsibility for economic development. Article 119 declared that "the law will regulate the progressive nationalization of mines, mineral deposits, and waterfalls or other sources of energy, as well as of the industries considered as basic or essential to the economic and military defense of the country."

The section on the rights and duties of labor revealed the importance Vargas attached to the imposition of a tutelage over the working class, a class to be courted through concessions but denied independence of action. The constitution of 1934 established a labor tribunal system, gave the government power to fix minimum wages, and guaranteed the right to strike. Subsequent decrees set the working day at eight hours in commerce and industry, fixed minimum wages throughout the country, and created an elaborate social security system that provided for pensions, paid vacations, safety and health standards, and employment security.

In exchange for these gains, obtained without struggle, the working class lost its freedom of action. The trade unions, formerly subject to harsh repression, but militant and jealous of their autonomy, became official agencies controlled by the Ministry of Labor. The workers had no voice in the drafting of labor legislation. Police and security agencies brutally repressed strikes not approved by the government.

The labor and social legislation, moreover, was unevenly enforced, and employers frequently took advantage of their employees' ignorance of the law. The legislation did not apply at all to the great majority of agricultural workers, who comprised some 85 percent of the labor force. Determined to maintain his alliance with the fazendeiro wing of his coalition, Vargas left intact the system of patrimonial servitude that governed labor relations in the countryside, just as he left intact the latifundio. The promises of agrarian reform made during the campaign of 1930 were forgotten.

Vargas's concessions to the Paulista oligarchy and the ouster of reformist tenentes from positions of power formed part of a rightward shift that grew more pronounced in 1934. This growing conservatism lost Vargas support among liberal tenentes, intellectuals, and radical workers and drew especially sharp criticism from the Communist party. Founded in 1922, the party gained growing influence after 1930 as a result of its anti-imperialist policies and the prestige of its most famous recruit, Luís Carlos Prestes. Prestes had refused to take advantage of the amnesty for political exiles proclaimed after the revolution but returned in 1934 to join the Communist party and become honorary president of the *Aliança*

Nacional Libertadora (National Liberation Alliance, or ANL), a popular front movement that attracted middle-class as well as working-class support with its slogans of liquidation of the latifundio, nationalization of large foreign companies, and cancellation of imperialist debts. The ANL was also sharply critical of the inadequacies of Vargas's labor and social legislation. Meanwhile, on the right there had arisen a fascist movement (*Integralismo,* or Integralism), complete with the trappings of its European models, including colored shirts (green), special salutes, and an ideology that denounced democrats, Communists, Masons, and Jews as "enemies of the state."

While tolerant of the Integralist movement, Vargas and an increasingly conservative Congress harassed the leftist opposition as "subversive." In March 1935, Congress enacted a National Security Act, which gave the government special powers to suppress "subversive" activities. It was clearly directed at the left. In July Prestes made a speech in which he attacked Vargas's failure to implement the tenente ideals and called for the creation of a truly "revolutionary and anti-imperialist government." Vargas responded by banning the ANL and ordering the arrest of many leftist leaders.

With the legal avenues of opposition for the left disappearing, the ANL and one wing of the Communist party began an armed uprising in November. Despite some initial successes, it was quickly crushed by government forces and followed by a savage repression. There were fifteen thousand arrests, and prisoners were tortured, some to death. Prestes and other leaders of the revolt were captured, tried, and sentenced to many years in prison. The Communist party was banned and went underground for a decade.

Vargas as Dictator

The repression of the left paved the way for the establishment of Vargas's personal dictatorship. A presidential election was scheduled for January 1938, but under the new constitution Vargas was barred from succeeding himself. He allowed candidates to emerge and campaign but carefully prepared for the coming coup by strategic "interventions" in the states and transfers in the army that filled key posts with reliable commanders.

On September 29, 1937, armed with the Cohen Plan, a crude forgery concocted by the Integralists that set out a detailed plan for a Communist revolution, War Minister General Eurico Dutra went on the radio and demanded the imposition of a state of siege. He had set the stage for the scrapping of what remained of constitutional processes. On November 10, Vargas made a broadcast in which he canceled the presidential elections, dissolved Congress as an "inadequate and costly apparatus," and assumed dictatorial power under a new constitution patterned on European fascist models. On December 2, all political parties were abolished.

The new regime, baptized the *Estado Novo* (New State), copied not only the constitutional forms of the fascist regimes but their repressive tactics. Strict press censorship was established, and prisons filled with workers, teachers, military officers, and others suspected of subversion. The apparatus of repression included a special police force for hunting down dissidents; its methods included torture. Yet there was little organized resistance to the regime. Labor, its most likely opponent, was neutralized by a paternalist social legislation and doped by populist rhetoric, and it remained passive or even supported Vargas.

The affinity between the Estado Novo and the European police states suggested to some observers that it was merely a Brazilian variant of the Continental fascist model. Brazil's growing trade and increasingly friendly relations with Germany and Italy also led to fears that the country was moving into the fascist orbit. Between 1933 and 1938, Germany became the chief market for Brazilian cotton and the second largest buyer of its coffee and cacao. German penetration of the Brazilian economy also increased, and the German Bank for South America established three hundred branches in Brazil.

But Brazil's economic rapprochement with Germany and Italy did not reflect sympathy with the expansionist goals of the fascist bloc; Vargas, the great realist, sought only to open up new markets for Brazil and to strengthen his hand in bargaining with the United States. Despite its authoritarian, repressive aspects, the Estado Novo continued the struggle against neocolonialism and the effort to achieve economic independence and modernization.

Indeed, under the new regime the state intervened more actively than before to encourage the growth of industry and provide it with the necessary economic infrastructure. Rejecting laissez faire, the Estado Novo pursued a policy of planning and direct investment for the creation of important industrial complexes in the basic sectors of mining, oil, steel, electric power, and chemicals. In 1940 the government announced a Five-Year Plan whose goals included the expansion of heavy industry, the creation of new sources of hydroelectric power, and the expansion of the railway network. In 1942 the government established the *Companhia Vale do Rio Doce* to exploit the rich iron-ore deposits of Itabira; in 1944 it created a company for the production of materials needed by the chemical industry; and in 1946 the National Motor Company began the production of trucks. In the same year, Vargas saw the realization of one of his cherished dreams: the National Steel Company began production at the Volta Redonda plant between Rio de Janeiro and São Paulo. Aware of the need of modern industry for abundant sources of power, Vargas created the National Petroleum Company in 1938 to press the search for oil.

By 1941, Brazil had 44,100 plants employing 944,000 workers; the comparable figure for 1920 was 13,336 plants with about 300,000 workers. Aside from some export of textiles, the manufacturing industries served the domestic market almost exclusively. State and mixed public-private companies dominated the heavy and infrastructural industries and private Brazilian capital predominated in manufacturing, but the 1930s also saw a significant growth of direct foreign investment as foreign corporations sought to enlarge their share of the internal market and overcome tariff barriers and exchange problems by establishing branch plants in Brazil. By 1940 foreign capital represented 44 percent of the total investment in Brazilian stock companies. Vargas made no effort to check the influx of foreign capital, perhaps because he believed that the growth of Brazilian state and private capitalism would keep the foreign sector in a subordinate status.

The Estado Novo banned strikes and lockouts but retained and even expanded the body of protective social and labor legislation. In 1942 the labor laws were consolidated into a labor code, regarded as one of the most advanced in the world. But it was unevenly enforced and brought no benefits to the great mass of agricultural workers. Moreover, spiraling inflation created a growing gap between wages and prices; prices rose 86 percent between 1940 and 1944, whereas between 1929 and 1939, they had risen only 31 percent. In effect, inflation, by transferring income from wages to capitalists, provided much of the financing for the rapid economic growth of the 1940s.

World War II accelerated that growth through the new stimulus it gave to industrialization. Brazil exported vast quantities of foodstuffs and raw materials, but the industrialized countries, whose economies were geared to war, could not pay for their purchases with machinery or consumer goods. As a result, Brazil built up large foreign exchange reserves, amounting to $707 million in 1945. Most of the economic advance of the war years was due to expansion and more intensive exploitation of existing plants or to the technical contributions of Brazilian engineers and scientists.

However, Vargas adroitly exploited Great Power rivalries to secure financial and technical assistance from the United States for the construction of the huge state-owned integrated iron and steel plant at Volta Redonda. U.S. companies and government agencies were notably cool to requests for aid for establishing heavy industry in Latin America. But Vargas's hints that he might have to turn for help to Germany removed all obstacles. Volta Redonda was a great victory for the Vargas policies of economic nationalism and state intervention in economic life. In return for its assistance, Vargas allowed the United States to lease air bases in northern Brazil even before it entered the war against the Axis. In August 1942, after German submarines had sunk a number of Brazilian merchantmen, Brazil declared war on Germany and Italy.

The paradox of Brazil's participation in an antifascist war under an authoritarian regime was not lost on Brazilians; the demands for an end to the Estado Novo grew stronger as the defeat of the Axis drew near. Ever sensitive to changes in the political climate and the balance of forces, Vargas responded by promising a new postwar era of liberty. In January 1945, he announced an amnesty for political prisoners, promulgated a law allowing political parties to function openly, and set December 2 as the date for presidential and congressional elections.

A number of new parties were formed to fight the coming elections, two by Vargas himself. They were the *Partido Social Democrático* (Social Democratic Party, or PSD) and the *Partido Trabalhista Brasileiro* (Brazilian Labor Party, or PTB). The PSD, the largest of the new parties, united pro-Vargas industrialists and rural machines, above all. The PTB had its base in the government-controlled trade unions and appealed to workers with a populist rhetoric proclaiming Vargas the "Father of the Poor." The *União Democrática Nacional* (National Democratic Party, or UDN) was the most conservative and chiefly represented neocolonial agrarian and commercial interests; it was strongly pro–North American. Of the other national parties, the most important was the Communist party, led by Prestes, which emerged from the underground with considerable prestige and strength.

A Military Coup

Vargas announced that he would not run for president but set the stage for a well-organized campaign by his supporters, called *queremistas,* (from the Portuguese verb *querer,* "to want"), who wanted Vargas to declare himself a candidate in the forthcoming election. Soon after issuing the decrees restoring political freedom,

Vargas moved to the left in economic policy. In June he authorized the expropriation of any organization whose practices were harmful to the national interest.

The authorization decree, which was aimed at keeping down the cost of living, inspired alarm in conservative foreign and domestic circles. Senior military officers regarded Vargas's political maneuvers and leftward move with growing uneasiness. The wartime alliance with the United States had accentuated their inherent conservatism and made them ready to accept the gospel of free enterprise and American leadership in the cold war against the Soviet Union and world communism.

On October 29, 1945, Generals Goes Monteiro and Eurico Dutra staged a coup, forced Vargas to resign, and entrusted the government until after the election to José Linhares, chief justice of the Supreme Court. The new government promptly indicated its tendency by repealing Vargas's antitrust decree and launching a suppression of the Communist party. Ostensibly, the military had acted to defend democracy by preventing Vargas from seizing power as he had done in 1937. But its democratic credentials were more than dubious; Goes Monteiro and Dutra were, after Vargas, the chief architects of Estado Novo and had supported Vargas's most repressive measures.

The military coup insured that Brazil would return to the parliamentary system under conservative auspices, with two generals as the major presidential candidates, Eurico Dutra for the PSD and Eduardo Gomes for the UDN. Dutra won, while Vargas had the satisfaction of winning election as senator from two states and congressman from six states and the Federal District. The newly elected Congress, sitting as a constituent assembly, framed a new constitution that retained both the federal system and the powerful executive created by Vargas and guaranteed civil liberties and free elections, but it still denied the vote to illiterates and enlisted men in the armed forces—more than half the adult population.

Under the mediocre, colorless President Eurico Dutra (1946–1951), neocolonial interests regained much of the influence they had lost under Vargas. In his foreign and domestic policies, Dutra displayed a blind loyalty to the anticommunist creed propounded by Washington. Alarmed by the growing electoral strength of the Communist party, Dutra outlawed the party, and Congress followed by expelling the party's elected representatives. Dutra exploited the resulting witch hunt to smash the independent, left-led labor movement; the Workers' Federation, organized in 1946, was declared illegal, and the government intervened in a large number of unions to eliminate "extremist elements." The imposition of a wage freeze and the failure to raise the officially decreed minimum wage caused the real income of workers to drop sharply.

With respect to economic development, Dutra pursued a laissez-faire policy that meant the virtual abandonment of the Vargas strategy of a state-directed movement toward economic independence. Dutra removed all import and exchange controls and allowed the large foreign exchange reserves accumulated during the war—reserves that Vargas had proposed to use for re-equipping Brazilian industry—to be dissipated on imported consumer goods, luxury goods in large part.

Attracted by the new economic climate, foreign capital flowed into Brazil. Meanwhile, seeking to curb inflation according to the prescription of American advisers, the government pursued a restrictive credit policy harmful to Brazilian entrepreneurs and industrial growth.

Vargas's Return to Power

In 1950, having assured himself of the neutrality of the armed forces, Vargas ran for president with the support of the PTB and a broad coalition of workers, industrialists, and members of the urban middle class. His campaign concentrated on the need to accelerate industrialization and expand and strengthen social welfare legislation. Riding a wave of discontent with the economic and social policies of the Dutra regime, Vargas easily defeated his two opponents.

Vargas inherited a difficult economic situation. After a brief boom in coffee exports and prices in 1949–1951, the balance of trade again turned unfavorable, and the inflation rate increased. In the absence of other major sources of financing for his developmental program, Vargas had to rely largely on a massive increase in the money supply, with all its inevitable social consequences. Meanwhile, his national program of state-directed industrialization, using state corporations as its major instrument, encountered increasing hostility from neocolonial interests at home and abroad. In the United States, the Eisenhower administration decided that the Vargas government had not created the proper climate for private investment and terminated the Joint United States–Brazilian Economic Commission. Within Brazil, Vargas's program faced sabotage at the hands of the rural forces that continued to dominate the majority of state governments and Congress. This hardening of attitudes signified that Vargas's options and his capacity for maneuvering between different social groups were greatly reduced.

In December 1951, Vargas asked Congress to approve a bill creating a mixed public-private petroleum corporation to be called *Petrobrás,* which would give the state a monopoly on the drilling of oil and new refineries. Petrobrás illustrated Vargas's belief that the state must own the commanding heights of the economy and represented an attempt to reduce the balance of payments deficit by substituting domestic sources of oil for imported oil. Vargas sought to appease domestic and foreign opponents by leaving the distribution of oil in private hands and allowing existing refineries to remain privately owned. Almost two years passed before Congress, under great popular pressure, passed the law creating Petrobrás in October 1953. However, Vargas's proposal to create a similar agency for electric power—to be called *Electrobrás*—remained bottled up in Congress.

Vargas's labor policy became another political battleground. Under Vargas, labor regained much of the freedom of action that it had lost during the Dutra years. In December 1951, the government decreed a new minimum wage that only compensated for the most recent price rises. In 1953, three hundred thousand workers went on strike for higher wages and other benefits. In June of that year, Vargas appointed a young protégé, João Goulart, minister of labor. Goulart, a populist in the Vargas tradition, was sympathetic with labor's demands. In January 1954, Goulart recommended a doubling of the minimum wage. This recommendation evoked a violent "manifesto of the colonels," in which a group of officers charged that the government was penetrated by communism and corruption, that the armed forces were being neglected, and that the recommended new minimum wage would demoralize the badly underpaid officer class. Under military pressure, Vargas dismissed Goulart, but in a May Day speech to workers he announced that the increased minimum wage would be enacted and praised the fallen minister of labor.

The battle lines between Vargas and his foes were being drawn ever more sharply. In speeches to Congress, Vargas attacked foreign investors for aggravating Brazil's balance of payments problem by their massive remittances of profits and claimed that invoicing frauds had cost Brazil at least $250 million over an eighteen-month period. Meanwhile, attacks on him by the conservative-dominated press and radio grew even more bitter; especially vituperative were the editorials of Carlos Lacerda, editor of the ultraconservative *Tribuna da Imprensa.*

An effort to silence Lacerda presented Vargas's enemies with a golden opportunity to destroy him. Unknown to Vargas, the chief of the president's personal guard arranged for a gunman to assassinate Lacerda. The plot miscarried, for Lacerda was only slightly wounded, but one of his bodyguards, an air force major, was killed. The resulting investigation revealed the complicity of palace officials and uncovered the existence of large-scale corruption in the presidential staff. The chorus of demands for Vargas's resignation was joined by the military, which informed him on August 24 that he must resign or

be deposed. Isolated, betrayed by the men he had trusted, the seventy-two-year-old Vargas found the way out of his dilemma by suicide. But he left a message that was also his political testament. It ended with the words:

I fought against the looting of Brazil. I fought against the looting of the people. I have fought bare-breasted. Hatred, infamy, and calumny did not beat down my spirit. I gave you my life. Now I offer my death. Nothing remains. Serenely I take the first step on the road to eternity and I leave life to enter history.

Reform and Reaction, 1954–1964

The death of Vargas foreshadowed the demise of the nationalist, populist model of independent capitalist development over which he had presided for the better part of a quarter-century. That model, based on a strategy of maneuver and compromise, of reconciling the clashing interests of the national bourgeoisie, fazendeiros, foreign capitalists, and the working class, of avoiding such structural changes as agrarian reform, had about exhausted its possibilities.

Two options remained. One was for Vargas's political heirs to mobilize the working class and the peasantry for the realization of a program of structural changes, including agrarian reform, that could impart a new dynamic to Brazilian national capitalism. The alternative was for Vargas's political enemies to impose a streamlined neocolonial model based on the denationalization and modernization of Brazilian industry, on its transformation into an extension of the industrial park of the great capitalist powers, accompanied by a shift in emphasis from the export of raw materials to the export of manufactured goods. Since such a course entailed immense sacrifices for the Brazilian people, it also required the imposition of a dictatorship of the most repressive kind. The balance of forces in

1954 already favored the second option. For a decade, however, Brazil would sway uncertainly between the two alternatives.

The right-wing military and civilian conspirators who spearheaded the movement for Vargas's removal had hoped to use it as a springboard for the establishment of a right-wing dictatorship. But the massive outpouring of grief and protest caused by Vargas's death and suicide message frustrated their plans. Vice president João Café Filho was allowed to serve Vargas's unexpired term. A conservative without sympathy for Vargas's economic nationalist policies, he pursued a course designed to attract foreign capital. One of his decrees exempted foreign firms in Brazil from the need to provide foreign exchange cover for importing machinery. The decree, which discriminated against national companies without foreign links, aroused the anger of nationalists.

The Kubitschek Era

The presidential election of 1955 took place under the watchful gaze of the military. The UDN nominated the conservative General Juarez Távora for president; the PSD and PTB jointly nominated Juscelino Kubitschek, governor of Minas Gerais, with João Goulart as his running mate. Their platform stressed the defense of democracy and the acceleration of economic growth. Kubitschek was not an economic nationalist in the Vargas mold, but the nationalist and reformist groups, knowing the limits of military tolerance, gave him their support. As the campaign progressed, there grew a clamor on the right for a coup to prevent the victory of Kubitschek and Goulart. However, they won the election in October, with the popular Goulart polling more votes than the president-elect.

Kubitschek took office in January 1956 with a promise of "fifty years of progress in five." But this progress was to be achieved with the aid of massive foreign investments, to which Kubitschek offered most generous incentives. Foreign capital flowed into Brazil; the total inflow between 1955 and 1961 amounted to $2.3 billion.

The bulk came from the United States, whose investments in Brazil reached the figure of $1.5 billion in 1960.

This influx of capital, which benefited from advantages denied to Brazilian enterprises, promoted a rapid foreign conquest of Brazilian national industry. In the process, the native entrepreneurs were frequently transformed into directors or partners of the foreign-controlled firms. The take-over concentrated on the most modern and fastest-growing industries (chemical, metallurgy, electrical, communications, and automotive). In 1960 foreign investment accounted for 70 percent of the capital invested in the 34 largest companies and more than 30 percent in the 650 corporations with capital of a million dollars or more.

The Kubitschek era was a heady time of unprecedented economic growth, with an average annual growth rate of 7 percent for the period from 1957 to 1961. By 1960, Brazil had been transformed from an agrarian country into an agrarian-industrial country with a base of heavy industry, for it could boast that it produced half its heavy-industry needs. Construction of a series of great dams provided much of the power needed by Brazil's growing industry. Kubitschek's decision to build a new capital, Brasilia, in the state of Goias, six hundred miles from the coast in an area still roamed by Indians, reflected his exuberant optimism about Brazil's future. Completed in three years, the new capital was inaugurated on April 21, 1960. A network of "highways of national unity" was constructed to link Brasilia with the rest of the country, but failed to solve the many difficulties—housing and resettlement problems, cultural isolation, and the like—that faced its inhabitants.

These triumphs of development had to be paid for, and their cost was high. A major source of financing was foreign loans, which swelled Brazil's already large foreign debt from $1.6 billion in 1954 to $2.7 billion in 1961. Service of the foreign debt took an ever-increasing share of the national budget, rising from $180 million to $515 million (more than half the value of Brazil's exports) in the same period. This source of financing had its limits; by 1959 the International Monetary Fund threatened to withhold loans if Brazil did not adopt a stabilization program and live within its means. Kubitschek responded by breaking off negotiations with the IMF and increasing the money supply. The result was an unprecedented inflation rate and a catastrophic decline in the value of the cruzeiro, whose exchange rate for the dollar fell from 70 to 210 between 1955 and 1961. This in turn greatly diminished the value of Brazil's exports. Inflation, like foreign loans, appeared to have reached its limits as a source of financing Brazilian development.

The Quadros Regime

The election of 1960 took place amid growing social unrest and intense debate over domestic and foreign policy. Inflation, corruption, and foreign control of the economy were major campaign issues. The campaign oratory and programs of all the principal candidates reflected the ascendancy that the nationalist, populist ideology had gained over public opinion. Even the conservative UDN recognized this fact by nominating as its candidate the flamboyant Jânio da Silva Quadros, former governor of São Paulo, whose campaign symbol was a broom with which he promised to "sweep out of the government the corrupt elements, the thieves and exploiters of the people." Although Quadros endorsed a balanced budget and stressed the need for a favorable climate for foreign investment, he also opposed the participation of foreign firms in Brazilian oil production, and he showed his independence in foreign policy by paying a visit to revolutionary Cuba at a time when the United States was bringing pressure on Latin American governments to sever diplomatic relations with Cuba.

Quadros's chief opponent was Marshal Henrique Teixeira Lott, who was endorsed by the UDN and the PTB, with Goulart as his running mate. A more authentic economic nationalist than Quadros, Lott favored sharply limiting profit remittances sent abroad by foreign firms and supported giving illiterates the vote. Quadros won the election but Goulart was re-elected vice president.

The short-lived Quadros administration was marked by a mixture of orthodox and unorthodox policies, by an essentially conservative posture in economic affairs and an independent posture in foreign policy. Without breaking with the traditional dependence on the capitalist countries for markets and loans, Quadros sought to reduce that dependence by developing new trade and diplomatic relations with the socialist countries and the Third World. Accordingly, he initiated negotiations for the resumption of diplomatic relations with the Soviet Union, sent a trade mission to the People's Republic of China, and denounced the CIA-backed Bay of Pigs invasion of Cuba in April 1961. Although he stressed the need for foreign investments and guaranteed their security, Quadros proposed to modify the "laws and regulations which place the Brazilian company in an inferior position" and to restrict the remittance of profits abroad.

However moderate, Quadros's foreign and domestic policies aroused the hostility of military and civilian conservatives. Quadros's problems were compounded by an increasingly recalcitrant Congress, in which the eighteen rural states, dominated by conservative fazendeiros, were overrepresented. Determined to break the legislative deadlock by some dramatic act, Quadros submitted his resignation on August 25, 1961, after only seven months of rule. His resignation message recalled Vargas's suicide note in its fervent nationalist tone and its claim that hostile foreign forces had obstructed his program of Brazil for the Brazilians. Convinced that the military would not permit the prolabor Vice President Goulart to succeed him, Quadros evidently believed that public clamor for his return would bring him back to office with the powers he needed to govern.

But he had miscalculated. His resignation caused great public excitement and perplexity, but the clamor that went up was not for his return but for a constitutional solution to the problem: the elevation of Goulart to the presidency. When the crisis broke out, Goulart was in China on a trade mission. The military cabinet officers, headed by war minister Odílio Denys, regarded Goulart, a wealthy rancher, as a dangerous demagogue and radical and announced that they considered his return to Brazil inadmissible for reasons of "national security."

A grave split developed within the military; in Goulart's home state of Rio Grande do Sul the commander of the Third Army announced his total support for Goulart, and the governor of the state rallied the population to defend the constitution and insure Goulart's elevation to the presidency. The threat of civil war loomed, but the military ministers, facing divisions within the armed forces and feeling the pressure of public opinion, agreed to a compromise. Goulart took office, but a constitutional amendment replaced the presidential system of government with a parliamentary one. Under this system, the president would share power with a council of ministers named by him, but drawn from and responsible to the legislature.

Goulart's Presidency

The right-wing military and its civilian allies had grudgingly accepted Goulart as president, but on probation. Taking office in September 1961, he began by steering a cautious course designed to allay conservative suspicions at home and abroad. In April 1962, he paid a visit to Washington. Addressing a joint session of Congress, he announced his opposition to the Castro regime and promised reasonable treatment of foreign-owned utilities in Brazil. The United States provided $131 million in aid for Brazil's depressed northeast, but the International Monetary Fund, whose approval was a condition for the cooperation of private bankers, remained skeptical of Goulart's intentions.

At the same time he courted foreign capital, Goulart continued Quadros's independent foreign policy of expanding Brazil's trade and diplomatic contacts with the socialist countries and the Third World. Goulart's refusal to join the United States in imposing sanctions against Castro's Cuba especially angered the right; Congress showed its displeasure with Goulart's able foreign minister, San Tiago Dantas, by refusing to approve his nomination as prime minister.

The first one and a half years of Goulart's rule under the parliamentary system saw few major legislative achievements. One was the passage of a long-delayed law establishing Electrobrás, the national agency proposed by Vargas for the control of the production and distribution of electric power. The other was a law requiring foreign capital to be registered with the Brazilian government and barring profit remittances abroad in excess of 10 percent of invested capital—certainly not a radical measure. Yet it produced a sharp drop in foreign investments, from $91 million in 1961 to $18 million in 1962. Lacking other sources for financing development, Goulart had to resort to the Kubitschek formula of a massive increase of the money supply. The new inflationary spiral brought the collapse of the cruzeiro and a wave of strikes and food riots, accompanied by a growing radicalization of labor and sections of the peasantry. But the economic slowdown apparent since 1961 continued. Import substitution as a stimulus to industrialization appeared to have reached its limits, and further advance was blocked by the small domestic market, the inequities of Brazilian income distribution, and the drain of capital through debt repayment and profit remittances (amounting to $564 million, or 45 percent of the value of Brazil's exports, in 1962).

With the advice of the brilliant young economist Celso Furtado, who had directed an ambitious effort to develop Brazil's backward, poverty-ridden northeast, Goulart drafted a program of structural reforms that was intended to impart a new dynamism to Brazil's faltering economy. The major proposed reforms were in the areas of land tenure, tax structure, and voting. Reform of the archaic land tenure system would expand the domestic market and increase agricultural production. Tax reform would reduce the inequities of income distribution and provide funds needed for public education and other social welfare purposes. The grant of votes to the illiterates would, it was hoped, drastically reduce the power of the rural oligarchy in the national and state legislatures.

To implement these changes, however, the legislative deadlock in Congress had to be broken. Accordingly, in mid-1962 Goulart launched a campaign for a plebiscite to let the people choose between presidential and parliamentary government. Under great public pressure, Congress agreed to the plebiscite; and on January 1, 1963, more than 12 million voters decided by a three to one majority to restore to Goulart his full presidential powers under the constitution of 1946.

But Goulart's victory did not change the balance of forces in Congress, which repeatedly voted down his reform proposals. Meanwhile, there was a growing polarization of opinion in the country, with the bourgeoisie and the middle class joining the landed oligarchy in opposition to Goulart's domestic program. Goulart's moderate reform proposals in reality favored the industrial bourgeoisie and should have enjoyed its support. But the dynamic industrialist class that had arisen and thrived under Vargas no longer represented a significant social force. The progressive foreign conquest of Brazilian industry had greatly reduced that class's influence as more and more national entrepreneurs gave up an unequal struggle and solved their personal problems by becoming directors or associates of foreign-owned firms. This dependent bourgeoisie shared the fears of social change of its foreign and rural allies. Those fears were also shared by the large urban middle class, battered by inflation and injected by the media with a virulent anticommunist prejudice.

The apprehension of these groups increased as a result of the extravagant rhetoric indulged in by the radical populists and by the spread of radical populism to the countryside. Under the leadership of the lawyer Francisco Julião, peasants in the bleak northeast, afflicted by drought, famine, and oppressive land tenure and labor systems,

began to join groups known as Peasant Leagues and agricultural unions and invade fazendas. Their activities seemed to threaten the existence of the latifundio, which was also threatened by Goulart's proposal to give the vote to illiterates and enact agrarian reform.

By the end of 1963, the forces on the right—the fazendeiros, the big bourgeoisie, the military, and their foreign allies—had begun to mobilize against the threat from the left. The military was especially angered by Goulart's proposal to give the vote and the right to hold office to enlisted men, regarding it as a fatal blow to the principle of hierarchy and discipline. The media launched a powerful attack on Goulart to convince the frustrated middle class that he was an agent of the international communist conspiracy and urging the military to intervene to safeguard "democracy" and "freedom." As 1964 began, Governors Adhemar de Barros of São Paulo and Carlos Lacerda of Guanabara announced the imminent military intervention to check what they called the "advance of communism and anarchy."

Defeated in his efforts to secure passage of his legislative program and under strong pressure from the impatient radical populists, Goulart moved to the left. Appearing at a mass rally in Rio de Janeiro in March 1964, he signed two decrees. One nationalized all private oil refineries. The other made liable to expropriation all large and "underutilized" estates close to federal highways or railways and lands of over seventy acres near federal dams, irrigation works, or drainage projects. At the same meeting, Goulart announced that he would shortly issue a decree on rent control. He asked Congress to pass reforms that included tax reform, the vote for illiterates and enlisted men, an amendment to the constitution providing for land expropriation without immediate compensation, and legalization of the Communist party.

By the middle of March, the military-civilian conspiracy for Goulart's overthrow was well advanced. The governors of a number of important states met with a view to transferring Congress to São Paulo, where a "legalist government" would be installed. An emissary returned from the United States with assurances from the State Department that the United States would immediately recognize the new government. Then, if it became necessary, the "legalist government" would solicit aid from the United States, and the dispatch of American troops would not constitute intervention but a response to a legitimate government's request for aid to suppress communism and subversion.

On March 31, the governor of Minas Gerais announced that he no longer accepted the president's authority. The same day, army units in Minas and São Paulo began to march on Rio de Janeiro. The U.S. ambassador to Brazil, Lincoln Gordon, was well informed of the conspiracy; five days before the coup he cabled Secretary of State Dean Rusk naming General Humberto de Alencar Castelo Branco as the probable head of the new military junta. Published documents also show that the United States was prepared to give military aid, if needed, to the rebels. But Operation Uncle Sam (its code name) proved unnecessary; the Goulart regime fell almost without a struggle on April 1, and the president fled into exile in Uruguay.

The ease with which the Goulart government was overthrown reflected the change in the alignment of forces in Brazil since 1945, and especially the movement of the Brazilian bourgeoisie and middle class into the camp of reaction, but it also revealed the weaknesses and divisions within the camp of Goulart's supporters. The working class, most of which was politically immature and accustomed to passively receiving favors and instructions from populist chieftains, failed to respond to Goulart's appeal for aid. The mass of the peasantry was still under the control of rural coronéis, while the Peasant Leagues and unions were weak and distant from the main theater of events. The left was badly split ideologically; there was little unity of program or coordinated direction of the groups making up the populist coalition.

Another cause of the passivity with which many received the coup was the widespread belief that it was simply another in a long series of military interventions; sooner rather than later

the military would return to its barracks and political life would return to normal. Events proved the error of this opinion. As the military regime consolidated its power, it became clear that the generals had come to install the alternative to the nationalist economic model—a neocolonial model based on the thorough integration of a dependent Brazilian economy into the international capitalist economy and the rapid modernization of Brazilian industry and agriculture without regard to its social consequences. Because of the regime's combination of brutally repressive policies with primary economic and political dependence on the United States, the Brazilian scholar Hélio Jaguaribe has aptly called it "colonial fascism."

Brazil's "Colonial Fascism"

The first acts of the military leaders of the self-proclaimed "democratic revolution" on April 1964 revealed their long-range intentions. On April 9, the Supreme Revolutionary Command issued the First Institutional Act, permitting the president to rule by decree, declare a state of siege, and deprive any citizen of civil rights for a period of ten years. A docile Congress approved the military's choice for president, General Humberto de Alencar Castelo Branco. Like many of his colleagues, Castelo Branco was a product of the *Escola Superior de Guerra* (School of Higher Military Studies), dominated in recent years by advocates of a *linha dura* (hard line), whose main tenets were fanatical anticommunism, favorable treatment of foreign capital, and acceptance of the leadership of the United States in foreign affairs.

Encouragement of Foreign Capital and Repression of Labor

It was in the area of economic policy that the new government most clearly defined its character and long-range aims. Roberto Campos, minister of planning, worked out a program for stimulating the entry of foreign capital by incentives that included the free export of profits, reduced taxes on the income of foreign firms, and a special type of exchange for the payment of external financing in case of devaluation. At the same time, internal credit was severely reduced in compliance with the anti-inflationary prescriptions of the International Monetary Fund, while the level of consumption of the domestic market fell as a result of a wage freeze and the decline in the real value of wages. These policies, placing Brazilian-owned companies in an unfavorable position, caused many to go under; 440 went bankrupt in 1966, 550 in 1967.

The new government's economic policies accelerated the foreign take-over of Brazilian industry. By 1968 foreign capital controlled 40 percent of the capital market of Brazil, 62 percent of its foreign trade, 82 percent of its maritime transport, 77 percent of its overseas air transport, 100 percent of its motor vehicle production, 100 percent of its tire production, more than 80 percent of its pharmaceutical industry, and 90 percent of its cement industry. The United States led, with about half of the total foreign investment, followed by Germany, Britain, France, and Switzerland.

To ensure foreign and domestic capital of an abundant supply of cheap labor, the government froze wages and banned strikes, with the result that workers' living standards fell sharply. In 1968 the minister of labor estimated that the real value of wages had fallen between 15 and 30 percent in the preceding four years. Labor was further shackled by the appointment of military interventors to oversee more than two thousand of the country's leading industrial unions.

Further, the government suppressed dissent in all areas of Brazilian life and suspended the political rights of thousands of so-called extremists. Thousands of federal employees were fired, and hundreds of nationalist military officers were arbitrarily retired or dismissed. The government shut down the Brazilian Institute of Higher Studies, a major center of nationalist economic theory, suppressed the National Student Union, and outlawed the Peasant Leagues.

Meanwhile, the military government unswervingly followed the lead of the United States in foreign policy. Brazil broke off diplomatic relations with Cuba, opposed the seating of the People's Republic of China in the United Nations, participated in the U.S. military intervention in the Dominican Republic, and actively supported the U.S. military effort in Vietnam.

In October 1965, after the government's candidates had suffered humiliating defeat in a series of local elections, President Castelo Branco issued the Second Institutional Act, which dissolved all political parties and instituted indirect elections of the president and vice president. The Third Institutional Act (February 1966) ended the popular election of governors of states and mayors of state capitals.

Yet for various reasons, probably including the wish to avoid embarrassing their principal patron, the United States, Brazil's military rulers chose to maintain a façade of democracy and representative government. They established two official parties, the *Aliança Renovadora Nacional* (National Renovating Alliance, called Arena) and a legal opposition party, *Movimento Democrático Brasileiro* (Brazilian Democratic Movement, or MDB). Since the ranks of the MDB were carefully screened to exclude subversives and its elected representatives held their mandates at the pleasure of the military, it had little or no impact on policy and legislation. However, it was the only legal channel for expressing and mobilizing dissent, and the vote for the MDB offered a measure of the growing discontent with the dictatorship.

Costa e Silva and a New Constitution

In March 1967, Castelo Branco turned over the presidency to Marshal Artur da Costa e Silva, who had been nominated by the military to succeed him and was duly elected by an obedient, purged Congress. On the day he assumed office, the government gave Brazil a new constitution, the sixth in its history, which incorporated the successive institutional acts. In general, Costa e Silva continued the policies of his predecessor but allowed a certain thaw in the climate of repression; this encouraged a revival of opposition activity and demands for changes in policy. Nationalists inside and outside the armed forces called for a return to the nationalist model of economic development, workers for an end to the wage freeze, intellectuals and students for an end to censorship and a return to academic freedom. A portion of the clergy, headed by the courageous archbishop of Recife and Olinda, Helder Câmara, added their voices to the general cry for social, political, and economic reforms.

Heartened by this show of popular resistance to the dictatorship, Congress and the Supreme Court gave signs of wanting to reassert their independence. The Supreme Court defied the military by granting a writ of habeas corpus for three student leaders who had been imprisoned for three months. Congress, after months of heated debate, rejected the government's demand that it lift the immunity of a deputy who had bitterly criticized the military for its brutal treatment of political prisoners and student dissenters.

These acts of defiance precipitated a governmental crisis and brought into the open a struggle within the regime between adherents of the hard line and a group of military officers who proposed to reduce foreign economic influence, pursue a more independent foreign policy, and make some concessions to the clamor for social and political reform. The hard-liners won out; under their pressure, Costa e Silva issued a Fifth Institutional Act in December 1968 that dissolved Congress, imposed censorship, suspended the constitution, and granted the president dictatorial powers.

The "coup within a coup" of December 1968 was accompanied by an increase in the use of terrorist tactics by a variety of police forces, local and national, against real or suspected opponents of the regime. The official security forces were joined by vigilante groups, operating with the covert approval of the government. The systematic use of torture by special units of the military police and the "death squads" reached a

level without precedent in Brazilian history. The victims included intellectuals, students, workers and even priests and nuns, as well as common criminals.

This intensified campaign of repression convinced some elements of the Brazilian left that there was no alternative to armed struggle against the dictatorship. There arose some half-dozen guerrilla groups whose activities included attacks on banks and armories, reprisal killings of notorious torturers, and kidnaping of diplomats and other prominent figures to secure the release of political prisoners. Their most sensational victory was the kidnaping in September 1969 of United States Ambassador Charles Burke Elbrick, was was later released in return for the freeing of fifteen political prisoners and the publication of an antigovernment manifesto by the press, radio, and TV.

But the guerrilla movement never achieved a mass character. The death of the most prominent guerrilla leader, Carlos Marighella, who was slain in an ambush by members of a death squad in November 1969, dealt a heavy blow to the movement, which gradually declined until it ceased to pose a serious problem for the regime.

In August 1969, a stroke incapacitated President Costa e Silva. Disregarding the constitutional provision that made Vice President Pedro Aleixo his successor, the three military ministers seized power in October and formed a triumvirate. When it became apparent that the ailing Costa e Silva could not return to his duties, they designated General Emílio Garrastazú Médici as his successor, and Congress confirmed their choice on October 22. A great landowner and former head of the secret police, Garrastazú Médici was completely identified with the hard line.

At the same time, the military junta presented the country with a new constitution. This document provided that the president would henceforth be chosen indirectly by an electoral college composed of Congress and delegates from state legislatures; it also weakened Congress by stripping its members of immunity against charges of libel or slander and making them liable to prosecution on the vague charge of endangering the public security. The junta also announced that instead of merely serving out the unexpired term of Costa e Silva, the new president was to have a full term of office, serving until March 15, 1974.

President Garrastazú Médici (1969–1974) was succeeded by General Ernesto Geisel (1974–1978), who continued in all essential respects his hard-line policies. Geisel proclaimed his desire for a détente with opposition elements and allegedly attempted to stop torture and arbitrary arrests, but Brazil remained a police state. Torture was routinely used against arrested political dissidents or suspects, who sometimes mysteriously disappeared or committed "suicide," and Geisel himself freely used the Fifth Institutional Act to strip elected representatives of the MDB of their political rights.

The Economy and Denationalization

Significant changes took place in the Brazilian economy. By 1970 the denationalization of key sectors of Brazilian industry was almost complete. One or a few giant multinational firms dominated each major industry. The automotive industry, which was dominated by three firms—Volkswagen, General Motors, and Ford—typified the concentration of industrial ownership and production. The military champions of free enterprise did not dismantle the state sector, however, as one might expect. Instead they assigned it the function of providing cheap steel, power, and raw materials to the profitable foreign-owned enterprises.

A counterpart of the concentration of production was the concentration of income. Brazil's gross national product grew at an average annual rate of 8 percent, one of the highest in the world, but there was no parallel growth of mass capacity to consume.

The contradiction between a highly productive, technologically advanced industrial plant and an extremely small domestic market had to be resolved somehow. The regime's economic planners found the answer by programming a vast increase in Brazil's exports. Primary products continued to dominate the export trade, but exports of manufactured goods increased at a rate of about 12 percent between 1968 and 1972. Most Brazilians lacked shoes and were poorly clad, but Brazil became a major exporter of shoes and textiles. Increasingly, however, primacy was placed on the export of durable consumer and capital goods, such as cars, electrical products, and machine tools.

Government planners hoped that exports would help to solve the problem of the balance of payments, a problem that grew ever more acute. But even as the volume of exports increased, so did the annual trade deficit. Meanwhile, the foreign debt, which stood at $12.5 billion in 1973, climbed to $17.6 billion in 1974 and stood at about $30 billion by the end of 1976. Service on this foreign debt, an important component of which was the increased cost of imported oil, amounted to nearly the total value of Brazil's exports in 1977. The problem was compounded by the heavy drain of interest and dividends in amounts considerably greater than the foreign investments that generated them. The deficits in the balance of payments contributed to a steep fall in the exchange value of the cruzeiro and an inflationary spiral that reached a rate of about 46 percent in 1976.

The recession that spread throughout the capitalist world in 1973–1974, combined with much higher oil prices, added to Brazil's economic difficulties. The passage of "antidumping" laws[1] in various countries, including the United States, cut into Brazil's exports of manufactured goods, creating overproduction and unemployment in various industries. By the mid-1970s, the bloom was off Brazil's "economic miracle." Official figures showed that the average indebtedness of Brazil's biggest five hundred companies had risen from 50 percent of net assets in 1971 to 63 percent in 1975, suggesting that many of these major

---

[1] These laws imposed duties designed to prevent the sale of goods in international trade at below-market prices.

Favelas (slums) ring Rio de Janeiro. (Paul Conklin)

Modern São Paulo. (Bruno Barbey/Magnum Photos, Inc.)

companies were dangerously overextended. The contraction in mass purchasing power as a result of the government's wage policies caused concern even in conservative capitalist circles.

The government's own figures documented the devastating effect of the "economic miracle" on the general welfare. By 1974, those figures revealed, the minimum wage was only half the minimum income required to buy food for subsistence. When the costs of rent, clothing, and transportation were added, a worker needed four times the minimum wage. Official data revealed an intolerable situation with respect to public health. Nearly half the population over the age of twenty suffered from tuberculosis and about 150,000 people died every year from the disease; about 42 million suffered from parasitic diseases that caused general debility and reduced working capacity. The great majority of Brazilian houses lacked running water and sanitary facilities, a condition that contributed to the prevalence of parasitic disease. According to the president of the National Institute of Nutrition, 12 million preschool children—70 percent of all children in that category—suffered from malnutrition in 1973.

These conditions prevailed not only in rural areas but in São Paulo, the hub of the "economic miracle." Infant mortality in the city increased between 1964 and 1974 and published studies linked this increase to the low income of workers. In rural areas, infant mortality reached a level of 168 deaths per 1,000 births. The situation was no better with respect to primary education. Of every 1,000 students who entered the first grade in 1968, only 301 finished the fourth grade.

In February 1969, the government announced a program of agrarian reform. Latifundia that had not been exploited for four years were to be expropriated, with compensation to the owners in cash or government bonds, and divided among the landless. It soon became clear that the "agrarian reform" was primarily directed at prodding and assisting semifeudal great landowners to transform their estates into agribusinesses at the expense of their tenants. The stress on "voluntary" adherence gave landowners time for delay and circumvention of the law by dividing the land among relatives or forming it into commercial enterprises exempt from the law's provisions. Thus, its principal result was to stimulate the development of capitalist large-scale agriculture, accelerating a process that had been under way since the 1930s. Sociologists warned that the so-called agrarian reform was spurring a new wave of rural emigration, throwing a new mass of cheap labor on an overstocked urban labor market.

Again, instead of correcting the profound regional contrasts of the Brazilian economy, the government had accentuated them. No serious effort was made to channel investment into the poorer areas of the north and northeast, and private investments naturally flowed into the developed south-central areas, widening the gap between the developed and the "submerged" zones. But official public investment policy also sharpened the tendency toward regional concentration of industry: in 1973 the Council for Industrial Development assigned about 90 percent of its resources to the southeast (of which 77 percent went to São Paulo), and only 3 percent to the northeast.

The Opposition and the Struggle for Rights

Ruled by a brutal military dictatorship, the Brazilian people expressed their dissent and discontent through the few available channels. In September 1974, in a massive repudiation of the regime, the voters gave 62 percent of their votes to the legal opposition party, the MDB, which secured 16 out of 22 seats in the Senate and 170 out of 364 seats in the Chamber of Deputies. The MDB also won majorities in the state assemblies of four of the largest states. Its program called for immediate amnesty for political prisoners, abolition of censorship, and reinstatement of habeas corpus and other traditional liberties, but its victory had little more than symbolic value, since the national legislature had been reduced to a "talking shop" without the power to influence official action. Nevertheless, the system offered a forum for guarded criticism of the government, and the size of the opposition vote provided some index of the government's unpopularity. In 1976, in the fifteen cities with populations of more than half a million, the MDB won in ten. The military government, however, continued to appoint the mayors of state capitals.

The Brazilian church occupied a leading place in the struggle for human rights and social justice in Brazil in the 1970s. A substantial minority of the hierarchy, led by Archbishop Helder Câmara, openly opposed capitalism and neocolonialism.

As the year 1978—the fourteenth year of the dictatorship—opened amid preparations for the election of a new president and a new Congress, there were many signs of an upsurge of democratic sentiment and resistance to the regime. With the government in firm control of the electoral college, the candidate of the MDB, retired General Euler Bentes Monteiro—who had played a major role in the coup of 1964 and now campaigned on a platform of immediate return to democracy—had virtually no chance to win against President Geisel's hand-picked successor, General João Baptista Figueiredo, former head of the secret police. But the campaign gave the opposition another means of agitation for change. Despite continuing though less frequent repression, including arrests, torture, and beatings of suspected "subversives," it made the most of its opportunities. Even some big businessmen who in the past had supported and financed political repression sensed the explosive potential of the rising popular discontent and joined the chorus for democratization. In September, thirty-three unions issued a manifesto demanding the right to strike, freedom to organize, and political amnesty. When all was said and done the official candidate was chosen president by the electoral college on October 15.

The next test of strength between the government and its opponents came in November, with the election of a new Congress. Once again, despite a new law that barred the opposition from using television and radio, the MDB made sweeping gains, with the biggest advances in the more developed southern parts of the country. Equally significant was the clear preference shown by the electorate for the more radical candidates of the MDB. Thanks to a bag of political tricks that included the selection of one-third of the senators by government-controlled electoral colleges and a gerrymander that reduced the representation of the more populous states in the Chamber of Deputies, the government retained a narrow control of the Congress. But the elections reflected the immense discontent of Brazilians with the economic and social results of fourteen years of dictatorial rule and the growing strength of an opposition that united ever wider sections of the population.

The Dictatorship in Crisis, 1978–1983

There were three major developments on the Brazilian scene between 1978 and 1983. First, a weak recovery from the recession of 1974–1975 soon gave way to an even more severe recession, culminating in a balance of payments crisis that brought Brazil to the verge of national bankruptcy. Second, the living standards of the masses continued to decline as a result of mounting unemployment, skyrocketing inflation, and the government's austerity measures, caus-

ing increased discontent and resistance on the part of the working class and the peasantry. At the same time, opposition to the military regime grew among the middle class and sections of the capitalist class. Third, in an effort to defuse the growing opposition, the regime applied the policy of *abertura,* or "opening toward democracy." This policy of limited political concessions left real power in the hands of the military and allowed it to continue the economic and social policies that led to the debacle of 1981–1983. Taken together, these developments defined a general crisis of the Brazilian model of dependent development.

Brazil's recovery from the recession of 1974–1975 was not strong or lasting. Between 1976 and 1979 the industrial growth rate hovered about 5 or 6 percent, compared with an average growth rate of 13 percent between 1967 and 1974. By 1980 Brazil had relapsed into an even more severe slump. Despite the downturn, inflation reached an unprecedented annual rate of 120 percent in mid-1981 and was running at about 95 percent at the end of 1982. By then many companies, including some of Brazil's biggest firms, had failed. Even the powerful multinational companies suffered losses, but some were able to strengthen their hold over the economy by the acquisition of national companies in trouble. In 1981, under pressure from foreign creditors to reduce public spending, the government announced a plan to sell many of the country's 564 state-owned companies to the private sector. Since local capital was insufficient to buy more than a few of these companies, the program tended to strengthen the hold of multinationals on the economy.

The economic crisis resulted from the interplay of domestic and external factors. An important cause was the inability of the domestic market to absorb the growing output of Brazilian industry. For almost two decades, the dictatorship had pursued a policy of promoting the growth of profits and capital by keeping wage increases below the cost of living; this policy sharply limited the purchasing power of the people. The economic downturn of the 1970s and the

1980s, however, also reduced the purchasing power of the middle classes, who provided a major part of the market for cars, television sets, and other durable consumer goods.

The most direct cause of the crisis was an unmanageable balance of payments and debt service problem. By 1980, Brazil had a foreign debt of $55 billion, largest in the Third World, and service of the debt absorbed 40 percent of the nation's export earnings. President Figueiredo complained that, because of the drain of interest, Brazil had "nothing left over for development." The high interest rates caused by the monetarist tight money policies of the Reagan administration added to Brazil's debt service burden. The export of a considerable part of the profits made by multinational companies in Brazil also increased Brazil's trade deficit. By 1980 these companies controlled 40 percent of the major industrial and mining enterprises of the country and were sending home 55 percent of their profits.

The military planners had counted on a great increase in exports to help solve the balance of payments problem. But each increase in exports was accompanied by an even greater increase in the imports of goods needed to maintain the export drive. In 1980, exports increased 24 percent, but imports grew by 50 percent. Brazilian exports also suffered from protectionist measures taken by the governments of industrialized countries under pressure from manufacturers' lobbies and trade unions worried about unemployment. Brazil's relations with the United States, in particular, deteriorated as a result of differences over trade.

This trade conflict, adding to the resentment caused by the Carter administration's earlier criticism of Brazilian violations of human rights, its ban on the shipment of arms to Brazil, and its refusal to sell Brazil nuclear reactors, reinforced a tendency on the part of Brazil to go its own way in foreign policy. Seeking to expand and diversify its markets, Brazil widened its ties with black Africa, including Marxist states like Angola and Mozambique, with the Arab world, and especially with the Soviet Union. Brazil also distanced itself

from the Central American policy of the United States by maintaining friendly relations with the Sandinist government of Nicaragua, a special target of United States destabilization efforts.

By December 1982, the balance of payments problem had reached a critical point. Brazil had almost run out of the foreign exchange it needed to meet its financial obligations. The foreign debt stood at about $89 billion, and many of the approximately 1,400 banks that had lent money to Brazil, grown suddenly nervous, were refusing to renew outstanding loans to Brazilian entities. A Brazilian default, however, could send shock waves that might topple the international banking system. Once more, as in the similar Mexican emergency, the self-interest of the Western financial community dictated a rescue operation. The plan was organized by the IMF, with strong support from the United States government and major United States banks, Brazil's biggest creditors. Brazil would receive a total of $6 billion from the IMF, an emergency credit of over $1 billion from the United States, and pressure would be brought on the uneasy private bankers to restore reductions in outstanding credit and make new loans to Brazil. Having reached agreement with the IMF, on December 20 Brazil asked the country's main creditors for a rescheduling of its debts. Brazil had gained a momentary respite, but the social costs of the relief operation to Brazil were high. The IMF's insistence on removal of subsidies meant that the price of gasoline, bread, wheat, and sugar rose substantially. Small and medium-sized companies and farmers were required to pay higher interest rates on their loans. Cuts in government spending swelled unemployment and increased bankruptcies. The new loans gave Brazil a breathing space, but the balance of payments problem remained as intractable as ever, and the financial juggling act of 1982 could not be indefinitely repeated.

The austerity program imposed by the IMF was a new blow at popular living standards that had sharply declined since the establishment of the military dictatorship in 1964. In mid-1978, one study concluded that at least 70 percent of the population lived below the officially calculated economic survival level. The state-decreed minimum wage lagged substantially behind inflation levels. In 1982 the minimum monthly wage was 23,000 cruzeiros, about $95. According to Brazilian sociologists, however, a family of five needed three times that amount to survive. The superexploitation of Brazilian workers took its heaviest toll on the weakest group of the population—its children. A partial census taken in 1982 indicated that half of all Brazilian children over ten worked.

Despite the official ban on strikes, with the threat of long prison sentences and other severe penalties for strike organizers, Brazilian unions waged many strike struggles and wrested partial gains from employers, especially for the skilled sectors of the work force. If the level of violence and repression gradually declined in industrial labor conflicts, the same was not true of the situation in rural areas, especially in the northeast and the Amazon. The number of violent land conflicts increased in those years.

A major cause of these conflicts was an explosion of land concentration and land-grabbing. In part this process of land concentration reflected the growth of capitalist, mechanized agriculture producing such crops as soya beans or sugar cane[2] on land formerly devoted to coffee or subsistence crops. In part it was due to the pattern of occupation of the new lands opened up for settlement in the Amazon by the construction of the Transamazonian Highway and other roads. Instead of taking advantage of the new agricultural frontier to settle thousands of landless peasant families, the Amazon development agency gave big companies large sums of money to set up vast cattle ranches. As a result, some 95 percent of the new landholdings in the Amazon were of 10,000 hectares or more. Unlike coffee plantations, the large new soya bean and sugar cane farms and cattle estates employed little labor.

Many of the dispossessed or discharged tenants and rural laborers migrated to the cities, swelling the ranks of the unemployed and underemployed and aggravating all the urban social problems. Thousands of others drifted to the Amazon frontier, becoming *posseiros* (squatters) who raise subsistence crops of rice, cassava, and maize on their small plots. They enjoyed considerable rights under Brazilian law, but these rights had little value on the violent frontier. The posseiros were (and are) frequently threatened with eviction by powerful land-grabbers, who arrive with their gunmen and sometimes enjoy the open or covert support of the local military or other officials. The posseiros have responded by organizing rural unions and defending their land by all the means at their disposal; they have found allies in courageous Catholic clergy who have on occasion been arrested, tortured, and even murdered for their humanitarian activities. Because the countryside is a major remaining bastion of reactionary forces, the struggle for land and human rights in the rural areas is crucial for the future of Brazil.

Discredited and isolated on account of its failed economic policies and corruption, the military regime sought a way out of its impasse by a strategy of détente with the opposition. This policy was begun under President Geisel as *distensão,* or "decompression," and expanded under President Figueiredo as abertura. Its successive steps included the lifting of most censorship; an amnesty that permitted the return of political exiles and the restoration of their political rights; and an overhaul of the political system that allowed the formation of new parties in addition to the two official government and opposition parties. The process was capped in 1980 by a congressional measure, approved by President Figueiredo, that provided for the direct election of all municipal officials, state governors, and members of the federal Congress. This meant that in the general election of 1982, for the first time since 1967, all members of the federal Congress and state and municipal officials would be elected directly by the voters.

[2] A major factor in the expansion of sugar cane cultivation is the success of Brazil's program for developing alcohol as a fuel. This fuel is now used in one-third of the country's large vehicle fleet.

368

These concessions were certainly not without significance, but their limited, calculated character must be understood. They were hedged about by constitutional amendments, replaced or added as the political situation required. These amendments were designed to ensure the continuation of military rule. In preparation for the election of 1982, the government introduced two such provisions. One banned party coalitions, thus severely limiting the possibilities of unity among the opposition parties. Another, designed to compensate for the expected loss of the larger industrial states by the government party, changed the electoral college that would elect the new president; under the new rules, a vote cast in a remote, sparsely settled Amazonian state would have as much weight as twenty-two votes cast in São Paulo!

Yet the election of November 15, 1982, in which 55 million Brazilians participated, was a major event, a plebiscite that rendered a decisive verdict on the military regime. The major opposition party was the Brazilian Democratic Movement party (PMDB), an informal coalition of bourgeois liberal and left-wing groups supported by many capitalists, at one end of the political spectrum, and by the still illegal Communist party, at the other end. Avoiding controversial issues that might divide its followers, its program stressed the need to carry the process of democratization to its logical conclusion. Two labor parties—one led by the trade union leader known as Lula, the other by the veteran populist leader of the Vargas-Goulart era, Leonel Brizola—also took part in the elections. Despite all the legal and illegal maneuvers of the regime the opposition took 62 percent of the vote and won the governorships of ten of the twenty-three states. A major surprise was the election of Brizola as governor in the state of Rio de Janeiro. The opposition gained control of the lower house of Congress, but the government party (the Democratic Social party, an outgrowth of the old Arena) retained control of the senate, and had a comfortable majority in the electoral college.

The opposition had made large gains, but under the constitution imposed by the military, the all-powerful president controlled both the federal budget and the operating funds of the states. Even before the election, the government was preparing changes in the tax collection system that would limit even further the power of the state governments. It seemed certain that a military man or a nominee of the military would be the next president of Brazil.

The Transition to Democracy, 1983–1991: "The New Republic"

The march of events upset the calculations of the military rulers. The dictatorship had counted on an easy victory of the conservative Paulo Maluf, candidate of the Social Democratic party (PDS), the government party, over Tancredo Neves, candidate of the PMDB on the Democratic Alliance ticket. In the course of the campaign, however, a stream of defections from the regime's unpopular candidate by PDS dissidents joined the Liberal Front party (PFL), a junior partner of the PMDB. On January 15, 1985, Neves easily defeated Maluf in the electoral college, receiving 480 votes to Maluf's 180, but died on the eve of his inauguration after emergency surgery. His successor, Vice President José Sarney, had left the PDS to join the PFL, and therefore represented the more conservative minority wing of the Democratic Alliance. He took office, however, vowing to carry out Neves's program of structural reforms, which included land reform and the grant of a larger voice in government to workers and unions.

The transition to democracy and civilian rule, made under the watchful eyes of the military, was a gradual process, and in 1991 is still incomplete. Behind the scenes, the military continued to influence the decision-making process on all major issues. The political life of the "New Republic" proclaimed by Neves during his campaign lacked significant popular input. The major parties, the PMDB and the PFL, were controlled by small cliques representing the dominant Brazilian elites. The PMDB, to be sure, had a varied make-up, including a left wing of middle-class intellectuals and liberals, but its dominant sector represented a national industrial bourgeoisie that proposed to create a modern and relatively independent capitalism. The PFL spoke for more traditional commercial and landed elites. To the left of these majority parties stood the Democratic Labor party (PDT) of Leonel Brizola, populist and reformist in the tradition of Vargas and Goulart; and the leftist Workers' party (PT), which sought to expand from its limited trade union base in São Paulo. The Communist party, legalized by Congress in 1985 after many years in the underground, enjoyed some influence in the labor movement but little on the national political scene. A total control of the mass media by elite interests hindered the development of independent political action and ideological independence on the part of the workers and peasants who form the overwhelming majority of Brazil's population.

This is not to minimize the importance of the return to democracy in Brazil. In 1991 most Brazilians live under a regime that respects civil liberties and human rights (but in the vast interior of the country, where there is little respect for law, great landowners and their hired thugs continue to terrorize peasants and their allies). The new civilian government extended the franchise to the illiterate, established direct elections on all levels, permitted parties of all political creeds to operate freely, and allowed workers to form unions, bargain collectively, and strike.

After two years in office, however, the Sarney administration had not seriously tackled the task of solving Brazil's great social and economic problems, the chief of which was land reform. This was not simply a question of redistributive justice; it was a prerequisite for the creation of a modern national capitalism based on a large domestic market. A report titled *Brazil 2000,* written by Brazilian scholars commissioned by Sarney, noted that 65 percent of Brazil's 135 million inhabitants were malnourished and 30 percent illiterate. Stressing the urgency of the problem, it concluded that Brazil "has reached the limits of peaceful coexistence between rich and poor."

In November 1985 the Brazilian Congress passed and Sarney signed into law an agrarian reform bill that provided for the distribution of 88 million acres of land to 1.4 million families through 1989. Under a new Ministry of Agrarian Reform and Development, the National Institute of Colonization and Agrarian Reform (INCRA) was to implement the plan on the regional level through mixed commissions of landowners, government officials, and landless peasants. A decree of May 1986 limited the land available for distribution and expropriation to state-owned lands and to private holdings whose production was below the land-use standards set by government agronomists.

So sluggish was the program's implementation that Minister of Agrarian Reform and Development Nelson Ribeiro resigned in protest. The major obstacle to land reform was the fierce resistance of the landowners. Organized under the Rural Democratic Union (UDR) and the Brazilian Society for the Defense of Tradition, Family, and Property, the landowners hired thousands of former military personnel to staff private militias, paying, it was reported, salaries three times higher than those of the army. The landowners enjoyed the support and protection of local officials and police. Their thugs compiled hit lists of landowners' perceived enemies.

The agrarian reform, so vital to modernizing Brazil's economic and social structures, had little prospect of success without a decisive change in direction. But President Sarney limited his response to defiance and aggression from the great landowners to delivering warnings that agrarian reform might become a "holy war between right-wingers and communists" and to ordering the confiscation of arms from landowners and peasants in the countryside. Both of these efforts proved ineffective in ending the "atmosphere of impunity."

If land reform was the most acute, violence-ridden issue of the "New Republic," Brazil's greatest external problem remained the immense foreign debt, which in 1990 stood at about $120 billion. The continuous drain of foreign exchange had a profoundly negative impact on Brazil's efforts to achieve social reform and economic growth. To many Brazilians, it appeared that the nation must choose between paying the interest and supporting social and economic development.

The new civilian government defined its position on the debt in a speech made by President Sarney to the United Nations General Assembly in September 1985: "Brazil will not pay its foreign debt with recession nor with unemployment, nor with hunger . . . a debt paid for with poverty is an account paid with democracy."

These were brave words, in sharp contrast to the docility with which military governments had accepted the debt status quo. In the same vein, Dilson Funaro, Sarney's finance minister, said that Brazil would no longer accept IMF monitoring of the Brazilian economy as a condition for debt-rescheduling operations, that the nation could not continue debt-servicing on the level of 1985, when debt service took about 5.2 percent of the Gross Domestic Product, and that in the future Brazil would limit payments to about half that amount. In February 1987, Brazil announced a suspension of interest payments to private banks. But this revolt by a timid, conservative president did not last long. Under pressure from foreign bankers and right-wing domestic groups, Sarney lifted the moratorium and in February 1988 began negotiations with the banks for a conventional rescheduling.

On taking office the Sarney administration found the economy in recession, racked by galloping inflation and high unemployment, although 1984 had seen a partial recovery fueled by a sharp increase in exports. In February 1986, Sarney announced the Plan Cruzado. This program for economic stabilization consisted of measures designed to halt triple-digit inflation through a freeze on wages, prices, and rents, and the replacement of Brazil's monetary unit, the cruzeiro, with a new and strong monetary unit, the cruzado. The Plan Cruzado immediately encountered strong labor opposition. The plan provided for wage increases only if prices rose over 20 percent; following the wage freeze in February prices rose at a rate of just above 10 percent. Workers' resentment at what they regarded as patently unfair policies produced a wave of

strikes that were partly successful in achieving the unions' demands, despite government threats and some acts of repression, including the arrest of some union leaders.

Despite fissures in the wage-price structure, the relative success of the Plan Cruzado in halting inflation and a consumer boom fueled by massive government spending inspired confidence and produced large political rewards for the government in the election of November 15, 1986. The PMDB won governorships in twenty of the twenty-three states and gained some 60 percent of the seats in the new congress. Both major opposition parties, the PDT and the PT, saw voter support drop from their showings in the 1985 municipal elections. These results meant that the PMDB majority would have a decisive voice in shaping Brazil's new constitution, the nation's eighth.

Even as voters were going to the polls, the government prepared to announce an abrupt shift in economic policy. Sarney's economic team, alarmed by a recent upsurge in inflation and a sharp decline in Brazil's trade surplus and foreign exchange reserves, put together a package of measures designed to cool down the overheated economy, slow economic growth, and balance the budget by increasing government revenues. Plan Cruzado II, unveiled five days after the 1986 election, provided for a series of devaluations to maintain export effectiveness; the immediate closing or merger of fifteen state companies and of thirty-two more in the coming months; and, most painful of all, large increases in postal rates, the cost of utilities, fuel, and sugar, and 100 percent increases in taxes on cigarettes and alcoholic beverages.

An explosion of popular wrath followed the announcement of Cruzado II; the fact that the government had concealed its plans until shortly after the November 15 election made it appear like a deliberate act of betrayal. In December the two labor federations, the leftist *Central Unica dos Trabalhadores* (CUT) and its rival, the more conservative *Central Geral dos Trabalhadores* (CGT), joined in a general strike designed to bring about the total repeal of the austerity program; organizers claimed that the strike brought 70 percent of the nation to a standstill. Although shaken by the strike, Sarney rejected the proffered resignation of his finance minister and insisted that what had been done could not be undone.

The austerity program, closely resembling programs imposed on Third World countries by the IMF as a condition for new loans or rescheduling of debt payments, came shortly before negotiations on the foreign debt started, during which creditor governments and banks were expected to demand that Brazil accept IMF guidance in formulating its economic policies. The parallel in programs was not lost on many Brazilians, and there was growing pressure on the new PMDB-dominated Congress to declare a moratorium on debt payments that would halt "the foreign exchange hemorrhage."

In fact, as noted above, in February 1987 the Sarney government announced a temporary suspension of interest payments to private banks until access to new loan facilities had been assured, but made clear it had no intention of defaulting on its debts. By this time the economic impact of Sarney's policies had virtually exhausted his reservoir of popular good will, and many called for his resignation. Assured of military support, Sarney responded to such demands in a tough speech by promising to serve out his five-year term. In the same speech he announced a ninety-day freeze on wages to take effect in mid-June 1987. Taken together with other provisions, including a devaluation of the cruzado, the plan was calculated to please foreign creditors by reducing domestic demand and expanding exports, thereby improving Brazil's balance of trade, but it angered Brazilian wage-earners, whose purchasing power, already slashed 30 percent since November 1, faced another decline of 29 percent. It was a foregone conclusion that the end of the freeze would see another wave of strikes.

In another sign of a rightward policy shift, Finance Minister Funaro resigned and was replaced by Luis Carlos Bresser Pereira. The resignation of Funaro, held responsible for the February 1987 suspension of interest payments, was interpreted by the *Wall Street Journal* (April 15, 1987) as a success for the commercial banks' policy of isolating Brazil by reaching rescheduling agreements with a series of other major debtor nations.

By mid-1987 Sarney's popularity had declined to the vanishing point. The widespread disillusionment with his promises and performance extended to the promise of "The New Republic." Brazilian slum dweller Janet Genilhoud, aged twenty-eight, gave voice to this disillusionment: "What good is freedom of speech if you can't feed your children?"[3] Janet's despair reflected a steadily worsening economic situation, with an inflation rate that rose from 230 percent in 1985 and 366 percent in 1987 to 988 percent in 1988. The U.S. banker David Rockefeller observed in 1988: "In all my visits to Brazil, I have never before come across such desperate poverty."

In October 1988, the National Congress, acting as a constituent assembly, gave the country a new democratic constitution that represented a sweeping rejection of all the late military regime had stood for. It provided for popular election of the president and mandated that Brazilians should vote in 1993 to choose between the presidential and parliamentary systems. Presidential rule by decree, so often used by the military regime, was abolished. The basic civil rights of freedom of assembly, speech, and the press were guaranteed, workers were given the right to strike and engage in collective bargaining, and the workweek was reduced from forty-eight to forty-four hours. Another provision nationalized oil- and mineral-mining rights. But critics on the left complained of the failure to adopt a radical agrarian reform and questioned an article that made the armed forces responsible for the maintenance of "constitutional order."

The constitution promised protection of Indian rights, but contained no concrete measures to

[3] *U.S. News and World Report,* July 13, 1987.

The survival of the Amazon rain forest, home to Brazilian Indian groups, is threatened by indiscriminate destruction caused by ranchers and mine companies. In the stretch of forest shown here, charred remains of trees can be seen next to pastureland. (Mike Nichols/Magnum)

prevent the destruction of the surviving Indian groups, their culture, and their habitat, the Amazon rain forest. With the approval and financial support of the military regimes and their civilian successors, big ranchers and mine companies, both Brazilian and foreign, have cut down or burned vast stretches of forest in order to graze cattle or strip-mine, threatening the livelihoods and very survival of the Indians and *seringueiros* (rubber tappers), who depend on the forests for their existence. Indians and rubber tappers who protest the exploitive practices of the ranchers and mine owners have often been murdered by hired gunmen, who are protected by corrupt and racist police, military, and officials. The survival of the Amazon rain forest, "the green lungs of Earth," and others like it concerns not only Bra-

zilians but all mankind, for they are the major source of the world's oxygen supply. Sarney displayed the same timidity in dealing with the problem as he did with agrarian reform.

His administration and the major parties received a stunning rebuff from Brazilian voters in the municipal elections in November 1988. In a sharp swing to the left, labor and socialist parties captured control of the major Brazilian cities and a majority of state capitals, and there was a rapid growth of left-wing parties, especially the Workers' Party, led by the militant trade union leader Luis Inacio da Silva (Lula), whose membership grew into millions.

The election results sounded an alarm bell to Brazil's elites and their political managers, preparing for the first popular presidential election in nearly thirty years, to be held in 1989. The new democratic environment required the Right to present a populist, charismatic presidential candidate who could convince the Brazilian people to swallow the ill-tasting free-market prescription of austerity and privatization, something Sarney had been unable to do.

Such a candidate was found in the person of Fernando Collor de Mello, former governor of Alagoa, but a relative newcomer to national politics. Collor, forty years old and dapper, a sportsman and athlete from a wealthy family, dissociated himself from the Sarney administration and ran as the candidate of the National Reconstruction party. Sharply critical of official corruption and inefficiency, his campaign focused on promises to reduce the bloated bureaucracy, attract foreign capital, and institute a free-market economy. In the first round of the election, he emerged as the winner, with Lula, candidate of the Workers' Party, as runner-up. Since neither candidate received a plurality of the votes, they faced each other in the run-off election.

Lula, born into a poor farm family, a steelworker and trade union leader and a veteran of major strike struggles against the military dictatorship, promised to raise wages and control prices, declare a moratorium on Brazil's huge foreign debt, and increase spending for health and public education. Collor, who traveled around the country in two private jets and a fleet of helicopters, obtained millions of dollars from wealthy backers. TV Globo, the fourth largest TV network in the world, created an attractive image of Collor as a crusading reformer, anti-Sarney and anticorruption. The major newspapers also supported him. Collor won with 37 million votes against Lula's 31 million, a result partly attributable to the fact that city voter turnout was 60 percent while it was 85 percent in rural areas. Brazil's elites greeted the result with rejoicing and the stock market shot up.

Collor took office in January 1990 and quickly displayed his own peculiar style of governing, one that combined populist initiatives—perhaps sincere, perhaps public relation shows—with others that reflected his hard-line free-market conservatism. Typical of his populist moves was his appointment of the most prominent ecologist in Brazil, Jose Lutzenberger, who won the Alternative Nobel Prize in 1988 for his commitment to conservation, as Secretary for the Environment. Time will tell if Lutzenberger retains Collor's support in his struggle to save the Amazon.

The basic thrust of Collor's program, however, conformed to the most traditional IMF recipes for economic solvency. Reduction of government spending and services, a halt to wage indexation (adjustment of wages to changing price levels), an end to collective bargaining except on the firm level, and wholesale privatization of state enterprises became the order of the day. A freeze of savings and banking deposits, designed to check inflation, helped to produce the desired effect but had major recessive results; by May 1990 industrial production had plummeted 25 percent and layoffs nationwide were well over 300,000.

By early December 1990 the economic picture had darkened on all fronts. "Eight months after Mr. Collor jolted Latin America's largest economy with a radical plan that cut inflation to single digits," wrote the *New York Times* correspondent James Brooke, "the rate has crept up to 17 percent, a healthy trade surplus has vanished and the economy has shrunk by 4 percent—the worst performance in a decade." Caught between the scissors of declining sales and interest rates of 6 percent a month, many companies filed for bankruptcy. Meanwhile talks with foreign commercial banks who held much of Brazil's $121 billion foreign debt had bogged down, the banks rejecting Brazil's proposal to tie debt service payments to its future "capacity to pay."

Responding to the devastating effects of the Collor program on wages, employment, and living standards, many unions went on strike and in some cases wrung concessions from employers and government. Collor's declining popularity was reflected in growing congressional and judicial resistance to his decrees. The first political fallout from Collor's economic program came in runoff elections in November, when voters elected opposition slates in ten of the fifteen states that held congressional and gubernatorial elections, including São Paulo. The chief gainers were left-of-center parties, the Democratic Labor party (PDT) of Leonel Brizola, who was elected governor of the state of Rio de Janeiro, and the Workers' party, led by Lula, which increased its seats in the Congress more than 100 percent. Another left-wing party, the Brazilian Socialist party (PSB), increased its seats from eight to eleven. Together with the representatives of the PMDB, left-of-center parties hold 246 votes in the New Congress, forming a strong opposition to President Collor.

In February 1991, almost one year after he took office with a pledge to "kill the inflationary tiger," Collor offered a new program of price and wage controls, called Collor Plan II, to a skeptical Congress and public. High inflation combined with a deepening recession to produce an atmosphere of crisis in the great Brazilian cities; official figures showed that almost a million workers were unemployed in Rio de Janeiro, São Paulo, and four other state capitals; this figure did not include workers in the so-called informal sector.

Meanwhile Brazil's land problem remains without solution. Amazonia continues to be the scene of violent clashes between great landowners who frequently acquired their land illegally and small farmers whose tiny plots will not support their families. Peasants who resist usurpation and exploitation face threats, harassment, and murder. Rent-a-killer agencies (*agências de pistolagem*) operate in many areas; they offer a sliding scale ranging from $600 for a peasant to $4000 for an elected official. In southern Pará state 172 rural activists have been killed since 1980. A judge in Rio Maria (Pará state) expressed surprise about the excitement caused by such killings; "they were only peasants," he said. The Collor government has done little to protect peasant leaders or punish their assassins. The conviction in December 1990 of a cattle rancher and his son for the murder of the celebrated Chico Mendes, an organizer of the rubber tappers and defender of the rain forest, appears to have been a response to international attention and pressure. When arrests are made, they rarely lead to prosecution and conviction.

Chapter 16

Storm over the Andes: Peru's Ambiguous Revolution

In the second half of the twentieth century, reform came at last to three countries whose economic and social structures were among the most archaic in Latin America, the Andean republics of Peru, Bolivia, and Ecuador. Here, as elsewhere on the continent, the movement for reconstruction fused the effort to modernize with the struggle for greater social justice for the masses: economic sovereignty, industrialization, and land reform were the main slogans of the Andean revolutions. But the presence of large, compact Indian-speaking groups, ranging from some 70 percent of the population of Bolivia to about 40 percent of the populations of Peru and Ecuador, gave a distinctive character to the nationalist, reformist movements in these countries.

Three Andean Revolutions

Bolivia, 1952–1991

Landlocked Bolivia, the most Indian of the three lands, a country where as late as 1976 only a minority of the population were monolingual speakers of Spanish, was the scene of the first true Andean social revolution. In 1952 the middle-class National Revolutionary Movement (MNR), led by Victor Paz Estenssoro, overthrew the rule of the great landlords and tin barons with the support of armed Indian miners and peasants. The Bolivian land reform, begun by the spontaneous rising of the peasantry and legitimized by the revolutionary government of President Paz Estenssoro, broke the back of the latifundio system in Bolivia. Like the Mexican land reform, however, the Bolivian reform created some new problems even as it solved some old ones. The former latifundia were usually parceled out into very small farms—true minifundia—and the new peasant proprietors received little aid from the government in the form of credit and technical assistance. Yet despite its shortcomings, the Bolivian land reform brought indisputable benefits: some expansion of the internal market, some rise in peasant living standards and, in the words of Richard W. Patch, "the transformation of a dependent and passive population into an independent and active population."

The new government also nationalized the principal tin mines, most of which were controlled by three large companies, and recognized its debt to the armed miners by placing the mines under joint labor-government management. It also abolished the literacy qualification for voting and thus enfranchised the Indian masses. But the new regime inherited a costly, run-down tin industry, while the initial disruptive effect of the agrarian reform on food production added to its economic problems.

Under strong pressure from the United States, which made vitally needed economic aid to the revolutionary government conditional on the adoption of conservative policies, the MNR leadership gradually moved to the right. The government of Paz Estenssoro offered generous compensation to the former owners of expropriated mines, invited new foreign investment on favorable terms, ended labor participation in the management of the government tin company, and reduced welfare benefits to the miners. Equally important, it agreed to the restoration of a powerful U.S.-trained national army to offset the strength of the peasant and worker militias. These retreats broke up the worker–middle class alliance formed during the revolution and facilitated the seizure of power in 1964 by right-wing generals.

In the violent ebb and flow of Bolivian politics since 1964, governments have risen and fallen, but a persistent theme has been the conflict between radical workers, students, and nationalist military and a coalition uniting remnants of the old landowning aristocracy, a new elite of businessmen and politicians grown wealthy through

U.S. aid, and conservative military. The peasantry, neutralized by the land reform that satisfied its land hunger, initially remained passive or even sided with the government in its struggles with labor, but later peasant unrest began to grow as a result of deteriorating economic conditions. There was a brief revival of social revolutionary and nationalist trends under President Juan José Torres González (1970–1971), who nationalized various foreign-owned enterprises and sought to promote Bolivia's economic independence by expanding economic ties with the Soviet Union and other socialist states. But in August 1971, his government was overthrown by a rightist army coup led by Colonel Hugo Banzer Suárez, whose dictatorial regime threw Bolivia's doors wide open to foreign investors and brutally repressed all dissidents. Massive financial aid from the United States enabled the Banzer government to survive despite growing popular opposition.

In July 1978, after a presidential election tainted by large-scale fraud in favor of Banzer's chosen successor, General Juan Pereda Asbun, Pereda seized power and proclaimed a government of "democratic transformation," promising new elections in 1980. Significantly, the peasantry, the regime's former ally, had voted heavily in favor of the presidential candidate of the united left parties. In an atmosphere of revival and mobilization of trade union, student, and other opposition movements, Pereda repealed various pieces of repressive legislation, yielded to the demands of various striking unions, and reopened the universities, closed arbitrarily by the Banzer regime. But a continuing wave of strikes and demonstrations revealed the fragility of Pereda's hold on power. In November a new military coup ousted Pereda and installed General David Padilla as president. Padilla continued to dismantle Banzer's repressive system, promised a return to civilian rule, and scheduled elections for July 1979.

Elections were duly held in July 1979, but produced no clear winner. Congress decided to hold new elections the next year, appointing a caretaker president pending their outcome. In November a military junta overthrew the provisional government, but itself fell within a few short weeks as a result of a general strike by the powerful Bolivian labor confederation and protests by virtually all sections of the population. Congress now elected a new caretaker president, Lydia Gueiler Tejada, the first woman president in Bolivian history. In June 1980, general elections gave victory to Hernán Siles Zuazo, presidential candidate of a coalition of leftist forces, the UDP (*Unidad Democrática Popular*), and a highly respected veteran of Bolivian politics. But Siles Zuazo was prevented from taking office when military hard-liners, led by General Luis García Meza Tejada, seized power in July and established a regime probably unprecedented in Bolivian history for brutality, corruption, and inefficiency. Contributing to the regime's discredit at home and abroad were its close links to the international drug traffic; under García Meza cocaine production became a major crop of the Bolivian economy, with prices for coca leaves rising from $50 to a reported $15,000 a ton in less than a year. Meeting stubborn resistance from the labor movement, the peasantry, all civilian parties, and even a section of the military, in August 1981 García Meza yielded power to another military junta, which then decided to convene Congress so that it might certify Siles Zuazo's election as president. In October 1982, Siles Zuazo took office amid large popular demonstrations of support in La Paz, which had become "the democratic capital of South America," while many officials of the previous regime took flight for right-wing havens in Paraguay and Argentina.

The new government faced a desperate economic situation. Tin prices were at their lowest level in twenty years and still falling. The peso had lost 90 percent of its value since February 1982, inflation stood at over 150 percent for the year, and 75 percent of the work force were unemployed or underemployed. In addition, 70 percent of Bolivia's income from exports went to service the foreign debt of $3.9 billion. The political turmoil of recent years, especially the strikes

against the military juntas, had drastically reduced production levels. To achieve even a modest recovery and begin the transition to a more balanced and independent development required cooperation and sacrifice from the masses, who had defeated the reactionary military and expected much from the new government.

The Siles Zuazo team's first task was to achieve control over a galloping inflation. This necessitated raising food prices for such staples as sugar, beef, and rice, but the government favored the poorer sectors by setting lower rates for electricity and cooking oil in working-class districts. In addition to granting small wage increases, the government implemented its promise to give labor representation on the boards of state companies by appointing three workers' delegates to the boards of the state mining corporation and the state oil company. The new government also displayed its nationalist temper by announcing plans to take over the U.S. and Canadian-owned *Electricidad de La Paz* (Bolivian Power Company). Foreign policy reflected the leftward shift, with resumed diplomatic relations with Cuba and expanded relations with other socialist countries.

Perhaps recalling the experience of President Allende in Chile, Siles Zuazo dismissed the entire military command in October 1982 and replaced it with reliable officers who supported democratic government. The "sudden Bolivian spring" had begun; whether it would continue largely depended on unity among the parties composing the ruling leftist coalition and its progress in the solution of Bolivia's formidable economic and social problems.

The government of Siles Zuazo proved unable to cope. An unstable coalition of leftist and centrist parties, it came under pressure from the left and the right. Meanwhile the economy steadily deteriorated as a result of a continuing slide in the price of Bolivia's major exports, tin and oil; by October 1984, inflation was running at an annual rate of 1,000 percent. The foreign debt stood at $5 billion, and debt payments had to be suspended. Siles Zuazo attempted to make

378

concessions to the right and the left but satisfied neither. In November 1984 he acknowledged defeat and yielded to rightist demands by calling presidential elections a year ahead of schedule.

With the left-wing parties unable to unite behind a single candidate, the election of July 1985 turned into a contest between the former dictator, General Hugo Banzer Suárez, candidate of the rightist National Democratic Action party (ADN), and Victor Paz Estenssoro, the 78-year-old leader of the National Revolutionary Movement and of the revolution of 1952. Disillusioned with politics, two-thirds of the electorate stayed away from the polls; a majority of the votes cast were divided between Banzer and Paz. Since neither candidate commanded more than 50 percent of the vote, the election was thrown into Congress, where leftist deputies and followers of Paz elected him president.

Under pressure from Banzer, who threatened a coup, and from the IMF, which demanded a severe austerity program as a condition for badly needed new loans, Paz veered sharply to the right. Accepting the IMF's terms, he slashed government subsidies for basic services and foods, froze wages, devalued the currency over 1,000 percent, removed all restrictions on foreign imports and investments, and resumed payments on Bolivia's foreign debt. When workers responded with a general strike in September 1985, it was crushed by the military, and more than a thousand labor and peasant leaders were arrested.

As 1986 began, the full dimensions of Paz's turn to the right became clear. In alliance with Banzer, some of whose followers Paz brought into his cabinet, he announced a plan designed to end hyperinflation and stabilize the economy. The plan, drafted by Harvard economist Jeffrey Sachs called for closing down as many as eleven unprofitable state-owned mines, laying off thousands of workers, selling other state enterprises to the private sector, making deep cuts in public services, and increasing taxes. Paz's decision to close down Bolivia's largest tin mine in August brought the conflict between the government and

the labor movement to a head. The miners' union called a general strike in the region of Oruro and Potosí, where thousands began a march on the capital of La Paz. The government imposed a state of siege, arresting hundreds of labor and community leaders, and sending troops, tanks, and planes to patrol the mining regions.

The mining crisis added to the tension caused by a July 1986 decision of Paz to invite U.S. troops into the country to work with the Bolivian military on "Operation Blast Furnace" in eradicating the country's cocaine laboratories. Ironically, the most dynamic sector of Bolivia's economy—despite well-publicized anti-narcotic raids and Operation Blast Furnace—was the cocaine trade; this chief source of dollars was compensating for the sharp decline in the country's export earnings. Sale of coca paste generated $600 million annually, one-third more than the nation's legal export earnings of $400 million. The cocaine trade, observed *Latinamerica Press* in 1986, had warped the Bolivian economy and way of life. Traditionally, peasants, miners, and workers chewed the coca leaf to dull hunger, thirst, and fatigue. The newly inflated price of coca in local markets put it beyond their reach. Meanwhile the incidence of drug addiction in Bolivia rose to the levels found in New York City or Los Angeles. The government proclaimed the anti-narcotic Operation Blast Furnace a total success. In fact, however, key figures in the nation's cocaine mafia, obviously forewarned, had fled the country long before the troops' arrival; their raids revealed only a few workers and dismantled laboratories.

The conflict between the miners and the government took a dramatic turn when some one thousand miners protested government mine-closing plans, the state of siege, and other repressive measures by occupying mine shafts and launching a hunger strike. The miners' plight and the stubborn refusal of the government to negotiate a solution to the conflict caused growing public sympathy and demonstrations of support for the miners. Aware of the unpopularity of its position, in September 1986 the Paz government

In July 1986 in a joint Bolivian and U.S. military exercise, Bolivian jungle camps processing cocaine materials were raided. A Bolivian policeman is shown standing in front of a former cocaine-processing camp in the Bolivian jungle. (Wide World Photos)

accepted the offer of church mediation in its dispute with the miners. Eleven days of talks produced an agreement providing for the release of a hundred labor, peasant, and community leaders, a halt to government efforts to close mines, new jobs or compensation for miners who lost jobs, a lifting of the blockade on the flow of supplies to the mining regions of Oruro and Potosí, and consultations with the union on further decisions regarding mines.

The miners, the backbone of the *Central Obrera Boliviana* (COB), historically Latin America's strongest labor movement, had beaten off government efforts to destroy their union. But

there was no indication of a change in the government's overall economic policy, a neoliberal, free-market policy that sought to eliminate or sell off state-owned industries, remove tariff barriers to foreign imports, and lift all restrictions on foreign investment. The fruits of that policy were apparent in the decline of traditional industries, a drop in consuming power of some 40 percent in 1985–1986, and an unemployment rate of 30 percent. By the end of 1986, 25,000 miners had already lost their jobs and 7,000 more expected layoffs.

Paz and Sachs could point to a drastic decline in the inflation rate as proof of the success of

380

their program. However, free-market theory assumed the tens of thousands of unemployed miners and others who had lost their jobs as a result of the Sachs plan would find work in the private sector. But the only expanding private sector economic activity in Bolivia was coca and cocaine production. Thousands of miners, finding no alternative employment, invested the indemnification money they received from the government in land and began to grow coca. Bolivian coca-leaf production increased 60 percent—from 50,000 metric tons before the Sachs plan to 80,000 afterward—making Bolivia the second largest producer of coca. It is also the second largest producer of cocaine. An estimated 500,000 Bolivians are now dependent on the coca economy, which makes cocaine "like a cushion that is preventing a social explosion."

In August 1989, after the first round of the presidential election had failed to give a plurality to the two leading candidates, a deal struck between the former dictator Banzer and Jaime Paz Zamora, candidate of the social democratic Movement of the Revolutionary Left (MIR), led to Paz Zamora's selection as president by Congress. In office he continued the policies of his predecessor, closing down or privatizing state-owned enterprises and proclaiming states of siege to deal with work stoppages by miners, doctors, and teachers, among others to protest his economic policies.

Although President Paz Zamora had initially rejected a United States offer to increase military aid to Bolivia on condition that the Bolivian armed forces be brought into the war on drugs, he appeared to be yielding to U.S. pressure on him to reconsider. Joint U.S.–Bolivian sorties now regularly occur in the Chapare region where most of Bolivia's coca is cultivated. But by spring 1991 there was no evidence that the sorties, the destruction of access roads, and other military measures were winning the Bolivian war on drugs. Increasing or declining supplies of coca from the Chapare region seemed above all to reflect the movement of peasants into and out of coca cultivation according to fluctuations in coca leaf prices.

Ecuador, 1972–1991

Ecuador, the smallest of the Andean republics, experienced the faint beginnings of a social revolution in 1972, when a group of nationalist military headed by General Guillermo Rodríguez Lara ousted the aging, demagogic President José María Velasco Ibarra, who had dominated Ecuadorian politics for the previous four decades. The new military junta promised social reform, including radical land reform, and offered a program of rapid economic development that stressed industrialization and the modernization of agriculture. It also promised to reverse the previous official policy of surrender of the country's rich oil resources in the Oriente, the Amazonian lowlands, to foreign companies. The new government counted on revenue from oil to finance the planned reforms and program of economic development.

Five years later, the advance of the Ecuadorian Revolution appeared to be stalled. Opposition from the still-powerful hacendado class had almost completely paralyzed agrarian and tax reform. Some land had been distributed to the peasants, but big landowners controlled 80 percent of the cultivated area. The military government appeared virtually to have abandoned land redistribution in favor of cooperating with the hacendados to increase production and revenues by mechanization, greater concentration of landownership, and the ouster of peasants from the land. The result was growing peasant agitation for true land reform, accompanied by invasions of estates and clashes between peasants and security forces.

Industrialization continued the advance begun in the 1960s, but it was a dependent industrialization based on massive importation of foreign capital and goods. By the early 1970s, foreign interests controlled some 35 percent of all industrial enterprises, nearly 60 percent of all commercial enterprises, and half of all banking assets in Ecuador. Under pressure from foreign oil companies for lower taxes and wider profit margins—a pressure exerted through a boycott on oil exports—the military regime retreated from its insistence on tight control over prices, profits, and the volume and rate of oil production. These concessions represented a defeat for the nationalist left wing of the military junta and sharpened the divisions within it.

In Ecuador, as in other Latin American countries under military control, the late 1970s saw a growing movement for a return to civilian rule. Aware of their economic failures and especially their failure to relieve the dismal poverty of the Ecuadoran masses—official figures showed that the wage earners' share of the national income had declined from 53 percent in 1960 to less than 46 percent in 1973 and that 7 percent of the population received more than 50 percent of the national income—the military appeared quite willing to abandon the burden of governing the country. In July 1978, Jaime Roldós, the populist candidate of the Concentration of Popular Forces, handily won the first round of a presidential contest presided over by the armed forces. During the campaign, the young, energetic Roldós promised a new deal that would include a revived agrarian reform and an end to foreign economic control. In April 1979, his victory was confirmed by the second round of the presidential elections. But a conflict with the congressional leader of his own party, who consistently blocked legislation proposed by Roldós, prevented him from implementing his program until May 1980, when he was assured of the support of a majority in Congress.

Central to that program was the use of large amounts of Ecuador's oil earnings to modernize agriculture, promote industrialization, and construct a network of roads to expand the internal market. Roldós's Five-Year Plan called for investment of $800 million in rural development that would bring some 3 million acres of coastal, highland, and Amazonian farmland into new production. The pace of agrarian reform was to be accelerated, with almost 2 million acres to be distributed to landless peasants by 1984. Roldós's foreign policy stressed greater independence of the United States, reflected in his maintenance of friendly relations with Cuba, expansion of diplomatic and commercial ties with socialist

countries, and support for Central American revolutionary movements. But Roldós's ambitious reform and development program had hardly begun when he was killed in a plane crash in May 1981. He was immediately succeeded by Vice President Oswaldo Hurtado Larrea of *Democracia Popular,* a Christian Democratic party.

This transition took place amid deteriorating economic conditions as a result of a developing recession and declining prices for Ecuadoran oil. Hurtado, more conservative than Roldós, reversed his foreign policy, abandoned much of his reform and development program, and adopted austerity measures, including the removal of subsidies on wheat and gasoline. Such moves were designed to ease the burdens of servicing a massive $4.7 billion foreign debt and to compensate for declining revenues from oil exports. These measures, it was hoped, would pave the way for an IMF loan. But the austerity program encountered intense opposition from the trade unions, who responded with strikes. In Congress Roldós's Concentration of Popular Forces secured votes of censure against the oil minister and the finance minister, who were forced to resign. While the stalemate between Congress and the president continued, the economic situation steadily deteriorated. By the end of 1982, the foreign debt stood at around $5.5 billion, and payments took 25 percent of the budget. Especially alarming was the rapid decline in Ecuador's oil reserves, fallen by early 1982 to as low as 650 million barrels according to some estimates; unless new reserves were discovered in the country's Amazonian region, it was predicted, Ecuador's oil wealth and chief exchange earner would be gone in a decade.

The economic slump sharpened the social problems created by advances in industrialization and the modernization of agriculture. From 1970 to 1980 the proportion of peasants in the population had fallen from 68 percent to 52 percent. The agrarian reform, stressing mechanization and concentration of landownership rather than distribution of land to the landless, had ended semiservile relations in the countryside but aggravated the problem of landlessness and also rural unemployment. The result was to swell the number of rural people fleeing to the cities in search of work that only few found. By the early 1980s the great port city of Guayaquil had a population of 1 million; an estimated two-thirds of its inhabitants were unemployed or underemployed and lacked adequate shelter, food, or medical care. Thus, in an atmosphere of economic and political crisis, social problems and tension accumulated with little prospect that solutions would soon be found.

In the mid-1980s, Ecuador, like Bolivia, became the scene of a determined effort to implement the free-market, neoliberal policies for which the United States under the Reagan administration provided a model. In 1984 León Febres Cordero, candidate of a coalition of six rightist parties, won a narrow victory in the presidential race over the candidate of a center-left coalition, Rodrigo Borja Cevallos. It soon became apparent that Febres intended to carry out the conservative economic program that he had stressed in the first round of the election and then muted, on the advice of his political consultants, in the second runoff. In late 1984 Febres reached an agreement with the IMF for the deferment of payment on Ecuador's foreign debt, which stood at about $7 billion and took between 30 and 40 percent of Ecuador's export earnings for interest payments. The price exacted and willingly accepted by Febres was that usually demanded of Third World countries by the IMF: Ecuador must take steps to encourage foreign investment and restrict domestic consumption, to lower tariffs on foreign imports, and to modify the monetary exchange system in favor of exporters. In this and in other ways Febres justified the tribute paid to him by President Reagan when he visited Washington in January 1986: Febres, declared Reagan, was "an articulate champion of free enterprise."

Febres also followed the United States in his foreign policy, declaring in October 1985 that peace could not come to Central America until "legitimate elections" without "clubbings and violence," were held in Nicaragua. Nicaraguan President Ortega responded by branding Febres "a tool of the United States" and calling attention to Febres's own dubious political tactics. The next day Ecuador broke off diplomatic relations with Nicaragua, barely one week after joining the Latin American nations endorsing the Contadora peace process.

In fact, Ortega was not alone to voice such criticism of Febres. *Latinamerica Press* in 1986 observed that one reason for Febres's popularity with the Reagan administration was that "Ecuador's government is democratic but authoritarian. It does not trouble itself with democratic niceties when they get in its way, and has demonstrated an extraordinary talent for neutralizing congressional opposition." In 1984, when Congress, in conformity with the constitution, named eighteen members to the Supreme Court, Febres rejected the appointments and ordered the court building sealed off to prevent appointees from taking their seats. Eventually the congressmen bowed to Febres's wishes and selected another group of appointees more satisfactory to the president. When Febres came to office, he faced a congress in which the center-left opposition had a three-vote margin. In the summer of 1985 Febres succeeded in knocking together a majority by enticing a number of minor party deputies into his coalition. Thereafter Congress routinely approved Febres's legislative proposals, and the flamboyant president appeared to be well on the way toward achieving his program.

There was a darker, more repressive side to Febres's domestic policy. Former President Osvaldo Hurtado Larrea, viewed as no radical, charged that Febres had committed "grave and systematic violations of human rights and laws protecting democracy." Febres, declared another observer, "treats all the opposition as subversive."

Febres's apparently irresistible march toward absolute power suffered a crushing setback on June 1, 1986, when Ecuadorans went to the polls. Voters decisively defeated Febres's congressional candidates and rejected proposals for electoral changes that would have reshaped the constitution to his liking. Overall, Febres's majority of 41 was changed to a minority of 10, while the left emerged with a majority bloc of 43, and the other 7 seats were held by centrist parties.

Given the irreconcilable differences between the left majority and the rightist president, all signs pointed to impasses like those between President Roldós and his congress and between President Hurtado and his congress. The most divisive issue was the debt problem, with Congress demanding a ceiling on debt service equal to 25 percent of Ecuador's oil earnings. Meanwhile the economic situation continued to worsen, with a 44 percent decline in earnings from oil in 1986. In early March 1987, earthquakes that left over a thousand dead and tens of thousands homeless destroyed a stretch of Ecuador's major oil pipeline, ending exports of the country's main hard-currency earner. On March 17 the government announced a moratorium on debt interest payments but made clear this was only temporary and simultaneously announced an 80 percent hike in fuel prices. The government also announced there would be no wage raises in 1987.

A balance sheet of the impact of President Febres Cordero's economic and social policies on Ecuadoran living standards made dismal reading. A study by Ecuador's Catholic University disclosed that foreign corporations took three dollars out of the country for every dollar they invested. Between 1981 and 1984, workers' wages fell from 32 percent to 20 percent as a percentage of national income and employers' profits rose from 60 percent to 70 percent. Ninety percent of school children suffered from parasitic diseases, and the infant mortality rate according to various estimates stood at between 150 and 250 per thousand.

As the 1988 general elections approached, the Febres administration and the opposition prepared for a struggle for the presidency. The country's trade unions mobilized behind a program calling for the nationalization of the oil industry, the rescinding of price hikes, a 100 percent increase in the country's $80-per-month minimum wage, and the impeachment of Febres. In the first

round of the elections (January 1988), two left-of-center candidates ran first and second, with Febres's choice for president a poor third. In the run-off election in May, Rodrigo Borja Cevallos of the Democratic Left party (ID) won and took office with a comfortable majority of seats held by left and center-left parties in Congress.

Borja had run on a platform of greater independence from the United States, renewal of ties with Nicaragua, and giving priority to social needs over debt interest payments to foreign banks. In fact he pursued a more independent foreign policy than Febres, joining other Latin American states in criticism of the United States invasion of Panama; he also renewed relations with Nicaragua. But Borja faced what he called "the worst economic crisis" in Ecuador's history. In the last four years food prices had jumped 240 percent, and half the labor force was unemployed or underemployed. The crisis sharply limited Borja's options in economic and social policy. A moderate leftist in the social democratic mold, Borja assured businessmen that his government would carry out no nationalizations but would seek to regulate the economy and support the private sector. His efforts to achieve debt payment relief met with resistance from the foreign banks: Ecuador was forced to accept IMF demands for a devaluation of its currency, a commitment to raise fuel prices, and other austerity measures as a condition for starting debt rescheduling talks with creditor banks. As a result, as the Borja regime approached its mid-term mark, it faced growing opposition both on the right and among its former supporters on the left. Denouncing Borja's economic policies as unjust and dictated by the IMF, the socialist parties joined conservatives in voting censure of the ministers responsible for the austerity measures, forcing their resignation under the country's parliamentary rules. As a result of these defections, Borja lost his working majority in the legislature. In an apparent move to prove his progressive credentials and strengthen his party's electoral prospects, Borja asked the legislature to approve a constitutional amendment that would enable the executive to increase the budget allocation for public health from 7 to 20 percent.

The growing militancy of Ecuadorian labor, reflected in a general strike in January 1991, was matched by that of the Indians who make up more than 40 percent of the country's population. In June 1990 their organization spearheaded a protest that mobilized hundreds of thousands of Indians from eight provinces in the sierra and several in the Amazon. The Indian demands included land redistribution and a constitutional declaration that Ecuador was a multi-ethnic country. Although the government agreed to dialogue with the Indian leaders, pressure from the great planters and ranchers resulted in the government's abandoning its promises. The new militancy of the Indians, traditionally reputed to be peaceful and docile, caused alarm among the country's landed elite.

Peru's "Ambiguous Revolution"

A revolution of a unique kind began in Peru in October 1968. Developments in that country between 1968 and 1975 exposed the fallacy of the common assumption that the Latin American military constitutes one reactionary mass. Moving with greater speed and vigor than any civilian reformist regime in Latin American history, a military junta headed by General Juan Velasco Alvarado decreed the nationalization of key industries and natural resources, a land reform that transferred great estates to peasant and worker cooperatives, and the creation of novel new forms of economic organization that should be "neither capitalist nor communist." In 1975 the Peruvian Revolution halted its advance and began a retreat that threatened even its major conquests—the agrarian reform and the great nationalizations—with erosion and even destruction. Yet it must rank among the more serious recent Latin American efforts to achieve a breakthrough in the struggle against backwardness and dependency. Despite its mistakes and failures, it has already made an indelible mark on Peruvian society. The study of those mistakes and failures should help Peruvians as they search

for new approaches to the solution of their country's great national problems.

Peru's "ambiguous revolution" poses some intriguing questions. Why should a group of military officers, a class commonly regarded as the staunchest defenders of the old order in Latin America, launch a major attack on that order in Peru? What economic and social interests did the Peruvian military reformers represent? In the last analysis, was the Peruvian Revolution a "bourgeois revolution" designed to promote the rise of an autonomous native capitalism? If the military reformers failed to make a clean break with the past, with the model of dependent development and the problems it generates, what were the reasons for that failure? An attempt to answer these questions requires an examination not only of the revolution itself but of its remote origins, going back to the establishment of an independent Peru.

Peru: From Independence to the War of the Pacific

The liberation of Peru from Spanish rule came from without, for the creole aristocracy, whose wealth was derived from the forced labor of Indians and black slaves in mines, workshops, and haciendas, rightly feared that revolution might set fire to this combustible social material. The elite, although eager for the economic and political benefits of self-rule, would have preferred a peaceful settlement through negotiation and the grant of autonomy within a reformed Spanish Empire. The process of Peruvian liberation began when an army of Argentinians and Chileans under General José de San Martín landed on the coast near Lima in 1820 and occupied the capital. It ended when Bolívar's lieutenant, General Antonio José de Sucre, at the head of a mainly Colombian army, accepted the surrender of José de la Serna, the last Spanish viceroy on the South American continent, on the field of Ayacucho in December 1824.

The liberators, San Martín and Bolívar, attempted to reform the social and economic institutions of the newly created Peruvian state. San Martín decreed a ban on slave importation, the automatic emancipation of all children born of slaves in Peru, and the abolition of Indian tribute, the mita, and all other kinds of Indian forced labor; he also proclaimed that all inhabitants of Peru, whether Indians or creoles, were Peruvians. Since these reforms did not conform to the interests of the creole elite, they were never implemented. When Bolívar assumed power in Peru in 1823, he enacted reforms reflecting the same liberal ideology. Wishing to create a class of independent small-holders, he decreed the dissolution of the Indian communities and ordered the division of the communal lands into parcels of land; each family was to hold its plot as private property, with the surplus to become part of the public domain. While attacking communal property, Bolívar left alone feudal property, the great haciendas serviced by yanaconas, or colonos (Indian sharecroppers or serfs) who had to pay their landlords a rent that amounted to as much as 50 to 90 percent of the value of their crops, in addition to *pongueaje* (free personal service).

The well-intentioned Bolivarian land reform played into the hands of hacendados, public officials, and merchants, who took advantage of Indian weakness and ignorance to build up vast estates at the expense of Indian communal lands; the process began slowly but gathered momentum as the century advanced. Bolívar's efforts to abolish Indian tribute had no greater success. After he left Peru in 1826, the Peruvian government reinstituted the tribute for the Indians of the sierra under the name *contribución de indígenas,* and for good measure reintroduced the *contribución de castas* for the mestizo population of the coast.

The heavy dependence of the new government on Indian tribute as a source of revenue reflected the stagnant condition of the Peruvian economy. The revolution completed the ruin of the mining industry and coastal plantation agriculture, both declining since the close of the eighteenth century, and the scanty volume of exports could not pay for the much greater volume of imports of manufactured goods from Britain. As a result, the new state, already burdened with large wartime debts to English capitalists, developed a massive deficit in trade with Great Britain, its largest trading partner. There was some growth of export of wool after 1836, and in 1840 a new economic era opened on the coast with the beginnings of exploitation of guano, but in its first stage the guano cycle failed to provide the capital accumulation needed to revive the coastal agriculture.

The Military Caudillos

The backward, stagnant state of the Peruvian economy, the profound cleavage between the sierra and the coast, and the absence of a governing class (such as arose in Chile) capable of giving firm and intelligent leadership to the state produced chronic political turbulence and civil wars. Under these conditions, military caudillos, sometimes men of plebeian origin who had risen from the ranks during the wars of independence, came to play a decisive role in the political life of the new state. Some were more than selfish careerists or instruments of aristocratic creole cliques. For example, the mestizo general Andrés de Santa Cruz had a vision of Peru and Bolivia united into a powerful modern state; as president of the Peruvian-Bolivian Confederation from 1836 to 1839, he made a serious effort to reform its institutions.

The ablest and most enlightened of the military caudillos was the mestizo general Ramón Castilla, who served as president of Peru from 1845 to 1851 and again from 1855 to 1862. Castilla presided over an advance of the Peruvian economy based on the rapid growth of guano exports. This export trade was dominated by British capitalists who obtained the right to sell guano to specified regions of the world in return for loans to the Peruvian government (secured by guano shipments). Exorbitant interest and commission rates swelled their profits. Although Castilla gave some thought to direct government exploitation of some guano deposits, to setting controls over the amount and price of guano to be sold, and to plowing guano revenues into development projects, he did nothing to implement these ideas. However, the guano boom stimulated some growth of native Peruvian commerce and banking and created the nucleus of a national capitalist class. Many of the guano producers were also landlords on the coast and utilized profits from guano to restore their plantations, and some Peruvian firms also participated in the guano trade as exporters. Guano prosperity also financed the beginnings of a modern infrastructure; thus, in 1851 the first railway line began to operate between Lima and its port of Callao.

The rise of guano revenues enabled Castilla to carry out a series of social reforms that also contributed to the process of modernization. In 1854 he abolished the Indian tribute, relieving the natives of a heavy fiscal burden, and that same year he freed the remaining black slaves, numbering some twenty thousand, with compensation to the owners of up to 40 percent of their value. Abolition had an initial disruptive effect on coastal agriculture, but in the long run it was very advantageous to the planter aristocracy. With the indemnities for their freed slaves, planters could buy seeds, plants, and Chinese coolies brought to Peru on a contract basis that made them virtual slaves. Meanwhile, the freed slaves often became sharecroppers who lived on the margins of the hacienda and supplied a convenient unpaid labor force and a source of rent. Stimulated by these developments, cotton, sugar cane, and grain production expanded on the coast. Highland economic life also quickened, though on a smaller scale, with the rise of extensive cattle breeding for the export of wool and leather through Arequipa and Lima.

The upward movement of the Peruvian economy after 1850 was briefly interrupted in the 1860s by two crises. In 1864, Spain, which had not totally abandoned its imperial ambitions, seized the Chincha Islands, Peru's richest guano area, in a dispute caused by alleged mistreatment of Spanish immigrants by the Peruvian government. There followed a short war that ended with Spanish surrender of the islands and final recognition of Peru's independence. In 1865 a liberal revolt broke out, reflecting the discontent of the new

commercial and planter aristocracy with the rule of conservative military caudillos. This revolt merged with a great Indian uprising in the sierra, caused by ruthless exploitation of the Indians by local governors, who compelled the natives to exchange their wool for poor-quality manufactured goods sold at vastly inflated prices. Both revolts ended in failure, and the conservative military was again in full control by 1868.

Freed from these crises, the Peruvian economy resumed its advance. Aided by such favorable factors as the temporary dislocation of the cotton industry of the southern United States and large inflows of foreign capital, exports of cotton and sugar increased sharply. The coastal latifundia continued to expand at the expense of sharecroppers and tenants, who were expelled from their lands, and of the remaining Indian communal lands. This process was accompanied by the modernization of coastal agriculture by the introduction of cotton gins, boilers, refinery equipment for sugar, and steam-driven tractors.

While profits from the agricultural sector enabled the commercial and landed aristocracy of Lima to live in luxury, the Peruvian state sank even deeper into debt. The guano deposits, Peru's collateral for its foreign borrowings, were being depleted at an ever-accelerating rate, and the bulk of the proceeds from these loans went to pay interest on old and new debts. In 1868, during the administration of the military caudillo José Balta, his minister of the treasury, Nicolás de Piérola, devised a plan for extricating Peru from its difficulties and providing funds for development. The project eliminated the numerous consignees to whom guano had been sold and awarded a monopoly of guano sales in Europe to the French firm of Dreyfus and Company. In return, the Dreyfus firm agreed to make Peru a loan that would tide it over immediate difficulties and in addition to service its foreign debt. The contract initiated a new flow of loans that helped to create a boundless euphoria, an invincible optimism, about the country's future.

A U.S. adventurer and entrepreneur, Henry Meiggs, who had made a reputation as a railway builder in Chile, easily convinced Balta and Piérola that they should support the construction of a railway system to tap the mineral wealth of the sierra. As a result, much of the money obtained under the Dreyfus contract, and a large part of the proceeds of the dwindling guano reserves, were poured into railway projects that could not show a profit in the foreseeable future.

Pardo and the Civilianist Party

The good fortune of Dreyfus and Company displeased the native commercial and banking bourgeoisie that had arisen in Lima. A group of these men—including former guano consignees who had been eliminated by the Dreyfus contracts—headed by the millionaire businessman Manuel Pardo, challenged the legality of the contract before the Supreme Court, arguing that assignment of guano sales to a corporation of native consignees that they proposed to form would be more beneficial to Peru's economic development. The native bourgeoisie suffered defeat, but in 1871 they organized the *Civilista,* or Civilianist party (in reference to their opposition to military caudillos), which ran Manuel Pardo as its candidate for president. An amalgam of "an old aristocracy and a newly emerging capitalist class," the Civilianist party opposed clerical and military influence in politics and advocated a large directing role for the state in economic development. Pardo won handily over two rivals and took office in 1872.

Pardo presided over a continuing agricultural boom, with exports reaching a peak in 1876. Foreign capital poured into the country. In those years, an Irish immigrant, W. R. Grace, began to establish an industrial empire that included textile mills, a shipping line, vast sugar estates, and Peru's first large-scale sugar-refining plants. While private industry prospered, the government sank ever deeper into a quagmire of debts and deficits. The guano cycle was nearing its end, with revenues steadily declining as a result of falling prices, depletion of guano beds, and competition from an important new source of fertilizer, nitrates, being exploited by Anglo-Chilean capitalists in the southern Peruvian province of Tarapacá. In 1875, wishing to control the nitrate industry and make it a dependable source of government income, Pardo expropriated the foreign companies in Tarapacá and established a state monopoly over the production and sale of nitrates. This measure angered the Anglo-Chilean entrepreneurs whose holdings had been nationalized and who were indemnified with bonds of dubious value. Meanwhile, due to unsatisfactory market conditions in Europe, the nationalization measure failed to yield the anticipated economic benefits.

In 1876, Peru felt the full force of a worldwide economic storm. In a few months, all the banks of Lima had to close; by the following year, the government had to suspend payments on its foreign debt and issue unbacked paper money. The economic collapse was followed by a military disaster: the War of the Pacific. Despite heroic resistance, Peru suffered a crushing defeat at the hands of a Chilean state that enjoyed a more advanced economic organization, political stability, and the support of British capitalists. The war completed the work of economic ruin begun by the depression. The Chileans occupied and ravaged the economically advanced coastal area; they levied taxes on the hacendados and dismantled equipment from the haciendas and sent it to Chile; they also sent troops into the sierra to exact payment from hacendados, towns, and villages. Their extortions infuriated the Indian peasantry. Led by General Andrés Cáceres, those Indians began to wage an effective guerrilla war of attrition against the Chilean occupiers. The war was finally ended by the 1883 Treaty of Ancón.

Neocolonial Peru: The English and North American Connections, 1883–1968

The war left a heritage of political and social turbulence as well as economic ruin. Military and civilian leaders disputed one another's claims to be the legitimate president and mobilized *montoneros* (bands of guerrillas and outlaws) for their armed struggles. In some areas, the Indian peasantry, having acquired arms during the war with Chile, rose in revolt against oppressive hacendados and local officials. Banditry was rife in parts of the sierra; on the coast, conflicts took place between bands armed by landowners or their agents for control of irrigation canals or over property boundaries.

From the struggle for power the militarists once again emerged victorious: in 1884 the guerrilla leader General Andrés Cáceres battled his way into Lima and seized the National Palace. Two years later, he was elected president for a four-year term. Under Cáceres, a slow, painful process of economic recovery began. His first concern was the huge foreign debt. In 1886 the Peruvian government negotiated the so-called Grace Contract with British bondholders. This agreement created a Peruvian Corporation, controlled by the British bondholders, that assumed the servicing of Peru's foreign debt and received in exchange Peru's railways for a period of sixty-six years. The agreement confirmed British financial domination of Peru but also initiated a new flow of investments that hastened the country's economic recovery. Particularly important was the resulting rehabilitation of the railways and their extension to important mining centers, especially into La Oroya, whose rich silver, zinc, and lead mines began to contribute to the economic revival.

Economic recovery strengthened the political hand of the planter aristocracy and the commercial bourgeoisie, who were increasingly impatient with the arbitrary ways of the military caudillos. Their leader was the flamboyant Piérola, founder of the Democratic party, which united various *Civilista* factions in an effort to bring the military under civilian control. In 1895, Piérola led a successful revolt against Cáceres when that guerrilla fighter sought to impose himself as president for a second time. The same year, Piérola, running unopposed, was elected president and presided over four years of rapid economic

recovery. On the coast, the sugar plantations expanded at the expense of small landholders and Indian communities and underwent intensive modernization. In the Andes, the economic revival spurred a renewed drive by hacendados to acquire Indian communal lands, a drive extended to regions hitherto free from land-grabbing. A new law (1893) that in effect re-enacted Bolívar's decree concerning the division and distribution of communal lands facilitated the process of land acquisition. In this period there also arose a new contract labor system, the *enganche,* designed to solve the labor problem of coastal landlords now that Chinese contract labor was no longer easily available. By this system, Indians from the sierra were recruited for prolonged periods of labor on coastal haciendas, sometimes under conditions of virtual serfdom.

The Indian Problem

Yet the postwar period also saw the birth of a new sensitivity to the Indian question and a movement in behalf of the Indians. The rise of this indigenismo was closely connected with the crisis of conscience caused by the disastrous War of the Pacific. By exposing the incompetence and irresponsibility of a creole elite that had totally failed to prepare Peru materially and morally for its greatest ordeal, the war led many intellectuals to turn to the Indian peasantry as a possible source of national regeneration. At the University of San Marcos in Lima there arose a generation of teachers who rejected the traditional positivist tendency to brand Indians as inherently inferior. The apathy, inertia, and alcoholism of the Indians, these scholars claimed, resulted from the narrow, dwarfed world in which they were forced to live. But as a rule these bourgeois reformers ignored the economic aspect of the Indian question and focused on a program of education and uplift that would teach Indians ways to help them to enter the new capitalist society.

The great iconoclast Manuel González Prada (1848–1918) rejected this gradual, reformist approach to the Indian problem. The Indian question is an economic and social question rather than one of pedagogy," he wrote. Schools and well-intentioned laws could not change a feudal reality based on the economic and political power of the *gamonales* (great landowners) lords of all they surveyed. Elimination of the hacienda system, therefore, was needed to solve the Indian question. But that change would never come through the benevolence of the ruling class: "The Indian must achieve his redemption through his own efforts, not through the humanity of his oppressors." And González Prada advised Indians to spend on rifles and cartridges the money they now wasted on drink and fiestas.

Splendid on the attack, sound in his general diagnosis of the Indian question, González Prada proved incapable of working out a well-defined political and economic program for its solution. But his powerful indictment of the oppressors of the Indians, his faith in the creative capacity of the Indian masses, and his rebellious spirit, expressed in prose that flowed like molten lava, profoundly influenced the next generation of intellectuals, who revered the master but went beyond his unsystematic radicalism in their search for solutions to Peru's problems.

The Return of Pardo

The Indian question was Peru's gravest social problem, but the rapid economic advance that began under Piérola produced the emergence of a working class whose demands also threatened the peace and security of the ruling class. By 1904 an organized labor movement had arisen, and strikes broke out in Lima's textile mills and other factories. Guillermo Billinghurst, a self-made millionaire and leader of the Democratic party who won election as president in 1912, was convinced that the stubborn refusal of employers to make reasonable concessions to the workers threatened the very existence of capitalism. Accordingly, as president he decreed the eight-hour day for some worker groups, legalized strikes, and pushed through Congress a law requiring collective bargaining between workers and management in individual plants. But Billinghurst's reform proposals and his tactic of mobilizing the workers in support of his program antagonized conservative interests, and in 1914 he was overthrown by an army coup. The next year, elections organized by a military junta again gave the presidency to the former president, Manuel Pardo.

Pardo's second term spanned the years of World War I. Although Peru remained neutral, the conflict had a large impact on the country's economy. After an initial brief recession, a boom developed as the belligerents sharply increased their demand for Peruvian oil, copper, cotton, rubber, and guano. Since the importation of consumer goods virtually came to a halt, there was a mushrooming growth of light industry. The profits of planters, mine owners, and merchants swelled, but a catastrophic inflation imposed great hardships on workers; food prices, in particular, soared as landowners abandoned food production in favor of such export commodities as cotton and sugar.

In 1918 miners, port workers, and textile workers went out on strike. Armed clashes took place between the strikers and the troops sent out to disperse them, and many strikers were arrested. News of the success of the Russian Revolution contributed to the workers' militancy. The strike movement culminated in a three-day general strike in January 1919; the workers demanded the implementation of currently unenforced social legislation, the reduction of food prices, and the imposition of the eight-hour workday. Under pressure from the workers, Pardo granted part of their demands, including the eight-hour day for the manufacturing and extractive industries. The labor struggles of that stormy year merged with the struggle of university students for the reform of an archaic system of higher education that made the university the preserve of a privileged few and denied students any voice in determining policies and faculty appointments.

As his turbulent term drew to a close, Pardo designated a conservative landowner, Antero Aspillaga, as his political heir. But sections of the oligarchy were convinced that the new and unstable political and social atmosphere required a different way of ruling. An astute businessman and politician, Augusto B. Leguía, who had served as minister of finance in the early 1900s and as president from 1908 to 1912, offered a new political model that could be called Caesarist: it combined unswerving fidelity to the dominant domestic and foreign interests with severe repression of dissidents and a demogogic program of nationalism and social reform designed to disarm the workers and achieve class peace. Charging that Aspillaga was a reactionary who did not understand the needs of the masses, Leguía presented himself as a candidate for president and easily defeated Aspillaga in the election of May 1919. Instead of waiting to be formally installed in office, he seized power in July, sent his predecessor Pardo into exile, and established a personal dictatorship that lasted eleven years (1919–1930).

The Leguía Regime: North American Investment and Peruvian Disillusionment

Leguía encouraged by every means at his disposal the influx of foreign—especially North American—capital. This was the cornerstone of his economic policies. Oil and copper were major fields of North American investment in Peru in this period. The fruits of Leguía's policy of opening the doors wide to foreign capital soon became evident; in 1927 a vice president of the First National City Bank wrote that "Peru's principal sources of wealth, the mines and oil-wells, are nearly all foreign-owned, and excepting for wages and taxes, no part of the value of their production remains in the country." Perhaps the most scandalous example of Leguía's policy of giving away Peru's natural resources was his cession of the oil-rich La Brea–Pariñas fields near the northern coastal town of Talara to the International Petroleum Company (IPC), a subsidiary of Standard Oil of New Jersey, in return for a min-

imal tax of about 71 cents a ton. This cession and a 1922 arbitral award confirming the dubious claims to the area in question of an English oil company, whose rights had passed to the IPC, became an abiding source of Peruvian nationalist resentment.

Peru under Leguía received a plentiful infusion of North American bond loans, amounting to about $130 million. The bankers were aware of the risks involved, but the prospects of extremely large profits made these transactions extremely attractive. A trail of corruption, involving Leguía's own family, followed these deals; Leguía's son Juan, acting as agent for Peru, received more than half a million dollars in commissions.

Leguía used the proceeds of these loans and the taxes on foreign trade and foreign investment operations for a massive public works program (including a large road-building program carried out with forced Indian labor) that contributed to the boom of the 1920s. During those years, Lima was largely rebuilt, provided with modern drinking water and sanitation facilities, and embellished with new parks, avenues, bank buildings, a racetrack, and a military casino. But these amenities did not improve the living conditions of Andean Indians or dwellers in the wretched *barriadas* (shantytowns) that began to ring Lima.

However, convinced that the threat of communism required some concessions to the masses, Leguía did make some gestures in the direction of reform. The constitution of 1920, framed at his bidding by a congress summoned for that purpose, had some striking resemblances to the Mexican constitution of 1917. It declared the right of the state to limit property rights in the interest of the nation, vested ownership of natural resources in the state, and committed the state to the construction of hospitals, asylums, and clinics. It empowered the government to set the hours of labor and to insure adequate compensation and safe and sanitary conditions of work. It also offered corporate recognition of the Indian communities, proclaimed the right of the Indians to land, and promised primary education to their children. But these and other provisions of the constitution were, in the words of Fredrick Pike, a "model for the Peru that never was."

That same contrast between promises and performance marked Leguía's labor policy. During his campaign for the presidency, he denounced "reactionaries" and made lavish promises to the workers. Indeed, on seizing power in July 1919 he immediately freed the labor leaders imprisoned under Pardo. He also permitted a congress of workers to meet in Lima in 1921 and form a Federation of Workers of Lima and Callao. But when the labor movement began to display excessive independence, he intervened to crush it. A second workers' congress, organized in 1927, was abruptly ended by repression, its leaders arrested, and the federation itself dissolved. Workers were forced to accept token reforms and a program of government- and church-sponsored paternalism, crumbs from the well-laden table of the wealthy.

Leguía's performance was especially disillusioning to the university students. Impressed by his promises of educational reform, they had proclaimed Leguía "Mentor of the Youth" and supported his presidential campaign in 1919. Once in power, however, he sought to drive a wedge between students and workers, jailing student leaders and outlawing the Popular University of González Prada, organized by the students to provide the workers with political education. Frequent jailings and deportations of dissident journalists and professors brought Leguía into chronic confrontation with students and faculty, who often went on strike, while the University of San Marcos was repeatedly closed down by the government.

Indianism and Socialism

The surrender to the dictator of what remained of the traditional oligarchical parties, the Democrats and the Civilistas, and the weakness and immaturity of the young Peruvian working class meant that the leadership of the movement of opposition to Leguía fell to middle- and lower-middle-class intellectuals who sought to mobilize the peasantry and the workers for the achievement of their revolutionary aims. Socialism, anti-imperialism, and Indianism provided the ideological content of the movement that issued from the struggles of the turbulent year of 1919, but Indianism was the most important ingredient.

From the writings of the revered González Prada, these intellectuals had learned that the revolution that would regenerate Peru must come from the sierra, from the Andean Indians, who would destroy age-old systems of oppression and unify Peru again, restoring the grandeur that had been the Inca Empire. Common to most of the indigenistas was the belief that the Inca Empire had been a model of primitive socialist organization (a thesis rejected by modern scholars) and that the Indian community had been and still was the "indestructible backbone of Peruvian collectivity" (in fact, by the 1920s almost all land in Peru was individually owned and worked). The mission of the intellectuals, they believed, was to blow life into the coals of Indian rebellion and link the Indian revolution to the urban revolution of students and workers.

An influential indigenista of this period was Luis E. Valcarcel, author of the widely read *Tempest in the Andes* (1927). In ecstatic prose, Valcarcel hailed the Indian revolts of the sierra as portents of the coming purifying revolution. For Valcarcel, the Indians only awaited their Lenin.

A more important and systematic thinker, José Carlos Mariátegui (1895–1930), attempted the task of wedding Indianism to the scientific socialism of Marx and Engels. His major work was the *Seven Interpretive Essays on Peruvian Reality* (1928), which apply the Marxist method to the Indian and land problems, public education, the religious factor, regionalism, and literature. Basing his theory on Indian communal practices and traditions, on the revolutionary experience of other lands, and on his study of history and economics, Mariátegui concluded that socialism offered the only true solution for the Indian problem.

Like other Indianists of his time, Mariátegui idealized the Inca Empire, which he regarded as the "most advanced primitive communist organ-ization which history records." But he opposed a "romantic and anti-historical tendency of recon-struction or re-creation of Inca socialism," for only its habits of cooperation and corporate life should be retained by modern scientific social-ism. Moreover, he stressed that the coming rev-olution must be led by the urban proletariat. Be-fore his untimely death, Mariátegui founded in 1929 the Peruvian Communist party, which affili-ated the next year with the Communist Interna-tional. Despite recent efforts to save Mariátegui from himself by stressing his tactical differences with the Communist International, it is clear that he was in basic agreement with its policies and admired the Soviet achievements.

Indianism was a major plank in the program of the *Alianza Popular Revolucionaria Americana,* or APRA, as it is more commonly known, a party founded in Mexico in May 1924 by Víctor Raúl Haya de la Torre, a student leader who had been exiled by Leguía. Haya de la Torre proclaimed that it was the mission of APRA to lead the Indian and proletarian masses of Peru and all "Indo-America" in the coming socialist, anti-imperialist revolution. Despite the high-sounding rhetoric of *Aprista* propaganda, the party's first concern was and remained Peru's middle sectors—artisans, small landowners, professionals, and small capi-talists. These groups' opportunities for develop-ment diminished as a result of the growing con-centration of economic power in Peru by foreign firms and a dependent big bourgeoisie.

In a revealing statement in the mid-1920s, Haya de la Torre declared that the Peruvian working class, whether rural or urban, lacked the class consciousness and maturity needed to qualify it for the leadership of the coming revolution. He assigned that role to the middle class. To this opinion he joined a belief in the mission of the great man (himself) who "interprets, intuits, and directs the vague and imprecise aspirations of the multitude."

Haya de la Torre early assumed an ambiguous position on imperialism. Standing on its head Le-nin's theory that imperialism was the last stage of capitalism, he argued that in weak, underde-veloped countries like Peru, imperialism was not the last but the first stage of capitalism, for there it provided the capital needed to create industry, a powerful working class, and the middle class that would lead the nation in a socialist revolu-tion. From this to the position that imperialism must be encouraged and defended was an easy step, one that Haya de la Torre eventually took. Mariátegui, who was associated with Haya de la Torre in the student and labor struggles of the early 1920s, soon perceived the inconsistencies and ambiguities of his position and assailed APRA for its "bluff and lies" and its personalism. Despite or precisely because of its opportunism and the vagueness of its ideology, APRA managed to win over an important section of the Peruvian middle class, especially the students, during the three decades after 1920 and to gain great influ-ence over groups of peasantry and urban work-ers, whom it organized into unions that were its main political base.

APRA versus the Military

The onset of a world economic crisis in 1929, which caused a serious decline of Peruvian ex-ports and dried up the influx of loans, brought the collapse of the Leguía dictatorship. But neither the small Communist party nor the stronger APRA movement was able to take political advan-tage of Leguía's downfall. An army officer of *cholo* (Indian) background, Luis Sánchez Cerro, seized power and became the dominant figure in a rul-ing military junta. In 1931, Sánchez Cerro ran for president on a populist platform that proclaimed the primacy of the Indian problem, the need for agrarian reform through expropriation of uncul-tivated lands, and the aim of regulating foreign investments in the national interest. In effect, Sánchez Cerro had stolen much of APRA's thun-der, to the annoyance of Haya de la Torre, who had returned from exile to run for president; his campaign featured demagogic attacks on capital-ism, the church, and the aristocracy but was vague with regard to specifics.

Sánchez Cerro was pronounced the winner, but the Apristas refused to accept the election results and prepared a revolt; in July 1932 they launched the revolt, seizing the garrison and town of Trujillo. Before the arrival of government reinforcements forced them to flee, the Aprista leaders ordered the execution of some sixty officers and soldiers who had been held as hostages. On breaking into the city, the government forces took summary vengeance, sending perhaps a thousand residents of Trujillo before firing squads. On April 30, 1933, in apparent retaliation, an Aprista assassin shot down Sánchez Cerro. This chain of events created a vendetta between the army and APRA that helps explain the long, stubborn opposition of the Peruvian armed forces to APRA's assumption of power, whether by force or peaceful means.

Congress chose Oscar Benavides, a representative of the financial and landed oligarchy, to fill Sánchez Cerro's unexpired term; in 1936, when an Aprista-backed candidate for president appeared to have won the election, the government canceled the election and announced that Benavides would rule for a full six years from the time he had taken power. Under Benavides, the economy gradually emerged from the depths of the depression; his term of office was also marked by some attempts to provide housing projects and other social services to the workers and by an intensive effort to suppress APRA, which continued to operate underground and organized several abortive coups.

In 1939, Benavides was succeeded by his political heir, the banker Manuel Prado, who had run virtually unopposed; at the same time, the voters approved a constitutional amendment extending the presidential term to six years. Prado presided over a boom based on growing wartime demand and high prices for Peru's exports. Prosperity and Peru's alignment on the side of the democracies in World War II (Peru broke off relations with the Axis countries in 1942 and declared war on them in 1945) helped to achieve a thaw in the repressive climate created by Benavides; in particular, Prado made overtures to APRA, which began to change its policies. Without abandoning their drive for exclusive power, the movement's leaders apparently had determined that they could

better achieve this end through negotiation and integration with the militarist-oligarchical establishment than through revolution. Certain shifts in Aprista ideology reflected this change of strategy. The notion that imperialism was the first rather than the last stage of Peruvian capitalism now assumed a new prominence in Aprista theory, and capitalism itself came in for praise, while the perspective of a socialist revolution receded into an increasingly dim and distant future.

Prado left office in 1945, succeeded by the law professor José Luis Bustamante y Rivero, who was elected as the candidate of a broadly based National Democratic Front that took in the outlawed Communist party and even APRA, renamed the Party of the People. Bustamante accelerated the process of liberalization that had begun under Prado. He expanded civil rights, legalized the Communist party, and attempted to institute some social reforms.

But he confronted immense political and economic problems. The Apristas, commanding a majority in Congress, accepted posts in Bustamante's cabinet but soon made clear that their first loyalty was to Haya de la Torre and that they expected Bustamante to function as a figurehead. Bustamante wished to cooperate with the newly legalized APRA movement but refused to become its puppet. When he resisted their demands, the Apristas increasingly resorted to violence, and when the press criticized their acts of terrorism, the APRA majority in Congress introduced a law calling for press censorship. Meanwhile, although Haya de la Torre and his party had championed land reform for decades, they failed to initiate any significant agrarian reform legislation or any other fundamental economic reform.

To add to Bustamante's woes, the country fell into a postwar slump characterized by sharp declines in the prices and exports of copper, cotton, lead, and wool, while a serious food shortage sent food prices soaring. Searching for new sources of revenue, Bustamante signed a contract with the International Petroleum Company that turned over to the company oil lands that had been set aside as a national reserve. The contract had the support of the Apristas, who had become warm friends of the United States and even supported a measure for compensation of American investors for the worthless bonds they had bought in the 1920s. At this time, the State Department decided that APRA was its favorite Peruvian party. The oil contract encountered strong opposition from nationalist businessmen and officers, however, and was defeated in the Senate.

Odría: A Shift to the Right

By 1948, in a stormy atmosphere of Aprista rioting, abortive revolts, and economic crisis, the oligarchy and the military decided that they had had enough of Bustamante. In October a "restorative revolution" overthrew him and proclaimed General Manuel A. Odría its leader. Two years later, having suppressed all opposition from APRA, the left, and Bustamante's followers, Odría organized his own unopposed election to the presidency. Thus, he stayed in power for eight years (1948–1956).

The "restorative revolution" produced a sharp shift to the right. The movement of rural unionization, which had assumed great strength under Bustamante, was forcibly halted; unions under APRA or leftist control were liquidated or taken over by Odría's supporters, strikes were broken with the use of troops, and a Law of Internal Security empowered the government to use whatever means were judged necessary to maintain public order. Meanwhile, foreign investors were treated with a generosity that recalled the days of Leguía. Their taxes were lowered, and exchange controls were removed. *Fortune,* a journal reflecting the viewpoint of U.S. businessmen, congratulated Peru on its "scrupulous respect for private property and the principle of free markets and convertibility."

Gradually, thanks in part to the stimulus of the Korean war (1950–1953), Peru emerged from its recession and even experienced a boom. Again imitating Leguía, Odría used part of the increased government revenues for a vast public works program and for a paternalistic program of social assistance to urban workers that recalled the similar program of Juan Domingo Perón in Argentina. With the ending of the Korean war, however, exports and revenues once more declined, and Odría found it increasingly difficult to continue his ambitious public works program. In 1954–1955, with unemployment and inflation both rising, strikes and unrest grew, and Odría even came under hostile criticism from oligarchical elements who were displeased with his arbitrary methods of rule. Under strong pressure for a return to democratic processes, Odría consented to repeal of the Law of Internal Security and promised free elections in 1956.

The two main contenders for the presidency in that year were former president Manuel Prado, who was supported by a coalition of conservatives and APRA, which he promised to legalize, and Fernando Belaúnde Terry, candidate of the National Front of Democratic Youth, a middle-class group that included many disillusioned Apristas and had taken over much of the APRA's program, especially its promise of agrarian reform and incorporation of Indians into national life. The victorious Prado proceeded to restore civil rights and trade unions and allowed the technically illegal Communist party as well as APRA to operate quite freely. In the economic sphere, however, Prado and his conservative finance minister, Pedro Beltrán, continued the policies of Odría: laissez faire; reduction of taxes on business, foreign and domestic; and promotion of foreign investments. The net result was that by the end of Prado's second term, the inequities of Peru's income distribution had markedly increased. In regard to the agrarian problem, Prado and Beltrán limited themselves to setting up commissions to study means of fostering small and medium-sized private property in the countryside, which meant that nothing was done.

As a result, the agrarian problem in the sierra had reached an acute stage by 1960, with unrest spreading like wildfire. Collisions between the hacendados and increasingly militant and well-organized peasants became ever more frequent. In some cases, peasants were revolting against precapitalist labor systems (like the yanacona system, which often required free personal service); in others, violence arose as a result of the efforts of landowners to evict their tenants and sheep in favor of wage labor and cash rent systems. These evictions increased landlessness and population pressure in the Indian communities and accelerated the flow of emigrants to the coast, swelling the population of city slums and shantytowns.

The election of 1962, then, took place against a background of growing social unrest in both the cities and the countryside. The three major candidates were Haya de la Torre, supported by the Prado administration as the "sort of conservative we need in Peru"; Belaúnde, supported by a middle-class party called *Acción Popular* (Popular Action); and Odría, candidate of another new party called the *Odrista* National Union, hastily created for the occasion.

None of the three candidates obtained the required one-third of the votes cast, which meant that Congress had to choose among them. Amid loud charges of Aprista electoral fraud, Haya de la Torre negotiated a deal with Odría, the former persecutor of Apristas, that, in the words of Fredrick Pike, "shocked and disgusted even the most sophisticated and cynical of the Peruvian electorate." Knowing that the military would most likely bar his own assumption of the presidency, Haya de la Torre formed an alliance with Odría that provided for his election as president and the seating of a large bloc of Aprista senators and deputies; Odría was to serve as a figurehead, with real power vested in the Aprista congressional group in alliance with other groups.

But the armed forces spoiled Haya de la Torre's game. Proclaiming that the elections were tainted with fraud, they intervened to nullify them, assuring that truly honest and free elections would be held in one year. During that year, the military government headed by General Ricardo Pérez Godoy initiated a number of reform measures that suggested some change in the military mentality. They included an institute for economic planning, a housing agency for slum-

clearance projects, and some pilot land reform projects.

Belaúnde: Broken Promises

In June 1963, elections organized by the military gave the presidency to the Popular Action candidate, Fernando Belaúnde, whose campaign had a decided indigenista tinge. Visiting the remotest Andean villages, Belaúnde extolled the Inca grandeur, called on the natives to emulate the energy and hard work of their ancestors, and proclaimed the right of the landless peasantry to land. But his performance in the field of agrarian reform did not match his promises. The agrarian law that issued from Congress the following year stressed technical improvement rather than expropriation and division of latifundia, with the hope that hacendados would adopt modern methods to improve production. As amended in Congress by a coalition of Apristas and rightist followers of Odría, the law exempted from expropriation the highly productive coastal estates, whose workers had been unionized by APRA, reserving for land distribution the archaic haciendas of the sierra. But the loopholes or exceptions were so numerous that the results of the law were very modest.

Meanwhile, Belaúnde's election after an indigenista campaign of lavish promises to the peasantry had given great impetus to peasant land invasions. By October 1963, invasions had multiplied in the central highlands and were spreading to the whole southern part of the sierra. The land-invasion movement also changed its character; whereas before the peasants had seized only uncultivated lands, they now occupied cultivated lands, arguing that they had paid for it with their unpaid or poorly paid labor of several generations. Militant peasant unions under radical leadership appeared, and a guerrilla movement arose in parts of the sierra. Meanwhile, a wave of strikes broke out in the cities, and workers occupied a number of enterprises in Lima and Callao.

These outbreaks took the Belaúnde administration by surprise. The extreme right, supported by APRA, demanded the use of the armed forces to repress the peasant movement. Indeed, APRA—once so "revolutionary"—called for the harshest treatment of the rebellious peasants. At the end of 1963, after some vacillation, the Belaúnde government decided to crush the peasant movement by force—a task that the armed forces apparently assumed with reluctance, preferring "civic action" programs of a reformist type. By 1966 the peasant and guerrilla movements had been suppressed. According to one estimate, the repression left 8,000 peasants dead and 3,500 prisoner, 14,000 hectares of land burned with fire and napalm, and 19,000 peasants forced to abandon their homes. Among the military, the conviction grew that only radical structural reforms could definitively end the rural climate of revolutionary violence.

Belaúnde had failed to solve the agrarian problem. He also failed to keep his promise to settle in ninety days after his inauguration the old controversy between Peru and the International Petroleum Company over the La Brea–Pariñas oil fields, claimed by Peru to have been illegally exploited for some forty years. Finally, under strong pressure from United States interests, who delayed large planned investments in Peru, Belaúnde's government signed a pact that represented a massive surrender to the IPC. Peru regained the now almost exhausted La Brea–Pariñas oil fields, but in return agreed to the cancellation of claims for back taxes and illegal profits amounting to almost $700 million. IPC also received a concession to exploit a vast area in the Amazon region and was allowed to retain the refinery of Talara, to which the government agreed to sell all the oil produced from the wells it had regained at a fixed price. A scandal rocked the country when the government, forced to publish the document, claimed to have "lost" the page setting the price that the IPC must pay the state oil company for its crude oil. As public indignation grew, the armed forces issued a statement denouncing the agreement. Opposition parties demanded annulment of the pact, and even the

Catholic church joined the chorus of disapproval. As a result, Belaúnde's Popular Action party and its APRA allies were completely isolated.

For Peru's military leaders, the pact, known as the Pact of Talara, was the last straw. For some years, those leaders had engaged in intense soul-searching over the past and future of their country; now they were convinced that Belaúnde's government and the social forces that supported it were incapable of solving the great national problems. In October 1968 the armed forces seized the presidential palace; sent Belaúnde into exile, and established a military governing junta that began a swift transformation of Peru's economic and social structures.

The Peruvian Revolution, 1968 to the Present

The Military About-Face

The first impression of the news of the military seizure of power in October 1968 was that it was but one more in a long series of military coups that punctuate the history of Peru and other Latin American countries—coups that change the occupant of the presidential palace but leave the existing order intact. Typical of this initial reaction was the Communist party statement that the coup had been hatched in Washington to protect vested United States interests. The error of this opinion became evident as the self-proclaimed "Revolutionary Government of the Armed Forces," under the leadership of General and President Juan Velasco Alvarado, decreed the nationalization of oil, a sweeping agrarian reform law, and a law providing for workers' participation in the ownership and management of industrial concerns.

Observers found these events as startling, in the words of Fidel Castro, "as if a fire had started in the firehouse," for the Latin American military had traditionally been regarded as loyal servants of the area's oligarchies. In Peru, however, a social and ideological gulf had been developing between the military and civilian elites for decades. The typical army officer came from a military family or from the lower middle class; very few officers had links with latifundistas or big business.

Faced with growing evidence of the incapacity of the bourgeois APRA and Popular Action parties to solve the great national problems during the 1950s and 1960s, the leadership of the armed forces undertook intensive study of those questions. At the Center for Advanced Military Studies, founded in 1952, emphasis was placed on economics, sociology, and research techniques. Officers studied topics ranging from the agrarian problem in a sierra valley to the development of the Amazonian jungle area. The dominant ideology at the center reflected the developmentalist theories of the United Nations Economic Commission for Latin America; it stressed the need for planning, industrialization, land reform, and an expanded directing role for the state. The Pact of Talara, regarded by the military as a sellout of Peruvian national interests, appeared to give decisive proof of the incompetence or corruption of the civilian politicians and triggered the coup in October 1968. Within a week, the Velasco junta had nationalized the IPC's oil fields and its refinery at Talara, and soon after it seized all its other assets. Having settled the IPC question, the junta went on to tackle the country's most burning economic and social questions.

Land Reform and Nationalization of Resources

Land reform was the key problem: Peru could not achieve economic independence, modernization, and greater social democracy without liquidating the inefficient, semifeudal latifundio system, the gamonal political system that was its corollary, and the coastal enclaves of foreign oligarchical power. Major specific objectives were to expand agricultural production, and to generate capital for investment in the industrial sector; thus landowners were to be compensated for expropriated

lands with bonds that could be used as investment capital in industry or mining. On June 24, 1969, President Velasco announced an agrarian reform designed to end the "unjust social and economic structures" of the past. The program deviated from orthodox Latin American reform policies in two respects: first, it did not retain the homestead or family-sized farm as its ideal; second, it did not exempt large estates from expropriation on account of their efficiency and productivity. Indeed, the first lands to be expropriated were the big coastal sugar plantations, largely foreign-owned and constituting highly mechanized agro-industrial complexes. These enterprises were transferred to cooperatives of farm laborers and refinery workers.

Next came the turn of the haciendas of the sierra. The reform applied to most highland estates above 35 to 55 hectares, but delays in implementing the law allowed many landowners to evade it by parcelling their holdings among family members and others. The initial aim was to encourage division of estates into small or medium-sized commercial farms, but this would have reduced the number of potential beneficiaries. Under pressure from militant, unionized peasants, who were demanding employment and the formation of cooperatives, the junta moved from parcellation toward cooperative forms of organization. Eventually fully 76 percent of the expropriated lands were organized into cooperatives, the remainder was distributed in individual plots. As noted above, expropriated estates were compensated with bonds that could be used as collateral for industrial development; the recipients of land were required to pay the purchase price over twenty years.

Observers agree that the agrarian reform produced some undeniable immediate and long-range benefits. To begin with, it ended the various forms of serfdom that still survived in the sierra in 1968. Second, food production increased, though not substantially or to the level required by Peru's growing population. Third, according to a 1982 field study of the agrarian reform, it "proved a major economic and political benefit to a significant sector of the peasantry," at least in the case of cooperatives with an adequate capital endowment. "In such cooperatives, members' wages and quality of life improved, often dramatically."[1]

But these gains were offset by the failure of the agrarian reform to raise the general material and political level of the Peruvian peasantry—a failure stemming from incorrect planning and methods on the part of the well-meaning military reformers.

First, the reform was neither as swift nor as thorough as the dimensions of the problem required. As noted above, delays in implementing the program and the ruses employed by landowners meant that a considerable amount of land escaped expropriation. As a result, the reform made only a slight impact on the problem of landlessness and rural unemployment and underemployment, especially in the sierra.

Second, the military reformers lacked a coherent strategy for the general development of the agricultural sector within an overall plan of balanced, inwardly directed national development. Basically, the agricultural sector was viewed as a means of pumping out food and capital to promote development in the urban-industrial area. This was reflected in the military government's food-pricing policy, which was to keep food prices low in order to check inflation and keep the urban working class and middle class content. In the absence of compensating subsidies for small farmers, this policy "served to perpetuate the long-run unfavorable trend of the rural-urban terms of trade." Within the agricultural sector, the allocation of resources and credit was skewed in favor of the already well endowed and efficient coastal estates producing for export, with the bulk of agricultural investment going into large-scale irrigation projects. The needs of highland small farmers for small-scale irrigation

works, fertilizer, and technical assistance were neglected. As a result, the coastal sugar, cotton, and coffee cooperatives tended to become "islands of relative privilege in a sea of peasant poverty and unemployment."

The same lack of a coherent strategy for the development of the agricultural sector as a whole was reflected in the method of distributing hacienda lands. The land was generally transferred to the workers who had been employed full time on the estates. They alone were eligible to be members of the new cooperatives. This left out the temporary laborers and the neighboring peasant villagers who eked out subsistence livings from tiny plots and small herds of sheep. This often led to serious tension and conflict, with the cooperatives defending their privileges and land against invasions by the *comuneros* (peasant villagers). Combined with the failure to distribute all the land subject to expropriation, this pattern of distribution contributed to the continuing flight of *campesinos* to the coastal cities where they swelled the ranks of a large unemployed or underemployed population.

Finally, a major flaw of the agrarian reform was that it was a "revolution from above," with little input from below. Despite lip service to participatory ideology and the creation of a National System of Support for Social Mobilization (SINAMOS), which was supposed to form links between the armed forces and the masses, the military technocrats made the final decisions with respect to work conditions, income policy, crop selection, and the like. Since the government's economic policy tended to subordinate peasant interests to the drive for rapid industrial growth, many peasants became disillusioned with the cooperative model. In some cases, particularly after 1975 when the nationalist reformist Velasco wing of the military was ousted from power by a conservative group stressing private enterprise and a free market, the disillusionment led to peasant demands for dismantling of the cooperatives and parceling out of the land.

After land reform, the nationalization of key foreign-owned natural resources and enterprises

[1] Cynthia McClintock, "Post-Revolutionary Agrarian Politics in Peru," in Stephen M. Gorman, *Post-Revolutionary Peru: The Politics of Transformation* (Boulder, Colorado, Westview Press, 1982), p. 135.

and of domestic monopolies that the military regarded as obstacles to development was the most important objective of the junta's program. When the revolution began, foreign firms controlled the commanding heights of the Peruvian economy. Eight years later, state enterprises had taken over most of these firms. The process began with the nationalization of the IPC, whose assets passed into the control of *Petroperu,* the state-owned oil company. Later, the national telephone system, the railroads (the Peruvian Corporation), and Peru's international airline came under state ownership. The cement, chemical, and paper industries, defined as basic and reserved to the state, were taken over. The important fishmeal industry, in which large amounts of foreign capital were invested, was nationalized. The sugar industry, in large part controlled by the Grace interests, and the cotton industry, dominated by the U.S. firm of Anderson, Clayton, were seized under the agrarian reform law. After the failure of efforts to prod the foreign-owned mining companies into making new investments and developing their unworked concessions, the government decided to enter the field for itself. Nationalization of the giant United States–owned mining complex of Cerro de Pasco in 1974 gave the state ownership of four thousand concessions and vested control of the bulk of mining and refining of copper, lead, and zinc in two state companies, *Minoperu* and *Centrominperu;* nationalization of Marcona Mining in 1975 gave the state control of iron ore and steel. In addition to the take-over of these primarily extractive and manufacturing firms, state companies obtained marketing monopolies of all major commodity exports and most food distribution. Through stock purchases, the government nationalized most of the banking and insurance industries. Thus the state came to control decisive sectors of the Peruvian economy.

The great nationalizations were accompanied by the development of new forms of economic organization—the industrial community and social property—that were conceived by President Velasco and his aides. They were to lay the foundations for a new society that would be "neither capitalist nor communist." The industrial community was a profit-sharing scheme designed to harmonize the interests of employers and workers and stimulate production. The law creating the new system required every industrial firm with six or more workers to allocate 15 percent of its gross earnings annually to the industrial community (comprising all employees, including management). These funds would be used to buy shares in the firm until the industrial community had acquired 50 percent of the stock. Another 10 percent of gross earnings was to be paid out to employees in cash. In addition, the industrial community was to be represented on the board of directors in proportion to the size of the shares it controlled. By 1975 there were 3,446 industrial communities with approximately 200,000 members, representing less than 4.3 percent of Peru's economically active population.

The social property program was viewed by President Velasco as the first step toward a unique Peruvian socialism. According to the law establishing this economic form, a social property firm consisted exclusively of workers, who participated fully in the direction, management, and economic benefits of the firm. However, the firm belonged not to the workers of a given enterprise but to the workers of the social property sector as a whole. Part of the income produced by the firm went into wages, new housing, and other benefits, but part was to be used for expansion and investment in other industries—in other words, for the benefit of society as a whole. This program had barely begun when it was virtually scrapped in the conservative "Second Phase" of the revolution that began in 1975.

The original intent of the military reformers was not to substitute the state for local private capital but to promote its formation by removing such impediments as the latifundio and foreign monopolistic firms and by the creation of an industrial infrastructure to be financed through the export of minerals and agricultural exports. But the radical rhetoric of the nationalistic military only frightened the local bourgeoisie, who were generally satisfied with their technological and financial dependence on foreign capital, and they failed to respond to the incentives for industrial investment. As a result the government itself had to assume the role of the economy's main investor and by 1972 accounted for more than half the total investment in the economy.

But the cost of this investment, added to the large sums expended for compensation for expropriated estates and foreign enterprises, came very high. Tax reform offered one possibility of mobilizing considerable amounts of previously untouched wealth. Such a move, however, would have antagonized the local bourgeoisie, whom the military was wooing, and the middle class, which formed its principal mass base. Because of disputes over expropriation, Peru could not apply for loans to the United States and the multinational agencies it controlled. Accordingly Peru had to turn to foreign private banks. Encouraged by the high price of copper and other Peruvian exports and by the prospect of rich oil strikes in the Amazon Basin, the banks willingly complied with Peru's requests for loans. They lent $147 million in 1972 and $734 million in 1973, making Peru the largest borrower among Third World countries in the latter year.

By early 1975, a new cyclical crisis had begun to ravage the capitalist world. Rising prices for oil and imported equipment and technology, combined with falling prices for Peru's raw material exports, undermined the fragile prosperity that had made President Velasco's reforms possible. These circumstances created unmanageable balance of trade and debt service problems. The model of development based on export expansion and foreign borrowing had again revealed its inherent contradictions.

The experience of the Peruvian Revolution shows the difficulty of escaping from dependent development without radical structural changes in class and property relationships and income distribution. Like the Mexican Revolution, Peru's experience suggests that the revolution that does not advance risks stagnation and loss of whatever gains have been made.

The Revolution Under Attack, 1975–1983

The economic crisis of 1975 provoked a sharp struggle within the military between radical nationalists, grouped around the ailing President Velasco, who proposed to extend the social and economic reforms, and centrists and conservatives, who called for a halt to the reforms and for measures that would win the confidence of native and foreign capitalists, thereby making possible a revival of private investments and the foreign loans needed to refinance existing debts. In August 1975, a peaceful coup replaced President Velasco with his conservative prime minister, Francisco Morales Bermúdez; this was followed by a gradual purge of radical nationalists from the government and the forced resignation of leftist officers from the armed forces. The so-called First Phase of the revolution had ended. To appease foreign and domestic capitalists, the new government introduced a package of severe austerity measures that called for sharp reductions in government investments in state enterprises, steep increases in consumer prices, and a 44 percent devaluation of the currency, only partly offset by wage increases of from 10 to 14 percent. These measures provoked widespread strikes and rioting, which were crushed by the government with a full-scale military operation.

By mid-1976, the process of liquidating the revolutionary changes of the First Phase was in full swing. In June the government announced that the agrarian reform was at an end, although only about one-third of the land subject to expropriation had been distributed. Implementation of the industrial community and social property programs, created by President Velasco and his planners in the heady springtime of the revolution, was abandoned for all intents and purposes. The industrial community program, seriously undermined by changes made in 1977 by the Morales Bermúdez government that deemphasized the law's collective aspect, barely held its own after that date. Students of the program agree that it had little redistributive effect and did not significantly increase production or reduce labor strife. The social property program, bitterly opposed by the private sector and denied government support, languished after 1975.

In early 1978, after long negotiations, Morales Bermúdez capitulated to the IMF and accepted its conditions for a new loan, including reduction of the state economic sector, heavy cuts in budgets and subsidies, large price increases, and severe restraints on wage increases. When the workers again protested with strikes and demonstrations, the government sent troops to break strikes and repress dissidence.

For the thoroughly discredited military junta, the prime concern was how to make a smooth transfer of power to a civilian regime that could be trusted to continue its conservative policies. In July 1977, Morales Bermúdez announced that a constituent assembly would be elected in June 1978 to frame a new constitution to replace the 1933 constitution as the first step toward a restoration of constitutional civilian rule. An electoral law published in November 1977 provided that all citizens who had reached the age of eighteen and could read and write should have the right to vote in the election of the constituent assembly. Preparations for the election immediately got under way, with heavy campaigning by parties on the right and the left.

The election, held in June 1978, reflected widespread discontent with the economic policies of the military junta. APRA, the self-proclaimed party of the "democratic left" with an essentially conservative record, gained the largest number of seats, followed by the right-wing *Partido Popular Cristiano* (PPC); together, these two parties had a working majority in the assembly. The leftist parties, operating under difficult conditions because of government harassment and repression, with many of their leaders in jail or in exile, held the balance of the hundred seats in the assembly and formed a strong opposition. The Popular Action party of former President Belaúnde, whom the military had deposed and sent into exile in 1968, boycotted the election to symbolize its opposition to the military seizure of power.

The document that emerged from the constituent assembly differed little from the constitution of 1933. It established a bicameral Congress, both elected, like the president, for five years. Rejecting efforts by the left to incorporate such reforms of the First Phase as the social property enterprise, the APRA-PPC coalition secured the adoption of language ensuring that the foundations of the Peruvian economy would be the free market and the primacy of the private sector. The constitution guaranteed the right to strike and collective bargaining—but those rights were subject to parliamentary regulation. The biggest novelty was the grant of the right to vote to illiterates.

Even before the assembly had completed its work, the political parties had begun to campaign for the elections scheduled for May 19, 1980. The biggest surprise of their outcome was the relatively poor showing of APRA, which won only 27 percent of the vote, an 8 percent decline from the 1978 level. The result was attributed to divisions in the party between a conservative and a populist wing, the leadership problem created by the illness of Haya de la Torre (he died August 2), and the hostility engendered by its use of violence against other parties during the campaign. But APRA's losses did not benefit the left, which was fragmented into many small groups and hopelessly divided over doctrinal and tactical issues; its vote fell from one-third of the total in 1978 to less than 21 percent in 1980. The big winner was the Popular Action party (AP), whose presidential candidate, Fernando Belaúnde Terry, a master of populist rhetoric who was surrounded by an aura of martyrdom thanks to his ouster by the military in 1968, obtained over 45 percent of the vote. On July 28, 1980, Belaúnde for a second time was inaugurated president of Peru. On the same day the major daily newspapers of Lima, controlled by oligarchical interests and expropriated in 1974 because of their bitter opposition to the reform program, were formally returned to their original owners.

It soon became clear that Belaúnde and Manuel Ulloa, who served as his prime minister and finance minister, intended to continue and extend the "counterreformation" begun by the Morales Bermúdez government of the "Second Phase." Export expansion and debt repayment were the great priorities, to be achieved with the familiar arsenal of austerity measures and devaluation, combined with wage freezes. The resulting decline in living standards caused an unprecedented popular protest; in January 1981, for the first time in Peruvian history, all the major labor groups joined in a general strike. Despite these austerity measures, the economic situation continued to deteriorate in 1981–1982 as the prices and demand for Peru's exports fell while imports rose as a percentage of the GNP. By the end of 1982 Peru's foreign debt, which stood at about $9 billion when Belaúnde took office, had risen to $11 billion, and the government vainly struggled to contain a growing balance of payments problem. Inflation at this time was running at an annual rate of 70 percent, and the currency had lost about 80 percent of its value during the year.

Meanwhile the Belaúnde government had begun to dismantle the major reforms of the Velasco era. A principal objective was to restore a free market in agricultural land, frozen by Velasco, through the dissolution of the cooperative system. A new agricultural promotion and development law gave the government the power to divide cooperative land into small individual plots and turn them over to cooperative members. The plots could then be bought, sold, or mortgaged. The law was condemned by the major peasant federations, which feared that it would lead to the reconcentration of land in a few hands. At the same time, despite much rhetoric about the priority of agriculture, its share of the budget fell sharply.

Other proposed legislation would empower the government to sell off many state-owned companies and increase private participation in many publicly owned firms, through stock issues and other programs. The government's legislative program also included a law banning general and sympathy strikes, and a 1983 budget that featured drastic reductions in public works and the

phasing out of subsidies on basic foods and fuel. These proposals caused bitter wrangling in parliament between the government and the opposition parties; indeed, they provoked rifts within the ruling AP-PPC coalition. In late December 1982, reflecting the disarray within the government's ranks and its failure to cope with the country's grave economic and political problems, Ulloa and his cabinet resigned. A new cabinet representing the same political forces was soon formed.

Thus, fifteen years after the military seized power in Peru, the nation again faced a crisis of unprecedented proportions. Unemployment climbed to new heights; strikes succeeded each other in industry, the railroads, and the banks; and the rural exodus continued to swell the population of the barriadas that ringed Lima. An ominous development in late 1982 and 1983 was a rapid expansion of a guerrilla movement known as the *Sendero Luminoso* (Shining Path), of Maoist inspiration, in the central highlands. In 1982, as he had done in 1963, Belaúnde sent the armed forces to crush an uprising in the Andes.

APRA in Power, 1983–1991

By the early 1980s, Belaúnde appeared increasingly out of touch with his country's realities. His government suffered a severe defeat in the municipal elections of November 1983. Left-of-center parties gathered over 60 percent of the vote; Alfonso Barrantes, candidate of the Marxist-led *Izquierda Unida* (IU) was elected mayor of Lima, whose 6 million inhabitants comprised one-third of Peru's population. The defeat came in response to the economic crisis, blamed by most Peruvians on the Belaúnde government's policies and especially on its debt payment and austerity programs.

These electoral results foreshadowed the outcome of the presidential election of April 1985. Since the centrist and right-wing parties were almost completely discredited, the election turned into a race between the APRA candidate, thirty-six-year-old Alán García Pérez, a disciple of the late Haya de la Torre, and Alfonso Barrantes of the IU. García campaigned on a populist, reformist program, promising to defend the agrarian and industrial reforms of the Velasco era and to reject the free market policies of the Belaúnde regime. In the first electoral round García fell short of the required 51 percent of the vote, gathering 48 percent, followed by Barrantes with 22 percent. The AP and the right-wing parties were virtually annihilated. In a show of good will and cooperation with García, Barrantes declined to take part in a run-off election. In July 1985 García assumed the office of president.

In his inaugural address García proclaimed that henceforth Peru would not deal with the IMF but directly with the creditor banks. He also announced that he would limit interest payments on Peru's foreign debt of about $14 billion to 10 percent of Peru's export earnings—about $400 million. "Peru," García declared, "has one overwhelming creditor, its own people." Other parts of his economic program included measures to halt capital exports, freeze the price of necessities, and raise the minimum wage by 50 percent—all measures opposed by the IMF and the foreign financial community.

García's economic plan aroused alarm in the United States. Treasury Secretary James Baker and Federal Reserve Chairman Paul Volcker attacked the proposed limit on interest payments and hinted at trade reprisals. In his foreign policy García pursued an equally independent line that was also bound to displease the Reagan administration. He expressed support for Nicaragua in its dispute with the United States and declared that he would break diplomatic relations with the United States if it invaded Nicaragua.

García's restrictions on foreign debt payments and his measures to prevent the flight of capital, prevent luxury imports, and raise wages formed part of a coherent program to revive the sluggish Peruvian economy. The long-term goal was promoting the development of an autonomous Peruvian capitalism based on expanded import-substitution industrialization and reduced dependence on imported raw materials. The re-striction on debt repayments and the controls on foreign trade were designed to make capital available for development; the substantial wage increases were expected to expand purchasing power and demand for Peruvian-made goods. In a speech marking the anniversary of his first year in office, he took care to reassure businessmen, declaring that even as he rejected devaluation and new indebtedness as a regression to "the colonial recipes of the IMF," so he rejected nationalization. His path, he said, led to "a strong state redirecting the structure of Peruvian industry toward less import-dependent options."

The results of the first year and a half of the García administration gave grounds for cautious optimism. The signs of economic revival included a projected 6.5 percent rate of economic growth in 1986, an annual inflation rate of some 70 percent (compared to a 200 percent rate when García took office), and an increase in real wages of about 10 percent. These advances inspired confidence and yielded political rewards. APRA made new gains in the municipal elections of November 1986, capturing Lima and some other strongholds of Izquierda Unida.

Ahead, however, lay serious economic problems. Resistance to the price freeze on the part of businessmen, reflected in shortages of consumer items, had forced the government to relax price controls, allowing some prices to rise. If the fissures in the price-freeze structure widened without corresponding wage increases, García's popularity could evaporate. García had banned devaluation as a "colonial recipe" of the IMF, but in November 1986 his government announced that it would soon devalue the currency in an effort to stimulate exports.

A closely related problem was the growing gap between the costs of the recovery program and government income from all sources, including export earnings and the savings obtained by limiting debt payments. García had few options. He could try by tax reform to tap the large wealth of the Peruvian elites, left untouched by the military reformers, but this was an unacceptable solution given the moderate nature of his program. Printing money or a slowdown in economic growth were equally unacceptable. There remained the option of going to foreign banks for loans, but García had ruled out "new indebtedness" as a colonial recipe of the IMF, which had in any case declared him ineligible for new credits.

A major obstacle to the sound, balanced economic growth envisaged by García was the continuing cleavage between the sierra and the coast; the contrast between the poverty and backwardness of the highlands (largely populated by Quechua- and Aymara-speaking Indian peasants) and the relative prosperity of the coast. Landlessness and unemployment or underemployment continued to be burning problems of the sierra. The military reformers had not made a thorough land reform; many great landowners, employing various ruses, had escaped expropriation. When the government expropriated great haciendas and turned them into cooperatives, most peasants were left out. The result was that the highlands became the scene of a struggle between the landless peasantry and the giant cooperatives, often controlled by elite groups of managers, engineers, and bureaucrats. The landless peasants and their organizations were supported by Izquierda Unida, other leftist movements, and often by the Catholic church; the cooperative bureaucrats had the support of government officials, the police, and the local APRA political machines. Typical of the position of many church leaders is the statement of Gustavo Gutiérrez, Peru's leading liberation theologian,[2] that the church must support the peasants' nonviolent struggle for land: "*Campesinos* know that land is life. When they call for land they are necessarily calling for life."

Into this struggle over land, with all its potential for violence, entered the Sendero Luminoso, a guerrilla organization that claimed to derive its inspiration from the ideas of Mao and José Carlos Mariátegui. This group was repudiated by Izquierda Unida and other left-wing movements, which viewed it as terrorist and mistaken in its effort to polarize Peruvian society into militarists and *senderistas*. For the most part led by radicalized students and other middle-class individuals, the Sendero Luminoso emerged in May 1980 with a program of terrorist activity against all who supported the existing bourgeois order; it also encouraged peasants to invade, occupy, and loot cooperatives. The Belaúnde government, it will be recalled, responded to this threat in 1982 by launching a counterinsurgency campaign and by placing nineteen of Peru's twenty-three provinces under a state of emergency with the military in overall control and most civil rights suspended. That situation remained unchanged in 1990. The García government claimed that thousands of officials, police, members of other security forces, and uncooperative peasants had been killed by the Sendero Luminoso, but church authorities and other independent observers asserted that the security forces had themselves committed many repressive acts, and that many killings of peasants ascribed to the guerrillas were the work of these forces.

On assuming office García promised to end the abuses of human rights by the military and other security forces, and appointed a peace commission to end the ongoing conflict in the highlands. But his claim as a champion of human rights suffered a damaging blow in June 1986 when the president acting as commander-in-chief sent troops and marines to end riots by Sendero Luminoso inmates of three prisons in Lima and Callao. The prisoners had demanded improved conditions for themselves and their relatives. These operations, made with no apparent effort to end the riots peacefully, resulted in a bloodbath that killed 267 prisoners, many of whom had not yet been sentenced by the courts. The deaths appeared to be a premeditated job of extermination. Efforts to investigate the situation on the spot were frustrated when the three prisons were declared militarized zones to which lawyers and relatives were denied access; the prisoners' bod-

[2] For a fuller discussion of "liberation theology"—a doctrine that frequently combines the church's "preferential option" for the poor with Marxist analysis of economic and social problems—see the section on "The Catholic Church" in Chapter 21.

ies were buried clandestinely. García promised punishment for "any excess" but also strongly defended the military. In a protest against the handling of the prison situation, García's peace commission resigned. It seemed doubtful that any sanctions would be taken against the parties responsible for the massacre. The episode suggested that the conservative military who had ousted President Velasco in 1975 retained much of their power under García.

Meanwhile the six-year-old guerrilla war continued. The Sendero Luminoso vowed reprisals and made good their promises, assassinating Admiral Gerónimo Cafferata in October 1986, killing or wounding members of the security forces and APRA officials, and carrying out numerous acts of terrorism in Lima and elsewhere.

To end the Sendero Luminoso threat a thoroughgoing agrarian reform was needed that could liquidate the festering poverty and landlessness of the highlands and simultaneously increase agricultural production; such reform would reduce the country's dependence on costly food imports (in 1987 more than 60 percent of the country's basic foods, including vegetables, beans, and wheat, was being imported). The progressive Velasco military regime had begun this reform when it shattered the hacienda system, but by the mid-1970s the reform had ground to a halt and Velasco had been ousted by conservative military. When the military reform ended, only 39 percent of all agricultural land had been transferred and less than 25 percent of the rural population had profited from the reform. The principal model of land distribution (the state-controlled cooperatives) adopted by the military suffered from many weaknesses: it failed to benefit a vast number of landless peasants and subsistence minifundista farmers; it pursued a policy of keeping farm prices low to avoid urban discontent; it failed adequately to capitalize the co-ops or provide them with needed technical advice; and it imposed a bureaucratic military management, typical of a model imposed from above. As a result, many cooperatives remained as unproductive as before,

and workers failed to develop a cooperative psychology.

When Peru returned to civilian rule under Belaúnde, he announced development based on laissez-faire principles as his agricultural priority, but did little to assist the cooperatives. The campesino communities continued to suffer from a lack of land, water, credit, and technical assistance. Belaúnde's 1980 Agricultural Promotion and Development Law offered nothing to the communities, authorized the sale of agricultural lands, and in the name of efficiency allowed the cooperatives to divide their land into privately owned plots. As a result, some 300 of the 600 cooperatives had been parceled out. The fruits of this policy can be seen in the rich Cañete valley south of Lima; where 16 cooperatives have been divided into more than 2,000 small farms, and 15,000 temporary farmhands have lost their jobs.

During and after his election campaign, García had promised new land redistribution and protection for the cooperatives: little came of these promises. Finally in November 1986, Congress passed the Land Irreversibility Law; this did not forbid but made more difficult the division of cooperatives. Then, on April 13, 1987, the government promulgated a law that officially recognized 3,642 (out of an estimated 4,560) peasant communities, many existing since Inca times. The new law also permitted the communities to enter into business contracts and exempted them from burdensome taxes. Congress also approved a National Fund for Communal Development and an institute to help the communities increase their agricultural output. All this, however, remained in the future; meanwhile the influx of imported food continued.

Meanwhile, the industrial community and social property programs, regarded by Velasco as laying the foundations of a unique "Peruvian socialism," were neglected and languished; they appeared to play no role in García's program for developing an autonomous Peruvian capitalism.

As his term of office drew to an end, a balance sheet of García's record in power could point to some positive initiatives and accomplishments,

406 including his decision to limit debt interest payments to a certain proportion of export proceeds, thereby making more funds available for development purposes, and his independent foreign policy, reflected in his opposition to U.S. intervention in Central America. García's debt strategy marked an advance over that of the military reformers, but it was not enough. Peru needed a program of structural economic and social change: the creation of a self-sufficient industrial base that would lessen dependency on foreign imports and capital; a more thoroughgoing agrarian reform that would attack the age-old problem of Andean poverty and backwardness, overcome the need for food imports, and expand the domestic market; and a reduction of the immense inequities in income distribution.

But these changes were not made. As a result, by 1987 García's project for creating an autonomous Peruvian capitalism was running out of steam; the country had a serious trade deficit, its foreign reserves were declining, and the business class, despite generous incentives from the government, was not increasing its level of investment. In July 1987, seeking to channel capital into priority areas and halt capital flight, García announced that he would nationalize the banks, which caused a storm of abuse by the right, Mario Vargas Llosa, the famous novelist turned apostle of laissez-faire, leading the pack.

The last two and a half years of García's presidency were an unmitigated disaster. From 1988 to 1989 the per capita gross economic product declined by 20 percent—the biggest decline in the region. As if the economic crisis were not enough, the war with the Maoist Sendero Luminoso movement, raging since 1980, grew more intense, with García seemingly powerless to prevent the spread of the Shining Path or to curb the well-documented atrocities committed by his own military.

Amid the economic gloom, the only light and cheer was provided by Peru's illicit coca trade, which has grown vastly in the last five years. In Peru, as in Bolivia, the jobs and dollars generated by the coca boom have served to cushion the impact of a devastating economic crisis. The heart of Peru's coca empire is the immense Upper Huallaga Valley. Coca acreage has been expanding here at the rate of about 10 percent a year, with unlimited possibilities for expansion along the eastern slopes of the Andes. With opportunities for employment in the legal economy shrinking, in recent years thousands of migrants have joined the "white gold rush" to the Upper Huallaga Valley. The coca, processed into a white paste, is sold to Colombian dealers, who daily arrive in small planes. Most of the proceeds of the traffic accrue to the drug barons in Colombia and the United States, but it is estimated that Peru's share comes to about $1.2 billion annually, roughly 30 percent of the value of all Peru's legal exports. Without these illicit dollars, according to one Peruvian economist, the exchange rate would nearly double, making vitally needed imports much more expensive. Like Paz in Bolivia, García liberalized Central Bank rules to permit the purchase of coca dollars, no questions asked.

A complicating factor was the alliance between the coca growers and the Sendero Luminoso, which provides them with protection in return for payment of "taxes" on their production. Against this background the announcement by the Bush administration in April 1990 of a proposed new $35 million program to aid the Peruvian military in its struggle against the guerrillas caused concern in the United States, where it raised fears of a new Vietnam, and Peru. In the event, García rejected any drug-fighting agreement that did not include economic aid for crop substitution and debt relief.

With APRA in total disgrace as a result of García's economic fiasco and failure to end the civil war and the Izquierda Unida (the left) greatly weakened by internal splits and the turmoil in eastern Europe, the favored contender on the eve of the first round of the presidential elections in April 1990 appeared to be Vargas Llosa, whose main campaign plank was "shock therapy" for the moribund Peruvian economy through the immediate introduction of a free-market economy. Backed by the conservative Fredemo Alliance, he

Alberto Fujimori, shown in this photograph, had no political experience when he defeated famed novelist Mario Vargas Llosa in Peru's presidential runoff in 1990. (Wide World Photos)

spent an estimated $70 million campaigning. His main opponent was an obscure agronomist, Alberto Fujimori, the son of poor Japanese immigrants, who ran a low-key campaign that avoided offering specific solutions for Peru's problems but strongly opposed "shock therapy," insisting that people's basic needs must be met before any economic adjustment was begun. Although polls in February showed Fujimori with barely 0.5 percent of the vote against Vargas Llosa's 42 percent, on April 8 they were almost tied, with Fujimori receiving 29 percent against Vargas Llosa's 30 percent. Assured of Aprista and left-wing support, Fujimori won by a large margin in the runoff election in early June and assumed office in July.

Following his election, Fujimori caused consternation among his followers by enacting severe austerity measures akin to those proposed by Vargas Llosa. "Fujishock," as the program was immediately dubbed, included the removal of customer subsidies. The result was soaring price increases, with the price of such staple foods as milk and bread nearly tripling. The program provoked widespread rioting and looting in Peru's shantytowns. In contradiction of the pledge that he would not privatize major public enterprises, Fujimori, hoping to attract foreign capital, offered to sell the controlling shares of the state-owned copper mines. Despite their many problems, these firms currently provide one-half of Peru's foreign exchange earnings.

Fujimori inherited a comatose economy kept alive only with large injections of coca dollars. At least 40 percent of the population is unemployed. Of Lima's 6 million people, 4 million live in shantytowns. The infant mortality rate, 89 per 1,000 births, is the third highest in the region. Twenty percent of children over the age of five years suffer severe brain damage from malnutrition. In these conditions, the austerity measures proposed by Vargas Llosa and implemented by Fujimori were, in the words of one Peruvian economist, "like performing stomach, kidney, and lung surgery all at the same time on a patient who hasn't eaten in three years." To add to the country's woes, in spring 1991 a cholera epidemic made thousands sick, killed hundreds, and threatened to deprive Peru of hundreds of millions of dollars in exports and tourism revenue.

Despite the failure of its economic policies to revive the moribund economy, the Fujimori team continued along its free-market road, announcing a new series of measures that included a reduction of import duties—a measure that, some businessmen feared, could destroy some parts of domestic industry—and the privatization of 23 state companies.

Chapter 17

The Cuban Revolution

In 1959 the island of Cuba—ninety miles from Key West, permeated by North American capital and culture, and long ruled by one of the region's most firmly entrenched dictatorships—became the scene of perhaps the first and certainly the most successful social revolution in Latin America during the twentieth century. Under the banner of Marxism and with the military, economic, and political support of the Soviet Union, the government led by Fidel Castro has made great progress toward the elimination of such problems as illiteracy, mass unemployment, and unequal distribution of income and wealth in the decades since taking power.

It is a historical irony that the first socialist state in the Americas has arisen in Cuba, a country bound by the strongest economic and political ties to the United States. In preserving their hard-won gains against the opposition of the United States, the Cuban revolutionaries have survived a CIA-backed invasion, diplomatic isolation, and an economic embargo; they have also overcome the consequences of their own serious miscalculations and inefficiency.

Cuba Under Spanish Rule

Cuba's development differed markedly from that of most other Latin American countries. For three centuries after its discovery by Christopher Columbus in 1492, the island served primarily as a strategic stopover for the Spanish treasure fleet. Without precious metals or a large indigenous population to exploit, Cuba remained a neglected, sparsely populated outpost of the empire. The island's inhabitants engaged, for the most part, in small-scale farming for domestic consumption. Unlike the other sugar-producing islands of the Caribbean, at the end of the seventeenth century, Cuba had few slaves (its colored population of 40,000 was only one-tenth that of Haiti), many of whom worked in non-agricultural occupations, often as skilled craftsmen.

Economic and Social Change

The second half of the eighteenth century, however, brought profound economic and social change. Spurred by the short-lived British occupation of Havana in 1762 and further stimulated by United States independence in 1783, the island experienced a commercial awakening. Most importantly, Cuba developed into a major sugar producer and slave importer in the aftermath of the Haitian Revolution of the 1790s, which ruined that island as a sugar producer. During the next half-century, sugar production in Cuba skyrocketed, and nearly 600,000 African slaves arrived on its shores. From 1774 to 1861, the island's population leaped from 171,620 to 1,396,530. Havana and Santiago de Cuba became large, busy urban centers and ports, and no fewer than eight other cities attained populations exceeding 10,000. Immigrants from Santo Domingo and Spain brought an infusion of new technology and capital to the sugar industry. Perceiving new opportunities in agriculture, the creole landowning class began to construct a latifundio-based economy.

The expansion and diversification of trade and the introduction of large-scale sugar production created a fantastic economic boom and delayed the development of the spirit of rebellion against Spanish rule that swept the rest of Spanish America. Cuba stayed loyal to Spain during the Spanish-American wars of independence, for its creole leaders saw no reason to tamper with their new-found prosperity. Discontent grew among the slaves and free blacks, however, as a result of tensions caused by the rise of an increasingly harsh plantation system; major slave rebellions, led by free blacks, erupted in 1810, 1812, and 1844. Meanwhile, the wealthy creoles became increasingly resentful of the arbitrary ways of the corrupt Spanish officialdom, which was determined to enforce continued obedience by Spain's last and richest colony in the New World.

As the colony grew increasingly dissatisfied with repressive Spanish rule, it became less dependent economically on the mother country. By 1776 the British colonies already provided one-third of the island's imports and purchased about one-half of its exports; after the United States achieved independence, Cuba turned more and more toward it as a market for its products and a source of needed imports. As a result of these growing economic ties, schemes for the annexation of Cuba to the United States emerged both in the island and in some North American circles. In Cuba, conservative creole planters saw in annexation an insurance policy against the abolition of slavery; in the United States, some proslavery groups regarded annexation as a means of gaining a vast new area for the expansion of plantation slavery. Some of these groups even dreamed of carving Cuba up into three or five states that would give the South increased power in the national government. The Civil War put an end to these projects.

During the 1860s, creole discontent grew, heightened by a developing national and class consciousness. The creole elite rejected various reform proposals offered by a weak Spanish government that was battered by internal dissension and economic difficulties. It became increasingly clear to the creoles that Spanish economic and political policies were severely restricting Cuban development—a feeling sharpened by a serious economic downturn in the 1860s. On October 10, 1868, in the small town of Yara in Oriente Province, a group of landowners proclaimed Cuban independence and initiated a struggle that was to continue for ten years.

The Ten Years' War

The Ten Years' War, a long, bitter, devastating guerrilla struggle, ended in 1878, when the Cubans accepted a peace that granted them some concessions but withheld independence. (The Spanish crown, desperate to retain the last vestige of its New World empire, sent ten times as many troops to quell the Cuban insurrection as it sent to all of South America from 1810 to 1828.) The Pact of Zanjón ended hostilities, but some rebel leaders, like the black revolutionary Antonio Maceo, the "Bronze Titan," rejected the settlement because it did not achieve the main goals of the revolution—independence and the abolition of slavery. Ironically, the Spanish government, hoping to win the loyalty of the black population, abolished slavery in 1880, with provision for an eight-year patronato, or period of apprenticeship for the liberated slaves. The abolition of slavery removed the last major factor tending to keep creole planters loyal to Spain. Thereafter, the prospect of independence, offering free, unlimited trade with the United States, became increasingly attractive.

The Ten Years' War had a far-reaching impact on the development of Cuban society. It decimated the creole landowning class, hindering the formation of a traditional Latin American landed elite on the island. Entrepreneurs from the United States came to fill the vacuum created by the ruin of the creole aristocracy and the bankruptcy of Spanish interests by the war. Thousands of North Americans accompanied their investment dollars to the island to run the sugar mills and merchant houses. The McKinley Tariff Act of 1890, which abolished import duties on raw sugar and molasses, greatly increased American trade with and economic influence in Cuba; by 1896, U.S. interests had invested $50 million in Cuba and controlled the sugar industry. By the early 1890s, Cuba supplied one-tenth of all products imported into the United States, ranking third behind Britain and Germany. The United States purchased 87 percent of Cuba's exports. The growth of United States investment in Cuba also brought about an increasing concentration of sugar production, a trend signaled by the entry of the "Sugar Trust" (the American Sugar Refining Company of Henry Q. Havemeyer) into the island in 1888.

Independence and the Spanish-Cuban-American War

The Revolutionary Movement

By the early 1890s, the movement for independence had revived, partly as a result of a worldwide depression that struck heavy blows at the Cuban economy. The spiritual, intellectual, and organizational leader of the revolutionary movement was José Martí (1853–1895). As a lad of sixteen, Martí was arrested on a charge of supporting the 1868 revolt and sentenced to six years in prison at hard labor, but in 1871 he was sent into exile. In 1880, Martí came to New York, his home for the next fourteen years. In the United States, he earned his living in brilliant journalistic and literary activity that won him fame throughout Latin America.

Meanwhile, Martí worked tirelessly to establish and unite Cuban émigré revolutionary groups. In 1892 he founded *El Partido Revolucionario Cubano* (the Cuban Revolutionary party), which proposed to obtain, "with the united effort of all men of good will, the absolute independence of the island of Cuba, and to foment and aid that of Puerto Rico." He then set about recruiting such military veterans of 1868 as Máximo Gómez and Antonio Maceo, in preparation for an invasion of the island. In April 1895, Martí himself landed on a Cuban beach with a group of insurgents; a little more than a month later, he was killed in a skirmish with a Spanish patrol.

Despite the loss of its ablest, most charismatic leader, the revolution spread and achieved major successes with the aid of time-proven guerrilla tactics. At the beginning of 1896, a new Spanish commander, General Valeriano Weyler, instituted counterinsurgency measures of the type that would later be employed against twentieth-century rebels in the Philippines, Algeria, and Vietnam. He set up population concentration centers and free-fire zones, which resulted in enormous hardships and losses to the peasantry. But his successes were transient and counterproductive, serving mostly to intensify popular hatred for

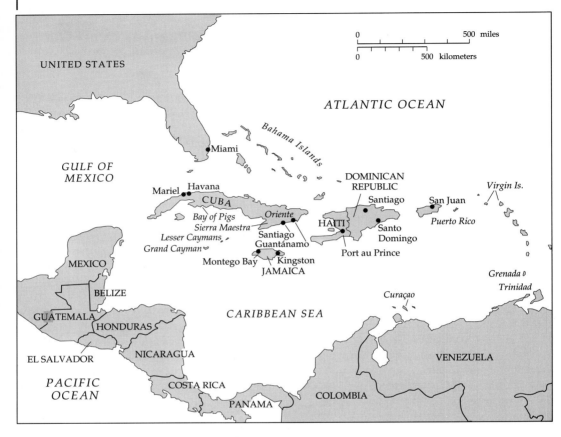

MODERN CARIBBEAN NATIONS

Spanish rule, and whole provinces remained under the absolute control of the liberating army. The failure of Weyler's military policies and growing pressure from the United States led Spain to make a promise of autonomy to Cuba in late 1897.

Involvement by the United States

As the rebellion spread over the land, it became an increasingly volatile issue in the United States. Inevitably, property was destroyed or damaged in the fighting, and this brought complaints from powerful U.S. businessmen and financiers with interests in Cuba. In addition, the Cuban struggle

for independence struck a sympathetic chord with the American people, particularly among the working class. William Randolph Hearst and Joseph Pulitzer, then engaged in a newspaper circulation war in New York City, helped to keep popular interest high by running lurid stories of Spanish brutality.

Meanwhile, within the McKinley administration as well as among enthusiastic expansionists like Theodore Roosevelt there was a growing feeling that the Cuban situation was getting out of control, that the autonomy proposal sponsored by the United States was failing, and that if the United States did not intervene an unmanageable Cuban revolutionary government might take over

General Calixto Garcia, shown with his staff during the Spanish-American War. (Courtesy of the National Archives)

from the collapsing Spanish regime. In the midst of this ferment, the U.S.S. *Maine* blew up in Havana Harbor on February 15, 1898, with a heavy loss of life. This incident helped spur McKinley to a more belligerent stance; he demanded that Spain terminate the concentration camp policy, offer an armistice to the rebels, and accept the United States as a final arbiter between the parties. There was no mention of Cuban independence. When Spain delayed its response to U.S. demands, McKinley sent a message to Congress asking it to authorize military intervention by the United States in Cuba. Congress, after considerable debate, adopted a joint resolution to that ef-

fect. It should be noted in passing that almost every major Cuban revolutionary figure—José Martí, Antonio Maceo, Máximo Gómez—opposed American entry into the war, fearing that it would result in direct or indirect U.S. political and economic control of Cuba. All they sought from the United States was recognition of Cuban belligerency and the right to purchase arms in the United States.

The ensuing war was short and nasty. United States commanders ignored their Cuban counterparts, excluding Cuban generals from decision making and relegating Cuban soldiers to sentry and cleanup duties. Incompetence was the key feature of both Spanish and American war efforts. United States military actions were ill prepared and badly led. The only major land battle of the war, the famous charge up San Juan Hill, which helped to catapult Theodore Roosevelt to national prominence, was very nearly a defeat for the United States. Spain, to some extent, defeated itself, for its generals believed the war lost from the beginning and sought above all to minimize their losses. Thus, in a bizarre little war, the United States Army—wretchedly led, scandalously provisioned, and ravaged by tropical disease—swiftly defeated a demoralized, dispirited Spanish army and snatched the fruits of victory from the *mambises,* the Cuban guerrilla fighters who had fought gallantly in a struggle of three years' duration. The exclusion of Cuban leaders from both war councils and peace negotiations foreshadowed the course of Cuban-American relations for the next sixty years.

The First United States Occupation, 1899–1902

The United States Army occupied Cuba from January 1899 to May 1902. The occupation had three basic goals. First, the United States sought to make Cuba into a self-governing protectorate, an arrangement designed to achieve political stability without the administrative burdens and costs of an outright colonial occupation. To this end, the American military sought to pacify the island without serious conflict with the Cuban army, which was still intact and in control of much of rural Cuba. The revolutionary army, however, did not resist the American take-over, as did Emilio Aguinaldo and his insurgent forces in the Philippines at the same time. Cuban passivity in part reflected the fact that the years of struggle had taken their toll—the leading Cuban generals, such as Calixto García and Máximo Gómez, were tired old men, and many of the younger men who could have led a resistance movement had died in battle. In addition, the Americans bought off the army by offering to purchase its arms, an offer that hungry, unemployed soldiers found diffi-

cult to refuse. They also offered key rebel leaders well-paid positions. At the same time, the occupation government established a Rural Guard, not only to eradicate banditry but, in the words of General Leonard Wood, to put down the "agitators who began to grow restive at the presence of the Americans."

After political stability, necessary to attract American capital, the second major American goal was to repair the destruction wrought by the war and provide the sanitation and other services needed for economic recovery. General Leonard Wood, appointed governor general in 1899, launched a program of public works and sanitation that led to a major achievement of the occupation—the conquest of yellow fever. Taking its lead from a Cuban doctor, Carlos Finlay, whose theory correctly attributed the transmission of the dread disease to the mosquito, the American Sanitary Commission succeeded in eliminating it. Another major accomplishment of the Wood administration was the creation of a Cuban national education system, vastly superior to what had existed under Spain but designed to inculcate American principles; even the textbooks were translations of American textbooks. All these programs and reforms, as well as the expenses of the United States troops, were paid for from the Cuban treasury.

Ruling with arbitrary methods and largely ignoring the former revolutionaries in favor of Spaniards and conservative planters who had opposed independence, Wood presided over the election of a convention to frame a constitution for Cuba. The convention, elected in June 1899, began its work in November and after several months of bitter debate adopted a document that, under intense American pressure, included the so-called Platt Amendment. This amendment limited the ability of independent Cuba to conduct foreign policy and to borrow money abroad, gave the United States the right to maintain a naval base at Guantánamo Bay and, most important, gave the United States the right to intervene in Cuba for the "preservation of Cuban independence" and for the "maintenance of a government adequate for the protection of life, property, and individual liberty."

The third goal of the occupation was to absorb Cuba into the economic sphere of influence of the United States. Since the Platt Amendment assured American businessmen of protection and a generally favorable investment climate on the island, capital poured into sugar and railroad construction. A reciprocal trade agreement signed by the two nations in 1903 was the final step in bringing Cuba under American hegemony. This treaty cut by 20 percent the tariff on Cuban sugar exported to the United States; in return, Cuba reduced the duties on imported American goods.

The Politics of Corruption, 1902–1953

Instability and Intervention, 1902–1924

Cuba's political life, afflicted by its status as a United States protectorate and suffering from interventions, had a weak and stunted growth. At the end of 1901, Tomás Estrada Palma was elected the first president of Cuba, and the Americans left the following May. Although he had not lived in Cuba for twenty-five years, Estrada, who headed the Cuban government-in-exile after the Ten Years' War, began his presidency with considerable popularity. However, his administration produced only scandals.

The 1904 elections to Congress were fraudulent and marked by sporadic violence. Local government was even more turbulent and corruption-ridden. The Estrada presidency established the pattern of Cuban politics for the next fifty years.

In 1905, Estrada, with his adherents in control of the electoral machinery and the opposition boycotting the election, ran for re-election and won. In the summer of 1906, the Liberal party, led by José Miguel Gómez, rose in revolt against the Estrada regime. Unable to suppress the rebellion, the president called for American intervention and left Cuba.

President William Howard Taft responded by sending in the marines, and shortly afterward appointed Charles Magoon, a judge from Minnesota, to preside over an American provisional government. Magoon's solution for the problem of factional violence was to divide the patronage among contending Cuban groups. As a result, the corruption that had emerged during the Estrada regime was institutionalized with the apparent blessing of the United States. The provisional government also took the first steps toward creating a permanent standing army, whose presence, it was hoped, would prevent insurrections of the kind that had toppled Estrada. During the second occupation, Cuban resistance to American domination virtually disappeared. The decline of national consciousness and protest against foreign control was due in large part to the workings of the system of institutionalized corruption, which united all sections of the elite in the eager pursuit of American favor and protection.

Two parties contested the presidential election of 1908, the Conservative party, made up of former supporters of Estrada, and the Liberal party, which had rebelled in 1906. There were no real ideological differences between the parties; the only issue was who should enjoy the spoils of office. The Liberal José Miguel Gómez won and took over the reins of government from Magoon; the United States withdrew its troops on April 1, 1909. Reestablishment of the lottery and legalization of cockfighting were among the highlights of Gómez's presidency.

The Conservative General Mario Menocal succeeded Gómez in 1912 and won re-election in 1916. Menocal continued the tradition of gross political corruption; a millionaire when he took office, he reportedly accumulated $40 million during his two terms. Having formerly managed one of the gigantic American-owned *centrales* (sugar mills), he was closely linked to U.S. economic interests in the island. In the spring of 1917, the Liberals again rebelled, this time in protest against Menocal's re-election. The revolt failed because the United States would not permit disruption of Cuban sugar production during World War I. United States troops landed and remained until 1923.

In 1920, Alfredo Zayas, a former Liberal who had participated in the unsuccessful revolt of 1917, won the presidency with Conservative support. Troubled over the crash of sugar prices in the second half of 1920 and the resulting political unrest in Cuba, President Warren Harding sent General Enoch Crowder to Cuba in January 1921 as his special representative. In effect, Crowder ruled Cuba from his headquarters on board the battleship *Minnesota* until 1923, when he became United States ambassador.

The sad pattern of corruption dominated Cuban politics from 1902 to 1924. Control of graft and patronage was the goal of all factions; party labels meant nothing. Four times during this period (1908, 1917, 1919, 1921), the losers of presidential elections staged or threatened revolts, alleging fraud (with good reason). In each instance, and in 1912 when there was a minor black rebellion in Oriente Province, United States troops landed to restore order and prevent property damage.

In the last two years of the Zayas administration, Cuban nationalism revived. Crowder's blatant meddling in Cuban politics and the postwar collapse of Cuban sugar revealed the disastrous consequences of foreign domination and monoculture. Searching for solutions for these problems, Cuban university students entered the political arena in the postwar period. Believing that to change society they must change the university, they directed their first attacks against inept and corrupt professors and administrators; in 1922 students at the University of Havana demonstrated for reforms along the lines of the recent university reform in Argentina. Students would henceforth play an important role in Cuban politics until the fall of Batista in 1959.

Machado, 1925–1933

Taking advantage of growing nationalistic sentiment, Gerardo Machado y Morales emerged as

the Liberal candidate in the presidential election of 1924. Running against the corruption of Zayas, on a platform of national regeneration, he defeated ex-president Menocal. Despite his nationalistic declarations, Machado had very close links to American economic interests, for he had been until his election vice president of an American-owned utility in Havana. Even before he took office, Machado visited the United States to assure President Calvin Coolidge of his government's good intentions.

Machado began his term auspiciously. He embarked on an ambitious program of public works and attempted to institute a system of controls for sugar production designed to protect small and medium-size producers against severe price declines. He also tried to encourage the diversification of agriculture by raising the tariffs on fruits, rice, and cacao; this program effectively increased production of these crops. Machado took steps to institute a merit system for the public bureaucracy and established new technical and commercial schools. He even sought, with little success, to reform the prostitutes of Havana. Thanks to these efforts, Machado enjoyed unparalleled popularity and faced virtually no opposition for two years.

Already, however, there were disturbing signs of tyranny. The number of political assassinations increased alarmingly. A wave of strikes during 1925 was broken by police shooting down strikers. The nation's most prominent Communist leader, Juan Antonio Mella, was murdered in his Mexican exile by a Machado gunman in 1929. Machado's secret police routinely eliminated his opponents by throwing them to the sharks in Havana Harbor.

Machado secured his re-election in 1928 by the simple expedient of outlawing the party of his main rival, Carlos Mendieta. Until the onset of the world depression in 1930, Machado maintained an iron grip on Cuba, despite mounting opposition from university students, the Communists, labor unions, and many old-line politicians led by Mendieta. The economic crisis had particularly catastrophic consequences for Cuba because of its heavy reliance on exports. Machado responded to the growing political unrest engendered by the economic conditions with increasingly harsh repression. A general strike failed in May 1930. In September, after the killing of a student leader, students at the University of Havana organized a large demonstration, which was followed by the firing of hundreds of teachers and the closing of the university.

In August 1931, Mendieta led a group of old-line politicians in an unsuccessful revolt, a last effort to revive the old strategies and leadership of Cuban politics. Late in 1931, a new secret organization, the ABC, sprang up among young members of the middle class and intellectuals as a moderate alternative to the more radical university students' group, the Student Directory. Machado answered these challenges with tightened censorship and stepped-up terror tactics on the part of his secret police, the *Porra*.

By the beginning of 1933, the United States government had become seriously concerned by the spreading violence, which appeared to threaten U.S. economic interests. In April, incoming President Franklin Roosevelt dispatched Sumner Welles as ambassador to attempt to negotiate some sort of understanding between Machado and his opponents. For several months, Welles unsuccessfully tried to mediate between Machado and the opposition, but Machado would not compromise, while the opposition was disunited and unable to agree on a course of action.

In the summer, a bus drivers' strike in Havana mushroomed into a general strike that nearly paralyzed the city. After the police massacred several demonstrators in August, Machado's position seriously deteriorated, for he had lost the support of Welles and the army. On August 12, Machado resigned and fled into exile.

The Revolution of 1933

For the next three weeks, a provisional government headed by Carlos Manuel de Cespedes struggled unsuccessfully to end the escalating violence. On September 4, a group of army ser-geants, one of whom was Fulgencio Batista, overthrew the government. The Student Directory immediately allied itself with the sergeants, and together they formed a revolutionary junta.

The new junta had no organized political backing, and its two main components, the noncommissioned officers and the Student Directory, had sharply divergent aims. The sergeants were concerned only with defending their newly won dominant position against any challenge. While the students sought genuine reforms but were unsure just how to achieve them. Within a week, the junta turned over the reins of government to Dr. Ramón Grau San Martín, a well-known physician and long-time opponent of Machado. Grau, Antonio Guiteras Holmes, a leader of the Student Directory, and Batista were dominant figures in the new alignment.

The first move of the new government was to abrogate the onerous Platt Amendment. A flurry of decrees produced more social legislation than all the previous history of independent Cuba: an eight-hour day for labor, a labor department, an end to the importation of cheap labor from other islands in the Caribbean, and greater access for children from lower-income groups to the university. There were also measures to redistribute land to peasants, eliminate usury, and give women the vote.

Ultimately, the Grau government was caught in the classic bind of the reformer: the left was dissatisfied because the reforms were not of sufficient scope, and the right opposed all reform. Grau also alienated American financial and agricultural interests when he suspended repayment of several loans owed to the Chase National Bank of New York and seized two mills of the Cuban-American Sugar Company. The United States government adamantly refused to recognize the Grau government.

The revolutionary coalition disintegrated. The ABC would not cooperate with Grau because his program had become too radical. He had earlier lost the support of the more radical elements of the Student Directory, and the Communists attacked him as a "petty bourgeois."

The behavior of Sumner Welles throughout the Grau interregnum was extraordinarily similar to the conduct of U.S. Ambassador Henry Lane Wilson in Mexico during the Madero administration. Welles persistently falsified reports and misrepresented the Cuban government to Secretary of State Cordell Hull and President Roosevelt. As Wilson had befriended Huerta and helped him to power, so Welles allied himself with Batista. Eventually (in November 1933), Welles was recalled, but he had seriously undermined the provisional government. As the economic and political situation worsened, Welles's successor, Jefferson Caffery, maneuvered with Batista to form a new government acceptable to the United States. In January 1934, Grau, unable to rule effectively in the face of American opposition, went into exile and was replaced by Carlos Mendieta.

The Era of Batista, 1934–1944

Fulgencio Batista y Zaldivar, the sergeant-stenographer mulatto son of a sugar worker, dominated Cuban politics for the next decade, ruling the island through puppet presidents from 1934 to 1940 and as elected president from 1940 to 1944. Although Batista alienated many of the "respectable" elements of the middle and upper classes, he was extremely popular among the masses. During the first two years after his successful coup, he presided over a mild reform program with some effort at land redistribution. In 1937, he moved leftward and openly courted the support of labor unions and the Communists.

The Auténtico Interlude, 1944–1952

At the end of 1939, Batista permitted the election of a constituent assembly to draft the constitution of 1940. Grau and his Cuban Revolutionary, or *Auténtico* party (founded in 1934) and other moderate parties won the election and produced a liberal document with provisions for the protection of labor and limitations on the right of property when it conflicted with the public good. It was Batista, however, who won the presidential election of 1940.

Choosing to observe the constitutional provision that the president should not succeed himself, Batista, to the general surprise, allowed honest elections to take place in 1944. As a result, Grau defeated Batista's hand-picked choice. Grau, who earlier had been the symbol of Cuban regeneration and democracy, presided over an unparalleled reign of corruption. Violence accompanied the corruption, and the University of Havana became a nest of political gangsterism. True, the Grau government initiated some minor reforms, but it made no attack on such key problems as agrarian reform and monoculture.

In 1947, a charismatic populist leader, Eddie Chibás, launched a new campaign against government oppression and corruption. A former ardent supporter of the Auténticos, Chibás had become disillusioned and formed his own Cuban People's, or *Ortodoxo,* party, which featured a mild program of social reform and clean politics, in the spring of 1947. Extremely popular, he posed a serious threat to the Auténticos. In 1948, Chibás opposed the Auténtico presidential candidate, Carlos Prío Socorrás, former leader of the Student Directory. Prío, who won easily because he controlled the election machinery and had the advantage of four years of economic prosperity, became another in a long line of Cuban country club presidents. He spent much of his time serving his guests daiquiris at his opulent farm in the suburbs of Havana. There was no letup in the corruption, gangsterism, and spoils system characteristic of his predecessor's regime. As under Grau, the prosperity brought on by high sugar prices concealed the mismanagement of the Prío administration.

Chibás was the leading candidate for the presidency for the upcoming election when Batista reappeared in Cuba after a long retirement to announce that he would be a candidate for president in 1952. Cuban politics were thrown into complete disarray when Chibás, in an apparent effort to awake the Cuban public to the extent of political corruption, killed himself on a nationwide radio broadcast in August 1951. In any event, in March 1952, before the election could take place, Batista headed a conspiracy of low-ranking army officers that overthrew Prío. Thoroughly disillusioned with politics, the Cuban people offered little protest.

The Return of Batista as Dictator, 1952–1959

Batista ruled Cuba for the second time until he was overthrown by Fidel Castro in 1959. Like his contemporaries, Carlos Ibañez in Chile, Getúlio Vargas in Brazil, and Juan Perón in Argentina, Batista found the second time around more difficult than the first. A new generation of revolutionaries rose to replace the discredited leaders of 1933. Unlike Grau or Prío, they would not be bought off or collaborate with the dictator. Several groups opposed Batista, including the Auténticos, who plotted from their havens in Florida; the 26th of July Movement led by Fidel Castro, which unsuccessfully tried to overthrow the government in 1953 by assaulting the Moncada army barracks; and the Federation of University Students (FEU). Despite the activities of the students and Castro's guerrilla group, the dictator seemed to be firmly entrenched. The instability and corruption of the Cuban political system was matched in its ill effects by the structural weakness of the economy, produced by reliance on a single crop, sugar.

The Export Economy: Sugar as King

Cuba is a classic case of monoculture—a nation dependent on the production and export of a single crop for its economic livelihood. Like the other Latin American nations we have examined (Argentina, Brazil, Chile, and Mexico), Cuba has suffered from the cyclical nature of world market demand for its product. Moreover, Cuba suffered the additional burden of almost total economic domination by the United States.

The Early History of Sugar

The Cuban sugar industry dates from the early 1790s, when revolution wrecked the sugar production of Haiti, then the world's leading sugar exporter. At the same time, the United States won its independence from Great Britain, thereby furnishing a ready nearby market for Cuban sugar. Cuban agriculturalists took advantage of their opportunity to shift to sugar and to import cheap slave labor from Africa.

Initially, the transfer to sugar did not stimulate the creation of the latifundio; first, because much of the land converted to sugar was the underused acreage of large cattle haciendas, and second, because many farmers did not change over to sugar, preferring instead to produce coffee and tobacco, which then enjoyed high prices resulting from the abolition of the royal monopoly on these commodities. Furthermore, the sugar mills themselves stimulated demand for livestock (to turn the mills) and food crops for the slaves. During the first decades of the nineteenth century, the number of farm proprietors increased markedly, and from their ranks came the leaders of Cuban society for the next century.

The boom that followed the destruction of Haitian sugar production ended by the turn of the century because other Caribbean islands expanded and initiated production in response to the same stimuli, thereby creating an enormous glut on the market. Just as the industry recovered from this setback, diplomatic maneuvering during the Napoleonic wars closed U.S. ports. Shortly thereafter, two new challenges to the Cuban economy arose: the introduction of beet sugar in Europe and the British campaign to end the slave trade. (England forced Spain to end the trade in 1821.) Further impediments resulted from the restrictions imposed by Spanish hegemony: high tariffs, scarce and expensive credit, and the disruptions brought on by the Spanish-American wars of independence.

By 1820 the first of a series of technological innovations began to transform the character of the sugar industry in Cuba. Mill owners had to

Ingenio (sugar mill) in Cuba. (Courtesy of the Organization of American States)

invest heavily in steam-operated machinery in order to compete with beet sugar. Modern machinery allowed the mills to expand in size, but they could do so only gradually because of the limited transportation facilities that were available. Since railroads were enormously expensive, and in any case there was not sufficient capital on the island or in Spain for large projects of this type, they did not become important until much later.[1] The mills also carried a huge overhead, because they were largely unused during the off season. Slaves and livestock had to be fed and sheltered even when the harvest was completed. The problem of fuel for the mills also slowed

their expansion. The forests close to the mills were quickly consumed, and transport of wood to the mills proved prohibitively costly. As a result, sugar production was expanded in the first half of the century by increasing the number of mills. In 1827 there were 1,000 mills, by 1846 there were 1,442, and by 1860 there were 2,000.

The Development of the Latifundio

Large plantations developed in Cuba in response to the necessity of building bigger and bigger mills. Sugar technology was continually improving, and Cuban mills had to expend huge sums to remain competitive. The larger the mill the more sugar it could process, the more fuel it consumed, and the more employees it needed.

[1] The first railroad in Cuba was built in 1836.

Smaller and less efficient mills were at a severe competitive disadvantage.

Sugar production was set up in one of two ways: the land might be cultivated by resident or temporary labor, or the land might be parcelled out to farmers, known as colonos, who would work the land for a salary or a share of the crop. The landowners, in either situation, might or might not also be the mill owners. As the number of mills grew smaller, the colonos became the main suppliers of sugar to the mills. They planted and harvested the cane and brought it to the mill to be processed. They paid for the processing in sugar. By the 1870s, sugar production was specialized into these components, colonos and centrales. The number of large plantations did not increase; instead, the number of colonos gradually rose.

The shake-out of mills during the war, the financial crisis of 1885–1890, and the expansion of the island's railroad network combined to stimulate the spread of the latifundio. As the mills grew, they required more cane and sought it over a wider geographic area than previously. At the same time, the introduction of cheap rails spurred railroad construction in Cuba (and all over the world). In their quest for more cane, centrales began to lay their own track in an effort to draw it from a greater area. Competition between centrales for cane, a condition previously unknown because of transportation limitations, resulted.

The centrales confronted the necessity of guaranteeing enough cane at the lowest possible prices for the *zafra* (harvest). They could do this either by reducing the independence of the colonos or by acquiring their own cane land. The first method transformed the once-free farmers into satellites of the giant mills. The second led to the creation of latifundia. Small and medium-size growers fell by the way, to be replaced by tenants or day labor. The colonos managed to hold their own until independence, after which time the massive influx of foreign capital into the sugar mills overwhelmed them. With their lesser financial resources, they were doomed.

The end of Spanish rule and the American oc-

cupation removed the final obstacles to the development of the latifundio in Cuba. The island, at peace at last, could repair the damage done by forty years of guerrilla warfare. The United States military and the new Cuban Rural Guard would prevent new revolutionary outbreaks, and the Platt Amendment guaranteed a favorable climate for investment. The elimination of yellow fever allowed foreigners to live on the island without fear for their health. The successive occupation governments and their Cuban successors furnished subsidies and other inducements for railroad construction and utilities. At a time when antitrust laws began to restrict industry in the United States, Cuba had no such inhibitions. Finally, Cuban sugar was an attractive investment because the United States was a close and growing market in which it had a competitive advantage because of the reciprocal trade treaty of 1903, which cut the tariff on Cuban sugar by 20 percent.

Two processes worked hand in hand in the following decades: the concentration of land and mills and the proletarianization of the sugar workers. The two wars of independence had devastated small mills: the total number fell from 2,000 in 1860 to 1,000 in 1877 to only 200 in 1899. The rapid and huge influx of foreign—mostly American—investment into sugar enabled the larger mills to buy up surrounding cane land. The colono was reduced to circumstances close to slavery. Ramiro Guerra y Sánchez has estimated that the great mills owned perhaps 20 percent of the island's area in 1927. A quarter of all the land owned by the mills was owned by four companies. Guerra y Sánchez calculates that as much as 40 percent of Cuba's land may have fallen under the control of the latifundia. Cuba was reduced to a "large sugar plantation producing sugar for the benefit of foreign consumers."

The expansion of the latifundio impoverished the rural masses of the island. The colonos were kept at subsistence levels, deeply indebted to the mill and in constant fear of eviction. The wages of rural workers were kept low because the mills imported cheap labor from other Caribbean islands. As a result, a considerable reserve pool of labor was available; even those lucky enough to get work worked only four months of the year during the harvest period. Displaced farmers had two choices. They could remain and work for small wages on a seasonal basis for the centrales, or they could emigrate to the cities, where jobs were also scarce. Small independent growers were at a severe disadvantage, for the mills squeezed the price paid for their cane to a minimum. In addition, the mills controlled the transportation network.

The ruin of the small mills and farmers and the low wages paid rural labor, which reduced the purchasing power of the masses, sharply limited the domestic market for manufactured goods and commercial services. There was thus little Cuban industrialization. Sugar companies monopolized the railroads and operated them solely for their own benefit, often without regard to the public interest. Although Cuba's railroad network exceeded that of most Latin American nations, it was inadequate to develop an internal market.

American companies poured money into Cuban sugar during the first occupation. By 1913, Americans had invested $200 million in Cuba, predominantly in sugar. This accounted for nearly one-fifth the total U.S. investment in all of Latin America.

World War I and the Dance of the Millions

Cuba's greatest sugar boom and bust took place as a consequence of World War I. The fighting in Europe, which disrupted sugar production on the Continent, from the first caused large price increases: prices nearly doubled in the first two months alone. Eventually, the Allies became totally dependent on Cuban sugar production, since they were fighting their major former supplier, Austria-Hungary. This demand spurred further expansion of Cuban sugar production, with planters moving into previously uncultivated land. The last great surge of mill construction also occurred. As production spread into virgin land, centrales were built and new towns sprang up.

The Allies attempted to keep commodity prices from skyrocketing by establishing purchasing committees to handle the acquisition of raw materials and food. Nonetheless, Cuban production rose in 1916 to 3 million tons at an average price of 4 cents a pound. Expansion created a severe labor shortage on the island, and laborers were imported from Jamaica and other Caribbean islands to fill the void. The colonos staged a comeback, and a few actually prospered.

The war accelerated the trend toward the concentration of the industry in American hands. By 1919 approximately half the island's mills were owned by U.S. companies, and these controlled more than half the total production. The boom also led to the integration of sugar mills and plantations with distributors and companies that were large sugar users. Giants such as Coca-Cola, Hershey (chocolate), and Hires (root beer) bought up producers in order to guarantee their supplies. Producers in turn purchased distributors and refiners.

The postwar years of 1918 to 1920 brought unprecedented prosperity to Cuba, as sugar prices soared and eastern European sugar areas were slow to recover from the war. After the Allied committee deregulated prices in 1920, they began an incredible upward spiral called the "Dance of the Millions." In February 1920, the price of sugar stood at 9.125 cents per pound. By mid-May, the price had climbed to 22.5 cents. Soon, however, prices collapsed as a result of a worldwide depression and Europe's agricultural recovery; by December the Cubans were getting 3.75 cents per pound, which was the prewar price level.

The precipitous rise and equally sudden collapse of sugar prices caused chaos in the Cuban economy. Mills had contracts to buy large quantities of sugar at high prices, prices that were now far higher than the world market. Producers and processors had taken out loans to expand—loans based on anticipated high prices. Banks began to call in these loans. In April 1921, the island's largest bank, the *Banco Nacional,* closed, and others throughout the country followed suit.

Simultaneously, the United States raised its tariff on sugar by one cent, thereby inflicting another blow on the already devastated industry. In 1921 the First National City Bank of New York—long heavily involved with American sugar interests in Cuba—took over nearly sixty bankrupt mills. The harvest reached 4 million tons in 1922, but prices stayed low. The following year, prices rose to 5 cents a pound as a result of the crisis over the French invasion of the Rhineland. Prices were not to reach that level again for three decades.

An Industry in Decline

During the 1920s, the sugar industry entered a long period of stagnation and decline, which lasted until the Castro revolution in 1959. It became clear that the Cuban economy was painfully vulnerable not only to world market fluctuations but to political conditions in the United States. During this decade, Cuba lost much of its U.S. market because it encountered the powerful interests of the sugar beet farmers of the American West. To make matters worse, sugar consumption stayed constant as competition grew more intense. In absolute terms, sugar consumption rose as the population rose, but per capita consumption, which had increased enormously since the 1890s, actually declined over the next forty years (from the 1920s).

In 1926 the harvest reached nearly 5 million tons but brought only an average of 2.2 cents per pound. That same year, the last sugar mill was built in Cuba. For the rest of the decade, the price of sugar stayed below 3.0 cents. After 1928 sugar became a major issue in the U.S. Congress; as a result, the Hawley-Smoot Tariff Act levied a duty of 2.0 cents per pound on Cuban imports two years later. In 1929, Cuban sugar sold for 1.79 cents, and the tariff therefore doubled the price! From then on, Cuba's share of the U.S. market shrank steadily, from 49.4 percent in 1930 to 25.3 percent in 1933. By 1931 the price for sugar was barely a penny a pound, and the next year it fell to 0.72 cents. Mills closed, and people were thrown out of work all over the island.

In 1937 the world's sugar-producing nations met in London to try to reach an agreement that would divide up the market and limit production. They formed an International Sugar Council, which allotted Cuba 29 percent of the U.S. market, half its share in 1929. It should be noted that the bulk of the profits generated by Cuba's sugar economy continued to flow out of the country because foreign companies accounted for 80 percent of Cuban production (American companies controlled 56 percent), while Cubans owned barely 20 percent.

World War II brought on another boom. In 1944 production reached its highest level since the depression. In 1946, as part of its efforts to aid European recovery, the United States agreed to purchase the entire harvest for 3.7 cents a pound. During the Korean war, the price of sugar soared to 5.0 cents. Inevitably, however, Cuba's competitors, especially the Philippines, expanded production. The market soon became glutted with sugar, and prices fell.

Thus, on the eve of the 1959 revolution, Cuba's sugar industry had stagnated for the better part of thirty years, and its malaise spread throughout the economy. Agriculture did not become diversified because the land was concentrated in a very few hands—twenty-two companies held one-fifth the island's farmland. Much of the land was kept idle in case sugar prices should ever boom. Industry was almost nonexistent, for a series of reciprocal trade agreements with the United States—which guaranteed Cuba's sugar market—made it impossible to compete with American imports. These same treaties also stunted agriculture by permitting a flow of agricultural products from the United States whose low prices barred potential Cuban competition. Because of its stagnant economy and the peculiar nature of the sugar industry, Cuba suffered from structural unemployment and underemployment. Most sugar workers were needed only during the harvest; even if well paid during this four-month period, they went jobless and often hungry during the other eight months. It was these structural deficiencies and the economic injustices created by them that helped lay the foundation of the Cuban Revolution.

The Revolution:
The Odyssey of Fidel Castro

The Cuban Revolution was deeply rooted in the history of the island, for the movement headed by Fidel Castro continued the revolutionary traditions of 1868, 1898, and 1933. By no coincidence, both before and after gaining power, Castro often cited the ideals of José Martí and the principles of the liberal constitution of 1940. Yet profound disillusionment accompanied those traditions, for Cuba's past revolutions had invariably failed—either its leaders had succumbed to the temptations of great wealth, or the United States had intervened to thwart their programs. In large part, the complex development of the Cuban Revolution reflected a combination of loyalty to those liberal traditions and a fear of falling into their errors. Castro desperately sought to avoid past mistakes.

Fidel Castro Ruz, the son of a wealthy Spanish farmer in northwest Cuba, was born in 1927. He attended the famous Jesuit school of Belén in Havana and acquired a reputation as a fine athlete. In 1945 he went off to the University of Havana, where he soon became involved in the frequently violent politics that then plagued the university. In 1947 he participated in an ill-fated invasion of the Dominican Republic, sponsored by student political groups that sought to overthrow dictator Rafael Trujillo. Later he became a follower of Eddie Chibás, to whose Ortodoxo party he belonged from 1947 to 1952.

In 1953, Castro headed a small band of lower-middle-class and working-class rebels that attacked the Moncada army barracks near Santiago de Cuba on July 26 in the hope of sparking a rebellion against the Batista dictatorship. Their program called for a return to the constitution of 1940, land reform, educational reform, and an end to the vast waste caused by government corruption and large weapons expenditures. The attack failed, and most of the attackers were killed or captured and tortured. Castro himself was captured several days after the disaster and later

put on trial. Although the assault failed, with heavy casualties, the drastic acts of repression the government carried out in its wake, and Castro's eloquent defense speech at his trial ("History Will Absolve Me") made him a national hero.

Fidel spent the next nineteen months in prison on the Isle of Pines, where he read, wrote, and continued to plan the overthrow of Batista. During this period, his *History Will Absolve Me* appeared clandestinely and enhanced his reputation. He also grew increasingly dissatisfied with the programs of the groups then opposing the dictator. Batista's general amnesty freed him in 1955 and shortly thereafter, he went to Mexico to organize a new attack on the dictatorship. While in Mexico, Castro's group received support from ex-president Prío and Venezuelan exile Rómulo Betancourt (later president of Venezuela). Late in 1955, Fidel met Ernesto (Che) Guevara, who was to become the revolution's second-in-command and its greatest martyr.

Castro was determined to return to the island to renew the struggle. In 1956 he purchased the yacht *Granma,* and he and his band left Mexico City in November. The *Granma* sailed from Mexico with eighty-two persons aboard. Among them were Guevara, Raúl Castro (Fidel's brother), and Juan Almeida, all of whom were to become major figures in the revolution.

Originally, Castro had planned to coordinate the *Granma's* landing in Oriente Province with an uprising in Santiago. As happened with the Moncada attack, however, the landing encountered logistical and scheduling problems, and Castro and his followers were betrayed. He and a small group of other survivors barely escaped to the Sierra Maestra. From the mountains, Castro and his rebels carried out guerrilla raids and beat off attacks by vastly superior forces.

In February 1957, Castro granted an interview in his mountain hide-out to Herbert Matthews, a well-known reporter for the *New York Times.* His articles gave Castro credibility in the United States and also gave notice to the Cuban people that Castro was still alive, despite government claims to the contrary, and that opposition to the regime existed in the mountains. The articles overstated the numerical strength and success of the movement and thereby helped to win adherents to the rebel cause all over the island. The guerillas continued to conduct raids throughout the spring of 1957, picking up recruits and gaining increased sympathy and support from the peasants of Oriente, who rendered invaluable assistance in the form of supplies and intelligence information about government forces.

By mid-1957, violence, especially in Havana, had become endemic as various groups, most unaffiliated with Castro's 26th of July Movement, attacked the regime and met with brutal retaliation. Life in Santiago and Oriente Province was completely disrupted by terrorism and strikes. The island was increasingly gripped by civil war. In the fall, there was an abortive uprising of junior naval officers at Cienfuegos. Batista used bombers and other military equipment to crush the revolt; this alienated some of his American support because the terms of Cuba's military assistance agreement with the United States expressly forbade using this equipment for domestic purposes.

After the New Year, the trend of events turned decisively against Batista. The United States suspended arms shipments to the Cuban government in March 1958. The rebels suffered a minor setback in April when a planned general strike met with little response, but Castro continued to gain support as Batista's situation worsened. Some elements of the church actively supported Castro (there had been several priests in the mountains with him for months). The middle class abandoned the dictator. In May, Batista launched a major effort to dislodge Castro from his base in the Sierra Maestra, and the resulting defeat doomed his regime. Rebel forces inflicted heavy losses on the government troops. Withered by corruption and led by incompetent cronies of Batista, the army was no match for the guerrillas.

In August the rebels began their final push. Three columns led by Castro, Guevara, and Camilo Cienfuegos set out to cut the island in two.

In the meantime, Castro dispatched emissaries to the various anti-Batista groups, seeking particularly the cooperation of the Communists and the labor unions they controlled.

As Batista's plight grew desperate, frantic negotiations involving the U.S. embassy began with a view to staving off Castro's victory by the creation, through a coup or fraudulent elections, of a new government, which the United States government would recognize and give military assistance to. Batista actually held presidential elections, printing up filled-in ballots in advance, and readied a president to take office in February. But the strong drive of the rebel forces frustrated these maneuvers; by the end of December 1958, the *barbudos* (bearded ones) were on the outskirts of Havana. On January 1, 1959, abandoned by his American allies, Batista and his closest aides fled to Miami. The remaining threat to the *Fidelistas* came from the remnants of the old army. Colonel Ramón Barquín, who had unsuccessfully attempted a coup in 1956 and had been released from prison soon after Batista fled, surfaced as a possible alternative to Castro. Barquín, however, retreated when he realized the overwhelming superiority of the 26th of July Movement and its armed forces. On January 1 and 2, Guevara and Cienfuegos entered Havana and occupied key military points. Simultaneously, Castro called for a general strike in support of the revolution. He arrived in the capital a week later amid the cheers of its inhabitants.

Thus, a rebel band, numbering fewer than three hundred until mid-1958 and scarcely three thousand when the old regime fell, won a great victory. The rebels won because they were persistent and disciplined and gained the sympathy of all the people—peasants, workers, and the middle class—and because they faced an army wracked by favoritism and incompetence, led by a dictator who preferred to play canasta than to plan antiguerrilla strategy. The rebels had conscientious, competent commanders and were motivated both by idealism and the knowledge that capture meant torture and death. Batista's army, put to the test, proved able to terrorize

Fidel Castro has ruled Cuba for more than thirty years. (Jean-Claude Francolon/Gamma-Liaison)

unarmed citizens but disintegrated when confronted with a formidable insurgency.

The Revolution in Power, 1959–1991

During its first four years (1959–1962), the revolution consolidated its domestic political position, began the socialization of the economy, and established a new pattern of foreign relations. In 1959, Castro and his lieutenants made a series of decisions that determined the course of the revolution for the next decade. First, they concluded that parliamentary democracy was inappropriate for Cuba at that time. The Fundamental Law of the Republic, decreed in February 1959, concentrated legislative power in the executive. As

prime minister and, later, as first secretary of the Communist party, Castro held the decisive posts in the government and the ruling party of the Cuban state. Within eighteen months, the revolutionary regime had suppressed the right of free press and the centuries-old autonomy of the University of Havana. The revolutionaries conducted public trials of former *Batistianos,* and a large number of Batista's henchmen were executed.

Second, Castro moved the revolution leftward in order to accomplish his economic goals—land reform, income redistribution, agricultural diversification, and economic independence from the United States. The radicalism of his economic program and the concentration of political power in the hands of the close-knit 26th of July Movement alienated much of his middle-class support. President Manuel Urrutia, who fell into this category, resigned in July 1959, and was replaced by

Osvaldo Dorticós. In October, Major Huber Matos, one of the foremost military leaders of the revolution and a violent anticommunist, was charged with treason and imprisoned; his case symbolized the moderate-radical split. At the same time, Castro moved toward an alliance with the Popular Socialist (Communist) party, seeking its help in administering the country.

In January 1960, Castro purged the moderate elements from the leadership of Cuban labor unions. He had long foreseen that conflict with the United States was inevitable and viewed the Soviet Union as Cuba's most logical potential ally and protector. The Soviet Union's deputy premier, Anastas Mikoyan, visited Cuba in January and agreed that his government would purchase 425,000 tons of Cuban sugar in 1960 and 1 million tons the next year. In May Cuba resumed diplomatic relations with the Soviet Union.

United States–Cuban Relations

Meanwhile, Cuban relations with the United States, already suffering from the unfavorable publicity brought by the trials and the expropriation of large estates, reached a crisis in May 1960. The Cuban government requested that the major petroleum refineries, owned by Texaco, Standard Oil, and Royal Dutch Shell, process Soviet crude oil, which the Cubans had obtained at a lower price than the three companies charged for their oil. At the urging of the U.S. State Department, the companies refused. At the end of June, Castro expropriated the refineries. In response, President Dwight Eisenhower withdrew the Cuban sugar quota. Castro in turn expropriated numerous American-owned properties.[2] In October, Eisenhower banned all U.S. exports to Cuba—an embargo that has not yet been lifted. This action set off a new wave of expropriations of American property, including Sears, Roebuck, Coca-Cola, and the enormous U.S. government-owned nickel deposits at Moa Bay.

[2] The government had previously taken over only the operation of these properties.

As relations between the two nations deteriorated, the Central Intelligence Agency began to funnel money to various exile groups for arms and training. During the summer of 1960, the CIA set up a training camp in Guatemala for an invasion force. On January 3, 1961, the outgoing Eisenhower administration severed diplomatic relations with Cuba. Three months later, President John F. Kennedy gave the go-ahead to the exile expeditionary force, which landed at the Bay of Pigs beginning on April 15. The revolutionary army swiftly crushed the invasion. Poorly planned and executed, the invasion was based on the false assumption that the Cuban people would rise in revolt as soon as they heard the exiles had landed. The Bay of Pigs fiasco immeasurably increased Castro's prestige and gave new impetus for radical reconstruction of the Cuban economy and society.

This process was accompanied by ideological changes. What had begun as a program of social and political reform within a framework of constitutional democracy and capitalism evolved into a Marxist revolution. One month after the Bay of Pigs, Castro proclaimed allegiance to socialism.

In the wake of the Bay of Pigs invasion, the Soviet Union pledged to defend Cuba in the event of an attack by the United States and stepped up its flow of arms to the island. These included missile emplacements and aircraft capable of delivering atomic weapons throughout most of North and South America. The United States claimed that these were offensive weapons; Cuba and the Soviet Union argued that they had a defensive, or deterrent, character. On October 22, 1962, President Kennedy ordered a quarantine on all offensive military equipment bound for Cuba and demanded the dismantling of the missile sites. For a time it appeared as if Kennedy was losing control of his military, who were pressing for the use of force against Cuba. After several days, during which the world came close to nuclear war, the two superpowers reached a compromise by which the Soviet Union agreed to remove its missiles from Cuba in return for a pledge from the

United States not to invade Cuba and to remove its own missiles from Turkey. However, efforts by the United States to subvert and harass the Cuban Revolution with the aid of counterrevolutionary Cuban exiles continued: They included CIA-sponsored raids against refineries and ports, infiltration of enemy agents, and even some bizarre attempts to assassinate Castro.

Revolutionary Economics

The Cuban Revolution benefited from advantages few other socialist revolutions have enjoyed. The guerrilla war (in contrast to that of China or Vietnam) was relatively short and caused little destruction of human life or property. Moreover, Cuba possessed well-developed communications and transportation systems, including an extensive railroad network and excellent primary roads. The character of Cuba's rural population promised to make the process of socialist land reform easier than it had been in Russia, for example. Since the sugar industry had proletarianized much of the agricultural work force, farm workers did not demand their own land but rather sought improved working conditions and wages. Cuba also had considerable unused land and industrial capacity, which could be quickly employed to raise living standards and increase productivity. Finally, by 1959 there existed a number of developed socialist states that could offer Cuba substantial assistance, thus offsetting the severe negative effects of the U.S. embargo on exports.

But the revolution also faced serious problems. To begin with, the revolutionaries, inexperienced in economic affairs, made mistakes. The socialist reorientation of the economy inevitably caused disruptions, and the American embargo caused crippling shortages of parts and other difficulties, which the development of new patterns of trade with countries in the socialist camp (and with some capitalist countries) only gradually overcame. Also, many of Cuba's ablest technicians joined the first wave of refugees that fled to the United States. Finally, Castro and his chief

aide, Ernesto (Che) Guevara, initially spurned material incentives, endorsed by more traditional Marxists as the best spur to production, in favor of moral incentives which would give rise to the "new socialist man." Application of this theory caused considerable economic damage before it was replaced in 1969 by a more pragmatic mix of material and moral incentives.

The first goal of the revolutionary government was to redistribute income to the rural and urban working class. During the first three years, it met with considerable success, raising wages 40 percent and overall purchasing power 20 percent. Unemployment was virtually wiped out. These benefits accrued predominantly to areas outside Havana, for the revolutionaries were determined to reverse the trend toward superurbanization, characteristic of most of Latin America.[3]

Castro decreed the first Law of Agrarian Reform in May 1959. This law restricted the size of landholdings and gave the government the right to expropriate private holdings in excess of stated limits; the owners would be indemnified depending on the assessed value of the property for tax purposes. The government distributed the expropriated land in small plots or established cooperatives, which the Institute of Agrarian Reform (INRA) administered. Much of the land redistribution took place in Oriente Province, where the peasants had provided early and crucial support for the 26th of July Movement. Eighty-five percent of all Cuban farms fell under the jurisdiction of the reform law, because landownership was so highly concentrated under the old regime.

The land reform began slowly, but its tempo accelerated in response to domestic and foreign pressures. The estates of Batistiano government officials were taken over immediately, followed by seizure of the great cattle estates when their owners resisted Castro's policies. The timing of the expropriation of the American-owned sugar

---

[3] *Superurbanization* is used to describe the vast expansion through internal migration and concentrated industrialization of one city, usually the capital.

lands was in obvious response to the elimination of Cuba's sugar quota from the American market (1960).

Industrial reforms also began slowly; the government at first took over the management of only one major foreign company, the extremely unpopular telephone company. But conflict with the United States over the initial interventions, the abrogation of the sugar quota, and the refusal of the American oil refineries to process Soviet oil led to sweeping expropriations of American-owned refineries, factories, utilities, and sugar mills. Next, the government took over the banking system and most urban housing. Finally, the revolutionary regime began to expropriate native-owned businesses.

During the first year of its rule, the Cuban government experimented with different types of agrarian holdings. Eventually, all became *granjas del pueblo* (state farms). Administered by INRA, they usually employed the same workers who had toiled on them before the revolution but paid better wages and offered improved working conditions.

The redistribution of income to workers and peasants resulted in some long-range problems. With more money to spend, Cubans demanded more food, especially meat, consumption of which rose 100 percent. This rising demand led to the overkilling of cattle, which seriously damaged the ability of the government to supply meat in later years. The government lowered rents and utility rates and supplied many services free of charge, which increased disposable income even more. Inevitably, shortages arose, because Cuba no longer imported consumer goods and foodstuffs. The government began rationing in March 1962. The revolutionaries also poured large sums into rural housing, roads, and other improvements, but poor planning wasted scarce resources.

Two other important programs had mixed success during the first three years: agricultural diversification and industrialization. The revolutionary government sought to become more self-sufficient by transferring cane land and idle fields to the production of cotton, vegetable oils, rice, soybeans, and peanuts, which would save badly needed foreign exchange on these previously imported commodities. Industrialization proved too difficult, and the program was officially put off in 1963.

The revolutionaries encountered serious problems in agriculture after 1961 because of their inability to organize, plan, and administer the economy. Although Castro set up a central planning agency, JUCEPLAN, in February 1961, more often than not he ignored or circumvented it with his personal "special" plans. For a long time, the government also ignored the private agricultural sector, a critical oversight because more than half the farmland remained in private hands. In early 1961, in an effort to overcome this neglect, the government established the National Association of Small Farmers (ANAP), which tried to coordinate the production of small farms with national goals. It also furnished credit, set up stores, and organized various associations.

From 1962 to 1970, Cuba put a remarkable portion of its gross national product into investment, but that achievement was largely wasted through inefficient administration and poor planning. Many projects were abandoned unfinished, and those that were completed were often improperly maintained and rendered useless.

The Return to Sugar, 1963–1970: The Ten-Million-Ton Harvest

Experience had shown that Cuba lacked the resources and the administrative and technical expertise to industrialize. As a consequence, Castro decided in 1963 to re-emphasize agriculture and return to intensive sugar production, while continuing the diversification program. Increased agricultural production, it was hoped, would generate large earnings and eventually underwrite future industrialization.

The symbol of this effort was the goal: 10 million tons of sugar to be harvested in 1970. Unfortunately, agriculture, especially sugar, had suffered enormously from well-intentioned but short-sighted policies. The sugar harvests of 1960 and 1961 were extraordinarily successful because they benefited from very favorable weather and because the island's cane was at the age of peak yield. Also, for the first time in a decade, the entire crop was harvested. The sugar harvest of 1962 was the worst since 1955, and subsequent harvests continued to be disappointing. The essential problem was that the revolutionaries, in their fervor to diversify, had ripped up some of the best cane land. They had not replanted cane in two years, and as a result most Cuban cane was well past its peak yield. Moreover, equipment and manpower were badly administered. Transportation and distribution were in chaos.

Sugar mills were damaged and left unrepaired for years. The great effort of the 1970 "ten-million-ton harvest" proved too much for many mills. They were old and mostly American-built; the usable facilities were capable of producing perhaps 6 million tons. Furthermore, in 1968 there were only one-fifth the number of professional cane cutters that there had been a decade before. From 1962 to 1969, agricultural production fell 7 percent. After a slight recovery in 1970, a new slump followed.

The government made considerable efforts to correct the situation. The regime decreed the second Agrarian Law in October 1963; under this law, it expropriated thousands of medium-size farms. State farms became the dominant form of agriculture, controlling 70 percent of the land and taking responsibility for all the major export crops. The government also forced those small farmers who remained to sell their crops to it at low cost.

From 1965 to 1967, Castro launched a new campaign of socialization that centralized the administration of the economy and stressed moral incentives to increase productivity. In effect, the campaign sought not only to achieve economic objectives but also to create the "new socialist man," an ideal communist society. Part of this strategy involved increased aid from the Soviet Union. In 1963 and 1964, Castro visited Moscow and came away with important trade

agreements. The Soviets subsidized the Cuban economy by absorbing over $1 billion in trade deficits between 1961 and 1967.

Cuba and Latin American Guerrilla Movements

During the mid-1960s, the Cuban government, proclaiming its unity with other revolutionary struggles, launched a campaign of support for guerrilla warfare against those Latin American regimes it regarded as reactionary and pro-imperialist. The Cuban government gave much support to guerrilla fighters throughout the continent. The policy of exporting revolution elsewhere came to an end when Castro's chief aid Che Guevara was hunted down and killed by U.S.-trained counterinsurgency forces while trying to establish a guerrilla movement in Bolivia in October 1967.

Failure and Reassessment, 1970–1975

The ballyhooed "ten-million-ton harvest" of 1970 failed to reach its acclaimed goal and in the process did extensive damage to the Cuban economy as a whole. To get the 8.5 million tons they eventually harvested, the revolutionaries virtually ruined the sugar industry, and subsequent harvests were generally poor. Resources and manpower were siphoned off from other sectors, causing disruption and turmoil.

The failure of the harvest was the most severe setback suffered by the revolution, and Castro, whose personal decision it had been, lost some of his prestige. On July 26, 1970, however, he addressed his countrymen and admitted his failure. He vowed that changes would be made and re-emphasized that sacrifice and hardship lay ahead, but the revolution would go on.

During the next five years, Castro depersonalized the government and institutionalized the revolution. He delegated authority to a new executive committee of the Council of Ministers and gave the bureaucracy wider scope of action and more influence. President Osvaldo Dorticós and Carlos Rafael Rodríguez, a veteran Communist who had fought with Castro in the Sierra

Maestra, took charge of Cuba's economic development. Castro reorganized the government so as to draw clear lines of separation between the armed forces, the bureaucracy, and the Communist party. The militia was disbanded and merged into the army. The military was restructured along traditional hierarchical lines, and Cuba got its first revolutionary generals. The judicial system was revamped. In addition, an attempt was made to broaden the popular base of the regime and to strengthen the Communist party. The labor movement was revitalized; a larger role was assigned to the trade unions and the workers' tribunals that saw to the enforcement of labor laws and workers' rights. Steps were taken to involve the workers more actively in the formulation of production goals and plans.

The Cuban leadership also drastically overhauled the revolution's policy of economic development. Sophisticated computerized planning techniques were introduced, and a system of material incentives for workers and managers was inaugurated. A work quota system was implemented between 1971 and 1973 resulting in a 20 percent increase in productivity in just one year (1972). The government also began to differentiate between jobs for pay purposes. No longer were people paid according to their need but rather according to the productivity and complexity of their job. These and other economic reforms led to a dramatic rise in productivity. From 1971 to 1975, the gross national product grew at an annual rate of more than 10 percent, compared with an annual growth rate of 3.9 percent for the period from 1966 to 1970.

The Institutionalized Revolution

The first Communist party congress in December 1975 ushered in a new era, completing the formal institutionalization of the revolution. The congress adopted Cuba's first socialist constitution, which was approved by nationwide referendum in February 1976. The constitution, which was an attempt to depersonalize government and make it more responsive to the people, provided for a pyramid of elected bodies. At the bottom are popularly elected members of municipal assemblies, who elect delegates to provincial assemblies and to the National Assembly of People's Power. Most of these representatives are Communist party members. Fidel Castro remained entrenched at the top as president of the Council of State (elected from the National Assembly), First Secretary of the Communist party, and Head of Government. The second congress of the Communist party reaffirmed him in these offices in 1980.

Despite (or perhaps because of) its institutionalization, the revolution encountered severe economic difficulties. Inefficiency and low productivity proved intractable problems and Cuba continued to be heavily dependent on sugar for its economic well-being. From 1976 to 1980 the economic growth rate averaged a disappointing 4 percent a year. At the root of the problem were the lack of professional management, quality control, and labor discipline, all of which added up to poor productivity. Many goods, from shoes to televisions, were poorly manufactured.

Cuba depends on sugar to as great an extent in the early 1990s as any time in its history. Consequently, the government has invested heavily in modernizing the industry. Most sugar cane is now harvested by machine, and new mills—the first in decades—have been built. Although the sugar harvests have produced over 8 million tons in each year since 1982, they have consistently fallen well below planned goals. These shortfalls adversely affect the balance of trade and foreign exchange earnings. Moreover, reliance on its major money crop of sugar ties Cuba inextricably to fluctuating world market prices, ranging from a high of 60 cents a pound in 1974 to 7 cents in 1982 (actually below Cuban production costs).

In order to maintain its development program and consumer consumption, Cuba has borrowed heavily abroad. It owes about $7 billion to Western countries. The government has been unable to meet these obligations, and repeatedly rescheduled repayment. Also, repayment of Cuba's $10 billion debt to the Soviet Union was postponed until 1991, after the original due date of 1986 proved an impossible one to meet. Given the

The tug boat shown here is filled with more than 800 Cubans headed for Key West. During the "Mariel exodus," more than 125,000 Cubans sought refuge in the United States and other nations in the region. (UPI/ Bettman News Photos)

island's size and resources, Cuba's total debt is colossal.

Persistent economic problems led to a massive emigration of Cubans, primarily to the United States, from April to September 1980. The so-called Mariel exodus began when Fidel Castro, angered at the Peruvian Embassy's refusal to turn over six Cubans who had taken refuge there, declared that anyone who wanted to leave the island was free to go. He ordered the Cuban guards from the embassy. Within days 10,000 people crowded into its grounds. Various nations in the region, including the United States, offered to take the refugees. More than 125,000 Cubans left,

mostly through the port of Mariel, many aboard dangerously overcrowded, leaky boats. Before drawing certain conclusions from this exodus, it should be remembered that all great political and social upheavals cause similar flights of disaffected people; it is estimated that after the American Revolution 10 percent of the population left for Canada or England rather than live under the new republican rule.

Achievements

Despite its mixed economic record, the revolution's achievements in the areas of employment, equitable distribution of income, public health, and education are remarkable. Cuba has the lowest rate of joblessness in Latin America. Inequalities in the standard of living have been dramatically reduced from the days of Batista. The lower classes in particular have benefited from government policies: rents are controlled, limited to no more than 10 percent of income, as are staple commodities' prices. The regime has periodically resorted to rationing some food products, but it has carried it out fairly. Rural income, which was $100 per year in 1959, jumped to between $550 and $850 in 1977. Agricultural workers on state farms get furnished houses with televisions and community recreational centers. Cuban city streets have virtually no beggars and sidewalk vendors, which sets them apart from their Latin American counterparts. Hunger and starvation do not exist, slums are almost wiped out, and the government provides free medical care and education. Cuba has the lowest doctor-to-patient ratio in Latin America. Cuba's infant mortality rate in 1989, 11.9 per 1,000 live births, was among the lowest in the world, and equal with that of the United States. Life expectancy had risen to seventy-five years, compared to average life expectancy of 58.2 years in the underdeveloped world. A recent study in the *Latin American Research Review* (1990) concludes that Cuba "has transformed itself into a world-class health-care provider, an extraordinary achievement." Sophisticated medical procedures now performed in Cuba include heart transplants, heart-lung transplants, and microsurgery. The educational budget amounts to 7 percent of the nation's GNP, the highest in Latin America. The population has an average of ninth-grade education, and illiteracy has been wiped out. Undoubtedly, most Cubans have benefited from the revolution.

Cuba and the World

From its early years, the Cuban revolutionary government has sent military aid to other Third World countries. It helped the Algerian independence movement and guerrilla groups in Zaire, the Portuguese African colonies, and Tanzania during the 1960s. With the capture of Che Guevara and the economic disasters of the late 1960s, this activity lessened. During the 1970s, as the danger of U.S. invasion diminished and the economy improved, Cuba again took an important role in Africa. Eleven thousand Cuban troops assisted Ethiopia in repelling the 1978 invasion of the Ogaden region by Somalia and fifty thousand Cuban soldiers helped Angolan forces in their fourteen-year struggle against counter-revolutionary rebels supported by the United States and South Africa and in thwarting a South African invasion of Angola across its southern border. At Cuito Cuanavale, in one of the decisive battles of modern African history, a joint Cuban-Angolan army inflicted a crushing defeat on the South African invaders, which led to the signing of an agreement in 1988 between Angola, Cuba, and South Africa for the mutual withdrawal of Cuban and South African troops and for the independence of Namibia.

Cuba now sponsors what the *New York Times* called "perhaps the largest Peace Corps style program of civilian aid in the world," with some 16,000 doctors, teachers, construction engineers, agronomists, economists, and other specialists serving in twenty-two Third World countries. The Cuban international aid program includes free education in Cuba. In addition to the motive of "international solidarity," Cuban international aid has the objective of providing the country with much-needed hard currency. Fees are charged on the basis of ability to pay, and poor countries receive aid free. Cuba's foreign construction projects have been a major income producer.

Cuba's international role has steadily grown in recent years. Its high standing in international opinion is suggested by its 1989 election for a two-year term to the United Nations Security Council by the largest majority ever obtained by a candidate country. Despite past hostilities and rancors, it now maintains good relations with virtually all other Latin American states. Despite the continuing American trade embargo and other indications of the fixed hostility with which U.S. government has long regarded Cuba, the

Castro regime has persistently sought to normalize its relations with the United States, but its efforts have not been reciprocated. The Guantanamo Naval Base stands as an ever-present reminder of the continuing U.S. military threat to socialist Cuba.

What Lies Ahead?

The chain of events set in motion by Mikhail Gorbachev's launching of *perestroika* (reconstruction) in the Soviet Union—the rapid collapse of Stalinist-type governments in central and eastern Europe and the headlong slide of some of the new democratic regimes toward capitalism—created major political, economic, and ideological problems for Cuba. Castro, speaking on a visit to Brazil in 1990, expressed his profound concern about these developments. Noting that even before perestroika Cuba had begun an effort to improve its own socialism and correct past mistakes in a process of *rectificación* (rectification) and conceding the good intentions of the Soviet leadership, Castro made plain his belief that Gorbachev's reforms had led to a dismantling of socialism in a number of east European countries. According to Castro, these developments, and the Soviet Union's striving for peace and good relations with the United States had only encouraged American imperialism. He claimed that the U.S. government interpreted peace as meaning its right to intervene and wage war anywhere in the Third World.

Ideological questions aside, the dramatic changes in eastern Europe have created difficulties for Cuba. As part of their transition toward a market economy, some of the eastern European countries with which Cuba has had the bulk of its trade have begun to demand that that trade be based on international prices and conducted in hard currency. But Cuba needs its limited stock of hard currency to pay interest on its foreign debt and purchase certain vital products from the West. Anticipating increased difficulties with some of its former socialist trading partners, Cuba has recently begun to diversify its trade links, doubling its trade with China and increasing its trade with Latin America by 20 percent. It is also giving top priority to exports that bring in hard currency and to import substitution. In 1989 two of its major hard currency earners, sugar and tourism, did well; sugar production increased by 7.5 percent and tourism by 25 percent. Medicinal supplies and biotechnological products, however, may become a major category of Cuban exports. In the 1980s Havana's center for genetic engineering produced interferon, an important drug in the treatment of cancer. Cuban scientists have scored important breakthroughs in the field of vaccines, and in 1990 Cuba signed a $140 million contract to supply Brazil with the vaccine against meningitis.

The Soviet Union's move toward a market economy and criticism in some Soviet circles of the country's preferential trade with Cuba, led some observers to suggest that a crisis was brewing in Soviet-Cuban relations. But the signing of an agreement to increase trade between the two countries in 1990 by 7.5 percent and talks to work out a five-year economic cooperation plan appeared to disprove such speculation.

The collapse of socialism in a number of east European states, the success of the U.S. invasion of Panama in December 1989, and the victory of the U.S.-supported opposition in the Nicaraguan elections of February 1990 produced gloating in Washington and predictions that Cuba was next; some Miami exiles prepared to pack their bags and return in triumph to Havana. But reports of the imminent demise of the Cuban Revolution are probably greatly exaggerated. Short of a massive United States invasion—which of course cannot be excluded from calculations—there is very little prospect that Cuba's socialist regime can be overthrown from within or without. In Cuba, unlike eastern Europe, socialism did not arrive in the wake of a victorious Red Army; it was created by an indigenous popular revolution that linked the ideals of socialism and independence, and it enjoys overwhelming popular support. Despite many economic problems, the Cuban Revolution has a record of social achievement without parallel in Latin American history that presents a vivid contrast to the economic and social crises gripping most of the capitalist societies of Latin America.

The process of rectification has been accompanied by efforts to democratize still further Cuba's political and economic structures and widen popular participation in decision-making and by greater tolerance for expressions of dissidence in various fields. In recent years the great majority of the "prisoners of conscience" in Cuba's prisons have been freed and those who chose to emigrate and could obtain visas were permitted to do so. According to Wayne S. Smith, director of Cuban studies at Johns Hopkins University School of Advanced International Studies, the principal obstacle to liberalization has been the Bush administration's policy of raising tensions with Cuba to their highest level since 1962. "As long as U.S.–Cuban relations are tense, Castro demands greater internal discipline. Only with a reduction of tensions can there be a relaxation that would benefit the Cuban people." Further progress in liberalization—perhaps including the introduction of a multiparty political system—must await a lessening of those tensions and especially removal of the threat posed by the unwanted presence of U.S. armed forces on Cuban soil.

Chapter 18

Revolution in Central America: Twilight of the Tyrants?

The July 1979 victory of the *Frente Sandinista de Liberación Nacional* (Sandinista Front for National Liberation) over one of Latin America's oldest tyrannies—the Somoza family dynasty of Nicaragua—was an extraordinary event that reverberated throughout Latin America and the United States. Like the Cuban Revolution of 1959, it challenged the geopolitical doctrine that the United States would not allow the success of a social, anti-imperialist revolution in its Caribbean backyard, a part of the world that for almost a century had been its own secure preserve. In Washington, the Sandinista triumph caused gloom and disarray as to how to deal with the new Nicaragua and prevent the spread of the revolutionary virus to its Central American neighbors. It heartened Latin American revolutionaries, their supporters, and all the democratic forces of the region, ending the discouragement caused by a long series of defeats for radical and progressive causes—from the Brazilian counterrevolution of 1964 to the destruction of Chilean democracy in 1973. Some unique aspects of the Nicaraguan revolution—its blend of Marxism and progressive Catholic thought, its effort to maintain a mix of state and private enterprise—gave room for thought to all who were concerned with the problem of achieving social change in Latin America.

The Carter administration tried to come to terms with the Sandinista regime in the hope of moderating its policies, efforts that ended after the election of Ronald Reagan to the presidency in 1980. Reagan's administration adopted a posture of fixed hostility toward the Nicaraguan government, accompanied by efforts to isolate and overthrow it by an economic blockade and by using Honduras as a base for CIA-organized destabilization activities and armed incursions into Nicaragua by former soldiers of Somoza's National Guard. After almost a decade of massive destabilization had taken its toll, in February 1990 the Nicaraguan people, weary of war and privation, gave Washington the conservative government it wanted in the freest elections in Nicaraguan history. But the Sandinistas remained the strongest, best-organized force in the country and successfully resisted efforts by the incoming regime of Violeta Chamorro to dismantle their basic social reforms.

In El Salvador, meanwhile, guerrilla activities against a repressive military-civilian junta had developed into a full-scale civil war by the spring of 1980. The guerrillas had created a revolutionary government (the *Frente Democrático Revolucionario*) with its own army, the *Frente Farabundo Martí de Liberación Nacional* (FMLN). Ten years later, despite massive infusions of U.S. military and economic aid (over $4.5 billion) to the government, rebel forces held much of the country and showed themselves capable of disrupting the economic life of the country and launching powerful offensives at will. By the spring of 1990, popular discontent with the U.S.-supported government, revulsion in the United States at the atrocities committed by the Salvadoran military, and the demonstrated strength of the guerrillas had forced the government to accept the rebel proposals for peace talks without preconditions.

Guerrilla movements had risen and waned in Guatemala since 1954, when a counterrevolutionary coup organized and armed by the CIA overthrew a reformist regime and the social changes that it had instituted. The guerrilla struggle gained in intensity and popular support in the late 1970s, even as the level of violence on the part of government security forces and death squads reached new heights. After the Guatemalan military government adopted a scorched-earth policy, accompanied by massacres of Indian villagers thought to have supported the guerrillas, the rebels faded into the mountains and jungles. The roots of revolution—massive poverty, injustice, and repression—remained,

however, even after the civilian government of Vinicio Cerezo took office in 1986. By the spring of 1990 the guerrilla war had revived and rebel units maintained a presence only thirty miles from the capital, Guatemala City. Here too peace talks had begun, but their success was in grave doubt.

Why should Central America, a region so richly endowed by nature—where United States economic, political, and cultural influence has been so strong—be such a violent land and present such immense contrasts of wealth and poverty? An attempt to answer this question requires a review of the historical background of the area and a more detailed survey of the history of three countries, Guatemala, Nicaragua, and El Salvador, where revolutionary movements have come to power or are in progress.

Independence and the Failure of Union, 1810–1865

On the eve of independence, the five republics—Guatemala, El Salvador, Honduras, Nicaragua, and Costa Rica—that are traditionally included in the region called Central America,[1] were provinces of the captaincy general of Guatemala, with its capital at Guatemala City. Under the captain general and his audiencia, a small group of wealthy creole merchants, organized in a powerful consulado, dominated the economic, social, and political life of the colony. The guild ruled over trade in Central America, and a tribunal named by the consulado settled all commercial disputes. Through their control of credit, goods, and the system of fairs to which farmers and cattle raisers had to bring their wares, the merchants forced the producers of indigo—the area's most important export—and other staples to sell

---

[1] For descriptive convenience, Belize, Panama, and the Panama Canal Zone are usually included in Central America.

Chapter 18   Revolution in Central America: Twilight of the Tyrants?

438

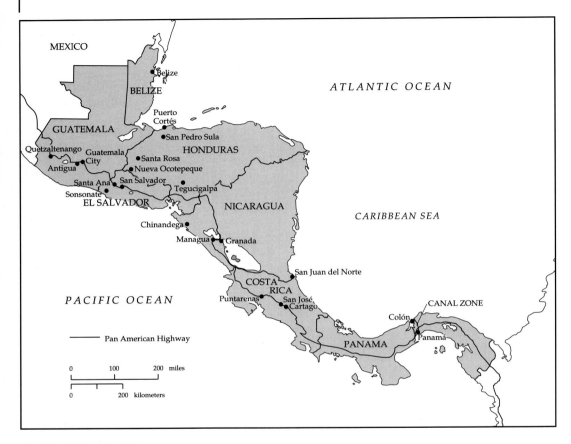

MODERN CENTRAL AMERICA

to them at low prices. Farmers, ranchers, and miners depended on the merchants to supply credit for production and to export their goods to foreign markets. As a result, they fell into debt, and when prices declined—as indigo prices did between 1800 and independence—many went bankrupt. Tied into the dependency network of Guatemala City and the world, producers concentrated on export products, neglecting subsistence crops, so food had to be imported. Resentment of this dependent relationship engendered bitter hostility by other provinces toward Guatemala and its dominant merchant clique.

The large Indian (chiefly Maya) population came under increasing pressure during the Bour-

bon period to enter the money economy. Tribute in kind was no longer acceptable. It had to be paid in money, and new taxes were assessed. The need to pay tribute in coin forced many Indians to become hacienda peons or migrant laborers, wandering from estate to estate. The crown also sought to solve its chronic money problems by tapping Indian community and cofradía funds, which the Indians had used in time of trouble to pay tribute; having lost these defenses, the Indians often had to resort to hacienda labor or debt peonage to meet their obligations. Despite the Bourbon dislike for repartimiento and efforts to reduce its use, forced labor drafts were freely used when needed to make Indians and the castas work in haciendas, obrajes, and mines and on public works.

Spain's hold over its American colonies weakened after 1800 as a result of its involvement in European wars, the resulting disruption of trade, and growing political turmoil at home. Central America drifted toward independence. When Mexico declared its independence in 1821, Central America followed suit. City after city declared its independence, not only from Spain, but from Guatemala and rival cities and towns. The captaincy general dissolved into a multitude of autonomous cabildo governments. The transition to independence was complicated by the efforts of Agustín de Iturbide to incorporate Central America into his Mexican empire, efforts supported by Central American conservatives and opposed by many liberals. In 1822 a majority of cabildos voted in favor of union with Mexico, but Iturbide's overthrow the next year permanently ended the Mexican connection.

Despite provincial rivalries and resentment against Guatemalan domination, a tradition of Central American unity remained and attempts were made to restore that unity. In 1823 a constituent assembly met and created the federal republic of Central America out of the five former provinces: Guatemala, Honduras, Nicaragua, Costa Rica, and El Salvador. The form of government provoked much debate, with the Guatemalan merchant oligarchy favoring a centralized political structure and representatives of the other provinces demanding a loose federal system. The compromise provided for a federal government with free and independent state governments. The constitution had a strong liberal tinge: it abolished slavery and the special privileges of the clergy and established the principles of laissez faire, free trade, and free contract of labor. The next year a Salvadoran liberal, Manuel José Arce, was elected as first president of the republic. Meanwhile, the states were forming their own governments. On the state as on the federal level, conservatives and liberals struggled for power: conservatism—the ideology of the old monopolistic merchant clique, many great landowners, and the church—had its base in Guatemala; liberalism was the dominant doctrine among many large and small landowners of the other states and the small middle class of artisans, professionals, and intellectuals. Behind the façade of elections and universal male suffrage, power throughout the area was held by great landowning and mercantile families who often mobilized their private armies of retainers and tenants in a struggle for control of regions and states.

The superficial unity of Central America soon dissolved as it became clear that the states were neither willing nor able to finance both their own governments and the federal government in Guatemala City. Efforts by the federal government to assert its prerogatives by the establishment of a strong army and the collection of taxes led to a destructive civil war between 1826 and 1829. The struggle ended with the defeat of the national government and its conservative leadership by liberal forces headed by Francisco Morazán and the reorganization of the union on a basis of liberal hegemony.

Morazán, elected president of the federal republic and commander of its armed forces, both based in San Salvador, defended it against conservative plots and attacks. At the same time, a former conservative turned liberal, Mariano Gálvez, governor of Guatemala, launched a program for the economic and social reconstruction of his state. The program included the establishment of civil marriage and divorce and secular schools on all levels, anticlerical measures that allowed nuns to leave their orders and reduced the number of church holidays, large land concessions to British companies that were to colonize the land with foreign immigrants and provide it with an infrastructure, and even an agrarian reform that allowed squatters to buy land for half its value and permitted Indians to settle on vacant land. Gálvez also sought to reform Guatemala's judicial system by basing it on the Livingston Code,[2] which provided for trial by jury and habeas corpus and vested power to appoint all judges in the

---

[2] An influential code of legal and penal reform completed by U.S. lawyer and statesman Edward Livingston in 1824.

440

governor of the state. This last feature alienated powerful landed interests who often served as jefes políticos, local officials who combined judicial and administrative functions and were permitted to keep a share of tax collections.

The loss of support of local landed interests combined with the ravages of a cholera epidemic that spread over Central America in 1837 to bring down the Gálvez regime and its ambitious reform program. Stirred up by local clergy who proclaimed the epidemic divine retribution for the heresies of civil marriage and divorce, the Indian and mixed-blood masses rose in revolt against Gálvez's radical innovations in law and taxation, attacks on their landholdings by creole landowners, and sanitary measures instituted to prevent the spread of disease. The principal revolt was led by the mestizo Rafael Carrera. In February 1838, at the head of an army of Indians and castas whose cry was "Long live religion and death to all foreigners!" Carrera took Guatemala City. In return for a bribe of money for himself and his followers, he agreed to leave but soon threatened to return and sack the city again. The Guatemalans now called on Morazán and the federal army to protect them. Through 1838 and 1839 Morazán continued to battle and defeat Carrera, who retreated into the mountains to prepare for a new attack on the capital. Amid the chaos, the federation of Central America expired. In 1839 Carrera again occupied Guatemala City, this time for good. Morazán, defeated in a last effort to oust him, was forced to flee. Two years later Morazán returned to Central America with a plan to restore the federation, briefly took over Costa Rica, but was captured by his enemies and put to death (1842).

From 1839 until his death in 1865 Carrera dominated Guatemala, either as dictator-president or through his puppets. In 1854, dispensing with the formality of elections, he had Congress name him president for life. Until his death he tried to dominate the rest of Central America, installing conservative puppet presidents in El Salvador and Honduras and generally meddling in the affairs of the other republics. In Guatemala he imple-

mented a reactionary social revolution that revived the authority of the church, returned church and Indian communal properties to their original owners, brought back Indian forced labor, and even changed the title of local officials from jefe político to the old colonial title of corregidor. But what had begun as a lower-class protest against radical innovations and the spoliation of Indian communal lands was soon taken over by the conservative merchant oligarchy who provided the taxes Carrera needed to pay his army and foreign loans. Conservative ministers drawn from the elite surrounded the dictator. Alongside the traditional labor arrangements, there existed free labor and a money economy, with landless Indians and mestizos working, sometimes under debt peonage, on the plantations.

Similar trends prevailed throughout Central America in the age of Carrera, although labor was freer in most of the area than it was in Guatemala. By the 1850s, a rising world demand for coffee stimulated expansion of the crop (it had been grown on a large scale in Costa Rica since the 1830s), and spurred attacks on Indian communal lands and individual peasant plots. Coffee in Costa Rica and indigo and coffee in El Salvador made for relative political stability in those countries. In the more backward republics of Nicaragua and Honduras, where cattle barons warred with each other, little centralized authority existed.

Foreign interventions and territorial claims added to the instability created by economic backwardness and political turbulence. In Nicaragua, the British laid claim to the Atlantic Mosquitia coast. The discovery of gold in California gave a new importance to Central America as a transoceanic transit route and sharpened the rivalry of the United States and Great Britain in the area. The threat to the sovereignty and territorial integrity of the Central American republics grew acute as a result of the folly of Nicaraguan liberals, who in 1855 invited William Walker, an adventurer from the United States, to help them overthrow a conservative regime. Having brought the liberals to power, Walker, supported by a band of some three hundred countrymen, staged a coup, proclaimed himself president, legalized slavery, and made English the official language. By mid-1856, in a rare display of unity, Nicaraguan liberals and conservatives, joined by all the other Central American republics, had combined in a National War against the Yankee intruders, but the Central American army opposing Walker was essentially a conservative army. Defeated in 1857, Walker returned to the United States. He nevertheless made two other attempts to conquer Central America, the last ending in his death before a Honduran firing squad in 1860.

The National War revived the moribund movement for Central American unity. The liberal Salvadoran president Gerardo Barrios was a leading advocate of federation. His efforts to realize Morazán's dream provoked Carrera, who was determined to maintain conservative domination over Central America, to send troops into El Salvador and its ally Honduras. The war ended with Barrios's defeat and exile; there were conservative regimes in every Central American republic. In 1865 Barrios attempted to make a comeback but was captured and executed by his enemies. Carrera died in the same year. With his death the violence-filled formative period of Central American history came to an end.

In the last third of the nineteenth century, the three countries selected for special study—Guatemala, Nicaragua, and El Salvador—underwent major economic changes in response to the growing world demand for two products that the area was ideally fitted to produce: coffee and bananas. The changes included a "liberal" reform that sought to modernize economic and social structures but left intact the existing class and property relations; the rise of a new dependency based on the export of one or two products, foreign control of key natural resources and much of the infrastructure; and acceptance of U.S. political hegemony. Because these changes were accompanied by concentration of landownership in very few hands, intensified exploitation of labor, and a growing gulf between the rich and the poor, they planted the seeds of today's Central American revolutions.

Guatemala

Liberal Reform and a New Dependency, 1865–1944

Carrera's death in 1865 was followed by six years of continuous political and military challenge to conservative rule. The liberals who opposed them were more responsive to changes in the world economy, in particular to the mounting foreign demand for coffee, and the adjustments this required in Guatemala's economic and social structures. In 1871, the liberals seized power; two years later, the energetic Justo Rufino Barrios became president and launched a many-sided reform program. Although a hard, dictatorial man, Barrios had a genuine passion for reform and was an apostle of Central American unity; he died in battle in 1885 in an attempt to unify Central America by force. Under his successors the liberal tradition rapidly lost whatever redeeming qualities it originally possessed. The liberal leaders grew increasingly cynical, corrupt, and repressive, and their professions of faith sounded thin and hollow. Manuel Estrada Cabrera, who held power from 1898 to 1920, because famous for his cruelty. He was finally removed when Congress declared him insane. After eleven years of instability, another strongman, Jorge Ubico, seized power and held it until he, too, was overthrown in 1934.

The liberal reform program included major economic, social, and ideological changes. The ideological reform involved the rejection of clerical and metaphysical doctrine in favor of a firm faith in science and material progress. This called for the secularization and expansion of education. The shortage of public funds, however, greatly limited public education; as late as 1921 the Guatemalan illiteracy rate was still over 86 percent. Seeking to reduce the power and authority of the church, the liberal governments nationalized its lands, ended its special privileges, and established freedom of religion and civil marriage.

The economic transformation encompassed three major areas: land tenure, labor, and infrastructure. A change in land tenure was necessary for the creation of the new economic order. The old staples of Guatemalan agriculture, indigo and cochineal, were grown by thousands of small and medium-sized producers; coffee, however, required large expanses of land concentrated in relatively few hands. Under Barrios, there began an "agrarian reform" designed to make such land available to the coffee growers. Church and monastery lands, confiscated by Barrios, were the first target. Next came uncultivated state holdings, which were divided and sold cheaply or granted to private interests, and Indian communal lands. Legislation requiring titles to private property provided the legal basis for expropriation of Indian lands. The principal native beneficiaries of this process were small and medium-sized coffee growers who could purchase or otherwise obtain land from the government. But foreign immigrants, warmly welcomed by the liberal regimes, also benefited by the new legislation. By 1914, foreign-owned (chiefly German) lands produced almost half of Guatemala's coffee. By 1926, concentration of landownership had reached a point where only 7.3 percent of the population owned land.

The land reform helped achieve another objective of the liberal program—the supply of a mass of cheap labor to the new group of native and foreign coffee growers. Many highland Indians who had lost their land migrated to the emerging coffee-growing areas near the coast. Before Ubico, the most common labor system was debt peonage—legal under Guatemalan law—in which Indians were tied to the *fincas* (plantations) by hereditary debts. This was supplemented by the recruitment of Indians who came down from the mountains to work as seasonal laborers on haciendas and plantations to add to their meager income from their own tiny landholdings. Under

Barrios, there was also revived the colonial system of mandamientos, under which Indians were required to accept offers of work from planters. The registers of Indians maintained by local officials for this purpose were also used to conscript Indians for military service and public works. Indians who could not pay the 2-peso head tax—the great majority—were required to work (two weeks a year) on road construction.

In 1934 Ubico abolished debt peonage, replacing it with a vagrancy law that required all persons owning less than a stipulated amount of land to carry cards showing that they had worked at least 150 days a year on the haciendas. Indians who failed to comply with this obligation to do "useful work" were jailed.

A third necessity for the new economic order was an infrastructure, particularly road and port facilities for transporting and shipping coffee. Although begun and initially financed with Guatemalan resources, the financing and construction contracts for this infrastructure soon passed into the hands of foreign, predominantly U.S. companies. The nation's electrical facilities, constructed by German interests and nationalized during World War I under U.S. supervision, were taken over by the U.S. company Electric Bond and Share. Another U.S. firm, International Railways of Central America (IRCA), which was linked to the United Fruit Company (UFCO) through interlocking directors, acquired monopolistic control over land transport in Guatemala and virtual ownership of the major Atlantic port of Puerto Barrios. The UFCO secured a contract in 1901 to carry Guatemalan mail from Puerto Barrios to the United States in its "Great White Fleet" and to carry bananas, obtained from producers at fixed prices, to the North American market. In time the company acquired vast banana holdings of its own on very favorable terms from the Guatemalan government.

The enormous U.S. economic influence based on direct investments, loans, and control over Guatemala's chief foreign market was translated into a growing U.S. tutelage over Guatemala. After World War I, the U.S. embassy became in effect a branch of the Guatemalan government; American ambassadors were approached for favors in return for cooperation with American corporations.

The depression of the 1930s created a crisis for the monocultural economy. During the 1930s, coffee prices declined to less than half the 1929 level. By cutting off European markets, World War II deepened dependence on the United States market and further depressed coffee prices. The crisis in foreign trade led to rising unemployment, wage cuts, and business failure for many small producers. Other Latin American countries, particularly the larger ones, took advantage of the crisis of the 1930s and the 1940s to try to reduce their dependence on the advanced capitalist countries by programs of import-substitution industrialization and expansion of the domestic market. The Guatemalan planter oligarchy and associated export-import interests, closely linked to U.S. enterprises, made the masses pay for the depression through wage cuts, intensified exploitation, and reduced government expenditures. In the 1930s, the level of official repression rose; in 1933 alone the government executed some one hundred labor leaders, students, and political dissidents.

The fall of the detested Ubico regime came as a result of the anti-fascist climate of opinion created by United States and Latin American participation in the war against the Axis powers. Although Guatemala, under U.S. pressure, had declared war on the Axis in December 1941, Ubico's pro-fascist views and the ties of many of his close advisers and ministers to German interests were well known. In June 1944 a general strike and antigovernment demonstrations forced Ubico to resign. A triumvirate of two army officers and a civilian took over and organized congressional and presidential elections to be held in December 1944. The overwhelming victory of Juan José Arévalo, a prominent educator and scholar who had spent many years in exile, confirmed the demand of the Guatemalan people for the establishment of a government pledged to democracy and social progress.

Revolution and Counterrevolutions, 1944–1983

The Guatemalan democratic revolution of 1944 was largely the work of a coalition of urban middle-class groups and discontented junior military, with the small working class as junior partner and the peasantry in a marginal role. The revolutionary leadership favored a capitalist course of development and was friendly to the United States. The program of the Arévalo administration (1945–1951) reflected its desire for a capitalist modernization. An ambitious social welfare program was launched that stressed construction of schools, hospitals, and housing as well as a national literacy campaign. The 1945 constitution abolished all forms of forced labor, and the 1947 labor code established workers' rights to decent working conditions, to social security coverage, and to collective bargaining through trade unions of their own choosing; it also provided for compulsory labor-management contracts. These reforms spurred a rapid organizing drive among urban, banana, and railroad workers, who made a number of limited gains. Labor organization made slower progress in the countryside, and Arévalo made no move toward agrarian reform.

Following the example of many Latin American governments in this period, Arévalo began a program of industrial development and diversification, employing the newly created state bank and other agencies for this purpose. As for the existing foreign economic enclaves (chiefly UFCO and IRCA), Arévalo's policy was not to nationalize but to regulate their operations in the national interest. The government insisted, for example, that UFCO submit wage disputes to arbitration. New laws stipulated that in the future the state or predominantly national companies should exploit natural resources; in industry, foreign investors could operate on the same terms as nationals.

Arévalo's agrarian program was equally moderate. Government programs offered state support to cooperatives and provided agricultural credit and technical assistance. A new law

444 protected tenants from arbitrary ouster by landlords, but the latifundia remained intact, although the constitution of 1945 permitted expropriation of private property.

The pace of reform quickened with the election of Major Jacobo Arbenz to the presidency in 1950. Arbenz defined his objectives thus: "To convert Guatemala from a dependent nation with a semi-colonial economy into an economically independent country; second, to transform our nation from a backward nation with a predominantly feudal economy into a modern capitalist country; and, third, to accomplish this transformation in a manner that brings the greatest possible elevation of the living standard of the great masses of the people."

Arbenz's major strategy to achieve these objectives was import-substitution industrialization, to be accomplished by private enterprise. But the creation of a modern capitalist economy was impossible without an expansion of the internal market—of mass purchasing power—through agrarian reform. The 1952 agrarian reform law provided for the expropriation of holdings over 223 acres and their distribution to the landless, with compensation made through twenty-five-year bonds. By June 1954, approximately 100,000 peasant families had received land, together with credit and technical assistance from new state agencies. The agrarian reform inevitably affected UFCO. No more than 15 percent of its holdings of over 550,000 acres were cultivated; the company claimed that it needed these large reserves against the day when its producing lands were worn out or ruined by banana diseases. The land expropriation, coming on top of a series of clashes between the government and UFCO over its labor and wage policies, brought their relations to the breaking point.

The moderate Arévalo had already been attacked in the U.S. media as procommunist. Arbenz's deepening of the revolution, threatening the profits and properties of UFCO, evoked a much angrier reaction in the United States and caused UFCO's friends in high places to prepare for direct action against Guatemala. By 1953,

President Dwight D. Eisenhower had approved a CIA–State Department plan for the removal of Arbenz. He was to be replaced by the rightist Colonel Carlos Castillo Armas, exiled to Honduras in 1950 for his part in a right-wing coup attempt. Deeply involved in the conspiracy against Guatemala were Secretary of State John Foster Dulles and his brother, CIA director Allen Dulles (both former partners in UFCO's legal counsel), United Nations Ambassador Henry Cabot Lodge, and Assistant Secretary of State for Latin America John Moors Cabot, both UFCO stockholders. A CIA official served as field commander for the operation. He set up headquarters in Miami and funneled guns and ammunition through a dummy armaments firm to Castillo Armas's "Liberation Army" of Central American mercenaries. The "Liberation Air Force" consisted of U.S. pilots flying CIA planes. The man in charge of psychological warfare was E. Howard Hunt, later of Watergate fame.

The arrival in Guatemala of a shipment of Czech arms in May 1954 (the United States had imposed an arms embargo against Guatemala) provided a pretext for implementing "Operation Success." In June, Castillo Armas advanced six miles from the Honduras border into Guatemala and waited for his U.S. allies to do the rest. While CIA planes dropped propaganda leaflets and incendiary bombs on the capital, the Guatemalan army remained passive, refusing to turn over arms to the workers and peasants who wanted to defend the revolution. Under intense pressure from his military colleagues, Arbenz resigned and turned over the government to a three-man junta, but the United States ambassador to Guatemala, John E. Peurifoy insisted on the installation of Castillo Armas, the CIA candidate, as president. On July 3, Castillo Armas arrived in the capital in a U.S. embassy plane. Assuming the presidency, he promptly launched a campaign of terror against supporters of the revolution. According to one estimate, eight thousand persons were executed. The land reform of 1952 was revoked, UFCO and other landowners regained holdings that had been expropriated, and Castillo

Armas surrounded himself with an entourage that has been described as a gang of "grafters and cutthroats."

The counterrevolution returned power and property to its traditional holders, the landed oligarchy and their foreign allies. The process of land reform was not only checked but reversed; since 1954 the size of the average peasant landholding has decreased, while the percentage of land devoted to commercial farming has increased. But the Guatemalan economy has not stood still since 1954. Two important developments have been the rise of a small dependent industry and some major shifts in the composition of agricultural exports.

Like the Arévalo and Arbenz governments, post-1954 Guatemalan regimes advocated industrialization as a solution to the problems caused by falling prices for coffee and increased competition for the U.S. market from even less developed countries. But there were fundamental differences between the two industrialization programs. The revolutionary governments sought an industrialization based on expansion of the domestic market through agrarian reform and other redistributive reforms and on safeguards against foreign penetration and domination of the national industry. The policy of the counterrevolutionary governments was to industrialize without such reforms or safeguards. The 1961 treaty among Guatemala, Honduras, El Salvador, and Costa Rica that established the Central American Common Market, combining the upper- and middle-class markets of the area, appeared to provide an adequate consumer base. During the 1960s, in the hopeful climate of the Alliance for Progress, U.S. officials and advisers supported the industrialization program and the Common Market idea, believing that they would promote economic and political stability in the area.

In the absence of controls over the composition of capital and the remittance of profits, however, the net result of the program was a dramatic foreign take-over of Guatemalan industry. By 1968, more than 62 percent of all major manufacturing establishments were controlled by foreigners. Moreover, since much of the new industry was capital- rather than labor-intensive, it contributed very little to solving the acute problem of unemployment. Thus, although the contribution of manufacturing to the gross national product rose from 10 percent in 1950 to 16.3 percent in 1979, industrial employment as a percentage of overall employment remained almost stable during that period. The shift of foreign investment to manufacturing reflected a general tendency of foreign corporations to eliminate the risks involved in direct investment in agriculture, transport, and utilities, whose visibility made them easy targets of nationalist resentment. The new strategy was illustrated by UFCO's 1958 decision to divest itself gradually of its banana lands (while retaining control over the marketing of bananas).

Since 1954 Guatemala's small industrial working class has been subjected to chronic governmental repression as well as to intimidation and violence by employers using gunmen and private armies.

Despite a modest advance of industry, Guatemala remained basically a producer of foodstuffs and raw materials. The composition of its exports changed considerably as a result of declining coffee prices. Coffee was still the leading export in 1980, but cotton, sugar, and cardamon ranked second, third, and fourth in value. While commercial agriculture gained, basic grains (wheat and maize) had to be imported from the United States. This reflected the continuing concentration of the best lands in the hands of latifundistas, often by usurpation of the plots of mestizo and Indian smallholders, with army and security forces present to prevent armed resistance. Since peasant unions were forbidden by law and the minimum wage laws ignored, extremely low wages ($1.12 a day in most jobs in the 1970s) were the rule. A system of debt contracting, similar to that abolished by Ubico, turned many peasants into temporary slaves; the contractor, often assisted by army and police units, rounded up indebted peasants and sold their labor for the harvest to sugar, coffee, or cotton plantations.

Under prodding from the United States, the counterrevolutionary governments periodically announced programs of "agrarian transformation" (the subversive term *reform* was carefully avoided). Such programs would distribute uncultivated state-owned lands and provide credit and technical assistance to landless peasants. The areas selected for these resettlement programs were usually inaccessible jungle lands of poor quality, and sometimes the programs resulted in increased spoliation of Indian and mestizo smallholders.

The narrow social base of the post-1954 regimes and the fact that they owed their existence to a flagrant foreign intervention explain their militaristic, repressive character. In the thirty-four years after 1954, there was only one civilian president—Mario Méndez Montenegro, elected in 1966—and he was allowed to take office only after he had assured the military that he would not interfere with them. It was under Méndez, in fact, that repression and counterinsurgency operations directed as much against peasants as guerrillas reached a climax. Aided by United States military advisers, an estimated fifteen thousand persons were slaughtered in the department of Zacapa alone between 1966 and 1968.

Despite the crushing blows inflicted by this and subsequent counterinsurgency campaigns, the guerrilla movements survived and reached a new height of activity in the mid-1970s, with the formation of the *Ejercito Guerrillero de los Pobres* (Guerrilla Army of the Poor). The resurgence was marked by growing cooperation between the guerrilla movements and trade union and peasant organizations. Another significant development was a cleavage in the church between the conservative Archbishop Mario Casariego, firmly loyal to the regime, and many working clergy and some bishops who were sympathetic to liberation theology and active in the Catholic *comunidades de base* (grass-roots communities). Their involvement in the daily struggles of the poor brought charges of subversion and attacks by government and paramilitary forces against them; in 1981 alone, twelve priests were killed and many others, including some bishops, were threatened with death. A not unrelated development, perhaps, was a large increase of missionary activity in Guatemala by U.S. Protestant fundamentalist ministers strenuously opposed to the revolutionary movements.

The guerrilla struggle achieved a high point of organizational unity in 1981 following the decision of the three major guerrilla organizations and the Guatemalan Communist party to form a unified command to coordinate their military operations. By the end of 1981 they had scored considerable successes. The widespread violence and the growing power of the guerrillas intensified the flight of capital, adding to the economic gloom brought on by low commodity prices and declining industrial activity.

The guerrilla advances produced discord among the military. One group of officers favored a more defensive strategy, controlling what was feasible; others favored an aggressive policy, including "scorched earth" tactics against the areas that were supposed to support the guerrillas. This group gained the upper hand in March 1982 when a military coup nullified the presidential election held in March. Claiming that the victorious official candidate had won by fraud, the rebels installed General Efraín Ríos Montt as head of a new three-man junta. Ríos Montt, a born-again fundamentalist Protestant, implemented a "scorched earth" policy. As explained by the *Latin America Weekly Report* in 1982, its aim was to clear the mainly Indian population out of the guerrillas' support areas: "Troops and militias move into the villages, shoot, burn, or behead the inhabitants they catch; the survivors are machine-gunned from helicopters as they flee. Any survivors are later rounded up and taken to special camps where Church and aid agencies cope as best they can." These conditions did not deter the Reagan administration from informing Congress that the human rights situation in Guatemala had improved and that therefore he would renew military aid and arms sales to its government.

Return to Democracy, Guatemalan Style, 1983-1991

In August 1983 Ríos Montt, who had alienated many Catholics by his fervent fundamentalist Protestantism, was overthrown by a coup headed by his defense minister, General Oscar Mejía Victores. The desperate state of the economy, the country's international isolation, and the pressure from the Reagan administration—anxious to prove that Nicaragua was the only nondemocratic nation in Central America as well as to overcome congressional objections to military aid for Guatemala—persuaded the military to turn the reins of government over to civilians. But the return to democracy was hedged with conditions. It was well understood that no future civilian government could hope to survive if it interfered with the military's conduct of the ongoing counterinsurgency war or attacked the oppressive land system.

The first step in the transition to this curious democracy was the election of a constituent assembly on July 1, 1984. The election gave the largest number of seats to the mildly reformist Christian Democratic party (DCG), which was closely followed by another moderate party, the National Center Union (UCN). The assembly produced a constitution that provided for a run-off election for the presidency, but it made no other significant political changes and avoided all reference to social problems.

The assembly set November 3, 1985, as the date for congressional and presidential elections. Vinicio Cerezo Arévalo of the DCG and Jorge Carpio Nicolle of the UCN were the leading candidates for the presidency. Cerezo's campaign promised a curb on inflation, the creation of jobs, respect for human rights, and an expansion of democracy. Carpio countered with charges of communist influence within the DCG. The military distrusted Cerezo, for he and his party had often criticized the army's violations of human rights; death squads linked to the army and the security forces had killed hundreds of DCG members and had even threatened Cerezo's own life. But the military were aware that a Christian Democrat government, with its connections to powerful sister parties in Europe and its patrons in Washington, had the best chance of securing urgently needed foreign aid. Besides, Cerezo gave the military assurances that he would not interfere with their conduct of the counterinsurgency or bring to justice senior officers charged with violations of human rights (like those held in Argentina). Consequently the army, although favoring Carpio, did not manipulate the elections in his favor.

The last civilian president, Julio César Méndez Montenegro (1968–1970), is reported to have said that during his term of office Guatemala had two presidents, himself and his minister of defense, who "kept threatening me with a machine gun." Guatemalans therefore regarded with skepticism the military's promises of a return to democracy after three decades of tyranny; a majority of qualified voters did not trouble to vote. The DCG won a narrow majority of seats in Congress. Cerezo won an impressive victory but knew well the limits of his power.

Under Cerezo the military retained effective control of rural Guatemala, scene of the prolonged counterinsurgency war. Thousands of highland Indians have been uprooted and resettled in so-called model villages, also known as "poles of development." In Phase One of the process, carried out under Ríos Montt and his predecessor, General (and President) Romeo Lucas, the army burned down Maya villages, laid waste fields, and killed over 30,000 villagers, according to estimates. Phase Two was designed to separate the Indians from guerrilla influence, "winning their hearts and minds"; it consisted of resettling the surviving Indians and those who had returned home after fleeing and living like hunted animals in the mountains. In model villages, the Indians now live by nearby military garrisons.

The military reorganization of Indian society included forced participation by hundreds of thousands of Mayans in a civil defense patrol program. Israel, a major supplier of arms to Guatemala, provided it with a wide range of sophisticated hardware, and also furnished advisers on counterinsurgency. Guatemala's counterinsurgency program caused an immense flow of

448

Indian refugees, an estimated 10 percent of the population, chiefly to Mexico. Meanwhile the guerrilla struggle, after suffering severe defeats that drove the partisans into remote parts of the mountains and jungles, has revived. Many model villages are surrounded by guerrilla territory; the guerrilla presence is particularly strong in three zones: the Petén, Quiché and Huehuetenango, and Solola. Despite the increase in guerrilla activities, the *Unidad Revolucionaria Nacional Guatemalteca* (URNG), which leads and coordinates the guerrilla movement, sent Cerezo an open letter expressing willingness to discuss peace talks. In April 1989 preliminary talks were held between a reconciliation commission approved by the government and rebel leaders, a second meeting was held in May 1990, and the talks have continued under Cerezo's successor, Jorge Serrano Elías. But the dominant influence of the military in the government made the prospect of reaching a settlement doubtful, at best.

The army's influence explains Cerezo's failure to keep his promise to initiate an official investigation of the many cases of "disappeared" persons, demanded by their relatives, organized in a support group. This group also called for repeal of an amnesty law, approved by the last military government before it left office, that protects military officers from prosecution for innumerable violations of human rights committed under that regime. Cerezo responded by advising relatives of the "disappeared" to forget the dark past. Death squads continued to operate with impunity; the Guatemalan Human Rights Commission, based in Mexico City, reported a dramatic increase in violence and repression in 1989.

Nor was the Cerezo administration able to deliver on its economic promises. Both unemployment and inflation remained high. Economic aid from the United States and European countries remained below expectations. The economy continued to stagnate. Cerezo responded to the crisis with an economic austerity program reflecting the dominant influence of landowning and business interests. The trade union movement, weakened by three decades of repression and its own

divisions, revived and enjoyed greater freedom of action under Cerezo, at least in urban areas, but was unable to mount an effective challenge to the austerity program. As growing numbers of Guatemalans began to doubt that Cerezo had the will or power to implement a true reform program, his reformist image began to dim.

Cerezo's most positive achievement was his foreign policy of "active neutrality" toward Central American conflicts. He opposed U.S. military aid to the Nicaraguan contras, strongly supported the proposals of the Contadora group of Latin American nations for a peaceful solution to the Nicaraguan war, and made a gesture of good will to the Sandinista regime, inviting President Daniel Ortega to his inauguration. Under Cerezo's auspices, in 1987 five Central American countries signed a peace plan in Guatemala City that finally brought peace to Nicaragua, followed by the most free elections in the country's history in February 1990.

As Cerezo's term drew to a close, campaigning began for the election of his successor. Alfonso Cabrera Hidalgo of the DCG, Cerezo's handpicked successor and protégé, ran under a cloud of suspicion that he was personally involved in drug trafficking. The Cabrera case called attention to the growing importance of Guatemala in the drug trade. It has become a leading producer of opium poppies and a major transshipment point for Colombian cocaine. Evidence has recently surfaced that drug traffickers have infiltrated army and military intelligence units. In January 1991 the conservative, born-again Christian Jorge Serran Elias won a run-off election in which less than half of the country's registered voters cast ballots. Although Serrano promised to work for peace and end human rights abuses, his promises were contradicted by a wave of assassinations in the following days and weeks. The U.S.-based Council on Hemispheric Affairs found that Guatemala, closely followed by El Salvador, was the worst human rights violator in Latin America in 1990. In that year, according to one human rights organization, there were 773 killings, including the murders of dozens of street children, mostly at the hands of the military, the national police, and right-wing civilian death squads.

Nicaragua

Modernization, American Intervention, and Sandino, 1857–1934

The history of Nicaragua for two decades after the collapse of the Central American federation in 1838 was dominated by a struggle between liberals and conservatives. Their responsibility for inviting William Walker to assist them, followed by Walker's attempt to establish his personal empire in Central America, so discredited the liberals that the conservatives were able to rule Nicaragua with very little opposition for more than three decades (1857–1893).

Although coffee was grown commercially as early as 1848, the principal economic activities in Nicaragua until about 1870 were cattle ranching and subsistence agriculture. Indian communities still owned much land, there existed a class of independent small farmers who lived on public land, and peonage was rare. The sudden growth of the world market for coffee created a demand by some members of the elite for land suitable for coffee growing and for a supply of cheap labor. Beginning in 1877, a series of laws required the Indian villages to sell their communal lands; these laws also put the national lands up for sale. These laws effectively drove the Indian and mestizo peasants off their land, gradually transforming them into a class of dependent peons or sharecroppers. The passage of vagrancy laws and laws permitting the conscription of Indians for agricultural and public labor also ensured the supply of cheap labor needed by the coffee growers. These laws provoked a major Indian revolt, the War of the Comuneros (1881); its defeat was followed by a ferocious repression that took five thousand lives.

The new class, made up of coffee planters, was impatient with the traditional ways of the con-

servative cattle raisers who had held power in Nicaragua since 1857. In 1893 the planters staged a revolt that brought the liberal José Santos Zelaya to the presidency. A modernizer, Zelaya ruled for the next seventeen years as dictator-president. He undertook to provide the infrastructure needed by the new economic order through the construction of roads, railroads, port facilities, and telegraphic communications. He reorganized the military, separated church and state, and promoted public education. Like other Latin American liberal leaders of his time, he believed that foreign investment was necessary for rapid economic progress and granted large concessions to foreign capitalists, especially U.S. firms. By 1909 North Americans controlled much of the production of coffee, gold, lumber, and bananas—the principal sources of Nicaragua's wealth.

But Zelaya was an ardent nationalist: he successfully asserted Nicaragua's claim to sovereignty over the Atlantic Mosquitia coast, where the British exercised a protectorate from 1678 to 1894; he was a champion of Central American federation; and he angered the United States by turning down its canal treaty proposal and negotiating with other countries for construction of a Nicaraguan canal that would have competed with the United States–controlled route in Panama. Like Porfirio Díaz in Mexico in the same period, Zelaya had become alarmed over the extent of U.S. economic influence in his country; he sought to reduce that influence by granting concessions to nationals of other countries.

These signs of independence convinced the United States, where imperialist attitudes and policies had flowered since 1898, that Zelaya must go. With American encouragement, a conservative revolt broke out in 1909. The United States Marines landed at Bluefields on the Atlantic coast and protected the conservative forces there against government attack. Under military and diplomatic pressure from the United States, Zelaya resigned and in 1910 the conservatives came to power. Their triumph represented a victory for the traditional landed oligarchy and a defeat for its progressive wing, who sought a capitalist modernization.

The conservatives installed Adolfo Díaz, an obscure bookkeeper in an American mining firm in eastern Nicaragua, as president of a puppet regime that hastened to satisfy all the U.S. demands. An American banking firm made loans to the Nicaraguan government, receiving as security a controlling interest in the national bank and state railways and the revenues from the customhouse.

The servility and unpopularity of Díaz and his puppet regime provoked a liberal revolt in 1912, led by the young liberal Benjamín Zeledón. The rebels were on the brink of victory when American marines were again sent in at the request of the conservative government. Ordered by U.S. officials to end his revolt, Zeledón fought on, warning the U.S. commander that he and his country would bear "a tremendous responsibility and eternal infamy before history . . . for having employed your arms against the weak who have been struggling to reconquer the sacred rights of their fatherland." Zeledón, fighting to the last, suffered defeat and was executed by the conservatives with the apparent approval of the United States. There followed the first U.S. occupation of Nicaragua, with the United States ruling the country through a series of puppet presidents from 1912 to 1925. In return for U.S. protection, the conservative regimes made a number of important concessions, notably the Bryan-Chamorro treaty of 1916, which gave the United States the exclusive right to construct an interoceanic canal across Nicaragua (since the Panama Canal already existed, its real purpose was to prevent any other country from doing the same).

In August 1925, convinced that the conservatives could maintain themselves in power without American assistance, the United States withdrew the marines. Two months later fighting again broke out, and in 1926 the marines returned, ostensibly to protect American and other foreign property. This time they stayed until 1933. The new U.S. strategy was to arrange a peace settlement between cooperative conservative and liberal politicians that would give the

latter an opportunity to share in the political spoils. With Henry L. Stimson, President Coolidge's personal representative, as mediator, such a settlement was reached in 1927. Under U.S. supervision, presidential elections held in 1928 and 1932 gave victory to the liberals. But real power remained in American hands.

Only one liberal officer, Augusto César Sandino, refused to accept the U.S.-sponsored peace treaty of 1927. The mestizo son of a moderately well-to-do, ardently liberal landowner and an Indian servant girl, Sandino had worked as a mechanic and had lived in postrevolutionary Mexico between 1923 and 1926. There he was exposed to radical nationalist and social revolutionary ideas. He returned to Nicaragua in 1926 to join the liberal struggle against a conservative puppet regime. He met with a cool reception from José María Moncada, the head of the liberal army, who later claimed that he immediately distrusted Sandino because he heard him speak of "the necessity for the workers to struggle against the rich and other things that are the principles of communism." Although no Marxist, Sandino had profound sympathy with all the disinherited and planned to make far-reaching social and economic changes after achieving his primary goal of the departure of U.S. troops.

Unable to convince the liberal leaders that he should be given an independent command, Sandino organized his own force, consisting mainly of miners, peasants, workers, and Indians. "I decided," he wrote, "to fight, understanding that I was the one called to protest the betrayal of the Fatherland." For seven years (1927–1933), Sandino's guerrilla army waged war against the United States Marines and the U.S.-sponsored Nicaraguan National Guard. Learning from early defeats and heavy losses when he attempted to meet the enemy in frontal combat, Sandino developed a new kind of warfare based on hit-and-run attacks, ambushes, temporary occupation of localities and, most important of all, close ties with the peasantry, who provided a supply base for the guerrillas and gave them accurate information about enemy movements and other assistance.

In the United States, meanwhile, the war was

General Sandino (third from left) and his staff. To his right is Salvadoran Agustín Farabundo Martí. (Courtesy of the National Archives)

growing increasingly unpopular, and eventually Congress cut off all funding for it. The new Hoover administration decided to extricate itself from the Nicaraguan quagmire but without loss of control. The instrument of that control would be a powerful National Guard, created by the marines in 1927 and trained and equipped by them. In February 1932, Secretary of State Stimson announced the withdrawal of one thousand marines in Nicaragua, the rest to be recalled after the American-supervised presidential election in November. The conservative Adolfo Díaz, widely regarded as a U.S. puppet, was pitted against Juan B. Sacasa, generally regarded as a more independent and genuine liberal than his predecessor

Moncada. The election results gave Sacasa a substantial majority, and on January 1, 1933, he was sworn in as president. Meanwhile, the U.S. minister to Nicaragua had picked a new director of the National Guard to replace its American head. That replacement was Anastasio Somoza García, a liberal general who had links to the prominent Moncada and Sacasa clans, and who had served as foreign minister and in other official capacities under Moncada.

After Sacasa's election, he wrote Sandino, proposing a peace conference. The election and postelection developments created a dilemma for Sandino. He had promised to lay down his arms after the marines left, and the last marines left on

January 2, 1934. But he profoundly mistrusted Sacasa's entourage, especially Somoza, who demanded that Sacasa order the total disarmament of the Sandinistas. In February 1934, Sacasa invited Sandino to Managua for negotiations, giving assurances for his security. In these negotiations Sandino demanded that the National Guard be disbanded—a demand that angered Somoza—but as the talks ended the president and Sandino appeared to be moving toward agreement. On February 21, the president held a farewell dinner, but as Sandino, his brother, and two Sandinist officers were leaving they were arrested by Somoza's officers, taken to the airfield, and shot. Questioned by Sacasa, Somoza protested his innocence; he later assumed full responsibility for the murders. It was his first step toward the establishment of a tyranny that would oppress the Nicaraguan people for well over four decades.

The Somoza Era, 1934–1979

Following the assassination of Sandino, Somoza gradually consolidated his political power, more and more openly defying President Sacasa. With the aid of a fascist-type paramilitary force known as the Blue Shirts, Somoza easily secured election to the presidency as the liberal candidate in 1936, taking care to combine the post with that of director of the National Guard. Since the Guard not only represented the military power of the country but controlled its communications and many other vital services, the Guard was official Nicaragua. With the Guard at his disposal, Somoza had no difficulty extending his term of office indefinitely, ruling directly as president or indirectly through puppet presidents until 1956, when he was assassinated, or *ajusticiado* (brought to justice) as Nicaraguans see it, by the young poet Rigoberto López Pérez, who was killed on the spot. Thoroughly cynical and self-seeking, Somoza represented the total degeneration of the liberal ideology that had inspired the progressive acts of a Barrios or Zelaya. Always obsequiously pro-U.S., he cut his ideas to fit the prevailing American style; a warm admirer of Hitler and Mussolini, he became a great friend of democracy when the United States moved toward war with the Axis powers in the 1930s. President Franklin D. Roosevelt professed admiration for Somoza's democratic and progressive ideas. The saying ascribed to Roosevelt, "Somoza is a S.O.B. but he is our S.O.B." may be apocryphal, but it accurately sums up the U.S. official posture toward the Nicaraguan despot. American friendship for Somoza brought him loans and assistance in establishing a military academy to turn out officers for the National Guard. Graduates of the school usually spent their senior year at the School of the Americas, the United States military training center in Panama.

Following Somoza's assassination in 1956, his elder legitimate son and vice president, Luis Somoza Debayle, took over. Somoza's younger son, Anastasio Somoza, Jr., a West Point graduate, assumed the post of director of the National Guard. Luis was president from 1956 to 1963, then allowed puppet presidents to rule from 1963 to 1967, when he died. In that year Anastasio Somoza, Jr., had himself elected president for a term that was to have lasted until 1971. Once in office, however, he amended the constitution to allow himself another year, then retired for two years while a puppet junta presided over the writing of a constitution that permitted him to be re-elected for another term, which was supposed to run until 1981.

Differences between the Somozas' ruling styles reflected their adaptations to the changing phases of U.S. Latin American policy. The relative mildness of Luis's rule appeared to reflect the reformist and developmentalist stress of the Alliance for Progress of the 1960s. In fact, all three dictators ruled Nicaragua as a personal estate for their benefit and that of their domestic and foreign allies. By 1970 the Somoza family controlled about 25 percent of the agricultural production of the country and a large proportion of its industry; the total wealth of the family was estimated to be $500 million. United States firms also enjoyed profitable investment opportunities in the food-processing industry and mining. Both foreign and domestic employers benefited from the repressive labor policies of the regime, but native capitalists grew increasingly unhappy with the monopolistic propensities of the Somoza family. The church, originally aligned with the Conservative party, shifted its support to the first Somoza and generally remained loyal to the family until the 1960s, when it joined the Christian Democratic party in opposition to Anastasio Jr.'s plans for his perpetual reelection. From first to last, however, the ultimate foundation of the family's power was the National Guard, whose top command always remained in the hands of a Somoza.

While the dynasty and its allies prospered, the economic and social condition of the Nicaraguan people steadily worsened as a result of the unchecked exploitation of rural and urban labor and the developmental programs of the Somoza era. Responding to growing world demand for new products, especially cotton, the Somozas opened up new lands to the planter class. Once again, as during the coffee boom a century earlier, many peasant families were driven from the land and into the cities. Nicaragua under the Somozas had one of the worst income distributions in Latin America; in 1978 the lower 50 percent of the population had an annual per capita income of $256.

Resistance to the Somoza dictatorship had begun in the 1950s, with a series of unsuccessful revolts led by the irrepressible Pedro Joaquín Chamorro, publisher of the highly respected *La Prensa* and son of parents from two of the most powerful conservative clans—a fact that explains why he was pardoned and allowed to return to Managua after each revolt. A more serious threat to the dictatorship arose with the formation in 1961 of the Sandinista Front for National Liberation (FSLN) founded by Carlos Fonseca, Silvio Mayorga, and Tomás Borge and composed largely of students. Its initial efforts to organize guerrilla warfare in the mountains met with defeat, but the rebels gradually improved their tactics and organization, attracting a growing number of recruits, especially among students.

It is estimated that 80% of Managua, the capital of Nicaragua (shown here), was destroyed by the devastating earthquake that hit the nation in 1972. (Henri Bureau/Sygma)

A turning point in the recent history of Nicaragua was the devastating earthquake in 1972, which killed 10,000 Nicaraguans and reduced the entire center of Managua to rubble, wiping out almost all businesses. There was immense public indignation over the shameless behavior of the Somozas, who diverted large amounts of foreign international aid into their own pockets and those of the National Guard. The center of Managua remained "an unreconstructed moonscape," for Somoza and his cronies had bought large parcels of land on the periphery of the city where they built new houses and shops, profiting from the disaster.

In December 1974, the FSLN scored a major political and propaganda coup when a group of Sandinistas stormed a party in Managua attended by leading figures of the regime and seized forty of the guests. They were held as hostages until the Sandinistas obtained a ransom of $5 million, freedom for fifteen political prisoners, and a flight to Havana. Somoza responded by declaring a state of siege and launching brutal repression in the rural areas where the FSLN was believed to be operating. In November 1976 the FSLN suffered a heavy loss when the Guard ambushed and killed its founder and principal ideologist, Carlos Fonseca.

In January 1978 the Somozas committed an act of folly that largely contributed to their downfall. Stung by a series of articles in *La Prensa* about the commercial blood-plasma operation through which Somoza sold the blood of his people in the United States, the family or one of its members ordered Pedro Joaquín Chamorro's liquidation. The murder of a much-loved and courageous journalist provoked an effective general strike that only ended after considerable violence and repression by the National Guard, but its repercussions continued. The crime alienated from the regime sections of the elite who could tolerate the murder, jailing, and torture of peasants and Sandinistas, but who were shocked at the killing of a member of an old privileged family like Chamorro. "If Pedro Joaquín Chamorro could be killed," writes Professor Thomas Anderson, "then everyone was in danger, and the Somozas would have to go. This became the thinking of the Nicaraguan elite."

The Chamorro affair, the general strike, and a brutal National Guard attack on an Indian community that was commemorating the forty-fourth anniversary of Sandino's assassination with a Catholic celebration strengthened the FSLN and contributed to a general broadening of the resistance movement. In August 1978 the Sandinistas launched their most audacious operation to date. Invading the National Palace, twenty-five guerrillas seized as hostages most of the members of the Chamber of Deputies and some 2,000 public employees. After frantic negotiations, Somoza agreed to most of the Sandinista demands: release of fifty-nine Sandinista prisoners, a huge ransom, and a safe flight for the guerrillas and released prisoners to Panama. This development was soon followed by another prolonged general strike and a spontaneous uprising in the city of Matagalpa by *muchachos* (youngsters), who forced the National Guard to retreat to their barracks and held out for two weeks. On September 8, the FSLN launched uprisings in five cities. With their headquarters surrounded by civilian and FSLN combatants, the Guard called in Somoza's air force for a ferocious bombing of the cities before government ground forces retook the cities one at a time. This was followed by a house-to-house search in a genocidal "Operation Cleanup," with a death toll of some 5,000 persons.

Alarmed by the September uprisings, the United States attempted to mediate a compromise between Somoza and his traditional elite opponents through a committee of the Organization of American States (OAS). The U.S. initiative was frustrated by Somoza's obstinate refusal to resign and the withdrawal of liberal factions from the mediation process, charging that the OAS commission wanted "*Somocismo* without Somoza." Meanwhile the FSLN, overcoming the differences over insurrectionary tactics of three groups within it, created a nine-man directorate.

The September uprisings were followed by a mobilization of both sides for a final struggle. Somoza prepared for the worst by liquidating his vast assets and shipping his capital abroad. Meanwhile the FSLN, aided by the Social Democratic parties of Western Europe and governments as diverse as those of Costa Rica, Panama, Venezuela, and Cuba, restocked its arms supply with weapons purchased on the international arms market. The regular FSLN army expanded from a few hundred to several thousand. Throughout the country the network of neighborhood defense committees established after the September revolts worked feverishly to prepare for the coming struggle by stockpiling food and medical supplies. Comunidades de base (Catholic grass-roots organizations) took an active part in these preparations.

In June 1979 the FSLN announced a general strike and the launching of a final offensive. On June 8, having infiltrated Managua, the Sandinistas launched their offensive in the capital, occupying barrios on both sides of the central zone. Somoza, retreating into his recently constructed bunker in the fortress of La Loma, ordered a counterattack that included a massive air and artillery bombardment of the city. "The devastation of June 1979 finished what the earthquake had spared," wrote Professor Thomas Anderson.

By July 5, the Sandinistas had encircled the capital leaving only one way out via the airport six miles east of the city. The Sandinistas could have taken it at will but allowed it to remain in the government's hands, perhaps to give the Somozas and their entourage an opportunity to leave the capital and thus avoid another bombardment and battle. With victory in sight, the Sandinista directorate named a provisional government, a five-member junta that included three Sandinistas; Alfonso Robelo, the leader of the businessmen's opposition to Somoza; and the widow of the martyred Pedro Joaquín Chamorro.

Meanwhile the United States made last-minute efforts to prevent the coming to power of a radical revolutionary regime. It called on the OAS to send a "peace-keeping" force to Managua but was unanimously rebuffed. Then it sent a special representative to Nicaragua to try to persuade the FSLN to broaden the base of the new junta. But the Sandinistas pointed out that they had already made a large concession by including the conservative Robelo and the moderate Violeta Chamorro in the junta; inclusion of the persons nominated by the United States—one was a general of the National Guard and another a personal friend of Somoza—would ensure the preservation of "*Somocismo* without Somoza."

Under intense pressure from Archbishop Miguel Obando y Bravo and people in other influential quarters to accept his inevitable defeat and to spare the capital a new assault, Somoza agreed on July 16, 1979, to go into exile in Florida. The next day he drove to the airport and left Nicaragua forever. Two days later the FSLN and its government entered Managua.

The Sandinistas in Power, 1979–1990

The cost of the Sandinista victory in lives and material destruction was enormous. Estimates of the dead ranged up to fifty thousand, or a loss of 2 percent of Nicaragua's population. The material damage was estimated at $1.3 billion; the national debt, a large part of which represented sums that Somoza had diverted into his foreign bank accounts, stood at $1.6 billion.

The government that presided over the immense task of national reconstruction consisted of four parts. The official government included the five-member junta, its cabinet or ministries of state, and the council of state, a legislative and consultative assembly in which a broad variety of mass and economic organizations were represented. The composition of these bodies reflected the sincere desire of the Sandinista leaders to maintain a pluralistic system and approach to the solution of the country's problems. In the first cabinet, in addition to Marxists like Tomás Borge, minister of the interior, and Jaime Wheelock Román, minister of agriculture, sat two bankers and two Catholic priests, the Maryknoll Father Miguel D'Escoto and the Trappist monk Ernesto Cardenal, "making Nicaragua probably the only country in the world with Catholic priests in the cabinet." From the first, however, it was understood that these formal organs of government were responsible to the nine-member directorate of the FSLN that had created them. The directorate had direct control of the Sandinista armed forces and police. Elections had been promised, but the state of war in which Nicaragua soon found itself as a result of CIA-organized efforts to destabilize and overthrow the Sandinist regime delayed elections until 1984.

Economic problems dominated the agenda of the new government. One immediate problem was that of repairing the ravages of war and the earthquake of 1972, a task mainly entrusted to the municipalities and the Sandinist Defense Committees. It was completed with such speed that visitors to Nicaragua in the fall of 1979 marveled at the relatively normal appearance of the country. Food shortages were another serious problem and required the importation of great quantities of foodstuffs, mostly financed with foreign donations. Meanwhile emergency food crops were sown so that domestic supplies of food would be available by the middle of 1980. The work of repair was combined with food-for-work schemes to provide a temporary solution for the vast unemployment that was a legacy of the war.

What to do about the national debt was a vexing question for the new government, for it knew well that many of the more recent loans had served only to swell the bank accounts of Somoza and his cronies. It decided, however, to agree to pay all the loans, even the corrupt ones, for both economic and political reasons. The Sandinistas wanted to retain access to Western loans and technology; they also wished to disprove the charge that the new Nicaragua was a Soviet or Cuban "puppet," solely dependent on the socialist bloc for economic and political support. The socialist countries, particularly the Soviet Union and Cuba, in fact gave considerable aid in the form of food shipments and other supplies. Cuba also sent large numbers of teachers and doctors to assist in the work of reconstruction.

The international lending agencies and Western governments hoped financial aid to Nicaragua would enable the private sector of the country to survive and keep the economy pluralistic. The principal difficulty in renegotiation arose with the United States. The Carter administration agreed to make a new loan of $75 million, chiefly for aid to the private sector. When Ronald Reagan came to the presidency, however, he froze the remaining $15 million of the loan, alleging that Nicaragua was sending arms to the rebels in El Salvador. Thereafter Nicaragua had to rely for aid on the socialist countries, friendly social democratic governments of Western Europe, and Third World countries, including Brazil.

The Sandinista government was avowedly socialist, but it recognized that private enterprise had a vital role to play in the reconstruction of the national economy. The state, however, became the most decisive and the most dynamic element in the economy and in the provision of social services, particularly health, education, and housing. The strengthening of the state sector was a direct result of the take-over of the enormous properties of the Somoza dynasty and its allies. These properties became the basis of the People's Property Area, including half the large farms over 500 hectares, a quarter of all industry, large construction firms, hotels, real estate, an airline, a fishing fleet, and more. The expropriation of the holdings of Somoza and his supporters placed approximately 40 percent of the gross national product in the hands of the state. The banking system and foreign trade were completely nationalized.

These expropriations, however, left 60 percent of the GNP in the hands of the Nicaraguan capitalist class, which continued to control 80 percent of agricultural production and 75 percent of manufacturing. The policy of the Sandinista government was to avoid radical changes that might cause a rupture with the "patriotic bourgeoisie," the results of which would be disastrous for the economy. At the same time the government insisted on safeguards with respect to working conditions, wages, hours, and the like that would at least modestly improve the life of Nicaraguan workers. It also encouraged the trade unions to watch over the proper functioning of factories so as to prevent decapitalization, slowdowns in production, and other sabotage by capitalists hostile to the revolution. The result was a built-in tension between the government and a section of the bourgeoisie. Partly because of this tension, partly because of objective conditions—lack of foreign exchange to buy inputs, obsolete machinery, and other problems—private businessmen began dropping out of manufacturing or failing to invest.

The growth of the public sector was most marked in agriculture. Land reform was placed under the *Instituto de Reforma Agraria* (INRA), which by the end of 1979 had confiscated without compensation over one-fifth of Nicaragua's cultivable land that belonged to persons or corporations affiliated with the Somoza regime. The government proposed to maintain these estates as productive units rather than to divide them into small parcels. Most of these lands were large farms that had been operated as capital-intensive enterprises, so parcelization would have resulted in heavy production losses. The decision was made to convert many of these estates into state farms, combined into 170 productive complexes, which in turn formed 27 agricultural enterprises. Others were organized as production cooperatives, called Sandinist Agricultural Communes. In late 1980 there were about 1,327 of these cooperatives. INRA simultaneously tried to improve the living conditions of state-sector workers through the establishment of clinics, schools, and housing projects. In 1980 more than fifty thousand workers worked full time in the state sector.

Although the government favored state farms and production cooperatives as basic agricultural units, small independent farmers were not neglected. Agricultural credit for small producers was greatly expanded, and they were encouraged to form credit and service cooperatives. In 1979–1980, there were 1,200 of these co-ops organized; they received over 50 percent of the agricultural credit extended by the government in the same period.

Even after the confiscation of the estates of the Somozas and their supporters, large commercial farms producing such crops as cotton, coffee, cattle, and sugar still held 66.5 percent of Nicaragua's cultivable land. The relationship between this private agricultural sector and the revolutionary government was an uneasy one. Most of the large landowners despised the Somozas, resented their hoggish propensities, and welcomed their overthrow. But the rules of the game had changed, and the new rules were not always to their liking. Landowners could no longer mistreat their workers; they must comply with reform legislation defining the rights of tenants and workers. Despite the government's assurances that it wanted to preserve a private sector, large landowners were understandably nervous about their

future. The commercial farmers and cattle ranchers defended their interests through their own associations, which negotiated with the government over prices, acreage quotas, and the like. The commercial farmers had access to credit at low interest rates, and a coffee stabilization fund was established to protect growers against fluctuations in the world market. The economic importance of this sector is evident from the fact that in 1979–1980 it accounted for 62 percent of the production of cotton and 55 percent of the production of coffee.

The difficulties of Nicaraguan agriculture were not due primarily to inadequate volume of production but stemmed above all from falling world prices for its major export crops. Sugar, which sold for 24 cents a pound in 1981, sold for 9 cents in 1983. Natural disasters also hurt production of staple foods in 1982. In May flooding destroyed 20,000 acres of just-planted basic grain crops, destroyed $3.6 million in stored grains, and caused $350 million in damage to the national economic infrastructure according to a United Nations survey. A drought in July and August caused estimated losses of $47 million. Finally, the greatly increased scale of CIA-organized counterrevolutionary activity that began in 1981, diverting manpower and resources to military purposes, caused serious damage to Nicaraguan agriculture and to the economy in general—probably a major aim of the U.S. destabilization program.

The implacable pressure of the Reagan administration on Nicaragua represented a threat not only to its economy but to the existence of the revolutionary government. Although the Carter administration's policy was "more than a little schizophrenic," once the FSLN was firmly in power it made a serious effort to come to terms with the revolution, hoping thereby to enable capitalism to survive in Nicaragua. With the election of Reagan, the U.S. attitude changed drastically. *Newsweek* (November 8, 1982), quoted an insider as reporting that the driving forces behind the operation were Alexander Haig, Reagan's secretary of state, and Thomas Enders, then assistant secretary of state for Latin America. To further the plan, General Vernon Walters, Haig's ambassador at large, was sent to discuss possible joint operations with conservative Latin American governments, including Argentina, Guatemala, and Honduras.

The Reagan administration authorized formation of a paramilitary force of ex-National Guardsmen, with an acknowledged budget of $19 million. In a move recalling the 1954 coup against Guatemala, Honduras was converted into a staging area for Nicaraguan operations. Beginning in 1981, Argentine and U.S. advisers trained the *Somocistas* (familiarly called the *contras* by both sides) and assisted them in making raids into Nicaragua, killing hundreds of Nicaraguan soldiers and civilians and destroying bridges and construction equipment.

The "secret war" against Nicaragua quickened its pace when Ambassador John Negroponte arrived in Honduras in 1982. Although Honduras formally returned to civilian rule in January 1982 when liberal President Roberto Suazo Córdova assumed office after nine years of military rule, real power was held by General Gustavo Adolfo Álvarez, who took his orders from Negroponte. With Negroponte masterminding the operation, the CIA station in Honduras grew to an admitted fifty employees, plus a large number of secret agents, including many Vietnam veterans who were now mercenaries under contract to the CIA. United States military aid to Honduras, under $2 million in 1980, grew to $10 million in 1981, and may have reached as high as $144 million in 1982–1983, with some of it coming from a hidden budget.

In March 1983, the operation moved into high gear when several thousand Somocistas and other mercenaries, supported by Honduran troops, invaded Nicaragua at several points on its northern border with Honduras. Simultaneously, in a gesture of "gunboat diplomacy" several U.S. warships were sent to Nicaragua's Pacific coast, ostensibly to monitor suspected movements of arms from Nicaragua to rebels in El Salvador. By the end of March, despite claims of victory from the invaders' radio, the Nicaraguan armed forces

and militia had crushed the counterrevolutionary attacks, although the contras continued to make raids, mostly of the hit-and-run variety.

By mid-July 1983, it appeared that what some called the Reagan administration's Bay of Pigs had aborted. The Sandinistas had driven the major counterrevolutionary force, the so-called *Fuerza Democrática Nicaragüense* (FDN), back into its Honduran sanctuaries, and probably only the wish to avert an open war with Honduras prevented their pursuit and total rout of the contras. A smaller group of guerrillas operating from the south along Nicaragua's border with Costa Rica, headed by the former Sandinista commander Edén Pastora, announced that it was ceasing its activities.

The international reaction to the March crisis reflected the fact that, despite the U.S. efforts to isolate Nicaragua economically and politically, its international prestige had steadily grown. In October 1982, for example, Nicaragua won a major diplomatic victory with its election to the U.N. Security Council as representative of the Latin American area. Nicaragua received 104 votes, while the U.S. candidate—the Dominican Republic—received 50. None of the other Central American republics voted for Nicaragua, but the great majority of the South American states voted in its favor. Some observers commented that the vote was an international plebiscite on the Nicaraguan Revolution.

Under the hardest conditions, Nicaragua's Sandinista leadership continued its difficult struggle to stabilize the economy, expand social reforms, replace the revolutionary government with a parliamentary democracy, and solve such major problems as a bitter church-state conflict and the demand for autonomy from the Miskito and Sumo peoples of Nicaragua's Atlantic coast. In the same period the United States intensified its "covert" war against Nicaragua, with an expanded role assigned to the Central Intelligence Agency. The CIA provided the contras with trainers and advisers, used CIA-controlled planes to make air drops of supplies to contras in Nicaraguan territory, mined Nicaraguan harbors, and even issued a manual for use within Nicaragua instructing the contras in terrorist methods—including the liquidation of government officials and progovernment activists. The "covert" war flouted U.S. laws, treaty obligations, and international law. In June 1986 the World Court, acting on a complaint by Nicaragua, ordered the United States to halt all its military and paramilitary actions against Nicaragua, but the Reagan administration, refusing to accept the jurisdiction of the court, disregarded the order.

Despite hundreds of millions of dollars' worth of U.S. financial and military aid of the United States to the contras, by the beginning of 1986 Nicaraguan President Daniel Ortega could speak of the rebels' "strategic defeat" as an accomplished fact. Shortly before the House of Representatives yielded in June 1986 to the arm-twisting pressures of President Reagan and voted by a razor-thin majority to give the contras another $100 million in aid, the House Intelligence Committee concluded that even with $100 million the Somocistas could not win.

A major factor in the military decline of the contras, despite stepped-up U.S. aid, was growing Sandinista military effectiveness. In the war's first stage, poorly trained militia bore the brunt of the fighting. But beginning in 1984, Irregular Warfare Battalions (BLIs) were deployed. Composed chiefly of draftees, they were well trained and armed, led by veterans, and made large use of helicopters to ferry troops to battle areas. The Sandinista army also dotted the rugged interior of the country with artillery fire bases that could saturate contra build-up with artillery fire and could launch air strikes from attack helicopters; BLIs were then carried in to mop up. As a result, the contras shifted their strategy within Nicaragua to operations by bands of from five to thirty soldiers. In 1986, for the first time the Somocistas were unable to disrupt the crucial coffee harvest.

The superior morale of Sandinista troops also contributed to the "strategic defeat" of the contras. The bulk of the contra forces consisted of mercenaries and an unknown number of forcibly recruited peasants. Contra commanders and U.S.

advisers often complained that the contra rank-and-file lacked stomach for fighting.

There was a growing belief among students of the war in Nicaragua that even the Reagan administration did not take seriously the prospect of a contra military victory. The guiding concept in the administration's policy of support for the contras appeared to be one of maintaining a "low-intensity conflict" designed to wear down the Nicaraguan government and economy, to undermine popular support for the regime by causing hardships and war weariness and by constantly threatening overt U.S. military intervention, and thereby eventually produce an internal collapse.

The war, which diverted manpower and resources to nonproductive uses and caused large-scale destruction of assets by the contras, contributed to a sharp decline in the Nicaraguan economy between 1983 and 1986. The Gross Domestic Product fell by 30 percent in 1985 alone, inflation reached an annual rate of 300 percent, and severe shortages of goods of every kind prevailed. But the war was not the sole factor responsible for the economic decline. Other causes included deterioration in the terms of trade for Nicaragua's exports; the U.S. trade embargo of May 1985, which isolated Nicaragua from its traditional export market and from a source of goods and technology difficult to replace; and the unwillingness of some private sector interests to invest in maintaining and expanding Nicaragua's production.

The Nicaraguan government responded to the economic crisis with measures to stimulate production by increasing prices paid for basic grains and other staples, while protecting the real value of salaries and wages by periodic adjustments to compensate for inflation; by expanding trade with the European Economic Community and the socialist bloc to compensate for the loss of the U.S. market; and by redesigning the agrarian reform to make more land available to individual peasants as a means of stimulating basic grains production.

The Sandinistas had promised in 1979 that

elections would be held by 1985, but the need to refute U.S. charges that their regime was undemocratic and illegitimate led to a decision to accelerate the timetable for elections. In November 1984, Nicaraguans went to the polls to vote for a president, a vice president, and a ninety-member national assembly that would frame a constitution for the country. Opposition poll watchers and a large number of foreign observers, including a task force of the Latin American Studies Association (LASA), the major organization of teachers and students of Latin American affairs in the United States, found no evidence of irregularities in the voting or the vote-counting process. The Sandinista Front received 67 percent of the vote, the rest going to opposition parties. In January 1985 Daniel Ortega Saavedra and Sergio Ramírez Mercado took office as president and vice president, respectively, of Nicaragua.

A year of intense discussion and debate at mass meetings throughout the country and in the national assembly, supplemented by consultations with foreign authorities on constitutional law, preceded the adoption of Nicaragua's first constitution since the Sandinista victory. The document established political pluralism, a mixed economy, and nonalignment as its guiding principles, and divided power among the executive, legislative, judicial, and electoral branches. It guaranteed individual and social rights, including the rights to a job, education, and health care, free expression of opinion and association; the right to strike; and the right to a fair trial. The constitution also sought a definitive solution for the troubled relations between the central government and the indigenous peoples of the Atlantic coast.

Self-determination for the Peoples of the Atlantic Coast

The Sandinistas inherited a long history of government neglect of coastal peoples and a resulting distrust of government on the part of the native peoples. The Sandinistas acknowledged that they had made serious errors in their effort to integrate indigenous peoples into the revolution because the government failed to take account of their unique culture and traditions. The problem was complicated by the fact that the United States and the contras sought to exploit those errors and misunderstandings and draw the Atlantic coast peoples to the side of counterrevolution, and by the continual contra raids into the coastal area from neighboring Honduras. In response to those raids, in 1981 the Nicaraguan government forcibly evacuated thousands of Miskito and Sumo Indians from their land along the Coco River, destroyed their villages to deny their use as bases by the contras, and resettled the refugees in camps away from the threatened coastal area. Although the camps provided improved health care, food subsidies, education, and improved housing and electricity, the Indians, who were strongly attached to their villages and lands, tended to view the camps as prisons. As a result, several antigovernment Indian-based guerrilla groups arose on the Atlantic coast. However, U.S. efforts to pressure the Miskitos into an alliance with the major contra groups, as a condition of military and financial aid, produced splits that the Sandinistas exploited to negotiate cease-fire agreements with individual Indian commanders.

Two major initiatives by the Nicaraguan government paved the way for a solution of the Atlantic coast problem. First, in 1985 Interior Minister Tomás Borge announced that the Miskitos living in relocation camps would be allowed to return to the Coco River area. Second, in 1984 the government created a commission to define an autonomous status for the Atlantic coast peoples under the new constitution. Thus, a dialogue began between the two factions. The new constitution incorporated the results of the dialogue; it recognized the right of the Atlantic coast peoples to autonomy, and guaranteed the preservation of their languages, religions, cultures, and social organization. They would elect their own representatives to the national Congress and use their resources to satisfy their own needs as determined by a regional assembly.

Government and Church Relations

A major problem of the Nicaraguan regime concerned its relations with the church hierarchy, headed by the extremely conservative and combative Archbishop Miguel Obando y Bravo, and through the hierarchy with the Vatican. Until shortly before the revolution, the hierarchy had excellent relations with the Somoza dynasty; on the occasion of the first Somoza's funeral, the then-archbishop of Managua proclaimed Anastasio a "Prince of the Church." As the Somozas' fall grew imminent, the church sought to distance itself from the regime and began to criticize its violations of human rights, but never expressed support for the FSLN. After the triumph of the revolution, the hierarchy made some effort to come to terms with the new order and even issued a pastoral letter that supported the revolutionary process. In 1980, however, a major split occurred within the governing junta marked by the resignations of conservative businessman Alfonso Robelo and of Violeta Chamorro (widow of the martyred editor of *La Prensa*); simultaneously the church hierarchy moved into the opposition to the Sandinista regime. Archbishop Obando y Bravo (a close friend of Robelo) began to criticize priests who occupied posts in the government or who defended government policies from their pulpits, and to remove priests identified with the so-called popular church from their parishes.

The developing church-state conflict took place in the context of a larger struggle of the Vatican, headed by John Paul II, the conservative Polish pope, to eliminate the influence of liberation theology in Latin America. Well primed by Obando y Bravo during the archbishop's visit to Rome, the pope used the occasion of a brief twelve-hour visit to Nicaragua to make a frontal attack on the Christian grassroots movement and the many priests (about half of the Catholic priesthood) who supported it. At an open-air mass attended by between 500,000 and 700,000 people John Paul II lashed out at the "popular church," criticized priests who served in the San-

dinista government, and called for obedience to the bishops. This was not the message of peace and condemnation of U.S. intervention and contra atrocities that the crowd expected, and it made its feelings known with chants of "We want peace." Three times the angry pope shouted back, "Silencio!" The atmosphere of confrontation was visible to the whole world of television, which showed the pope reprimanding and shaking his finger at Father Ernesto Cardenal, poet, priest, and Nicaraguan minister of culture, as he genuflected and tried to kiss the pope's ring.

In the wake of John Paul II's stormy visit, church-state tension markedly increased in Nicaragua. The ever-more militant antigovernment stance of the hierarchy coincided with increasing U.S. economic and military pressure on Nicaragua. In 1985, Obando y Bravo, now a cardinal, returned from Rome to tour Nicaragua, calling on the government to dialogue with the contras—a position identical with that of the Reagan administration. Other church leaders visited the United States in 1986 to campaign for aid to the contras. The Nicaraguan government responded by refusing to permit one priest to return to the country and expelling another on his return; it also expelled ten foreign priests who expressed support for the contras. Other government responses to procontra activities by church spokesmen or media included the closing of the church newspaper *Iglesia* in October 1985 and the shutdown of *Radio Católica* in January 1986. These closures and all media censorship were lifted by the government in compliance with the Guatemala City peace agreements of August 1988.

The Quest for Peace and the Election of 1990

By the end of 1986 the Sandinista government had achieved a "strategic victory" over the contras, who were reduced to hit-and-run raids into Nicaragua across the long, densely wooded or mountainous border with Honduras. In the wake of the U.S. congressional election of November 1986, which handed a heavy defeat to President

Reagan, his administration suffered another blow due to the revelation that part of the proceeds of a sale of arms to Iran, in a supposed swap for U.S. hostages in Lebanon, had been illegally diverted to the contras through the use of secret Swiss bank accounts. The scandal, which daily brought new revelations—such as the involvement in drug smuggling of the crews of CIA-connected planes used to drop arms to the contras—increased opposition to the additional contra aid that President Reagan requested. By the end of the Reagan presidency Congress had rejected an administration request for military aid and voted to limit funding to so-called humanitarian aid.

The Iran-contra scandal and its repercussions created a favorable atmosphere for new peace negotiations. An earlier peace initiative by the Contadora group of Latin American nations had produced a draft regional peace treaty, which Nicaragua in September 1984 offered to sign immediately, without further modifications, but U.S. pressure on its Central American allies caused them to reject it on various pretexts. The new peace process was initiated by Costa Rica and Guatemala, whose governments had no love for the Sandinistas but feared that the Nicaraguan conflict might provoke a direct U.S. intervention, with unforeseeable consequences for the entire region. In August 1987, in Guatemala City, the presidents of Guatemala, El Salvador, Honduras, Nicaragua, and Costa Rica signed a set of agreements first proposed by Costa Rican President Oscar Arias, whose efforts won him the Nobel Peace Prize. The treaty barred outside assistance to insurgent forces, provided for the release of political prisoners, and called for steps toward democratization and the holding of honest elections in all countries, with particular reference to Nicaragua. Evidently fearing that the Sandinistas would win fair elections, the Reagan administration placed every possible obstacle in the way of the peace process initiated by President Arias.

Thanks to the desire of the Sandinista government for peace and its full compliance with the conditions set by the Guatemala City agreements, elections were held on schedule in Feb-

ruary 1990, with more than 1,000 observers from other countries present at polling stations. The FSLN faced the National Opposition Union (UNO), an unlikely coalition of fourteen small parties, ranging from the far right to the Communist party (PC de N). The overwhelming majority of foreign observers found that the elections were free and fair, but some noted that they took place "within a climate of United States–generated military and economic pressure."

Up to the day of the elections, the most reliable international polls showed a victory for the FSLN. But as the results began to come in, stunned observers became aware that an upset was in progress. The final results gave 55 percent of the vote in the presidential race to the UNO candidate, Violeta Chamorro, 41 percent to FSLN's Daniel Ortega. In the National Assembly, the UNO coalition captured 51 of 92 seats, the FSLN won 39 seats.

What had brought about the upset UNO victory? Most observers agreed that the election results did not represent a popular repudiation of the Sandinista program of social reforms. There is general agreement that the key factors in the Sandinista defeat were the war and the disastrous state of the economy. In a country of less than 4 million people, the war had left 60,000 dead, 28,000 wounded, and thousands of others kidnapped. For years, more than half the national budget was directed to military needs. UNO campaign literature had concentrated on the war-weariness and opposition to the draft, omitting mention that the contra war was the cause of the draft. UNO campaign rhetoric also blamed the Sandinista government alone for the economic crisis: an inflation rate in 1988 of 30,000 percent, an acute shortage of basic foods, a fall of purchasing power since 1980 of 90 percent.

Washington's strategy of bringing Nicaragua to its knees by a combination of economic blockade and low-intensity warfare had finally achieved its goal. But the aftermath of the election produced new surprises. In a stinging defeat for the extreme right wing in the UNO coalition, Chamorro announced that General Humberto Ortega, chief of the Sandinista army and brother of the outgo-

Violeta Chamorro's stunning upset victory over FSLN's Daniel Ortega was viewed by most observers as a result of the long civil war and desparate economic conditions. Here she receives the presidential sash from former President Ortega. (Wide World Photos)

ing president, would remain. In another blow to UNO's extreme right wing, headed by Vice President Virgilio Godoy, Chamorro loyalists joined FSLN deputies in electing a slate of National Assembly officers that included two Sandinista deputies. Chamorro's moderation irritated Bush administration officials, who warned that $300 million in U.S. aid would be endangered if she made appointments that did not meet with Washington's approval.

The spirit of amity soon vanished as the Chamorro government began to implement a harsh austerity program, including periodic devaluations that weakened the earning power of workers, an end to subsidized prices for staple products, massive layoffs of government workers, and efforts to dismantle the agrarian reform and other social conquests of the Sandinista revolution. The first major confrontation between the Chamorro government and the Sandinista unions ended in victory for the latter. A ten-day general strike was settled on July 10 on terms that were very favorable to the strikers, including wage increases and major political concessions like union consultation on economic policies, assurances of no large-scale layoffs of government workers, and the abandonment of a program for returning confiscated land to its former owners. But the actions of the government soon cast doubt on its sincerity, and strikes and squabbling continued in an atmosphere of growing tension and economic crisis. The quest for *concertacíon* (consensus) finally ended on October 26 with the signing by government, labor, and business leaders of a pact outlining plans for economic reconstruction and social reconciliation. Admitting noncompliance with past accords, the government pledged to respect all previous agreements with the National Workers Front (FNT) and never to return state properties to Somocistas or threaten Nicaraguans who had benefited from agrarian or urban reform before February 25, 1990. The agreement gave the government a breathing space to seek relief from its desperate economic crisis through foreign loans and U.S. aid.

Signing of the pact was followed by an uneasy calm, with no assurance that the pact would hold. The principal immediate threat to the Chamorro government, however, came from the far right, from Godoy, Obando y Bravo, leaders of the ultraright Private Enterprise Council (COSEP), who criticized Chamorro's yielding to Sandinista pressure, and from demobilized contras, who, angry over the government's failure to satisfy their demands, began taking over an increasing number of villages and cooperatives.

The Sandinista leadership and rank-and-file, meanwhile, regrouped their forces, critically examined the reasons for their electoral defeat, and prepared to try to regain power in the 1996 elections.

El Salvador

The Coffee Cycle and Peasant Revolts, 1850–1932

The history of El Salvador, the smallest and most densely populated country in Central America,

presents in exaggerated form all the economic and social problems of the area: an extreme dependence on a single crop, making the economy very vulnerable to fluctuations in price and the demand of outside markets; a marked concentration of land and wealth in a few hands; and intolerable exploitation of the peasantry, accompanied by ferocious repression of all attempts at protest or revolt.

By the mid-nineteenth century, El Salvador had already passed through two economic cycles. The first was dominated by cacao, whose prosperity collapsed in the seventeenth century; the second by indigo, which entered a sharp decline in the latter half of the nineteenth century, first as a result of competition from other producing areas and then as a result of the development of synthetic dyes. The search for a new export crop led to the enthronement of coffee. Coffee cultivation began about the time of independence but it did not expand rapidly until the 1860s. As elsewhere in Central America, the rise of coffee was marked by expropriation and usurpation of Indian lands—carried out in the name of private property and material progress—since most of the land best suited to coffee cultivation was held by Indian communities. Unlike indigo, which was planted and harvested every year, coffee trees did not produce for three years. Producers, therefore, had to have capital or credit, and the persons who had capital or access to credit were the hacendados who had prospered from the growing of indigo. To help these hacendados in their search for land, a government decree of 1856 declared that if two-thirds of a pueblo's communal lands were not planted in coffee, ownership would pass into the hands of the state. This pressure was replaced by a more direct attack on Indian landholdings: an 1881 law ordered that all communal lands be divided among the co-owners (which opened the way for their acquisition by legal or illegal means by the expanding coffee growers); and thirteen months later a decree abolished all communal land tenure. The new legislation harmed not only the Indian communities but *ladino* (mestizo) small farmers as well. These farmers often relied on municipal *tierras comunes* (the free pasture and woodlot where they could graze their stock) for an important part of their subsistence.

The result of this new legislation was a rapid concentration of landownership in the hands of a landed oligarchy often referred to as "the Fourteen Families." The number, while not an exact figure, expresses symbolically the reality of the tiny elite that dominated the Salvadoran economy and state. As late as September 1979, 0.85 percent of the landowners held 77.3 percent of the cultivable land, while 99.15 percent of the landowners owned 22.7 percent of the land.

Throughout most of the nineteenth century the great landowners used their own private armies to deal with the problem of recalcitrant peasants. Governmental decrees of 1884 and 1889 made these private armed forces the basis of the public Rural Police, later renamed the National Police. In 1912 the *Guardia Nacional* (National Guard), modeled after the Spanish National Guard, was established. Like the National Police, the National Guard patrolled the countryside and offered police protection to haciendas. The national army, created in the 1850s, did not become an instrument of repression until the late twentieth century.

For the rural poor, the social consequences of the coffee boom were disastrous. A few of the dispossessed peasants were permitted to remain on the fincas, or new estates, as colonos—peons who were given a place to live and a milpa, or garden plot, where they could raise subsistence crops. Unlike the old indigo or sugar latifundia, however, which required a large permanent labor force, the need for labor on the coffee plantations was so seasonal that for the most part planters relied on hired hands. This circumstance determined the pattern of life of the typical Salvadoran campesino. He might farm a small plot as a squatter or a colono on a plantation, but his tiny plot did not as a rule provide subsistence for his family. He would therefore tend to follow the harvests, working on coffee fincas during the harvest season, moving on to cut sugar cane or harvest cotton during August and September, and finally returning to his milpa, hopeful that the maize had ripened. This unstable migratory pattern created many social problems.

The economic and social problems generated by the coffee monoculture became more acute with the advent of the Great Depression in 1929. Campesinos who made 50 cents a day before the depression had their wages reduced to 20 cents a day. The price of coffee was cut in half between July 1929 and the end of the year, ruining many small producers who were forced to go out of business and sell their lands. High unemployment and below-subsistence-level wages added to the discontent caused by harsh treatment by overseers and frauds practiced by company stores.

Even before the depression, there had been scattered peasant revolts in the twentieth century; they were always put down by the National Guard. In the 1920s urban workers and some of the peasantry began to form unions. In 1925 a small Communist party began to operate underground; its leader was Agustín Farabundo Martí, who had been introduced to Marxism at the national university. Expelled from El Salvador in 1927 for his radical activities, Martí joined Augusto César Sandino, who was fighting the United States Marines in Nicaragua. Martí returned to El Salvador in 1930 and again plunged into political activity. Aided by a small group of youths, mostly university students, he carried on propaganda and organizational activity among peasants in the central and western parts of the country. He was soon jailed but was released after going on a hunger strike.

Against this background of depression and growing left-wing agitation, a presidential election, perhaps the first free election in Salvadoran history, was held. The winner was the wealthy reformer Arturo Araujo, who had formed his own Labor party (he was a great admirer of the British Labour party and its policies). This event caused much disquiet among the coffee planters and the military. The new president immediately ran into storms: teachers and other public servants clamored for back pay, peasants demanded land and other reforms, while the coffee oligarchy and the military pressed him to make no concessions. On

December 21, 1931, a military coup ousted Araujo and installed his vice president, General Maximiliano Hernández Martínez, as president. The coup signified the end of direct rule by the oligarchy and the beginning of a long era of military domination.

The fall of the liberal Araujo and the rise of Hernández Martínez to power closed the door to popular participation in politics. Convinced that the new regime had no intention of allowing reforms or free elections, Martí and other radical leaders decided on insurrection. Simultaneous uprisings were set to take place in several towns on January 22, 1932. But the authorities got wind of the plot several days in advance, and Martí and two of his aides were seized. Other rebel leaders then tried to call off the revolt, but communications had broken down, and the revolt began without its leadership.

In town after town, the campesinos, including many full-blooded Indians, rose up, often armed only with machetes. Having taken over much of the western area of the country, they attacked the regional center of Sonsonate. The unequal combat between peasants armed with machetes and the garrison, supported by the Guard and other police units, all armed with modern weapons, ended in total defeat for the insurgents. In a few days the captured towns were retaken. Then the oligarchy began to take its revenge, relentlessly hunting down the "communists," defined as any peasant who was not vouched for by a landowner as not having taken part in the revolt. Estimates as to the number of killed range from ten thousand to forty thousand. The commonly accepted figure is thirty thousand. Ferocious repression was the oligarchy's way of teaching the peasantry a lesson, of ensuring that there would be no repetition of the revolt. The history of El Salvador since 1932 shows how vain was that expectation.

Oligarchs and Generals, 1932–1979

The coup that installed General Hernández Martínez in the presidency marked a turning point in modern Salvadoran history. Terrified by the peasant uprising of 1932, the oligarchy struck a bargain with the military that allowed the military to hold the reins of government while the oligarchy directed the economic life of the country. A network of corruption that permitted the officer class to share in the oligarchy's wealth cemented the alliance between the two groups. Nevertheless, the persistence of reformist tendencies among junior officers periodically produced strains and tensions within the alliance that threatened its existence.

General Hernández Martínez, known as *El Brujo* (the Witch Doctor) because of his dabbling in the occult, maintained a tight rule over the country through his control of the army and the National Guard until 1944. In addition, power and access to wealth were concentrated in a clique of Hernández Martínez's cronies. The discontent that this engendered in many junior officers, combined with the political and ideological ferment of the war years, led to his overthrow in 1944. Between that year and 1961, governments came and went. Juntas of reformist junior military and liberal civilians, alternated with governments dominated by conservative military and oligarchs. In 1961 the friendly posture of the military-civilian junta toward the Cuban Revolution as well as its reformist program earned it the distrust of the oligarchy, the conservative military, and the U.S. embassy. The coup that ousted the junta was led by Colonel Julio Adalberto Rivera, who promptly announced that his revolution was anticommunist and anti-Cuban.

Rivera established a system, patterned on the Mexican idea of a single dominant party that would perpetuate itself in power, holding elections every five years and employing fraud, coercion, and co-optation to maintain control. On this basis, Colonel Rivera was succeeded as president in 1967 by Colonel Fidel Sánchez Hernández, who was replaced by Colonel Armando Molina in 1972, and he in turn by General Carlos Humberto Romero in 1977. While maintaining his control of the political system, Rivera allowed a number of opposition parties to exist. The most important were the Christian Democratic party, *Partido Demócrata Cristiano* (PDC), headed by José Napoleon Duarte, mayor of San Salvador from 1964 to 1970; a Social Democratic party, *Movimiento Nacional Revolucionario* (MNR), led by Guillermo Manuel Ungo; and the *Unión Democrática Nacionalista* (UDN), a front for the Communist party, which had been illegal since 1932. In the first phase of the system, opposition parties were allowed to win some mayoral contests and even a number of seats in the National Assembly.

As the economic difficulties of the country multiplied during the 1960s and 1970s, however, the strains within the system grew and it became increasingly unworkable. The roots of the problem lay in the monoculture that made the country dependent on a world market over which it had no control and a system of land tenure and use that progressively reduced the land area available to small landowners and staple food production.

Land monopoly and the prevailing system of land use led to population pressure on land, a problem that was greatly aggravated by the population explosion. Thanks to the eradication of yellow fever and malaria and to the successes of preventive medicine, the population shot up from 1,443,000 in 1930 to 2,500,000 in 1961 and 3,549,000 in 1969. By 1970 the population density was about 400 per square mile. The swelling population put great pressure on wage levels: the average daily wage for a field hand in the early 1960s was about 62 cents a day, for an overseer or *mayordomo,* a little over a dollar a day. Since labor on coffee plantations was seasonal and a peon was lucky to get 150 days of work a year, the labor of an entire family for that period might yield a total yearly cash income of $300.

With land reform ruled out as a solution for land hunger and population pressure, Rivera attempted another remedy: industrialization and economic integration through the creation of the Central American Common Market (CACM) in 1961. The underlying reasoning was that the unrestricted flow of goods and capital throughout

the area would stimulate an expansion of markets and industrialization, relieving population pressure and unemployment. Unfortunately this industrial expansion took place without a corresponding growth in employment, for the new industries were capital-intensive and required relatively few workers. Also, much of the new industry was foreign-owned and geared to exports; much of it was designed to assemble imported components. U.S.-based companies in El Salvador like Texas Instruments and Maidenform could greatly enlarge their profit margins because the U.S. tariff law assessed duty only on the "value added" to the product, that is, the cost of labor. Since salaries in El Salvador averaged $4 a day, these companies' exports to the United States grew from a value of $12 million in 1975 to a value of about $26 million four years later.

The problem of population pressure on the land grew much more acute as a result of a bitter dispute between El Salvador and Honduras that culminated in the so-called Soccer War between the two countries in 1969—a war that took several thousand lives and left at least 100,000 Salvadorans homeless. Called the Soccer War because it followed a series of hotly contested games between teams representing the two countries in the qualifying rounds of the 1969 World Cup, the conflict had more pragmatic causes. One was a border dispute of long standing. Another was Honduran resentment over the marked imbalance of trade between the two countries as a result of the operations of CACM, to which both countries belonged. Honduras, an extremely underdeveloped country whose economy was largely based on bananas, lumber, and cattle, felt that it was subsidizing the industrial development of El Salvador. The third and decisive cause of the war was the presence in Honduras of some three hundred thousand illegal Salvadoran settlers. In April 1969, following adoption of an agrarian reform law, Honduras ordered the departure of some of the settlers within thirty days; eventually about eighty thousand were expelled. El Salvador retaliated in July 1969 by invading Honduras and destroying most of its

468   air force on the ground. The war was over in five days, largely due to U.S. pressure on El Salvador in the form of threatened economic sanctions. The war, which was very popular in El Salvador, momentarily diverted popular attention from its great problems, but the effects on the country were entirely negative: El Salvador lost the Honduran market for its manufacturers for over a decade, and the return of Salvadorans from Honduras swelled the number of landless and homeless peasants.

These developments contributed to the ever-growing economic and social crisis of the 1970s. Population growth continued to outstrip the food supply; among the Latin American countries, only Haiti's people had a lower caloric intake than El Salvador's. By the early 1970s, unemployment was running at 20 percent and underemployment at 40 percent; in 1974 the annual inflation rate reached 60 percent. The proportion of landless peasantry rose from 11.8 percent in 1950 to 41 percent in 1975. The calamitous economic situation gave the opposition parties hope for victory in the presidential election of 1972; in September of that year the Christian Democratic party, the *Movimiento Nacional Revolucionario,* and the Communist UDN formed a united front, the *Unión Nacional Opositora* (UNO). Its candidate for president was José Napoleon Duarte. Although Duarte had clearly won the election by some 72,000 votes, the electoral commission found that the official candidate, Colonel Molina, had won by about 100,000 votes. The flagrant electoral fraud provoked a revolt by reformist junior military, and for a few days it appeared to have succeeded. But the National Guard and the air force remained loyal to the regime, and by the end of March the rebels had been forced to surrender. Duarte, the candidate of the united opposition, was arrested, tortured, and exiled to Venezuela.

The Molina government continued the oscillation between concession and repression that had characterized military rule since 1932. In 1975, hoping to promote the emerging tourist industry, Molina decided that El Salvador should play host to the 1975 "Miss Universe" pageant and spent about $30 million on the show. In a country with so many unfilled social needs, this impressed many Salvadorans as a scandalous extravagance. Units of the National Guard—without any provocation—fired on students attending a protest rally in San Salvador. At least thirty-seven died and an unknown number of others "disappeared." The massacre was part of a pattern of growing violence—from the right and from the left. With increasing frequency, guerrilla organizations that had sprung up since 1970 kidnaped and held members of the oligarchy for ransom. In the countryside, the National Guard, aided by right-wing paramilitary organizations like ORDEN (*Organización Democrática Nacionalista*), conducted sweeps against "subversive" peasants, surrounding and destroying villages, killing many villagers, and abducting others who "disappeared."

Although convinced that the familiar pattern of fraud would be repeated in the 1977 presidential election, the UNO decided to run a symbolic candidate, a hero of the Honduran war, Colonel Ernesto Claramount Rozeville. The election was in fact marked by widespread fraud, with rampant stuffing of the ballot boxes for Romero and armed ORDEN thugs on hand to discourage close scrutiny by the opposition at the polls. The outcome was never in doubt. A massive protest demonstration held on February 15 in the main square of San Salvador and addressed by Claramount and other speakers was attacked by army and police units and by members of ORDEN. More than two hundred people were killed by machine-gun fire. Claramount and other leaders sought sanctuary in the cathedral; later Claramount was permitted to go into exile. As he departed for the airport he uttered a prophetic comment: "This is not the end, it is only the beginning."

The fraudulent election of 1977, ending all hope of reform via the electoral process, and the spiral of violence that followed it marked the opening of a new phase that may be called the prerevolutionary stage of development in Salvadoran politics. On the left, the revolutionary organizations that had sprung up since 1970 began to mobilize their forces and attempted to overcome their ideological and tactical differences. All these groups robbed banks, seized radio stations in order to broadcast propaganda, kidnaped oligarchs for ransom, and assassinated persons identified with official or unofficial repression. There was a rapid growth of labor and peasant unions and other mass movements, known collectively as *Fuerzas Populares* (Popular Forces), and of umbrella organizations, such as FAPU (Front for United Popular Action), which united many groups for joint action against the government. On the right, meanwhile, there was increased repressive activity by the National Guard, the National Police, and other security forces as well as by the death squads of ORDEN and another terrorist organization, the White Warrior Union.

A major development of this period was the changing posture of the church toward the Salvadoran crisis. Prior to the Second Vatican Council (1962) and the Medellín Bishops' Conference, the church in El Salvador—as elsewhere in Latin America—supported the regime and the oligarchy. Although most of the hierarchy maintained that position, Archbishop Luis Chávez y González and his successor Oscar Romero, with Vatican II and Medellín as their guides, committed themselves to what Romero called "the preferential option for the poor." One result of this ferment in the church was the formation in a few short years of hundreds of comunidades de base, which combined Bible study with attention to the economic and social problems of their localities. Between 1970 and 1980, seven centers trained approximately fifteen thousand persons who had been selected by the groups to be catechists and leaders. The message the priests brought to their parishioners was that God is "a God of justice and love who acts on the side of the poor and oppressed," that the people "have a basic human right to organize in order to begin taking control of their own lives." Their social activism inevitably marked the priests as targets of right-wing death squads and security forces. The Jesuit Fa-

ther Rutilio Grande was murdered by a death squad of the White Warrior Union in March 1977, and three other Jesuits who had been working with him were expelled from the country. By May 1977, leaflets urging Salvadorans to "Be a Patriot! Kill a Priest!" were circulating in San Salvador. Altogether, seven priests were killed by death squads or security forces between 1977 and 1979. The death of Father Grande, three weeks after Romero was installed as archbishop, contributed to what the archbishop referred to as his "transformation." "Once you pose the question of the defense of the poor in El Salvador," he said in 1977, "you call the whole thing into question. That is why they have no other recourse than to call us subversives—that is what we are." From then on, during his three years and one month as archbishop, Romero used his position to denounce the regime's human rights violations and to plead for social justice. His sermons, transmitted via radio to almost every part of the country, "became the single most listened-to program in the nation."

As the crisis deepened month after month, a differentiation also began to take place within the military. A group of reformist junior military watched with profound anxiety the revolutionary course of events in Nicaragua in July–August 1979; they became convinced that a coup offered the only alternative to a solution of the Nicaraguan type. Planning for a coup began in July 1979, with regular consultations with Archbishop Romero and representatives of the Christian Democratic party as well as contacts with the U.S. embassy, which indicated it would not oppose such an action. On October 15 the coup went off almost without a hitch, with virtually no resistance from any garrison, and President Romero meekly accepted exile. A military-civilian junta was formed. The civilians included two moderate leftists, Román Mayorga Quiroz, rector of the Central American University, and the Social Democrat Guillermo Ungo; the military representatives were the authentically democratic Colonel Adolfo Majano and the rightist Colonel Jaime Abdul Gutiérrez, head of the Military

School, who owed his inclusion to U.S. pressure. The junta's program called for dissolution of the terrorist ORDEN organization, respect for human rights, agrarian reform, freedom for the Popular Forces to operate, and improvement of relations with Nicaragua.

Although Gutiérrez gave his nominal approval to the program, he decided, without consulting his colleagues, to change the balance of forces in the government by appointing another conservative, Colonel José Guillermo García, as defense minister in the cabinet that was to assist the junta. It was a fateful decision.

The left and the Popular Forces, meanwhile, regarded the junta with an intense suspicion that time was to justify. On October 28, a demonstration by several organizations demanding to know the fate of the many persons who had "disappeared" was met with gunfire by the National Guard, leaving twenty-five people dead. In fact, the October 15 coup did not end repression by the security forces; more people were killed by them in the three weeks after the coup than had died in any similar period under Romero. Efforts by civilian junta members Román Mayorga and Guillermo Ungo to restrain the official violence were totally ineffective, for the armed forces listened to no one but García. A meeting of the junta and the cabinet with the chiefs of the various armed forces was futile. "We have been running this country for fifty years, and we are quite prepared to keep on running it," the chief of the National Guard is said to have arrogantly declared.

The fall of the junta in fact occurred not at Christmas but on New Year's Day 1980. It followed demands by liberal members of the junta and cabinet that the military recognize the supremacy of the junta and carry out its orders. Failing to receive such assurances, Mayorga and Ungo resigned; all the cabinet, except García, followed their example. After three days of turmoil and street clashes between the military and the Popular Forces, a new government was announced, the product of a secret deal between the military and the Christian Democratic party.

Two Christian Democrats replaced Mayorga and Ungo. The military committed itself to a program of agrarian reform and nationalization of the banks; all repression would cease; and the armed forces would open a dialogue with the Popular Forces. Barely one week after accepting these conditions, the security forces fired on a massive demonstration of the Popular Forces, the largest in Salvadoran history, killing about twenty persons. This and similar repressive acts, demonstrating the bad faith of the military, caused a split in the Christian Democratic party. One of its representatives, Héctor Dada, resigned from the junta and was replaced by José Napoleón Duarte. At least 60 percent of its membership resigned from the party by November 1981. To add to the junta's problems, a rightist coup led by Roberto d'Aubuisson, head of the White Warrior Union, was barely averted by Defense Minister García and other high military officers. The agrarian reform promulgated with dramatic suddenness by the junta in March 1980 resulted from intense pressure by the United States, eager to give a reformist face to its protégé, even as James Cheek, the American chargé d'affaires, advised the junta to conduct a "clean counter-insurgency war." Typical of its strategy of reform and repression, the junta announced a state of siege on the same day that it promulgated the agrarian reform.

The agrarian reform was to be implemented in three stages. Phase I, promulgated in March 1980, nationalized 376 estates of more than 500 hectares, belonging to 244 owners and largely consisting of pasture and cotton land. The owners were to be compensated with thirty-year bonds, and the estates were to be converted into cooperatives with 29,755 peasant members. As of January 1, 1983, only 22 cooperatives had received final title, although 130 of the owners had been paid for their farms. Phase II, which would have affected about 200 farms of between 100 and 500 hectares, including most of the coffee fincas, "died before it was born," postponed for an indefinite period.

Phase III, called "land to the tiller," promulgated in April 1980, allowed peasants who rented up to 42 hectares of land to buy it from the owner. As of January 1983, 58,152 applications had been received, roughly half of the number that were possible under Phase III provisions. By June 1982, no permanent titles had been issued to applicants; the number rose to 251 in August of that year, and to 1,050 by January 1983. The Salvadoran Peasants' Union charged that the increase resulted from the need to provide the Reagan administration with proof for certifying to the U.S. Congress that El Salvador was making progress in essential economic reform and had therefore fulfilled the requirements for continued economic and military aid.

This curious land reform was accompanied by a wave of repression directed above all against the peasantry. Responsibility for seizure and distribution of land was assigned to the army and the security forces, who used their authority in several ways. Often they distributed land to members of the terrorist ORDEN organization whether or not they were entitled to it. They also used ORDEN members to identify peasants who belonged to the Popular Forces or to the guerrilla movements; these peasants were then killed by the military. Sometimes they collaborated with landowners who evicted tenants from lands they had recently acquired under land reform provisions. In December 1981 the Peasants' Union reported to junta President José Napoleón Duarte (he had been named president in a leadership reshuffle in November 1980) that the "failure of the agrarian reform is an immediate and imminent danger." The union claimed that at least ninety of its officials and "a large number of beneficiaries" of the agrarian reform had died during 1981 at the hands of ex-landlords and their allies, who were often members of the local security forces. The report also charged that twenty-five thousand former *aparceros,* or sharecroppers, had been evicted from their plots before they could obtain provisional titles. Duarte's inability to carry out the agrarian reform or to check the terror in the countryside proved that the junta was in fact "a rightist military regime with a civilian facade"; it also showed that Duarte himself was an "orna-

ment," in the words of one observer, needed by the United States to maintain the reformist image of the junta, and accepted by the military in order to pacify the U.S. State Department.

The most prominent victim of the terror that accompanied the promulgation of the agrarian reform was Monsignor Oscar Romero, archbishop of San Salvador. For years his attacks on the military and the security forces for their violations of human rights had been a thorn in the government's side. Increasingly disillusioned with the role of the Christian Democratic party in the junta, he gradually moved toward supporting armed struggle as the only remaining resort. In a sermon on February 2, 1980, he proclaimed: "When all peaceful means have been exhausted, the church considers insurrection moral and justified." On March 23, responding to the repression that accompanied the land reform, he appealed to soldiers not to turn their guns on unarmed civilians. The next day, as he celebrated mass in a chapel in San Salvador, he was gunned down, probably by a military officer. The National Guard celebrated his death with a savage attack on his hometown of Ciudad Barrios that left ten dead. According to the judge appointed to investigate his death—who made these revelations after he had fled for his life to Costa Rica—the assassination was planned by General José Alberto Medrano, founder of ORDEN, and Major Roberto d'Aubuisson. Robert White, former U.S. ambassador to El Salvador, informed a congressional committee that there was "compelling" evidence that d'Aubuisson was involved in the killing. Romero's martyrdom was to have profound political and military repercussions.

The Salvadoran Revolution, 1980–1991

"If I am killed," Archbishop Romero had prophesied shortly before his death, "I shall rise again in the struggle of the Salvadoran people." His death, in fact, served as a powerful catalyst for the growth of that struggle. In particular, it hastened the breakup of the Christian Democratic party and the unification of its center and left wings with Social Democratic and Marxist-led groups in opposition to the junta. In April 1980, a broad coalition of political parties, professional associations, trade unions, and revolutionary groups formed the *Frente Democrático Revolucionario* (Democratic Revolutionary Front, FDR). In January 1981, the FDR set up a kind of government-in-exile, called a "political commission," headed by the Social Democratic leader Guillermo Ungo.

As important as achieving the political unity of the opposition was the unification of the various guerrilla movements. By mid-summer of 1980 the five major guerrilla groups had united in a single command, which was given the name *Frente Farabundo Martí de Liberación Nacional* (FMLN), in honor of the leader of the abortive 1932 revolt. In January 1981, the FMLN launched its first general offensive and achieved significant successes. Eventually, however, the offensive ran out of steam and the guerrillas were forced to retreat to their bases in the thinly populated northern part of El Salvador.

The ensuing military stalemate ended in the middle of 1982, when the scales began to tip in favor of the insurgents. A turning point was the battle of Mt. El Escandón (June 5), where the army massed 4,000 troops, supported by Honduran troops who crossed into Salvadoran territory, in an effort to encircle and destroy a guerrilla force. Despite intense bombardment and shelling of the rebel positions, the guerrillas succeeded in putting an elite battalion of government troops out of action and captured the army's chief of staff, Colonel Francisco Adolfo Castillo. Beginning in October 1982 a series of FMLN offensives, accompanied by systematic destruction of bridges, power lines, trucks, and other elements of the infrastructure, greatly weakened the government's military and economic potential.

Thereafter, the almost uninterrupted series of government defeats provided an answer to the much disputed question of the source of the FMLN's arms. Contrary to the Reagan administration's claim, based largely on fabricated or dubious data, that the bulk of these arms came from Cuba, Nicaragua, or other external sources, the evidence seems overwhelming that the most important source of weapons was the capture of U.S.-supplied government arms. This explains why the U.S.-supplied M16s virtually became the FMLN's standard weapon. Between June and October 1982 alone the rebels captured six hundred fifty firearms, over twenty guns, mortars, and heavy machine guns, and about eighty thousand rounds of ammunition.

Although the guerrillas invariably evacuated the large population centers captured in their offensives, by the spring of 1983 they had considerably expanded the zones of their control. They dominated areas inhabited by some two hundred thousand people; in these areas, political power was based on a self-governing system called the *Poder Popular Local* (PPL). While guerrilla self-assurance and confidence in victory grew, the morale of government troops, poorly led and lacking conviction in the justice of what seemed increasingly a lost cause, continued to decline. Desertions became more frequent, and more and more government soldiers surrendered as soon as the first shots were fired.

The rebel successes sowed dissension within the officers' ranks and spurred demands for the removal of Defense Minister García by critics who wanted a more aggressive conduct of the war. The crisis within the military broke out into the open in January 1983 with a mutiny by a field commander who refused to obey García's orders and demanded his resignation. The dispute was patched up, but broke out afresh in April when the head of the air force threatened to mutiny. This time García agreed to step down, and Provisional President Alvaro Magaña immediately appointed General Carlos Vides Casanova, former head of the National Guard, as his successor. The move pleased hard-liners and U.S. military advisers, impatient with García's inept direction of the war.

Increased military aid was one pillar of Reagan's Salvadoran policy; the other was a plan to improve the image of the regime by holding elections that would legitimize it, giving it a "democratic" face. The elections, it was assumed, would give victory to the Christian Democratic party and its leader José Napoleón Duarte. He would then preside over a modest reform and civic action program that would win "hearts and minds" for the government; Duarte's reforms, combined with expanded military aid, should lead to a speedy pacification of the country. In compliance with U.S. wishes, elections for a sixty-member Constituent Assembly were held in El Salvador in March 1982. Boycotted by the left and the guerrillas, who pointed out that there was no possibility of fair elections under existing conditions (the army had recently published a hit list marking leaders of the FDR and the FMLN for death), the elections were largely organized and dominated by the right-wing parties and the military.

In any event, the outcome of the elections did not conform to the expectations of the Reagan administration. With only 35 percent of the vote, Duarte and the Christian Democrats proved unable to form a majority government. The fascist Nationalist Republic Alliance (ARENA) of Roberto d'Aubuisson garnered one-fourth of the vote and pressed for a coalition with other right-wing parties that would leave the Christian Democrats out in the cold. Thus, instead of legitimating Duarte and the Christian Democrats, as projected in the Reagan administration scenario, the elections appeared to legitimate D'Aubuisson and ARENA. The chagrin of the Washington policy makers can be imagined. Finally, by applying immense pressure, in August 1982 the United States managed to convince the three major parties—ARENA, the right-wing Party of National Conciliation, and the Christian Democrats—to sign a pact for cooperation in the transition to a new constitutional government. As part of the deal, the U.S.-supported "moderate" banker Alvaro Magaña was elected provisional president of the republic and D'Aubuisson president of the Constituent Assembly.

The Reagan administration's policy in El Salvador had one overriding purpose: at all costs to prevent the FMLN-FDR from coming to power. To ensure congressional support for the large infusions of military and economic aid needed to achieve this objective, the Reagan administration strongly supported the 1984 presidential candidacy of José Napoleón Duarte, who was identified by many in El Salvador and the United States with social reform. At the same time that it backed the supposed reformer Duarte, Washington demanded a more aggressive strategy in the war against the rebels, with massive use of air power and large-scale sweeps into rebel territory to force out the civilian population, to isolate the insurgents, and thus to deny them the material and logistical support they needed to survive. This more aggressive strategy was to be combined with civic action programs designed to win the rural population's support.

Duarte promised peace through negotiations with the rebels, expansion of agrarian reform, and improved conditions for urban workers (his main political base). In May 1984 he defeated Roberto d'Aubuisson, the candidate of the extreme right, in a run-off election. Following the election it was revealed that the CIA had spent several million dollars to promote the Salvadoran electoral process; a large part of the funds went to Duarte's campaign. Duarte consolidated his victory in the congressional and mayoral elections of March 1985, which gave the Christian Democrats a clear majority of seats in Congress.

Soon it became evident that Duarte lacked the power, the resources, and perhaps the will to carry out his promises. He initiated peace talks with the FMLN in late 1984, but broke them off; the talks were probably intended above all to prove his good will regarding peace to his domestic supporters and his congressional backers in Washington. Duarte's promises of social and economic reform proved equally illusory. He presided over a moribund economy that survived only due to the immense largesse of the United States. (Between 1981 and 1987 U.S. government military and economic aid to El Salvador totaled $2.7 billion.) Duarte faced a dilemma. His promises and election had encouraged the labor movement to organize, call strikes, and engage in political activity; the right responded with repression, including a revival of death-squad killings and disappearances. Even if he had the means, Duarte could not satisfy labor's economic

An old woman—a member of the committee of mothers of missing political prisoners in El Salvador—holds a picture of her missing grandson during a demonstration denouncing the Duarte government in the San Salvador cathedral in 1984. (UPI/Bettmann Newsphotos)

leftist federation, the National Union of Salvadoran Workers (UNTS). In October 1986, Duarte introduced another economic austerity package that levied steep taxes on basic goods and services and reduced already minimal social services. The package, described as an act of "political suicide" by a rebel leader, set off a fresh wave of strikes and demonstrations that drew ever-larger numbers of workers. By the end of 1986, Duarte's labor base had virtually collapsed. He could not even count on the support of the business sector, which organized a twenty-four-hour strike on January 22, 1987, that was said to be 90 percent successful in San Salvador. Of great significance, the strikes and demonstrations increasingly linked economic demands to calls for an end to the civil war through negotiations; these calls were strongly supported by the head of the Salvadoran church, Archbishop Arturo Rivera y Damas.

As if to give a *coup de grace* to the battered Salvadoran economy, a powerful earthquake hit San Salvador on October 10, 1986, killing about 1,000 people, leaving 400,000 homeless, and destroying large sectors of the nation's infrastructure. Nearly 50 percent of all buildings within a twenty-block radius of the center were leveled or heavily damaged. The destruction of the capital's major hospitals left 4 million Salvadorans without medical care. A proposal of the FMLN for an indefinite truce during the period of reconstruction was rejected by the Salvadoran army.

Washington's 1984 strategy of depopulating areas of the countryside under guerrilla control by saturation bombing created a large population of internal refugees living in relocation camps at government expense, an added strain on the country's threadbare economy. Under prodding from the United States, the Salvadoran army also stepped up use of a sophisticated pacification program that incorporated civil action and psychological warfare operations. U.S. military advisers assisted with planning, procurement of materials, and training of the Salvadoran personnel. Evidence gathered from different parts of El Salvador suggested that this effort to win "hearts

and social demands over the opposition of the oligarchy, the army, and even the Reagan administration. On the other hand, he could not openly support repression without losing his base in the labor movement. Duarte solved the problem by denouncing repression in words, while tolerating and even sanctioning it in practice.

In January 1986 the Duarte government announced an economic austerity program to help pay the costs of the war against the FMLN-FDR; the program included a 100 percent devaluation of the currency and large increases in fuel prices, measures that hit workers the hardest. Thousands of angry workers responded by leaving the trade union federation, controlled by the Christian Democrats, and joining a newly organized and minds" was less than a brilliant success. "In a country that suffers from deep structural problems for generations," one government development worker remarked, "it won't work to offer a bit of food when three years ago you perhaps killed the [family's] grandmother."

The massive influx of new U.S. military aid, including gunships and helicopters, and a considerable increase in the size of the Salvadoran army undoubtedly changed the balance of forces in the civil war. U.S. reconnaisance flights from Honduras and the Panama Canal Zone helped pinpoint rebel columns and command posts, using infrared tracking systems. Unable to compete with the army in numbers and firepower, the FMLN developed a new strategy. The large battalion-size units were broken up into small units of classic guerrilla warfare; these moved out of the way of the army's sweeps and returned after the army had left. However, the rebels were still capable of launching major surprise attacks. Other new FMLN tactics included using mines, which caused perhaps as much as 70 percent of the army's casualties; another was economic sabotage through efforts to destroy the country's electrical grid by downing power lines and blowing up installations and dams, and through the destruction of coffee-processing plants. U.S. sources estimated the 1979–1985 loss through economic sabotage at $1.2 billion.

Of particular importance to the promise of victory, the insurgents believed, were the upsurge of the labor movement in the cities, Duarte's increasing isolation, and the growing movement for peace that embraces more strata of the population. These developments, the FMLN-FDR claimed, had given a new dimension to the civil war that strongly favored their cause.

The war in El Salvador in mid-1987 was commonly described as at an impasse. The insurgents, however, denied that a stalemate existed and insisted that their tactics of sapping the army's strength by ambushes and lightning strikes, of wearing down the government and the country's economy, and of exploiting the resentment that this generated among the people, were

working and bringing the FMLN-FDR ever closer to victory. In an important assessment of the military situation, Joaquín Villalobos, a leading figure of the FMLN, claimed that the rebels already had effective control of almost one-third of the country, areas in which the army's presence was limited to short-term incursions or operations.

By the beginning of 1988 the failure of the U.S. counterinsurgency strategy in El Salvador was apparent to all. The economy was in ruins, with industry operating at 40 percent of capacity. Riddled with corruption, the Duarte administration had proved unable to end the war, implement serious reforms, or check the repression. The results of the congressional and local elections of March 1988, carried out under the guns of the military, represented a repudiation of both Duarte and his American sponsors. Most of El Salvador's eligible voters stayed away from the polls; a majority of those who voted cast their ballots for D'Aubuisson's fascist ARENA, which gained control of parliament and most of the country's local governments.

One year later, in elections marked by a massive abstention of voters and charges of widespread fraud by the Christian Democrats and other opposition parties, ARENA completed its sweep of political offices with the election of Alfredo Cristiani as president. The FMLN, which had called for a boycott of the elections, paralyzed traffic across the country with a transport stoppage and waged battles with government troops throughout the country.

Cristiani, a big coffee grower, was a man in the Duarte mold: a graduate of an American university, who spoke perfect English and presented an appearance of moderation, claiming he wanted to negotiate with the rebels. But his apparent moderation, which convinced some liberal U.S. senators like Christopher Dodd and John Kerry to vote more money for El Salvador, was another case of window-dressing. Behind Cristiani stood D'Aubuisson, widely suspected of being the author of the murder of Archbishop Romero and four American nuns in 1980. This alliance did not deter Vice President Dan Quayle from making a ceremonial call on D'Aubuisson when he attended Cristiani's inauguration in June 1989.

Cristiani complied with his campaign promise to initiate talks with the FMLN guerrillas following his inauguration but demanded their virtual surrender by insisting they lay down their arms as a condition for a cease-fire. As a result the peace talks were suspended and fighting resumed, accompanied by an escalation of death squad killings and torture of civilians. Cristiani's intransigent attitude, it was widely believed, reflected the decisive influence of the so-called *Tandona,* an elite group of extreme right-wing military from the cadet class of 1966 that included the defense minister, the army's chief of staff, and the chiefs of the air force, the national police, and the national guard. This tight-knit group regarded Roberto d'Aubuisson as its leader.

Prospects of peace suffered a shattering blow on October 31, 1989, when bombings of the headquarters of the National Federation of Salvadoran Workers (FENESTRAS) killed ten persons, including its president, Febe Elizabeth Velasquez, the most prominent woman unionist in the country, and wounded many others. In response to the bombings, the FMLN announced that it would not resume talks with the government as long as "guarantees for the labor movement are not achieved"; then, on November 11, 1989, it launched its most powerful offensive since 1981, striking at a number of cities, including San Salvador. Its main objectives were the working-class quarters in the city's densely populated northern outskirts. By the following morning the guerrillas, assisted by thousands of civilians who built barricades, provided food and information, and took up arms, were in control of the north's perimeter. The government responded with a ferocious aerial bombing of the working-class barrios. The FMLN held sections of the city for up to two weeks before withdrawing.

The concentrated bombardment of densely populated working class barrios, causing many civilian casualties, provoked an international outcry. The bombardment was accompanied by

a new wave of repression directed against church and labor critics of the government. Six Jesuit priests and professors at San Salvador's Central American University, whom the military regarded as the "brains" of the uprising, together with their housekeeper and her daughter, were shot in cold blood. One year later, thanks to stonewalling by President Cristiani and the military, the "investigation" of the crime had reached a dead end.

The FMLN's offensive was designed to prove to the Cristiani government and to the United States that after nine years of war the FMLN was stronger than ever and could not be defeated militarily, and thereby to bring the ARENA regime to the bargaining table for serious negotiations.

Moved by this demonstration of rebel power, and even more, perhaps, by the threat of a congressional halt to U.S. aid to El Salvador in reaction to the murder of the six Jesuits and other human rights abuses (in the fall of 1990 Congress voted to freeze half of the allocated aid), the Cristiani government agreed to resume negotiations with the FMLN, without preconditions, with the United Nations as mediator. By mid-May 1990 the two sides had agreed to a timetable which called for a cease-fire by September. The FMLN also agreed to take part in elections if certain conditions were met, including a purge of the army by removal of officers who had been guilty of torture and assassination and a gradual process of demilitarization that would ultimately dismantle both armies and replace them with a civilian police force. Not unexpectedly, the military, who have grown rich through a decade of massive U.S. support, proved unyielding on both points. As 1990 drew to a close, the peace talks were deadlocked and fighting had resumed. In January 1991, after rebel fire downed a U.S. military helicopter and three servicemen died (two apparently executed after the crash), President Bush released all the approved 1991 military aid to the Cristiani government. Meanwhile the human rights situation in El Salvador worsened. According to the Human Rights Commission of El Salvador, of 355 civilians killed between July and November 1990, all but ten were killed by the military. In February 1991 a group of U.S. senators wrote President Cristiani, expressing their concern over an apparent escalation of terror backed by the military; they specifically referred to a massacre of fifteen peasants and the destruction by an arson attack of the opposition paper *Diario Latino.*

Against this unpromising background, legislative and municipal elections were held in March 1991. The FMLN had announced that it would not permit voting in the regions it controlled but would not interfere with elections in government-controlled territory. Although marked by repression, intimidation, and massive fraud, the elections produced some significant political changes. The ruling ARENA failed to win a majority in the legislature, and the left opposition, headed by the Democratic Convergence (CD), won 20 percent of the votes and took third place after ARENA and the Christian Democratic party. On May 1, in a major political turnabout, ARENA deputies joined in electing the leftist leader Rubén Zamora, one of the vice presidents of the Legislative Assembly. These developments coincided with some forward movement in the U.N.-sponsored peace talks. But a FMLN commander cautioned against excessive optimism, warning that "we will not lay down our arms until we win the guarantees of democracy and social justice."

Chapter 19

Lands of Bolívar: Venezuela and Colombia in the Twentieth Century

Modern Venezuela and Colombia are often cited as oases of democratic and economic stability in a turbulent, poverty-ridden continent. A closer look at their recent history, however, suggests they have not escaped the general crisis of Latin American dependent capitalism. Its effects are clearly evident in the devastating impact of Venezuela's foreign debt on a country whose oil wealth once made it the envy of the continent. In February 1989, after Venezuelan President Carlos Andrés Pérez announced drastic increases in the prices of basic goods and services in order to satisfy the requirements of the International Monetary Fund for loans to his government, the country exploded into riots that were crushed with the loss of hundreds of lives. Between 1981 and 1987 the number of Venezuelans living in poverty had risen from 22 to 54 percent of the population.

Neighboring Colombia presented an even darker picture. Colombia was the home of the Medellín and Cali drug cartels, which accounted for an estimated 76 percent of the refined cocaine smuggled into the United States. Under an ostensibly democratic and moderate regime, death squads linked to the army, security forces, and the drug mafia operated with impunity against leftists, trade union activists, and even against conservative elite opponents of the drug cartels. In the decade ending in 1989 the mafia's death squads had murdered scores of judges attempting to investigate the activities of the Medellín cartel. Meanwhile a twenty-five-year guerrilla war—the longest continuing insurgency in Latin America, reflecting the vast accumulation of unsolved social problems in this oligarchical democracy—raged in Colombia's jungles and mountains and even spread into more densely inhabited areas.

Bolívar and the State of Colombia

The early history of Venezuela and Colombia is inseparably linked to the name of the Liberator Simón Bolívar. Venezuela was his homeland; Colombia (then called New Granada) and Venezuela were the theaters of his first decisive victories in the war for Latin American independence. Bolívar sought to unite Venezuela and New Granada into a single large and powerful state; beyond this he looked toward the creation of a vast federation of all the Spanish-American republics, extending from Mexico to Cape Horn. In 1819 the Congress of Angostura (in Venezuela) approved the formation of the state of Colombia (later called Gran Colombia or Greater Colombia) that would combine Venezuela, New Granada, and Ecuador (then still in Spanish hands). In 1821, at Cúcuta on the Venezuelan-Colombian border, the union was formalized with the adoption of a centralized constitution drafted according to Bolívar's wishes, and he was elected provisional president of the new state. But he soon went off to launch a campaign for the liberation of Peru and Bolivia and entrusted the administration of the new state, with its capital at Bogotá, to his vice president, Francisco de Paula Santander, a veteran revolutionary leader whose policies in general conformed to Bolívar's.

Santander presided over the implementation of a liberal reform program that included the gradual abolition of slavery, the abolition of Indian tribute and the division of Indian communal lands into private parcels (a "reform" that opened the door to land-grabbing at the Indians' expense), the suppression of smaller male convents and the seizure of their property for the

support of public secondary education, and a general expansion of education.

The major threat to Gran Colombia's survival came from its geographic, economic, and social realities. Immense distances separated its component parts, and a mountainous terrain made communication very difficult; it took about a month for a letter to reach Bogotá from Caracas. These conditions also hindered the development of economic ties between Venezuela and New Granada, and also Ecuador; Caracas and other Venezuelan coastal cities communicated more easily with Europe than overland via the Andes with Bogotá. Finally, the Venezuelan elite of cacao planters and merchants, joined by a new elite of military leaders or caudillos, had little sympathy for Bolívar's idea of fusing several independent Spanish-American republics into one and even less for his vision of a confederation that would unite all the Spanish-American states.

The latent conflict broke out into the open in 1826, when José Antonio Páez, the principal Venezuelan military commander, refused to appear before Congress in Bogotá to answer charges that he had violated the rights of citizens by sending soldiers to round them up for militia service. Supported by his army of *llaneros* and other caudillos, Páez proclaimed a revolt against the Bogotá government. Bolívar finally returned to deal with Páez's rebellion and the growing unrest.

In 1826, Bolívar worked out a compromise with Páez in Venezuela by which Páez recognized Bolívar's supreme authority in return for amnesty for the rebels, the title of Supreme Chief of Venezuela for himself, and a promise of constitutional reform that would grant the Venezuelans most of the autonomy they sought.

In Bogotá, however, Bolívar came under fire from Congress and Santander, "the Man of Laws," for his leniency with Páez and allegedly unconstitutional conduct. By 1828, amid growing turbulence as pro-Santander and pro-Bolívar factions struggled for power, Bolívar was convinced that only a strong government along the lines of the constitution that he had framed for Bolivia—a document that provided for a three-chamber congress and a powerful life-time president who could choose his successor—could save Colombia from destruction. Reclaiming the authority he had delegated to Santander, Bolívar gradually established a personal dictatorship that leaned for support on the old and new elites—the great landowners, the church hierarchy, and the military caudillos. Believing that Santander's reforms had gone too far and too fast, he annulled portions of the educational and religious reforms especially offensive to the clergy and even restored the Indian tribute, which he had recently abolished in Peru and Bolivia, over the opposition of their elites.

Bolívar's personal dictatorship failed to achieve the peace and stability he sought for Colombia. Santander's liberal supporters repeatedly rose up in arms; Bolívar's generals crushed these revolts, but the ferment continued. In Venezuela, meanwhile, the clamor for independence continued and Páez ruled supreme; in Ecuador, the Venezuelan caudillo Juan José Flores dominated.

Colombia's political troubles reached a crisis stage in 1829. In a vain effort to regain the initiative, Bolívar issued a call for meetings to be held where citizens could express their opinions about the future form of Colombia's government and elect members to a congress to be held in January 1830 (the suffrage was limited to free males who met a means test that excluded the vast majority of the population). Bolívar's gesture, meant to mobilize support, played into the hands of the separatists. In Venezuela, the "popular assemblies," carefully organized by the caudillos, voted overwhelmingly in favor of independence, for Páez against Bolívar. Nothing came of the Constitutional Congress on which Bolívar had pinned his hopes. In mid-1830 Ecuador followed the example of Venezuela and seceded from the union. Gran Colombia was dead. Months before, Bolívar, filled with despair, terminally ill with tuberculosis, had resigned from office. Attended by a retinue of faithful officers and soldiers, he left Bogotá and made his way to the coast, planning to go into self-imposed exile in Europe, but died near Santa Marta in 1830.

Venezuela: The Nineteenth-Century Background

The Reign of Páez, the Conservative-Liberal Cleavage, and the Federal War, 1830–1863

On May 6, 1830 a congress assembled in Valencia to provide the independent state of Venezuela with a constitution, the third in the country's short history. The document limited the suffrage to males who were twenty-one, literate, and had a high income. These requirements excluded most of the population, numbering under nine hundred thousand, from participation in political life. Of that number about half were *pardos* (free mulattos) and free blacks; slaves numbered about forty to fifty thousand, and over a quarter were whites. A tiny minority of whites, about ten thousand, composed the ruling class of wealthy merchants, great landowners, and high office holders and military officers, who usually were also landowners. The members of this class, often linked through family networks, dominated political life.

Military hero, long-time champion of Venezuelan independence, and former ranch hand José Antonio Páez was elected president, a post he combined with supreme army commander. His rise illustrates the renewal of the old colonial ruling class through the admission of a new elite of military caudillos, frequently of very humble origins.

The Venezuelan society and economy over which Páez presided essentially resembled the colonial social and economic order. The latifundio continued as the basic unit of economic activity; concentration of landownership increased after independence because of the rapid acquisition of royalist estates and public lands by a small group of military caudillos. A decree of October 15, 1830, compelling the sale of so-called uncultivated lands of Indian communities gave the latifundists more opportunities to expand their landholdings.

Labor relations in the countryside continued to be based on slavery, peonage, and various forms of tenancy, including sharecropping and obligatory personal service. Slavery in Venezuela, as in other parts of Latin America, had long been in decline. The Constituent Congress of 1830 adopted a manumission law freeing the children of slaves but requiring them to work for their masters until the age of twenty-one. Continuing a tendency that began in the late colonial period, however, many slave owners found it more profitable to free their slaves voluntarily, since they generally remained on their former masters' land as tenants or peons bound by debts and other obligations. By 1841, 14,000 had been freed this way and only 150 because they had reached the age of manumission.

The long revolutionary war had caused immense material damage and loss of life—the population had been reduced by 262,000—and destroyed the fragile economic links between the country's different regions. By the time Páez became president, however, a partial recovery had taken place, leading to a boom based on the switch from cacao to coffee as Venezuela's principal export and the country's integration into the capitalist world market, which henceforth absorbed about 80 percent of Venezuela's exports of coffee, cacao, indigo, tobacco, and hides.

The high coffee prices that accompanied the 1830s boom made planters hungry for credit to expand production by obtaining new land. Foreign merchant capitalists, the Venezuelan export-import merchants who were their agents, and native moneylenders obliged on the security of coffee crops and the planters' estates, but there was the obstacle of colonial legislation that regulated interest rates and punished usury. The Venezuelan congress removed this impediment by passing a credit law in 1834 that abolished all traditional Spanish controls on contracts. Henceforth the state would enforce a legally executed contract, no matter how exorbitant the interest rate.

By the late 1830s, with the world price of coffee in decline, the Venezuelan economy was in serious trouble. Creditors refused to refinance their debtors, and by the 1840s Venezuela was in a severe depression.

The economic crisis caused a rift in the elite, with the emergence of factions that turned into political parties in the 1840s. One called itself Conservative, but opponents dubbed its members *godos* (Goths) to identify them with the unpopular Spanish colonial rule. Páez was its acknowledged leader, and it represented the views and interests of the export-import merchants and their foreign partners, the moneylenders, the high civil and military bureaucracy, and some great landowners. The Liberal party was led by Antonio Leocadio Guzmán and was a loose coalition of debt-ridden planters, the urban middle class, artisans, intellectuals seeking reform, and disaffected caudillos resentful of Páez's long reign. In 1840 Guzmán founded a newspaper, *El Venezolano,* which bitterly attacked Páez's authoritarian rule and criticized the government for such policies as using the treasury surplus to pay foreign creditors instead of paying for public works to relieve unemployment and creating an agricultural land bank to make loans to planters at low rates of interest and other institutions for the public welfare.

Guzmán's rhetorical attacks on Conservative economic policies and on the elections of 1842 and 1846 as fraudulent contributed to a growing social tension. A series of popular uprisings, which Páez described as open warfare against private property, terrified the Conservatives, who raised the specter of a general social race war, waged by pardos and slaves, which they blamed on Guzmán's inflammatory propaganda. In fact, Guzmán and most Liberals feared social revolution as much as their opponents and had no links to the popular revolts of 1846–1847. But the government of President Carlos Soublette, who succeeded Páez, determined to crush these revolts at their supposed source, brought Guzmán to trial, found him guilty of instigating the revolutionary movements, and sentenced him to death. The sentence, breaking with the tradition of exiling aristocratic troublemakers rather than exe-

482

cuting them, caused great shock and focused attention on Páez's choice for president to succeed Soublette, since it would be up to him to carry it out. In 1848, war hero General José Tadeo Monagas, an eastern caudillo, became the Conservative president through the customary controlled election.

If Páez had expected to find a pliant executor of Conservative policies, he was disappointed. Monagas, determined to free himself from Páez's control and establish his own dynasty, favored moderate Liberals for posts in his cabinet and other government positions. His commutation of Guzmán's death sentence to exile was a virtual declaration of independence from Páez and the Conservatives.

Those Liberals who expected substantial social and political reforms from Monagas were also disillusioned. He paid his political debt to his planter allies by supporting congressional passage of several laws designed to give relief to distressed planters. Under his brother José Gregorio, slavery was abolished in Venezuela (March 23, 1854), with compensation to the slave owners. Slavery had been increasingly unprofitable as a result of falling coffee prices; even as Congress was discussing emancipation, some planters were voluntarily freeing their slaves to avoid paying their support.

Emancipation brought little change in the lives of most freedmen. In the absence of a modern factory system to provide alternative employment or any program for distributing land to them, most were doomed to remain on their former owners' estates as tenants burdened with heavy obligations or peons whose scanty wages were paid in *vales* (tokens) redeemable only for goods purchased in the estate store (*tienda de raya*) at inflated monopoly prices.

Hard times continued in the late 1850s: depressed coffee prices, the unwillingness of foreign capital to invest in Venezuela because the debt-relief legislation increased the risk of investment, elite fears of a social explosion, and general resentment of the greed and nepotism of the Monagas dynasty persuaded Conservatives

and Liberals to join forces in March 1858 in a revolution that overthrew the hated regime. But the coalition soon fell apart when a group of extreme Conservatives seized power and installed a government even more repressive than the Monagas regime, imprisoning or deporting many Liberals, who responded with an uprising that began the Federal War (1858–1863).

The term "Federal" here had different meanings for the Liberal elite and its rank-and-file followers. After their victory the Liberals gave the country a new constitution (1864) with many reforms, including universal male suffrage and increased autonomy for the twenty states. But without substantive social reform, these rights were virtually meaningless. "Federalism" under these conditions simply meant the continued supremacy of the local caudillo, who often was a great landowner as well, and whose arbitrary rule was tolerated by the Caracas government as long as he remained its loyal proconsul.

For the peasants and artisans who rose in spontaneous revolt against the reactionary Conservative regime and accepted Liberal leadership and their slogan of Federalism, the term had a different meaning. Their vague hopes were expressed in a manifesto of Ezequiel Zamora, the veteran guerrilla fighter who had been freed by the Revolution of 1858, then exiled by the Conservative regime, and who returned to Venezuela in February 1859 to open in Coro province another front of a rapidly expanding peasant war.

The advance of Zamora's troops was accompanied by the occupation of large estates by their former peons and tenants, the creation of federal states, and the election of local governments by the citizenry. Zamora's death by an assassin's bullet in 1860 cut short the life of a leader who represented a genuinely democratic, social revolutionary tendency in the Federal War. Conservatives rejoiced, and some moderate Liberals heaved sighs of relief. The war continued, but the Liberal leadership, although favored by the military balance of forces, preferred a negotiated peace to a fight to the finish. The 1863 Treaty of Coche, negotiated by Antonio Guzmán Blanco, son of the famous Liberal caudillo, ended the war. It had cost some 50,000 lives and inflicted immense damage on the economy. Many haciendas had been destroyed, and the cattle herds of the llanos had virtually disappeared as a result of wartime depredations and neglect.

Like the War of Independence, the Federal War produced some social changes. One loser of the conflict was the old Conservative oligarchy: a considerable part of this group had fled or died in battle, and their estates often fell into the hands of victorious Liberal military, some of plebeian background. These nouveaux riches sometimes became local caudillos or even governors of states or districts, but for the rank-and-file of the revolutionary armies, the war's end spelled disillusionment and betrayal. They had to surrender the parcels of land they had occupied and return as peons to the great estates. Instead of reversing the trend toward concentration of landownership, the war accelerated it.

Antonio Guzmán Blanco and the Maturing of Neocolonial Venezuela, 1870–1908

The government of Juan Crisóstomo Falcón, who became president in 1863, could not cope with the Federal War's legacy of economic bankruptcy and political instability. He was overthrown in 1868, and the ensuing turmoil ended in 1870 when Antonio Guzmán Blanco, the ablest of Venezuela's nineteenth-century rulers, seized power.

Like his father, Guzmán Blanco was a master of demagogic rhetoric. He was a self-proclaimed Liberal and foe of the oligarchy, an anticlerical and devout believer in the positivist creed of science and progress whose ambition was to create a "Practical Republic," a "civilized people." Peace and money were the means to achieve his goals. To secure them he forged pacts with the conservative merchant class of Caracas, which viewed him with suspicion when he came to power; with the regional caudillos, traditionally identified with the principle of local autonomy; and with foreign economic interests, whose support he

needed for his ambitious program to construct roads, railroads, and telegraph systems. In the end Guzmán Blanco's dream of a developed capitalist Venezuela proved to be a mirage; after two decades of his rule, Venezuela remained rural, monocultural, and dependent, a country in which caudillos again ran rampant as they struggled for power.

His system has been called "a national alliance of caudillos," but over this alliance "The Illustrious American," as he came to be called by his sycophantic Congress and press, presided as the supreme caudillo. The Constitution of 1864 was periodically replaced by new constitutions that reinforced the centralization of power. Although Guzmán's dictatorship was mild by comparison with some others in Venezuelan history, he did not hesitate to use repressive measures against his foes.

Political centralization went hand in hand with a fiscal unification that gradually eliminated the economic independence of the states, which had to surrender the collection of custom duties to the central government, receiving national subsidies in return. The state also took over the administration of mines, including the rich gold mines of Guayana. An 1871 law ended the existing monetary anarchy by creating a national money of gold, silver, and copper and prescribed rules for its coinage and circulation.

By his pact with the caudillos Guzmán secured a relatively stable peace (though there were several large-scale revolts against him between 1870 and 1888 and local uprisings were common throughout the period). Soon after coming to power he established a *Compañía de Crédito* with a powerful group of Caracas merchants. This gave him the resources needed to initiate a program of public works designed to improve transportation and communication. Between 1870 and 1874 fifty-one road-building projects were begun. But local funding did not suffice; Guzmán needed the cooperation of foreign capital, hesitant to invest in a country whose recent history had been marked by recurrent episodes of civil war. In 1879 he secured his first foreign contract, with a group of British investors for the construction of a railroad connecting Caracas with its major port, La Guaira. By the time he left office Venezuela had eleven railroad lines completed or under construction, all designed to serve the export-import trade by connecting Caracas and the major agricultural and mining areas with the ports. Given Venezuela's unfavorable terms of trade—the long-term tendency for the prices of its exports to decline and those of its manufactured imports to rise—the net result was to reinforce Venezuela's economic dependency, promote decapitalization, and leave the country a legacy of large unpaid foreign debt that in time posed a threat of foreign intervention and loss of sovereignty. But the astute Guzmán Blanco made this process pay handsome dividends by skimming the contracts and loans that his government undertook to pay back in years to come.

Guzmán Blanco believed that education was an indispensable instrument for creating a "civilized people," for freeing the Venezuelan nation from the reactionary influence of caudillos and the church. Accordingly he issued a decree for free, compulsory, primary education and created a Ministry of Public Instruction. His goal to provide a school for every locality with ten children remained largely on paper, but it appears that when he left office for the last time in 1887, Venezuela had almost the same number of schools it would have in 1930.

Guzmán Blanco's anticlerical policies led to a further weakening of the church. Tithing had already been abolished as "an excessive tax burden" on the citizenry. Under Guzmán Blanco the priestly fuero was ended, civil marriage and civil registration of birth and deaths established, and convents and seminaries closed. The church was also forbidden to inherit real estate, and many church estates were seized by the government.

For the rest, Guzmán Blanco's development programs caused little change in the country's economic and social structures. In 1894 the population, numbering some two and a half million, was overwhelmingly rural; only three cities had a population of more than 10,000. Most of the working population was employed in agriculture; what little modern industry existed was limited to light industry such as food processing and textiles. The artisan shop, employing some 50,000 workers, was economically much more important. In the virtual absence of a factory system, a proletariat in the modern sense hardly existed, but the severe depression of the 1890s gave rise to the first serious labor protests and attempts at organization.

In 1888 "The Illustrious American," whose interest in modernizing Venezuela appeared to flag, departed for Europe, leaving a hand-picked successor in charge. After a chaotic decade during which governments rose and fell, in 1899 Cipriano Castro, an energetic young caudillo from the Andean state of Táchira, seized power with his *compadre* (buddy) Juan Vicente Gómez, a prosperous cattle raiser and coffee grower. Castro's seizure of power reflected the growing economic importance of the Andean coffee-growing region. Announcing a program of "new men, new ideals, new methods," Castro formed a provisional government of national unity that included all political factions. In 1901 a constituent assembly elected him president and framed a constitution that extended the executive's term of office to six years.

Castro continued Guzmán Blanco's policy of centralization, appointing or confirming local officials and state governors, and sought to establish a strong national armed force that would replace the old-time personal armies and state militias. His program of military reform was handicapped by declining coffee prices that reduced state revenues, by a series of caudillo revolts repressed at heavy cost, and by a major conflict with foreign powers whose blockade of Venezuelan ports deprived the government of a vital source of income, custom duties.

Castro presided over a country in ruin due to devastating civil wars and a prolonged depression. Hard-pressed for funds, in December 1900 he demanded that Manuel Antonio Matos, Guzmán Blanco's brother-in-law and the country's wealthiest man, and his fellow financiers loan the government money. When they refused he paraded them through the streets of Caracas on the way to jail. The loan was made, but Matos took his revenge, organizing a large-scale revolt that brought together Caracas financiers, foreign investors, and regional caudillos. This *Revolución Libertadora* received considerable aid from foreign firms. Despite this assistance and Matos's own resources, Castro, leading the government forces in person, inflicted a decisive defeat on the rebels at La Victoria in November 1902.

The German and British governments chose this time to demand immediate settlement of their nationals' claims for unpaid debts and damages suffered in various civil wars. The government, having thrown all its resources into the struggle against the Matos revolt, could not pay these claims. In December 1902, despite Castro's offer to negotiate, the two powers sent an Anglo-German squadron of twelve warships into Venezuelan waters with orders to seize or destroy Venezuela's tiny fleet and blockade its ports. The powerful guns of the Anglo-German squadron soon silenced the answering fire of Venezuelan coastal batteries, and the aggressors occupied several Venezuelan ports. The unequal nature of the struggle, the catastrophic economic impact of the Anglo-German blockade, and the continuing Matos revolt in some areas of the country made a settlement necessary. Accordingly, Castro asked the U.S. ambassador to serve as mediator in negotiating a settlement. The terms required Venezuela to allocate 30 percent of its customs duties to the payment of claims and provided for an end to the blockade and re-establishment of diplomatic relations between the parties but denied Venezuela the right to demand compensation for its losses.

Castro's last years in power were troubled by new clashes with foreign states—France, Holland, the United States—usually caused by his insistence that foreign nationals were subject to Venezuelan courts and laws. As Castro's health declined, Juan Vicente Gómez conspired to take power. The regime divided into two bands, one supporting Castro, the other Gómez. Gómez also had the support of foreign powers, notably the United States, eager to get rid of Castro. On No-

vember 24, 1908, on the advice of his physicians, Castro left for Europe to seek medical aid. Gómez, assuming the duties of president, staged a coup d'état. Castro attempted to return but was blocked by U.S. warships off the Venezuelan coast and by French authorities on Martinique, who put him on board a ship sailing for Europe. He spent the rest of his life in exile, dying in Puerto Rico in 1924.

Venezuela in the Early Twentieth Century, 1908–1958

The Tyranny of Juan Vicente Gómez, 1908–1935

On taking power, Gómez tried to placate his foreign patrons and promote a flow of investments into Venezuela by nullifying Castro's nationalistic policies. In 1909 he signed agreements with the United States and France restoring to foreign companies the concessionary rights Castro had abrogated. In another move designed to reassure foreign investors, Gómez issued an executive decree allowing foreign nationals who did not like the arbitration of Venezuelan courts to appeal to their own national courts or to international tribunals.

Foreign oil companies were especially favored by Gómez. The explosive growth of the oil industry eventually transformed Venezuelan economy and society, but the process began slowly. The transformation of the economy by "black gold" did not reduce its dependence or broaden its base; the monoculture of coffee and cacao was replaced by the monoculture of oil. The oil industry pumped vast wealth into the hands of the foreign concessionaires—in 1928 three companies, Dutch Shell, Standard Oil, and Gulf, controlled 89 percent of the market—and of Gómez and the small native elite linked to the foreign oil interests, but little of this wealth trickled down to the masses nor did it generate significant industrial progress. Government subsidies failed to stem the decline of agriculture, a sector that traditionally resisted modernization. The agricultural crisis contributed to a wave of rural migration to the oil fields of the Maracaibo Basin and other petroleum areas and to the growing cities.

In the 1920s nationalist resentment of foreign economic domination and hostility toward Gómez began to pervade the growing middle class. Venezuelan professionals and would-be entrepreneurs chafed at the difficulties of operating in an economic climate dominated by monopoly, nepotism, and corruption. In 1928 a celebration of the "Week of the Student" turned into a protest against the dictatorship, as the students were joined by trade unionists and other *Caraqueños* (inhabitants of Caracas). The protest marked the public emergence of an anti-Gómez movement with future importance.

The student protest inspired the military revolt of April 1928, led by young officers of the Caracas garrison and joined by the majority of cadets of the *Escuela Militar* and a number of students. Grievances over the favoritism shown in pay and promotions to officers of unquestioned loyalty to Gómez, and awareness that the army had become a repressive force designed to maintain internal order, fueled their discontent. An informer revealed the conspiracy to the military authorities, and government troops easily crushed the revolt before it had well begun. One group of students, including Rómulo Betancourt, future president of Venezuela, managed to escape and make their way abroad.

In 1931 Gómez was at the peak of his power. But in the next few years his health began to decline and in 1935 the prospect of his early demise led to intense factional maneuvering in his inner circle. The principal contenders for Gómez's throne were two generals, Minister of War López Contreras and the dictator's cousin, Eustoquio Gómez, each supported by his own faction. Eustoquio Gómez's candidacy was supported by the most barbarous followers of the old dictator. López was a more ambiguous figure. Like Gómez, he was an *Andino* (from one of the Andean provinces) and seemed absolutely loyal to the dictator, in whose service he had steadily risen, marrying his daughter and becoming his most trusted aide and heir apparent.

In 1935, amid growing signs that Gómez's illness was terminal, López Contreras wove a network of alliances designed to isolate Eustoquio and ensure his own peaceful coming to power without a civil war or dangerous risings of the masses. López already had the solid support of most army commanders, so by the time of Gómez's death on December 17, 1935, López appeared to have established the necessary conditions for a relatively peaceful transfer of state power into his own hands.

The jubilation and the demands for vengeance and social and political reform that the news of Gómez's death provoked in the long-silent Venezuelan nation not only made a mockery of López's eulogy of the dead dictator but foreclosed the possibility of an easy transition to a social order resembling that of the old regime. The entrance of the Venezuelan middle classes and workers on the political scene opened two decades of complicated struggle, culminating in the victory of a new capitalist model of development and its associated political form of representative democracy.

Liquidating the Gómez Legacy, 1936–1945

Announcing Gómez's death, López proclaimed two weeks of public mourning. Venezuelans, however, responded to the announcement with rejoicing and, in Caracas, angry crowds sacked the palaces of Gómez's most prominent supporters. When police fired on crowds of demonstrators in the Plaza Bolívar, killing many, López Contreras removed the governor of the federal district who was held responsible for the massacre but replaced him with another member of Gómez's inner circle. On December 21 Eustoquio Gómez, who regarded himself as the late dictator's rightful heir and Venezuela as his family estate, attacked the presidential palace in a desperate bid for power and was killed. Nine days later López Contreras was chosen by the dead dictator's hand-picked Congress to fill his unexpired term.

In an atmosphere of great social and political effervescence, many exiles with different ideologies returned home and joined activists emerging from the underground in organizing trade unions, political parties, and professional organizations. López found himself under siege from the right and the left. He sometimes yielded to pressures for reform, then stubbornly resisted demands for change in the undemocratic Gómez political system. Under that system Gómez's hand-picked Congress elected López for a new term as president in April 1936.

In 1936 the country also received a new constitution, but López, as rabidly anticommunist as Gómez, insisted on retaining the Gómez clause that defined communism and anarchism as treason. In 1937 López conducted a wholesale purge of dissidents, expelling forty-seven leading figures in the political or labor opposition.

With the major opposition parties (the reformist *Partido Democrático Nacional* [PDN] led by Rómulo Betancourt and the Venezuelan Communist party of Gustavo Machado) outlawed and their leaders in exile, the outcome of the 1941 presidential election was never in doubt. López's hand-picked candidate, General Isaias Medina Angarita, won easily over novelist Rómulo Gallegos, the unofficial candidate of the PDN, whom López had dropped from his cabinet.

Medina, a Tachirense like López, proved more liberal than his predecessor. He created his own official government party, the *Partido Democrático Venezolano* (PDV) but permitted the political and labor leaders López had expelled to return and the PDN (renamed *Acción Democrática* [AD] in September 1941) and other opposition parties, including the Communists, to operate with complete freedom.

World War II, having created an insatiable demand for Venezuela's oil, enabled Medina's government to wrest more favorable terms from the oil companies than were in the old inequitable contracts. Other achievements of his administration included the passage of Venezuela's first so-

cial security and income-tax legislation. The government also encouraged the formation of trade unions, which gained considerable strength, particularly in the oil industry. Medina viewed favorably a movement toward a more democratic system, with direct popular election of the president and a broader suffrage, and discussed these reforms with the civilian politicians, but left their implementation to the president who would succeed him in 1946.

Medina also tackled the country's urgent agrarian problem. Near the end of his administration he asked his minister of agriculture, Angel Biaggini, to draft an agrarian reform bill that would distribute the extensive state landholdings to landless peasants. Congress passed the law, but one month after passage it died stillborn as a result of the overthrow of the Medina administration by a military-civilian revolt headed by two men who would dominate Venezuelan politics for the next two decades, Marcos Pérez Jiménez and Rómulo Betancourt.

Betancourt and the movement he headed deserve special analysis, for the ideology and the political system he created still dominate Venezuelan politics. Betancourt was the most influential personality among that famous generation of student leaders who in 1928 electrified Caracas by leading a public demonstration against Gómez. Of middle-class background, during his years of exile Betancourt had read widely in the classics of Marxist literature. But the most decisive influence on his thought was a nationalist, reformist ideological current best represented in Latin America by the Peruvian Victor Raúl Haya de la Torre, who argued that in Latin America's specific conditions, characterized by economic backwardness and a small, weak working class, the immediate historical task of social revolutionaries was to complete the unfinished bourgeois revolution. Because of the weakness and lack of consciousness of the working class, Haya de la Torre assigned to the middle class the task of leading a multiclass coalition in a national, antifeudal, anti-imperialist revolution.

Betancourt thus appears as the standard-bearer of the Venezuelan bourgeois revolution, which sought to end dependency on oil by diversifying the economy through industrialization, to expand the internal market by improving living standards, and to initiate land reform that would increase the productivity of agriculture. All these goals he hoped to achieve within the framework of parliamentary democracy. Betancourt assigned a decisive role in this process to the state, which should plan, regulate, and assist economic development.

The political instrument Betancourt and his colleagues created to achieve Venezuela's bourgeois, democratic revolution was *Acción Democrática* (AD), a multiclass party and a mass organization that enjoyed a large growth from 1941 to 1945, gaining a clear superiority in numbers and influence among workers, peasants, and the middle class over its closest rival, the Communist party.

A Strange Alliance: Betancourt and the Military in Power, 1945–1948

On October 18, 1945, a military-civilian coup overthrew the Medina regime as it was approaching its legal end and established a provisional government headed by Betancourt as president. The motives for this coup, born of an alliance between conservative young military officers and the AD's liberal leadership, continue to provoke historical debate. The fact that Medina's record was on the whole consistently progressive and that he had supported sweeping constitutional reforms, including universal suffrage, raises serious questions as to why AD supported the coup against him.

The dominant motive of the young officers, organized in the *Unión Patriótica Militar* (UPM), who planned the coup and obtained AD's support for it, appears to have been discontent over promotion, salary, and appointment policies within the military. The fighting to achieve the triumph of the less than lofty aims of these allies caused some 2,500 casualties. Once the fighting had ended, the military displayed little interest in

governmental affairs and appeared content to leave policy making and its implementation to the AD. Of the seven members of the ruling Revolutionary Junta, headed by Betancourt, only two were military men.

However dubious the motives that inspired the coup of October 18, 1945, it proved a milestone in Venezuelan history. The three years of government by the AD (between October 1945 and November 1948)—a period Venezuelans call the *Trienio*—represented the first serious effort to transform the country's archaic economic and social structures.

Betancourt, acting as the junta's provisional president, ruled by decree from October 1945 until the election of Rómulo Gallegos in December 1947. In March 1946 Betancourt issued two decrees that constituted a new electoral law and provided for universal suffrage. Since Acción Democrática was, in effect, the government and had a large nationwide network of party organizations to mobilize the population, it had a distinct advantage over its political rivals, the conservative Social Christian party, usually called COPEI, led by Rafael Caldera; the liberal, reformist Democratic Republican Union (URD), led by Jovito Villalba; and the Communist party, led by Gustavo Machado.

The AD won an overwhelming victory in the election for the Constituent Assembly, with almost 79 percent of the vote. The Constituent Assembly empowered the Revolutionary Junta to govern until a new constitution had been approved and a congress and president elected.

This period of whirlwind political activity was also marked by a major campaign to organize trade and peasant unions in which the AD played a leading role. AD control of the distribution of land and agricultural credits under the agrarian reform enabled it to build a clientele of peasant union leaders that gave it a commanding majority of the peasant vote. AD established a similar relationship of influence and leadership over most of the more than 500 trade unions organized in this period and affiliated with the Venezuelan Confederation of Workers, which included both trade and peasant unions.

The Constituent Assembly proclaimed the new constitution on July 5, 1947. The document guaranteed many civil and social rights, including labor's right to organize and strike and the principle that land should belong "to him who works it." The constitution established universal, secret voting for all persons over eighteen, with direct election of the president and both houses of Congress.

On December 14, 1947, presidential and congressional elections were held and the AD candidate for president, Rómulo Gallegos, was elected with almost 75 percent of the popular vote.

Among the economic issues with which the AD government had to deal, oil policy was most important, for it involved fundamental questions of dependency, economic sovereignty, and the revenues needed for economic diversification and modernization. In December 1946 the government had imposed a supertax of 26 percent on all company profits over 28 million bolivars; the law was aimed primarily at the oil companies. This tax alone increased government income in 1947 by 230 percent over its income in 1938.

In view of the great importance the AD program attached to agrarian reform, the junta's approach was timid. Evidently fearing the political and economic repercussions of a frontal attack on the latifundio, the government preferred to distribute land to the peasants from the extensive state holdings taken over on Gómez's death, Venezuela's premier latifundist. Out of a landless peasant population estimated at about 330,000, only between 55,000 and 80,000 received land during the Trienio. Since the average peasant received only 2.2 hectares of land to cultivate, "the problem," as Judith Ewell points out, "then changed from *latifundia* to *minifundia.*"

The creation of an independent national economy through industrialization was a major government goal. The *Corporación Venezolana de Fomento* (CVF) (Venezuelan Development Corporation) was formed in 1946 to promote this process through loans to private entrepreneurs and direct investment in state corporations. Between January 1946 and December 1948 it lent nearly 50 million bolivars to industrial enterprises.

By the Trienio's end, the program of "sowing the petroleum" to diversify and modernize the economy had achieved only modest results. More impressive progress was made in health and education. Under Gallegos the budget for the ministry of education for 1948 tripled and that for the ministry of health quadrupled by comparison to 1945. Important advances were also made in eliminating the country's principal health scourge, malaria, by spraying with DDT the breeding grounds of mosquitos, which carried the disease.

The principal danger to the regime came from the military. The conservative officers gradually became disenchanted with what they regarded as the radical excesses of their civilian partners. In November 1948 a group of officers headed by Colonel Pérez Jiménez presented an ultimatum to Gallegos demanding that COPEI be given representation in the government, that several officers be included in the cabinet, and that Betancourt be exiled. Although Gallegos rejected these demands, he made no effort to discipline the military and turned down offers by the labor movement and his own party to organize civilian resistance to the upcoming coup. On November 24 the government was overthrown by a virtually bloodless coup, and Minister of Defense Carlos Delgado Chalbaud took power as president of a military junta. Many of the leading members of the AD regime were arrested and imprisoned. Betancourt escaped and took refuge in the Colombian Embassy; later he, Gallegos, and other prominent AD leaders were permitted to go into exile.

The Military Dictatorship, 1948–1958

In a proclamation issued on November 25, Delgado Chalbaud, who had personal and political differences with Pérez Jiménez, declared that the junta was a provisional government and did not intend to destroy Venezuelan democracy or prohibit the activities of political parties. Unlike Pérez Jiménez, who favored the immediate imposition of a military dictatorship, Delgado Chalbaud sought to maintain a façade of democracy to exploit the rivalry between AD and COPEI and URD by inviting AD's rivals to operate as legal parties and even participate in the new government, thereby splitting the opposition. URD and COPEI took the bait, and members of those parties served the junta in various official capacities during the first few years.

The junta's actions contradicted its claims of democratic intentions. Soon after the coup it dissolved Congress, annulled the 1947 Constitution, and voided the petroleum law and other progressive measures of the Gallegos administration. The agrarian reform program and the school construction program initiated by the AD regime were abandoned or suspended. The junta also imposed a strict censorship, forbidding any criticism of the regime. In January 1949 the junta launched an offensive against the unions, arresting leaders of the Venezuelan labor confederation, forbidding union meetings, and freezing the funds of most of the unions.

Initially resistance to the junta and its repressive policies was largely limited to student protests and the activities of the illegal Communist party, whose members played a leading role in the organization of the resistance movement. In 1949 AD leaders who remained in the country formed an underground organization. Against the objections of the strongly anticommunist Betancourt and other AD leaders in exile, the AD underground cooperated with the Communists and other groups of the resistance movement in the struggle against the dictatorship.

The assassination of Delgado Chalbaud, kidnapped in November 1950 in a Caracas street in full daylight and taken to the outskirts of the city where he was murdered, ended the first phase of the military dictatorship. The government claimed the crime was committed by opposition parties, but its author turned out to be a confidant of Pérez Jiménez, the chief beneficiary of Delgado Chalbaud's death. A civilian puppet of Pérez Jiménez, Germán Suárez Flamerich, now became president of the military junta, and announced that elections would be held and the constitutional order restored as soon as possible.

Simultaneously, however, the military regime intensified its repressive activity. By the fall of 1952, the regime, evidently convinced that the repression had intimidated the Venezuelan people into accepting its rule, decided it would be safe to hold elections for a Constituent Assembly. AD and the Communist party were outlawed but the COPEI and URD were permitted to offer candidates. The junta presented its own slate under the party name of the *Frente Electoral Independiente* (FEI).

Despite the repressive conditions and the call issued by the exiled AD leadership to abstain from voting—a position it reversed at the last moment—Venezuelans gave a two-thirds majority of the popular vote to the opposition parties, 54 percent to the URD, 15 percent to the COPEI, and only 25 percent to the FEI. Furious at this outcome, Pérez Jiménez nullified the election, arrested and deported the leaders of the URD, and announced he was taking office as provisional president in the name of the armed forces. Presently a recount of the vote, made at his orders, showed an "overwhelming victory" for the government party. An obedient Constituent Assembly gave the dictator the constitution he wanted and named him "Constitutional President."

For the next five years (1953–1958) Pérez Jiménez was the absolute ruler of Venezuela. A brutally efficient repression, whose principal instrument was *Seguridad Nacional,* the secret police, made antigovernment activities very difficult. A resistance movement, however, uniting persons of all political tendencies survived and continued its struggle against the dictatorship.

The social and economic policies of the regime generated discontent among ever wider sections of the population. Its limitations on the right to organize and strike contributed to a decline of labor's share of the national income. Venezuelan industrialists were angered by the U.S.-Venezuelan commercial treaty of 1952, which denied protection to the country's infant industries and reduced custom duties on a wide range of imported products. As a result some native companies were forced to go out of business or were absorbed by subsidiaries of American-based multinationals.

Pérez Jiménez's reversal of the AD's petroleum policy not to issue new concessions to the foreign oil companies led to a scramble for new concessions by the oil companies, resulting in a nearly doubled national budget. The increased revenues allowed Pérez Jiménez to continue his wasteful program of "pyramid building," accompanied by corrupt contracting practices that served to enrich the dictator and other public officials. In place of the AD's focus on education, health, agrarian reform, and balanced economic development, the Pérez Jiménez regime emphasized grand works of infrastructure—highways, urban freeways, and port improvements, and urban constructions, some of little or no social utility, like the Officers Club in Caracas or the many-storied shopping center built on the side of one of Caracas's hills.

Signs of defection from the regime multiplied in 1957. Especially significant was the increasingly critical attitude of the conservative Catholic hierarchy, which issued statements deploring the government's disregard for the interests of the poor. Disaffection also grew among national capitalists, who complained of the government's neglect. With the end of the oil export boom in the late 1950s, the regime's capacity to generate business activity and employment through public works programs began to run out of steam. Within the armed forces there was growing resentment of Pérez Jiménez's arbitrary ways and his reliance on the secret police to watch over the loyalty of officers.

By mid-1957, an underground organization called the Junta Patriótica had been formed to unite the principal political parties—AD, COPEI, URD, and the Venezuelan Communist party. This group became the principal motor of the resistance movement and its preparation for a popular revolt. In October Pérez Jiménez, approaching the end of his constitutional term as president and fearing the results of an election, announced that a plebiscite would be held instead to determine whether the people wished him to continue in power. This brazen announcement and the farcical plebiscite that followed caused an explosion of mingled ridicule and wrath. On January 21 the Junta Patriótica proclaimed a general strike that was overwhelmingly effective and was accompanied by clashes between the people and the regime's security forces. Barricades appeared in the streets of Caracas. The next day the insurgents seized key strategic points in the capital. The majority of military units refused to obey Pérez Jiménez and fraternized with the rebels. On January 23 a military junta headed by Admiral Wolfgang Larrazábal met with Pérez Jiménez and demanded that he resign; within a few hours the dictator had fled the country for the Dominican Republic.

The military junta, enlarged by the addition of two prominent businessmen, became a provisional government: its first decrees proclaimed the restoration of all democratic freedoms, amnesty for all political prisoners and exiles, and legalization of all political parties. Almost ten years of rule by a repressive military dictatorship had ended.

Venezuela's Representative Democracy, 1958–1991

The military-civilian junta headed by the popular Larrazábal presided over the transition to democratic elections, set for December 1958. Larrazábal defeated a number of conspiracies by reactionary military and he was supported by most of the armed forces and thousands of workers and students, who took to the streets in protest.

Chastened by experience, the Betancourt who returning from exile was politically more moderate than the aggressive leader who presided over the reforms of the Trienio. Betancourt's efforts to reassure Venezuela's economic elite about his intentions and his decision to choose the right-leaning COPEI as his principal political ally reflected his new caution.

On October 31, 1958, the three centrist parties—AD, COPEI, and URD—formally endorsed the Pact of Punto Fijo which provided that whatever the election results, the three parties would form a coalition government to carry out a program of democratic socioeconomic and political reforms.

The Pact of Punto Fijo was important far beyond its impact on the 1958 elections because it created a unique Venezuelan model of representative democracy that still functions today. The Venezuelan government was consciously tailored to isolate the Marxist left, making it virtually impossible for Marxists to wield political power. Secondly, although the Pact of Punto Fijo provided for a three-party coalition, the system evolved toward hegemonic control of political life by two parties, the social democratic AD and the social Christian COPEI, whose reformist programs were broadly similar.

A third distinctive feature of the Venezuelan model of representative democracy was the major role that it assigned to the state as regulator and arbiter of relations between the classes and interest groups. The massive influx of petroleum revenues over most of the past three decades strengthened the state and endowed it with the financial resources to perform this role, which required it to balance and mediate the conflicting demands and interests of all the major classes and pressure groups—labor, the peasantry, capitalists, the middle class, the armed forces, the church, the political parties.

Finally, the architect of the Venezuelan model of representative democracy, Rómulo Betancourt, viewed the state as an instrument for the gradual recapture of the nation's natural resources from foreign control, the reform of its socioeconomic structures, and the promotion of a balanced economic development. Betancourt hoped that, in time, economic development would lead to the rise of an autonomous Venezuelan capitalism capable of providing Venezuelans with a high standard of living and culture. Indeed, over the last three decades Venezuela has made large advances in such problem areas as health and literacy. But the vast sums expended in "sowing the petroleum" over those decades have not achieved Betancourt's main goals; poverty has not declined but increased, income distribution is as inequitable as in Mexico and Brazil, and today's Venezuela, burdened with an unpayable foreign debt, is more deeply dependent than it was in the time of Juan Vicente Gómez.

A Decade of AD Rule, 1959–1969

Although the three centrist parties had approved a common program of economic, social, and political reform broadly similar to the one carried out during the Trienio, they could not agree on a presidential candidate acceptable to all, and so each ran its own in the December 1958 election. AD's candidate, Betancourt, won with 49 percent of the popular vote and formed a coalition government that included cabinet positions for URD, AD, COPEI, and independents but excluded the Communist party.

Differences within and between the parties over domestic and foreign policy, aggravated by the continuing economic crisis and Betancourt's own contentious nature, soon placed serious strains on the coalition. The victory of the Cuban Revolution in January 1959 and Cuba's gradual turn toward socialism created an especially divisive issue. Younger AD and URD activists hailed the revolution as a model that Venezuela could well emulate. But Betancourt, virulently anti-Communist, regarded the Cuban socialist regime as a direct challenge to his own reformist philosophy and program and fully supported U.S. efforts to isolate Castro's regime economically and politically. As a result of Betancourt's position, AD's left wing broke away in April 1960 and formed the Movement of the Revolutionary Left (MIR), which soon proclaimed itself a Marxist-

Leninist party. A few months later Betancourt's decision to break off diplomatic relations with Cuba led to the departure of the URD from his government. He responded to these defections by strengthening his ties with the conservative COPEI, the armed forces, with the church, and with the economic elite.

The new constitution promulgated in February 1961 proclaimed the government's responsibility for its citizens' social well-being, provided for proportional minority representation in Congress, and prohibited the president from succeeding himself, but gave him significant powers to suspend constitutional guarantees of personal and civil liberties.

Betancourt's tactics in his struggle against the left strongly suggest a calculated effort to goad the leftist opposition into resorting to violence that would discredit it and that the armed forces could easily repress. The MIR and the Communist party played into Betancourt's hands and initiated an insurgency movement in 1961. At first primarily an urban movement whose participants were recruited from MIR and PCV youth, by April 1962 the insurgency included rural guerrilla bands operating in at least eight of the country's twenty states. Poorly organized and unskilled militarily, most of the bands were soon wiped out by the government's counterinsurgency operations.

During his 1958 election campaign Betancourt laid heavy stress on the need for agrarian reform, and his promise to give land to the landless helped him gain an overwhelming majority of the peasant vote. But the results of the agrarian reform were mixed, at best, and fell far short of solving Venezuela's acute agrarian problem.

By 1969 only some 150,000 out of the 350,000 peasant families without land in 1960 had received plots. Combined with the estimated 200,000 new families formed in those eight years, there remained 400,000 families without land. Government investments in irrigation, roads, and credit and technical assistance primarily benefited large and medium-sized commercial farms, which produced the lion's share of profitable crops and accounted for most of the 150 percent increase in agricultural production during the years between 1959 and 1968.

More significant, perhaps, were the large advances made in health and public education during the Betancourt administration. Nearly 9 percent of the national budget was assigned to the Ministry of Health and Social Assistance. A concerted attack on the problems of endemic disease, infant mortality, and malnutrition resulted in a decline of infant mortality from 64 per 1,000 live births in the 1955–1959 period to 46.5 in 1966.

The Betancourt years also saw a significant growth of public education. Avoiding clashes over regulation of private schools that had embittered its relations with the church during the Trienio, the AD government concentrated on expansion of the public school system. More than 3,000 new primary schools, and nearly 200 secondary, normal, and technical schools were constructed. There was a parallel expansion of teacher training institutes and the university system.

A major objective of the Betancourt regime was to increase its share of oil profits in order to make more funds available for development. A tax law of December 1958 raised the tax rate on oil profits to 65 percent.

Agrarian reform and industrialization were the two keystones of the new Venezuela Betancourt wished to build. The slogan "Venezuela must industrialize or die" expressed the militant spirit of the new campaign to industrialize that began in 1958. The principal instrument of the import-substitution strategy pursued by the AD government was the Venezuelan Development Corporation (CVF), created during the Trienio. The CVF transferred large resources generated by oil exports to the industrialization process in the form of loans and direct subsidies.

The campaign for "economic independence," however, had a peculiar outcome; it fastened more firmly the chains of dependence on Venezuela. Confronted with high tariff walls, unwilling to lose the large consumer market created by oil wealth, a growing number of U.S. and other foreign firms chose to establish branches in Venezuela, frequently in association with local capital. The label "Made in Venezuela" increasingly came to mean an article made with raw materials and intermediate materials imported from the United States and finished or assembled in Venezuela.

Between 1958 and 1970 the number of plants producing such items as cans, foodstuffs, clothing, automobiles, auto tires, paint, and cigarettes mushroomed. The alliance of foreign and native capital achieved the goal of import substitution and the proportion of industrial goods produced locally rose from 65 percent in 1960 to 85 percent in 1970. But since the dominant partner in the alliance was foreign capital, most of the profits flowed back to the home offices of foreign firms. By 1971 Venezuela had the largest gross accumulated foreign investment in any Third World country: $5.57 billion.

The drive for import-substitution industrialization was accompanied by the incorporation of labor as a less-than-equal partner in an alliance with the state and industry. In 1958 labor leaders signed a pact with management that committed the unions to seek conciliation of conflicts with employers. The subordination of labor was completed during the following decade of AD rule.

Raul Leoni, AD's nominee for president, won over COPEI's Rafael Caldera and five other candidates in the election of December 1963. But the AD margin of victory had markedly declined and his government had to rely on a shifting alliance of parties.

Although Leoni continued Betancourt's policy of state-supported import-substitution industrialization, the outcome was a dependent industrialization dominated by foreign-based multinationals. During Leoni's presidency the export of profits reached an annual average of $672 million. Venezuela, observes one economist, had become "a fiscal paradise of foreign monopoly capital."

Caldera in Power, 1969–1973

Internal division contributed to the loss of the AD candidate to COPEI nominee Rafael Caldera in 1968. Responding to growing nationalist sentiment and charges that the foreign oil companies were withholding further investment in Venezuela in reprisal for higher taxes and increased government control, Caldera had called for the reversion to the nation of all existing oil concessions after 1983. With the support of all the parties in Congress, the Hydrocarbons Reversion Law was passed in 1971. This law called for the reversion to the state of all existing oil concessions beginning in 1983 and stipulated that unexploited concessions be ceded to the CVP in 1974. In addition, the oil companies were required to post bonds guaranteeing that their plant and machinery would be turned over in good condition. Also enacted in 1971 were bills nationalizing the foreign-owned natural gas industry and giving the government power to control oil production levels.

Finally, during his last months in office, Caldera issued a decree that forbade foreign interest in radio and television stations and electric companies.

Despite the establishment of representative democracy in 1958 and the reforms initiated by Caldera in 1969 a survey of Venezuela's economic and social conditions made in 1973 gave no cause for satisfaction with either of the country's two ruling parties. No basic change in economic structure had occurred; the government remained heavily dependent on oil income. True, import-substitution industrialization had achieved some economic diversification, but it was a dependent industrialization largely based on foreign capital, inputs, and technology. Despite the agrarian reform, agriculture remained the most backward branch of the national economy. In 1971 Venezuela still imported 46 percent of its basic foodstuffs. The failure of the agrarian reform to correct fundamental problems was also reflected in the continuing high concentration of landownership; 1.4 percent of the large estates held 67 percent of all privately owned land in 1973.

Thanks to the eradication of such scourges as malaria and improved health care, the Venezuelan population had grown rapidly, increasing from 7,524,000 in 1958 to 10,722,000 in 1971. But it is doubtful whether the quality of life for the majority of Venezuelans had improved after fifteen years of democratic rule. In 1974, 30 percent of all Venezuelan children suffered from malnutrition; 12 percent of all adults suffered from mental retardation from the same cause, combined with other difficult living conditions. In the early 1960s a United Nations study described Venezuela's income distribution as one of the most unequal in the world. A decade later the situation had not improved.

The Dilemmas of a Petroleum Republic, 1974–1991

From the election of December 1973 the AD candidate, Carlos Andrés Pérez, a Betancourt protégé, emerged an easy winner over the COPEI nominee. The flamboyant Pérez, a master of populist rhetoric, had promised a "war on poverty" and against "privilege." Despite his rhetoric, his program did not differ substantially from those of his predecessors.

Pérez took office under the most favorable auspices: the Arab oil embargo of 1973 had brought a rapid rise in the price of oil, going from $2.01 a barrel in 1970 to $14.26 in January 1974. The resulting vast increase in state revenues appeared to give Venezuela the means to solve all its major social and economic problems. Pérez promised to "manage abundance with the mentality of scarcity," but the flood of oil riches and the irresistible drive to modernize overwhelmed his administration and frustrated his good intentions.

On August 29, 1975 Pérez signed a law nationalizing the Venezuelan oil industry, taking effect January 1, 1976. A state oil company, *Petroven,* was created to control a sector of the economy whose annual sales volume exceeded $10 billion. In addition to a generous compensation of $1 billion to the foreign companies, the nationalization agreement authorized the state to enter into contracts with those companies for the provision of technological assistance and equipment, as well

as marketing agreements for the international transshipment of Venezuelan oil exports.

Even earlier President Pérez had signed a law (effective January 1, 1975) that nationalized the iron industry. In addition to financial compensation to the former owners (subsidiaries of U.S. Steel and Bethlehem Steel), Venezuela agreed to sell iron to the parent companies for as long as seven years.

Pérez's economic program called for the creation and expansion of heavy industries, especially petrochemicals, steel, and shipbuilding, that would supply the needs of Venezuela's consumer goods industry. Gradually other projects—a fishery industry, a national rail system, the Caracas metro, and modernized port facilities—were added to this list.

During his campaign Pérez had pledged he would direct "priority attention to the needs of Venezuelan agriculture as the essential motor of economic development." But like his predecessors, Pérez understood those "needs" as the needs of large commercial farmers. Although Pérez claimed in 1975 to have achieved an "agricultural miracle," the reality was very different. Domestic food production increased, but imports of the country's basic foodstuffs rose from 46 percent in 1971 to almost 70 percent by the close of his administration. The rapid growth of the urban population contributed to this increased food dependence.

The immense revenues that flowed to the state from 1974 to 1979 proved inadequate to cover the costs of the government's ambitious development program. Increasingly Pérez had to resort to foreign loans; between 1974 and 1978 Venezuela's foreign debt grew by almost $10 billion.

In foreign policy, Pérez continued an initiative begun by Caldera and resumed diplomatic relations with Castro's government in December 1974. Pérez also supported Panama's efforts to gain control of the Panama Canal and the Sandinista struggle against the dictatorship of Anastasio Somoza.

Pérez cultivated a populist image that did not correspond to his social policies. As a result of the orgy of state spending in the Pérez years, the economy heated up and inflation cut deeply into workers' living standards. For the business, financial, and political elites, however, the boom created vast opportunities for enrichment resulting in an explosion of conspicuous consumption by these classes as the standard of living for peasants and workers deteriorated. The intimate ties between the state, the ruling party, and the economic elites generated corruption on an unheard-of scale.

Finally, the Pérez economic program had clearly failed to solve the dilemma of dependency that continued to plague Venezuela. Measured by the yardsticks of foreign indebtedness and the degree of its reliance for revenue on a single resource—oil—Venezuela was more dependent in 1980 than it had been in 1974. In 1980 the Inter-American Development Bank ranked the Venezuelan economy as fifth in terms of dependence among twenty-three Latin American and Caribbean nations.

In 1978, the electorate chose COPEI nominee Luis Herrera Campins to lead the nation out of the economic morass.

The COPEI leadership advanced a conservative economic program including privatization of many state enterprises, reduction of state expenditures, tight credit policies, and the removal of price controls on a wide range of consumer products. Instead of stimulating domestic production, however, as predicted, the measure caused another surge in prices.

If the Herrera economic team failed to reduce the level of inflation below that of the Pérez years, its recessionary monetary policy certainly achieved the goal of cooling off the economy with a vengeance. The unemployment rate, which was 4.3 percent at the close of 1978, rose to almost 15 percent in 1981. Venezuela was at once plagued with high inflation, high unemployment, and an economy sliding from stagnation into recession.

By the spring of 1981 the disastrous state of affairs had forced Herrera to change course and adopt an expansionary policy. The Iranian Revolution of 1979 and the Iran-Iraq war produced a

sharp rise in oil prices, giving Herrera abundant revenues to finance his new policies. However, a worldwide recession in 1982 forced down the price of oil and resulted in dwindling revenues for Venezuela. To cover his deficits Herrera was compelled to borrow on a massive scale and increased the nation's indebtedness to $27 billion. By mid-1983 more than 70 percent of the country's food had to be imported, and severe shortages had arisen.

Not surprisingly, the inability of COPEI leadership to master Venezuela's economic woes resulted in its defeat in the 1983 election. The AD candidate, Jaime Lusinchi, won with the largest margin of victory since 1947.

Lusinchi, who took office in February 1984, tackled the nation's most urgent problem—foreign debt—by insisting on faithful payment of interest to foreign bankers. Between 1985 and 1988 he sent $15 billion in interest and principal out of the country assuming that the foreign bankers would reward his compliance by rescheduling the debt on generous terms and providing new loans to aid economic recovery. But Venezuela's dwindling oil revenues proved inadequate to meet the payments required by the rescheduling agreement signed in February 1986, and the large new loans were not forthcoming.

In a New Year's Eve 1989 address to the nation Lusinchi, proclaiming that the debt "is strangling our country's social and economic development and that of the majority of the world's people," announced a payment moratorium on the principal of all debts accumulated with foreign banks before 1983.

The combined effects of a drop in oil prices in 1988 and the massive outflow of funds to service the foreign debt were devastating. Inflation climbed from 12.3 percent in 1986 to 36.1 percent in 1987. Although unemployment dropped from 16 percent in 1984 to 7 percent in 1988, an estimated 40 percent of the work force were underemployed.

A series of price freezes on basic products and services and a slight increase in the minimum wage of the poorest urban and rural workers, decreed by Lusinchi as part of a so-called social pact designed to protect the interests of all social groups, did little to halt the decline in living standards of the masses. Not even the rich escaped the impact of the crisis: a government report declared that 51 percent of Venezuela's richest families had been wiped out in the past few years.

The 1988 election saw the return of AD candidate Carlos Andrés Pérez to the presidency. Pérez, who had denounced Lusinchi's subservience to the foreign bankers, inaugurated an economic austerity program in response to the conditions demanded by the IMF in exchange for a $4.5 billion loan over a three-year period. The program included a massive currency devaluation, the lifting of controls and subsidies on a wide range of products and services, such as gasoline, bread, and electricity, and a rise in interest rates. The price increases were announced in advance of their application; as a result goods vanished from the shelves as shopkeepers prepared to take advantage of the higher prices.

On February 27 and 28, 1989, a popular explosion rocked Caracas when a significant rise in bus fares was announced. For many Venezuelans, whose wage increases were cut in half by this measure alone, it was the last straw. Tens of thousands of people took to the streets, rioting and looting shops; from Caracas the rioting spread to the poor barrios surrounding the city, then to the nearby port of La Guaira, and later to more distant cities and towns.

The Pérez government responded with a display of force that many observers found excessive; in contrast to the officially admitted death toll of around 300, unofficial estimates placed the number of dead at twice or three times that number, with some 2,000 wounded. The shock waves of the explosion in Venezuela soon reached Washington, where the U.S. Treasury hastened to make a $453 million "bridging loan" to the Pérez government in advance of the signing of an economic adjustment program by Venezuela and the IMF. In another apparent reaction to events in Venezuela U.S. Treasury Secretary Nicholas Brady announced a plan providing for a partial

When an increase in bus fares was announced in Caracas during February 1989, tens of thousands of angry Venezuelans took to the streets in protest. (Wide World Photos)

reduction of the Latin American debt. Pérez continued to insist that his "six-month shock" economic program was correct in its essentials and would in time create "a new Venezuela."

In the meantime, however, that program was deepening the recession Pérez had inherited from Lusinchi and causing a growing amount of economic pain. As a result of the currency devaluation and the lifting of price controls and subsidies, by May prices for many basic foods and household items, transport, and electricity had risen between 50 and 100 percent. Real wages had fallen between 20 and 50 percent. In March alone the inflation rate reached 21.3 percent.

Pérez faced a dilemma. He was caught between the demands of the IMF, the World Bank, and the foreign bankers that he continue his austerity program as a condition for obtaining the new loans needed to reactivate the economy and the counterdemands of labor and the middle class

498

that he change course and relieve the suffering caused by his economic adjustment program and a deepening recession. He decided to continue with his economic adjustment plan, which included the privatization of a large number of state-owned enterprises. Not the least irony was that it was Pérez himself who had nationalized the iron and steel industries and proclaimed "evolutionary socialism" his long-term goal.

In December Venezuela held its first direct elections of 269 mayors and 20 state governors. The elections showed the highest rate of abstention in Venezuelan history, reflecting widespread cynicism about the ruling AD and COPEI parties. Also significant was the election of left-wing candidates for governor in two important industrial states, Bolívar and Aragua, where opposition to privatization was very strong.

Critics of Pérez's program for selling off publicly owned enterprises to the private sector in the name of "industrial reconversion" and "rationalization" warned that it would cause significant loss of employment in a country already burdened with large unemployment and that ownership of those enterprises would most likely pass into the hands of foreign multinationals. Despite the opposition within and without his own party López vowed to press ahead with the program in the second half of 1990. But the volume of criticism and the many technical problems involved ensured that the progress of privatization would be slower than he had expected.

Colombia: The Nineteenth-Century Background

The Santander Regime and the Birth of a Two-Party System, 1830–1850

Following the secession of Venezuela and Ecuador from Gran Colombia in 1830, the remaining territory went its separate way under the name of the Republic of New Granada (present-day Colombia plus Panama). Struggles for control of the governmental apparatus in Bogotá between followers of Bolívar and Santander ended in the latter's victory. He returned from exile in 1832 to become the first president of an independent New Granada under a constitution that provided for a president elected for four years, a bicameral Congress, and provincial legislatures. The constitution granted suffrage to all free males who were married or aged twenty-one and were not domestic servants or day laborers. In practice, political life was dominated by a small aristocratic ruling class.

The geographic, economic, and social conditions of the new state posed even greater obstacles to the creation of a true national society than those facing Venezuela. The country's difficult geography, dominated by the towering Andean cordillera whose ranges, valleys, and plateaus were the home of the overwhelming majority of a population numbering less than one and a half million, offered formidable barriers to communication and transport; as late as the end of the nineteenth century it was cheaper to transport goods from Liverpool to Medellín than from Medellín to Bogotá.

This geography contributed to the formation of an economic structure that has been called an "economic archipelago," consisting of a number of isolated regions having little contact with each other. The economy of some of these regions was characterized by traditional haciendas mainly dedicated to growing wheat, barley, potatoes, and raising cattle. Their labor force usually consisted of mestizo peons or tenants who paid rent in labor or in kind for the privilege of cultivating their own small parcels of land; their freedom of movement could be restricted by debts, and sometimes they owed personal service to their patrón.

Alongside these haciendas and on marginal lands and mountain slopes lived other peasants whose precarious independence came from subsistence farming and supplying food to nearby towns. The northwest region of Antioquia, with its rugged terrain and low population, had few haciendas and numerous small and medium landholdings; a more independent peasantry had also arisen in neighboring Santander. Slave labor was chiefly employed on plantations and gold-mining districts in the western states and on the Caribbean coast, but the institution, greatly weakened by the revolutionary wars and legislation providing for the freedom of the children of slaves, was in decline.

The 1821 Congress of Cúcuta had ordered the division of *resguardos* (Indian communal lands) to conform with the prevailing liberal ideology, but the natives resisted. In 1839, however, dissolution of the resguardos was again ordered and a large part of the remaining Indian lands was divided; much of it was acquired for low prices by white landowners and merchants. Some of the former Indian owners became peons or tenants on haciendas; others became minifundio farmers.

New Granadan industry in 1830, like agriculture, displayed many precapitalist features. Most industrial activity (weaving and spinning, the making of pottery, shoeware) was done in the home, chiefly by women. The 1830s saw numerous state-sponsored efforts to establish factories making soap, glassware, textiles, and iron in Bogotá, but most ended in failure. By the 1840s sizable artisan groups had arisen in larger towns like Bogotá, Medellín, and Cali, but despite moderate tariff protection for local industries they had difficulty in competing with imported foreign goods.

The backwardness of economic life was most apparent in transportation; in parts of the country porters and pack mules were used for transport well into the twentieth century. Even after steamboat navigation became regular on the Magdalena River in the 1840s, it took between four and six weeks to make the voyage from Atlantic ports to Bogotá. The low development of productive forces, and the sluggish tempo of economic activity, were reflected in the modest wealth of even the upper classes. In the first half of the nineteenth century the income of Bogotá's upper class came to about $5,000 per capita, and the number of persons whose capital exceeded $100,000 could be counted on the fingers of one hand.

The lack of a dynamic export base to stimulate the economy and provide resources for a strong nation-state was a major factor in the economic and political difficulties of Colombia in its first half-century. Efforts to replace gold production—which had been in decline even before independence—with tobacco, cotton, cinchona bark, and other products as export staples produced a series of short booms that soon collapsed because of declining markets and prices, competition from foreign producers whose prices or quality Colombia could not match, or exhaustion of resources. The absence of an export base and a nationally dominant elite helps explain the "economic archipelago" or regional isolation and self-sufficiency that developed. A corollary of this economic autarchy was political autarchy, an almost permanent instability punctuated by frequent civil wars or threats of war and even secession by hacendado-generals, who could mobilize private armies of peons to settle scores with rival caudillos or the weak central government.

President Santander was more successful than some of his successors in keeping the peace during his term (1832–1837). A stern, inflexible figure mindful of constitutional legalities, he moved swiftly to crush a number of conspiracies, but generally reined in his Enlightenment passion for liberal economic and social reform. An exception was his educational policy, which reinstated the utilitarian philosophy of Jeremy Bentham, whose works Bolívar had banned in his last conservative phase.

Under Santander's successor, José Ignacio de Márquez (1837–1841), whose policies continued Santander's brand of moderate liberalism, the political climate turned stormy. Responding to a measure of Congress that closed some small convents in the fervently Catholic province of Pasto in the far South, the population rose up in arms. The revolt was crushed but revived in 1840 by a regional caudillo, General José María Obando, who had in turn been a royalist guerrilla leader and a fervent liberal republican and had unsuccessfully sought command of the forces sent to crush the Pasto rebellion before becoming its leader. He was soon joined by other military caudillos, who called themselves liberals and supreme chiefs of their regions; they formed a

500   strange alliance with the Pasto reactionaries in "The War of the Convents" or "The War of the Supremes." What motivated these caudillos was the desire for greater provincial autonomy and the hope of gaining control of the central government with its attendant political spoils. By 1841 the revolt had been defeated, but it had one lasting effect; its contribution to the formation of the classic Colombian two-party system: liberals versus conservatives.

Until the late 1840s the difference between the ideologies and programs of the two groups was far from absolute. Actually both had more in common with the moderate liberalism of Santander than Bolívar's late conservatism. Both represented upper-class interests but accepted the formal democracy of representative, republican government; both had faith in social and technological progress, believed in freedom of speech and the press and other civil liberties, and in economic policy accepted laissez-faire and liberal economics. Neither party cared about the agrarian problem or other problems of the rural and urban masses. The only genuine issue separating them was the relation between church and state and the church's role in education. The emergent Liberal party was distinctly anticlerical, regarding the church as hostile to progress; they did, however, favor freedom of worship and separation of church and state. The nascent Conservative party endorsed religious toleration but favored cooperation between church and state, believing that religion promoted morality and social peace.

This difference between the parties was reflected in the policies of the Conservative administration of Pedro Alcántara Herrera (1841–1845), which sought to ban secular ideologies like the Benthamite while stressing the teaching of practical technical subjects. The reform was capped in 1844 by recalling the Jesuits—banished from the Indies by Charles III in 1767—so that they might resume their educational mission in New Granada.

If Herrera's administration reflected the proclerical side of conservatism, the succeeding administration of Tomás C. Mosquera (1845–

1849) reflected its "positivist and modernizing" side. He presided over an ambitious program of public works, including the construction of roads, canals, and railroads. Signing of the 1846 Bidlack-Mallarino Treaty paved the way for the construction of a railroad across the Isthmus of Panama and guaranteed New Granadan sovereignty over Panama. In higher education Mosquera stressed the need to form a technical elite, founding a military school that was in effect an engineering school. Other measures included a sharp reduction of tariffs and the liquidation of the state tobacco monopoly, which reflected Mosquera's general agreement with Liberal laissez-faire doctrine.

As the Liberal and Conservative parties prepared for the 1849 election, their ideological gap widened and a coalition of three liberal groups emerged. One cause of this was a partial quickening of the economy due to the rapid expansion of tobacco cultivation, the beginnings of the coffee cycle, internal improvements of the Conservative administrations, and a resulting growth of foreign and domestic trade. The economic change was accompanied by important social and intellectual changes.

As the population increased, reaching two million in 1850, the merchant class grew in numbers and self-consciousness. The sons of this class and of some landowners, well educated and influenced by French romanticism, utopian socialism, and the 1848 French Revolution, developed a peculiar sentimental brand of liberalism based on a romantic interpretation of Christianity in which Christ appeared as a forerunner of nineteenth-century secular reformism. Because of their frequent references to Christ as the "Martyr of Golgotha," they came to be known as the Gólgotas. This ideology's practical essence was its demand for the abolition of slavery, the ecclesiastical and military fuero and compulsory tithing, and the removal of all restraints on free enterprise.

The second element in the Liberal coalition that took shape in 1849 was the urban artisan group, whose numbers had increased in the past decade. Competition with foreign imported manufactures had caused serious unemployment among the artisans, who attributed their distress to the lower tariffs enacted under Mosquera; perhaps an equally important cause was the recent establishment of permanent steam navigation on the Magdalena River, which ended the protective isolation of their markets from the outside world. The artisans created a network of "Democratic Societies," beginning with the Democratic Society of Bogotá (1847), which had almost 4,000 members. These clubs were mutual aid societies and carried on educational and philanthropic activities, but they also served as important political vehicles for the Liberal leadership in the 1849 election.

A third faction in the Liberal coalition was the *"Draconianos,"* military from the lower officer ranks, who would later align themselves with the artisans.

In the election of 1849 the Conservatives were seriously handicapped by divisions within the party. The general affinity of Mosquera's program with that of the moderate Liberals troubled some Conservatives, who suspected Mosquera of being a crypto-Liberal. The voters thus were presented with two Conservative candidates for president, representing the pro- and anti-Mosquera factions. The Liberals had their own division between moderates and Gólgotas but put aside their quarrels until after the election. With the help of the artisans, the Liberal candidate and wealthy landowner General José Hilario López, won the presidency. His election opened one of the strangest chapters in the history of Latin American nineteenth-century political history, featured by "a veritable frenzy of reform activity" as the new merchant elite, with large support from regional landed oligarchies, sought to achieve the triumph of laissez-faire and modernity. This noisy revolution, although full of drama, produced little change in the basic structures of the Colombian economy and society.

The Liberal Hegemony, 1850–1885

Dominating the presidency and Congress, the Liberals began to establish the reign of liberty and reason in New Granada. The new constitution of 1853 provided for universal male suffrage—a provision that troubled some Liberals who knew that illiterate pro-clerical peasants were most likely to vote Conservative. As a matter of fact, since in most areas voters continued to vote the wishes of the local gamonales, or bosses, the new electoral law did not significantly change anything. The new constitution also expanded provincial autonomy by permitting the people of each province to elect their governor, previously appointed from Bogotá.

In economics, the Liberals sought a decisive break with the colonial tradition of restriction and monopoly. The abolition of the state tobacco monopoly, enacted during the Mosquera administration, finally took effect in 1850. An 1850 law ceded to the provinces revenues from tithes (hitherto collected by the state but used for support of the church), the *quinto* tax on gold and other precious metals, and other traditional sources of state revenue. The provinces were also empowered to abolish these taxes. To compensate for the resulting loss of state revenues, Congress adopted a tax on individuals.

Slavery was completely abolished in 1851, and slave owners were compensated. The measure, freeing about twenty-five thousand individuals, had its most severe impact on gold-mining areas, which generally relied heavily on slave labor. Some of the freedmen became peons on haciendas; others turned to subsistence farming.

The Liberals intensified the attack on resguardos, Indian communal lands, and land "liberated" by forced division often passed into the hands of neighboring hacendados by legal or illegal means. Indians made landless by such means often became peons serving the hacendados.

The abolition of compulsory tithes and of ecclesiastical fuero formed part of a larger campaign waged by the Liberals against the church, regarded as a state within the state that must be stripped of its economic and ideological power. The Jesuits, recalled to New Granada by the Conservatives in the 1840s, were again expelled in 1850. The 1853 constitution formally established freedom of worship and the separation of church and state. Still to come was the seizure and sale of church wealth and the outlawing of all religious orders.

The alliance between the Gólgotas and the artisans was now coming apart; the Liberal elite, having achieved their ends with artisan support, ignored their allies' demands for tariff protection. The Draconianos were disgruntled over the dismantling of the army under Liberal rule and resented the Gólgotas' wealth and intellectual pretensions. A crisis arose under López's successor, José María Obando. In April 1854 a group of Draconianos staged a coup, overthrew Obando, and installed General José María Melo. Melo, promising to raise tariff rates, received the full support of the artisans, who formed workers' battalions to defend the revolution. But Liberal and Conservative generals, putting aside their differences, raised private armies and defeated Melo in a brief campaign. His artisan allies were imprisoned and 300 were deported to Panama. The economic, political, and military rout of the artisans was complete.

In 1857 a Conservative, Mariano Ospina Rodríguez, was elected president but held office only long enough to bring back the Jesuits and preside over the adoption of a new constitution (1858) that was more explicitly federalist than the old one. In 1860 a Liberal revolt ousted Ospina and the victors carried their religious and political reforms to their extreme and logical conclusions. Not only the Jesuits but all other religious orders were suppressed, all convents and monasteries closed, and all church wealth was seized by the government and sold. The transfer of massive amounts of church land into private hands produced little or no change in the land tenure system; clerical latifundia simply became lay latifundia, contributing to a further concentration of landownership. The principal buyers were Liberal merchants, landowners, and politicians, but Conservatives also participated in the plunder of church land.

In 1863 Liberal political reform reached its climax when a new constitution changed the country's name to the United States of Colombia and carried the principle of federalism to great lengths. The nine sovereign states became, in effect, independent nations, each with its own armed forces, possessing all the legislative powers not explicitly granted to the central government, which was made as weak as possible.

The Liberals remained in power from 1863 to 1885 in a political climate that approximated institutionalized anarchy, as the central government was powerless to intervene against the local revolutions that toppled and set up state governments.

The economic movement and its quest for the export base that could firmly integrate Colombia into the capitalist world economy continued. By the 1870s tobacco exports were down sharply, but this decline was made up by exporting coffee, quinine, and other products. Coffee was emerging as the country's major export product, but its development lagged behind that of Brazil, which relied increasingly on European immigrant free labor. In Colombia coffee production in its principal centers of Santander and Cundinamarca, was based on traditional haciendas worked by peons and tenants who lived and labored under oppressive conditions. A more satisfactory situation existed in Antioquia and Caldas, characterized by a mix of haciendas with more enlightened forms of sharecropping and smallholdings, operations marked by high productivity. It was in these states that the twentieth-century takeoff of the Colombian coffee industry occurred.

The development of coffee as the major export, the growing ties between foreign and domestic merchants and coffee planters, and the stimulus given to trade and speculation by the expropriation of church lands created economic interests that required a new political model—a strong state capable of imposing order and creating the railroads and the financial infrastructure needed for the expansion of the coffee industry. The Liberal reform had removed many obstacles to capitalist development but had created others by its federalist excesses. By the early 1880s not only Conservatives but many moderate Liberals were convinced that political and social stability required making peace with the church and restoring its traditional role. The unlikely instrument for the creation of this new conservative, unitary order was the poet and intellectual Rafael Núñez, whom his party elected president in 1879.

Rafael Núñez, the "Regeneration," and the War of a Thousand Days, 1880–1903

Núñez began political life as a radical Liberal and had spent thirteen years in the consular service in Europe. His studies and observations of political and social trends in Europe convinced him that Colombia needed a conservative restoration. He returned home in 1875, and was elected president in 1879, governing with a coalition of right-leaning elements from both the Liberal and Conservative parties. Elected again, in 1884, he swiftly crushed a radical Liberal revolt and announced that the 1863 constitution had "ceased to exist." In 1886 he presented the country with a new constitution that replaced the sovereign states with departments headed by governors appointed by the president, extended the presidential term to six years, established literacy and property qualifications for voting for representatives, and provided for indirect election of senators. Under that constitution, personally or through surrogates, Núñez ruled Colombia until his death in 1894.

Like the religious skeptic Bolívar, Núñez believed the authority of religion and the church was the foundation of the social order and must be fully supported by the state. The 1886 constitution made Catholicism the official religion and entrusted education to the clergy. A concordat signed with the Holy See provided that education on all levels must be organized in conformity with Catholic doctrine and gave the clergy the right to inspect and approve all textbooks.

The other foundations of Núñez's authoritarian republic were a strong standing army and a national police force. The Liberal regimes had virtually dismantled the regular army; the revolts and civil wars of the federal period had been fought by private armies formed by the great landowners with their tenants and peons. The existence of these regional private armies and militias was incompatible with Núñez's unitary project. The 1886 constitution created a permanent army and reserved to the central government the right to possess arms and ammunition. The national police, organized in 1891, kept under vigilance political suspects and disrupted most plots against the government.

Núñez is credited with two major economic innovations. Claiming that the Liberal policy of free trade or low tariffs was the cause of economic decadence and poverty, which had caused the civil war, he proposed to use tariff protection to stimulate the growth of certain industries. He believed that this would create a new middle class that would form a buffer between the governing social class and the unlettered multitude. But his implementation of this program was timid and inconsistent, since import duties were the state's principal source of income, and the new policy, opposed by merchants and landowners, was actively supported only by the politically powerless artisans. The new policy succeeded, however, in providing a modest level of protection for domestic industry.

Núñez's other innovation was the creation in 1881 of a National Bank designed to relieve the financial distress of a government always on the verge of bankruptcy. The bank had the exclusive right to issue money; this monopoly enabled the state to provide for its needs and was managed prudently until 1890. Then its uncontrolled emissions of paper money caused a galloping inflation. The expensive civil war of 1899 provoked the emission of paper money on such a scale that the printers could not keep up with the demand, and the country was flooded with millions of pesos of depreciated currency.

The "Regeneration," as the Núñez era is known, represented an effort to achieve national unification from above, under reactionary auspices; it has been compared with Bismarck's project for German national unification, a com-

504

pound of feudal and capitalist elements. Under Núñez the conditions for the rise of a modern, capitalist state began. An important step in this direction was his creation of a permanent army and the assumption of a monopoly of the use of force by the state. His removal of internal barriers to trade and his policy of tariff protection, however modest, contributed to the formation of an internal market; his national bank, despite its later scandalous mismanagement, represented an initial effort to create a national system of credit; and he gave impulse to the construction of internal improvements, especially railroads. These policies, combined with the coffee boom, contributed to a growth of capitalism in Colombia. But other policies had profoundly negative effects. By entrusting control of education and civil society to the church Núñez created an environment inimical to technical and scientific progress and strengthened the hold of clericalism over the peasant masses and their subjection to the great landowners. His muzzling of the press and exiling of political and ideological dissidents contrasted sharply with the lively debate and intellectual ferment that prevailed under earlier Liberal and Conservative administrations. His efforts to create a permanent control of Colombian politics by a coalition of reactionary elements from both major parties represented an ominous precedent for later efforts.

When he died in 1894, Núñez's leadership was assumed by Conservative politicians who lacked his intelligence and iron will. Their corruption, flagrant rigging of elections, and division over freedom of the press and electoral reform collided with Liberal anger at their long exclusion from power and an economic slump caused by a sharp decline of coffee prices. The result was a political crisis followed by a resort to arms. Confident of victory over a thoroughly unpopular government, the Liberals launched a revolt in 1899 that ushered in the disastrous War of a Thousand Days. It raged for three years, caused an estimated loss of 100,000 lives, and immense material damage, but ended in a government victory.

Colombia in the Twentieth Century

The Conservative Republic, 1903–1930

The War of a Thousand Days and the loss of Panama dealt a profound psychological shock to Colombians. At the war's end both parties asked the government to reform the political system. The Conservative government disregarded these appeals. New elections, attended by the customary frauds, gave victory to the Conservative General Rafael Reyes (1904–1909), and produced a Congress in which the Liberals had only two seats. But Reyes proved more conciliatory than the party traditionalists, invited Liberals to join his cabinet, and proposed reforms. When Congress balked at his reforms, Reyes dissolved it and established his personal dictatorship, ruling by decree through a puppet national assembly in which one-third of the seats were occupied by Liberals. Despite his dictatorial methods, Reyes's policies of enforcing peace and order, construction of railroads and highways, encouragement of export agriculture, and protection and subsidies for industry initially attracted much elite support.

Reyes's downfall came when he attempted to conclude a treaty with the United States under which Colombia was to receive an indemnity of $2,500,000 in return for its recognition of Panama's independence. Colombia's governing class, aware of the growing importance of the North American market for its coffee and hopeful of attracting North American capital, accepted the new relations. But the wound of Panama was still too fresh, and news of the treaty aroused a public fury of which Reyes's enemies took advantage to force his resignation.

Both parties now organized a constituent assembly to reform the constitution of 1886. The problem for Conservatives was how to create more political space for the Liberals without jeopardizing the supremacy they had just consolidated in the War of a Thousand Days. The reforms included weakening the executive, increasing the powers of Congress, and ensuring minority representation in elective bodies. Other changes included direct election of the president, establishment of elected departmental assemblies, and abolition of the death penalty. These reforms left intact, however, property and literacy qualifications for voting that excluded 90 percent of the adult male population from the suffrage, and the privileged position of the church as the state church.

Although the constitutional reforms made the total hegemony of one party more difficult, control of the electoral process remained in government hands. The constitutional changes also left intact the *gamonal* system under which landowners, public officials, and priests exerted influence on rural voters, and that usually favored the Conservatives.

The characteristic blandness of Colombian politics between 1910 and 1930 contrasted sharply with the sometimes stormy developments in economic and social life. These developments, reflecting the rapid overall growth of Colombian capitalism, included the upsurge of coffee exports, centered in Antioquia, with its system of free labor; the accumulation of capital and its transfer from commerce to industry, with the formation of many new companies; a partial shift from the old semiservile forms of rural labor to free, capitalist wage labor, accompanied by a wave of strikes, land invasions, and clashes between landowners and peasants; and the emergence in cities and plantation areas of the first true trade union movements, left-wing parties, and struggles between workers and employers.

In this period U.S. capital began to flow into Colombia, facilitated by the 1914 treaty by which the United States paid Colombia for its loss of Panama. One of the first U.S. firms to enter modern Colombia was the United Fruit Company, which in the early 1900s began to cultivate bananas in the tropical Santa Marta zone. Direct loans to the Colombian government formed the bulk of North American investments in Colombia. The "dance of the millions" began in 1921–1922 and was fueled initially by the first installment of

a $25 million U.S. indemnity. Between 1922 and 1928 the U.S. government and private investors poured $280 million into Colombia, most of which was expended for a vast, chaotic program of public construction. The boom, luring workers from agriculture into the cities, reduced food production and raised living costs, leaving workers worse off than before.

The golden shower ended in 1929 with the New York stock market crash and the start of a great depression that soon spread to Colombia. Growing unemployment, food shortages, and the government's severe fiscal problems completed the discredit of a regime weakened by political scandals, public outrage over a massacre of banana workers in the tropical Santa Marta zone by government troops, and its own internal divisions. Alarmed by an upsurge of peasant and worker unrest, urban strikes, land invasions by peasants organized in leagues and unions,[1] and the rise of new radical ideologies moderate Conservatives decided the best hope for avoiding revolutions was to support the candidacy of the moderate Liberal Enrique Olaya Herrera, a man of their own kind, close to the oligarchs of both parties, in the election of February 1930. Olaya's election ended almost half a century of Conservative rule but ushered in no major changes; his government was one of transition to an era of sweeping reform still to come.

The New Liberalism: "The Revolution on the March," 1934–1946

Olaya's term was spent waiting for the Depression to end and the infusions of United States loans and investments to resume. His failure to respond to popular expectations for change caused growing tension. In departments where the problem of latifundismo and landlessness

[1] The land invasions were spurred by a 1926 Supreme Court ruling that the only proof of ownership was the original title stating the government had ceded title to the land. Many peasants knew that the estates on which they worked had no such titles and had been formed through illegal acquisition of public lands.

506 was particularly severe, such as Cundinamarca, Tolima, and Cauca, clashes between peasants and landowners and police were frequent. The 1934 election occurred against this troubled background. The divided and demoralized Conservatives abstained from putting up a candidate, and the left-wing Liberal Alfonso López won. He promptly announced a program called *La Revolución en Marcha* (The Revolution on the March). In 1936 he obtained the congressional majority needed to implement his policies.

López and other Liberal reformers knew that social justice and national economic interest required land reform. The advance of Colombian capitalism was blocked by the backwardness of agriculture, especially the food-producing sector, which could not even provide enough food for the growing urban population. The 1936 agrarian reform law provided for reversion to the state of lands not rationally exploited by their owners but gave the latifundists ten years to make the transition to efficient land exploitation based on wage labor. The lengthy grace period and the hostility of the Conservative administrations that succeeded López to land reform assured that reversion and redistribution of land rarely took place. The law also prohibited payment of rent in labor or in kind; this had the effect of speeding up the spread of wage labor and the rise of a land market. The law annulled the 1926 Supreme Court decision and thus confirmed the property titles of the great landowners, but it also gave peasants "squatters' rights" on unused public and private lands that they had improved. The eviction of squatters thus became more difficult and dropped sharply.

Other legislation adopted during López's administration defined the rights of labor. To implement these rights Congress passed a law that established a minimum wage and paid vacations and holidays, forbade the use of strikebreakers, set up the eight-hour day and the forty-eight-hour week, and created a special tribunal to provide arbitration in labor disputes. With López's support, the number of organized workers quadrupled between 1935 and 1947. Equally important

was the formation in 1936 of the Colombian Confederation of Labor (CTC), headed by syndicalists, Communists, and liberals.

One of the most revolutionary innovations of the López reform era was a new progressive tax law. Before 1936 tax laws had been ineffectually enforced. The new tax law, effectively enforced, almost doubled the state's revenue-raising capacity.

Despite the moderate character of the reforms, they came under bitter attack from all reactionary elements, and López began to retreat. He announced in December 1936 a "pause" in reform. This "pause" was accentuated by López's successor, the moderate Liberal Eduardo Santos (1938–1942), editor of the influential journal *El Tiempo.* Santos had been chosen by the Liberal nominating convention in 1937 against López's wishes. Santos's selection created a bitter division within the Liberal ranks between moderates and reformers. In office, Santos failed to implement many of the López reforms. López responded by founding his own newspaper, *El Liberal,* in which he assailed Santos's conservative views and announced his intention of resuming the presidency in 1942.

These Liberal divisions infused new life into the demoralized Conservative party, now under the direction of the right-wing ideologue and admirer of Hitler, Mussolini, and Franco, Laureano Gómez, who fanned the flames of Liberal discord. If López returned to power, Gómez announced, he would personally lead an armed revolution against him.

López won the Liberal nomination for president and easily defeated a candidate of the moderate Liberal faction, but Lopez's second term brought his Revolution on the March to an inglorious close. He began with immense popular support but faced a hostile legislature in which moderate Liberals banded together with Conservatives to defeat his proposals. The world was at war, and Colombia felt the impact in shortages, loss of its coffee markets, and growing unemployment. Meanwhile Laureano Gómez's mouthpiece, *El Siglo,* poured a steady stream of vituperative attacks on López. Behind Gómez was an array of reactionary forces, including great landowners, the church hierarchy, and industrialists angered by López's concessions to labor, who sought a counterrevolutionary *Reconquista*.

In 1943, weary and discouraged, with one year of his term remaining, López resigned. Congress appointed Alberto Lleras Camargo to head a one-year interim government. He ruled with a coalition cabinet composed of moderate Liberals and Conservatives.

With López's departure the leadership of the Liberal party's left wing passed to Jorge Eliécer Gaitán, who had held various political posts. As mayor of Bogotá, he had been regarded as the best the capital ever had.

Conservatives and many moderate Liberals denounced Gaitán as a demogogue. He was in fact a magnetic speaker of burning sincerity, capable of presenting his economic and social ideas to audiences of peasants and workers in a clear way, but there was nothing exotic or extravagant about those ideas. Although he used socialist terminology, the essence of Gaitán's program was the need for state intervention in the economy in order to democratize capitalism, control the great private monopolies, and ensure that peasants owned the land they cultivated. In 1945 he proposed limiting landownership to a maximum of 1,000 hectares and suggested a minimum size of four hectares for landholdings to avoid the low productivity of minifundios.

As the 1946 elections approached, party leaders met to decide on their strategy and candidates. The Liberal nominating convention, with moderates in firm control, nominated Gabriel Turbay, a wealthy, conservative follower of Santos. Angered by the rejection of their champion, the party's left wing advanced Gaitán. In view of the split in the Liberal party, it was widely believed that the Conservatives would not field a candidate of their own, but would throw their support to Turbay. Instead, the party convention chose Mariano Ospina Pérez as its nominee. With only 42 percent of the vote, Ospina was elected

president. The Conservative reconquest of power had begun.

Counterrevolution on the March, 1946–1958

After his inauguration, in a conciliatory gesture to the Liberal party, Ospina Pérez invited six Liberals into his cabinet, thus establishing parity in the twelve ministries and implementing his campaign promise to form a National Union government. He made no effort to consult Gaitán. The snubbing of Gaitán suggests a design on the part of Ospina Pérez to isolate him politically, deepen the rift between Liberal moderates and reformists, and form a bipartisan coalition of conservative elements to barricade against Gaitán's program of radical social and economic change. It was, in fact, a Liberal congressional majority that had defeated Gaitán's legislative program, including steps to implement López's agrarian reform and establish a State Planning Commission to improve conditions for the peasants and workers. These defeats for Gaitán and his reform program occurred during a time of worsening economic conditions. High inflation, static wages, and growing unemployment in the postwar period added to the anger and frustration of workers as they saw their hopes for change crushed by what they perceived as a conspiracy of the "double oligarchy"—Liberal and Conservative— that controlled the government.

The Conservative leadership in 1946 presented two faces. Ospina Pérez represented its conciliatory aspect, the desire for a peaceful coexistence of the two traditional parties and their collaboration in a National Union government of sound conservative views. But this aspect was contradicted by the supreme chief of the Conservative party, Laureano Gómez. Gómez, soon to be appointed Ospina's foreign minister, emerged as the new government's Gray Eminence, the power behind the throne and made no effort to conceal his scorn for the National Union policy.

Gómez quickly had the Liberal general who commanded the national police force dismissed, and then followed with a wholesale purge of Liberal police officers, who were replaced by officers known for their fanatical conservatism. The pace of events quickened in 1947. In an evident effort to gain the advantage in the March congressional elections armed bands organized by Conservative landowners and officials began to attack and persecute Liberals in many rural areas. The outcome of the elections, however, was a clear victory for the Liberals; equally significant was the predominance of radicals over moderates on the Liberal slate. Claiming the need to restore law and order, Ospina organized a new security force, the *policía política,* or political police, that soon became an extension of the Conservative party and an additional instrument of terror against Liberals; it was widely known as the "creole Gestapo." Beatings, killings, and outrages of every kind spread throughout the countryside provoking a growing polarization and armed responses by the Liberal peasantry, middle class, and landowners.

As 1948 opened the violence in some areas began to assume the proportions of a civil war, with battles taking place between Conservative and Liberal towns. The church, with its immense power, also instigated violence and persecution of Liberals. Some rural churches were decorated with portraits of Laureano Gómez and copies of his speech against the supposed "Liberal fraud." In March the Liberal convention called on party members to resign from every public office under the Conservative administration. The Conservatives rejoiced; one of their journals exulted: "At last we are alone."

In an atmosphere of growing tension the government prepared to host the Ninth Inter-American Conference in April. Although efforts were made to clean up the city, to banish beggars, vagrants, and street vendors, the government could not dispel the uneasiness caused by the continual arrival of peasants and other political refugees fleeing the violence in the countryside.

On April 9, 1948, as Gaitán was on his way to lunch, he was approached by a stranger who fired four bullets into him. Mortally wounded, Gaitán collapsed on the sidewalk. The man regarded by the masses as the sole hope for their liberation, generally expected to run and win the election for president in 1950, died the same day he was shot. The assassin was an obscure figure with a history of mental trouble.

Gaitán's murder was the signal for a formidable popular insurrection that tore Bogotá apart and spread to the provinces before it was put down by the army at the cost of thousands of lives. The spontaneous rising of the masses, accompanied by peasant expropriation of haciendas, establishment of revolutionary committees and workers' control over foreign-owned oil installations, and other radical measures, frightened Conservative and Liberal elites. Liberal leaders, faced with the choice of joining the insurrection or accepting Ospina's offer to reconstitute a National Union coalition, chose the latter. In the Liberal party, the dominant influence now shifted from the Gaitán to the Santos, or moderate, wing.

During 1949 the coalition government began to come apart as the official and unofficial violence in the countryside, directed above all at Liberals of all classes, continued and widened; it had become a persistent, widespread phenomenon generically called *la Violencia.* In May, after Ospina fired several Liberal governors from departmental posts and the repressive activity of rural police forces increased, Liberal leader Carlos Lleras Restrepo announced the irrevocable end of his party's collaboration with the Ospina government. In June a crucial election again gave victory to the Liberals on the municipal, departmental, and congressional levels. That month Laureano Gómez, Conservative candidate for president, returned from Spain to greet the assembled Conservatives with the Fascist salute and announce that it was "incumbent upon the Conservative party to save the republic."

As the presidential election drew nearer, the threatening, repressive atmosphere visibly deepened. In the countryside goon squads, backed by the military, compelled Liberal peasants to turn in their voting cards and register as Conservatives. In some areas landowners took revenge for the land invasions of the 1930s, using hired thugs to kill or expel peasant occupants. In this stage of the Violencia, however, the conflict had primarily a political character and was based on the peasants' loyalty to political bosses on each side. Ospina, discarding his previous conciliatory manner, began to use the army and the security forces to harass Liberals. Finally, in response to a move by the Liberal congressional majority to impeach him, Ospina issued a series of decrees providing for a state of siege, the dissolution of Congress and all departmental legislatures and municipal councils, the grant of extraordinary powers for the governors, and national censorship of the press and radio.

In the face of these dictatorial measures the Liberals caved in completely, withdrawing their presidential candidate and leaving the field to Laureano Gómez, who received all but 14 of the 1,140,034 votes supposedly cast. He was inaugurated as president in August 1950.

Ideologically, the Gómez regime (1950–1953) appears "feudal" in its effort to restore the intellectual atmosphere of sixteenth-century Spain. In its economic policies, however, the regime showed itself quite favorable to modern corporate capitalism. In the spirit of economic liberalism, all import and export restrictions were removed and foreign investment was encouraged in all possible ways. Riding a wave of prosperity based on a doubling of exports between 1949 and 1953, coffee growers and other elite groups made large gains, reflected in the rapid increase in such indices as capital formation and bank deposits. For labor, however, it was the worst of times. Wages lagged behind prices, and the state regularly intervened in labor struggles in favor of employers, permitting the use of strikebreakers and blacklists and annulling the López law that barred parallel unions. This made it possible for employers to form so-called confessional or church-dominated unions that were in effect company unions.

In foreign policy Gómez made a complete volte-face from his shrill denunciations of the United States during World War II. He now proclaimed his friendship for the United States, praised its involvement in the Korean war, and "gave Colombia the dubious honor of having been the only Latin American country to have veterans of the Korean war" by sending a battalion of 3,200 men to participate in that struggle. The United States in turn saw Gómez as a worthy ally in the anti-Communist struggle and gave him its full support.

In the Colombian countryside, meanwhile, the Violencia gained in intensity and expanded into new regions. But the conflict now increasingly assumed the nature of a class struggle as peasants resisted the efforts of landowners and their hired thugs to eject them from their parcels and Communist party activists as well as peasant leaders loyal to the Liberal party became active in organizing strongholds of self-defense among uprooted peasants. Thus the period between 1949 and 1953, in addition to a growth of landowner and official terrorism and banditry, saw the rise of an extensive, well-organized resistance in guerrilla zones inhabited by peasants and other fugitives from regions marked by anarchy or terror. Some of these zones had an elaborate political, economic, and social organization. The most stable and successful zones were areas with productive structures that could support large contingents of men for relatively long periods. One such zone was the eastern Llanos, with its cattle wealth and a soil that yielded quick food crops. These guerrilla enclaves may have held 20,000 armed men, of whom about half were based in the Llanos. Each zone had its own commander or commanders, some of whom soon became legends.

The failure of the Conservative dictatorship to achieve a military solution to the guerrilla problem contributed to its gradual weakening and eventual collapse. In late 1951 a heart attack forced President Gómez to retire and name Roberto Urdaneta Arbeláez, his minister of war, who had directed the struggle against the so-called bandits, as acting president. The illness of the old lion brought to the surface all the contradictions and clashing personal ambitions within the ruling party.

Two other developments caused growing disarray in the Conservative camp and discredited the regime at home and abroad. In September, after a ceremony in Bogotá honoring five policemen who had been killed by bandits in Tolima, a mob, shouting "down with the Liberals, down with the assassins," gutted and set fire to the offices of the Liberal journals *El Tiempo* and *El Espectador,* did the same to the offices of the Liberal party headquarters, and went on to destroy the homes of the Liberal leaders Alfonso López and Carlos Lleras Restrepo. The Liberal party closed its offices and suspended operations. These outrages upset many Conservatives, who joined the Liberals in protests to the government.

Many members of both parties found equally disturbing a project of Gómez to give Colombia a new reactionary corporate constitution that would ensure the indefinite extension of Conservative rule. This project, clearly influenced by the Falangist ideology and political system of Franco's Spain, widened the breach between the Gómez group and more traditional Conservatives of the Ospina type. Thus a series of factors led to Gómez's isolation and created conditions for a "Bonapartist" solution for the developing political crisis. General Gustavo Rojas Pinilla, who formed part of an officer group sympathetic to the Ospina faction, became the instrument of the coup d'état. A countermove by Gómez to arrest Rojas backfired; the old caudillo was placed under arrest and sent into exile. Amid general rejoicing, on June 13, 1953 the national radio announced that Rojas Pinilla had assumed the presidency with the support of the armed forces and representatives of both parties.

Rojas Pinilla assumed power on June 13 1953 in a social and political crisis: a reign of terror prevailed over a large area, and the peasant insurgency dominated another extensive area. Thus his slogan of "Peace, Justice, Liberty" evoked a warm response among the population. One of his first initiatives was to proclaim an unconditional amnesty to all guerrillas who would return to civilian life. Several thousand accepted the amnesty, surrendered their weapons, and returned to their old homes, but the leaders of

some guerrilla fronts, especially the Communist leadership in southern Tolima and the Sumapaz region of southern Cundinamarca, distrusted Rojas Pinilla's sincerity, recalled his role as army commander in a famous massacre of Liberals in Cali in 1949, and warned their comrades not to "believe the false promises of propaganda thrown from planes of the dictatorship." These guerrilla fronts preferred to maintain an armed truce and await further developments.

Events proved the skeptics right. The honeymoon between Rojas Pinilla and the elites and the nation as a whole began to wane as it became evident that instead of restoring the traditional political arrangements he was moving toward the establishment of a personal dictatorship with some populist features, not unlike Argentina's Peronist system. One of his reformist measures was giving women the vote in 1954.

Despite some reforms, the essence of Rojas Pinilla's policies was reactionary. One sign of this was the revival of the Violencia as the president gave a free hand to notorious *pájaros* (hired assassins), Conservative vigilante gangs, and army-police forces to wreak vengeance on veterans of the guerrilla war who had accepted amnesty. As a result many former guerrillas left their farms and rejoined the surviving guerrilla fronts. In April 1955, after a hundred guerrillas nearly wiped out an army infantry company, Rojas Pinilla declared Sumapaz, embracing portions of Tolima and Cundinamarca, a "war zone" and prepared a major offensive, using jet fighters, bombers, and tanks.

The renewal of the civil war combined with other repressive measures and with the effects of a deepening depression to unify all elite elements against Rojas Pinilla. In July 1956 the Liberal leader Alberto Lleras Camargo met Conservative Laureano Gómez in the little Spanish town of Benidorm and signed a pact to form a coalition of their parties for joint action in the "reestablishment of liberty and constitutional guarantees." On May 7 1957 a commercial strike, supported by the middle classes, entrepreneurial class, and the student movement, was followed by a denunciation of the dictatorship by Cardinal

Luque, who condemned the regime for "murder" and "sacrilegious profanation" of churches. The next day Rojas Pinilla's military colleagues prevailed on him to resign and power passed to a five-man caretaker military junta.

In July 1957 Lleras Camargo and Laureano Gómez again met and signed an agreement creating a National Front coalition, which in effect provided for a monopoly of shared power for sixteen years by the two parties. There would be parity in legislative positions on both national and local levels and alternation of the presidency between the two parties. A plebiscite held on December 1, with all citizens of twenty-one or over eligible to vote, approved the agreement. In March 1958 congressional elections were held and the Liberals outpolled the Conservatives by 58 to 42 percent; Lleras Camargo was elected president in May and inaugurated in August, with the oath of office given by Laureano Gómez, "rehabilitated" and transformed overnight from a right-wing fanatic who had lit the fires of civil war into a sturdy apostle of democracy. The Colombian experiment in bipartisan rule and "controlled democracy" had begun.

The National Front: Reform and Repression, 1958–1974

The constitutional pact creating the Colombian National Front in 1958 bears an obvious resemblance to the pact signed between Venezuela's centrist parties the same year. In both cases the intent was the same: to prevent interparty rivalry from reaching a level of conflict that might create situations—like the Violencia and the Rojas Pinilla dictatorship in Colombia or the Pérez Jiménez dictatorship in Venezuela—that the dominant elites could not control and to marginalize or isolate political movements that might pose such threats. Both may therefore be called variants of a type of representative democracy that has been called "controlled democracy" or, more correctly, "restricted democracy." The Colombian power-sharing pact, providing for a monopoly of political power (and a corresponding division of political spoils) for the Conservative and

Liberal parties, excluded existing parties like the Communist and the Christian Democratic or new parties that might be formed later. Thus the electorate was denied the opportunity to reject the policies of the National Front coalition or exercise its sovereign right to change the government. The relative absence of issues between the parties promoted voter apathy and alienation, reflected in low turnout rates; participation in congressional elections fell from a high of 68.9 in 1958 to a low of 36.4 percent in 1972.

The rules of the political game established by the National Front, designed to prevent the hegemony of either party, tended to immobilize its governments. Their social policies reflected their fundamentally conservative orientation and did nothing to alter the great inequalities in income distribution. Although the unions gained legal recognition, the government repeatedly intervened in labor conflicts on the employers' side.

In 1958 President Lleras Camargo issued an amnesty—to expire in 1959—for all guerrillas who would return to peaceful life. The establishment of the National Front coalition is usually regarded as marking the end—or at least the beginning of the end—of the Violencia, a conflict estimated to have taken between 200,000 and 300,000 lives. Between 1958 and 1965 the army and police hunted down the remaining outlaw bands. But the continued existence of the latifundio, an estimated one million landless peasants, and landowner and official repression of land-hungry peasants continued and continues to generate violence in the Colombian countryside.

In 1961, evidently fearing that failure to act might produce a Cuban-style revolution, Congress adopted an agrarian reform law. Inaugurated with much fanfare, the law vested apparently limitless power to expropriate and redistribute inefficiently exploited land in a new state agency (INCORA). In Tolima, the site of the first program, only 1,115 out of 90,000 landless agricultural workers had received titles to land by 1969. Although 4.2 percent of the landowners in Tolima possessed 57.7 percent of the farmland in the department, only 4.5 percent of INCORA's acquisitions came through the expropriation or purchase of large holdings; the rest, points out James Henderson, "was acquired from *baldio* [unsettled] lands that no one else wanted. Such tracts were either too far removed from transportation routes to be desirable or were of such poor quality as to be of dubious value to farmers."

This innocuous agrarian reform coincided with the launching of a large-scale military effort to destroy the guerrilla zones established under Communist party leadership in eastern and southern Tolima. Like the agrarian law, this offensive seems to have been inspired by the anticommunist strategy of the Kennedy administration's Alliance for Progress, a program combining reform and repression. The success of this and many other later offensives can be gauged by the fact that twenty years later the few guerrilla bases had grown into a network of thirty guerrilla fronts in the Colombian backcountry, with their own military organization, the Communist-led Revolutionary Armed Forces of Colombia (FARC). In addition to the FARC, the largest of the guerrilla groups, created in 1966, whose membership and leadership were primarily peasant, the 1960s and 1970s saw the emergence of other revolutionary organizations, such as the National Liberation Army (ELN), inspired by the Cuban example, and the April 19 Movement (M-19), both largely composed of radical students and other urban elements.

In summary, the National Front's political, economic, and social policies produced basically negative results. Its economic policies successfully promoted the accumulation of foreign and domestic capital, but neglected the interests of workers and peasants, whose living standards sharply declined. In 1964, 25 percent of the total labor force, 24.6 percent of the urban labor force, and 25.4 percent of the rural labor force lived below the absolute poverty line. By 1973 those percentages had risen to 50.7 percent, 43.4 percent, and 67.5 percent. Clearly, instead of contributing to the solution of grave socioeconomic problems, the sixteen years of National Front rule sharpened them.

Drug Lords, Guerrillas, and the Quest for Peace, 1974–1991

The end of the National Front period ushered in a general crisis of Colombian society that it is still struggling to overcome.

Beginning with the 1974 elections, Colombia returned to the political system of electoral competition, except for vestiges of the power-sharing system. Article 120 of the constitution extended bureaucratic parity for the presidential term of 1974 to 1978 and declared that after that term the president had to offer "adequate and equitable" participation in his government to the largest party other than his own. The vagueness of the words "adequate and equitable" allowed the president to determine precisely how many cabinet posts and other patronage-controlling positions the minority party should receive. Despite the renewal of competition, the political system remained a restricted, oligarchical democracy designed to limit the level of conflict between elites and to "keep the masses in their place," with a system of electoral mobilization based on machine politics and payoffs, known as *clientelismo.*

In addition to their loss of credibility, post–National Front governments faced economic problems of unprecedented proportions. The quadrupling of oil prices in 1974, coming at a time when Colombia ceased to be self-sufficient in oil production, dealt a very heavy shock to the economy. Against the background of a general world recession, Colombian industry, which had been the motor of the economy since 1945, experienced a decline reflected in the loss of foreign and domestic markets and employment. One cause was the technological backwardness of key sectors of Colombian industry; another was a "neoliberal" low tariff policy pursued by post–National Front governments. Other negative economic factors were lower prices for coffee and the burden of servicing a foreign debt that reached $9.4 billion in 1982—still small by contrast with the foreign debts of other major Latin American countries. By 1982 Colombia had not only severe inflation but its worst recession in fifty years.

In this time of economic gloom, some relief came from an unexpected quarter: the drug traffic with the United States. Until recently that traffic was negligible, mostly confined to the export of marihuana. It began to mushroom in the 1970s, most likely as a result of antidrug campaigns in Turkey and the Middle East. Skyrocketing prices as a result of effective antidrug efforts and high transportation costs forced the international drug cartels to seek closer sources of supply for the U.S. market. Colombia, with its access to both U.S. coasts, and cocaine, lower in price than heroin or opium, and easier to carry in short plane trips to the Florida coast, provided a solution. An efficient distribution system made the new drug available to the ever-swelling U.S. market. A division of labor and profits emerged between the Colombian producers and exporters, centered in Medellín and Cali, and North American domestic wholesalers, bankers, and money launderers. Contrary to a common misconception, Colombia is not a large grower of coca but processes the substance that comes from Peru, Bolivia, Ecuador, and Brazil. By the mid-1980s, with cocaine prices dropping, a new product—crack—known as *bazuco* in Colombia and packaged in small quantities costing only a fraction of cocaine powder, created a large new class of consumers.

Colombia's Medellín and Cali cartels, it is estimated, make $4 to $6 billion annually in cocaine traffic. Of this amount, according to the economist Salomón Kalmanovitz, between $1 and $1.5 billion enters the Colombian black market. Without this "cushion" for the country's balance of payments, he suggests, an exchange crisis would have broken out in 1983 or 1984 at the latest. This contribution of Colombian narco-capitalism to the country's financial stability and the close ties established between the drug lords and landowners, businessmen, government officials, and members of the police and the armed forces help to explain the singular immunity that the drug mafias enjoyed until recently.

This situation changed as a result of two developments. One was increased U.S. pressure on the government of Liberal President Virgilio Barco (1986–1990) to wage a more effective war on drug trafficking. This pressure was accompanied by the offer of financial aid that was difficult to refuse.

The second reason was a growing concern on the part of sectors of the elite that the drug traffickers had gotten out of control and their violence was threatening the monopoly of power the elite had enjoyed since Colombia achieved independence from Spain. For years death squads (the government acknowledged the existence of 149 paramilitary groups) recruited and trained by the drug mafia, in alliance with the police and the armed forces, had murdered, with complete impunity, thousands of trade union and peasant union leaders, left-wing activists, judges, and others who opposed their activities or sought to make Colombia a functioning democracy.

In the course of 1989, however, the mafia went too far and began killing prominent members of the elite who were their known enemies. The victims included the governor of Antioquia, the country's attorney general, Medellín's police chief, and, on August 18, Liberal party senator and presidential candidate Luis Carlos Galán. The murder of the popular Galán, identified with the reformist wing of his party, shocked the Bogotanos. Tens of thousands marched through the streets on the day of his funeral, shouting "Death to the drug traffickers."

Within hours after Galán's death the Barco government had already ordered the searches and seizures of dozens of mansions, hundreds of cars, and more than a hundred airplanes and helicopters claimed to belong to the drug traffickers. A few days later Barco ordered the confiscation of a chain of drugstores and other businesses belonging to the drug cartels. To give these confiscations a firm legal basis Barco issued a decree making "illicit enrichment" a crime punishable by five to ten years in prison. He also reinstated, by decree, the extradition of drug traffickers to the United States—declared unconstitutional by the Colombian Supreme Court in 1987

Luis Carlos Galán, shown here, was a popular political figure and presidential candidate when he was murdered by the Colombian drug mafia in 1989. His death fueled a massive government response against the drug cartels. (El Espectador/Sygma)

and opposed by many Colombians as a surrender of the state's autonomy and an admission of the impotence of its judicial system.

The drug lords promptly responded to Barco's offensive. *Los Extraditables,* as they called themselves, issued a communiqué announcing total war on Barco's government and all their other foes and promising that their retaliation would include the destruction of the elite's estates, homes, and businesses. In December a leading Medellín drug lord, José González Rodriguez Gacha, his son, and some followers were killed in a clash with security forces. As 1989 drew to a close the drug war heated up, with a string of se-

lective killings of judges, trade union leaders, and other foes of the drug mafia, leading observers to conclude that the government's offensive against the cartels had only made a temporary impact and that the basic structure of the paramilitary groups remained intact. Support for a negotiated solution began to grow in some political quarters.

There is reason to believe, in fact, that without major social and economic reforms in Latin America, the principal supplier of cocaine, and in the United States, its principal consumer, the drug wars cannot be won. Without new policies that provide Latin American peasants with a viable alternative to growing coca as a cash crop, its cultivation will continue, no matter how many fields are burned or sprayed with defoliants. If the laboratories that process the coca are destroyed in one part of the region, they will be moved to another. In both the United States and Latin America, where the cocaine epidemic is growing dangerously, its principal social roots are mass poverty, despair, and frustration. Neither the supply side nor the demand side of the problem, in the last analysis, can be solved by military means alone.

The Colombian war against the cartels coincided with the first serious effort to end the thirty-year-old guerrilla war by peaceful means. The fact that the peace process was initiated by a Conservative president reflects a growing awareness on the part of sections of the elite as well as the middle classes, workers, and peasants that the war could not be won by either side, that the atmosphere of senseless violence it had created posed an insuperable obstacle to economic and social progress.

The drug and guerrilla problems were indissolubly linked, for it had long been common knowledge that there exists a network linking government agencies, elements of the armed forces and police, landowners, industrialists, and the drug lords. The primary target of this alliance is Colombia's left-wing movement, the guerrillas first but also trade unions, peasant unions, and the opposition parties.

It is significant that Barco's offensive against the drug traffickers was not accompanied by any sanctions against the military, which had been charged in judicial investigations with acts of torture, disappearances, and executions. Under these conditions, it should cause no surprise that the guerrillas objected to surrendering their arms and disbanding their forces before they had evidence of a change in the attitude and conduct of the military and security forces.

In 1984, after the forced resignation of Defense Minister Fernando Landazábal Reyes, who had strenuously opposed a cease-fire with the guerrillas, Conservative President Belisario Betancur (1982–1986) negotiated a series of historic truce agreements with three of the four major guerrilla movements that did not require them to surrender their arms. The accord with the FARC, the largest of the insurgent groups, stipulated that the government would recommend to Congress adoption of an agrarian reform, legislation for improvements in public health, education, and housing, and a law permitting local elections of mayors and city councils in order to broaden popular participation in government, but only legislation permitting local elections was passed by Congress. Despite a boycott of the agreements by the armed forces, which repeatedly attacked guerrilla zones, and the refusal of some smaller guerrilla groups to negotiate a truce, the peace process somehow survived. Barco, Betancur's successor, had little sympathy for the peace project, which came under greater strain as military attacks on the guerrillas and death squad killings multiplied.

In 1985 the FARC decided to form a political movement called the Patriotic Union (UP), a coalition of leftist parties including the Communist party and the Workers Socialist party, and announced it would participate in the 1986 elections. In those elections the UP received over 400,000 votes, won 14 seats in Congress and representatives on 187 city councils, often in coalitions with Conservative and Liberal leaders. It had become a major political force in Colombia, but at a fearful price; over 1,000 of its members, including its first presidential candidate, Jaime Pardo León, have been killed by death squads. Its presidential candidate in the 1990 election, Bernardo Jaramillo, was gunned down in Bogotá's international airport on March 22. Carlos Pizarro, the candidate of a party formed by the small guerrilla movement M-19 after it had signed a peace pact with the government and surrendered its weapons, was murdered one month later. The elaborate precautions taken by the Liberal party candidate and winner of the May presidential election, César Gaviria—in public appearances he was accompanied by hundreds of bodyguards and a physician carrying several pints of blood, and he always wore a bulletproof vest—tell much about the political and social climate of contemporary Colombia. The abstention rate in the election—67.8 percent of the eligible voters—also reveals the precarious state of Colombian democracy. The country's greatest writer, Gabriel García Márquez, says, "The Constitution, the laws . . . everything in Colombia is magnificent, everything on paper. It has no connection with reality."

Part of that reality is that Colombia is the scene of two wars. One is the drug war. From the official U.S. point of view this is being waged to stem the tide of cocaine flowing into the United States. For the Colombian elite, however, it is a private quarrel with that section of the "cocaine nouveau riche," centered in Medellín, that seeks too aggressively to join it in the seats of power. It is noteworthy that the Cali cartel, which in general shuns violence and is more discreet in its dealings with the traditional oligarchy, has experienced little interference by the government.

The other war is the "dirty war" waged by an alliance of the military, the security services, drug lords, great landowners, and businessmen against Colombia's left-wing movement, trade unions, and peasant leagues. The military has made no secret that it is far more interested in fighting guerrillas than in fighting drugs. It repeatedly thwarted Betancur's sincere efforts to achieve a cease-fire with the guerrilla movements and continued its repressive activity—bombardments, disappearances, torture, and murder—under Barco, who appeared unable or unwilling to control his armed forces. The majority of the victims have not been guerrillas but peasants, workers, and left-wing activists.

It is too early to tell whether the May 1990 elections have tipped the scales in Colombia in favor of reform and peace or renewed reaction and war. The May presidential ballot included a proposal for a national constituent assembly that was overwhelmingly ratified. The assembly was charged with reforming the Colombian political system by ending the Liberal-Conservative "duopoly" of power and the emergency "state of siege" that has been in place for over forty years, providing a cover for countless human rights abuses. The assembly was also expected to revamp the electoral and judicial systems and public administration. Elections of delegates to the assembly were held in December 1990, and the body was to convene between February and July 1991. A decree issued by Gaviria limited guerrilla participation in the constituent assembly to delegates of insurgent groups that had disbanded and surrendered their arms. M-19 and two other small guerrilla groups complied, and one of the surprises of the December elections was the strong showing of the socialist-oriented Democratic Alliance (the disbanded M-19), which emerged as the second strongest national party, with nineteen of the seventy-three delegates making up the assembly. But the two largest guerrilla groups, the Revolutionary Armed Forces (FARC) and the National Liberation Army (ELN), while declaring their support for the peace process and the constituent assembly, said they would not negotiate with the government unless there were "positive signs of changes" in the country.

At present the "signs" are mixed and contradictory. President Gaviria appeared to show his good will toward the left by appointing the former M-19 leader Antonio Navarro Wolf (who replaced his slain comrade Carlos Pizarro as presidential candidate in the May election and made a remarkably strong showing) as minister of health in his cabinet. On the other hand, the period before, during, and after the election was marked by a stepped-up counterinsurgency campaign by the military, with a marked increase in aerial bombardments by U.S.-supplied planes and helicopters of rural communities throughout the Santander region and other areas. Ostensibly launched to protect the electoral process from "narco-terrorism," the operation actually targeted rural areas where the guerrilla forces were active. There was widespread belief that the offensive represented an effort by an alliance of military hard-liners and drug traffickers to disrupt the peace process and damage the prestige of Gaviria. The guerrillas responded with a counteroffensive that included a campaign of economic sabotage, blowing up sections of oil and gas pipelines, and destroying communications and energy towers. Under pressure from assembly delegates to negotiate with the guerrillas, Gaviria softened his stand that he would not talk to them until they stopped military actions, and in February 1991 his interior minister said he would meet with them at any time.

In December 1990 truce talks began between the new government and the major drug traffickers, centering on a proposal that the traffickers should surrender in return for lenient treatment, immunity from extradition, and security for their wealth. The new extradition policy was a serious blow to Washington's "war on drugs." Colombians appeared to give overwhelming approval to the peace plan. By mid-February 1991 members of the major Ochoa clan had turned themselves in, but Pablo Escobar, head of the Medellín cartel, was reportedly holding out for better terms.

In July 1991, the constitutional convention completed its work. The new charter, replacing the constitution of 1886, was designed to open up Colombia's political system, ending the monopoly of power long held by a handful of Liberal and Conservative clans. The document provided for the dissolution of congress three years early, with new elections to be held in October 1991. Until the new congress is installed in December 1991, President Gaviria will govern with the aid of a multiparty legislative commission with veto powers. In addition to a series of measures designed to prevent political fraud and corruption, the new constitution provided for the popular election of state governors, limited the president to one term, granted congress the right to veto cabinet members, limited presidential state-of-siege powers to 90 days, established the office of a "people's" defender to investigate human rights abuses, recognized the authority of traditional courts on Indian *resguardos* or reserves, ensured representation for political minorities in congress, and banned the extradition of native-born Colombians. Within hours after the adoption of the extradition ban, the head of the Medellín drug cartel, Pablo Escobar, and his associates, surrendered for trial.

The new constitution offered a blueprint for a more just and humane Colombia, but it remains to be seen whether the still powerful forces of reaction, including great landowners, drug barons, and elements of the military, will permit that blueprint to become a reality. Widespread distrust was reflected in the continuing difficult negotiations between the government and the two largest guerrilla groups for their disarmament and incorporation into the political process.

Meanwhile Colombia continues to be a violent land. The drug traffic has generated a huge criminal substructure, including a large number of youthful killers who are willing to murder for small sums, with $500 the going rate. A recent Colombian movie, *Rodrigo D (No Future)*, set in Medellín in 1988, chillingly portrays the life of these young thugs, who are "amoral murder machines," who "know that life is cheap" and "that they are going to die soon." In February 1991 alone the murders included the killing of the president's cousin, a prominent Liberal politician, and the death of at least twenty people, including seven members of the police intelligence unit, in a car bomb explosion. Fear of kidnapping has caused many journalists to leave the country and many papers to stop investigating the drug traffic.

Chapter 20

The Two Americas: United States–Latin American Relations

Two consistent themes appear when the relations of the United States with Latin America over the past one hundred and eighty years are examined. First and foremost, the United States has sought to protect and expand its economic interests in the region. Ever since the administration of James Monroe, the United States has attempted to establish and maintain Latin America as an economic appendage. U.S. policy makers have displayed resourcefulness and flexibility in pursuit of this goal, adapting their methods to meet the varying domestic political pressures, the changing requirements of American economic enterprise, and the shifting conditions in Latin America. Second, the United States has generally subordinated Latin America to its other concerns abroad. Consequently, American policy makers have tended to deal with Latin America either by employing frameworks formed for other regions or by grouping the nations of the area under one heading and ignoring their individual problems and needs.

United States Policy

American policy toward Latin America has changed over time to accommodate burgeoning American economic activities in the region. During the early years of the nineteenth century, U.S. commerce with its southern neighbors demanded little more than policing the Caribbean for marauding pirates. As the United States grew into a commercial, industrial, and, eventually, financial power, its foreign policy broadened in scope. The hunt for new markets brought it into competition with European nations, especially Great Britain. As a result, it became one of the major aims of American policy to check the further penetration of European commerce and capital into Latin America.

By the turn of the century, Latin America had become not only a substantial market for American products but an important source of raw materials and a major area for capital investment as well. Having recently built a powerful navy, the United States assumed the responsibility of protecting American commerce and investment by forcibly maintaining order in the region. Uninvited, it assumed the role of policeman of the Western Hemisphere. In this capacity, the United States focused its attention on the weak and chaotic nations of the Caribbean and Central America, where American economic activity was concentrated.

At mid-century, South America replaced the Caribbean as the focus of American economic expansion. Geography, logistics, and the anti-imperialist temper of the times required the United States to abandon the old policies of military intervention in favor of more subtle and sophisticated ways of achieving its ends; these new methods included the lure of grants and loans, the threat of economic sanctions, and subversion. When these methods failed, however, as they did in Guatemala in 1954, in Cuba in 1959, and in the Dominican Republic in 1965, the United States did not hesitate to resort to the open or covert use of force.

Ideology has always figured in United States policy toward Latin America. Thus, Theodore Roosevelt vowed to "civilize," Woodrow Wilson to "democratize," and John F. Kennedy to "reform" Latin America. But ideology has always been subordinated to the material needs of United States–Latin American policy, and the presidents who made these pious professions were ready to use force in defense of the U.S. empire in Latin America. They were also ready to support the most oppressive regimes in the area as long as they cooperated with the United States.

The two Americas, both born in wars of national liberation, have followed very different historical paths. In two centuries, the United States has risen to become the industrial and financial giant of the capitalist world; despite its many economic and social problems, it provides the majority of its people with a high material standard of living. Latin America has fallen far behind the other America and belongs to the underdeveloped world.

Many Latin Americans are convinced that these divergent trends are not unrelated, that Latin American underdevelopment is the other side of North American development, that Latin American poverty and misery have accumulated as the economic and political power of foreign (chiefly North American) multinational corporations has grown. A growing number of Latin Americans also believe that they must recapture their national resources from foreign control if they wish to make the structural economic and social changes needed by the area. How the United States adjusts its policies to this trend may well determine the substance of Latin American relations in the future.

Prelude to Empire, 1810–1897

Manifest Destiny, 1810–1865

During the early decades of the nineteenth century, westward expansion and nascent commerce brought the United States into its first contact with its southern neighbors. However, American military weakness, lack of information, and British predominance in the area limited U.S. activities in Latin America. U.S. trade with Latin America began in earnest in 1797, when Spain opened the ports of its New World colonies to foreign trade. By 1811 the Spanish colonies accounted for 16 percent of all U.S. trade. A dozen years later, despite the disruptions of the War of 1812, the figure had increased to 20 percent.

With only a small navy and few funds at its disposal, the U.S. government could offer little aid or comfort to the Spanish-American nations during their wars of independence (1810–1826). During the first stage of these wars, the War of 1812 consumed the attention and resources of the

520

United States. From 1817 to 1821, it undertook delicate negotiations with Spain for the purchase of Florida and did not choose to jeopardize these dealings by helping the Spanish-American insurgents.

When it was clear that the Latin American independence movements had succeeded, the United States acted to prevent other European nations from acquiring colonies or undue influence in the region, developments that could shut off U.S. access to potentially lucrative markets. In his message to Congress on December 2, 1823, President James Monroe declared that as a matter of principle, "the American continents, by the free and independent condition they have assumed and maintain, are henceforth not to be considered subjects for future colonization by any European powers. . . . We should consider any attempt on their [the European powers'] part to extend their system to any portion of this hemisphere as dangerous to our peace and safety." Monroe went on to say that the United States would not interfere with existing colonies, nor would it meddle in European affairs.

The Monroe Doctrine was ineffective for much of the nineteenth century because the United States had neither the resources nor the inclination to back it up. The doctrine, furthermore, failed to prevent repeated European interventions in Latin America. Following the accepted practice of the time, French and British gunboats regularly bombarded or blockaded Latin American ports to force payment of debts or reparations. The United States, too, adopted this practice, landing troops in the Falkland Islands, Argentina, and Peru during the 1830s, in Argentina, Nicaragua, Uruguay, Panama, Paraguay, and Mexico during the 1850s, and in Panama, Uruguay, Mexico, and Colombia during the 1860s.

Westward territorial expansion involved the United States in two wars during the nineteenth century. After the purchase of Louisiana (1803) and Florida (1821), the country began to cast covetous looks toward the northern provinces of Mexico, where U.S. citizens had begun to conduct flourishing commerce. In 1825, President John Quincy Adams authorized the United States min-

ister to Mexico to negotiate the purchase of Texas. The Mexican government rejected the proposal. During the early 1830s, American settlers poured into Texas and quickly found themselves at odds with Mexican authorities over the issues of local autonomy and the illegal introduction of slavery into the area. In 1836 the settlers rebelled, defeated Mexico in a short war, and won their independence. Texas remained an independent nation for ten years, for the bitter debate over the extension of slavery prevented its annexation to the United States until 1845.

In 1845, President James Polk sent an emissary, James Slidell, to Mexico to arrange the acquisition of California. Outraged at the annexation of Texas, the Mexicans refused to cede any of their territory. Consequently, Polk trumped up a border incident along the Rio Grande, provoking a military clash that led to the Mexican-American War (1846–1848). The victorious United States took the territories of Arizona, New Mexico, and California. Barely a half-century old, the United States had successfully waged a war of territorial acquisition.

Commerce and the Canal

From 1815 to 1860, U.S. foreign commerce increased dramatically; exports grew by nearly 400 percent and imports by 300 percent. The nature of U.S. trade was transformed, for instead of re-exporting foreign-made goods, U.S. merchants exported agricultural commodities and manufactured goods produced in the United States. Because of the increased economic activity in the Caribbean, especially Cuba and Central America, the United States began to pay close attention to the region. Cuba became one of the most important U.S. overseas markets, ranking third behind Great Britain and France in total American trade. Throughout the 1850s, there was a strong sentiment, particularly among southerners, to annex the island. President Millard Fillmore tried unsuccessfully to purchase Cuba from Spain in 1852.

Central America became important because of the prospect of a canal through the region. Americans had talked of a canal through the Central American isthmus as early as 1825. In 1846 the United States signed an agreement with New Granada (Colombia) that guaranteed American access to any canal built in Panama, then a province of New Granada. This concern over a canal and its commercial interests in Central America brought the United States into direct confrontation with Great Britain, which had colonies in the region. Each nation sought to keep the other from dominating the area or controlling any canal that would be built. As a result, in 1850 they agreed to the Clayton-Bulwer Treaty, which provided that neither would try to dominate Central America or any part of it or would acquire exclusive rights to a canal. Thus, they eliminated a potential cause of hostilities.

The gold rush to California in 1849 increased the importance of transportation across the isthmus. American entrepreneurs invested heavily in steamships and railroad construction in the region to satisfy the demand for cheap and fast transport across the isthmus to California. Despite the treaty with Britain and these heavy investments in transportation, U.S. interest in a canal continued.

The Awakening Giant, 1865–1887

In the two decades after the Civil War (1861–1865), U.S. policy makers focused their concerns on territorial expansion and increased trade in Latin America, finding little success in either. The major diplomatic triumph of the era came in 1866 when Secretary of State William H. Seward, belatedly invoking the Monroe Doctrine, demanded that France remove its troops from Mexico, where they propped up the rule of the Emperor Maximilian, the Austrian Archduke. Emperor Napoleon III of France complied the following year, more because of growing tensions with Prussia in Europe than because of fear of the United States.

A succession of U.S. presidents and secretaries of state attempted to acquire new territories, but they were inevitably thwarted by Congress. There were also major efforts to expand U.S.

trade to Latin America through the negotiation of reciprocal trade treaties and establishment of inter-American diplomatic conferences. The United States signed bilateral reciprocal trade agreements with six Latin American nations during the 1880s but no real benefits accrued. The first Inter-American Conference met in Washington, D.C., in 1889. It resulted in little more than the airing of long-simmering grievances and mistrust.

Adventures in Latin America, 1888–1896

U.S. adventurism in Latin America in the last years of the nineteenth century stemmed from severe domestic economic and social problems and from the country's growing stake in commerce and investment in the region. The United States experienced a deep depression from 1893 to 1898, the third such downturn in twenty-five years (the others occurred in 1873–1878 and 1882–1885). It became evident that the domestic market could not absorb the rapidly growing output of U.S. agriculture and industry. American leaders unanimously agreed that the answer to the problem was to expand foreign markets. The depression of 1893 created deep-seated social unrest as well, resulting in a series of bitter and bloody strikes. Businessmen and politicians alike feared that continued depression would lead to class warfare.

At the same time, U.S. capitalists increased their investment in Latin America. Paradoxically, despite the depression, U.S. banks had surplus funds to invest. Because investments in the United States were unattractive, the bankers turned to potentially more lucrative foreign enterprises. These investors poured millions of dollars into Cuban sugar and Mexican mining and railroads. By 1900 the U.S. stake in Mexico alone had reached $500 million.

American interest, however, was not limited to areas like Mexico and Cuba, where the United States already had large investments. The United States was willing to go to great lengths, even at the risk of war, both to protect potential markets and to reinforce its political dominance in the region. This was particularly true of the Caribbean, which leaders tended to view as an "American lake." Thus, in 1888 the United States intervened in a civil war in Haiti to secure a favorable commercial agreement and a naval base at Môle St. Nicolas. The U.S. fleet actually broke a blockade to bring about the victory of the faction it favored. Once entrenched in power, however, this group reneged on its promises to the Harrison administration (1887–1893). Then Secretary of State James G. Blaine also tried unsuccessfully to obtain Samaná Bay from Santo Domingo.

As the depression of 1893 deepened, U.S. leaders looked southward with growing anxiety. President Grover Cleveland declared in his annual message to Congress in 1893 that unrest and European meddling had threatened American interests in Nicaragua, Guatemala, Costa Rica, Honduras, and Brazil in 1892; the United States fleet was finding it difficult to keep up with its "responsibilities." Markets desperately needed by the United States were threatened by disorders and competition from European nations, particularly Britain.

In 1894 the United States became involved in another revolution when it intervened in Brazil to protect a potentially important market and to check British influence there. The United States had signed a reciprocal trade agreement with the newly proclaimed republic of Brazil in 1891, but the rebels who rose up in 1893 opposed the pact. The main strategy of the rebel forces was to blockade the harbor of Rio de Janeiro, the nation's principal city; they hoped to strangle the government by denying it the all-important customs revenue. The United States helped to undermine this strategy by refusing to recognize the blockade. U.S. vessels unloaded their cargoes without interference.

Late in 1894, however, with clandestine aid from the British, the rebellion regained momentum. At this time, important mercantile and oil (Rockefeller) interests, fearing the loss of their Brazilian market, brought pressure on the State Department to intervene. The United States responded by sending most of the Atlantic fleet to

the harbor of Rio de Janeiro. By maneuvering to prevent rebel bombardment of the capital, the American warships played a crucial part in the defeat of the revolt.

Shortly thereafter, the United States intervened in Nicaragua to protect American rights to an isthmian canal and the substantial holdings of American investors. In 1893 a nationalist government, headed by General José S. Zelaya, took power in Nicaragua; it threatened to cancel a concession granted by a previous administration to the Maritime Canal Company to build a canal through Nicaraguan territory. Later, Zelaya also threatened the prosperous U.S.-run banana plantations in the Miskito Indian reservation (an area claimed by Nicaragua but controlled by the British) by invading the reservation in 1894. In response, British troops landed and quickly subdued the Nicaraguan force. U.S. interests, with a $2 million stake in the Miskito region, were unwilling to accept either British or Nicaraguan rule. To protect American property, the United States stationed two warships off the coast and in July dispatched marines to restore order. United States troops landed three more times, in 1896, 1898, and 1899, to protect American lives and property.

The Turning Point: Venezuela, 1895–1896

The Venezuelan crisis of 1895–1896 ended in full British recognition of U.S. hegemony in the Western Hemisphere. The United States intervened in a boundary dispute between Venezuela and Great Britain that had festered for over half a century. The controversy concerned the region at the mouth of the Orinoco River, the major artery for northern South America, which was claimed by both Venezuela and the British colony of Guiana (present-day Guyana). In the 1880s, Britain extended its claims, causing Venezuela to break off diplomatic relations.

During 1893 and 1894, the Venezuelan government, confronted with mounting economic difficulties and political unrest, appealed to the

United States to help settle the controversy. President Cleveland's entrance into the dispute reflected his deep concern about the apparent resurgence of European intervention in Latin America. Between 1891 and 1895, the British had actively intervened in Chile, Brazil, and Nicaragua. The French had become involved in a dispute with Brazil over the boundary of their colony of Guiana and had threatened intervention in Santo Domingo to obtain satisfaction for the killing of a French citizen. The simultaneous scramble for territories in Africa magnified the threat; what the European rivals did on one continent, they could do on another. Specifically, President Cleveland feared that British control of the mouth of the Orinoco would exclude American commerce from northern South American markets.

In 1895, in an obvious effort to intensify U.S. support, the Venezuelan government granted a lucrative concession to an American syndicate for the exploitation of rich mineral resources located in the disputed zone. In July 1895, Secretary of State Richard Olney spelled out the American attitude toward European meddling in Latin America. Citing the Monroe Doctrine, he declared that the United States would intervene whenever the actions of a European power in the Western Hemisphere posed a "serious and direct menace to its own integrity and welfare." In effect, Olney claimed hegemony for the United States in Latin America.

The British initially responded to Olney's claims with disdain; the English foreign secretary denied the validity of the Monroe Doctrine in international law and brushed aside the American assertion of supremacy in the Western Hemisphere. President Cleveland, however, firmly supported Olney's position and made it clear that the United States was willing to go to war to uphold it. Meanwhile, international developments worked to soften the British stand; the threat of a war with Germany and British problems in South Africa took precedence. Accordingly, in late 1896, the British agreed to submit the dispute to arbitration. The government of Venezuela neither participated in nor was informed of this agreement.

The Venezuelan affair marked the end of British military predominance in Latin America. Its attention now focused on the growing German power and the competition for territory in Africa, Britain could no longer commit substantial resources to the region. With the growing threat of a general war in Europe, British leaders could also not afford to alienate the United States, a powerful potential ally. Thus, the British formally recognized U.S. hegemony in Latin America with the signing of the Hay-Pauncefote Treaty of 1901, which allowed the United States unilaterally to build, control, and fortify an isthmian canal. In 1906, Britain withdrew its fleet from the Caribbean. Great Britain retained its predominant economic position in southern South America but was fated to lose that also to the United States after World War I.

An Imperial Power, 1898–1933

By 1898 the United States had emerged as an industrial, financial, and naval power. It surpassed Great Britain as the world's leading manufacturing state. Giant U.S. banks and corporations invested heavily overseas. Increasingly, the nation looked abroad for markets, raw materials, and profits. Recurring economic difficulties and mounting social unrest spurred American leaders to seek solutions in overseas economic expansion and foreign adventures.

The War with Spain

The war with Spain in 1898 established the United States as a full-fledged imperial power. The primary goal of its Cuban policy during the 1890s was to protect the very large (over $50 million) U.S. investment in the island by stopping the chronic political disorder there. When Spain proved unable to end the turmoil, and it appeared that ungovernable native rebels might

524

take over, the United States intervened. In declaring war against Spain, the United States Congress pledged to free Cuba from Spanish tyranny and in the Teller Resolution disavowed any intention to annex the island. But the U.S. government proceeded to conduct the war and negotiate the peace without consulting the Cubans.

The United States occupied and ruled the island from 1898 to 1902, departing only after the Cubans agreed to include in their constitution the notorious Platt Amendment, which made the country a virtual American protectorate. American forces occupied the island three more times, 1906 to 1909, 1912, and 1917 to 1922. As noted in Chapter 17, instead of bringing the Cubans liberty and economic progress, U.S. intervention promoted and perpetuated corruption, violence, and economic stagnation.

An "American Lake":
The "Big Stick" and "Dollar Diplomacy"
in the Caribbean

From 1898 to 1932, the United States intervened militarily in nine Caribbean nations[1] a total of thirty-four times. Its occupation forces ran the governments of the Dominican Republic, Cuba, Nicaragua, Haiti, and Panama for long periods; Honduras, Mexico, Guatemala, and Costa Rica experienced shorter invasions. Military intervention was not the only method employed by the United States to control the region; other effective means included threats, nonrecognition, and economic sanctions.

The U.S. economic stake in the Caribbean was substantial. Moreover, the nature of this investment, which was concentrated primarily in agricultural commodities, mineral extraction, oil production, and government securities, made it particularly vulnerable to political disorders. From 1987 to 1914, U.S. investment in Cuba and the West Indies rose almost sevenfold, from $50

million to $336 million. Investment in Central America more than quadrupled, from $21 million to $93 million. By 1914, U.S. investment in Mexico had risen to over $1 billion. In 1914, 43 percent of this investment was in mining, 18.7 percent in agriculture, and 10 percent in oil. An additional 13 percent was invested in railroads, which were built to transport the export products to market. The owners of these enterprises often had considerable influence on American policy.

The United States justified its actions in the Caribbean by the so-called Roosevelt Corollary (1904) to the Monroe Doctrine, so named because President Theodore Roosevelt maintained that the United States, as a "civilized" nation, had the right to end "chronic wrongdoing" and thus could intervene in the Caribbean to maintain order. The Roosevelt Corollary was a logical outgrowth of the increasingly aggressive policies successively advanced by Seward, Grant, Cleveland, and Olney.

The Panama Canal

United States interest in a canal across Central America to join the Atlantic and Pacific oceans intensified as the nation filled out its continental boundaries and expanded its commercial activities throughout the Western Hemisphere. A group of New York businessmen initiated a project to build a canal in 1825 but failed to obtain financial support. In 1846 the United States signed a treaty with New Granada to assure American access to any future canal constructed in the province of Panama. The California gold rush three years later created a large demand for transportation across the isthmus en route to the West Coast gold fields. In response, a group of New York capitalists constructed a railroad across the 48-mile width of Panama between 1851 and 1855. No sooner was the railway finished than U.S. troops landed to protect American interests from Panamanian insurgents rebelling against Colombian rule. In 1865, U.S. troops again landed to protect American lives and property during another rebellion.

---

[1] The Caribbean nations include the West Indies, Cuba, Central America, and Mexico.

Americans were not the first to attempt to build a canal. Ferdinand de Lesseps, the Frenchman who had constructed the Suez Canal, began a project to dig a sea-level canal across Panama in 1878. After eleven years of effort, de Lesseps, thwarted by tropical disease and engineering problems, gave up the project. Throughout this period, the United States pressured France to abandon the undertaking; it asserted its "rightful and long-established claim to priority on the American continent." The growth of a large United States Navy, which had two coasts to defend, added to the urgency of constructing an isthmian passageway.

In the 1880s and 1890s, support grew for building a canal through Nicaragua. In 1901 a presidential commission endorsed the Nicaraguan route, despite the more favorable engineering and logistical characteristics of the Panamanian alternative, because the French company that controlled the canal concession in Panama wanted the fantastic sum of $109 million for its rights. At this point, two extraordinary entrepreneurs, William N. Cromwell, an influential New York attorney, and Philippe Bunau-Varilla, chief engineer of the de Lesseps project and an organizer of the New Panama Canal Company (the French company that had rights to the canal) acted to change the course of U.S. policy. Cromwell, as lawyer for the canal company, bribed the Republican party to end its support of the Nicaraguan route. He and Bunau-Varilla then convinced the company to lower the price for its concession to a more reasonable $40 million.

The two men were faced with the problem of convincing the United States to purchase their company's concession before it expired in 1904. In 1902, Bunau-Varilla and Cromwell managed to push through Congress the Spooner Amendment, which authorized President Roosevelt to buy the New Panama Canal Company's rights for the asking price of $40 million if he could negotiate a treaty with Colombia. In 1903, Secretary of State John Hay pressured the Colombian ambassador to the United States to sign a pact that gave the United States a 99-year lease on a strip of land across the isthmus in return for $10 million and an annual payment of $250,000. The Colombian Senate, demanding more money, rejected the proposal.

In the meantime, Bunau-Varilla undertook to exploit the long tradition of Panamanian nationalism and rebelliousness for his own end. From the time that Colombia won its independence from Spain in 1821, it had never been able to establish its rule in Panama. During the nineteenth century, the Panamanians revolted fifty times against their Colombian masters. On two occasions, when the Panamanian rebels seemed near success (1855–1856 and 1885), the United States intervened militarily to protect American interests and end the revolts. After a terrible civil war (1899–1902) had severely weakened Colombia, Panamanian nationalists again prepared to rise in revolt. Working closely with the U.S. State Department and the Panamanians, Bunau-Varilla triggered a successful uprising in early November 1903. With the help of the United States Navy and bribes paid to the Colombian officers who were supposed to crush the revolt, Panama won its independence.

The Panamanians, to their own undoing, entrusted to Bunau-Varilla the subsequent negotiations with the United States over the canal concession. Feverishly working to complete the arrangements before the New Panama Canal Company's rights expired, he produced a treaty that gave the United States control over a ten-mile-wide canal zone "as if it were a sovereign of the territory." The United States was to have "in perpetuity the use, occupation, and control" of the zone. In return, the United States was to pay Panama $10 million and assume a virtual protectorate over the new nation. The Panamanian government indignantly protested the terms of the agreement but eventually accepted the pact, fearing that the United States might either seize the canal with no compensation or build one in Nicaragua instead.

United States Marines were stationed in Panama from late 1903 until 1914 to protect American interests while the canal was built. During

The construction of the Panama Canal. (Courtesy of the National Archives)

this period, the United States disbanded the Panamanian army and assumed the responsibility of defending Panama against any external threat. The United States established its own postal system, custom houses, and commissaries in the Canal Zone, privileges that seriously undermined the Panamanian economy and badly injured Panamanian pride. The canal was completed in 1914.

The Dominican Republic, Haiti, and Nicaragua

The United States occupied and administered the governments of the Dominican Republic (1916–

1924), Haiti (1915–1934), and Nicaragua (1912–1925 and 1926–1933) to the detriment of these nations' long-range political and economic development.

President Ulysses S. Grant had sought to annex the Dominican Republic (then known as Santo Domingo) in 1869; only rejection of the agreement by the United States Senate prevented him from acquiring the nation, which shares the island of Hispaniola with Haiti. In the decades that followed, a series of venal and brutal dictators, often supported by loans from American banks, produced a debilitating cycle of repression and rebellion. In 1893 the Santo Domingo Improvement Company, a U.S. firm, purchased the country's heavy foreign debt in return for the right to collect its customs revenue. In both 1903 and 1904, the United States dispatched marines to protect the interests of the influential New York financiers who were principals in the company. In 1905, the United States government assumed the administration of Dominican customs.

Unrest, however, persisted. In 1916, President Woodrow Wilson sent in the marines after the Dominican government refused to accept broader U.S. control over the nation's internal affairs, and the United States Navy maintained a military dictatorship until 1924. The marines brutally repressed guerrilla activities, which threatened American-owned sugar plantations. In addition, several American officers were subsequently court-martialed for the commission of atrocities.

The U.S. occupation forces attempted administrative and fiscal reforms and built some roads, but these projects were abandoned when the soldiers departed. One institution that remained intact after the occupation ended was the *Guardia Nacional,* the national police force. Rafael Trujillo, with U.S. support, rose through the ranks of the Guardia to become dictator of the Dominican Republic in 1928. His rapacious rule, extending over three decades (he was assassinated in 1961) was the bitter legacy of intervention by the United States.

Events in Haiti followed a similar course. For a century after winning independence from France in 1804, Haiti experienced ruinous political turmoil. Reacting to the brutal murder of the Haitian president in 1915, Woodrow Wilson sent in the marines, ostensibly to prevent Germany from taking advantage of the chaos to establish a base on the island, which would endanger U.S. commerce and the access routes to the Panama Canal. A treaty signed the next year placed the United States in full control of the country. Although Haitians held public office, they served only at the pleasure of the American authorities. Here, too, American troops committed atrocities while engaged in the suppression of rural guerrillas, and civil liberties were ignored. U.S. control lasted until 1934.

The United States also intervened in Nicaragua to protect the interests of American companies operating there. The U.S. investment totaled only $2.5 million, but the largest American company, the United States–Nicaraguan Concession, had considerable influence in the Taft administration (1909–1913); Secretary of State Philander C. Knox had been the company's legal counsel. In 1909, General José Zelaya, an old nemesis of the United States, canceled a concession to one American company and threatened the Nicaraguan Concession. The same year, the United States backed a revolution that overthrew Zelaya. In 1912, at the request of the Nicaraguan government, U.S. President William Howard Taft sent in the marines to crush a new rebellion; the marines remained for thirteen years. In 1916 the United States and Nicaragua agreed to the Bryan-Chamorro Treaty, which gave the United States sole rights to build a canal through Nicaragua in return for payment of $3 million.[2] President Calvin Coolidge withdrew American troops for a short period in 1925, but dispatched them again to subdue yet another revolution the following year; the soldiers stayed until 1933.

Puerto Rico

The United States became a colonial power with the conquest and acquisition of the island of Puerto Rico in 1898 during the Spanish-American-Cuban War. From December 1898 until May 1900, U.S. military governors ruled the island. In 1900, the United States Congress passed the Foraker Act, which established a new civilian government for the island with a governor and an executive council appointed by the U.S. president. In 1917 this government was modified by replacing the executive council with an elected Senate. But the president maintained the power to veto legislation passed by the Puerto Rican Congress. The same year the U.S. Congress granted Puerto Ricans United States citizenship in time to make them eligible for the military draft for World War I.

---

[2] This treaty gave the United States control over the two best routes for a canal in Central America.

United States occupation cost Puerto Ricans dearly politically. At the time of the Spanish-American War, the island had won a large degree of autonomy from Spain. The new colonial regime stripped that from them and ruled Puerto Rico with tactless, condescending mainlanders, who had no experience in dealing with different cultures. When Puerto Ricans protested against unresponsive government, U.S. authorities reacted harshly. In 1909, for example, members of the Puerto Rican House of Delegates refused to pass the year's appropriation bill because of their objections to the indifference shown in the court system to struggling coffee growers. President William H. Taft angrily demanded that the right of appropriations be taken from the House of Delegates, and the United States Congress enacted this legislation in the so-called Olmstead Amendment. Puerto Rico did not have a native-born governor until 1947, nor an elected governor until 1948.

Puerto Rico also underwent drastic economic changes as a result of the United States occupation. In 1898 its leading crop, coffee, was exported to Europe. United States policies transformed the island into a monocrop sugar economy with landownership concentrated in very few hands, mostly absentee foreign corporations. Puerto Ricans became dependent on the U.S. sugar quota. The decline of sugar prices during the 1920s and their collapse during the depression of the 1930s brought chronic economic problems. By 1929, near starvation prevailed in many parts of the island. New Deal agencies, such as the Puerto Rican Emergency Relief Administration and the Puerto Rican Reconstruction Administration, poured some $230 million into the island from 1933 to 1941.

A series of disastrous governors ruled the island during the 1920s. Its plight improved with the arrival of Theodore Roosevelt, Jr., as governor in 1929. Roosevelt even learned Spanish! In the 1930s, President Franklin D. Roosevelt appointed mediocre political hacks or men of no experience to the governorship until 1941, when he installed Rexford Tugwell.

Despite the lack of autonomy and the exclusion of natives from the highest echelons of government, Puerto Rico maintained a vibrant politics. The Unionist party dominated from 1904 to 1924. It was led for much of the era by Luis Muñoz Rivera. In 1924 the political parties realigned as the Unionists combined with the Republicans to form the *Alianza* (Alliance), and the Socialists joined with dissident Republicans to form the Coalition. These groups disintegrated by the end of the decade.

During the 1930s and for decades thereafter, the influence of two Puerto Ricans, Pedro Albizu Campos and Luis Muñoz Marín, dominated Puerto Rican politics. Harvard-educated Albizu became the foremost spokesman for independence. He formed the Nationalist party and took an ardently anti-U.S. stand. He spent many years in prison for supporting violent confrontation with the island's colonial master. Muñoz Marín, whose father had led the Unionists in the early years of United States rule, was also educated in the United States. He did not live in Puerto Rico permanently until 1931. During the dark depression days of the 1930s, Muñoz Marín became the star protégé of the New Deal.

The terrible plight of Puerto Rico during the depression led to a re-evaluation of its status by policy makers in the United States in the late 1930s. It was, as historian Arturo Morales Carrión has said, "a crisis of the whole colonial system." North Americanization had brought the "rise of absentee landownership, the collapse of coffee culture, the migration to growing slums, and shocking poverty in rural areas." United States rule had been a "mixture of paternalism and neglect, self-righteousness and condescension." The U.S. administrators of the island reacted harshly to this criticism.

In March 1937 during a parade of the Nationalist party in San Juan, police killed seventeen protesters in an unprovoked attack. This incident, known as the "Ponce Massacre," was the most obvious illustration of the darkest side of U.S. colonialism.

In the crisis that followed in the aftermath of

the massacre, old political coalitions realigned and Muñoz Marín emerged as the leading political figure. Based on his grassroots organization in the countryside, Muñoz Marín's Popular Democratic party (PPD) rose meteorically, sweeping elections from 1944 until 1968. With help from Washington, he was able to lead Puerto Rico into a new era of industrialization and economic development.

The first substantial change in Puerto Rico's status took place after World War II. When Tugwell left office in 1947, President Harry S Truman appointed Jesús T. Pinero, the first native governor. A year later Muñoz Marín became the first elected governor of the island. This did not satisfy all Puerto Ricans' desire for self-rule, however. In November 1950, two Puerto Rican nationalists invaded Blair House in Washington, D.C., Truman's temporary home, in an assassination attempt on the president. In March 1954, three Puerto Rican men and a woman entered the U.S. House of Representatives with guns and wounded five congressmen. But self-rule was not desired by the majority of Puerto Ricans. In June 1950, the island held its first plebiscite on its status, voting by 70 percent for commonwealth status; the Constitution of Puerto Rico, establishing the commonwealth, took effect in 1952. In 1967 another plebiscite showed 60 percent in favor of remaining a commonwealth.

Tugwell and Muñoz Marín engineered the diversification of the Puerto Rican economy under the auspices of Operation Bootstrap. The plan attracted mainland manufacturing companies to the island with special tax inducements and low labor costs. Thus, Puerto Rico enjoyed an economic boom during the 1950s and 1960s; unemployment was also reduced in part by the migration of hundreds of thousands of Puerto Ricans to the mainland, particularly to New York City. By the 1970s, however, Operation Bootstrap had broken down; companies left the island for the Far East or other regions that offered even cheaper labor and lower taxes, leaving many islanders without jobs. Puerto Ricans became almost totally reliant on federal help, much of it in the form of food stamps and other assistance programs. By 1980, over half the island's population was eligible for these programs. Then the cutback of federal welfare funds under the Reagan administration badly hurt the Puerto Rican economy. An estimated 25 percent of the labor force was unemployed in the early 1980s.

Muñoz Marín stepped aside for his protégé Roberto Sánchez Vilella, who was elected governor in 1964. In 1968 a split occurred in the ranks of the ruling Popular Democrats, allowing the pro-statehood New Progressive party to elect Luis A. Ferré as governor. The Popular Democrats regained control in 1972 with Rafael Hernández Colón, but New Progressive Carlos Romero Barceló won in 1976 and was re-elected in 1980. The New Progressives obtained their strongest support among younger voters in the larger urban areas. Rafael Hernández Colón won a second term as governor in 1984 and was re-elected in 1988. The island's voting rolls doubled in size from 1960 to 1980. Elections reflected a highly competitive two-party system with an independent electorate, fully prepared to elect a governor from one party and a legislature controlled by the other.

Puerto Rico's status remains a crucial issue. Though U.S. presidents have repeatedly supported the island's self-determination, "the truth is that, beyond the realm of rhetoric, that right has never been recognized for Puerto Rico."[3] Puerto Rico has been placed in an in-between world. Heated debates are now taking place in Puerto Rico concerning a United States proposal for a plebiscite on the island's status, to be held in 1991. The ruling party, the Popular Democratic Party, supports a "permanent union" with the United States as a "Free Associated State," or Commonwealth. The New Progressive Party (PNP), the second largest party, favors statehood. The small but growing Puerto Rican Inde-

---

[3] Puerto Rico's Supreme Court Chief Justice Jose Trías Monge, quoted in Jorge Heine and Juan M. García-Passalacqua, *The Puerto Rican Question* (New York: Foreign Policy Association, 1983), p. 59.

530 pendence Party (PIP), supported by organizations on the left, proposes a formula providing for a transition to independence, with a commission of representatives of Puerto Rico and the United States to oversee the transfer of power from federal agencies to Puerto Rico. But the U.S. Congress must approve the plebiscite before a vote is taken, and Congress will have to specify what it is ready to offer Puerto Rico with each status choice. In October 1990 the House of Representatives approved a bill calling for a referendum to be held in September 1991, but a Senate version of the bill was stalled in committee.

U.S. economic policy has tied Puerto Rico ever more tightly to the mainland, first as the primary market for its monocrop, sugar, then as the major investor in its industrialization, and finally as the main supporter of the welfare state.

The Mexican Revolution

We have already discussed some aspects of United States policy toward the Mexican Revolution (1910–1920) in Chapter 12. That policy was directed above all at safeguarding the vast U.S. investment below the border and securing the favorable political and economic climate required by American interests in Mexico. The specific policies and tactics employed by the administrations of Presidents Taft and Wilson varied with the shifting conditions in Mexico, political pressures in the United States, and the changing international background. We recall that the United States twice resorted to military intervention in Mexico. In 1914, United States Marines occupied the gulf ports of Veracruz and Tampico in an effort to bring down General Victoriano Huerta by denying his government the use of customs revenues and arms imports from Europe. The second intervention, General John J. Pershing's incursion into northern Mexico in 1916 in pursuit of Pancho Villa, served only to unite the Mexican nation behind the regime of Venustiano Carranza.

The United States exerted more decisive influence on the military course of the revolution by regulating the flow of arms and munitions across the United States–Mexican border. Through selective application of its neutrality laws, the U.S. government prevented "undesirable" factions from instigating disruptive activities on the American side of the border. Woodrow Wilson introduced a new tactic in United States relations with Mexico by announcing that he would withhold recognition of governments that did not measure up to his standard of "morality." Wilson used this ploy against Huerta, Carranza, and Obregón. Another United States tactic to influence the course of the revolution was the threat of invasion. President Taft's shift of American troops to the border area in Texas, a veiled threat of intervention, may have helped to convince Porfirio Díaz to abdicate in 1911.

United States efforts to control the course of the revolution were diluted by stubborn resistance on the part of nationalist Mexican leaders like Carranza, divisions among U.S. investors in Mexico—some favoring and others opposing military intervention—and, finally, America's growing involvement in World War I. America's entry into the war in 1917 sharply limited policy alternatives, since the country lacked the military resources to fight in both Mexico and Europe. The threat of a Mexican alliance with Germany—a threat strongly posed by the famous Zimmerman telegram[4]—forced the United States to adopt a more moderate policy toward its neighbor.

Wilson and Latin America

In the presidential election campaign of 1912, Woodrow Wilson disavowed the Republican policies of "gunboat" and "dollar" diplomacy. Yet he surpassed his predecessors in the use of military force to impose U.S. hegemony in Latin America.

---

[4] In this dispatch the German government, not yet at war with the United States, offered to return to Mexico the southwestern part of the United States (lost during the Mexican War, 1846–1848), if Mexico would invade the United States. This telegram was a major factor in President Woodrow Wilson's decision to go to war in 1917.

Under the banner of "morality" and "democracy," Wilson occupied most of the Caribbean, maintaining a harsh U.S. rule over five major Caribbean republics (Panama, Nicaragua, Haiti, Cuba, and the Dominican Republic).

Wilson's Secretary of State William Jennings Bryan, who had railed against "corporate interests," appointed as his main adviser on Latin America a former vice president of the New York City Bank, one of the biggest lenders to the governments of the Caribbean. Bryan, who later resigned in protest against Wilson's aggressive policy toward Germany, was the most ardent supporter of the U.S. intervention in Haiti in 1915.

Quiet Imperialism:
The Post–World War I Years

United States investment in Latin America grew rapidly in the period between 1914 and 1929. The world war enabled American entrepreneurs to buy up much of the large British and German investment in the region. Total U.S. investment in Cuba and the West Indies, for example, rose from $336 million in 1914 to $1.2 billion in 1929, nearly four times the amount. United States capital in Central America more than tripled, while investment in South America skyrocketed to about an eightfold increase; investment in South America doubled every five years. In 1929 total U.S. investment in Latin America had reached the staggering sum of $5.4 billion, or 35 percent of all U.S. foreign investment.

Much of the new investment went into oil: U.S. companies channeled $235 million to Venezuela, $134 million to Colombia, $120 million to Mexico, and $50 million to Peru for oil exploration and production. Another $163 million went to manufacturing enterprises in South America. U.S. companies also invested heavily in Chilean copper and nitrate, in Argentine beef, and in Cuban sugar.

This period marked the full-fledged involvement of large U.S. corporations, later called multinationals, in Latin America. Such giants as Standard Oil of New Jersey, the American Smelting and Refining Company, International Telephone and Telegraph, American Foreign Power, and Armour established or added to their vast stake in the region.

The basic goal of United States policy in Latin America did not change during the postwar period; it remained the protection of American economic interests. However, public opinion and realism dictated modifications. The American people were badly disillusioned by the negotiations over the Versailles treaty and the subsequent rejection of the treaty and the League of Nations by the U.S. Senate. Americans were weary of overseas adventures and crusades. The United States remained dominant in the Caribbean, exerting decisive influence in the affairs of Mexico and Cuba and continuing to occupy the Dominican Republic, Haiti, and Nicaragua during the 1920s, but there was growing opposition to the old-style imperialism.

Foreign policy makers in the U.S. also realized that growing anti-American feeling in Latin America, primarily a response to U.S. actions in the Caribbean, posed a serious long-term danger to American economic interests. An early sign of a shift in United States policy came in 1921, when the Colombian government threatened to cancel the concessions of American companies to explore and drill for oil. The United States responded by paying Colombia $25 million to compensate for the loss of Panama. This act had a dual meaning: it served to protect U.S. economic interests, and it symbolized a less aggressive policy toward Latin America. The shift in American tactics became even clearer when the United States removed its troops from Cuba in 1922, from the Dominican Republic in 1924, and from Nicaragua in 1925. Despite these actions, the United States encountered bitter criticism of its role in the hemisphere at the Pan-American conferences held in Santiago in 1923 and Havana in 1928.

The most important indication that the United States had largely abandoned military intervention as a major tactic was its restraint in dealing with Mexico, the biggest trouble spot in the hemisphere during the 1920s. The Mexican constitution of 1917, as noted previously, was a most radical document by contemporary standards. The constitution's provisions on landownership and ownership of subsoil rights seriously endangered U.S. investments. American oil companies, in particular, objected to the new laws, which sought to reclaim Mexico's rich natural resources from foreign control.

Throughout the 1920s, the United States and Mexico haggled over application of the constitution. Several times, they reached temporary compromises, but the basic disagreement inflamed relations until World War II. The United States did not intervene militarily to protect the very large U.S. investments in Mexico because three circumstances discouraged such action. First, public opinion opposed further foreign adventures. Second, a military invasion would have been prohibitively costly in terms of both manpower and finances. Finally, American entrepreneurs with interests in Mexico disagreed sharply over the proper course of action. The oil companies, who were most threatened by the constitution, favored intervention. The banks and the mining companies, whose interests would have been in greater danger in the event of war between the United States and Mexico, opposed intervention. The controversy abated during the late 1920s, when the Calles regime made significant concessions with regard to American oil interests in Mexico.

President Herbert Hoover and Secretary of State Henry L. Stimson continued to shift toward moderation and stepped up U.S. efforts to win good will in Latin America. During the interim between his election and inauguration, Hoover toured Latin America. On taking office, he abandoned Wilson's policy of denying recognition to "unworthy" governments. The Clark memorandum, published in 1930, was a milestone in Hoover's efforts. It declared that the Roosevelt Corollary had no support in the Monroe Doctrine; consequently, the United States would no longer interfere in the internal affairs of Latin American nations under the provisions of the doctrine. But

the president carefully refrained from rejecting intervention outright. In 1933 he withdrew United States troops from Nicaragua and would have removed them from Haiti as well had the Haitians not objected to the withdrawal terms.

A New Era: The Good Neighbor in Depression and War, 1933–1945

Franklin D. Roosevelt assumed the presidency in 1933 amid a severe economic depression. Rejecting "interference in the internal affairs of other nations" and proclaiming the United States to be a "good neighbor" to the rest of the world, Roosevelt built his relations with Latin America on the foundations laid by his predecessor. First, expanding Hoover's initiative, Roosevelt renounced the right to intervene in Latin American affairs. The following year, the United States reached an agreement with Cuba to abrogate the Platt Amendment, thus abandoning its protectorate over the island; the same year, it withdrew its occupation troops from Haiti. In 1937 the United States gave up its right to intervene militarily to protect transit across the Isthmus of Tehuantepec in Mexico.

The nonintervention policy was soon put to the test in Cuba. In 1933 political unrest there threatened the substantial American investment on the island. Roosevelt dispatched Sumner Welles to Havana to try to arrange an accommodation between dictator Gerardo Machado and his opponents. After several months of unsuccessful negotiations, Machado fled, and power fell into the hands of a disorganized and disunited junta. Eventually, Dr. Ramón Grau San Martín emerged as leader of the government. He quickly fell into disfavor with the United States when he suspended loan repayments to a large New York bank and seized two American-owned sugar mills. As a result, the United States refused to recognize the Grau government. With U.S.

warships lingering in Havana harbor, Grau was forced to relinquish his leadership. Supported by the United States, Fulgencio Batista emerged as the strongman of Cuba. Despite the protestations of the United States to the contrary, it was evident that it had not entirely abandoned the "big stick."

Nonintervention was put to another severe test in Mexico in 1938. The long dispute between the Mexican government and the oil companies culminated in the expropriation of foreign oil holdings when the oil companies defied an order of the Mexican Supreme Court in a labor dispute. While the oil companies clamored for reprisal, Roosevelt tried to settle matters peacefully. In the face of isolationist sentiment in the United States, intervention was unthinkable. Moreover, with war in Europe on the horizon, the United States did not want to endanger an important source of oil. A settlement was eventually reached during the 1940s.

Another aspect of Roosevelt's "good neighbor" policy toward Latin America was the effort to achieve reciprocal trade agreements as a means of increasing U.S. trade with the area. Secretary of State Cordell Hull ardently supported such agreements, believing they would help the United States emerge from the Great Depression. From 1934 to 1941, Hull succeeded in signing reciprocal trade treaties with fifteen Latin American nations. Had these treaties succeeded in significantly increasing U.S. trade, which they did not, they would have adversely affected Latin America's nascent industrialization, which was critically dependent on protective tariffs for its survival. In this area, therefore, United States policy was in direct conflict with the goal of Latin American economic development.

In the 1930s, the United States grew increasingly concerned over the spread of German economic and political influence in Latin America. The large communities of German and Italian immigrants in Argentina, Chile, and southern Brazil were viewed as potential foci for the growth of German influence in the area. Both the Chilean and Argentine military establishments had long-standing ties with Germany. In the early 1930s, moreover, Germany began to compete for Latin American trade with the United States through barter agreements.

In response to this growing German economic and political activity, the United States pushed for closer cooperation among the nations of the Western Hemisphere by promoting a series of meetings to consider common problems. In December 1936, the participants in the Inter-American Conference for the Maintenance of Peace agreed to consult in the event of war among themselves or outside the hemisphere. Two years later, the eighth Pan-American Conference met in Lima, Peru; the conferees decided that the mechanism for consultation would be foreign ministers' meetings. In September 1939, shortly after the German invasion of Poland, the First Meeting of Foreign Ministers of the American Republics approved a joint declaration of neutrality and established the Inter-American Financial and Advisory Committee to consider common problems brought on by the war. The foreign ministers proclaimed the existence of a safety zone around the hemisphere and warned belligerents not to wage war within it. In July 1940, after the fall of France, the Second Meeting of Foreign Ministers was held in Havana; the representatives agreed to administer French and Dutch colonies in the Western Hemisphere in the event they were in danger of Nazi takeover. They also proclaimed that an attack on any of the conferring nations would be construed as an attack on all.

As war approached, Latin American nations were generally very cooperative with U.S. efforts to establish mutual defense. The Dominican Republic offered land for bases in 1939; Panama did the same in 1941. Several Latin American nations agreed to sell their raw material production to the United States.

The Third Meeting of Foreign Ministers was held shortly after the Japanese attack on Pearl Harbor in early 1942. The ministers agreed to cooperate against the Axis; most Latin American nations severed diplomatic relations with the Axis powers. During the war, Brazilians fought

534

with distinction in Italy, and a Mexican air squadron served in the Philippines. With the exception of Argentina, every Latin American country contributed to the Allied war effort.

The war strengthened the economic links between the United States and Latin America. The United States served as the sole market for the region's exports and the only supplier of its requirements of arms, munitions, industrial equipment, and manufactured goods. North American investment diversified geographically, going increasingly into South America whereas it had previously focused on the Caribbean. A growing proportion of U.S. capital went into manufacturing enterprises instead of raw material extraction. By the end of the war, Argentina accounted for 16 percent of U.S. investment in Latin America, Chile 16 percent, Brazil 13 percent, and Peru 4 percent. For the first time, South America accounted for over half the total U.S. investment in Latin America.

Defending the Empire and Capitalism, 1945–1981

In the postwar era, three factors determined United States–Latin American relations: the need for the United States to protect large investments in the region, the desire of Latin American nations to industrialize and diversify their economies, and the rivalry between the United States and the Soviet Union.

American Investment and Trade

Several important trends characterized U.S. investment in and trade with Latin America after World War II. First, the amount of investment increased enormously. Furthermore, the type of investment changed from mostly extractive industries, such as mining and oil, to manufacturing. Also, this investment became concentrated in the hands of a few large corporations and banks. Last, although the amount of U.S. trade with Latin America grew substantially, the relative importance of this trade to the economies of the United States and individual Latin American nations decreased.

All these trends did not mean that the United States had changed its policies. Its policy makers continued to base their decisions on U.S. economic interests in the region, as trade and investment represented huge sums, despite declining importance. Thus, every overt or covert U.S. intervention in Latin America during this period—in Guatemala, Cuba, the Dominican Republic, and Chile, for example—took place in countries where the security of large American investments appeared to have been endangered.

Post–World War II Adjustments

Despite the high degree of wartime cooperation, sharp differences between the United States and Latin America surfaced in the immediate postwar years. These disagreements emerged initially at the Chapultepec Conference (Inter-American Conference on the Problems of War and Peace) in February 1945. Latin American leaders felt they should be rewarded for their contributions and sacrifices during the war. The United States, however, regarded European recovery as its first priority. There were also major disagreements over trade, industrialization, the overall direction of Latin American economic development, and the role of the United States in this development. The United States insisted on an open door to Latin American markets and investment opportunities but was unwilling to make any concessions that might injure its own producers. Latin Americans, however, feared that such free access to Latin American markets would destroy much of the industrial progress the region had made in the preceding two decades.

United States and Latin American interests were clearly opposed. The United States wanted to protect and maintain its markets and investment in Latin America, whereas Latin American nations sought to industrialize and diversify their economies. Whereas U.S. leaders regarded private capital investment and free trade as the best routes to development, Latin American nations favored a massive government role in industrialization and restrictions on foreign trade and investment as the only means of modernizing and regaining control over their economies.

After the war, Latin America vainly sought help from the United States to finance industrialization and access to American manufactured goods, especially capital equipment in order to further industrialization. These efforts were hindered further in the next few years as high prices for manufactured products dissipated the dollar reserves Latin American nations had accumulated during the war, while declining prices for raw materials eroded Latin America's terms of trade even further.

There was increasing evidence, moreover, that the United States had reverted to its traditional disregard for Latin American sensitivities and to intervention in the internal affairs of nations of the region. Latin America was pointedly snubbed in the meetings at Dumbarton Oaks (1944) that led to the formation of the United Nations. In addition, President Franklin Roosevelt would not permit Latin American participation in the San Francisco Conference, which organized the United Nations, until every nation of the region declared war against the Axis. This position deeply offended Latin Americans, who objected to being forced to dance to the tune of the United States. In 1946 the United States interfered in the internal political affairs of three South American nations. It meddled disastrously in the Argentine presidential campaign of that year, assuring the election of Juan Perón; it forced the González Videla government in Chile to oust the Communist members of its coalition cabinet; and it helped to undermine a revolutionary regime in Bolivia that had been accused of fascist tendencies.

The Cold War

Alarm in the United States over the vast expansion of Communist influence in Eastern and Central Europe as a result of World War II, the Communist victory in the Chinese civil war, and the gains of Communist parties in Western Europe as a result of their leading role in wartime resis-

tance movements had the effect of pushing Latin America to the back burner. In this initial stage of the cold war, which lasted into the 1950s, the United States focused its attention on checking the further spread of communism in Western Europe by aiding the revival of the shattered capitalist economy of that region through the Marshall Plan. From 1950 to 1954, the United States fought in the Korean war, designed to stem the invasion of the Communist North Koreans.

During this first stage of the cold war, U.S. leaders tended to view the world as two camps, one committed to the United States and its free enterprise system, the other loyal to communism. Since it regarded the world in such black and white terms, the United States viewed with implacable hostility governments and movements that disagreed with its policy or attempted to institute structural social and economic reforms. On two occasions, in Guatemala and Iran, the United States helped to topple such governments through the subversive activities of the CIA.

A second stage of the cold war began in the mid-1950s, when a "third world" emerged, made up of the many newly independent states of Africa and Asia, which proclaimed themselves unaligned in the struggle between the blocs led by the Soviet Union and the United States. The two superpowers, faced with the unacceptable consequences of nuclear war, fought out the cold war in the Third World. In this second stage, the United States became intensely concerned with Latin America only after the 1959 Cuban Revolution led to the establishment of the first socialist state in the Americas. U.S. preoccupation with the threat of more Cubas in the hemisphere produced the Alliance for Progress as an alternative to the Cuban model.

The third stage of the cold war followed the disastrous U.S. experience in Vietnam and lasted until Ronald Reagan took office as president of the United States in 1981. Losing the Vietnam war and its tragic cost brought home to the U.S. government and its people the limitations of U.S. power and the dangers involved in trying to prevent social revolutions. Nonetheless, the United States remained determined to maintain its he-

Salvadoran officer candidates are trained at Fort Benning, Georgia. U.S. advisers also train the Salvadoran army in El Salvador. (Randy Taylor/Sygma)

gemony in the Western Hemisphere and in order to achieve its goals adapted its methods to suit new conditions.

A fourth stage of the cold war brought to the late 1980s the renewal of provocative, anticommunist rhetoric, the simplistic 1950s division of the world into "them" and "us," the return to using force as a policy tool, and a revival of illegal, covert activities. The rise of perestroika under Mikhail Gorbachev in the Soviet Union, the collapse of the Stalinist-type communist regimes in eastern and central Europe, and the resulting demise of the cold war created a problem for the military-industrial complex that had flourished in the cold war's protective shadow and for United

States Latin American policy by depriving it of its traditional enemy, "international communism." In the 1990s, it seems likely the drug trafficker may replace that traditional enemy as a convenient pretext for intervention in Latin America.

The Latin American Policies of Truman and Eisenhower

The Truman administration (1945–1953) focused its attention on fighting communism in Europe and the Far East. But, as we have seen, it meddled with mixed success in the political affairs of Chile, Bolivia, and Argentina in 1946. Under Truman, the movement for hemispheric cooperation continued, at least outwardly. The Rio Treaty of

1947 brought Central and South America into a military alliance with the United States. The ninth International Conference of American States, held in Bogotá the following year, resulted in the formation of the Organization of American States (OAS). The OAS was to provide collective security, with an attack against one member being viewed as an attack on all. The organization also was to be a mediator in disputes between members. Truman and his chief advisers were primarily concerned with maintaining the status quo in the region.

The Eisenhower presidency (1953–1961) marked a revival of strong corporate influence in U.S. foreign policy. Eisenhower took office in the middle of the Korean war and at the height of the McCarthy "Red Scare." His administration, particularly the fanatical anticommunist Secretary of State John Foster Dulles, divided the world into two categories: nations that supported the United States and those that did not. Any foreign government that restricted the activities of U.S. corporations under its jurisdiction was adjudged to be communist and a threat to the security of the United States. During his two terms, Eisenhower faced four challenges of this kind in Latin America: Bolivia, British Guiana, Guatemala, and Cuba. In each case, his administration reacted according to the scale of the American economic interests involved and the prevailing domestic and international conditions.

In Bolivia in 1952, a successful revolution headed by Victor Paz Estenssoro and the National Revolutionary Movement (MNR) ushered in sweeping economic and political reforms; in its first year, the new government nationalized the nation's tin mines, wiped out the latifundio system, replaced the old army with workers' and peasants' militias, and greatly increased the number of eligible voters. The MNR, however, encountered serious economic difficulties that arose from the obsolescence of the tin industry, the disruption to agricultural production caused by the land reform, and massive inflation. The outgoing Truman administration, anxious over the radicalism of the regime, withheld recogni-

tion and aid from Bolivia. The middle-class leadership of the MNR eventually managed to convince the Eisenhower administration that it was not communist; as a result, Bolivia received millions of dollars in grants and loans and substantial technical assistance over the next decade. U.S. aid had a significant moderating influence on the MNR reform program. Indeed, U.S. assistance decisively altered the whole course of Bolivian development; the United States re-established, equipped, and trained the Bolivian army, which overthrew Paz Estenssoro in 1964, ushering in a period of conservative rule that continued almost uninterruptedly until 1981.

The United States employed different tactics to achieve the same general results under the differing conditions of another Latin American country. In 1953, Cheddi Jagan, an avowed Marxist, was elected on a program of structural reform to head the government of the British colony of Guiana. Guiana, however, was an important source of bauxite and other metals; several large U.S. companies, including Reynolds Metals and Kennecott Copper, had substantial holdings in the colony. Alarmed at the prospect of nationalization of these holdings by a Marxist regime, the United States urged the British to nullify the election; the British government duly sent troops to Guiana and deposed the new government.

The Eisenhower administration employed yet other tactics in Guatemala in 1954; conspiring to overthrow a democratically elected government whose reforms threatened the interests of a large and influential American corporation. In 1944 a revolution toppled the oppressive regime of Jorge Ubico, who had ruled Guatemala since 1931. The victorious middle-class revolutionaries favored a capitalist course of development and were friendly to the United States. However, the reform programs of Presidents Juan José Arévalo (1945–1951) and Jacobo Arbenz (1951–1954) provoked the hostility of the United Fruit Company (UFCO) and Dulles. UFCO had operated in Guatemala since the 1890s, when it acquired a virtual monopoly on banana production and distribution. It was Guatemala's largest employer, with ten thousand workers, and its largest landowner. The company also controlled the nation's main transportation artery, the International Railways of Central America (IRCA), and major port facilities on the Gulf of Mexico.

The Guatemalan government clashed with UFCO over labor and land reform. Arévalo enacted a new labor code in 1947. The company, charging that it was being discriminated against, protested sharply. The ensuing labor agitation severely hampered banana production for several years. In 1952 the Guatemalan Congress enacted a land reform program, expropriating large tracts of uncultivated land for distribution among landless peasants. Again, UFCO charged the government with discrimination.

Unfortunately for the Guatemalan government, UFCO enjoyed great influence with the United States government. It was a client of Dulles's law firm. In addition, the company's headquarters were in Boston, which made it a constituent of three of the most powerful men in the United States Congress: Senator Henry Cabot Lodge, Speaker of the House Joseph Martin, and Democratic party leader John McCormack. What was more, the family of the assistant secretary of state in charge of Guatemalan relations, John Moors Lodge, was a major stockholder in United Fruit.

Guatemala's independent foreign policy sharpened its differences with the United States. The Guatemalan labor movement, closely linked to the Arévalo and Arbenz administrations, refused to cooperate with the American Federation of Labor's anticommunist international labor organization. Guatemala was critical of the United States at both the Rio (1947) and Bogotá (1948) conferences; the United States responded by cutting off arms supplies to Guatemala in 1948. In both the United Nations and the Organization of American States, Arbenz resisted American efforts to make it mandatory for members to send troops to Korea.

Seizing on allegations of communist participation in the Arbenz government to justify its actions, the United States trained and outfitted a

rebel group under the command of Carlos Castillo Armas. Castillo Armas invaded Guatemala through UFCO property and overthrew Arbenz in June 1954. His repressive regime, which lasted until his assassination in 1957, erased all of the postwar reforms and restored UFCO's privileges.

The Cuban Revolution and United States–Latin American Relations

Eisenhower's successful interventions in Bolivia, British Guiana, and Guatemala produced bitter criticism of the United States in Latin America and contributed to the hostile and violent reception accorded Vice President Richard Nixon on his tour of the region in 1958. No major change in policy, however, occurred until the victory of Fidel Castro in Cuba in 1959.

After an initial period of confusion over the goals of the new revolutionary government, the United States embarked on a two-pronged program designed to destroy Castro and avert new Cubas. American policy makers simultaneously sought to undermine the rebel regime and to placate the rest of Latin America with various concessions. The United States imposed economic sanctions on Cuba and began clandestinely to train an invasion force of Cuban exiles. To insure Latin American backing, the United States committed limited funds to a new Social Trust Fund for the region and agreed to support plans for common markets in the area, such as the Latin American Free Trade Association (LAFTA) and the Central American Common Market, proposals which it had long opposed.

Cuba was the first major crisis to confront the new administration of John F. Kennedy in 1961. Fearing a proliferation of Cuban-style revolutions throughout Latin America, the administration responded with a comprehensive plan for the region, the Alliance for Progress. The United States pledged to spend $10 billion in the region, over ten years, to build badly needed transportation facilities and to buy technology and industrial equipment. In return, Latin American governments were to institute programs of social and political reform. The United States proposed to foster democracy and economic justice in Latin America through a program of incentives. To guard against more radical movements like the Castro-led guerrilla movement in Cuba, the American government also undertook to strengthen the military forces of the region with arms and training.

The Alliance for Progress, however, brought neither economic development nor democracy to Latin America. In the first place, the program was not intended to be philanthropic but rather to foster capitalist, private-sector development and to expand U.S. trade and investments. Much aid to the region was in the form of loans that eventually had to be repaid. Moreover, aid money had to be used to buy U.S. products transported on U.S. ships; by eliminating competition, such restrictions added greatly to the cost. Although the U.S. government and private sources pumped $10 billion into Latin America during the 1960s, more than that amount of capital flowed out from the area. Debt service payments ate up an increasing share of the budgets of Latin American nations, leaving little for social welfare expenditures and economic development. Often, these nations had to obtain new loans just to pay off their old debts. Unfortunately, too, a significant percentage of aid funds was dissipated through corruption and inefficiency.

American support for the Latin American military was the most effective program of the Alliance. Officers from the region received the most modern training in counterinsurgency tactics against both rural and urban guerrillas and were indoctrinated in the U.S. world view. Allegedly, sophisticated torture techniques formed part of the curriculum. One indication of the thoroughness of the training was the success of U.S.-trained and equipped Bolivian rangers in hunting down Che Guevara and his comrades. The United States also urged Latin American military leaders to take a more positive role in their nations' development by participating in civic action programs in which military personnel built roads and other public facilities.

It was clear, however, that despite the Kennedy administration's avowed goal of helping Latin America "strike off the remaining bonds of poverty and ignorance," its major concern was to maintain friendly capitalist regimes in the region. Kennedy continued to interfere in the internal affairs of countries in the area, even after the debacle of the Bay of Pigs. In 1961 he attempted to destroy the regime of Cheddi Jagan in British Guiana for a second time by refusing to grant much-needed aid and pressing the British to overturn the democratically elected premier. The CIA also helped to subvert the Jagan government. Kennedy was involved in attempts to rid the Dominican Republic of Rafael Trujillo, and there are allegations that the CIA was responsible for the assassination of the dictator in 1961.

Like its predecessors, the Kennedy administration supported dictatorial regimes in Latin America when U.S. policy makers considered them the only alternative to disorder and possible revolution. In March 1962, the United States made no protest when the Argentine military overthrew the democratically elected President Arturo Frondizi. Four months later, the U.S.-trained and equipped Peruvian army seized power to prevent a democratically elected president from taking office. For a time, the United States withheld recognition and cut off aid, but it soon reached an understanding with the military regime. Like its predecessors, the Kennedy administration preferred order, even at the expense of democracy.

President Lyndon Johnson carried on Kennedy's Latin American program, although he increasingly shifted the emphasis of American policy from reform to the maintenance of order. Johnson was determined that he, unlike Kennedy, would not "lose" any nation in any part of the world to communism. In the Dominican Republic in 1965, Johnson faced a rebellion against a reactionary military regime that less than two years before had overthrown the nation's first democratically elected president. Johnson claimed that the United States had the right to intervene unilaterally in Latin America to prevent

540

what he feared would be a Castro-like communist take-over. He dispatched the marines to suppress the rebellion. Johnson was undoubtedly worried about another Cuba in the Dominican Republic, but there is considerable evidence to indicate that his administration's main concern was to assure Dominican sugar production for several important American firms. Not coincidentally, several of Johnson's key foreign policy advisers, including Ellsworth Bunker and W. Averell Harriman, had close links to the sugar industry.

Under Johnson, the United States also played a major role in the military overthrow of the leftward-leaning regime of João Goulart in Brazil in 1964. Disapproving of Goulart's proposed "radical" reforms—which included a mild land reform and the grant of the vote to illiterates—the United States cut aid to Brazil to a minimum in 1963 and began to channel funds instead to pro-U.S. state governors. In April 1964, the Brazilian military toppled Goulart and instituted fifteen years of brutal, repressive dictatorship. The Johnson administration immediately recognized the new government. In the next five years, the United States poured more than $1.5 billion in economic and military aid into Brazil, one-quarter of all U.S. aid to Latin America.

The lavish aid funneled to the Brazilian military helped to persuade the Argentine military that they should overthrow the faltering regime of President Arturo Illia in June 1966. The United States gave the military government $135 million in aid during the three years following the coup.

In political as well as socioeconomic terms, the results of the Alliance under Kennedy and Johnson were dismaying. When Kennedy took office, Alfredo Stroessner in Paraguay was the only dictator in power in South America. By 1968 military dictators ruled in Argentina, Brazil, and Peru, as well as in Paraguay. In Bolivia and Ecuador, civilian-elected governments served as figureheads for the military. In Central America, the record was worse. Rightist military overthrew democratically elected governments in Honduras, Guatemala, and El Salvador. The Somozas tightened their grip on Nicaragua. In 1968

a military coup ousted the elected president of Panama. More importantly, by every measure, the Alliance failed to stimulate economic development or rectify the immense economic and social inequalities of Latin America.

The Vietnam Era

From the late 1960s until 1981, the repercussions of the disastrous U.S. experience in Vietnam and related developments produced readjustments in U.S. foreign policy toward its southern neighbors. But the main goal of this policy—to protect and expand North American economic interests and maintain capitalism as the dominant economic system in the region—has remained constant.

In the aftermath of Vietnam, U.S. policy makers did not regard overt military intervention as a realistic option. They relied on such indirect methods as economic sanctions and subversion. The United States used these methods in Chile from 1970 to 1973 to undermine and ultimately to topple a democratically elected Socialist government.

The story began in 1958, when the Socialist Salvador Allende narrowly missed victory in the Chilean presidential election. For the next fifteen years, the American government poured millions of dollars into Chile, first to prevent Allende from winning subsequent elections, and then, after his election in 1970, to subvert his administration. The scare caused by Allende's near victory in 1958 led the United States to channel funds into the 1964 campaign of the Christian Democratic candidate, Eduardo Frei, a moderate reformer, helping him win the presidency. During Frei's term (1964–1969) the United States sent an average of $130 million a year in aid to Chile. Despite this enormous effort, the mild success of Frei's reform program, and the injection of more millions of dollars in the 1970 campaign, Allende was elected president in 1970.

The United States then imposed economic sanctions on the Allende government, cutting aid by 90 percent and denying credit. Meanwhile, the

CIA cooperated with opposition groups to destabilize the Chilean economy. Amid growing economic difficulties and political turmoil, the Chilean military overthrew Allende in a bloody coup in September 1973. The United States promptly recognized the military junta and resumed aid and credit.

The U.S. economic stake in Chile, as we saw in Chapter 14, was large and concentrated primarily in copper mining. The first act of the Allende government, supported by the unanimous vote of the Chilean Congress, had been to expropriate the holdings of the American copper companies without compensation. Later, it expropriated the International Telephone and Telegraph Company, whose president enjoyed considerable influence in the Nixon administration. The United States intervened both to protect these investments and to teach a salutary lesson to other Latin American nations that might wish to construct a socialist society in the future.

Carter's Latin American Policy: Nationalism, the Canal, and Human Rights

President Jimmy Carter took office in 1977 proclaiming a "new approach" for United States foreign policy based on "a high regard for the individuality and sovereignty of each Latin American and Caribbean nation . . . our respect for human rights, . . . [and] our desire to press forward on the great issues which affect the relations between the developed and developing nations." He immediately put these principles into practice in two major initiatives: the reopening of negotiations with Panama over the canal and the beginning of talks with Cuba about normalization of relations.

Periodically since the signing of the original canal treaty, Panamanians violently protested the U.S. presence in the middle of their country; serious anti-American riots erupted in 1931, 1947, 1959, and 1964. These riots occurred in times of economic hardship in Panama and wrung minor concessions from the United States. One such

concession came in 1936 in the form of the Hull-Alvaro Treaty, which ended the United States protectorate over Panama.

In the 1950s, the Panamanians began a new effort to renegotiate the canal treaty, and talks toward that end opened in 1954. However, it took two major riots, the Castro revolution, and ten years to push the United States into serious negotiations. Lyndon Johnson renewed talks after the bloody riots of 1964. There was a plan afoot at the time to build a new canal through Nicaragua to replace the already obsolete Panama Canal, but when this plan fell through, consideration of a new treaty was also abandoned. Ten years later, General Omar Torrijos, head of a revolutionary military junta in Panama, renewed the push for a new pact. After four years of sometimes bitter negotiations, the United States and Panama agreed to a new treaty that should gradually hand over control of the Canal Zone to Panama by the year 2000. The United States Senate ratified the treaty in April 1978. Although Panamanians were unhappy with a Senate reservation to the treaty that gave the United States the right to intervene to maintain the operation of the canal, it was received with general satisfaction in Panama and throughout Latin America.

During the Torrijos administration (1968–1981), moreover, there was an upsurge of reformist activity, marked by the adoption of a Labor Code (1972) that improved the condition of the working class and by the beginnings of agrarian reform. After Torrijos's mysterious death in an airplane crash, however, power was taken by Manuel Noriega, whose corrupt and brutal reign eroded the reforms and paved the way for the return of the traditional oligarchy.

Negotiations with Cuba led eventually to the opening of United States and Cuban Interest Sections in Havana and Washington in September 1977. These initiatives were short-lived, however, for the two nations came into conflict early in 1978 over Cuba's extensive military involvement in Africa, particularly in Angola and Ethiopia. The Carter administration strenuously objected to the presence of upwards of 35,000 Cuban troops

542

and advisers in Africa and broke off further talks as a result. Relations worsened during 1980 as a consequence of the exodus of 125,000 Cuban refugees to the United States.

Relations with Mexico also proved thorny. Two difficult issues—the terms under which Mexico would supply gas and oil to the United States and the influx of undocumented workers from Mexico into the United States—troubled relations between the two nations. All of this was complicated by Carter's embarrassing lack of sensitivity to Mexican national pride and his inability to establish a working rapport with Mexican President José López Portillo. With the discovery of Mexico's vast petroleum reserves and its development into the United States' third largest trading partner (behind Canada and Japan), Mexico took on increased importance.

Carter's pursuit of human rights proved to be the most controversial aspect of his foreign policy. He centered his attention on Chile, Argentina, and Brazil, the harshest practitioners of repression in the region. The United States instituted sanctions against all of these nations, ending or reducing economic and military aid and impeding their ability to obtain credit from international lending agencies. In the last two years of his term, as a result of stepped-up pressure from American business and concern about growing communist influence in Central America, Carter backed off his human rights activism. His earlier efforts, however, had shown some success. In 1978, nine Latin American nations held elections (though some, like Stroessner's re-election in Paraguay, were pro forma). Carter's criticism of Chile helped bring about some lessening of oppression there; the ruling junta released many political prisoners and disbanded the hated secret police, DINA. The intensity of repression eased in Brazil as the military dictatorship pursued its process of *abertura* (political opening), proclaiming an amnesty in 1979. Carter's greatest human rights triumph was in assuring the democratic transfer of power in the Dominican Republic in 1978. That year when it became clear that Antonio Guzmán would defeat the conser-

vative, long-time incumbent and U.S. ally Joaquín Balaguer (who had ruled since the U.S. intervention in 1965), the army stopped the balloting. The United States, however, quickly made it clear that it would not tolerate a coup. Guzmán subsequently took office peacefully.

Nicaragua proved to be Carter's most difficult and pressing problem in Latin America. The growing insurrection of the Sandinista Front for National Liberation, a broad coalition movement, against the U.S.-backed dictator Anastasio Somoza brought Nicaragua to crisis in 1978. Carter, worried about leftist elements in the Sandinista coalition, sought a more moderate alternative, proposing at one point that the Sandinistas include members of the hated national guard in the post-revolution Nicaraguan government. Following the Sandinista victory in 1979, the United States offered economic aid to rebuild the nation devastated by civil war. After considerable debate the United States Congress approved $75 million. The rise of guerrilla insurgency in neighboring El Salvador, however, alarmed the Carter administration and it backed off from full support for Nicaragua's Sandinistas. The question as to whether or not the Nicaraguan revolutionaries were sending arms to the Salvadoran guerrillas became a major issue in the Carter-Reagan presidential campaign during 1980.

Ronald Reagan, George Bush, and the Return to "Gunboat Diplomacy," 1981–1991

Ronald Reagan became president in 1981 determined to turn back "communism" in Latin America. In the process he openly courted repressive right-wing regimes in Argentina and Chile and committed substantial amounts of U.S. money and military advisers to the antiguerrilla war in Central America. The anticommunist saber rattling was reminiscent of the early 1950s.

The Malvinas/Falklands War

One of the biggest disasters of the Reagan administration's Latin American policy was the war between Argentina and Great Britain over the Malvinas Islands in the South Atlantic. Encouraged by Ambassador to the United Nations Jeane Kirkpatrick, an expert on Latin America, Reagan sought to repair relations with both military regimes in the southern cone, Argentina and Chile. Argentina became an important ally in Central America, providing military advisers to the government of El Salvador.

Misinterpreting the Reagan administration's friendly overtures as a blank check, the shaky military junta in Argentina (see Chapter 13) sought to divert attention from its domestic woes by settling an old dispute with Britain over possession of the Malvinas. A last-minute telephone call from President Reagan to President Galtieri failed to deter the Argentines, who believed the United States would remain neutral in the conflict. On April 2, 1982, the Argentines invaded the islands. Secretary of State Alexander Haig vainly tried to mediate as the British fleet made its way 8,000 miles south to retake the islands. When he failed to bring an end to the war, the United States shifted to full support of the British. In a short, bloody war the British recaptured the Falklands. The Malvinas war badly undermined Latin American trust in the United States as a reliable ally.

Grenada

On October 25, 1983, the United States invaded the tiny island nation of Grenada in the southern Caribbean in order to oust its allegedly Communist, pro-Cuban government. With the event the Reagan administration proclaimed its greatest triumph in Latin American policy. The invasion took place hard on the heels of disastrous foreign-policy blunders in the Malvinas war and amid tragic events in Lebanon, where more than 200 U.S. Marines were killed in a terrorist attack.

In March 1979 the New Jewel Movement, led by Maurice Bishop, had overthrown the British and U.S.-backed government of Eric Gairy, who had dominated Grenadan politics since the early 1950s. After Grenada obtained its independence in 1974, Gairy had grown increasingly dictatorial and eccentric. Bishop proclaimed a revolution and set about establishing close ties with Cuba.

Bishop's program included a massive literacy campaign, the institution of free medical care, free secondary education, and an extensive rehabilitation of housing. He stressed agricultural independence, reducing Grenadan food imports. Bishop undertook to expand tourism, mainly by building a modern airport. In 1983, however, he was murdered during a coup led by Bernard Coard's radical faction in Bishop's own party.

The United States invaded Grenada on the pretext of rescuing U.S. medical students on the island and at the invitation of the Association of East Caribbean states whose members claimed to be threatened by their neighbor. The military operation was later revealed to have been marred by poor planning and faulty intelligence. Elections were held in Grenada in December 1984 that brought to power a middle-road coalition headed by Herbert Blaize. United States aid was $57 million until 1985 but declined considerably thereafter. Hoped-for private investment, widely ballyhooed after the invasion, never materialized. The economy has badly deteriorated and unemployment is rampant.

The invasion of Grenada showed clearly that the United States was as willing as ever to use force to protect its perceived interests in the Caribbean. The action also conveyed the message— as did U.S. policies in Central America—that the United States opposed far-reaching economic and social reform in its "backyard." Moreover, Grenada, like so many other "crises" in the region, was not seen as a nation struggling to overcome impoverishment, but as part of a worldwide communist threat or at the very least as "another Cuba."

Haiti

Barely two years after the Grenada invasion, the Reagan administration played a crucial role in the February 1986 ouster of the long-time dictator of Haiti, Jean Claude ("Baby Doc") Duvalier. The United States had grown increasingly apprehensive about Haiti because of the flood of unwanted immigration to Florida of Haitians, seeking escape from desperate poverty and tyranny. Also Reagan's policy makers feared that the notoriously corrupt and brutal regime would eventually be toppled by Communist forces, which they saw sweeping through Central America during the 1980s. As a result of widespread protests by Haitians of all classes against Duvalier, in January 1986 the United States cut off aid to the dictator's government. The Reagan administration then helped engineer a bloodless coup, easing the way for Duvalier's departure and even furnishing the airplane that took him and his retinue into French exile.

A civilian-military regime led by Lieutenant-General Henri Namphy took over the Haitian reins of government with the avowed tasks of ending oppression and beginning economic reconstruction. Increasingly, however, Namphy resorted to repression and violence to maintain his regime but made no progress in alleviating mass hunger and unemployment. In September 1989, he was toppled by a bloodless coup led by lower-ranking officers and soldiers who demanded democratization, an end to repression, and measures to relieve the terrible poverty of the people. A long-time associate of Duvalier, but regarded as a "moderate," General Prosper Avril, was installed in power and promised a purge of Duvalier elements and free elections in 1990. But Avril, alarmed by the upsurge of organized political activity by labor, peasant, and middle-class groups launched a repression that rivaled Duvalier's in ferocity and postponed elections to an indefinite future. But he continued to have the support of the United States, which regarded him as Haiti's best chance for democracy. Faced with a mounting wave of strikes and popular protest, Avril re-

signed the presidency in March 1990 and left the country. Supreme Court Justice Ertha Pascal-Trouillo was then named interim president, becoming the first woman president in Haiti's history; she promised to remain in office only long enough to organize elections and pass power to a democratically elected government.

In a tense atmosphere, clouded by the return of exiled Duvalierists, including a leader of the brutal Tontons Macoutes militia who appeared to enjoy official protection, and by fear of another army coup, Haitians prepared to elect a president on December 16, 1990. It soon became apparent that the front-runner was the populist priest Jean-Bertrand Aristide, an advocate of liberation theology, whose program of economic justice for the poor alarmed elements of the army, the large landowners, and the business class. A grenade explosion that killed seven of his followers at a rally raised fears for Aristide's life. In the first democratic elections in Haiti's history, he won a landslide victory with some 70 percent of the vote. The presence of a large contingent of international observers, including former President Jimmy Carter, undoubtedly contributed to the fairness and security of the elections, but questions remained as to what would happen after the observers left. As if to remove doubts about its attitude, the United States offered Aristide its assistance. Bolstered by overwhelming popular support, the president-elect was inaugurated in February 1991 and prepared to implement a program that included justice for victims of the Duvalier tyranny, removal of official corruption, land reform, and the protection of vital industries from foreign competition.

Reagan, Bush, and Central America

Ronald Reagan's campaigns against the leftist Sandinista regime in Nicaragua and the leftist Farabundo Martí Front for National Liberation (FMLN) guerrillas in El Salvador took on all the characteristics of a holy crusade against communist forces in Central America. From the beginning of his first term, President Reagan sought to overthrow the Sandinistas, employing tactics that included economic sanctions, a campaign of public misinformation, support of rightist counterrevolutionary armies (the contras), and covert terrorist operations aided by the CIA.

One of Reagan's first official acts in 1981 was to cut off the last $15 million in aid of the $75 million Congress had appropriated for Nicaragua at President Carter's request. More severe economic sanctions followed. By the end of 1985, the United States, by threatening to end its financial support, had effectively foreclosed any possibility of the Sandinistas obtaining loans from any of the major international lending agencies, such as the World Bank or the Inter-American Development Bank. The U.S. government closed Nicaragua's consulates and even forbade the Nicaraguan airline from landing in the United States. The misinformation campaign included unproven allegations against the Sandinistas of running arms to El Salvador, smuggling illegal drugs, and training terrorists.

By far the most damaging U.S. strategy against the Sandinistas was support of the armed opposition to the Nicaraguan government. Predominantly led by ex-Somocista National Guardsmen, the contras were the 1979 creation of the CIA, which recruited ex-guardsman Enrique Bermúdez as their leader. In Reagan's first year in office, he secretly funneled $40 million to support these counterrevolutionaries. The CIA forged the Nicaraguan Democratic Force in late 1981, unifying, temporarily, the contra factions.

Frustrated with Reagan's policy, the United States Congress passed the so-called Boland Amendment, which forbade the use of funds to overthrow the Sandinistas; this legislation was in effect from December 1982 until December 1983. Congress subsequently voted the contras $24 million for 1984. In early 1984 the CIA mined Nicaraguan harbors and staged several helicopter attacks inside Nicaragua. Later that year a CIA manual became public that advised the contras to employ terrorist tactics, including assassinations. The ensuing furor led the Congress to cut

off aid to the contras in October. During the next several months White House aides found private sources for supporting them. Eventually, the Congress gave in to White House pressure and approved $27 million in "humanitarian" aid. In June 1986 Congress appropriated $100 million for the contras.

The Sandinistas drove the contras out of Nicaragua in 1985, reducing their activity to hit-and-run raids across the border from Honduras, which the United States transformed into an enormous military base. By 1987 the United States had invested $200 million in support of the contras and had little to show for it. The counterrevolutionaries were corrupt and quarrelsome, their civilian and military leaders hopelessly divided, and they had made no military headway in overthrowing the Nicaraguan government.

Evidently fearing that the Sandinistas would win a free and fair election in Nicaragua, the Reagan and Bush administrations placed obstacles in the way of the peace process initiated by the Guatemala City accords of August 1987 and continued to provide "humanitarian" aid to the contras in Honduras up to February 25, 1990, the date of the elections. The United States gave millions of dollars in aid to the anti-Sandinista coalition (UNO). Exhausted by almost ten years of U.S.-supported contra war and the U.S. economic blockade, Nicaraguans by a large majority voted in the UNO candidate for president, Violeta Chamorro, and a UNO-dominated congress. But the UNO suffered from serious divisions, and the Sandinistas remained the strongest, best-organized political force in the country.

In the process of taking over the counterinsurgency war in El Salvador, the United States took over the nation's economy and politics as well. The United States consistently interfered in Salvadoran politics, successfully keeping the far right, led by Roberto D'Aubuisson, from taking power in 1989 and shoring up the tottering centrist government of President José Napoleon Duarte, from 1984.

The United States poured some $4.5 billion from 1979 to 1990 into a futile effort to defeat the

FMLN guerrillas. This included massive military assistance in the form of equipment and training. Between 50 and 100 U.S. advisers planned the counterinsurgency campaign, sometimes accompanying Salvadoran government troops in anti-guerrilla forays. For a time, during 1984 and 1985, the Salvadoran army kept the guerrillas at bay because of its advantages in equipment. By early 1987, however, the FMLN was again striking at government forces and installations in almost every part of the country at will. Under domestic and U.S. pressure, both Duarte and his successor, Alfredo Cristiani, initiated peace talks with the guerrillas but appeared to believe their purpose was to negotiate an FMLN surrender. The formidable November 1989 offensive by the FMLN shattered that delusion and forced the government back to the bargaining table without preconditions. By the spring of 1991, despite continuing efforts by hard-line military to obstruct the peace talks, some progress toward agreement had been made and both President Cristiani and the FMLN leadership declared the peace process was "irreversible."

The Invasion of Panama

On his election as president in 1988, George Bush vigorously continued Reagan's Latin American policy of maintaining and reinforcing U.S. dominance over the region. The new noninterventionist course pursued by the Soviet Union, which withdrew its troops from Afghanistan and made no effort to prevent the collapse of Stalinist-type regimes in eastern and central Europe, was interpreted by Washington to mean that its freedom of action was no longer hampered by the possibility of a Soviet response. Most Latin American countries, mired in the greatest depression in the continent's history and heavily indebted to U.S. banks, were unlikely to make more than token protests against U.S. interventionist actions. If the end of the cold war deprived American imperialism of its stock in trade, the bogeyman of "international communism," a new villain, the Latin American *narcotraficante,* the drug traf-

ficker, provided a convenient pretext for an armed intervention that could also distract attention from the failure of the United States to cope with its drug problem at home.

Bush justified the December 1989 invasion of Panama by the need to protect U.S. citizens (a U.S. marine had been killed in a shooting incident), defend democracy, seize dictator Manuel Antonio Noriega on drug charges, and protect the canal. These arguments convinced few foreign governments; the great majority denounced or deplored the invasion as a violation of the UN charter, the Organization of American States treaty, and the Panama Canal Treaty. But they were accepted without questioning by the U.S. press, which "did little more than parrot the Bush administration's transparent legal justifications for the invasion." The press ignored the fact that until he began to display an inconvenient nationalist independence and stopped being "our man in Panama," Noriega was a prized ally of the United States, receiving, by conservative estimates, more than $1.2 million in payoffs from the CIA just during the last ten years of his thirty-year connection with the agency. As regards his drug connections, as recently as February 1987 Noriega received a letter from the U.S. Drug Enforcement Administration (DEA), expressing its gratitude for his traditional position of support for the DEA and the cooperation of his army. The notion that Bush, the former CIA director, did not know of Noriega's drug links strains one's credulity.

The press overlooked, too, long-standing Republican objections to the Carter-Torrijos canal treaties, which provided that in the year 2000 the canal will become Panamanian territory and the U.S. military bases will be dismantled. A document titled "Santa Fe II: A Strategy for Latin America in the Nineties," issued during the 1988 campaign and reflecting the views of the Republican right, in effect provided a blueprint for the invasion, stressing the need for the replacement of Noriega by a "democratic regime" with which the United States would hold talks concerning "the United States' retention of limited facilities in Panama . . . for proper force projection

The capture of General Manuel Noriega, dictator of Panama, was one of President Bush's stated goals of the 1988 U.S. invasion of Panama. Noriega is shown here during his extradition to Miami. (Sygma)

throughout the Western Hemisphere." These and other recommendations in the Santa Fe document closely conform to the Bush administration's Panama policies.

The administration, echoed by the media and the overwhelming majority of the public, which knew only what it read in the papers or saw on television, proclaimed "Operation Just Cause" a huge success. Panamanian Defense Forces resistance was soon broken by intense bombardment;

Noriega escaped death (the U.S. government had placed a bounty of $1 million on his head) but eventually surrendered and was taken off in triumph to be displayed on U.S. television and then imprisoned to await trial on drug charges. Twenty-four American soldiers were killed; estimates of the Panamanian death toll ranged from Washington's figure of 516 to the figure given by an Independent Commission of Inquiry of between 3,000 and 4,000, the great majority being

548 civilians. The areas hardest hit by the invasion were the poorest neighborhoods of Panama City, inhabited primarily by black and mixed-blood people. Thousands were made homeless and re-settled in refugee camps that often lacked medical care, sanitary facilities, and food. In the wake of the invasion the Panamanian Defense Forces were disbanded and replaced by a *Fuerza Pública* (police force), auxiliary to and under the control of the U.S. military command. Hundreds of members of the former ruling Revolutionary Democratic party, of the PDF, and of the volunteer Dignity Battalions organized by Noriega were arrested, and thousands of state employees were dismissed. It was estimated that the invasion had cost $2 billion in damages and reduced the country's economic life, already moribund as a result of U.S. economic sanctions, to paralysis.

In the midst of the invasion, a new president and two vice presidents were sworn in, fittingly enough at a military base of the U.S. Southern Command. The new president, Guillermo Endara, had been leading in the presidential elections of May 1989 (the United States had contributed at least $10 million to his race) when Noriega annulled the election. Endara and his vice presidents represented the traditional oligarchy of very wealthy white families (90 percent of Panama's 2,200,000 population is black, mulatto, or mestizo) who lost their political but not their economic power as a result of the reformist, nationalist revolution of 1968, led by Omar Torrijos. This handful of families, linked by intermarriage and corporate boards, control some 150 of Panama's principal businesses.

One year after the invasion the economic and political situation showed no improvement. With unemployment at almost 30 percent and underemployment at 25 percent, massive layoffs of government employees (the government bureaucracy had more than doubled under Noriega) have aggravated the country's economic and social problems. Pleas that the United States compensate victims of the invasion for loss of property and family have been rejected by the Bush administration. Meanwhile the fragile coalition

supporting Endara's government appeared to be disintegrating due to growing tensions and rivalries between the parties.[5]

The larger issue troubling many Panamanians is continuing U.S. intervention in Panamanian affairs and what it portends for the future. Drug Enforcement Administration agents, for example, have launched operations in various provinces without seeking official Panamanian consent. What many Panamanians fear is that "Washington will use its efforts to oust Noriega as an excuse to declare the Canal treaties void and to continue to maintain a military presence in the isthmus, something ruled out by the Carter-Torrijos treaties." Even if sanctioned by Panama's government, such an action would certainly produce a new explosion of Panamanian nationalism, like that which occurred in the years before the signing of the treaties.

Latin America and the Gulf War

Latin America felt the impact of the crisis that began with the Iraqi invasion of Kuwait in August 1990 and erupted into the short but destructive Gulf War in February 1991. For most countries of the region, heavily dependent on oil imports, the economic effects of the dramatic rise in oil prices were profoundly negative. Brazil, the largest oil importer, was particularly hard hit, for it had a barter arrangement with Iraq whereby it paid for oil with manufactured goods, and U.N. sanctions against Iraq forced Brazil to use its limited hard

[5] A few indicators of the change in Panamanian public opinion since the December 1959 invasion: One year later President Endara's approval rating in the polls had fallen from 90 percent to 14 percent. In special elections held in January 1991 in nine legislative districts three parties tied to the Noriega regime won five seats, while President Endara's party won none. According to the *New York Times* (February 11, 1990) "hopes among the poor and lower middle class who made up two-thirds of the population have evaporated . . . In interviews they say they resent the lawyers and bankers who hold the top posts in the government as descendants of the oligarchy overthrown in 1968 by Mr. Torrijos, then a colonel in the national Guard."

currency to buy oil from other sources at world market prices. The region's oil exporters—Venezuela, Mexico, Ecuador, Colombia, and Trinidad and Tobago—profited by increasing their oil exports to compensate for the loss of Iraqi and Kuwaiti supplies and by the sharp rise in crude oil prices. But even they stood to lose in the long run—the unexpectedly quick ending of the war left them with large oil surpluses, forcing prices down to much lower levels.

Although most Latin Americans condemned Iraq's invasion of Kuwait, polls showed that they opposed the war option by equal or even greater majorities. In Argentina, whose government was the only one to give military aid to the coalition led by the United States, 91 percent of those questioned opposed Argentina's participation in the war and demanded the return of the two warships sent to join the multinational force. In general, editorial opinion was strongly critical of President Bush's haste to abandon reliance on sanctions against Iraq in favor of war, his rejection of various peace proposals, and the massive destruction of life and material resources caused by the war. There was widespread skepticism, too, regarding Bush's professions of concern for self-determination by critics who recalled the U.S. invasions of Panama and Grenada and the covert war against Nicaragua. Many regarded Bush's call for a "new world order" as a thin disguise for the vision of a unipolar world dominated by the United States, the only superpower.

Chapter 21

Latin American Society in Transition

By the early 1990s, Latin America's economic, social, and political problems had reached explosive proportions. The signs of crisis were everywhere, but the imbalance between the area's burgeoning population and the sluggish rate of growth or even decline of staple food production in most Latin American countries was especially disquieting.

Crises in the Twentieth Century

Economic Problems

By 1990 the population of Latin America was estimated to be 455 million; it was growing at a rate of almost 3 percent a year and was likely to exceed 600 million by the end of the century. In order to achieve even a modest improvement in Latin American living standards, per capita staple food production should grow considerably faster than population. In fact, Latin American agricultural production in absolute terms has greatly increased in recent decades, due to the expansion of acreage and the "green revolution," which has dramatically raised crop yields through increased use of tractors, fertilizers, and new hybrids. Between 1970 and 1977, agricultural production increased by 30 percent. The bulk of this increase is accounted for by increased production of such export crops as sugar, coffee, and soybeans. In the same period the importation of grains (wheat, maize, and rice) had grown at a rate of about 9 percent a year. Today only three Latin American countries—Argentina, Uruguay, and Guyana—are grain exporters. The dependence of all other countries on food imports has grown considerably. Countries that once were self-sufficient now suffer from food shortages. Mexico, which as late as 1969–1971 was a net exporter of grain, had to import 13 percent of its needs in 1978. In the same year, the share of imports in national food consumption rose to 21 percent for Brazil, 75 percent for the Caribbean area, almost 50 percent for Chile. The dependence on food imports is reflected in the price of staple foods, which has risen more rapidly than wages in eighteen of the twenty-one Latin American countries. At least half of the Latin American population cannot satisfy its basic food needs.

Chile, whose military dictatorship liquidated the agrarian reforms instituted by previous regimes, illustrates the dramatic decline in nutritional standards. In 1977–1979, food consumption of the population was 13 percent below the 1971–1973 level, while the poorest portion of the population (40 percent) consumed less than 1,900 calories a day, though the indispensable minimum to avoid malnutrition is 2,318 calories. The consumption of foods of high nutritive content has declined in recent years in some of the most favored countries of the area, such as Argentina and Uruguay.

Population pressure on limited land resources is not a major cause of the food problem. In 1980, of the total area of 570 million hectares suitable for cultivation, only 143 million hectares, or 28 percent, were actually worked. A major cause of the food crisis is an agricultural strategy that emphasizes export crops at the expense of internal consumption. According to the United Nations' Food and Agriculture Organization, if Latin America converted the coffee, cotton, sugar, and banana plantations—many owned by multinational companies—to food production for internal consumption, it could double its wheat yield or increase its rice crop by 250 percent. A closely related cause of the problem is an unjust system of land tenure and use, the latifundio. The new capitalist, highly mechanized type of latifundio in particular sharply limits employment opportunities and absorbs, by legal or illegal means, many small plots previously devoted to staple food cultivation.

By the late 1980s the problem of deficits in staple food production had grown instead of diminished. In Mexico, the production of maize, wheat, and sunflowers for local consumption was increasingly replaced by cultivation of strawberries and a wide variety of vegetables for sale in the United States during the winter months. Between 1983 and 1986 the production of maize in Mexico declined 15 percent and that of wheat grew only 4 percent; in the same period the population grew 9 percent. One study showed that in Mexico more grain is consumed by cattle than by peasants. In Brazil, extensive tracts of land that once produced traditional staples like black beans, rice, and manioc are now producing coffee, soybeans, and oranges for export. The growing dependency in Latin America on imports of basic grains, purchased at international market prices, means that larger sectors of the population find these imports prohibitively expensive. A 1983 study by the Latin American Economic System (SELA), an organization formed to promote economic ties in the region, projected from early 1980s trends an 86 percent decline in Latin America's basic grain self-sufficiency by the year 2000. The dangers of such extreme dependency on foreign grain producers are obvious. More and more Latin Americans are calling for a change in agricultural strategy based on different priorities that would place meeting the area's nutritional needs ahead of extracting wealth from the production of industrial crops, livestock feed crops, and luxury fruits and vegetables. Such a shift would have to take place within the context of a thorough, regionwide democratically controlled agrarian reform. It would be naive, however, to expect that most Latin American governments, presently controlled by and representing elite interests, will willingly adopt such new policies.

The income disparities of the region are growing instead of diminishing. Some of the preceding chapters on individual countries have already provided information on this point. It should be noted that high national per capita income figures may be deceptive, concealing a very skewed income distribution. It is interesting to note that the political system of a Latin American country, whether a dictatorship of the type that ruled Brazil in the 1960s and 1970s or a formal democracy of the Mexican or Venezuelan type, seems to have little bearing on the pattern of income distribution. The percentage of the national income received about 1975 by the poorest 20 percent of the population of Chile, Brazil, and Venezuela, was 5 percent, 5 percent, and 2 percent, respectively. For the area as a whole, the share of the total income received by the poorest 40 percent of the population fell from 8.7 to 7.7 percent between 1960 and 1975.

Social Problems

Housing is one of the area's gravest social problems. Throughout the area, much of the housing is improvised and lacks proper sanitary facilities. Often a whole family is crowded into a single room. The absence of adequate drinking water and sewage services contributes to a high incidence of parasitic and infectious diseases.

Adequate health care is one of the most pressing needs of Latin Americans, and it is the least available of public services. Malnutrition is the greatest health problem. Children are the principal victims. Recent UNICEF statistics indicate that in Latin America, 3,000 children under the age of five die every day; malnutrition is believed to account for half of these deaths. Commercial infant formulas, aggressively promoted in Latin America by such transnational corporations as Nestlé and Bristol Myers, have contributed to infant malnutrition because poor women have been persuaded to substitute bottled formula for breast milk. In areas without clean water, the mothers' frequent practice of watering the milk to save money on formula makes bottle feeding especially dangerous for newborns and "results in repeated epidemics of diarrhea—and the vicious cycle of diarrhea-malnutrition brings early death." Latin American infant mortality rates declined in the 1970s but increased in the 1980s, almost certainly as a result of deteriorating economic conditions.

The reappearance of diseases that had apparently been eradicated in the area provides other evidence that the health situation in Latin America is deteriorating. In 1985, for example, the incidence of malaria reached levels that had not been seen for twenty years. Again, the absence of clean drinking water and adequate sewage facilities are major causes of such infectious or contagious diseases as typhoid, hepatitis, malaria, cholera and the great killer diarrhea.

Rising health problems are clearly related to the present economic crisis, the worst since the Great Depression of the 1930s. Purchasing power has declined by 40 percent or more in many nations in recent years, in some countries half the working force is unemployed or underemployed. Such factors aggravate the incidence of malnutrition and disease in general. Too many Latin American governments have sharply reduced social services, including health services, as part of austerity programs designed to meet interest payments on foreign debt. In 1976, Latin American governments on the average assigned 15 percent of their budgets to health; by 1986 the figure fluctuated between 4 percent and 12 percent. These cutbacks are reflected in the deterioration of hospital care, fewer pharmaceutical imports, and reduced government support for medical schools.

Great disparities exist in the levels of health care available in different Latin America countries. Cuba and Haiti may serve to illustrate these differences. In 1986, Cuba had the following health indicators: its infant mortality rate was 15 deaths per 1,000 live births; life expectancy was 73.5 years; 99 percent of all expectant mothers delivered in hospitals or clinics; 100 percent of the infant population was vaccinated; 20,000 doctors and 35,000 nurses served an urban and rural population of 10 million; and the national health budget (1985) was $668 million, or $66 per capita. The corresponding 1986 indicators for Haiti are as follows: the infant mortality rate was 133 deaths per 1,000 live births; one-third of all children died before the age of five; life expectancy was 48 years; in rural areas there was one doctor for every 20,000 people and one dentist for every 100,000; and the national health budget (1985) was $18 million, or $3.44 per capita.

Latin America suffers from a tremendous shortage of educational facilities. In Brazil, for example, a majority of school-age children do not attend school because there are not enough schools and teachers or because the poverty of their parents forces them to join the work force. Almost everywhere the dropout rate is very high. Although official figures show that the illiteracy rate among persons fifteen years of age or over declined from 45 to 27 percent between 1950 and 1970, the number of illiterates actually increased by 13 million in those years because of the rapid population growth. In 1977, the illiteracy rates for Mexico, Brazil, and Peru were 35 percent, 33 percent, and 55 percent. Only socialist Cuba and more recently Nicaragua (until the effects of the contra war and the rightist electoral victory in 1990 reversed that trend) showed dramatic improvement in this area; Cuba's nationwide campaign to wipe out illiteracy had achieved its goal by 1982. The inadequacy of Latin America's educational system is reflected in the low technical level of its work force.

An accelerated urbanization, caused by a massive migration of rural dwellers to the city, has sharpened all these problems. This rural exodus results from the interplay of two forces: the "pull" of the city, which attracts rural people with the frequently illusory prospect of factory work and a better life, and the "push" of the countryside, where concentration of land and mechanization of agriculture are expelling millions of peasants from their farms and jobs. In 1959, 39 percent of the population lived in towns and cities; by 1960 the figure had risen to 47 percent, by 1970 to 54 percent, and by 1975 to an estimated 58 percent. The urban population is increasing at more than twice the rate of the population as a whole. A United Nations estimate foresaw that by the year 2000 the urban population (*urban* here refers to a settlement of more than 2,000 people) would form some 80 percent of the total population of the area.

Most striking, however, has been the growth in the number of cities with over 1 million inhabitants. Between 1950 and 1970 the number of such cities rose from six to seventeen, and their total population increased from 15 to 55 million. If these trends continue, in the year 2000 the cities will contain about 220 million inhabitants, or about 37 percent of the total Latin American population at that time.

Industrialization and the rural exodus have produced the phenomenon of hyperurbanization—the rise of vast urban agglomerations or zones of urban sprawl. About 80 percent of Brazil's industrial production is located in the metropolitan zones of São Paulo, Rio de Janeiro, and Belo Horizonte. Two-thirds of Argentine production is concentrated in the area between Buenos Aires and Rosario. More than half of the industrial production of Chile and Peru is located in the metropolitan zones of Santiago and Lima-Callao, respectively; Caracas accounts for 40 percent of the industrial production of Venezuela. Between 25 and 50 percent of the populations of Uruguay, Argentina, and Mexico now live in the capitals of those countries.

As these vast urban concentrations increase, life becomes more and more difficult for their inhabitants. All the urban problems—food, housing, transportation, schools, drinking water, and sanitation—are immensely aggravated. Mexico City is a case in point. In 1930 the city had 1 million inhabitants and extended over an area of 200 square kilometers; it reached 2.8 million inhabitants in 1950; by 1982 it had a population of 14 million persons spread over an area of 800 square kilometers. At the present rate of growth, the population will be 32 million by the end of the century. In 1950 the city accounted for 22 percent of the country's gross national product, 44 percent in 1975, and nearly 50 percent in 1982. The pollution caused by toxic agents generated by industry and the automobile (Mexico City has more than 2 million cars) has been denounced by medical specialists as a major danger to health and life. Shantytowns cover almost 40 percent of the urban area and house approximately

Rapid urbanization and rural exodus have created immense social problems throughout many Latin American nations. The living conditions of urban squatters outside Lima, Peru—shown here—reflect the poverty experienced by many who live in heavily populated areas. (Gamma Graphics)

4 million people, a large proportion of whom are unemployed or underemployed; in 1978, 1.2 million persons lacked potable water. With some variations, most large cities of Latin America have similar slum areas—called *favelas* in Brazil, *callampas* in Chile, *villas miseria* in Argentina—that present the same spectacle of extreme want and squalor.

In Europe and North America, urbanization, industry, and the demand for labor grew at a fairly even pace, but in Latin America, industrial growth and demand for labor lag far behind the explosive growth of the urban population. Much of the new industry, especially its foreign-owned sector, is highly mechanized and automated; it therefore generates relatively little new employ-

ment. In such a traditional Latin American industry as textiles, mechanization has actually produced a net loss of jobs. The low purchasing power of the masses also hinders the creation of new jobs, for the market for goods is quickly saturated, and industry chronically operates below capacity. Finally, many of the rural migrants are illiterate and lack the skills required by modern industry. As a result, an immense "reserve army" of labor has arisen both in the city and the countryside. According to the United Nations Economic Commission for Latin America, 40 percent of the area's labor force is completely or partly unemployed.

Industry's inability to absorb the supply of labor has produced an exaggerated growth of the so-called service sector. The growth of this sector considerably exceeds that of the industrial labor force, which grew from 20 to 24 percent of the labor force from 1960 to 1980, while the service sector rose from 33 to 45 percent in the same period. The service sector includes a great number of poorly paid domestic servants and a mass of individuals who eke out a precarious living as lottery ticket vendors, car watchers and washers, shoeshiners, and street peddlers of all kinds. As a result of the economic crisis of the 1980s, this service sector, also known as the "informal sector" of the economy, has grown considerably in the past decade.

Cuba alone has made a serious effort to check and reverse the hypertrophy of the city. On the eve of the revolution, Cuba's urban-rural structure closely resembled that of the rest of Latin America. One-fifth of the country's population and almost 53 percent of its industrial production were concentrated in Havana; there was an enormous economic, social, and cultural imbalance between the capital and the countryside. Almost from the day it took power, the revolutionary government undertook to redress the balance by shifting the bulk of its investments to the countryside and by raising rural living standards through the provision of adequate medical, educational, and social services; a more rational geographic distribution of the economic infrastructure; and the creation of planned new cities. Thanks to these policies, aided by the departure of thousands of middle-class dissidents for the United States, the growth of Havana's population had begun to decline by 1965, and a reverse current of migration began from the capital into a countryside that was itself becoming urbanized.

The New Class Structure

Industrialization, urbanization, and the commercialization of agriculture have significantly altered the Latin American social structure and the relative weight of the various classes. These changes include a partial transformation of the old landed elite into a new latifundista class with a capitalist character, the emergence of a big industrial and financial bourgeoisie with close ties to foreign capital, an enormous growth of the so-called urban middle sectors, and the rise of a small but increasingly class-conscious factory working class. A survey of these and other developments suggests the complexity of modern Latin American class alignments and the possible direction of future social and political change.

The Great Landowners

Although they have had to yield first place economically and politically to the big bourgeoisie, the great landowners, Latin America's oldest ruling class, retain immense power, thanks to their control over the land and water resources of the area. Over the last few decades, as earlier chapters show, there has been a major expansion of the latifundio, especially of the new type, which produces industrial and export crops with the use of improved technology and wage labor. This expansion was stimulated by rising prices for land, crops, and livestock; by the desire to forestall peasant claims to land under future land reform legislation; and by the prodding of governments that saw modernization as an alternative to radical land reform from below. The movement is gaining momentum throughout the continent and spreading even in countries like Mexico and Bolivia, which had experienced radical but not socialist land reforms.

The traditional hacendado is a vanishing breed. His successor is often a cosmopolitan, university-trained type who combines agribusiness with industrial and financial interests. But the arbitrary and predatory spirit of the old hacendados survives in the new latifundistas. The great landowners continue to be the most reactionary class in Latin American society.

The New Bourgeoisie

A native commercial bourgeoisie arose in Latin America after independence and consolidated its position with the rise of the neocolonial order after mid-century. In the second half of the nineteenth century, an industrialist class, largely of immigrant stock, appeared in response to the demand of a growing urban population for consumer goods. World War I further stimulated the movement for import-substitution industrialization. But the day of the industrial entrepreneur did not arrive until the great economic crisis of 1930 disrupted the trading patterns of the area. Aided by favorable international and domestic background conditions and massive state intervention, the native industrial bourgeoisie quickly gained strength and in many countries displaced the landed elite as the dominant social and economic force. However, as a rule, the new bourgeoisie avoided frontal collision with the latifundistas, preferring to form bonds of kinship and interest with the landed elite.

Meanwhile, foreign capital, attracted by the potential of the growing Latin American market, began to pour into the area, particularly after 1945. Possessing immensely superior capital and technological resources, foreign firms absorbed many small and middle-sized national companies and came to dominate key sectors of the economy of the host countries. Aware, however, that the survival of a native bourgeoisie was essential to their own security, foreign capitalists endeavored to form close ties with the largest, most powerful national firms through the formation of mixed companies and other devices. This dependence on and linkage with foreign corporations explains why the Latin American big bourgeoisie lacks nationalist sentiment.

Latin American big business, like its foreign counterparts, displays a clear tendency toward monopoly. The typical form of business organization in most countries is the family firm. In Brazil in the 1960s, six large family companies dominated the native private industrial sector. The Matarazzo family controlled more than three hundred enterprises (textiles, food, chemical, cellulose, construction, and oil, among others) with a labor force of over thirty thousand persons and an annual turnover of more than $300 million. In Argentina, the giant Bunge y Born firm employed more than seventeen thousand workers in its eighty-two enterprises and had an an-

nual turnover of more than $350 million. The large Tornquist family, which was active in cattle ranching, sugar refining, and industry, illustrated the fusion of industrial and latifundist interests in Argentina. In Chile, the Alessandri, Yarur, Matte, and Edwards families dominated the industrial scene. Here, too, three large holding groups—Banco de Chile, Banco Sud Americano, and the Edwards group—controlled about 70 percent of all capital in business corporations. Similar processes of concentration of capital were visible in Mexico, Colombia, and other countries of the region.

In its youth, some sections of the Latin American national bourgeoisie supported the efforts of such nationalist, populist chieftains as Cárdenas, Perón, and Vargas to restrict foreign economic influence and accepted, though with misgivings, their concessions to labor. Soon, however, the big bourgeoisie adopted the hostility of its foreign allies to restrictions on foreign capital and independent trade unionism. With rare exceptions, the big capitalists supported repressive military regimes in such countries as Brazil, Uruguay, and Chile until, convinced that the policies of those regimes threatened the stability of capitalism itself, they became converts to democracy.

The bourgeoisie, however, is not a monolithic bloc. Alongside the small group of big capitalists there exists in each country a much greater number of small and middle-sized firms that tend to favor state action to restrict foreign economic and political influence. Typical of the Latin American parties predominantly representing the interests of this capitalist group is *Acción Democrática* (Democratic Action) in Venezuela. Following its electoral victory in 1974, the Venezuelan government, headed by President Carlos Andrés Pérez, nationalized the foreign-owned oil industry and iron ore mines and began to broaden trade and diplomatic relations with the socialist countries and the Third World. But the commitment of the native capitalist group to nationalist economic policies is far from being firm and consistent; moreover, it tends to share the anti-working-class sentiments of the big capitalists.

The Urban Middle Sectors

The urban middle sectors are that great mass of urban dwellers who occupy an intermediate position between the bourgeoisie and the landed elite, on the one hand, and the peasantry and industrial working class, on the other. The boundaries of this intermediate group with other classes are vague and overlapping. At one end, for example, the group includes highly paid business managers whose lifestyle and attitudes identify them with the big bourgeoisie; at the other, it takes in store clerks and lower-echelon government servants, whose incomes are often lower than those of skilled workers.

The oldest urban middle sector consists of self-employed craftsmen, shopkeepers, and owners of innumerable small enterprises. The great number of small workshops in which the owner both works and employs other workers (90 to 95 percent of all enterprises) suggests the importance of this sector.

White-collar employees from another large urban intermediate sector. Urbanization, the growth of commercial capitalism, and the vast expansion of the state sector in recent decades have contributed to an inflation of both public and private bureaucracies. Public employees make up about one-fifth of the economically active population of the area.

University students compose a sizable urban middle sector. Between 1950 and 1970, their number rose from 250,000 to over 1 million. The great majority (some 90 percent) come from middle-class backgrounds, and many must combine work and study. Student discontent with inadequate curricula and teaching methods and the injustices of the social and political order have made the university a focal point of dissidence and protest. But the students are in the end transients; in Latin America, as elsewhere, their radical or reformist zeal often subsides after they enter a professional career.

Because of their great size, the ideology of the urban middle sectors and their actual and potential role in social change are issues of crucial importance. Following World War II, many foreign experts on Latin America, especially in the United States, pinned great hopes on the "emerging middle sectors" (to which they assigned the new industrialist class) as agents of progressive social and economic change. The history of the last few decades has not confirmed those expectations. The urban middle sectors have mushroomed, but with the exception of many students and intellectual workers—teachers, writers, scientists—they have not been a force for social change.

The error of the foreign experts consisted in confusing the Latin American middle sectors with their counterparts in Europe and North America. Unlike the European and North American middle classes, the Latin American middle sectors did not arise from a process of dynamic industrial development. They arose in the protective shadow of a neocolonial export-import economy that was gradually transformed into a dependent, deformed capitalism with strong ties to the latifundia. Very few self-made men have come from their ranks. Their ideology mirrors that of the ruling class, whose lifestyle they try to copy by keeping one or two servants and in other ways. They regard manual labor as degrading, resent forced contact with the lower orders in buses or trolleys, and look down on Indians and blacks. Confused and misinformed on economic and political issues, they are easy prey to rightist demagogy and anticommunist propaganda. These groups provided the mass base for the right-wing military coups in Brazil and Chile. However, the urban middle sectors should not be written off as hopeless reactionaries. By their very intermediate nature, they are capable of strong political oscillations, especially in response to the movement of the economy.

The Peasantry

The term peasantry refers here to all small landowners, tenants, and landless rural laborers. As noted, the current expansion of the new type of latifundio is creating an unparalleled crisis for the Latin American peasantry. The increased use of tractors and other kinds of mechanized farm

Contrasting statuses of Bolivian women; two peasants flank a middle-class shopper. (Paul Conklin)

equipment has already displaced millions of farm workers, and the process is accelerating. The growing surplus of labor, inflation, and the weakening of rural labor organizations by repressive military regimes have contributed to the decline of peasants' real income from wages and other forms of labor. The majority of the "land reforms" of Latin American governments have not checked the trend toward concentrations of land and agricultural income in the hands of a small elite. Out of a Latin American rural labor force of some 32 million, about 20 million are already landless. Lacking access to agricultural credits, machinery, and soil-improving inputs, the small farmer appears doomed.

An exaggerated individualism, political apathy, and religious fanaticism are traits commonly attributed to the Latin American peasantry, but these are stereotypes that most anthropological and sociological studies seem to disprove. The supposed attachment of the peasantry to private landownership is especially open to question. When given an option, as in Cuba, Peru, and Chile, campesinos have usually preferred collective or cooperative farming over small, private landholdings. The failure of capitalist agricultural models to solve the problems of rural poverty, employment, and food production makes it likely that the future of Latin American agriculture belongs in the main to a variety of socialist and cooperative forms of land tenure.

The Industrial Working Class

The rapid growth of capitalism in Latin America in recent decades has been accompanied by a parallel growth of the industrial working class. Although miners and factory workers form the best-organized and most class-conscious detachments of the army of labor, they are a minority of the labor force. Artisans, self-employed or working in shops employing less than five persons, constitute the largest group. The predominance of the artisan shop, whose labor relations are marked by paternalism and individual bargaining, hinders the development of workers' class consciousness and solidarity.

The recent peasant origins of great numbers of workers have also had a negative influence on the development of the labor movement, for rural migrants often bring with them traditions of dependence on and deference to the patrón and a general social and cultural backwardness. This backwardness made the new factory workers susceptible to the populist demagogy of leaders like Perón and Vargas, who offered them limited concessions in return for the abandonment of independent trade unionism and class struggle. Even more susceptible to such demagogy and marginal concessions are the large slum populations, composed of rural migrants who are often unemployed or irregularly employed.

These problems of growth delay but do not prevent the development of working-class consciousness, organization, and independence. The collapse of the nationalist-populist model of economic and social reform in countries like Argentina and Brazil and the equal failure of the Christian Democratic reformist model in Chile and elsewhere have tended to radicalize the Latin American labor movement. Today, socialism is probably the most influential ideology among the factory workers of such key countries as Chile, Argentina, and Brazil.

The industrial working class has played a key role in major recent movements for social and political democracy in Latin America. Armed Bolivian tin miners helped achieve the victory of the 1952 revolution and its program of land reform and nationalization of mines. Cuban workers gave decisive support to the guerrilla struggle against the Batista dictatorship. Their general strike in 1959 helped to topple it. The working class of Buenos Aires intervened at a critical moment (October 1945) to save Juan Perón from being overthrown by a reactionary coup, and its pressure broadened his reform program. In Chile the working class led the Popular Unity coalition that brought Salvador Allende to the presidency, ushering in a three-year effort (1970–1973) to achieve socialism by peaceful means.

These advances—especially the Cuban and Chilean revolutions—provoked a counterrevolutionary reaction that until recently was still ascendant. In many countries under military and personal dictatorships, all working-class parties were banned and trade unions abolished or placed under strict government control.

In the past, reactionary elites were able to play the peasantry against the working class, as happened in Bolivia in the 1950s, or the urban middle sectors against the peasantry and the working class, as occurred in Brazil in 1964 and in Chile in 1973. The price of this disunity appears to have been learned, and new interclass coalitions are being forged in which the working class will certainly play a large role.

Attitudes and Mentalities: Change and Resistance to Change

Change was in the air of Latin America as it entered the last quarter of the twentieth century. Economic modernization demanded changes in family life, race relations, education, and the whole ideological superstructure of society, but the old attitudes and mentalities struggled hard to survive. As a result, Latin America presented dramatic contrasts between customs and mores that were as new as the Space Age and others that recalled the age of Cortés and Pizarro.

Woman's Place

The status of women was a case in point. In some ways, that status had improved; the struggle to obtain the vote for women, for example, began

560 around World War I and ended successfully when Paraguay granted women suffrage in 1961. More and more Latin American women held appointive and electoral offices, and in increasing numbers they entered factories, offices, and the professions. By 1970 in some countries, notably Brazil and Argentina, the number of working women classified as professionals was higher than the number of men, a significant fact because the proportion of economically active women was much lower than that of men. In Brazil, out of every 100 women working in nonagricultural sectors in 1970, 18 were engaged in professional and technical operations, whereas for men the figure was only 6 out of every 100. The ratios were reversed, however, for positions of higher responsibility; this reflected the persistence of discriminatory attitudes.

The impact of recent economic and social changes on the place of women in the Latin American workplace has been complex and even contradictory. The commercialization and mechanization of agriculture have made it more difficult for women to find work in that area except in processing plants. At the same time, inflation, falling wages, and decline of living standards caused by government austerity programs have forced growing numbers of women to join the labor force to help support their families. In Brazil, for example, the number of economically active women almost doubled from 1970 to 1980.

The small movement for women's rights could claim much less progress in such areas as family patterns, divorce laws, and sexual codes. The traditions of the patriarchal family, of closely supervised courtship and marriage, remained dominant among the upper and middle classes. The ideology of machismo, the cult of male superiority, with its corollary of a sexual double standard, continued to reign almost everywhere in the continent. "The Mexican family," wrote sociologist Rogelio Díaz-Guerrero in 1967, "is founded upon two fundamental propositions: (a) the unquestioned and absolute supremacy of the father and (b) the necessary and absolute self-sacrifice of the mother." With small variations, Díaz-Guerrero's statement could be made about the family structure in almost every other Latin American republic.

Socialist Cuba has made great advances in abolishing sexual discrimination in law and practice; in 1976 it introduced the Family Code, which gave the force of law to the division of household labor. Working men and women are required to share housework and child care equally, and a recalcitrant spouse can be taken by the other to court. But Vilma Espín, head of the Cuban women's movement, admitted that the law was one thing and the way people lived was another. "Tradition is very strong. But we have advanced. Before, the machismo was terrible. Before, the men on the streets would brag about how their wives took care of them and did all the work at home. They were very proud of that. At least now we have reached the point where they don't dare say that. That's an advance. And now with young people you can see the difference."

Nicaragua is another country where a liberating revolution transformed the lives and roles of many women. Women, both rural and urban, took part in the struggle against the Somoza tyranny and made an immense contribution to its final triumph in July 1979. Women prepared for the final offensive by stockpiling food, gathering medical supplies, and organizing communication networks to send messages to Sandinista fighters and their families. By the time of the final victory, from one-quarter to one-third of the Sandinista People's Army were female—some as young as 13. Three women were guerrilla commanders; two served on the general staff of the People's Army. Following the triumph of the revolution, women assumed responsible positions at all levels of the Sandinist government. A similar process of women's liberation is taking place as part of the revolutionary struggle in neighboring El Salvador. As the Cuban experience shows, old ideologies die hard; neither in Cuba nor in Nicaragua have women achieved full consciousness of themselves as equals or full recognition of their equality by males, but significant progress has been made in that direction.

Race Prejudice

Notions of black and Indian inferiority are everywhere officially disapproved, but race prejudice remains strong, especially among upper- and middle-class whites. Socialist Cuba has made the largest progress in integrating its black minority into the national life and in combating the vestiges of racism.

The Indian remains the principal victim of racist exploitation and violence. In Brazil, according to one recent estimate, the number of Indians has dropped from 1 million to 180,000 since the beginning of the century. In the late 1960s, the Brazilian government revealed that hundreds of officials of its own Service for the Protection of the Indians had been implicated in crimes against Indians that included the liquidation of whole tribes. In one case, the Indians were machine-gunned and bombed from the air; in another, they were given presents of sugar mixed with arsenic. The process of destroying the Indians by relocation in the interests of economic development continues. Wanton killings of Indians have been reported from the jungle lowlands of Colombia, and murders of Indians by land-grabbing *hacendados* or their *pistoleros* (gunmen) have occurred in Mexico, Guatemala, and other countries with sizable Indian populations.

In some countries, the Indians are subjected to a many-sided economic, social, and cultural exploitation. "The Indian problem," writes the Mexican sociologist Pablo González Casanova, "is essentially one of internal colonialism. The Indian communities are Mexico's internal colonies. . . . Here we find prejudice, discrimination, colonial types of exploitation, dictatorial forms, and the separation of a dominant population, with a different race and culture."

The Catholic Church

The ideological crisis of Latin America is illustrated by the rifts that have emerged in two of the area's oldest and most conservative institutions, the Catholic church and the armed forces.

The new reformist and revolutionary currents that have emerged within the Catholic church since about 1960 have different sources: a more liberal climate of opinion within the church since the Second Vatican Council, convened in 1962 under Pope John XXIII; concern on the part of some elements of the hierarchy that the church's traditional collusion with the elites risked a loss of the masses to Marxism; and a crisis of conscience on the part of some clergy, especially working clergy whose experiences convinced them that the area's desperate dilemmas required drastic solutions.

The new ferment within the Latin American church found dramatic expression in the life and death of the famous Colombian priest and sociologist Camilo Torres. Born into an aristocratic Colombian family, a brilliant scholar and teacher, Torres, who became convinced of the futility of seeking to achieve reform by peaceful means, joined the Communist-led guerrilla National Liberation Army. He was killed in a clash with counterinsurgency forces in February 1966.

The proper stand for the church to take in the face of Latin America's structural crisis was hotly debated at the second conference of Latin American bishops, held at Medellín, Colombia, in 1968. The presence of Pope Paul VI at its opening session underlined the meeting's importance. Reflecting the leftward shift of portions of the clergy, the bishops at Medellín affirmed the commitment of the church to the task of liberating the people of Latin America from neocolonialism and "institutionalized violence." This violence, declared the bishops, was inherent in the economic, social, and political structures of the continent, dependent on what Pope Paul called "the international imperialism of money."

Even before Medellín, a group of Latin American bishops had taken a position in favor of socialism. Their leader was Helder Câmara, archbishop of Recife (Brazil). He and seven other Brazilian bishops had signed a pastoral letter issued by seventeen bishops of the Third World that called on the church to avoid identification of religion "with the oppression of the poor and the workers, with feudalism, capitalism, imperi-

562 alism." Rejecting violence as an instrument of revolutionary change, Helder Câmara expressed sympathy and understanding for those who felt that violence was the only effective tactic.

These developments were accompanied by the emergence and growing acceptance by many clergy of the so-called theology of liberation, the product of the study and reflection of leading church scholars in various Latin American countries. This doctrine taught that the church, returning to its roots, must again become a Church of the Poor. It must cease to be an ally of the rich and powerful and commit itself to the struggle for social justice, to raising the consciousness of the masses, to making them aware of the abuses from which they suffered and of the need to unite in order to change an oppressive economic and political system. Liberation theology rejected Marxism's atheist world view but drew heavily on the Marxist analysis of the causes of the poverty and oppression in the Third World. On the subject of revolution, while deploring all violence, liberation theologians taught that revolution, or counterviolence, was justified as a last resort against the greater violence of tyrants—an orthodox Catholic teaching that goes back to St. Thomas Aquinas. It was in this spirit that Archbishop Oscar Arnulfo Romero of San Salvador, in one of the last sermons he gave before he was murdered by a right-wing assassin in March 1980, declared: "When all peaceful means have been exhausted, the Church considers insurrection moral and justified."

In order to implement the teachings of liberation theology, progressive clergy set about developing a new type of Christian organization, the *comunidad de base,* or Christian grassroots organization. Composed of poor people in the countryside and the barrios of cities, assisted and advised by priests and students, these communities combined religious study and reflection with efforts to define and solve the practical social problems of their localities. The great landowners and the authorities frequently branded their activities as subversive, and both laity and priests were subjected to severe repression. This led to a growing politicization and radicalization of many communities and their involvement in revolutionary movements. In Nicaragua, the Christian communities were integrated into the revolutionary struggle led by the Sandinista Front for National Liberation to a degree not found elsewhere in Latin America.

This unity of rank-and-file Catholic clergy and laity with the revolution continued after the Sandinista triumph in July 1979. Five priests hold high office in the revolutionary government and defied a 1980 Vatican ruling barring direct priestly involvement in political life. Many priests and nuns enthusiastically supported and participated in the literacy campaign and other reconstruction projects of the new regime.

The church hierarchy, headed by Archbishop Miguel Obando y Bravo, grew increasingly critical of the Sandinist government, however. Before the revolution, the hierarchy, historically aligned with the wealthy class, gradually moved toward anti-Somoza positions, but never became pro-Sandinist. The bishops may have feared the gradual growth of atheism among the people and the loss of their influence over the faithful. The Sandinist government claimed that the hierarchy was again aligning itself with the rich and playing the game of the Reagan administration by trying to destabilize the revolutionary regime.

The conflict between traditionalists and progressives concerning the role of the church was high on the agenda of the third conference of Latin American bishops, convened at Puebla, Mexico, in March 1979. Unlike Medellín, where the progressives had the upper hand, a conservative faction controlled the preparations for the Puebla conference and clearly intended to put down the troublesome liberation theology and its supporters. The dominant conservative faction prepared a working paper that urged resignation on the part of the poor in the hope of a better hereafter and placed its trust for the solution of Latin America's great social problems in the failed reformist models of the 1960s. This document raised a storm of criticism among progressive bishops and other clergy.

The unknown element in the equation at Puebla was the position of the new pope, John Paul II, who was to inaugurate the conference. Seeking a guide for their deliberations, the bishops anxiously awaited his arrival in January 1979. But the apparent contradictions in his message made his position uncertain: some of his speeches appeared to emphasize personal devotion and religious discipline, to condemn priestly involvement in politics and—by implication—the theology of liberation; others could be considered favorable to liberation theology.

Despite their ambiguity, the pope's statements in general tended to reinforce the position of progressives and moderates at the Puebla conference. Its final document continued the line of Medellín, especially in its expression of overwhelming concern for the poor: "We identify as the most devastating and humiliating scourge, the situation of inhuman poverty in which millions of Latin Americans live, with starvation wages, unemployment and underemployment, malnutrition, infant mortality, lack of adequate housing, health problems, and labor unrest."

Since 1982 the pope's opposition to liberation theology and the so-called popular church appears to have hardened. He expressed this opposition during his visit to Nicaragua in 1983, a visit that produced an extraordinary confrontation between the pope and the mass of the faithful who came to hear his homily (see Chapter 18). Brazil—where many bishops accept the basic tenets of liberation theology, actively engage in the struggle for land reform and other reforms, and enjoy the support of many thousands of grass-roots communities—became another target of the pope's attack on the supposed subversive or heretical teachings of liberation theology. This attack took the form of sanctions against a very popular theologian, Leonardo Boff, and of efforts to weaken the majority of progressive Brazilian bishops by naming more conservative bishops. The struggle between the old and the new in the Catholic church goes on throughout the continent.

The recent rapid growth in membership and influence of Protestant evangelical or fundamentalist sects poses a major challenge to the religious supremacy of the Catholic church in Latin America. Between 1981 and 1987 the membership of these sects had doubled to 50 million. In Guatemala they claim 30 percent of the population; the most recent figures for Chile and Brazil are 15 and 10 percent of the population. The dramatic economic and social changes taking place throughout the continent have much to do with the phenomenal growth of these new churches. Their revivalist preaching and "pie-in-the-sky" message bring color, excitement, and hope to the lives of the uprooted rural immigrants of the shantytowns that ring every Latin American city. The churches' support networks often provide these "marginal" people with material assistance as well.

The fervently right-wing, anticommunist teachings of the fundamentalist sects have gained them the approval and support of sections of the Latin American oligarchy, who find in these teachings a useful foil for the radical social doctrines of Catholic liberation theology. In Guatemala, Efraín Ríos Montt, the general who directed the brutal suppression of Maya highland Indians, is a born-again Christian, as is Jorge Serrano, elected president in the 1991 election. Alberto Fujimori, the newly elected president of Peru, who has implemented a harsh free-market "shock therapy" for the country's economic problems, also belongs to a fundamentalist sect. But not all evangelicals are accomplices of the ruling classes; in Nicaragua, Ecuador, and other countries, mainstream Protestant churches and spin-offs from evangelical groups have found common ground with Catholic base communities in supporting agrarian reform and other progressive changes.

The Military

Within the Latin American armed forces, as within the church, a differentiation is taking place. The phenomenon of the reformist or even social revolutionary military officer is older than

564 is sometimes supposed. In Brazil, we recall, the tenente revolts of the 1920s paved the way for the triumph of Getúlio Vargas's reformist revolution of 1930. Juan Perón and other members of the Group of United Officers exemplified a similar tendency within the Argentine officer corps in the 1930s. In Guatemala in 1944, a group of progressive officers led by Colonel Jacob Arbenz overthrew the Ubico dictatorship and installed a government that enacted a sweeping land reform and other democratic changes.

The massive influx of North American capital into Latin America after 1945, accompanied by the growing political influence of the United States in the area, altered the balance of forces between conservatives and progressives within the Latin American military. Many high-ranking officers became fervent converts to the North American system of free enterprise and accepted the inevitability of a mortal struggle between "atheistical communism" and the "free world." By the Treaty of Rio de Janeiro (1947), the Latin American republics committed themselves to join the United States in the defense of the Western Hemisphere. In the context of the cold war, this commitment entailed collaboration with the United States in a global anticommunist strategy, to the extent of justifying military intervention in any country threatened or conquered by "communist penetration." Under the cover of this doctrine, in 1965 Brazilian troops joined United States forces in intervening in the Dominican Republic to crush the progressive revolutionary government of Colonel Francisco Caamaño. The integration of Latin American armies into the strategic plans of the Pentagon converted many into appendages of the North American military machine.

This integration was accompanied by the establishment of the technical and ideological tutelage of the Pentagon over the Latin American military, aimed particularly at the destruction of Latin American revolutionary movements. After the victory of the Cuban Revolution in 1959, this program of training and indoctrination was greatly expanded. Thousands of Latin American officers were sent to take courses in counterinsurgency warfare at Fort Bragg, Fort Knox, Fort Monmouth, and other installations in the United States and in the Panama Canal Zone. An especially important role was played by the School of the Americas, founded in 1949 and run by the United States Army at Fort Gulick in the Panama Canal Zone for the training of Latin American officers. During 1949–1986, 33,534 Latin American military personnel, including many future generals and some presidents, passed through its doors; one of its former students is General Augusto Pinochet, until lately the head of the Chilean military junta.

The formation of close ties between high-ranking officers and large foreign and domestic firms contributed to the making of a reactionary military mentality. In Argentina in the 1960s, 143 retired officers of the highest ranks held 177 of the leading posts in the country's largest industrial and financial enterprises, mostly foreign-controlled. Latin America thus developed its own military-industrial complex. Through all these means, the United States acquired an enormous influence over the Latin American military.

Pentagon influence over the Latin American military engendered not only an obsessive anticommunism but an implacable hostility to even moderate programs of social and economic reform. North American ideological influence undoubtedly played an important role in creating a favorable climate of military opinion for the wave of counterrevolutionary coups that swept over Latin America in the 1960s and 1970s.

Not all Latin American military, however, are reactionaries of the Pinochet type. Even in countries like Chile, Brazil, and Uruguay, until lately ruled by military dictatorships, a more or less subterranean struggle within the military continued between extreme rightists and moderates who favored the restoration of democracy. In other countries, the military seized power not to preserve the status quo but to change it. Although the military regimes in Peru (1968), Panama (1968), and Ecuador (1972) differed considerably in the scope and depth of their reforms, they demonstrated the existence of a reformist or even revolutionary officer class. In Panama, a group of officers of the Panamanian National Guard organized a revolt in 1968 that overthrew President Arnulfo Arias, a representative of the traditional oligarchy. The rebels formed a military junta, headed by General Omar Torrijos, which soon displayed an unexpected reformist and nationalist fervor: it demanded the liquidation of the American military presence in Panama and a revision of the ancient Treaty of 1902 that would restore Panamanian sovereignty over the Canal Zone.

The Flowering of Latin American Culture

By mid-century, Latin American culture had attained maturity in a number of fields. Art and scholarship drew closer to the people and its problems and at the same time displayed a growing mastery of the refinements of technique. The swelling output of Latin American art and scholarship has grown into a torrent; we can only note some major trends in each field, with special attention to literature, a faithful mirror of Latin American history and problems.

The Social Sciences

Latin American social scientists, continuing the tradition of such nineteenth-century enlighteners as Sarmiento, Alberdi, and Lastarria, for the most part reject an impossible neutrality and openly take sides in the political and social struggles of the area. In Latin America, even history, the most aristocratic of the social sciences, walks hand in hand with politics. The liberal current, which dominated nineteenth-century historiography, was represented in the twentieth century by such major figures as the Mexican Daniel Cosío Villegas, who directed and took part in the writing of a monumental *Modern History of Mexico* (1955–1972), and the Argentine Ricardo Le-

vene, who founded a historical school stressing archival research, rigorous critical method, and economic factors.

But there also existed a conservative current whose hallmarks were nostalgia for the colonial period and enthusiasm for such right-wing nineteenth-century caudillos as Alamán and Rosas. In Mexico this tendency was typified by José Vasconcelos, who proclaimed that Cortés was the creator of Mexican nationality; in Argentina it was represented by a group of revisionist historians who sought to rehabilitate the federalist caudillo Juan Manuel Rosas and bitterly criticized such fathers of Argentine liberalism as Mitre and Sarmiento.

Less involved in such historical quarrels were younger scholars who applied the new methods of social and quantitative history to the study of history, especially the colonial period; in Mexico this new school was represented by Enrique Florescano, in Chile by Mario Góngora, Alvaro Jara, and Rolando Mellafe. The Marxist historical method also had its able practitioners, such as Germán Carrera Damas in Venezuela, Caio Prado Júnior in Brazil, and Enrique Semo in Mexico.

The rise of Latin American anthropology was linked to that of nationalist, reformist movements whose programs stressed the redemption of the Indians and their integration in the national society. The triumph of the Mexican Revolution of 1910 gave a large impetus to such indigenismo. With modest official support, and in an atmosphere of widespread and sometimes emotional interest in Mexico's Indian past, Mexican anthropology made large quantitative and qualitative advances after 1920. The long roster of its distinguished names includes Manuel Gamio, Alfonso Caso, Wigberto Jiménez Moreno, and Miguel Covarrubias. In Peru the pro-Indian propaganda of APRA and other reformist or revolutionary movements stimulated a revival of interest in the study of Indians, past and present; two pioneers of Peruvian anthropology were Julio Tello and Luis Valcarcel. In the same period, Gilberto Freyre and Arturo Ramos in Brazil and Fernando Ortiz in Cuba began to explore the contributions made by blacks and attack racial myths. In recent decades, Latin American anthropology has combined a strong interest in the social, economic, and political structures of the ancient Indian peoples with much attention to the problems of contemporary Indian groups.

The first task of modern Latin American sociology was to rid itself of its nineteenth-century Spencerian heritage, which accounted for the area's disorder and backwardness by the racial inferiority of Indian and other nonwhite groups. Since about 1960 there has arisen a "new sociology" that rejects the "impartial," empirical sociology in vogue in the United States. The new school openly identifies itself with the struggle for radical social change. A Marxist perspective illuminates the writings of such scholars as Fals Borda, Rodolfo Stavenhagen, Pablo González Casanova (Mexico), Octávio Ianni, and Florestan Fernandes (Brazil). The new school has made contributions to the understanding of such problems as the causes of rural violence, internal colonialism, the social basis of Latin American populism, and race relations in Brazil.

Economics is a relatively young science in Latin America. Its rise is largely connected with the great crisis of 1930 and its disastrous impact on the economy of the area. In the 1940s, the UN's Economic Commission for Latin America (ECLA), led by the Argentine economist Raúl Prebisch, advanced a series of propositions, collectively given the name of structuralism, which attempted to explain Latin America's economic stagnation. Prebisch argued that countries of the "periphery," like those of Latin America, were at a permanent disadvantage in their terms of trade with the "center," the industrialized lands of Europe and North America. Two other alleged obstacles to growth were the traditional structure of agriculture, which led to the stagnation of agricultural output, and the excessive concentration of wealth and power in a few hands, which hampered social mobility, capital formation, and industrial development. The theories of the ECLA and Prebisch gave an important rationale and stimulus to the movement for Latin American in-

dustrialization, economic integration, agrarian reform, and social reform in general. A Brazilian economist, Celso Furtado, applied the structuralist thesis to Brazil in his scholarly *Economic Formation of Brazil* (1963).

Prebisch (who died in 1985) and Furtado appear to believe that Latin America can achieve economic independence and balanced development within a capitalist framework. Disappointment with the ECLA reform program and the Latin American economic performance in the 1960s and 1970s, however, produced a progressive radicalization of Latin American economists, whose writings increasingly stress Latin America's structural dependence on multinational corporations. Pointing to the deformed, dependent character of Latin American capitalist industrialization and the persistence of such problems as the latifundio, Marxist economists like Theotonio dos Santos argue that socialism alone can cure the area's economic ills.

Variants of economic dependency theory have flowered in the past two decades. One of the most influential was advanced by the Brazilian scholar Fernando Henrique Cardoso. Impressed by Brazil's rapid economic growth under a military regime that relied heavily on foreign loans and investment, Cardoso argued that development was not incompatible with foreign monopoly penetration of dependent economies. To this development, based on collaboration between international capital, the national bourgeoisie, and the state, he gave the name of "dependent capitalist development" or "associated dependent development." The collapse of the Brazilian "economic miracle" and incontrovertible evidence that foreign debt represents the greatest single obstacle to Latin American development have cast serious doubt on the validity of Cardoso's thesis, at least as far as a long-range solution for the problem of underdevelopment is concerned. Whatever the particular variants to which social scientists may subscribe, dependence theory remains the most influential contemporary model for all who wish to understand contemporary Latin America's problems.

Latin America by José Clemente Orozco, shown here, is an example of the national subject matter favored by artists in the Mexican school. (Courtesy of the Dartmouth Museum)

The Arts

The arts, like the social sciences, combined mastery of modern technical resources with increased use of national subject matter and local folk traditions. National schools of music arose that achieved a synthesis of those traditions with advanced European techniques and styles; examples of such synthesis are the compositions of Heitor Villa-Lobos in Brazil and Carlos Chávez in Mexico, the first two Latin American composers to achieve world renown. In painting, the Mexican school, led by Diego Rivera, José Clemente Orozco, and David Alfaro Siqueiros, won world acclaim with bold, socially conscious art. Almost equally famous are the monumental murals of the Brazilian Cándido Portinari, which portray with moving simplicity and sympathy the bleak lives of Brazilian workers and peasants.

In recent decades, however, there has been a movement in the plastic arts toward a more cosmopolitan aesthetic, illustrated by the magical paintings of the Mexican Rufino Tamayo, very different from the art of Rivera, Orozco, and Siqueiros in theme and technique, yet as intensely Mexican in their own way. Modern Brazilian architecture impresses foreign observers with its audacity and its skillful solutions of problems of light and air, as evidenced by the work of the architect Oscar Niemeyer, who planned and directed the building of the city of Brasilia.

It is in the field of literature, however, that Latin American culture of the twentieth century burns with the most brilliant flame. It may appear surprising that poor, backward countries with masses of illiterates and very small literary markets should produce such a multitude of distinguished poets and novelists, including four Nobel Prize winners in literature,[1] but the phenomenon has its reasons. In the first place, by the early decades of the twentieth century, the advance of the export-import economy had created the necessary economic and social conditions for the rise of literary circles whose members closely followed European artistic developments, plus a small reading public. Second, since colonial times literary culture has enjoyed much greater prestige in Latin America than in the United States, illustrated by the fact that many of Latin America's greatest men of letters have been rewarded with diplomatic posts, which were often sinecures. Finally, the dramatic contrasts of Latin American life—the extremes of wealth and poverty, the barbarous dictatorships, the rich variety of regional types, the still untamed nature—have stimulated the creative imagination of Latin American writers to an extent that has not occurred in happier countries. To a very considerable degree, Latin American literature is a literature of protest and struggle. In this, it continues the tradition established by such great nineteenth-century romantic writers as Sarmiento, Echeverría, Martí, and Montalvo.

Literature and Society, 1910–1930: The Search for Self-expression

After 1900 the art-for-art's-sake creed, of which Rubén Darío had given the supreme example, came under growing attack. Latin American intellectuals, increasingly concerned with backwardness, weakness, and disunity of their continent vis-à-vis its powerful neighbor, the United States, began to descend from Parnassus. In 1899, José Enrique Rodó had already argued that Darío, despite his great technical virtuosity, was

not "the poet of America." In a famous poem, "Wring the Neck of the Swan" (1910), the Mexican poet Enrique González Martínez (1871–1952) attacked Darío's proud swan, symbol of beauty as an end in itself. This poem foreshadowed the rise of a new spirit of sincerity, realism, and social consciousness in Latin American literature. By this time, Darío himself had turned away from escapism and had begun to write such powerful public poetry as his "To Roosevelt" (1905).

The intellectuals' concern about the destiny of the continent, about the growing gap in economic and political power between Latin America and the Colossus of the North, inspired numerous essays that probed the causes of the area's problems and suggested solutions. Particularly influential—no doubt because it expressed views Latin Americans wanted to hear—was the essay *Ariel* (1900) by José Enrique Rodó. One of its key themes was the opposition between Latin American spirituality and the materialism of the United States. However, contrary to a common misreading of Rodó, he did not wholly condemn North American utilitarianism; instead, he urged a fruitful fusion of Latin American spirituality and the practical, energetic spirit of the United States. Another important work of stocktaking was *Les democraties latines de l'Amérique* (1912) by the Peruvian Francisco García Calderón, published in France to inform Europeans about Latin America. The book deplores Latin American disunity and anticipates a modern complaint of Latin Americans by its statement that the "new continent, politically free, is economically a vassal." In the same period, there appeared a large number of books that analyzed the problems of individual countries and often found the origins of their malaise in the racial inferiority of Indians or mixed races; typical of such primitive sociological analysis was Alcides Arguedas's study of Bolivia, *A Sick People* (1909).

The essayists sometimes also stressed the need for artistic originality. García Calderón, for example, claimed that originality in art was as important as economic independence. In the 1920s, a time of preliminary skirmishes in some countries between traditional elites and emerg-

[1] They are the Chilean poet Gabriela Mistral (1945), the Guatemalan novelist Miguel Angel Asturias (1967), the Chilean poet Pablo Neruda (1971), and the Colombian novelist Gabriel García Márquez (1982).

ing bourgeois groups, Latin American writers began to try to express the essence of their lands in an original and truly native way. Struggle against an untamed nature, the Indians, the various regional forms of creole life, and the problems of the peon and the worker were among the varied subject matter of the new literature. Writers received guidance from one of Latin America's most eminent men of letters, Pedro Henríquez Ureña, who pointed out in his *Seven Essays in Search of Our Expression* (1928) that every formula of literary Americanism could be useful but that there was only one secret of expression: "To work for it profoundly, to seek to purify it, going to the roots of the things we wish to say, to polish, to refine, with a desire for perfection."

Two postmodernist poets, the Peruvian José Santos Chocano (1875–1934) and the Mexican Ramón López Velarde (1888–1921), illustrate the turning away of the new generation of writers from swans, eighteenth-century palaces, and princesses reclining on velvet divans to the reality of their own lands. Santos Chocano used a wide range of subject matter. He had a certain taste for exotic pre-Columbian and colonial themes: one of his finest poems evokes the ancient city of Cartagena de las Indias, dreaming behind her great walls. Pirates disturb her sleep, but she awakes serene, then softly closes her eyes; fanned by her palm trees and rocked in the hammock of the waves, she falls asleep again. But Santos Chocano could also sound a note of social protest:

Indian who toils without rest
on the lands that others own,
Do you not know that they are yours
by right of your blood and sweat?[2]

The intensely personal poems of Ramón López Velarde celebrated the provincial scenes of his youth in verse free from sentimentality. His most famous poem, however, is "Suave Patria" (1921), a poem in two tender, teasing "acts" in which the

poet expresses his love for Mexico with complete freedom from rhetoric. In the "intermezzo" between the acts, the poet invokes the Indian hero Cuauhtemoc—an early illustration of the indigenismo that is a major aspect of twentieth-century Mexican culture. The intermezzo opens: "Young forebear: hear me praise you, the only hero of artistic stature." But there are no heroics: the mood is subdued, tragic, compassionate. Upon the poet's spirit weigh the terrible losses and sufferings of the Mexican Revolution. His Cuauhtemoc is a Man of Sorrows; he is also an instrument for the fusion of Spanish and Indian elements into a Mexican synthesis.

The Mexican Revolution, which subtly colors "Suave Patria," also pervades the somber novels of Mariano Azuela (1873–1952). Their main theme is the betrayal by middle-class leaders and cynical intellectuals of the peasants and workers whose ignorance and valor they exploit. Azuela's best novel, *The Underdogs* (1916), tells the story of a peasant, Demetrio Macías, who organizes a guerrilla band, rises to the rank of general, and is killed fighting for Villa. He is the victim of blind forces he does not understand, over which he has no control. His simplicity and naiveté contrast with the cunning of the demagogic medical student Luis Cervantes, who carefully keeps out of harm's way and uses looted diamonds to lay the foundation of his future professional career.

The new cultural nationalism also found expression in the novels of the Colombian José Eustasio Rivera (1888–1928) and the Venezuelan Rómulo Gallegos (1884–1969). In Rivera's best work, *The Vortex* (1924), a violent tale of rubber collectors in the Amazonian jungle, the implacable wilderness joins the "rubber lords" in debasing men, in shattering their hopes and bodies. A novel of protest against the barbarism of his country, it is also a truly national novel, the first Colombian novel to depict the difficult lives of the cowboys of the plains and the rubber collectors of the jungle.

The novels of Rómulo Gallegos, an active opponent of long-time dictator Juan Vicente Gómez, depict the hitherto neglected life of Venezuela's *llanos* (plains and jungles) and suggest

[2] "Quién sabe," quoted in Jean Franco, *The Modern Culture of Latin America* (New York: Praeger, 1967), p. 49.

that the country's destructive regional conflicts can be solved by the fusion of the antagonistic elements: whites and blacks, indigenous and European cultures, barbarism and civilization. In *Doña Bárbara* (1929), the mulatta heroine whose name the novel bears embodies the barbaric vigor and lawless spirit of the people of the plains. Santos Luzardo, on whose land she has encroached, is a city-educated lawyer who finds that he himself must resort to violence to defeat her. Their duel is finally ended by Santos Luzardo's marriage to Doña Bárbara's daughter, a child of nature whom he carefully educates, with particular care that she drop the plebeian dialect of the llanos and learn to speak and act like the "exquisite young ladies of Caracas." The patent artificiality of the civilization-barbarism dichotomy, reflecting Gallegos's middle-class liberalism, weakens his works.

A different viewpoint on the quarrel between civilization and barbarism emerges in the gaucho novel *Don Segundo Sombra* (1926) by Ricardo Guiraldes (1886–1927). One of the most perfect of Latin American novels, it evokes with incomparable skill a regional type rapidly receding into the past, but the portrait is clearly touched with nostalgia. The gaucho hero emerges as a dignified and rounded individual, perfectly adapted to his milieu; he needs no transformation from without, for he is already a completely civilized human being.

Literature and Society, 1930–1991: A Social Consciousness

In the 1930s, a time of growing economic difficulties accompanied by the sharpening of class struggles in mines, factories, and plantations, the radicalization of Latin American writers gave rise to the novel of social protest, frequently influenced by Marxist ideology. Since the principal victims of capitalist exploitation in Latin America were Indians, the new novels of social protest were usually Indianist novels as well. Leading representatives of this genre were Jorge Icaza (b.

1906) in Ecuador, Ciro Alegría (1909–1967) and José M. Arguedas (1901–1969) in Peru, and Miguel A. Asturias (1899–1974) in Guatemala.

The early Indianist novels, like *Birds Without a Nest* (1889) by Clorinda Matto de Turner or *Race of Bronze* (1919) by Alcides Arguedas, had found the roots of Indian misery and exploitation in the personal vices or weaknesses of the ruling classes or of the Indians themselves. In the new Indianist novel, the destruction of the Indians flows inexorably from the operation of blind economic forces, of which the grasping landlord or exploitive foreign company (the Indianist novel is often an anti-imperialist novel as well) are mere instruments. The new Indianist novelists also made a more serious effort to enter the Indian mind and sometimes prepared themselves for their task by living with the Indians to learn their speech and customs.

Icaza's *Huasipungo* (1934) reports with blazing anger the brutal exploitation of a group of Ecuadorian Indians, which culminates in an effort to expel them from their parcels of land (*huasipungos*) to make way for the exploitation of the area by foreign oil companies. But the Indians are shown as so degraded by their servitude, so brutish even in dealing with one another, that it is difficult to sympathize with them. More successful in this respect is Ciro Alegría's *Broad and Alien Is the World* (1941), which also relates the destruction of an Indian community by a landowner bent on acquiring its lands. Alegría's idealized portrayal of Indian life and virtues borders on the sentimental, yet he convincingly portrays a communal society whose driving force is mutual aid and, therefore, engages the reader's sympathy with the Indians.

Land and labor struggles also characterize the Indianist novels of Arguedas, who knew Quechua before he knew Spanish and had a profound mastery of Indian culture and customs. His novels achieve an unusual penetration of the Indian mentality through his effort to reproduce the rhythm and syntax of Quechua and evoke the religious world view of the Indians.

The Guatemalan writer Miguel A. Asturias is

one of the founders of the school of magical realism, which attempts to depict Indian life as the Indians themselves might experience it, in terms of myth. In *Men of Maize* (1949), he records from this mythic perspective the losing struggle of the Indians to retain their land and way of life, using a style whose language and rhythms resemble those of the Maya language. The blend of fantasy and reality in Asturias's Indianist novels is far removed from the documentary tone of such regional novelists as Rivera, Gallegos, and Icaza.

In Brazil in the 1920s and 1930s, there arose a "northeastern school" that portrayed the varied social types and struggles of the drought-ridden sertão and the coastal sugar plantations. This group included Graciliano Ramos (1892–1953), José Lins do Rego (1901–1957), and Jorge Amado (b. 1912). In *Barren Lives* (1938), Ramos deals with the struggle of a cowherder against drought and starvation and his eventual flight to the city. The "sugar cane cycle" of Lins do Rego (1932–1943) chronicles the decline and fall of the old sugar aristocracy—the rise of the great *usina* (sugar mill) and the impact of economic change on planters, slaves, and their descendants. Partly based on Lins do Rego's own childhood and adult experiences, these novels reconstruct the social history of Brazilian sugar. In his *Cacao* (1933), Amado describes the life of the workers on the cacao plantations south of Bahia; in *The Violent Land* (1943), he records the bloody struggles for economic and political power of the cacao planters.

Cuban novelist Alejo Carpentier applies the method of magical realism to West Indian blacks in *The Kingdom of This World* (1949); set in Haiti in the time of the French Revolution, it presents the rise and fall of the black dictator Henri Christophe and the emergence of a new mulatto ruling class as seen through the eyes of a house slave. Revolution and the corruption of revolutionaries are major themes of Carpentier's *The Age of Enlightenment* (1962), which is also set in the period of the French Revolution but deals with the Caribbean as a whole.

Poetry, like prose, revealed a new social consciousness. At the same time, Latin American poets struggled to free their verse from rhetoric and the tyranny of old forms. The difficult poetry of Peruvian Cesar Vallejo (1892–1938), though concerned from first to last with human anguish, with the inherently tragic human condition, reveals in its later phase a compassion for the victims of war and exploitation, a vision of a possible better life, that reflects his new socialist ideology. For the Chilean poet Pablo Neruda (1904–1973), as for Vallejo, the Spanish Civil War was a turning point; in a poem written at the beginning of the war he declares that henceforth he will unite his "lone wolf's walk" to the "walk of man." At the end of the war, he joined the Communist party and combined his poetic career with political activism until his death in 1973. His major work is *Canto general* (1950), an epic attempt to tell the history of the Latin American continent from the point of view of figures neglected by textbooks—workers, peasants, and fighters for freedom. Another major poet of left-wing tendencies, the Cuban Nicolás Guillen (b. 1902), founded the Afro-Cuban poetry movement, based on the rhythms and images of Cuban black folk poetry. With the passage of time, his poetry acquired strong social revolutionary and anti-imperialist tones.

The period since 1940 has seen a continuing revolution in the technique of the novel. This technical revolution is marked by intensive use of such devices as stream of consciousness, flashbacks, symbolism, and fantasy. Some writers, like Argentina's Jorge Luis Borges in his *Ficciones* (1944), employ fantasy and other avant-garde techniques to demonstrate the absurdity and senselessness of life. Others, however, employ them to heighten awareness of an abhorrent social and political order. To one degree or another, these writers continue the Latin American tradition of employing literature as an instrument of social protest and change. Typical of such novelists is Mario Vargas Llosa, author of *Conversations in the Cathedral* (1970), whose structural and verbal disorder appears to re-enact the disorder of Peruvian life and geography.

Gabriel García Márquez, shown here accepting the Nobel literature award in 1982, uses magical imagery and fantasy to depict the violence and horror he sees in Colombian society. (Wide World Photos)

We noted Asturias's use of magical realism in such Indianist novels as *Men of Maize.* His powerful *Mr. President* (1941), deals with a sinister dictator who rules with a vast apparatus of repression. In it dreams, memories, and imaginings replace the truth the characters cannot speak. Fantasy and reality blend in Asturias's anti-imperialist trilogy, *Strong Wind* (1950), *The Green Pope* (1954), and *The Eyes of the Buried* (1960), which deal with the formation of a monopolistic banana company and the struggles of small farmers and workers against it. In *Strong Wind,* when those struggles fail, a hurricane summoned by an Indian witch doctor destroys the company's plantations.

Fantasy is the means employed by Gabriel García Márquez to attack a monstrous social and political order in *One Hundred Years of Solitude* (1967), which records the history of an imaginary town set in the remote Colombian *ciénaga* (swampland) where García Márquez grew up. The book describes extraordinary people and events in deadpan fashion; in this magical world, miracles occur in the most natural way. But many of the fantastic situations "are absurd but logical exaggerations of real situations." The fantasies are a parody of Colombian history itself. Indeed, no event depicted in the book is as fantastic as history's la Violencia, the civil war unleashed in the Colombian countryside by conservative repression in 1949, a war that took perhaps 300,000 lives in the course of a few years.

Accelerated urbanization and industrialization have placed their stamp on the new novel; frequently, it is set in the great city and deals with the psychological problems of the urban middle class. In the urban novels of the Mexican Carlos Fuentes (b. 1929), a major theme is the betrayal of revolutionary ideals by the men who made the revolution. In *Where the Air Is Clearer* (1958), *The Clear Consciences* (1959), and *The Death of Artemio Cruz* (1962), Fuentes skillfully depicts the life of a cynical, cosmopolitan society. Alienation and the emptiness of middle- and upper-class life are also common themes in the Argentine urban novel; a good example is *A November Party* (1938) by Eduardo Mallea (b. 1903).

Although the beginnings of the Latin American film go back to the first decades of this century, its emergence as a major art form dates from the 1960s, when a group of Latin American filmmakers initiated a reaction against the dominant commercial Hollywood model. Revolutionary Cuba took the lead in this process, producing a large number of excellent films in a variety of styles and relatively free from political constraints. Two such films were Gutierrez Alea's *Memories of Underdevelopment* (1968) and Humberto Solas's *Lucia* (1968). Working under more difficult, sometimes clandestine or semiclandestine conditions, Argentine, Bolivian, Brazilian, and Central American filmmakers have also produced first-class films that explore the history and the social and political problems of their nations.

Continuing a tradition established by the founders of Latin American culture, modern Latin American scholars, writers, and artists have often tended to view their work not only as a means of self-expression but as an act of social protest, an instrument of social and political change. To be sure, in Latin America as elsewhere, there are poets who write very private verse, novelists who deal with intensely personal themes, and painters whose abstract or surrealist art conveys no explicit social message. But to a greater extent than elsewhere, perhaps, the Latin American poet, novelist, painter, and filmmaker have also been the voice and the conscience of the people.

Appendix

A Statistical Profile of Latin America

The tables and figures in this profile offer statistical evidence for certain points made in the text. Table 1 documents the explosive growth of the Latin American population between 1960 and 1988. Note that in less than three decades the population of some countries, like Brazil and Mexico, doubled or more than doubled. Table 2 records the equally explosive growth of Latin American cities, a reflection of the massive migration of rural people to the city as a result of a "push and pull" process described in the text. Table 3 provides evidence of some of the grave social problems Latin America faces today. Note that the statistics understate the real extent of the problems, since they are averages. Similarly, since the middle and upper classes consume much more than their share, a very large part of the Latin American population receives less than the daily intake of 2,500 calories commonly regarded as the minimum requirement for a healthy life. Table 4 documents some striking changes in the distribution of the labor force between 1960 and 1980. Note the very sharp decline in the agricultural work force, reflecting the concentration of land and mechanization of agriculture in the countryside, the slowing increase or actual decline of the industrial labor force, and the sharp increase in the size of the service or "informal" sector, names that conceal a vast amount of marginal employment or even illegal activity like the growing of coca or the cocaine traffic. The Bar Chart shows The Inexorable Growth of the Foreign Debt, 1975–1987, a growth that has done incalculable damage to living standards and frustrated hopes for economic development in the region.

Table 1

Population Estimates, in Thousands, 1960–1988

Country	1960	1970	1980	1988
Argentina	20,616	23,962	28,237	31,354
Bolivia	3,428	4,325	5,570	6,918
Brazil	72,594	95,847	121,286	144,428
Colombia	15,538	20,803	25,794	30,568
Costa Rica	1,236	1,731	2,284	2,286
Cuba	7,029	8,572	9,732	10,322
Chile	7,614	9,504	11,145	12,748
Ecuador	4,413	6,051	8,123	10,203
El Salvador	2,570	3,588	4,525	5,031
Guatemala	3,964	5,246	6,917	8,681
Haiti	3,675	4,500	5,413	6,263
Honduras	1,935	2,627	3,662	4,829
Mexico	38,020	52,771	70,416	84,866
Nicaragua	1,493	2,053	2,771	3,622
Panama	1,105	1,487	1,956	3,622
Paraguay	1,774	2,351	3,147	4,039
Peru	9,931	13,193	17,195	21,256
Dominican Republic	3,231	4,423	5,696	6,867
Uruguay	2,538	2,808	2,908	3,081
Venezuela	7,502	10,604	15,024	18,757

SOURCE: Adapted from Economic Commission for Latin America and the Caribbean (ECLAC), *Statistical Yearbook for Latin America and the Caribbean,* 1989 edition, Santiago, Chile, February 1990. Used by permission.

Table 2

Population of Largest Cities, According to Recent Estimates or Censuses

Argentina (Buenos Aires) (1985)	10,728,000
Bolivia (La Paz) (1985)	992,592
Brazil (São Paulo) (1985)	10,099,086
Chile (Santiago) (1985)	4,099,714
Colombia (Bogotá) (1985)	4,208,000
Costa Rica (San José) (1983)	305,401
Cuba (La Habana) (1985)	2,014,806
Dominican Republic (Santo Domingo) (1981)	1,313,172
Ecuador (Guayaquil) (1984)	1,387,819
El Salvador (San Salvador) (1971)	335,990
Guatemala (Guatemala City) (1981)	754,243
Haiti (Port-au-Prince) (1984)	738,342
Honduras (Tegucigalpa) (1986)	597,512
Mexico (Mexico City) (1979)	14,750,182
Nicaragua (Managua) (1979)	608,020
Panama (Panama City) (1984)	424,204
Paraguay (Asuncion) (1982)	457,210
Peru (Lima) (1985)	5,008,400
Uruguay (Montevideo) (1975)	1,229,748
Venezuela (Caracas) (1981)	2,944,000

SOURCE: Adapted from James W. Wilkie and Enrique Ochoa, eds., *Statistical Abstract of Latin America*, Vol. 27 (Los Angeles: UCLA Latin American Center Publications. University of California. 1989), Table 633.

Table 3

Social Indicators

	Infant Mortality Per 1000 Live Births	Life Expectancy	Illiteracy, Age 15 and Over (%)	Daily Caloric Intake (1983–1985)
Argentina	36.0 (1984)	69.7 (1984)	4.5 (1985)	3,195
Bolivia	124.4 (1982)	54.0 (1984)	25.8 (1985)	2,114
Brazil	70.7 (1980–85)	63.5 (1980–85)	22.3 (1985)	2,629
Chile	21.9 (1983)	67.0 (1980–85)	5.6 (1985)	2,589
Colombia	45.7 (1981)	62.5 (1981)	17.7 (1985)	2,578
Costa Rica	18.8 (1984)	73.1 (1980–85)	6.4 (1985)	3,094
Cuba	11.9 (1988)	75.0 (1989)	1.9 (1980)	3,094
Dominican Republic	74.5 (1985)	62.6 (1980–85)	22.7 (1985)	2,468
Ecuador	69.5 (1985)	64.3 (1980–85)	17.6 (1985)	2,031
El Salvador	35.1 (1984)	64.8 (1980–85)	27.9 (1985)	2,163
Guatemala	71.5 (1983)	60.7 (1980–85)	40.5 (1985)	2,298
Haiti	117.1 (1980–85)	54.5 (1980–85)	62.4 (1985)	1,843
Honduras	81.5 (1985)	59.9 (1980–85)	40.5 (1985)	2,208
Mexico	53.0 (1985)	65.7 (1980–85)	9.7 (1985)	3,147
Nicaragua	76.4 (1984)	57.6 (1980–85)	13.0 (1980)	2,284
Panama	25.6 (1985)	70.7 (1980–85)	11.8 (1985)	2,420
Paraguay	45.0 (1985)	65.1 (1980–85)	11.8 (1984)	2,813
Peru	98.6 (1985)	59.1 (1980–85)	15.2 (1985)	2,144
Uruguay	30.0 (1983)	70.3 (1980–85)	6.1 (1975)	2,721
Venezuela	27.7 (1985)	67.8 (1980–85)	13.1 (1975)	2,550

SOURCE: Adapted from James W. Wilkie and Adam Perkal, eds., *Statistical Abstract of Latin America,* Vol. 27 (Los Angeles: UCLA Latin American Center Publications, University of California, 1989), and Economic Commission for Latin America and the Caribbean (ECLAC), *Statistical Yearbook for Latin America and the Caribbean,* 1990 edition.

Table 4

Sectoral Distribution of the Labor Force, 1960–1980 (%)

	Agriculture		Industry		Service	
	1960	1980	1960	1980	1960	1980
Argentina	20	13	36	28	44	59
Bolivia	61	50	18	24	21	26
Brazil	52	30	15	24	33	46
Chile	30	19	20	19	50	62
Colombia	51	26	19	21	30	53
Costa Rica	51	29	19	23	30	48
Cuba	39	23	22	31	39	46
Dominican Republic	67	49	12	18	21	33
Ecuador	58	52	19	17	23	31
El Salvador	65	58	17	22	21	27
Guatemala	67	55	14	21	19	24
Honduras	70	63	11	15	19	22
Mexico	55	36	20	26	25	38
Nicaragua	62	39	16	14	22	47
Panama	51	27	14	18	35	55
Paraguay	56	49	19	19	25	32
Peru	52	40	20	19	28	41
Uruguay	21	11	29	32	50	57
Venezuela	35	18	22	27	43	56

SOURCE: Adapted from James W. Wilkie and Enrique Ochoa, eds., *Statistical Abstract of Latin America,* Vol. 27 (Los Angeles: UCLA Latin American Center Publications. University of California. 1989), Table 1306.

Bar Chart

Latin America: The Inexorable Growth of the Foreign Debt, 1975–1987*
($ bn)

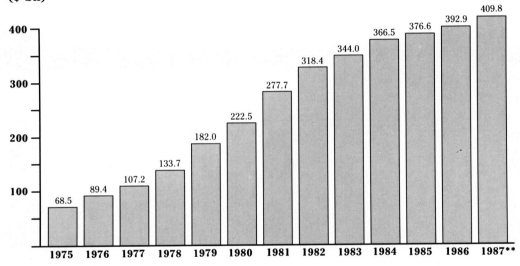

* Includes officially guaranteed public and private external debt, long- and short-term non-guaranteed debt with institutions reporting to the Bank for International Settlements.

** Preliminary Figures.

SOURCE: From Sue Branford and Bernardo Kucinski, *The Debt Squads: The U.S., the Banks, and Latin America,* copyright 1988. Used by permission of Zed Books Limited.

Glossary

Amo (Ah-mō) Master.

Amparo (Ahm-pah-rō) Writ of injunction.

Aprista (Ah-prees-tah) A follower of APRA (Alianza Popular Revolucionaria Americana), a twentieth-century Peruvian political movement.

Campesino (Cahm-pay-see-nō) A peasant.

Cangaçeiro (Cahn-gah-say-ro) A bandit or outlaw in rural Brazil.

Caudillismo (Cow-dee-yeez-mo) The system of rule by *caudillos.*

Caudillo (Cow-dee-yo); Port., **caudilho** (kaw-deel-oh) A military or political leader or strong man, especially prominent in the nineteenth century, whose power is often based on a combination of force and charisma.

Coronel (Cō-ro-nel), pl. **coroneis** (cō-ro-nees) A military title, often honorary, borne by a Brazilian large landowner or other influential individual.

Creole (Cree-ole) An American-born Spaniard in the Spanish colonies.

Ejidatario (Ā-hee-dah-tah-reeō) Member of an *ejido.*

Ejido (Ā-hee-doh) An agricultural community which has received land in accordance with Mexican agrarian laws.

Estancia (Es-tahn-see-ah) A cattle ranch in the Río de la Plata region of Argentina.

Estanciero (Es-tahn-see-ay-ro) The owner of an *estancia.*

Fazenda (Fah-sen-dah) A large estate (Brazil).

---

* Terms repeatedly defined or glossed in the text are not included in the Glossary.

† Aids to pronunciation of terms appear in parentheses after each term, and are phonetic approximations.

582

Gamonal (Gah-mo-nahl)   An oppressive great landowner and local boss (Peru).

Hacendado (Hah-sen-dah-doh)   The owner of a *hacienda.*

Hacienda (Ha-see-en-dah)   A large landed estate.

Jagunço (Ha-gun-so)   A hired gunman or mercenary soldier (Brazil).

Latifundio (Lah-tee-foon-deeō)   A great estate, often characterized by inefficient use of land and servile or poorly paid labor.

Latifundista (Lah-tee-foon-dees-tah)   The owner of a *latifundio.*

Mestizo (Mez-tee-zo)   A person of mixed Indian and white descent.

Moderados (Mow-day-rah-dose)   Individuals comprising the moderate wing of the Liberal party in nineteenth-century Mexico.

Patria (Pa-tree-ah)   The fatherland.

Patrón (Pah-trone)   Master.

Peso (Pay-so)   A monetary unit of eight *reales.*

Porfiriato (Pour-fee-reeah-toh)   The period of Mexican history (1876–1910) characterized by the domination of Porfirio Díaz and his policies.

Puros (Poo-rows)   Individuals comprising the radical wing of the Liberal party in nineteenth-century Mexico.

Real (Ray-ahl)   A monetary unit; one-eighth of a *peso.*

Sertão (Sayr-tah-ow)   The semiarid, isolated interior of the Brazilian northeast.

Tierras baldías (Tee-ay-rahs bahl-dee-ahs)   Vacant or public lands.

Bibliographical Aids

Suggestions for Further Reading*

The indispensable *Handbook of Latin American Studies,* published annually since 1936, attempts to digest published material on Latin America in the social sciences and humanities. C. C. Griffin, ed., *Latin America: A Guide to the Historical Literature* (University of Texas Press, Austin, 1971), "provides a selective scholarly bibliography, accompanied by critical annotations, covering the whole field of Latin American history."

Students can also keep abreast of the most recent writing in the field by consulting the review sections of *The American Historical Review* (1895–), the *Hispanic American Historical Review* (1918–1922, 1926–), *Revista de Historia de America* (1938–), *The Americas: A Quarterly Review of Inter-American Cultural History* (1944–), *The Review of Inter-American Bibliography* (1951–), *Latin American Research Review* (1965–), and the British *Journal of Latin American Studies* (1969–).

For well-informed coverage of current events in the area, see the *Latin American Weekly Report* and the *Latin American Regional Reports,* published by Latin American Newsletters Ltd. (London). For more extended coverage of particular topics and events, see the bimonthly *NACLA Report on the Americas,* published by the North American Congress on Latin America (1967–) and focusing on the political economy of the area. The articles in *Latin American Perspectives*

---

* This bibliographical essay represents a small sample of the vast literature on Latin American history, largely limited to books published since 1970. For more thorough coverage, students are urged to consult the bibliographical aids given below, especially the *Handbook of Latin American Studies* and the Griffin *Guide.*

(1973–) offer scholarly Marxist interpretations of past and present problems of the area.

General Works

Good recent surveys of the colonial period are James Lockhart and Stuart B. Schwartz, *Early Latin America: A History of Colonial Spanish America and Brazil* (Cambridge University Press, Cambridge, Eng., 1983), L. N. McAlister, *Spain and Portugal in the New World* (University of Minnesota Press, Minneapolis, 1984), and M. A. Burkholder and L. L. Johnson, *Colonial Latin America* (Oxford University Press, New York, 1990). Stanley J. and Barbara H. Stein, *The Colonial Heritage of Latin America: Essays on Economic Dependence in Perspective* (Oxford University Press, New York, 1966), shows the continuity of Latin American economic patterns from colonial times to the present. For a compact but comprehensive collection of source materials, see Benjamin Keen, ed., *Latin American Civilization: History and Society, 1492 to the Present* (Westview Press, Boulder, Colo., fifth ed., 1991).

David Bushnell and Neill Macaulay, *The Emergence of Latin America in the Nineteenth Century* (Oxford University Press, New York, 1988), is a readable, well-informed survey of the subject. Leslie Bethell, ed., *The Cambridge History of Latin America,* 6 vols. to date (Cambridge University Press, Cambridge, Eng., 1985–), provides an authoritative collaborative history of the region from pre-Columbian times to the present.

Chapter 9
Dictators and Revolutions

David Bushnell and Neill Macaulay, *The Emergence of Latin America in the Nineteenth Century,* and Tulio Halperin-Donghi, *The Aftermath of Rev-olution in Latin America* (both cited above), provide good overviews of developments in the first half-century after Independence. E. Bradford Burns, *The Poverty of Progress: Latin America in the Nineteenth Century* (University of California Press, Berkeley, 1980.) A provocative, but not altogether convincing, work argues that modernization put an end to a traditional, harmonious Latin American society.

M. C. Meyer and W. L. Sherman, *The Course of Mexican History,* 4th ed. (Oxford University Press, New York, 1990), supersedes all previous general histories of Mexico. C. A. Hale, *Mexican Liberalism in the Age of Mora, 1821–1853* (Yale University Press, New Haven, Conn., 1968), is a thorough analysis of the Mexican liberal creed. On the chronic financial problems of early Mexican republican governments, see Barbara Tenenbaum, *The Politics of Penury: Debts and Taxes in Mexico, 1821–1856* (University of New Mexico Press, Albuquerque, 1986). R. N. Sinkin, *The Mexican Reform, 1855–1876: A Study in Liberal Nation-Building* (Institute of Latin American Studies, University of Texas, Austin, 1979), argues that the Liberal leaders succeeded in establishing a nation-state, but at the expense of their professed libertarian ideals. For the key church issue, see Jan Bazant, *Alienation of Church Wealth: Social and Economic Aspects of the Liberal Revolution, 1856–1875* (Cambridge University Press, Cambridge, Eng., 1971). On the Caste War, see Nelson Reed, *The Caste War of Yucatan* (Stanford University Press, Stanford, Calif., 1964).

For the first half-century of Argentina's independent existence, see the reliable survey by H. S. Ferns, *Argentina* (Praeger, New York, 1969), and Miron Burgin, *The Economic Aspects of Argentine Federalism, 1820–1852* (Harvard University Press, Cambridge, Mass., 1946). On Rosas, see the fine biography by John Lynch, *Argentine Dictator: Juan Manuel Rosas, 1829–1852* (Oxford University Press, New York, 1981). For the social and political content of the liberal-conservative cleavage, see David Bushnell, *Reform and Reaction in the Platine Provinces* (University Presses of Florida, Gainesville, 1983). J. C. Brown, *A*

Socioeconomic History of Argentina, 1776–1860 (Cambridge University Press, New York, 1979), is an excellent history of trade and agriculture, but underestimates the emerging pattern of a new dependency. R. A. White, *Paraguay's Autonomous Revolution* (University of New Mexico Press, Albuquerque, 1978), is an important revisionist study of the Francia era.

For the first decades of independent Chile, see the relevant sections of Brian Loveman, *Chile: the Legacy of Hispanic Capitalism* (Oxford University Press, New York, 1979), and consult again Simon Collier, *Ideas and Politics of Chilean Independence, 1808–1833* (cited above). On the Chilean great estate and its social consequences, see Arnold Bauer's thorough study, *Chilean Rural Society from the Spanish Conquest to 1930* (Cambridge University Press, New York, 1975).

For independent Brazil's early history, see E. B. Burns's excellent *A History of Brazil* (Columbia University Press, New York, 1970). Leslie Bethell deals with a crucial issue in *The Abolition of the Brazilian Slave Trade: Britain, Brazil, and the Slave Trade Question, 1807–1869* (Cambridge University Press, Cambridge, Eng., 1971). Gilberto Freyre, *The Mansions and the Shanties: The Making of Modern Brazil,* tr. by Harriet de Onis (Knopf, New York, 1963), carries his study of Brazilian society and race relations into the period of the empire. On the crisis of slavery in this period, see the revisionist study of Robert Conrad, *The Destruction of Brazilian Slavery, 1850–1888* (University of California Press, Berkeley, 1973). Conrad's *The African Slave Trade to Brazil* (Louisiana State University Press, Baton Rouge, 1986), is a moving account of this detestable traffic. On the condition of slaves, see Katia M. de Queiros Mattos, *To Be a Slave in Brazil, 1550–1888* (Rutgers University Press, New Brunswick, N.J., 1986). Stanley Stein, *Vassouras: A Brazilian Coffee County* (Harvard University Press, Cambridge, Mass., 1957), is a model socioeconomic study. On Dom Pedro see Harry Bernstein, *Dom Pedro II* (Twayne, Boston, 1973). C. J. Kolinski, *Independence or Death! The Story of the Paraguayan War* (University of Florida Press, Gaines-

ville, 1965), is a good account of the war's military aspects.

Chapter 10
The Triumph of Neocolonialism

On the emergence and flowering of the neocolonial economy, see Celso Furtado, *The Economic Development of Latin America,* tr. by Suzette Macedo (Cambridge University Press, New York, 1970), and Roberto Cortes Conde, *The First Stages of Modernization in Spanish America* (Harper & Row, New York, 1974). For a study of peasant resistance to capitalist transformation of the countryside, see Florencia Mallon, *The Defense of Community in Peru's Central Highlands: Peasant Struggle and Capitalist Transformation, 1860–1910* (Princeton University Press, Princeton, N.J., 1983).

There is a good brief discussion of the Díaz era in M. C. Meyer and W. L. Sherman, *The Course of Mexican History* (cited above). J. K. Turner, *Barbarous Mexico* (C. H. Kerr, Chicago, 1910), is a blistering contemporary assessment of the result of Díaz's rule. J. M. Hart, *The Coming and Process of the Mexican Revolution* (University of California Press, Berkeley, 1987), has an illuminating background discussion of the Porfiriato, stressing foreign economic influence on the rise and policies of the regime. The Northern Illinois University Press has published a series of monographs on the Porfiriato; they include R. J. Knowlton, *Church Property and the Mexican Reform, 1856–1910* (Northern Illinois University Press, DeKalb, 1976), R. D. Anderson, *Outcasts in Their Own Land: Mexican Industrial Workers, 1906–1911* (Northern Illinois University Press, DeKalb, 1976), L. B. Perry, *Juarez and Díaz, Machine Politics in Porfirian Mexico* (Northern Illinois University Press, DeKalb, 1979), and J. H. Coatsworth, *Growth and Development: The Economic Impact of Railroads in Porfirian Mexico* (Northern Illinois University Press, DeKalb, 1981). For an ex-

586   cellent survey of intellectual dissent in the late Porfiriato, see J. D. Cockcroft, *Intellectual Precursors of the Mexican Revolution, 1900–1913* (University of Texas Press, Austin, 1968). For the mutations of positivist thought and other ideological developments in Porfirian Mexico, see Charles Hale's exemplary study, *The Transformation of Liberalism in Late Nineteenth-Century Mexico* (University of Princeton Press, Princeton, N.J., 1990). Monographs on particular regions or provinces have proliferated in recent years; two good examples are Mark Wasserman, *Capitalists, Caciques, and Revolution: The Native Elite and Foreign Enterprise in Chihuahua, Mexico, 1854–1911* (University of North Carolina Press, Chapel Hill, 1984), and Allen Wells, *Yucatan's Gilded Age: Haciendas, Henequen, and International Harvester, 1860–1915* (University of New Mexican Press, Albuquerque, 1985).

On Argentina in the same period, see H. S. Ferns, *Argentina* (Praeger, New York, 1969), and especially Thomas McGann, *Argentina, the United States, and the Inter-American System, 1880–1914* (Harvard University Press, Cambridge, Mass., 1957), for an excellent account of oligarchical politics in the period from 1880 to 1914. For the British connection, see H. S. Ferns, *Britain and Argentina in the Nineteenth Century* (Clarendon Press, Oxford, Eng., 1960). James Scobie, *Argentina: A City and a Nation* (Oxford University Press, New York, 1971), is especially good for economic and social developments; see also his *Revolution on the Pampas: A Social History of Argentine Wheat* (University of Texas Press, Austin, 1964). On the rise of Radicalism, see David Rock, *Politics in Argentina, 1890–1930* (Cambridge University Press, New York, 1975).

On the political and economic evolution of Chile in the same period, see again Brian Loveman, *Chile: The Legacy of Hispanic Capitalism* (cited above). On the agrarian structure, consult A. J. Bauer's excellent *Chilean Rural Society from the Spanish Conquest to 1930* (Cambridge University Press, New York, 1975). R. N. Burr, *By Reason or Force: Chile and the Balancing of Power in South America, 1830–1905* (University of Califor-

nia Press, Berkeley, 1965), studies Chile's international relations. For the War of the Pacific, see William Sater, *Chile and the War of the Pacific* (University of Nebraska Press, Lincoln, 1986). For opposing interpretations of the civil war of 1891, see Harold Blakemore, *British Nitrates and Chilean Politics, 1886–1896* (Athlone Press, London, 1974), and Maurice Zeitlin, *The Civil Wars in Chile (or the Bourgeois Revolutions That Never Were)* (Princeton University Press, Princeton, 1984).

For Brazil in the period under review, see especially E. B. Burns's *A History of Brazil* (Columbia University Press, New York, 1970). On the decisive slavery issue, again see Robert Conrad, *The Destruction of Brazilian Slavery* (cited above). Euclides da Cunha, *Rebellion in the Backlands,* tr. by Samuel Putnam (University of Chicago Press, Chicago, 1957), portrays the defeat of a major religious protest movement. P. L. Eisenberg, *The Sugar Industry in Pernambuco, 1840–1910* (University of California Press, Berkeley, 1974), studies the transformation of a major industry. Richard Graham ably discusses British economic and cultural influence in *Britain and the Onset of Modernization in Brazil, 1850–1914* (Cambridge University Press, New York, 1968). Warren Dean, *The Industrialization of São Paulo, 1880–1945* (University of Texas Press, Austin, 1969), is an important work on early Brazilian industrialization and its social aspects. On the so-called social question, see June Hahner, *Poverty and Politics: The Urban Poor in Brazil, 1870–1920* (University of New Mexico Press, Albuquerque, 1986). On the very different lifestyle of the elite, see Jeffrey D. Needell, *A Tropical Belle Epoque: The Elite Culture of Turn-of-the-Century Rio de Janeiro* (Cambridge University Press, New York, 1986).

Chapter 11
Society and Culture in the Nineteenth Century

Tulio Halperin-Donghi's book, *The Aftermath of Revolution in Latin America* (cited above), is excellent on social and cultural change in the post-independence period. For the process of social and cultural Europeanization, again see Richard Graham's book on British influence on Brazil, *Britain and the Onset of Modernization in Brazil* (cited above), and Frank Safford's excellent study, *The Ideal of the Practical: Colombia's Struggle to Form a Technical Elite* (University of Texas Press, Austin, 1976). The literature on nineteenth-century Latin American women is meager, but Silvia Arrom, *The Women of Mexico City, 1790–1857* (Stanford University Press, Stanford, Calif., 1985), is a valuable case study.

J. L. Mecham, *Church and State in Latin America: A History of Politico-Ecclesiastical Relations,* rev. ed. (University of North Carolina Press, Chapel Hill, 1966), is the standard work on the subject. The Mexican philosopher Leopoldo Zea ably discusses Latin American nineteenth-century thought in *The Latin American Mind* (University of Oklahoma Press, Norman, 1963) and *Positivism in Mexico* (University of Texas Press, Austin, 1974); see also Charles Hale, *The Transformation of Liberalism in Late Nineteenth-Century Mexico* (cited above). For a source book on the subject, see R. L. Woodward, Jr., ed., *Positivism in Latin America* (D. C. Heath, Lexington, Mass., 1971). On the rise of racist ideology, see Richard Graham, ed., *The Idea of Race in Latin America, 1870–1940* (University of Texas Press, Austin, 1990).

On Latin American literature in the nineteenth century, Jean Franco, *An Introduction to Spanish American Literature* (Cambridge University Press, London, 1969), is especially recommended for its perceptive treatment of the relations between literature and society. For a case study in the relations between historiography and politics, see Allen Woll, *A Functional Past: The Uses of History in Nineteenth-Century Chile* (Louisiana State University Press, Baton Rouge, 1982).

Chapter 12
The Mexican Revolution— and After

The past decade has seen the appearance of a number of important broad studies of the Mexican Revolution. R. E. Ruiz, *The Great Rebellion: Mexico, 1905–1924* (Norton, New York, 1980), argues unconvincingly that the Mexican Revolution was no such thing, but provides much useful new information, particularly on economic development. Friedrich Katz, *The Secret War in Mexico: Europe, the United States, and the Mexican Revolution* (University of Chicago Press, Chicago, 1981), illuminates all major aspects of the revolution, both foreign and domestic. Alan Knight, *The Mexican Revolution,* 2 vols. (Cambridge University Press, New York, 1986), a work written on a monumental scale, stresses the popular character of the revolution but questions the importance of economic factors. J. M. Hart's powerful *The Coming and Process of the Mexican Revolution* (cited above) emphasizes the nationalistic character of the revolution and sheds much new light on foreign economic and political influence in shaping its course.

There has been a flowering of regional studies of modern Mexican history in recent decades; good examples include Thomas Benjamin and Mark Wasserman, eds., *The Mexican Revolution: Essays in Regional Mexican History, 1910–1929* (University of New Mexico Press, Albuquerque, 1990); G. M. Joseph, *Revolution from Without: Yucatan, Mexico, and the United States, 1880–1924* (Duke University Press, Durham, N.C., 1988), and H. F. Salamini, *Agrarian Radicalism in Veracruz, 1920–1938* (University of Nebraska Press, Lincoln, 1971).

For the prerevolutionary background of intellectual dissent, again see James Cockcroft, *Intellectual Precursors of the Revolution* (cited above). On Madero, see Stanley Ross, *Francisco I. Madero, Apostle of Mexican Democracy* (Columbia University Press, New York, 1955); on Carranza, see C. C. Cumberland, *The Mexican Revolution: The Constitutionalist Years* (University of Texas Press, Austin, 1972). John Womack, *Zapata and the Mexican Revolution* (Knopf, New York, 1968), is the masterful standard life. M. C. Meyer attempts the difficult task of partially rehabilitating Huerta in *Huerta, A Political Portrait* (University of Nebraska Press, Lincoln, 1972).

Special topics are covered by R. E. Ruiz, *Labor and the Ambivalent Revolutionaries: Mexico: 1911–1923* (Johns Hopkins University Press, Baltimore, 1976); R. E. Quirk, *The Mexican Revolution and the Catholic Church, 1910–1929* (Indiana University Press, Bloomington, 1973); and Edwin Lieuwen, *Mexican Militarism: The Political Rise of the Revolutionary Army, 1910–1940* (University of New Mexico Press, Albuquerque, 1973). For a disillusioned assessment of Mexican political life a half-century after the revolution, see Pablo Gonzalez Casanova, *Democracy in Mexico,* tr. by D. Salti (Oxford University Press, New York, 1970). For equally critical judgments on Mexican official economic and social policies, see J. D. Cockcroft, *Mexico: Class Formation, Capital Accumulation, and the State* (Monthly Review Press, New York, 1983), Nora Hamilton, *Mexico: The Limits of State Autonomy* (Princeton University Press, Princeton, N.J., 1982), and J. M. Cypher, *State and Capital in Mexico: Development Policy since 1940* (Westview Press, Boulder, Colo., 1990).

Chapter 13
Argentina: The Failure of Democracy

J. R. Scobie, *Argentina: A City and a Nation,* 2nd ed. (Oxford University Press, New York, 1971), and David Rock, *Argentina, 1516–1982: From Spanish Colonization to the Falklands War* (University of California Press, Berkeley, 1985), are the best overviews of Argentine history and society. H. S. Ferns, *The Argentine Republic, 1516–1971* (Barnes & Noble, New York, 1971), is a comprehensive economic history. See also C. F. Díaz Alejandro, *Essays on the Economic History of the Argentine Republic* (Yale University Press, New Haven, Conn., 1970), and Laura Randall, *An Economic History of Argentina in the Twentieth Century* (Columbia University Press, New York, 1978).

Notable studies of the Argentine military are R. A. Potash, *The Army and Politics in Argentina, 1928–1945* (Stanford University Press, Stanford, Calif., 1969), and *The Army and Politics in Argentina, 1945–1961: Perón to Frondizi* (Stanford University Press, Stanford, Calif., 1982). P. H. Smith, *Politics and Beef in Argentina* (Columbia University Press, 1969), is a competent study of the landowning elite. S. L. Baily, *Labor, Nationalism, and Politics in Argentina* (Rutgers University Press, New Brunswick, N.J.), attempts to separate myth from reality in Argentine labor history.

P. H. Smith, *Argentina and the Failure of Democracy* (University of Wisconsin Press, Madison, 1974), employs sophisticated methods to produce some provocative hypotheses about Argentine politics. David Rock, *Politics in Argentina, 1890–1930: The Rise and Fall of Radicalism* (cited above), is the best study of the Radical era. Mark Falcoff and R. H. Dolkart, eds., *Prologue to Perón: Argentina in Depression and War, 1930–1943* (University of California Press, Berkeley, 1976), is a valuable collection of essays.

The Perón era has attracted much scholarly interest. G. I. Blanksten, *Peron's Argentina* (University of Chicago Press, Chicago, 1974), is a classic work. The best life of Perón is J. A. Page, *Perón: A Biography* (Random House, New York, 1983), but see also Roland Crassweller, *Perón and the Enigma of Argentina* (Norton, New York, 1987). J. R. Barager, ed., *Why Perón Came to Power* (Knopf, New York, 1968), is a useful reader. For a summing up of the Perón era, see F. C. Turner and J. E. Miguens, *Juan Perón and the Reshaping of Argentina* (University of Pittsburgh Press, Pittsburgh, 1983).

David Rock, ed., *Argentina in the Twentieth*

Century (University of Pittsburgh Press, Pittsburgh, 1975), contains some outstanding essays. D. C. Hodges, *Argentina, 1943–1976: The National Revolution and Resistance* (University of New Mexico Press, Albuquerque, 1976), studies Argentine guerrilla movements. Monica Peralta-Ramos and C. H. Waisman, *From Military Rule to Liberal Democracy in Argentina* (Westview Press, Boulder, Colo., 1987), documents the damage done to Argentine industry and living standards by the military rulers.

Two powerful indictments of the military rule after 1976 are Jacobo Timmerman, *Prisoner Without Name, Cell Without Number* (Knopf, New York, 1981), and *Never Again* (Farrar, Straus, New York, 1985).

Chapter 14
The Chilean Way

The best, most up-to-date survey of Chilean history is Brian Loveman, *Chile: The Legacy of Hispanic Capitalism* (cited above). For an excellent overall economic history, see M. J. Mamalakis, *The Growth and Structure of the Chilean Economy from Independence to Allende* (Yale University Press, New Haven, Conn., 1976). James Petras, *Political and Social Forces in Chilean Development* (University of California Press, Berkeley, 1969), is an excellent examination of the development of left-wing parties in Chile. Alan Angell, *Politics and the Labor Movement in Chile* (Oxford University Press, London, 1972), is the best study of Chilean labor. F. N. Nunn, *The Military in Chilean History* (University of New Mexico Press, Albuquerque, 1976), is objective and well researched. Maurice Zeitlin and R. E. Ratcliff, *Landlords and Capitalists: The Dominant Class of Chile* (Princeton University Press, Princeton, N.J., 1988), shows the overlap between landownership and industrial and finance capital in modern Chile.

Sound studies of the Chilean agricultural sector are R. F. Kaufman, *The Politics of Land Reform in Chile, 1950–1970* (Harvard University Press,

Cambridge, Mass., 1972); Brian Loveman, *Struggle in the Countryside: Politics and Rural Labor in Chile, 1919–1973* (Indiana University Press, Bloomington, 1976); and A. J. Bauer, *Chilean Rural Society from the Spanish Conquest to 1930* (cited above).

There is copious literature on the Allende regime and its overthrow. Edy Kaufman, *Crises in Allende's Chile* (Praeger, New York, 1988), is a comprehensive account of the Allende regime. Other useful studies include P. E. Sigmund, *The Overthrow of Allende and the Politics of Chile, 1964–1976* (University of Pittsburgh Press, Pittsburgh, 1977), and Barbara Stallings, *Class Conflict and Economic Development in Chile, 1958–1973* (Stanford University Press, Stanford, Calif., 1978). On the complicity of the United States in the revolt, see James Petras and Morris Morley, *The United States and Chile* (Monthly Review Press, New York, 1976).

Studies of Chile since the 1973 coup include J. Samuel Valenzuela and Arturo Valenzuela, eds., *Military Rule in Chile: Dictatorship and Oppositions* (Johns Hopkins University Press, Baltimore, 1986); see also J. R. Ramos, *Neo-Conservative Economics in the Southern Cone of Latin America, 1973–1983* (Johns Hopkins University Press, Baltimore, 1986). On resistance to the dictatorship, see Kenneth Aman and Cristina Parker, *Popular Culture in Chile: Resistance and Survival* (Westview Press, Boulder, Colo., 1990). Samuel Chavkin, *Storm over Chile: The Junta under Siege* (Lawrence Hill, Westport, Conn., 1985), is a poignant story of life under Pinochet.

Chapter 15
Republican Brazil

E. B. Burns's *A History of Brazil* (cited above) and Rollie Popino, *Brazil: The Land and the People* (Oxford University Press, New York, 1968), offer good brief accounts of developments since 1914, but the most thorough recent study of modern Brazil is Peter Flynn, *Brazil: A Political Analysis* (Ernest Benn, London, 1978). Good studies of the

590 Vargas era include J. M. Young, *The Brazilian Revolution of 1930 and the Aftermath* (Rutgers University Press, New Brunswick, N.J., 1967), R. M. Levine, *The Vargas Regime: The Critical Years, 1934–1938* (Columbia University Press, New York, 1970), and John Wirth, *The Politics of Brazilian Development, 1930–1954* (Stanford University Press, Stanford, Calif., 1970). T. L. Skidmore, *Politics in Brazil, 1930–1964: An Experiment in Democracy* (Oxford University Press, New York, 1967), is especially good on the events leading to the coup of 1964. On the role of the military, see Alfred Stepan, *The Military in Politics: Changing Patterns in Brazil* (Princeton University Press, Princeton, N.J., 1971), and T. L. Skidmore, *The Politics of Military Rule in Brazil, 1964–1985* (Oxford University Press, New York, 1988).

The apparent economic success of the Brazilian military regime focused much scholarly interest on it; studies that view it as an example of the "bureaucratic-authoritarian model" or from the perspective of corporatist theory include Alfred Stepan, ed., *Authoritarian Brazil: Origins, Politics, and Future* (Yale University Press, New Haven, Conn., 1973), and G. A. Fiechter, *Brazil since 1964—Modernization under a Military Regime* (Macmillan, London, 1978). For a collective effort to understand Brazil's recent past, see John Wirth, ed., *State and Society in Brazil: Continuity and Change* (Westview Press, Boulder, Colo., 1987).

Outstanding works on special topics in this period include Ralph della Cava, *Miracle at Joaseiro* (Columbia University Press, New York, 1970), a study of a religious protest movement and its leader; J. L. Love, *Rio Grande do Sul and Brazilian Regionalism* (Stanford University Press, Stanford, Calif., 1971), on the politics of a key Brazilian state; and Neill Macaulay, *The Prestes Column: Revolution in Brazil* (Franklin Watts, New York, 1974).

Chapter 16
Storm Over the Andes: Peru's Ambiguous Revolution

H. S. Klein, *Bolivia: The Evolution of a Multi-Ethnic Society* (Oxford University Press, New York, 1982), provides the best introduction to its subject. The best account of the events leading to the revolution of 1982 is H. S. Klein, *Parties and Political Change in Bolivia, 1880–1952* (Cambridge University Press, New York, 1969). For assessments of the revolution and its aftermath, see James Malloy, *Bolivia, The Uncompleted Revolution* (University of Pittsburgh Press, Pittsburgh, 1970), and James Malloy and Eduardo Gamarra, *Revolution and Reaction: Bolivia, 1964–1985* (Transaction Books, New Brunswick, N.J., 1988). June Nash, *We Eat the Mines and the Mines Eat Us: Dependency and Exploitation in Bolivian Tin Mines* (Columbia University Press, New York, 1979), is an innovative study of the culture of a Bolivian mining community.

The historical literature on Ecuador in English is very meager, but G. I. Blanksten, *Ecuador, Constitutions and Caudillos* (University of California Press, Berkeley, 1951), is a competent study of the country's modern political history. For social and economic conditions, see Carlos Luzuriaga C. and Clarence Zuvekas, Jr., *Income Distribution and Poverty in Rural Ecuador, 1950–1979* (Center for Latin American Studies, Arizona State University, Tempe, 1983); for a valuable collection of essays on indigenous cultures, see Norman E. Whitten, Jr., *Cultural Transformations and Ethnicity in Modern Ecuador* (University of Illinois Press, Champaign, 1981).

F. B. Pike, *The Modern History of Peru* (Praeger, New York, 1967), is the best general account. J. C. Mariátegui, *Seven Interpretive Essays on Peruvian Reality* (University of Texas Press, Austin, 1971), is a brilliant and influential Marxist analysis. On the economic and social origins of the Aprista movement, see P. F. Klaren, *Modernization, Dislocation, Aprismo: Origins of the Peruvian Aprista Party* (University of Texas Press,

Austin, 1973). On the Indian question, see T. M. Davies, Jr., *Indian Integration in Peru: A Half Century of Experience, 1900–1948* (University of Nebraska Press, Lincoln, 1974), and Howard Handelman, *Struggle in the Andes: Peasant Political Participation in Peru* (University of Texas Press, Austin, 1974).

The Peruvian revolution of 1968 produced an abundant literature. For a good collection of retrospective views, see Abraham Lowenthal and Cynthia McClintock, eds., *The Peruvian Experiment Revisited* (Princeton University Press, Princeton, N.J., 1983). Tom Alberts, *Agrarian Reform and Rural Poverty: A Case Study of Peru* (Westview Press, Boulder, Colo., 1983), shows the failure of the revolution to correct rural income inequities. There is an excellent discussion of the revolution's economic policies in Rosemary Thorp and Geoffrey Bertram, *Peru, 1890–1977: Growth and Policy in an Open Economy* (Macmillan, London, 1978).

Chapter 17
The Cuban Revolution

Hugh Thomas's monumental *Cuba: The Pursuit of Freedom* (Harper & Row, New York, 1971), remains the standard history of Cuba. There are several fine studies of Cuban society and political economy during the nineteenth century; they include Ramiro Sanchez y Guerra, *Sugar and Society in the Caribbean* (Yale University Press, New Haven, Conn., 1964); Fernando Ortiz, *Cuban Counterpoint: Tobacco and Sugar* (Knopf, New York, 1947); F. W. Knight, *Slave Society in Nineteenth Century Cuba* (University of Wisconsin Press, Madison, 1970); and R. J. Scott, *Slave Emancipation in Cuba: The Transition to Free Labor* (Princeton University Press, Princeton, N.J., 1985).

L. A. Perez, Jr., *Army Politics in Cuba, 1898–1958* (University of Pittsburgh Press, Pittsburgh, 1976), is the best work on the Cuban military.

P. S. Foner, *The Spanish-Cuban-American War, 1895–1906* (Monthly Review Press, New York, 1972), drastically revises the traditional historiography of the Spanish-American War. L. A. Perez, Jr., *Cuba Under the Platt Amendment, 1902–1934* (University of Pittsburgh Press, Pittsburgh, 1984), finds that the results of the U.S. presence were "debased political institutions, deformed social formations, and dependent economic relations." L. E. Aguilar, *Cuba 1933: Prologue to Revolution* (Norton, New York, 1974), is a fine monograph on the unsuccessful moderate revolution of 1933.

The Cuban revolution and Fidel Castro have attracted numerous studies that differ widely in their assessments of both. J. R. O'Connor, *The Origins of Socialism in Cuba* (Cornell University Press, Ithaca, N.Y., 1970), is a masterful study of the background of the Cuban revolution. Edward Gonzalez, *Cuba Under Castro: The Limits of Charisma* (Houghton Mifflin, Boston, 1974), is highly critical; Lee Lockwood, *Castro's Cuba, Cuba's Fidel,* 2nd ed. (Westview Press, Boulder, Colo., 1990), is highly favorable. Tad Szulc, *Fidel: A Critical Portrait* (Morrow, New York, 1986), is a recent provocative biography of the Cuban leader.

Cuban emigrant economists like Carmel Mesa-Lago, *The Economy of Socialist Cuba: A Two Decade Appraisal* (University of New Mexico Press, Albuquerque, 1981), dispute that Cuba has achieved economic growth, but Andrew Zimbalist and Claes Brundenius, *The Cuban Economy: Measurement and Analysis of Socialist Performance* (Johns Hopkins University Press, Baltimore, 1989), conclude that Cuba has outpaced its Latin American neighbors in distribution of income and economic growth. Jorge Dominguez, *Cuba: Order and Revolution* (Harvard University Press, Cambrddge, Mass., 1978), is an encyclopedic but critical effort to measure the achievements of the revolution. For more favorable views, see Sandor Halebsky and J. M. Kirk, eds., *Cuba: Twenty-Five Years of Revolution, 1959–1984* (Praeger, New York, 1985). Jorge Dominguez, *To Make a World Safe for Revolution* (Harvard University Press, Cambridge, Mass., 1988),

592

argues that the origins of Cuban foreign policy are to be found in the island, not in Moscow.

Chapter 18
Revolution in Central America: Twilight of the Tyrants?

R. L. Woodward, Jr., *Central America: A Nation Divided* (Oxford University Press, New York, 1976), and James Dunkerley, *Power in the Isthmus: A Political History of Modern Central America* (Verso, London, 1988), are two sound overviews of the area's history. T. L. Karnes, *The Failure of Union: Central America 1824–1975* (Arizona State University Press, Tempe, 1976), surveys the many failed efforts to unite the region. M. L. Wortman, *Government and Society in Central America, 1680–1840* (Columbia University Press, New York, 1982), is a carefully researched socioeconomic study. J. A. Booth and T. W. Walker, *Understanding Central America* (Westview Press, Boulder, Colo., 1989), is an excellent introduction to the area's problems.

Susanne Jonas and David Tobis, eds., *Guatemala* (NACLA, New York, 1974), is a good overview. For new light on the U.S. role in the 1954 coup in Guatemala, see R. H. Immerman, *The CIA in Guatemala: The Foreign Policy of Intervention* (University of Texas Press, Austin, 1982), and Stephen Schlesinger and Stephen Kinzer, *Bitter Fruit: The Untold Story of the American Coup in Guatemala* (Doubleday, Garden City, N.Y., 1982). On the consequences, particularly the terror against the Indian peasantry, see R. N. Adams, *Crucifixion by Power* (University of Texas Press, Austin, 1970), and C. A. Smith, ed., *Guatemalan Indians and the State, 1540–1988* (University of Texas Press, Austin, 1990), an important collection of essays that amounts to a social history of Guatemala.

T. W. Walker, *Nicaragua: The Land of Sandino*, 2nd ed. (Westview Press, Boulder, Colo., 1986), is a well-informed survey; see also T. W. Walker, *Reagan and the Sandinistas* (Westview Press, Boulder, Colo., 1987), for a critique of the Reagan policy in Nicaragua. On the Somoza era, see Richard Millett, *Guardians of the Dynasty: A History of the U.S.-created Guardia Nacional de Nicaragua and the Somoza Family* (Orbis, Maryknoll, N.Y., 1977). On Sandino, see Gregorio Selser's fine biography, *Sandino*, tr. by Cedric Belfrage (Monthly Review Press, New York, 1981), and Neill Macaulay, *The Sandino Affair* (Quadrangle Books, Chicago, 1967), which focuses on his military activity. For Sandino's social and political views, see D. C. Hodges, *The Intellectual Foundation of the Nicaraguan Revolution* (University of Texas Press, Austin, 1986). M. E. Conroy and M. E. Frenkel, eds., *Nicaragua: Profiles of the Revolutionary Public Sector* (Westview Press, Boulder, Colo., 1987), studies an important aspect of Sandinista economic policy.

Alastair White, *El Salvador* (Praeger, New York, 1973), provides much useful background information. T. P. Anderson has written model monographs on two milestones on El Salvador's road to revolution, *Matanza: El Salvador's Communist Revolt of 1932* (University of Nebraska Press, Lincoln, 1971), and *The War of the Dispossessed: Honduras and El Salvador* (University of Nebraska Press, Lincoln, 1981). T. S. Montgomery, *Revolution in El Salvador: Origins and Evolution* (Westview Press, Boulder, Colo., 1982), studies the development of the revolutionary movement in engrossing detail.

Chapter 19
Lands of Bolívar: Venezuela and Colombia in the Twentieth Century

J. V. Lombardi, *Venezuela: The Search for Order, the Dream of Progress* (Oxford University Press, New York, 1982), has for its main theme the progressive integration of Venezuela into the "North Atlantic world." Judith Ewell, *Venezuela: A Century of Change* (Hurst, London, 1984), examines in some detail political, socioeconomic, and cultural aspects, with a focus on the period since 1900. D. E. Blank, *Venezuela: Politics in a Petroleum Republic* (Praeger, New York, 1984), attempts to provide a conceptual framework for Venezuela's "controlled democracy." J. A. Peeler, *Latin American Democracies: Colombia, Costa Rica, Venezuela* (University of North Carolina Press, Chapel Hill, 1985), sees all three as representing "masked hegemony" by elites.

Good studies of special topics include Robert Gilmore, *Caudillism and Militarism in Venezuela, 1810–1910* (Ohio University Press, Athens, 1964); Edwin Lieuwen, *Petroleum in Venezuela: A History* (University of California Press, Berkeley, 1954); J. F. Petras, Morris Morley, and Steven Smith, *The Nationalization of Venezuelan Oil* (Praeger, New York, 1977); B. S. McBeth, *Juan Vicente Gomez and the Oil Companies in Venezuela, 1908–1935* (Cambridge University Press, Cambridge, 1983), and R. J. Alexander's informative but excessively reverential study of *Rómulo Betancourt and the Transformation of Venezuela* (Transaction Books, New Brunswick, N.J., 1982).

D. L. Herman, ed., *Democracy in Latin America: Colombia and Venezuela* (Praeger, Westport, Conn., 1988), provides a comparative analysis of the two regimes. Jonathan Hartlyn, *Politics of Coalition Rule in Colombia* (Cambridge University Press, New York, 1988), argues that coalition rule was a strategy for maintaining control by traditional elites. Robert Dix, *The Politics of Colombia* (Praeger, New York, 1987), attempts to reconcile the apparent vitality of republican institutions with high levels of violence and great social inequality. For economic history, see William McGreevey, *An Economic History of Colombia, 1845–1930* (Cambridge University Press, Cambridge, Eng., 1971).

Good studies of special topics include Charles Bergquist, *Coffee and Conflict in Colombia, 1886–1910* (Duke University Press, Durham, N.C., 1976), an economic interpretation of a tremendous civil war; James Park, *Rafael Núñez and the Politics of Colombian Regionalism* (Louisiana State University Press, Baton Rouge, 1985); and Catherine LeGrand, *Frontier Expansion and Peasant Protest in Colombia, 1850–1936* (University of New Mexico Press, Albuquerque, 1986); Herbert Braun, *The Assassination of Gaitán: Public Life and Urban Violence in Colombia* (University of Wisconsin Press, Madison, 1986), which deals with a major turning point in Colombian history; and James Henderson, *When Colombia Bled: A History of the Violencia in Tolima* (University of Alabama Press, 1985).

Chapter 20
The Two Americas: United States–Latin American Relations

Two recent general works, Harold Molineu, *U.S. Policy Toward Latin America: From Regionalism to Globalism* (Westview Press, Boulder, Colo., 1986), and Abraham Lowenthal, *Partners in Conflict: The United States and Latin America* (Johns Hopkins University Press, Baltimore, 1986), present overviews of United States–Latin American relations.

A. P. Whitaker, *The United States and the Independence of Latin America, 1800–1830* (Johns Hopkins University Press, Baltimore, 1941), and Dexter Perkins, *A History of the Monroe Doctrine*, rev. ed. (Little, Brown, Boston, 1963), are the standard studies of these related subjects. The best treatment of the Mexican war from the United States perspective is Otis Singletary, *The Mexican War* (University of Chicago Press, Chicago, 1960). Walter LaFeber's brilliant *The New Empire* (Cornell University Press, Ithaca, N.Y., 1963), stresses economic factors in U.S. relations with Latin America from 1865 to 1898. L. D. Langley, *The Banana Wars: An Inner History of American Empire, 1900–1934* (University Press of Kentucky, Lexington, 1983), shows how intervention in Mexico, Central America, and the Caribbean became an American way of life. J. R. Benjamin, *The United States and Cuba: Hegemony and Dependent Development 1880–1934* (University of Pittsburgh Press, Pittsburgh, 1974), and L. A. Perez, Jr., *Cuba Between Empires, 1878–1902*

(University of Pittsburgh Press, Pittsburgh, 1983), are two excellent studies of the U.S. role in Cuba.

On Puerto Rico, see two general studies, J. L. Dietz, *The Economic History of Puerto Rico* (Princeton University Press, Princeton, N.J., 1986), and A. Morales Carrion, *Puerto Rico: A Political and Cultural History* (Norton, New York, 1983). Amid other studies on "the Puerto Rican Question," see Raymond Carr, *Puerto Rico: A Colonial Experiment* (Vintage, New York, 1983); J. M. García Passalacqua, *Puerto Rico: Equality and Freedom at Issue* (Praeger, New York, 1984); and Jorge Heine, ed., *Time for Decision: The United States and Puerto Rico* (North-South Publishing, Lanham, Md., 1983), a collection of essays sharply critical of the island's political status and economic model. On that model, see also Richard Weiskoff, *Factories and Foodstamps: The Puerto Rican Model of Development* (Johns Hopkins University Press, Baltimore, 1985).

Bryce Wood, *The Making of the Good Neighbor Policy* (Columbia University Press, New York, 1961), offers a traditional view of New Deal policy toward Latin America; L. Gardner, *The Economic Aspects of New Deal Diplomacy* (University of Wisconsin Press, Madison, 1964), emphasizes the less altruistic goals of American policy.

For the post–World War II period, see S. L. Baily, *The United States and the Development of South America, 1845–1975* (New Viewpoints, New York, 1976), a dispassionate plea for a change in American policy. Cole Blasier, *The Hovering Giant* (University of Pittsburgh Press, Pittsburgh, 1986), assesses American responses to revolution in Latin America.

Walter LaFeber's superb *The Panama Canal* (Oxford University Press, New York, 1978), explains the issues in the negotiations over the canal treaties. For the background of the Panama invasion, see John Dinges, *Our Man in Panama: How General Noriega Used the United States— and Made Millions in Arms and Drugs* (Random House, New York, 1990). See also John Weeks and Phil Gunson, *Panama: Made in the USA* (Latin American Bureau, London, 1990). On Grenada, see G. K. Lewis, *Grenada: The Jewel Despoiled* (Johns Hopkins University Press, Baltimore,

1986); on Haiti, Michel-Rolph Trouillot, *Haiti: State Against Nation: The Origins and Legacy of Duvalierism* (Monthly Review Press, New York, 1990). For a general overview of U.S.-Mexican relations, see J. Zoraida Vasquez and Lorenzo Meyer, *The United States and Mexico* (University of Chicago Press, Chicago, 1986). See also Bryce Wood, *Dismantling of the Good Neighbor Policy* (University of Texas Press, Austin, 1986).

There is copious literature on U.S. involvement in Central America. Walter LaFeber's *Inevitable Revolutions: The United States in Central America* (Norton, New York, 1983) is the best overview. L. S. Etheredge, *Can Governments Learn? American Foreign Policy and Central American Relations* (Pergamon Press, New York, 1985), attempts to explain American failure to learn from past mistakes in its Central American and Caribbean policies. On policy toward Nicaragua, see E. B. Burns, *At War in Nicaragua: The Reagan Doctrine and the Politics of Nostalgia* (Perennial, New York, 1987), and Roy Gutman, *Banana Diplomacy: The Making of American Policy in Nicaragua, 1981–1987* (Simon and Schuster, New York, 1987).

Chapter 21
Latin American Society in Transition

The Economic Survey of Latin America, published annually since 1948 by the Economic Commission for Latin America of the United Nations, is a valuable source of information on economic and social conditions. The essays in James Petras, ed., *Latin America: Bankers, Generals, and the Struggle for Social Justice* (Rowman and Littlefield, Totowa, N.J., 1986), offer cogent analyses of current socioeconomic and political trends. M. S. Grindle, *State and Countryside: Development Policy and Agrarian Politics in Latin America* (Johns Hopkins University Press, Baltimore, Md., 1986), helps to explain the paradox of growing food production and growing hunger in Latin

America. Rachel Garst and Tom Barry, *Feeding the Crisis: U.S. Food Aid and Farm Policy in Central America* (University of Nebraska Press, Lincoln, 1990), reveals the negative effects of U.S. aid to Central America. For data on poverty and inequality, see Robert Ferber, ed., *Consumption and Income Distribution in Latin America* (Organization of American States, Washington, D.C., 1980). On urbanization and housing problems, see Jorge Hardoy, ed., *Urbanization in Latin America: Approaches and Issues* (Doubleday, Garden City, N.Y., 1975), and Alan Gilbert and P. M. Ward, *Housing; The State and the Poor: Policy and Practice in Three Latin American Cities* (Cambridge University Press, Cambridge, Eng., 1984).

On dependent development in Latin America, see the older but basic works of F. H. Cardoso and Enzo Faletto, *Dependency and Development in Latin America* (University of California Press, Berkeley, 1979), and Peter Evans, *Dependent Development: The Alliance of Multinational, State, and Local Capital in Brazil* (Princeton University Press, Princeton, N.J., 1979), and such recent works as Rhys Jenkins, *Transnational Corporations and Industrial Transformation in Latin America* (St. Martin's Press, New York, 1984); Richard Newfarmer, ed., *Profits, Progress, and Poverty: Case Studies of International Industries in Latin America* (University of Notre Dame Press, Notre Dame, Ind., 1985); and E. R. Stoddard, *Maquila: Assembly Plants in Northern Mexico* (Texas Western Press, El Paso, 1987).

Older but still useful works dealing with class structure and alignments are J. J. Johnson's classic *Political Change in Latin America: The Emergence of the Middle Sectors* (Stanford University Press, Stanford, Calif., 1958), S. M. Lipset and Aldo Solari, eds., *Elites in Latin America* (Oxford University Press, New York, 1967), and I. L. Horowitz, ed., *Masses in Latin America* (Oxford University Press, New York, 1970). On the peasantry, see Andrew Pearse, *The Latin American Peasant* (Frank Cass, London, 1975), and Alain de Janvry, *The Agrarian Question and Reformism in Latin America* (Johns Hopkins University Press, Baltimore, Md., 1981). On Latin American labor, see

the important studies of H. A. Spalding, *Organized Labor in Latin America: Historical Case Studies of Workers in Dependent Societies* (New York University Press, New York, 1977), and Charles Bergquist, *Labor in Latin America: Comparative Studies on Chile, Argentina, Venezuela, and Colombia* (Stanford University Press, Stanford, Calif., 1986). S. B. Liss, *Marxist Thought in Latin America* (University of California Press, Berkeley, 1984), surveys a topic of large importance.

On the status of women in contemporary Latin America, see June Nash and Helen Safa, eds., *Women and Change in Latin America* (Bergin and Garvey, South Hadley, Mass., 1986). For a case study in early feminism, see Ana Macias, *Against All Odds: The Feminist Movement in Mexico to 1940* (Greenwood Press, Westport, Conn., 1982). For a notable case study in race relations, see Florestan Fernandes, *The Negro in Brazilian Society* (Columbia University Press, New York, 1969). Richard Arens, ed., *Genocide in Paraguay* (Temple University Press, Philadelphia, 1976), documents the destruction of Paraguayan Indians, a situation with parallels in Brazil and other Latin American countries.

There is a large and growing literature on the new reformist and radical tendencies with the Catholic church. On the sources of liberation theology, see Philip Berryman, *The Religious Roots of Rebellion* (Orbis, Maryknoll, N.Y., 1984), and Enrique Dussel, *History and the Theology of Liberation* (Orbis, Maryknoll, N.Y., 1976); on the especially militant Brazilian clergy, see T. C. Bruneau, *The Church in Brazil: The Politics of Religion* (University of Texas Press, Austin, 1982). On the challenge of Protestantism, see David Stall, *Is Latin America Turning Protestant?* (University of California Press, Berkeley, 1990).

On the Latin American military, see the excellent country studies of F. M. Nunn and Robert Potash (cited above) and Nunn's *Yesterday's Soldiers: European Military Professionalism in South America, 1890–1940* (University of Nebraska Press, Lincoln, 1983). For the United States connection, see J. K. Black, *Sentinels of Empire: The United States and Latin American*

596 *Militarism* (Greenwood Press, Westport, Conn., 1986), which argues that the United States encouraged military rule in the 1960s and 1970s to maintain its own hegemony.

On Latin American economic thought, see the excellent survey of Cristobal Kay, *Latin American Theories of Development and Underdevelopment* (Routledge, New York, 1989). For statements and applications of dependency theory by Latin American and North American scholars, see R. H. Chilcote and J. C. Edelstein, eds., *Latin America: The Struggle with Dependency and Beyond* (Halstead Press, New York, 1974).

On twentieth-century literary trends, again see Jean Franco, *An Introduction to Spanish-American Literature* (cited above), and John King, ed., *Modern Latin American Fiction* (London, Faber and Faber, 1987). On the Latin American film, see E. B. Burns, *Latin American Cinema: Film and History* (UCLA Press, Los Angeles, 1978), and Julianne Burton, ed., *Cinema and Social Change in Latin America: Conversations with Filmmakers* (University of Texas Press, Austin, 1986).

Index